READINGS IN WESTERN CIVILIZATION

VOLUME ONE—FALL

SECOND EDITION

PROVIDENCE COLLEGE

Development of Western Civilization Program

Tapestry Press, Ltd.
Acton, MA 01720

Front Cover: "Aristotle Contemplating the Bust of Homer" by Rembrandt. The Metropolitan Museum of Art. Purchase, special contributions and funds given or bequeathed by friends of the Museum, 1961. (61.198) Photograph © 1993 by The Metropolitan Museum of Art. Used by permission.

All possible effort has been made to locate the copyright owner or holder of the copyrighted material included in this book. If any rights have been inadvertently infringed upon, the publisher asks to be excused, and agrees to make corrections to any subsequent editions or reprintings.

Acknowledgments:

Pp. 3–33: "Gilgamesh" from *The Epic of Gilgamesh*, translated by N.K. Sandars (Penguin Classics 1960, third edition 1972) copyright © N.K. Sandars, 1960, 1964, 1972. Reproduced by permission of Penguin Books Ltd.

Pp. 37–130: "The Iliad" by Homer from *The Iliad of Homer*, translated by Richmond Lattimore. Copyright © 1951 by The University of Chicago Press. Reprinted by permission of The University of Chicago Press.

Pp. 132–239: *The Oresteia* by Aeschylus, translated by Richmond Lattimore, from *The Complete Greek Tragedies*, ed. Grene and Lattimore. Copyright © 1983. Reprinted by permission of The University of Chicago Press.

Pp. 240–283: "Oedipus Rex" by Sophocles, from *Sophocles, The Oedipus Cycle: An English Version* by Dudley Fitts and Robert Fitzgerald, copyright 1949 by Harcourt, Inc. and renewed 1977 by Dudley Fitts and Robert Fitzgerald, reprinted by permission of the publisher. Caution: All rights, including professional, amateur, motion picture, recitation, lecturing, performance, public reading, radio broadcasting, and television are strictly reserved. Inquiries on all rights should be addressed to Harcourt, Inc., Permissions Department, Orlando, FL 32887-6777.

Pp. 284–316: "Antigonê" by Sophocles, from *Sophocles, The Oedipus Cycle: An English Version* by Dudley Fitts and Robert Fitzgerald, copyright 1939 by Harcourt, Inc. and renewed 1967 by Dudley Fitts and Robert Fitzgerald, reprinted by permission of the publisher. Caution: All rights, including professional, amateur, motion picture, recitation, lecturing, performance, public reading, radio broadcasting, and television are strictly reserved. Inquiries on all rights should be addressed to Harcourt, Inc., Permissions Department, Orlando, FL 32887-6777

Pp. 317–353: "Medea" by Euripides, translated by Rex Warner. From *Great Plays of Euripides* by Rex Warner. Copyright © 1986 by Penguin Putnam Inc. All rights reserved.

Pp. 354–400: "Trojan Women" from *Euripides—Ten Plays* by Euripides, translated by Paul Roche, copyright © 1998 by Paul Roche. Used by permission of Dutton, a division of Penguin Putnam Inc.

Pp. 401–435: "Lysistrata" by Aristophanes, translated by C.T. Murphy and Whitney A. Oates. Copyright © Longman Publishing Company. All rights reserved.

Pp. 436–446: "The Peloponnesian Wars" from *History of the Peloponnesian War* by Thucydides, translated by Richard Crawley. From Internet, http://classics.mit.edu/Thucydides/pelopwar.mb.txt All rights reserved.

Pp. 447–465: "The Apology" by Plato, translated by Benjamin Jowett. From the Internet, http://promo.net/pg/authors/platocircabc.html and ftp://sunsite.unc.edu/pub/docs/ books/gutenberg/etext99/crito10.txt All rights reserved.

Pp. 466–485: Selections from *The Republic* by Plato, translated by Benjamin Jowett. From Internet, http://promo.net/pg/authors/platocircabc.html#apology All rights reserved.

Pp. 489–508: Excerpts from "On Friendship" by Cicero, translated by Evelyn S. Shuckburgh. From Internet, http://www.fordham.edu/halsall/ancient/cicero-friendship.html All rights reserved.

Pp. 509–612: *The Aeneid* by Virgil from *The Aeneid of Virgil, A Verse Translation*, translated by Rolfe Humphries. Copyright © 1951 by Charles Scribner's Sons. All rights reserved.

Pp. 613–622: "Amores (Selections)" by Ovid from *The Erotic Poems* by Ovid, translated by Peter Green (Penguin Classics, 1982) copyright © Peter Green, 1982. Reproduced by permission of Penguin Books Ltd.

Pp. 623–656: *Metamorphoses* by Ovid, translated by Rolfe Humphries. Copyright © 1955 Indiana University Press. Reprinted by permission of Indiana University Press.

CONTENTS

Unit II: Greece (continued)

Unit III: Rome

Unit III: Rome (continued)

Unit IV: Early Middle Ages

Unit IV: Early Middle Ages (continued)

PROLOGUE

Readings in Western Civilization are three custom anthologies designed for the Providence College Western Civilization Program. The selected primary works represent an attempt to include the most obvious works and ideas which have shaped our western cultural identities.

As cultural studies in colleges and universities have expanded to be global, so too the commercial anthologies that service such courses have grown to include selections from world literatures, with the increased breadth accompanied by increased heft and cost. The western focus which these custom volumes contain, partial as it is, reflects a conscious effort to provide depth and focus on the western heritages by which we, in the west (regardless of race, ethnicity, or place of origin), have been historically shaped—at least up until the nineteenth century. The Providence College Western Civilization Program, and these volumes, trace that cultural bias, expanding the inclusions to the global as the past moves to the present and cultural influences are no longer contained by geography.

The idea of creating custom anthologies means that the selections can be altered and supplemented as needs, interests, and themes suggest. These volumes are not collections of perfect texts perfectly edited. Many translations are arguably the best to be had; many translations and texts are from public domain sources, and in these cases the editors tried not to sacrifice quality to cost. In this they may not have always succeeded. The volumes therefore constitute an open invitation to students and instructors to read carefully, question thoughtfully, and make suggestions for ongoing improvement of the present work.

Brian Barbour
Terrie Curran

I: MESOPOTAMIA

1. GILGAMESH
(c. 2000 BCE)

(trans. by Nancy K. Sanders)

The Mesopotamian epic of Gilgamesh *tells of a legendary king of Uruk who discovers the meaning of friendship and, upon its loss, journeys in search of immortality. His failure to achieve eternal life indicates Mesopotamian pessimism about the relationship of the gods and humans and recognition that the most they may hope for are limited earthly joys of family, food, and security within the strong walls of the city Gilgamesh built. Parts of the story can be traced back to Sumerian sources from the third millennium BCE, though the extant fragments we have are from seventh century BCE Akkadian clay tablets.*

PROLOGUE

Gilgamesh King in Uruk

I will proclaim to the world the deeds of Gilgamesh. This was the man to whom all things were known; this was the king who knew the countries of the world. He was wise, he saw mysteries and knew secret things, he brought us a tale of the days before the flood. He went on a long journey, was weary, worn-out
5   with labour, returning he rested, he engraved on a stone the whole story.
When the gods created Gilgamesh they gave him a perfect body. Shamash[1] the glorious sun endowed him with beauty, Adad the god of the storm endowed him with courage, the great gods made his beauty perfect, surpassing all others, terrifying like a great wild bull. Two thirds they made him god and one third man.
10   In Uruk[2] he built walls, a great rampart, and the temple of blessed Eanna for the god of the firmament Anu,[3] and for Ishtar the goddess of love. Look at it still today: the outer wall where the cornice runs, it shines with the brilliance of copper; and the inner wall, it has no equal. Touch the threshold, it is ancient. Approach Eanna the dwelling of Ishtar, our lady of love and war, the like of

---

[1]Also judge and lawgiver, with some fertility attributes; he is the husband and brother of Ishtar, goddess of love, fertility, and war and queen of heaven.

[2]City in southern Babylonia between Fara and Ur. Shown by excavation to have been an important city from very early times, with great temples to the gods Anu and Ishtar. After the Flood it was the seat of a dynasty of kings, among whom Gilgamesh was the fifth and most famous.

[3]Also father of the gods; he had an important temple in Uruk. Eanna was the temple precinct in Uruk, sacred to Anu and Ishtar.

15 which no latter-day king, no man alive can equal. Climb upon the wall of Uruk; walk along it, I say; regard the foundation terrace and examine the masonry: is it not burnt brick and good? The seven sages[4] laid the foundations.

1: THE COMING OF ENKIDU

Gilgamesh went abroad in the world, but he met with none who could withstand his arms till he came to Uruk. But the men of Uruk muttered in their
20 houses, "Gilgamesh sounds the tocsin[5] for his amusement, his arrogance has no bounds by day or night. No son is left with his father, for Gilgamesh takes them all, even the children; yet the king should be a shepherd to his people. His lust leaves no virgin to her lover, neither the warrior's daughter nor the wife of the noble; yet this is the shepherd of the city, wise, comely, and resolute."
25 The gods heard their lament, the gods of heaven cried to the Lord of Uruk, to Anu the god of Uruk: "A goddess made him, strong as a savage bull, none can withstand his arms. No son is left with his father, for Gilgamesh takes them all; and is this the king, the shepherd of his people? His lust leaves no virgin to her lover, neither the warrior's daughter nor the wife of the noble." When Anu had
30 heard their lamentation the gods cried to Aruru, the goddess of creation, "You made him, O Aruru, now create his equal; let it be as like him as his own reflection, his second self, stormy heart for stormy heart. Let them contend together and leave Uruk in quiet."
So the goddess conceived an image in her mind, and it was of the stuff of Anu
35 of the firmament. She dipped her hands in water and pinched off clay, she let it fall in the wilderness, and noble Enkidu was created. There was virtue in him of the god of war, of Ninurta himself. His body was rough, he had long hair like a woman's; it waved like the hair of Nisaba, the goddess of corn. His body was covered with matted hair like Samuqan's, the god of cattle. He was innocent of
40 mankind; he knew nothing of the cultivated land.
Enkidu ate grass in the hills with the gazelle and lurked with wild beasts at the water-holes; he had joy of the water with the herds of wild game. But there was a trapper who met him one day face to face at the drinking-hole, for the wild game had entered his territory. On three days he met him face to face, and the
45 trapper was frozen with fear. He went back to his house with the game he had caught, and he was dumb, benumbed with terror. His face was altered like that of one who has made a long journey. With awe in his heart he spoke to his father: "Father, there is a man, unlike any other, who comes down from the hills. He is the strongest in the world, he is like an immortal from heaven. He ranges over the hills
50 with wild beasts and eats grass; he ranges through your land and comes down to the wells. I am afraid and dare not go near him. He fills in the pits which I dig and

---

[4]Wise men who brought civilization to the seven oldest cities of Mesopotamia.
[5]tocsin: an alarm or urgent warning.

tears up my traps set for the game; he helps the beasts to escape and now they slip through my fingers."

55   His father opened his mouth and said to the trapper, "My son, in Uruk lives Gilgamesh; no one has ever prevailed against him, he is strong as a star from heaven. Go to Uruk, find Gilgamesh, extol the strength of this wild man. Ask him to give you a harlot, a wanton from the temple of love; return with her, and let her woman's power overpower this man. When next he comes down to drink at the wells she will be there, stripped naked; and when he sees her beckoning he will

60 embrace her, and then the wild beasts will reject him."

   So the trapper set out on his journey to Uruk and addressed himself to Gilgamesh saying, "A man unlike any other is roaming now in the pastures; he is as strong as a star from heaven and I am afraid to approach him. He helps the wild game to escape; he fills in my pits and pulls up my traps." Gilgamesh said,

65 "Trapper, go back, take with you a harlot, a child of pleasure. At the drinking-hole she will strip, and when he sees her beckoning he will embrace her and the game of the wilderness will surely reject him."

   Now the trapper returned, taking the harlot with him. After a three days' journey they came to the drinking-hole, and there they sat down; the harlot and the

70 trapper sat facing one another and waited for the game to come. For the first day and for the second day the two sat waiting, but on the third day the herds came; they came down to drink and Enkidu was with them. The small wild creatures of the plains were glad of the water, and Enkidu with them, who ate grass with the gazelle and was born in the hills; and she saw him, the savage man, come from far-

75 off in the hills. The trapper spoke to her: "There he is. Now, woman, make your breasts bare, have no shame, do not delay but welcome his love. Let him see you naked, let him possess your body. When he comes near uncover yourself and lie with him, teach him, the savage man, your woman's art, for when he murmurs love to you the wild beasts that shared his life in the hills will reject him."

80   She was not ashamed to take him, she made herself naked and welcomed his eagerness; as he lay on her murmuring love she taught him the woman's art. For six days and seven nights they lay together, for Enkidu had forgotten his home in the hills; but when he was satisfied he went back to the wild beasts. Then, when the gazelle saw him, they bolted away; when the wild creatures saw him they fled.

85 Enkidu would have followed, but his body was bound as though with a cord, his knees gave way when he started to run, his swiftness was gone. And now the wild creatures had all fled away; Enkidu was grown weak, for wisdom was in him, and the thoughts of a man were in his heart. So he returned and sat down at the woman's feet, and listened intently to what she said. "You are wise, Enkidu, and

90 now you have become like a god. Why do you want to run wild with the beasts in the hills? Come with me. I will take you to strong-walled Uruk, to the blessed temple of Ishtar and of Anu, of love and of heaven: there Gilgamesh lives, who is very strong, and like a wild bull he lords it over men."

   When she had spoken Enkidu was pleased; he longed for a comrade, for one

95 who would understand his heart. "Come, woman, and take me to that holy temple,

to the house of Anu and of Ishtar, and to the place where Gilgamesh lords it over the people. I will challenge him boldly, I will cry out aloud in Uruk, 'I am the strongest here, I have come to change the old order, I am he who was born in the hills, I am he who is strongest of all.'"

100 She said, "Let us go, and let him see your face. I know very well Gilgamesh is in great Uruk. O Enkidu, there all the people are dressed in their gorgeous robes, every day is holiday, the young men and the girls are wonderful to see. How sweet they smell! All the great ones are roused from their beds. O Enkidu, you who love life, I will show you Gilgamesh, a man of many moods; you shall look at him well

105 in his radiant manhood. His body is perfect in strength and maturity; he never rests by night or day. He is stronger than you, so leave your boasting. Shamash the glorious sun has given favours to Gilgamesh, and Anu of the heavens, and Enlil, and Ea the wise has given him deep understanding. I tell you, even before you have left the wilderness, Gilgamesh will know in his dreams that you are coming."

110 Now Gilgamesh got up to tell his dream to his mother, Ninsun, one of the wise gods. "Mother, last night I had a dream. I was full of joy, the young heroes were round me and I walked through the night under stars of the firmament, and one, a meteor of the stuff of Anu, fell down from heaven. I tried to lift it but it proved too heavy. All the people of Uruk came round to see it, the common people jostled and

115 the nobles thronged to kiss its feet; and to me its attraction was like the love of woman. They helped me, I braced my forehead and I raised it with thongs and brought it to you, and you yourself pronounced it my brother."

Then Ninsun, who is well-beloved and wise, said to Gilgamesh, "This star of heaven which descended like a meteor from the sky; which you tried to lift, but

120 found too heavy, when you tried to move it it would not budge, and so you brought it to my feet; I made it for you, a goad and spur, and you were drawn as though to a woman. This is the strong comrade, the one who brings help to his friend in his need. He is the strongest of wild creatures, the stuff of Anu; born in the grass-lands and the wild hills reared him; when you see him you will be glad; you will love

125 him as a woman and he will never forsake you. This is the meaning of the dream."

Gilgamesh said, "Mother, I dreamed a second dream. In the streets of strong-walled Uruk there lay an axe; the shape of it was strange and the people thronged round. I saw it and was glad. I bent down, deeply drawn towards it; I loved it like a woman and wore it at my side." Ninsun answered, "That axe, which you saw,

130 which drew you so powerfully like love of a woman, that is the comrade whom I give you, and he will come in his strength like one of the host of heaven. He is the brave companion who rescues his friend in necessity." Gilgamesh said to his mother, "A friend, a counsellor has come to me from Enlil, and now I shall befriend and counsel him." So Gilgamesh told his dreams; and the harlot retold them to

135 Enkidu.

And now she said to Enkidu, "When I look at you you have become like a god. Why do you yearn to run wild again with the beasts in the hills? Get up from the ground, the bed of a shepherd." He listened to her words with care. It was good advice that she gave. She divided her clothing in two and with the one half she

140   clothed him and with the other herself; and holding his hand she led him like a
child to the sheepfolds, into the shepherds' tents. There all the shepherds crowded
round to see him, they put down bread in front of him, but Enkidu could only suck
the milk of wild animals. He fumbled and gaped, at a loss what to do or how he
should eat the bread and drink the strong wine. Then the woman said, "Enkidu,
145   eat bread, it is the staff of life; drink the wine, it is the custom of the land." So he
ate till he was full and drank strong wine, seven goblets. He became merry, his
heart exulted and his face shone. He rubbed down the matted hair of his body and
anointed himself with oil. Enkidu had become a man; but when he had put on
man's clothing he appeared like a bridegroom. He took arms to hunt the lion so
150   that the shepherds could rest at night. He caught wolves and lions and the
herdsmen lay down in peace; for Enkidu was their watchman, that strong man
who had no rival.

    He was merry living with the shepherds, till one day lifting his eyes he saw a
man approaching. He said to the harlot, "Woman, fetch that man here. Why has he
155   come? I wish to know his name." She went and called the man saying, "Sir, where
are you going on this weary journey?" The man answered, saying to Enkidu,
"Gilgamesh has gone into the marriage-house and shut out the people. He does
strange things in Uruk, the city of great streets. At the roll of the drum work begins
for the men, and work for the women. Gilgamesh the king is about to celebrate
160   marriage with the Queen of Love, and he still demands to be first with the bride,
the king to be first and the husband to follow, for that was ordained by the gods
from his birth, from the time the umbilical cord was cut. But now the drums roll for
the choice of the bride and the city groans." At these words Enkidu turned white
in the face. "I will go to the place where Gilgamesh lords it over the people, I will
165   challenge him boldly, and I will cry aloud in Uruk, 'I have come to change the old
order, for I am the strongest here.'"

    Now Enkidu strode in front and the woman followed behind. He entered
Uruk, that great market, and all the folk thronged round him where he stood in the
street in strong-walled Uruk. The people jostled; speaking of him they said, "He is
170   the spit of Gilgamesh." "He is shorter." "He is bigger of bone." "This is the one
who was reared on the milk of wild beasts. His is the greatest strength." The men
rejoiced: "Now Gilgamesh has met his match. This great one, this hero whose
beauty is like a god, he is a match even for Gilgamesh."

    In Uruk the bridal bed was made, fit for the goddess of love. The bride waited
175   for the bridegroom, but in the night Gilgamesh got up and came to the house. Then
Enkidu stepped out, he stood in the street and blocked the way. Mighty Gilgamesh
came on and Enkidu met him at the gate. He put out his foot and prevented
Gilgamesh from entering the house, so they grappled, holding each other like bulls.
They broke the doorposts and the walls shook, they snorted like bulls locked
180   together. They shattered the doorposts and the walls shook. Gilgamesh bent his
knee with his foot planted on the ground and with a turn Enkidu was thrown.
Then immediately his fury died. When Enkidu was thrown he said to Gilgamesh,
"There is not another like you in the world. Ninsun, who is as strong as a wild ox

185   in the byre, she was the mother who bore you, and now you are raised above all men, and Enlil has given you the kingship, for your strength surpasses the strength of men." So Enkidu and Gilgamesh embraced and their friendship was sealed.

2: THE FOREST JOURNEY

Enlil of the mountain, the father of the gods,[6] had decreed the destiny of Gilgamesh. So Gilgamesh dreamed and Enkidu said, "The meaning of the dream is this. The father of the gods has given you kingship, such is your destiny,
190   everlasting life is not your destiny. Because of this do not be sad at heart, do not be grieved or oppressed. He has given you power to bind and to loose, to be the darkness and the light of mankind. He has given you unexampled supremacy over the people, victory in battle from which no fugitive returns, in forays and assaults from which there is no going back. But do not abuse this power, deal justly with
195   your servants in the palace, deal justly before Shamash."

The eyes of Enkidu were full of tears and his heart was sick. He sighed bitterly and Gilgamesh met his eye and said, "My friend, why do you sigh so bitterly?" But Enkidu opened his mouth and said, "I am weak, my arms have lost their strength, the cry of sorrow sticks in my throat, I am oppressed by idleness." It
200   was then that the lord Gilgamesh turned his thoughts to the Country of the Living; on the Land of Cedars the lord Gilgamesh reflected. He said to his servant Enkidu, "I have not established my name stamped on bricks as my destiny decreed; therefore I will go to the country where the cedar is felled. I will set up my name in the place where the names of famous men are written, and where no man's name is
205   written yet I will raise a monument to the gods. Because of the evil that is in the land, we will go to the forest and destroy the evil; for in the forest lives Humbaba whose name is 'Hugeness,' a ferocious giant." But Enkidu sighed bitterly and said, "When I went with the wild beasts ranging through the wilderness I discovered the forest; its length is ten thousand leagues in every direction. Enlil has appointed
210   Humbaba to guard it and armed him in sevenfold terrors, terrible to all flesh is Humbaba. When he roars it is like the torrent of the storm, his breath is like fire, and his jaws are death itself. He guards the cedars so well that when the wild heifer stirs in the forest, though she is sixty leagues distant, he hears her. What man would willingly walk into that country and explore its depths? I tell you,
215   weakness overpowers whoever goes near it: it is not an equal struggle when one fights with Humbaba; he is a great warrior, a battering-ram. Gilgamesh, the watchman of the forest never sleeps."

Gilgamesh replied: "Where is the man who can clamber to heaven? Only the gods live for ever with glorious Shamash, but as for us men, our days are
220   numbered, our occupations are a breath of wind. How is this, already you are afraid! I will go first although I am your lord, and you may safely call out, 'Forward, there is nothing to fear!' Then if I fall I leave behind me a name that

---

[6]The breath and "word" of Anu; he is also god of earth, wind, and spirit.

endures; men will say of me, 'Gilgamesh has fallen in fight with ferocious Humbaba.' Long after the child has been born in my house, they will say it, and
225   remember." Enkidu spoke again to Gilgamesh, "O my lord, if you will enter that country, go first to the hero Shamash, tell the Sun God, for the land is his. The country where the cedar is cut belongs to Shamash."

    Gilgamesh took up a kid, white without spot, and a brown one with it; he held them against his breast, and he carried them into the presence of the sun. He
230   took in his hand his silver sceptre and he said to glorious Shamash, "I am going to that country, O Shamash, I am going; my hands supplicate, so let it be well with my soul and bring me back to the quay of Uruk. Grant, I beseech, your protection, and let the omen be good." Glorious Shamash answered, "Gilgamesh, you are strong, but what is the Country of the Living to you?"

235   "O Shamash, hear me, hear me, Shamash, let my voice be heard. Here in the city man dies oppressed at heart, man perishes with despair in his heart. I have looked over the wall and I see the bodies floating on the river, and that will be my lot also. Indeed I know it is so, for whoever is tallest among men cannot reach the heavens, and the greatest cannot encompass the earth. Therefore I would enter that
240   country: because I have not established my name stamped on brick as my destiny decreed, I will go to the country where the cedar is cut. I will set up my name where the names of famous men are written; and where no man's name is written I will raise a monument to the gods." The tears ran down his face and he said, "Alas, it is a long journey that I must take to the Land of Humbaba. If this
245   enterprise is not to be accomplished, why did you move me, Shamash, with the restless desire to perform it? How can I succeed if you will not succour me? If I die in that country I will die without rancour, but if I return I will make a glorious offering of gifts and of praise to Shamash."

    So Shamash accepted the sacrifice of his tears; like the compassionate man he
250   showed him mercy. He appointed strong allies for Gilgamesh, sons of one mother, and stationed them in the mountain caves. The great winds he appointed: the north wind, the whirlwind, the storm and the icy wind, the tempest and the scorching wind. Like vipers, like dragons, like a scorching fire, like a serpent that freezes the heart, a destroying flood and the lightning's fork, such were they and Gilgamesh
255   rejoiced.

    He went to the forge and said, "I will give orders to the armourers; they shall cast us our weapons while we watch them." So they gave orders to the armourers and the craftsmen sat down in conference. They went into the groves of the plain and cut willow and box-wood; they cast for them axes of nine score pounds, and
260   great swords they cast with blades of six score pounds each one, with pommels and hilts of thirty pounds. They cast for Gilgamesh the axe "Might of Heroes" and the bow of Anshan;[7] and Gilgamesh was armed and Enkidu; and the weight of the arms they carried was thirty score pounds.

---

[7]Anshan—A district of Elam in southwest Persia; probably the source of supplies of wood for making bows.

The people collected and the counsellors in the streets and in the market-place
265   of Uruk; they came through the gate of seven bolts and Gilgamesh spoke to them in
the market-place: "I, Gilgamesh, go to see that creature of whom such things are
spoken, the rumour of whose name fills the world. I will conquer him in his cedar
wood and show the strength of the sons of Uruk, all the world shall know of it. I
am committed to this enterprise: to climb the mountain, to cut down the cedar, and
270   leave behind me an enduring name." The counsellors of Uruk, the great market,
answered him, "Gilgamesh, you are young, your courage carries you too far, you
cannot know what this enterprise means which you plan. We have heard that
Humbaba is not like men who die, his weapons are such that none can stand
against them; the forest stretches for ten thousand leagues in every direction; who
275   would willingly go down to explore its depths? As for Humbaba, when he roars it
is like the torrent of the storm, his breath is like fire and his jaws are death itself.
Why do you crave to do this thing, Gilgamesh? It is no equal struggle when one
fights with Humbaba, that battering-ram."

When he heard these words of the counsellors Gilgamesh looked at his friend
280   and laughed, "How shall I answer them; shall I say I am afraid of Humbaba, I will
sit at home all the rest of my days?" Then Gilgamesh opened his mouth again and
said to Enkidu, "My friend, let us go to the Great Palace, to Egalmah,[8] and stand
before Ninsun the queen. Ninsun is wise with deep knowledge, she will give us
counsel for the road we must go." They took each other by the hand as they went
285   to Egalmah, and they went to Ninsun the great queen. Gilgamesh approached, he
entered the palace and spoke to Ninsun. "Ninsun, will you listen to me; I have a
long journey to go, to the Land of Humbaba, I must travel an unknown road and
fight a strange battle. From the day I go until I return, till I reach the cedar forest
and destroy the evil which Shamash abhors, pray for me to Shamash."

290   Ninsun went into her room, she put on a dress becoming to her body, she put
on jewels to make her breast beautiful, she placed a tiara on her head and her
skirts swept the ground. Then she went up to the altar of the Sun, standing upon
the roof of the palace; she burnt incense and lifted her arms to Shamash as the
smoke ascended: "O Shamash, why did you give this restless heart to Gilgamesh,
295   my son; why did you give it? You have moved him and now he sets out on a long
journey to the Land of Humbaba to travel an unknown road and fight a strange
battle. Therefore from the day that he goes till the day he returns, until he reaches
the cedar forest, until he kills Humbaba and destroys the evil thing which you,
Shamash, abhor, do not forget him; but let the dawn, Aya, your dear bride, remind
300   you always, and when day is done give him to the watchman of the night to keep
him from harm." Then Ninsun the mother of Gilgamesh extinguished the incense,
and she called to Enkidu with this exhortation: "Strong Enkidu, you are not the
child of my body, but I will receive you as my adopted son; you are my other child
like the foundlings they bring to the temple. Serve Gilgamesh as a foundling serves
305   the temple and the priestess who reared him. In the presence of my women, my

---

[8]Egalmah—home of the goddess Ninsun.

votaries and hierophants,[9] I declare it." Then she placed the amulet for a pledge round his neck, and she said to him, "I entrust my son to you; bring him back to me safely."

And now they brought to them the weapons, they put in their hands the great
310   swords in their golden scabbards, and the bow and the quiver. Gilgamesh took the axe, he slung the quiver from his shoulder, and the bow of Anshan, and buckled the sword to his belt; and so they were armed and ready for the journey. Now all the people came and pressed on them and said, "When will you return to the city?" The counsellors blessed Gilgamesh and warned him, "Do not trust too much in
315   your own strength, be watchful, restrain your blows at first. The one who goes in front protects his companion; the good guide who knows the way guards his friend. Let Enkidu lead the way, he knows the road to the forest, he has seen Humbaba and is experienced in battles; let him press first into the passes, let him be watchful and look to himself. Let Enkidu protect his friend, and guard his
320   companion, and bring him safe through the pitfalls of the road. We, the counsellors of Uruk entrust our king to you, O Enkidu; bring him back safely to us." Again to Gilgamesh they said, "May Shamash give you your heart's desire, may he let you see with your eyes the thing accomplished which your lips have spoken; may he open a path for you where it is blocked, and a road for your feet to tread. May he
325   open the mountains for your crossing, and may the nighttime bring you the blessings of night, and Lugulbanda, your guardian god, stand beside you for victory. May you have victory in the battle as though you fought with a child. Wash your feet in the river of Humbaba to which you are journeying; in the evening dig a well, and let there always be pure water in your water-skin. Offer
330   cold water to Shamash and do not forget Lugulbanda."

Then Enkidu opened his mouth and said, "Forward, there is nothing to fear. Follow me, for I know the place where Humbaba lives and the paths where he walks. Let the counsellors go back. Here is no cause for fear." When the counsellors heard this they sped the hero on his way. "Go, Gilgamesh, may your
335   guardian god protect you on the road and bring you safely back to the quay of Uruk."

After twenty leagues they broke their fast; after another thirty leagues they stopped for the night. Fifty leagues they walked in one day; in three days they had walked as much as a journey of a month and two weeks. They crossed seven
340   mountains before they came to the gate of the forest. Then Enkidu called out to Gilgamesh, "Do not go down into the forest; when I opened the gate my hand lost its strength." Gilgamesh answered him, "Dear friend, do not speak like a coward. Have we got the better of so many dangers and travelled so far, to turn back at last? You, who are tried in wars and battles, hold close to me now and you will
345   feel no fear of death; keep beside me and your weakness will pass, the trembling will leave your hand. Would my friend rather stay behind? No, we will go down together into the heart of the forest. Let your courage be roused by the battle to

---

[9]hierophants—priests.

350 come; forget death and follow me, a man resolute in action, but one who is not foolhardy. When two go together each will protect himself and shield his companion, and if they fall they leave an enduring name."

Together they went down into the forest and they came to the green mountain. There they stood still, they were struck dumb; they stood still and gazed at the forest. They saw the height of the cedar, they saw the way into the forest and the track where Humbaba was used to walk. The way was broad and the going was 355 good. They gazed at the mountain of cedars, the dwelling- place of the gods and the throne of Ishtar. The hugeness of the cedar rose in front of the mountain, its shade was beautiful, full of comfort; mountain and glade were green with brushwood.

There Gilgamesh dug a well before the setting sun. He went up the mountain and poured out fine meal on the ground and said, "O mountain, dwelling of the 360 gods, bring me a favourable dream." Then they took each other by the hand and lay down to sleep; and sleep that flows from the night lapped over them. Gilgamesh dreamed, and at midnight sleep left him, and he told his dream to his friend. "Enkidu, what was it that woke me if you did not? My friend, I have dreamed a dream. Get up, look at the mountain precipice. The sleep that the gods sent me is 365 broken. Ah, my friend, what a dream I have had! Terror and confusion; I seized hold of a wild bull in the wilderness. It bellowed and beat up the dust till the whole sky was dark, my arm was seized and my tongue bitten. I fell back on my knee; then someone refreshed me with water from his water-skin."

Enkidu said, "Dear friend, the god to whom we are travelling is no wild bull 370 though his form is mysterious. That wild bull which you saw is Shamash the Protector; in our moment of peril he will take our hands. The one who gave water from his water-skin, that is your own god who cares for your good name, your Lugulbanda. United with him, together we will accomplish a work the fame of which will never die."

375 Gilgamesh said, "I dreamed again. We stood in a deep gorge of the mountain, and beside it we two were like the smallest of swamp flies; and suddenly the mountain fell, it struck me and caught my feet from under me. Then came an intolerable light blazing out, and in it was one whose grace and whose beauty were greater than the beauty of this world. He pulled me out from under the 380 mountain, he gave me water to drink and my heart was comforted, and he set my feet on the ground."

Then Enkidu the child of the plains said, "Let us go down from the mountain and talk this thing over together." He said to Gilgamesh the young god, "Your dream is good, your dream is excellent, the mountain which you saw is Humbaba. 385 Now, surely, we will seize and kill him, and throw his body down as the mountain fell on the plain."

The next day after twenty leagues they broke their fast, and after another thirty they stopped for the night. They dug a well before the sun had set and Gilgamesh ascended the mountain. He poured out fine meal on the ground and said, 390 "O mountain, dwelling of the gods, send a dream for Enkidu, make him a favourable dream." The mountain fashioned a dream for Enkidu; it came, an ominous dream; a cold shower passed over him, it caused him to cower like the mountain barley under a storm of rain. But Gilgamesh sat with his chin on his knees till the sleep which flows over all mankind lapped over him. Then, at

395 midnight, sleep left him; he got up and said to his friend, "Did you call me, or why did I wake? Did you touch me, or why am I terrified? Did not some god pass by, for my limbs are numb with fear? My friend, I saw a third dream and this dream was altogether frightful. The heavens roared and the earth roared again, daylight failed and darkness fell, lightning flashed, fire blazed out, the clouds lowered,

400 they rained down death. Then the brightness departed, the fire went out, and all was turned to ashes fallen about us. Let us go down from the mountain and talk this over, and consider what we should do."

When they had come down from the mountain Gilgamesh seized the axe in his hand: he felled the cedar. When Humbaba heard the noise far off he was enraged;

405 he cried out, "Who is this that has violated my woods and cut down my cedar?" But glorious Shamash called to them out of heaven, "Go forward, do not be afraid." But now Gilgamesh was overcome by weakness, for sleep had seized him suddenly, a profound sleep held him; he lay on the ground, stretched out speechless, as though in a dream. When Enkidu touched him he did not rise, when

410 he spoke to him he did not reply. "O Gilgamesh, Lord of the plain of Kullab,[10] the world grows dark, the shadows have spread over it, now is the glimmer of dusk. Shamash has departed, his bright head is quenched in the bosom of his mother Ningal. O Gilgamesh, how long will you lie like this, asleep? Never let the mother who gave you birth be forced in mourning into the city square."

415 At length Gilgamesh heard him; he put on his breastplate, "The Voice of Heroes," of thirty shekels' weight; he put it on as though it had been a light garment that he carried, and it covered him altogether. He straddled the earth like a bull that snuffs the ground and his teeth were clenched. "By the life of my mother Ninsun who gave me birth, and by the life of my father, divine Lugulbanda, let me

420 live to be the wonder of my mother, as when she nursed me on her lap." A second time he said to him, "By the life of Ninsun my mother who gave me birth, and by the life of my father, divine Lugulbanda, until we have fought this man, if man he is, this god, if god he is, the way that I took to the Country of the Living will not turn back to the city."

425 Then Enkidu, the faithful companion, pleaded, answering him, "O my lord, you do not know this monster and that is the reason you are not afraid. I who know him, I am terrified. His teeth are dragon's fangs, his countenance is like a lion, his charge is the rushing of the flood, with his look he crushes alike the trees of the forest and reeds in the swamp. O my Lord, you may go on if you choose into

430 this land, but I will go back to the city. I will tell the lady your mother all your glorious deeds till she shouts for joy: and then I will tell the death that followed till she weeps for bitterness." But Gilgamesh said, "Immolation and sacrifice are not yet for me, the boat of the dead shall not go down, nor the three-ply cloth be cut

---

[10]In Uruk.

435   for my shrouding. Not yet will my people be desolate, nor the pyre be lit in my house and my dwelling burnt on the fire. Today, give me your aid and you shall have mine: what then can go amiss with us two? All living creatures born of the flesh shall sit at last in the boat of the West, and when it sinks, when the boat of Magilum[11] sinks, they are gone; but we shall go forward and fix our eyes on this monster. If your heart is fearful throw away fear; if there is terror in it throw
440   away terror. Take your axe in your hand and attack. He who leaves the fight unfinished is not at peace."

       Humbaba came out from his strong house of cedar. Then Enkidu called out, "O Gilgamesh, remember now your boasts in Uruk. Forward, attack, son of Uruk, there is nothing to fear." When he heard these words his courage rallied; he
445   answered, "Make haste, close in, if the watchman is there do not let him escape to the woods where he will vanish. He has put on the first of his seven splendours[12] but not yet the other six, let us trap him before he is armed." Like a raging wild bull he snuffed the ground; the watchman of the woods turned full of threatenings; he cried out. Humbaba came from his strong house of cedar. He nodded his head
450   and shook it, menacing Gilgamesh; and on him he fastened his eye, the eye of death. Then Gilgamesh called to Shamash and his tears were flowing, "O glorious Shamash, I have followed the road you commanded but now if you send no succour how shall I escape?" Glorious Shamash heard his prayer and he summoned the great wind, the north wind, the whirlwind, the storm and the icy
455   wind, the tempest and the scorching wind; they came like dragons, like a scorching fire, like a serpent that freezes the heart, a destroying flood and the lightning's fork. The eight winds rose up against Humbaba, they beat against his eyes; he was gripped, unable to go forward or back. Gilgamesh shouted, "By the life of Ninsun my mother and divine Lugulbanda my father, in the Country of the Living, in this
460   Land I have discovered your dwelling; my weak arms and my small weapons I have brought to this Land against you, and now I will enter your house."

       So he felled the first cedar and they cut the branches and laid them at the foot of the mountain. At the first stroke Humbaba blazed out, but still they advanced. They felled seven cedars and cut and bound the branches and laid them at the foot
465   of the mountain, and seven times Humbaba loosed his glory on them. As the seventh blaze died out they reached his lair. He slapped his thigh in scorn. He approached like a noble wild bull roped on the mountain, a warrior whose elbows are bound together. The tears started to his eyes and he was pale, "Gilgamesh, let me speak. I have never known a mother, no, nor a father who reared me. I was born of the
470   mountain, he reared me, and Enlil made me the keeper of this forest. Let me go free, Gilgamesh, and I will be your servant, you shall be my lord; all the trees of the forest that I tended on the mountain shall be yours. I will cut them down and build you a palace." He took him by the hand and led him to his house, so that the heart of Gilgamesh was moved with compassion. He swore by the heavenly life, by the

---

[11]Unclear; perhaps the boat of the dead.
[12]Unclear; perhaps warlike attributes.

475 earthly life, by the underworld itself: "O Enkidu, should not the snared bird return to its nest and the captive man return to his mother's arms?" Enkidu answered, "The strongest of men will fall to fate if he has no judgement. Namtar, the evil fate that knows no distinction between men, will devour him. If the snared bird returns to its nest, if the captive man returns to his mother's arms, then you my
480 friend will never return to the city where the mother is waiting who gave you birth. He will bar the mountain road against you, and make the pathways impassable."

Humbaba said, "Enkidu, what you have spoken is evil: you, a hireling, dependent for your bread! In envy and for fear of a rival you have spoken evil
485 words." Enkidu said, "Do not listen, Gilgamesh: this Humbaba must die. Kill Humbaba first and his servants after." But Gilgamesh said, "If we touch him the blaze and the glory of light will be put out in confusion, the glory and glamour will vanish, its rays will be quenched." Enkidu said to Gilgamesh, "Not so, my friend. First entrap the bird, and where shall the chicks run then? Afterwards we
490 can search out the glory and the glamour, when the chicks run distracted through the grass."

Gilgamesh listened to the word of his companion, he took the axe in his hand, he drew the sword from his belt, and he struck Humbaba with a thrust of the sword to the neck, and Enkidu his comrade struck the second blow. At the third
495 blow Humbaba fell. Then there followed confusion for this was the guardian of the forest whom they had felled to the ground. For as far as two leagues the cedars shivered when Enkidu felled the watcher of the forest, he at whose voice Hermon and Lebanon[13] used to tremble. Now the mountains were moved and all the hills, for the guardian of the forest was killed. They attacked the cedars, the seven
500 splendours of Humbaba were extinguished. So they pressed on into the forest bearing the sword of eight talents. They uncovered the sacred dwellings of the Anunnaki[14] and while Gilgamesh felled the first of the trees of the forest Enkidu cleared their roots as far as the banks of Euphrates. They set Humbaba before the gods, before Enlil; they kissed the ground and dropped the shroud and set the head
505 before him. When he saw the head of Humbaba, Enlil raged at them. "Why did you do this thing? From henceforth may the fire be on your faces, may it eat the bread that you eat, may it drink where you drink." Then Enlil took again the blaze and the seven splendours that had been Humbaba's: he gave the first to the river, and he gave to the lion, to the stone of execration, to the mountain and to the dreaded
510 daughter of the Queen of Hell.

O Gilgamesh, king and conqueror of the dreadful blaze; wild bull who plunders the mountain, who crosses the sea, glory to him, and from the brave the greater glory is Enki's![15]

---

[13]Mountains in Lebanon.

[14]Gods of the underworld, judges of the dead, and offspring of Anu.

[15]Or Ea, god of the sweet waters and wisdom, a patron of arts, and one of the creators of humankind, toward whom he is usually well disposed.

3. ISHTAR AND GILGAMESH, AND THE DEATH OF ENKIDU

515   Gilgamesh washed out his long locks and cleaned his weapons; he flung back his hair from his shoulders; he threw off his stained clothes and changed them for new. He put on his royal robes and made them fast. When Gilgamesh had put on the crown, glorious Ishtar lifted her eyes, seeing the beauty of Gilgamesh. She said, "Come to me Gilgamesh, and be my bridegroom; grant me seed of your body, let me be your bride and you shall be my husband. I will harness for you a chariot of
520 lapis lazuli and of gold, with wheels of gold and horns of copper; and you shall have mighty demons of the storm for draft-mules. When you enter our house in the fragrance of cedar-wood, threshold and throne will kiss your feet. Kings, rulers, and princes will bow down before you; they shall bring you tribute from the mountains and the plain. Your ewes shall drop twins and your goats triplets; your
525 pack-ass shall outrun mules; your oxen shall have no rivals, and your chariot horses shall be famous far-off for their swiftness."

    Gilgamesh opened his mouth and answered glorious Ishtar, "If I take you in marriage, what gifts can I give in return? What ointments and clothing for your body? I would gladly give you bread and all sorts of food fit for a god. I would
530 give you wine to drink fit for a queen. I would pour out barley to stuff your granary; but as for making you my wife—that I will not. How would it go with me? Your lovers have found you like a brazier which smoulders in the cold, a backdoor which keeps out neither squall of wind nor storm, a castle which crushes the garrison, pitch that blackens the bearer, a water-skin that chafes the
535 carrier, a stone which falls from the parapet, a battering-ram turned back from the enemy, a sandal that trips the wearer. Which of your lovers did you ever love for ever? What shepherd of yours has pleased you for all time? Listen to me while I tell the tale of your lovers. There was Tammuz,[16] the lover of your youth, for him you decreed wailing, year after year. You loved the many-coloured roller, but still
540 you struck and broke his wing; now in the grove he sits and cries, "kappi, kappi, my wing, my wing." You have loved the lion tremendous in strength: seven pits you dug for him, and seven. You have loved the stallion magnificent in battle, and for him you decreed whip and spur and a thong, to gallop seven leagues by force and to muddy the water before he drinks; and for his mother Silili[17] lamentations. You
545 have loved the shepherd of the flock; he made meal-cake for you day after day, he killed kids for your sake. You struck and turned him into a wolf; now his own herd-boys chase him away, his own hounds worry his flanks. And did you not love Ishullanu, the gardener of your father's palm-grove? He brought you baskets filled with dates without end; every day he loaded your table. Then you turned
550 your eyes on him and said, 'Dearest Ishullanu, come here to me, let us enjoy your manhood, come forward and take me, I am yours.' Ishullanu answered, 'What are you asking from me? My mother has baked and I have eaten; why should I come to

---

[16]The dying god of vegetation.

[17]Silili—perhaps a divine horse.

such as you for food that is tainted and rotten? For when was a screen of rushes sufficient protection from frosts?' But when you had heard his answer you struck
555 him. He was changed to a blind mole deep in the earth, one whose desire is always beyond his reach. And if you and I should be lovers, should not I be served in the same fashion as all these others whom you loved once?"

When Ishtar heard this she fell into a bitter rage, she went up to high heaven. Her tears poured down in front of her father Anu, and Antum her mother. She said,
560 "My father, Gilgamesh has heaped insults on me, he has told over all my abominable behaviour, my foul and hideous acts." Anu opened his mouth and said, "Are you a father of gods? Did not you quarrel with Gilgamesh the king, so now he has related your abominable behaviour, your foul and hideous acts?"

Ishtar opened her mouth and said again, "My father, give me the Bull of
565 Heaven to destroy Gilgamesh. Fill Gilgamesh, I say, with arrogance to his destruction; but if you refuse to give me the Bull of Heaven I will break in the doors of hell and smash the bolts; there will be confusion of people, those above with those from the lower depths. I shall bring up the dead to eat food like the living; and the hosts of dead will outnumber the living." Anu said to great Ishtar,
570 "If I do what you desire there will be seven years of drought throughout Uruk when corn will be seedless husks. Have you saved grain enough for the people and grass for the cattle?" Ishtar replied, "I have saved grain for the people, grass for the cattle; for seven years of seedless husks there is grain and there is grass enough."

575 When Anu heard what Ishtar had said he gave her the Bull of Heaven to lead by the halter down to Uruk. When they reached the gates of Uruk the Bull went to the river; with his first snort cracks opened in the earth and a hundred young men fell down to death. With his second snort cracks opened and two hundred fell down to death. With his third snort cracks opened, Enkidu doubled over but
580 instantly recovered, he dodged aside and leapt on the Bull and seized it by the horns. The Bull of Heaven foamed in his face, it brushed him with the thick of its tall. Enkidu cried to Gilgamesh, "My friend, we boasted that we would leave enduring names behind us. Now thrust in your sword between the nape and the horns." So Gilgamesh followed the Bull, he seized the thick of its tail, he thrust the
585 sword between the nape and the horns and slew the Bull. When they had killed the Bull of Heaven they cut out its heart and gave it to Shamash, and the brothers rested.

But Ishtar rose up and mounted the great wall of Uruk; she sprang on to the tower and uttered a curse: "Woe to Gilgamesh, for he has scorned me in killing the
590 Bull of Heaven." When Enkidu heard these words he tore out the Bull's right thigh and tossed it in her face saying, "If I could lay my hands on you, it is this I should do to you, and lash the entrails to your side." Then Ishtar called together her people, the dancing and singing girls, the prostitutes of the temple, the courtesans. Over the thigh of the Bull of Heaven she set up lamentation.

595 But Gilgamesh called the smiths and the armourers, all of them together. They admired the immensity of the horns. They were plated with lapis lazuli two

fingers thick. They were thirty pounds each in weight, and their capacity in oil was six measures, which he gave to his guardian god, Lugulbanda. But he carried the horns into the palace and hung them on the wall. Then they washed their hands in Euphrates, they embraced each other and went away. They drove through the streets of Uruk where the heroes were gathered to see them, and Gilgamesh called to the singing girls, "Who is most glorious of the heroes, who is most eminent among men?" "Gilgamesh is the most glorious of heroes, Gilgamesh is most eminent among men." And now there was feasting, and celebrations and joy in the palace, till the heroes lay down saying, "Now we will rest for the night."

When the daylight came Enkidu got up and cried to Gilgamesh, "O my brother, such a dream I had last night. Anu, Enlil, Ea and heavenly Shamash took counsel together, and Anu said to Enlil, 'Because they have killed the Bull of Heaven, and because they have killed Humbaba who guarded the Cedar Mountain one of the two must die.' Then glorious Shamash answered the hero Enlil, 'It was by your command they killed the Bull of Heaven, and killed Humbaba, and must Enkidu die although innocent?' Enlil flung round in rage at glorious Shamash, 'You dare to say this, you who went about with them every day like one of themselves!'"

So Enkidu lay stretched out before Gilgamesh; his tears ran down in streams and he said to Gilgamesh, "O my brother, so dear as you are to me, brother, yet they will take me from you." Again he said, "I must sit down on the threshold of the dead and never again will I see my dear brother with my eyes."

While Enkidu lay alone in his sickness he cursed the gate as though it was living flesh, "You there, wood of the gate, dull and insensible, witless, I searched for you over twenty leagues until I saw the towering cedar. There is no wood like you in our land. Seventy-two cubits high and twenty-four wide, the pivot and the ferrule and the jambs are perfect. A master craftsman from Nippur has made you; but O, if I had known the conclusion! If I had known that this was all the good that would come of it, I would have raised the axe and split you into little pieces and set up here a gate of wattle instead. Ah, if only some future king had brought you here, or some god had fashioned you. Let him obliterate my name and write his own, and the curse fall on him instead of on Enkidu."

With the first brightening of dawn Enkidu raised his head and wept before the Sun God, in the brilliance of the sunlight his tears streamed down. "Sun God, I beseech you, about that vile Trapper, that Trapper of nothing because of whom I was to catch less than my comrade; let him catch least, make his game scarce, make him feeble, taking the smaller of every share, let his quarry escape from his nets."

When he had cursed the Trapper to his heart's content he turned on the harlot. He was roused to curse her also. "As for you, woman, with a great curse I curse you! I will promise you a destiny to all eternity. My curse shall come on you soon and sudden. You shall be without a roof for your commerce, for you shall not keep house with other girls in the tavern, but do your business in places fouled by the vomit of the drunkard. Your hire will be potter's earth, your thievings will be flung into the hovel, you will sit at the cross-roads in the dust of the potter's quarter, you will make your bed on the dunghill at night, and by day take your stand in the wall's shadow. Brambles and thorns will tear your feet, the drunk and the dry will strike your cheek and your mouth will ache. Let you be stripped of your purple dyes, for I too once in the wilderness with my wife had all the treasure I wished."

645   When Shamash heard the words of Enkidu he called to him from heaven: "Enkidu, why are you cursing the woman, the mistress who taught you to eat bread fit for gods and drink wine of kings? She who put upon you a magnificent garment, did she not give you glorious Gilgamesh for your companion, and has not Gilgamesh, your own brother, made you rest on a royal bed and recline on a couch

650   at his left hand? He has made the princes of the earth kiss your feet, and now all the people of Uruk lament and wail over you. When you are dead he will let his hair grow long for your sake, he will wear a lion's pelt and wander through the desert."

When Enkidu heard glorious Shamash his angry heart grew quiet, he called

655   back the curse and said, "Woman, I promise you another destiny. The mouth which cursed you shall bless you! Kings, princes and nobles shall adore you. On your account a man though twelve miles off will clap his hand to his thigh and his hair will twitch. For you he will undo his belt and open his treasure and you shall have your desire; lapis lazuli, gold and carnelian from the heap in the treasury. A

660   ring for your hand and a robe shall be yours. The priest will lead you into the presence of the gods. On your account a wife, a mother of seven, was forsaken."

As Enkidu slept alone in his sickness, in bitterness of spirit he poured out his heart to his friend. "It was I who cut down the cedar, I who levelled the forest, I who slew Humbaba and now see what has become of me. Listen, my friend, this is

665   the dream I dreamed last night. The heavens roared, and earth rumbled back an answer; between them stood I before an awful being, the sombre-faced man-bird; he had directed on me his purpose. His was a vampire face, his foot was a lion's foot, his hand was an eagle's talon. He fell on me and his claws were in my hair, he held me fast and I smothered; then he transformed me so that my arms became

670   wings covered with feathers. He turned his stare towards me, and he led me away to the palace of Irkalla, the Queen of Darkness,[18] to the house from which none who enters ever returns, down the road from which there is no coming back.

"There is the house whose people sit in darkness; dust is their food and clay their meat. They are clothed like birds with wings for covering, they see no light,

675   they sit in darkness. I entered the house of dust and I saw the kings of the earth, their crowns put away for ever; rulers and princes, all those who once wore kingly crowns and ruled the world in the days of old. They who had stood in the place of the gods like Anu and Enlil, stood now like servants to fetch baked meats in the house of dust, to carry cooked meat and cold water from the water-skin. In

680   the house of dust which I entered were high priests and acolytes, priests of the incantation and of ecstasy; there were servers of the temple, and there was Etana, that king of Kish whom the eagle carried to heaven in the days of old. I saw also

---

[18]Also Ereshkigal, queen of the underworld.

685   Samuqan, god of cattle, and there was Ereshkigal the Queen of the Underworld; and Belit-Sheri squatted in front of her, she who is recorder of the gods and keeps the book of death. She held a tablet from which she read. She raised her head, she saw me and spoke: 'Who has brought this one here?' Then I awoke like a man drained of blood who wanders alone in a waste of rushes; like one whom the bailiff has seized and his heart pounds with terror."

690   Gilgamesh had peeled off his clothes, he listened to his words and wept quick tears, Gilgamesh listened and his tears flowed. He opened his mouth and spoke to Enkidu: "Who is there in strong-walled Uruk who has wisdom like this? Strange things have been spoken, why does your heart speak strangely? The dream was marvellous but the terror was great; we must treasure the dream whatever the terror; for the dream has shown that misery comes at last to the healthy man, the end of life is sorrow." And Gilgamesh lamented, "Now I will pray to the great gods, for my friend had an ominous dream."

695

This day on which Enkidu dreamed came to an end and he lay stricken with sickness. One whole day he lay on his bed and his suffering increased. He said to Gilgamesh, the friend on whose account he had left the wilderness, "Once I ran for you, for the water of life, and I now have nothing." A second day he lay on his bed and Gilgamesh watched over him but the sickness increased. A third day he lay on his bed, he called out to Gilgamesh, rousing him up. Now he was weak and his eyes were blind with weeping. Ten days he lay and his suffering increased, eleven and twelve days he lay on his bed of pain. Then he called to Gilgamesh, "My friend, the great goddess cursed me and I must die in shame. I shall not die like a man fallen in battle; I feared to fall, but happy is the man who falls in the battle, for I must die in shame." And Gilgamesh wept over Enkidu.

700

705

With the first light of dawn he raised his voice and said to the counsellors of Uruk:

710   Hear me, great ones of Uruk,
          I weep for Enkidu, my friend,
          Bitterly moaning like a woman mourning
          I weep for my brother.
          O Enkidu, my brother,
715   You were the axe at my side,
          My hand's strength, the sword in my belt,
          The shield before me,
          A glorious robe, my fairest ornament;
          An evil Fate has robbed me.
720   The wild ass and the gazelle
          That were father and mother,
          All long-tailed creatures that nourished you
          Weep for you,
          All the wild things of the plain and pastures;
725   The paths that you loved in the forest of cedars

Night and day murmur
Let the great ones of strong-walled Uruk
Weep for you;
Let the finger of blessing
730 Be stretched out in mourning;
Enkidu, young brother. Hark,
There is an echo through all the country
Like a mother mourning.
Weep all the paths where we walked together;
735 And the beasts we hunted, the bear and hyena,
Tiger and panther, leopard and lion,
The stag and the ibex, the bull and the doe.
The river along whose banks we used to walk,
Weeps for you,
740 Ula of Elam and dear Euphrates
Where once we drew water for the water-skins.
The mountain we climbed where we slew the Watchman,
Weeps for you.
The warriors of strong-walled Uruk
745 Where the Bull of Heaven was killed,
Weep for you.
All the people of Eridu
Weep for you Enkidu.
Those who brought grain for your eating
750 Mourn for you now;
Who rubbed oil on your back
Mourn for you now;
Who poured beer for your drinking
Mourn for you now.
755 The harlot who anointed you with fragrant ointment
Laments for you now;
The women of the palace, who brought you a wife,
A chosen ring of good advice,
Lament for you now.
760 And the young men your brothers
As though they were women
Go long-haired in mourning.
What is this sleep which holds you now?
You are lost in the dark and cannot hear me.

765 He touched his heart but it did not beat, nor did he lift his eyes again. When Gilgamesh touched his heart it did not beat. So Gilgamesh laid a veil, as one veils the bride, over his friend. He began to rage like a lion, like a lioness robbed of her whelps. This way and that he paced round the bed, he tore out his hair and

770 strewed it around. He dragged off his splendid robes and flung them down as though they were abominations.

In the first light of dawn Gilgamesh cried out, "I made you rest on a royal bed, you reclined on a couch at my left hand, the princes of the earth kissed your feet. I will cause all the people of Uruk to weep over you and raise the dirge of the dead.
775 The joyful people will stoop with sorrow; and when you have gone to the earth I will let my hair grow long for your sake, I will wander through the wilderness in the skin of a lion." The next day also, in the first light, Gilgamesh lamented; seven days and seven nights he wept for Enkidu, until the worm fastened on him. Only then he gave him up to the earth, for the Anunnaki, the judges, had seized him.

Then Gilgamesh issued a proclamation through the land, he summoned them
780 all, the coppersmiths, the goldsmiths, the stone-workers, and commanded them, "Make a statue of my friend." The statue was fashioned with a great weight of lapis lazuli for the breast and of gold for the body. A table of hard-wood was set out, and on it a bowl of carnelian filled with honey, and a bowl of lapis lazuli filled with butter. These he exposed and offered to the Sun; and weeping he went
785 away.

4: THE SEARCH FOR EVERLASTING LIFE

Bitterly Gilgamesh wept for his friend Enkidu; he wandered over the wilderness as a hunter, he roamed over the plains; in his bitterness he cried, "How can I rest, how can I be at peace? Despair is in my heart. What my brother is now, that shall I be when I am dead. Because I am afraid of death I will go as best I can
790 to find Utnapishtim[19] whom they call the Faraway, for he has entered the assembly of the gods." So Gilgamesh travelled over the wilderness, he wandered over the grasslands, a long journey, in search of Utnapishtim, whom the gods took after the deluge; and they set him to live in the land of Dilmun, in the garden of the sun; and to him alone of men they gave everlasting life.

795 At night when he came to the mountain passes Gilgamesh prayed: "In these mountain passes long ago I saw lions, I was afraid and I lifted my eyes to the moon; I prayed and my prayers went up to the gods, so now, O moon god Sin, protect me." When he had prayed he lay down to sleep, until he was woken from out of a dream. He saw the lions round him glorying in life; then he took his axe in
800 his hand, he drew his sword from his belt, and he fell upon them like an arrow from the string, and struck and destroyed and scattered them.

So at length Gilgamesh came to Mashu, the great mountains about which he had heard many things, which guard the rising and the setting sun. Its twin peaks are as high as the wall of heaven and its paps reach down to the underworld. At
805 its gate the Scorpions stand guard, half man and half dragon; their glory is terrifying, their stare strikes death into men, their shimmering halo sweeps the

---

[19]A wise king and priest who, like the biblical Noah, survived the Flood along with his family and with "the seed of all living creatures." Afterward he was taken by the gods to live forever in Dilmun, the Sumerian paradise.

mountains that guard the rising sun. When Gilgamesh saw them he shielded his eyes for the length of a moment only; then he took courage and approached. When they saw him so undismayed the Man-Scorpion called to his mate, "This one who comes to us now is flesh of the gods." The mate of the Man-Scorpion answered, "Two thirds is god but one third is man."

810

Then he called to the man Gilgamesh, he called to the child of the gods: "Why have you come so great a journey; for what have you travelled so far, crossing the dangerous waters; tell me the reason for your coming?" Gilgamesh answered, "For Enkidu; I loved him dearly, together we endured all kinds of hardships; on his account I have come, for the common lot of man has taken him. I have wept for him day and night, I would not give up his body for burial, I thought my friend would come back because of my weeping. Since he went, my life is nothing; that is why I have travelled here in search of Utnapishtim my father; for men say he has entered the assembly of the gods, and has found everlasting life. I have a desire to question him concerning the living and the dead." The Man-Scorpion opened his mouth and said, speaking to Gilgamesh, "No man born of woman has done what you have asked, no mortal man has gone into the mountain; the length of it is twelve leagues of darkness; in it there is no light, but the heart is oppressed with darkness. From the rising of the sun to the setting of the sun there is no light." Gilgamesh said, "Although I should go in sorrow and in pain, with sighing and with weeping, still I must go. Open the gate of the mountain." And the Man-Scorpion said, "Go, Gilgamesh, I permit you to pass through the mountain of Mashu and through the high ranges; may your feet carry you safely home. The gate of the mountain is open."

815

820

825

830

When Gilgamesh heard this he did as the Man-Scorpion had said, he followed the sun's road to his rising, through the mountain. When he had gone one league the darkness became thick around him, for there was no light, he could see nothing ahead and nothing behind him. After two leagues the darkness was thick and there was no light, he could see nothing ahead and nothing behind him. After three leagues the darkness was thick, and there was no light, he could see nothing ahead and nothing behind him. After four leagues the darkness was thick and there was no light, he could see nothing ahead and nothing behind him. At the end of five leagues the darkness was thick and there was no light, he could see nothing ahead and nothing behind him. At the end of six leagues the darkness was thick and there was no light, he could see nothing ahead and nothing behind him. When he had gone seven leagues the darkness was thick and there was no light, he could see nothing ahead and nothing behind him. When he had gone eight leagues Gilgamesh gave a great cry, for the darkness was thick and he could see nothing ahead and nothing behind him. After nine leagues he felt the north wind on his face, but the darkness was thick and there was no light, he could see nothing ahead and nothing behind him. After ten leagues the end was near. After eleven leagues the dawn light appeared. At the end of twelve leagues the sun streamed out.

835

840

845

There was the garden of the gods; all round him stood bushes bearing gems. Seeing it he went down at once, for there was fruit of carnelian with the vine

850

hanging from it, beautiful to look at; lapis lazuli leaves hung thick with fruit, sweet to see. For thorns and thistles there were haematite[20] and rare stones, agate, and pearls from out of the sea. While Gilgamesh walked in the garden by the edge of the sea Shamash saw him, and he saw that he was dressed in the skins of

855 animals and ate their flesh. He was distressed, and he spoke and said, "No mortal man has gone this way before, nor will, as long as the winds drive over the sea." And to Gilgamesh he said, "You will never find the life for which you are searching." Gilgamesh said to glorious Shamash, "Now that I have toiled and strayed so far over the wilderness, am I to sleep, and let the earth cover my head

860 for ever? Let my eyes see the sun until they are dazzled with looking. Although I am no better than a dead man, still let me see the light of the sun."

Beside the sea she lives, the woman of the vine, the maker of wine; Siduri sits in the garden at the edge of the sea, with the golden bowl and the golden vats that the gods gave her. She is covered with a veil; and where she sits she sees

865 Gilgamesh coming towards her, wearing skins, the flesh of the gods in his body, but despair in his heart, and his face like the face of one who has made a long journey. She looked, and as she scanned the distance she said in her own heart, "Surely this is some felon; where is he going now?" And she barred her gate against him with the cross-bar and shot home the bolt. But Gilgamesh, hearing the

870 sound of the bolt, threw up his head and lodged his foot in the gate; he called to her, "Young woman, maker of wine, why do you bolt your door; what did you see that made you bar your gate? I will break in your door and burst in your gate, for I am Gilgamesh who seized and killed the Bull of Heaven, I killed the watchman of the cedar forest, I overthrew Humbaba who lived in the forest, and I killed the

875 lions in the passes of the mountain."

Then Siduri said to him, "If you are that Gilgamesh who seized and killed the Bull of Heaven, who killed the watchman of the cedar forest, who overthrew Humbaba that lived in the forest, and killed the lions in the passes of the mountain, why are your cheeks so starved and why is your face so drawn? Why is despair

880 in your heart and your face like the face of one who has made a long journey? Yes, why is your face burned from heat and cold, and why do you come here wandering over the pastures in search of the wind?"

Gilgamesh answered her, "And why should not my cheeks be starved and my face drawn? Despair is in my heart and my face is the face of one who has made a

885 long journey, it was burned with heat and with cold. Why should I not wander over the pastures in search of the wind? My friend, my younger brother, he who hunted the wild ass of the wilderness and the panther of the plains, my friend, my younger brother who seized and killed the Bull of Heaven and overthrew Humbaba in the cedar forest, my friend who was very dear to me and who endured

890 dangers beside me, Enkidu my brother, whom I loved, the end of mortality has overtaken him. I wept for him seven days and nights till the worm fastened on him. Because of my brother I am afraid of death, because of my brother I stray through

---

[20]haematite—a kind of iron ore.

the wilderness and cannot rest. But now, young woman, maker of wine, since I have seen your face do not let me see the face of death which I dread so much."

895 She answered, "Gilgamesh, where are you hurrying to? You will never find that life for which you are looking. When the gods created man they allotted to him death, but life they retained in their own keeping. As for you, Gilgamesh, fill your belly with good things; day and night, night and day, dance and be merry, feast and rejoice. Let your clothes be fresh, bathe yourself in water, cherish the little child 900 that holds your hand, and make your wife happy in your embrace; for this too is the lot of man."

But Gilgamesh said to Siduri, the young woman, "How can I be silent, how can I rest, when Enkidu whom I love is dust, and I too shall die and be laid in the earth. You live by the sea-shore and look into the heart of it; young woman, tell me 905 now, which is the way to Utnapishtim, the son of Ubara-Tutu? What directions are there for the passage; give me, oh, give me directions. I will cross the Ocean if it is possible; if it is not I will wander still farther in the wilderness." The wine-maker said to him, "Gilgamesh, there is no crossing the Ocean; whoever has come, since the days of old, has not been able to pass that sea. The Sun in his glory 910 crosses the Ocean, but who beside Shamash has ever crossed it? The place and the passage are difficult, and the waters of death are deep which flow between. Gilgamesh, how will you cross the Ocean? When you come to the waters of death what will you do? But Gilgamesh, down in the woods you will find Urshanabi, the ferryman of Utnapishtim; with him are the holy things, the things of stone. He is 915 fashioning the serpent prow of the boat. Look at him well, and if it is possible, perhaps you will cross the waters with him; but if it is not possible, then you must go back."

When Gilgamesh heard this he was seized with anger. He took his axe in his hand, and his dagger from his belt. He crept forward and he fell on them like a 920 javelin. Then he went into the forest and sat down. Urshanabi saw the dagger flash and heard the axe, and he beat his head, for Gilgamesh had shattered the tackle of the boat in his rage. Urshanabi said to him, "Tell me, what is your name? I am Urshanabi, the ferryman of Utnapishtim the Faraway." He replied to him, "Gilgamesh is my name, I am from Uruk, from the house of Anu." Then Urshanabi 925 said to him, "Why are your cheeks so starved and your face drawn? Why is despair in your heart and your face like the face of one who has made a long journey; yes, why is your face burned with heat and with cold, and why do you come here wandering over the pastures in search of the wind?"

Gilgamesh said to him, "Why should not my cheeks be starved and my face 930 drawn? Despair is in my heart, and my face is the face of one who has made a long journey. I was burned with heat and with cold. Why should I not wander over the pastures? My friend, my younger brother who seized and killed the Bull of Heaven, and overthrew Humbaba in the cedar forest, my friend who was very dear to me, and who endured dangers beside me, Enkidu my brother whom I loved, 935 the end of mortality has overtaken him. I wept for him seven days and nights till the worm fastened on him. Because of my brother I am afraid of death, because of

my brother I stray through the wilderness. His fate lies heavy upon me. How can I be silent, how can I rest? He is dust and I too shall die and be laid in the earth for ever. I am afraid of death, therefore, Urshanabi, tell me which is the road to
940 Utnapishtim? If it is possible I will cross the waters of death; if not I will wander still farther through the wilderness."

Urshanabi said to him, "Gilgamesh, your own hands have prevented you from crossing the Ocean; when you destroyed the tackle of the boat you destroyed its safety." Then the two of them talked it over and Gilgamesh said, "Why are you so
945 angry with me, Urshanabi, for you yourself cross the sea by day and night, at all seasons you cross it." "Gilgamesh, those things you destroyed, their property is to carry me over the water, to prevent the waters of death from touching me. It was for this reason that I preserved them, but you have destroyed them, and the *urnu* snakes with them. But now, go into the forest, Gilgamesh; with your axe cut poles,
950 one hundred and twenty, cut them sixty cubits long, paint them with bitumen, set on them ferrules and bring them back."

When Gilgamesh heard this he went into the forest, he cut poles one hundred and twenty; he cut them sixty cubits long, he painted them with bitumen, he set on them ferrules, and he brought them to Urshanabi. Then they boarded the boat,
955 Gilgamesh and Urshanabi together, launching it out on the waves of Ocean. For three days they ran on as it were a journey of a month and fifteen days, and at last Urshanabi brought the boat to the waters of death. Then Urshanabi said to Gilgamesh, "Press on, take a pole and thrust it in, but do not let your hands touch the waters. Gilgamesh, take a second pole, take a third, take a fourth pole. Now,
960 Gilgamesh, take a fifth, take a sixth and seventh pole. Gilgamesh, take an eighth, and ninth, a tenth pole. Gilgamesh, take an eleventh, take a twelfth pole." After one hundred and twenty thrusts Gilgamesh had used the last pole. Then he stripped himself, be held up his arms for a mast and his covering for a sail. So Urshanabi the ferryman brought Gilgamesh to Utnapishtim, whom they call the
965 Faraway, who lives in Dilmun at the place of the sun's transit, eastward of the mountain. To him alone of men the gods had given everlasting life.

Now Utnapishtim, where he lay at ease, looked into the distance and he said in his heart, musing to himself, "Why does the boat sail here without tackle and mast; why are the sacred stones destroyed, and why does the master not sail the
970 boat? That man who comes is none of mine; where I look I see a man whose body is covered with skins of beasts. Who is this who walks up the shore behind Urshanabi, for surely he is no man of mine?" So Utnapishtim looked at him and said, "What is your name, you who come here wearing the skins of beasts, with your cheeks starved and your face drawn? Where are you hurrying to now? For
975 what reason have you made this great journey, crossing the seas whose passage is difficult? Tell me the reason for your coming."

He replied, "Gilgamesh is my name. I am from Uruk, from the house of Anu." Then Utnapishtim said to him, "If you are Gilgamesh, why are your cheeks so starved and your face drawn? Why is despair in your heart and your face like the
980 face of one who has made a long journey? Yes, why is your face burned with heat

and cold; and why do you come here, wandering over the wilderness in search of the wind?"

Gilgamesh said to him, "Why should not my cheeks be starved and my face drawn? Despair is in my heart and my face is the face of one who has made a long
985 journey. It was burned with heat and with cold. Why should I not wander over the pastures? My friend, my younger brother who seized and killed the Bull of Heaven and overthrew Humbaba in the cedar forest, my friend who was very dear to me and endured dangers beside me, Enkidu, my brother whom I loved, the end of mortality has overtaken him. I wept for him seven days and nights till the worm
990 fastened on him. Because of my brother I am afraid of death; because of my brother I stray through the wilderness. His fate lies heavy upon me. How can I be silent, how can I rest? He is dust and I shall die also and be laid in the earth for ever." Again Gilgamesh said, speaking to Utnapishtim, "It is to see Utnapishtim whom we call the Faraway that I have come this journey. For this I have wandered over
995 the world, I have crossed many difficult ranges, I have crossed the seas, I have wearied myself with travelling; my joints are aching, and I have lost acquaintance with sleep which is sweet. My clothes were worn out before I came to the house of Siduri. I have killed the bear and hyena, the lion and panther, the tiger, the stag and the ibex, all sorts of wild game and the small creatures of the pastures. I ate
1000 their flesh and I wore their skins; and that was how I came to the gate of the young woman, the maker of wine, who barred her gate of pitch and bitumen against me. But from her I had news of the journey; so then I came to Urshanabi the ferryman, and with him I crossed over the waters of death. O, father Utnapishtim, you who have entered the assembly of the gods, I wish to question you concerning the living
1005 and the dead, how shall I find the life for which I am searching?"

Utnapishtim said, "There is no permanence. Do we build a house to stand for ever, do we seal a contract to hold for all time? Do brothers divide an inheritance to keep for ever, does the flood-time of rivers endure? It is only the nymph of the dragon-fly who sheds her larva and sees the sun in his glory. From the days of old
1010 there is no permanence. The sleeping and the dead, how alike they are, they are like a painted death. What is there between the master and the servant when both have fulfilled their doom? When the Anunnaki, the judges, come together, and Mammetun the mother of destinies, together they decree the fates of men. Life and death they allot but the day of death they do not disclose."

1015 Then Gilgamesh said to Utnapishtim the Faraway, "I look at you now, Utnapishtim, and your appearance is no different from mine; there is nothing strange in your features. I thought I should find you like a hero prepared for battle, but you lie here taking your ease on your back. Tell me truly, how was it that you came to enter the company of the gods, and to possess everlasting life?"
1020 Utnapishtim said to Gilgamesh, "I will reveal to you a mystery, I will tell you a secret of the gods."

5: THE STORY OF THE FLOOD

"You know the city Shurrupak, it stands on the banks of Euphrates? That city grew old and the gods that were in it were old. There was Anu, lord of the firmament, their father, and warrior Enlil their counsellor, Ninurta the helper, and Ennugi watcher over canals; and with them also was Ea. In those days the world teemed, the people multiplied, the world bellowed like a wild bull, and the great god was aroused by the clamour. Enlil heard the clamour and he said to the gods in council, 'The uproar of mankind is intolerable and sleep is no longer possible by reason of the babel.' So the gods agreed to exterminate mankind. Enlil did this, but Ea because of his oath warned me in a dream. He whispered their words to my house of reeds, 'Reed-house, reed-house! Wall, O wall, hearken reed-house, wall reflect; O man of Shurrupak, son of Ubara-Tutu; tear down your house and build a boat, abandon possessions and look for life, despise worldly goods and save your soul alive. Tear down your house, I say, and build a boat. These are the measurements of the barque as you shall build her: let her beam equal her length, let her deck be roofed like the vault that covers the abyss; then take up into the boat the seed of all living creatures.'

"When I had understood I said to my lord, 'Behold what you have commanded I will honour and perform, but how shall I answer the people, the city, the elders?' Then Ea opened his mouth and said to me, his servant, 'Tell them this: I have learnt that Enlil is wrathful against me, I dare no longer walk in his land nor live in his city; I will go down to the Gulf to dwell with Ea my lord. But on you he will rain down abundance, rare fish and shy wild-fowl, a rich harvest-tide. In the evening the rider of the storm will bring you wheat in torrents.'

"In the first light of dawn all my household gathered round me, the children brought pitch and the men whatever was necessary. On the fifth day I laid the keel and the ribs, then I made fast the planking. The ground-space was one acre, each side of the deck measured one hundred and twenty cubits, making a square. I built six decks below, seven in all, I divided them into nine sections with bulkheads between. I drove in wedges where needed, I saw to the punt-poles, and laid in supplies. The carriers brought oil in baskets, I poured pitch into the furnace and asphalt and oil; more oil was consumed in caulking, and more again the master of the boat took into his stores. I slaughtered bullocks for the people and every day I killed sheep. I gave the shipwrights wine to drink as though it were river water, raw wine and red wine and oil and white wine. There was feasting then as there is at the time of the New Year's festival; I myself anointed my head. On the eleventh day the boat was complete.

"Then was the launching full of difficulty; there was shifting of ballast above and below till two thirds was submerged. I loaded into her all that I had of gold and of living things, my family, my kin, the beast of the field both wild and tame, and all the craftsmen. I sent them on board, for the time that Shamash had ordained was already fulfilled when he said, 'In the evening, when the rider of the storm sends down the destroying rain, enter the boat and batten her down.' The time

1025

1030

1035

1040

1045

1050

1055

1060

1065
was fulfilled, the evening came, the rider of the storm sent down the rain. I looked out at the weather and it was terrible, so I too boarded the boat and battened her down. All was now complete, the battening and the caulking; so I handed the tiller to Puzur-Amurri the steersman, with the navigation and the care of the whole boat.

1070
"With the first light of dawn a black cloud came from the horizon; it thundered within where Adad, lord of the storm was riding. In front over hill and plain Shullat and Hanish, heralds of the storm, led on. Then the gods of the abyss rose up; Nergal pulled out the dams of the nether waters, Ninurta the war-lord threw down the dykes, and the seven judges of hell, the Annunaki, raised their torches, lighting the land with their livid flame. A stupor of despair went up to

1075
heaven when the god of the storm turned daylight to darkness, when he smashed the land like a cup. One whole day the tempest raged, gathering fury as it went, it poured over the people like the tides of battle; a man could not see his brother nor the people be seen from heaven. Even the gods were terrified at the flood, they fled to the highest heaven, the firmament of Anu; they crouched against the walls,

1080
cowering like curs. Then Ishtar the sweet-voiced Queen of Heaven cried out like a woman in travail: 'Alas the days of old are turned to dust because I commanded evil; why did I command this evil in the council of all the gods? I commanded wars to destroy the people, but are they not my people, for I brought them forth? Now like the spawn of fish they float in the ocean.' The great gods of heaven and of hell

1085
wept, they covered their mouths.

"For six days and six nights the winds blew, torrent and tempest and flood overwhelmed the world, tempest and flood raged together like warring hosts. When the seventh day dawned the storm from the south subsided, the sea grew calm, the flood was stilled; I looked at the face of the world and there was silence,

1090
all mankind was turned to clay. The surface of the sea stretched as flat as a roof-top; I opened a hatch and the light fell on my face. Then I bowed low, I sat down and I wept, the tears streamed down my face, for on every side was the waste of water. I looked for land in vain, for fourteen leagues distant there appeared a mountain, and there the boat grounded; on the mountain of Nisir the boat held fast,

1095
she held fast and did not budge. One day she held, and a second day on the mountain of Nisir she held fast and did not budge. A third day, and a fourth day she held fast on the mountain and did not budge; a fifth day and a sixth day she held fast on the mountain. When the seventh day dawned I loosed a dove and let her go. She flew away, but finding no resting-place she returned. Then I loosed a

1100
swallow, and she flew away but finding no resting-place she returned. I loosed a raven, she saw that the waters had retreated, she, she flew around, she cawed, and she did not come back. Then I threw everything open to the four winds, I made a sacrifice and poured out a libation on the mountain top. Seven and again seven cauldrons I set up on their stands, I heaped up wood and cane and cedar and

1105
myrtle. When the gods smelled the sweet savour, they gathered like flies over the sacrifice. Then, at last, Ishtar also came, she lifted her necklace with the jewels of heaven that once Anu had made to please her. 'O you gods here present, by the

lapis lazuli round my neck I shall remember these days as I remember the jewels of my throat; these last days I shall not forget. Let all the gods gather round the
1110 sacrifice, except Enlil. He shall not approach this offering, for without reflection he brought the flood; he consigned my people to destruction.'

"When Enlil had come, when he saw the boat, he was wrathful and swelled with anger at the gods, the host of heaven, 'Has any of these mortals escaped? Not one was to have survived the destruction.' Then the god of the wells and canals
1115 Ninurta opened his mouth and said to the warrior Enlil, 'Who is there of the gods that can devise without Ea? It is Ea, alone who knows all things.' Then Ea opened his mouth and spoke to warrior Enlil, 'Wisest of gods, hero Enlil, how could you so senselessly bring down the flood?

Lay upon the sinner his sin,
1120 Lay upon the transgressor his transgression,
Punish him a little when he breaks loose,
Do not drive him too hard or he perishes;
Would that a lion had ravaged mankind
Rather than the flood,
1125 Would that a wolf had ravaged mankind
Rather than the flood,
Would that famine had wasted the world
Rather than the flood,
Would that pestilence had wasted mankind
1130 Rather than the flood.

It was not I that revealed the secret of the gods; the wise man learned it in a dream. Now take your counsel what shall be done with him.'

"Then Enlil went up into the boat, he took me by the hand and my wife and made us enter the boat and kneel down on either side, he standing between us. He
1135 touched our foreheads to bless us saying, 'In time past Utnapishtim was a mortal man; henceforth he and his wife shall live in the distance at the mouth of the rivers.' Thus it was that the gods took me and placed me here to live in the distance, at the mouth of the rivers."

6: THE RETURN

Utnapishtim said, "As for you, Gilgamesh, who will assemble the gods for
1140 your sake, so that you may find that life for which you are searching? But if you wish, come and put it to the test: only prevail against sleep for six days and seven nights." But while Gilgamesh sat there resting on his haunches, a mist of sleep like soft wool teased from the fleece drifted over him, and Utnapishtim said to his wife, "Look at him now, the strong man who would have everlasting life, even now the
1145 mists of sleep are drifting over him." His wife replied, "Touch the man to wake him, so that be may return to his own land in peace, going back through the gate by

which he came." Utnapishtim said to his wife, "All men are deceivers, even you he will attempt to deceive; therefore bake loaves of bread, each day one loaf, and put it beside his head; and make a mark on the wall to number the days he has slept."

1150   So she baked loaves of bread, each day one loaf, and put it beside his head, and she marked on the walls the days that he slept; and there came a day when the first loaf was hard, the second loaf was like leather, the third was soggy, the crust of the fourth had mould, the fifth was mildewed, the sixth was fresh, and the seventh was still on the embers. Then Utnapishtim touched him and he woke.

1155 Gilgamesh said to Utnapishtim the Faraway, "I hardly slept when you touched and roused me." But Utnapishtim said, "Count these loaves and learn how many days you slept, for your first is hard, your second like leather, your third is soggy, the crust of your fourth has mould, your fifth is mildewed, your sixth is fresh and your seventh was still over the glowing embers when I touched and woke you."

1160 Gilgamesh said, "What shall I do, O Utnapishtim, where shall I go? Already the thief in the night has hold of my limbs, death inhabits my room; wherever my foot rests, there I find death."

     Then Utnapishtim spoke to Urshanabi the ferryman: "Woe to you Urshanabi, now and for ever more you have become hateful to this harbourage; it is not for
1165 you, nor for you are the crossings of this sea. Go now, banished from the shore. But this man before whom you walked, bringing him here, whose body is covered with foulness and the grace of whose limbs has been spoiled by wild skins, take him to the washing-place. There he shall wash his long hair clean as snow in the water, he shall throw off his skins and let the sea carry them away, and the
1170 beauty of his body shall be shown, the fillet on his forehead shall be renewed, and he shall be given clothes to cover his nakedness. Till he reaches his own city and his journey is accomplished, these clothes will show no sign of age, they will wear like a new garment." So Urshanabi took Gilgamesh and led him to the washing-place, he washed his long hair as clean as snow in the water, he threw off his
1175 skins, which the sea carried away, and showed the beauty of his body. He renewed the fillet on his forehead, and to cover his nakedness gave him clothes which would show no sign of age, but would wear like a new garment till he reached his own city, and his journey was accomplished.

     Then Gilgamesh and Urshanabi launched the boat on to the water and
1180 boarded it, and they made ready to sail away; but the wife of Utnapishtim the Faraway said to him, "Gilgamesh came here wearied out, he is worn out; what will you give him to carry him back to his own country?" So Utnapishtim spoke, and Gilgamesh took a pole and brought the boat in to the bank. "Gilgamesh, you came here a man wearied out, you have worn yourself out; what shall I give you to
1185 carry you back to your own country? Gilgamesh, I shall reveal a secret thing, it is a mystery of the gods that I am telling you. There is a plant that grows under the water, it has a prickle like a thorn, like a rose; it will wound your hands, but if you succeed in taking it, then your hands will hold that which restores his lost youth to a man."

1190   When Gilgamesh heard this he opened the sluices so that a sweet-water current might carry him out to the deepest channel; he tied heavy stones to his feet and they dragged him down to the water-bed. There he saw the plant growing; although it pricked him he took it in his hands; then he cut the heavy stones from his feet, and the sea carried him and threw him on to the shore. Gilgamesh said to

1195   Urshanabi the ferryman, "Come here, and see this marvellous plant. By its virtue a man may win back all his former strength. I will take it to Uruk of the strong walls; there I will give it to the old men to eat. Its name shall be 'The Old Men Are Young Again'; and at last I shall eat it myself and have back all my lost youth." So Gilgamesh returned by the gate through which he had come, Gilgamesh and

1200   Urshanabi went together. They travelled their twenty leagues and then they broke their fast; after thirty leagues they stopped for the night.

      Gilgamesh saw a well of cool water and he went down and bathed; but deep in the pool there was lying a serpent, and the serpent sensed the sweetness of the flower. It rose out of the water and snatched it away, and immediately it sloughed

1205   its skin and returned to the well. Then Gilgamesh sat down and wept, the tears ran down his face, and he took the hand of Urshanabi; "O Urshanabi, was it for this that I toiled with my hands, is it for this I have wrung out my heart's blood? For myself I have gained nothing; not I, but the beast of the earth has joy of it now. Already the stream has carried it twenty leagues back to the channels where I

1210   found it. I found a sign and now I have lost it. Let us leave the boat on the bank and go."

      After twenty leagues they broke their fast, after thirty leagues they stopped for the night; in three days they had walked as much as a journey of a month and fifteen days. When the journey was accomplished they arrived at Uruk, the strong-

1215   walled city. Gilgamesh spoke to him, to Urshanabi the ferryman, "Urshanabi, climb up on to the wall of Uruk, inspect its foundation terrace, and examine well the brickwork; see if it is not of burnt bricks; and did not the seven wise men lay these foundations? One third of the whole is city, one third is garden, and one third is field, with the precinct of the goddess Ishtar. These parts and the precinct

1220   are all Uruk."

      This too was the work of Gilgamesh, the king, who knew the countries of the world. He was wise, he saw mysteries and knew secret things, he brought us a tale of the days before the flood. He went a long journey, was weary, worn out with labour, and returning engraved on a stone the whole story.

7: THE DEATH OF GILGAMESH

1225   The destiny was fulfilled which the father of the gods, Enlil of the mountain, had decreed for Gilgamesh: "In nether-earth the darkness will show him a light: of mankind, all that are known, none will leave a monument for generations to come to compare with his. The heroes, the wise men, like the new moon have their waxing and waning. Men will say, 'Who has ever ruled with might and with

1230   power like him?' As in the dark month, the month of shadows, so without him there is no light. O Gilgamesh, this was the meaning of your dream. You were given the kingship, such was your destiny, everlasting life was not your destiny. Because of this do not be sad at heart, do not be grieved or oppressed; he has given you power to bind and to loose, to be the darkness and the light of mankind. He has given unexampled supremacy over the people, victory in battle from which no fugitive returns, in forays and assaults from which there is no going back. But do not abuse this power, deal justly with your servants in the palace, deal justly before the face of the Sun."

1235

The king has laid himself down and will not rise again,
1240   The Lord of Kullab will not rise again;
He overcame evil, he will not come again;
Though he was strong of arm he will not rise again;

He had wisdom and a comely face, he will not come again;
He is gone into the mountain, he will not come again;
1245   On the bed of fate he lies, he will not rise again,
From the couch of many colours he will not come again.

The people of the city, great and small, are not silent; they lift up the lament, all men of flesh and blood lift up the lament. Fate has spoken; like a hooked fish he lies stretched on the bed, like a gazelle that is caught in a noose. Inhuman Namtar
1250   is heavy upon him, Namtar that has neither hand nor foot, that drinks no water and eats no meat.
For Gilgamesh, son of Ninsun, they weighed out their offerings; his dear wife, his son, his concubine, his musicians, his jester, and all his household; his servants, his stewards, all who lived in the palace weighed out their offerings for
1255   Gilgamesh the son of Ninsun, the heart of Uruk. They weighed out their offerings to Ereshkigal the Queen of Death, and to all the gods of the dead. To Namtar, who is fate, they weighed out the offering. Bread for Neti the Keeper of the Gate, bread for Ningizzida the god of the serpent, the lord of the Tree of Life; for Dumuzi also, the young shepherd, for Enki and Ninki, for Endukugga and Nindukugga, for
1260   Enmul and Ninmul, all the ancestral gods, forbears of Enlil. A feast for Shulpae the god of feasting. For Samuqan, god of the herds, for the mother Ninhursag, and the gods of creation in the place of creation, for the host of heaven, priest and priestess weighed out the offering of the dead.
Gilgamesh, the son of Ninsun, lies in the tomb. At the place of offerings he
1265   weighed the bread-offering, at the place of libation he poured out the wine. In those days the lord Gilgamesh departed, the son of Ninsun, the king, peerless, without an equal among men, who did not neglect Enlil his master. O Gilgamesh, lord of Kullab, great is thy praise.

II: GREECE

2. THE ILIAD (SELECTIONS)
(c. 8th c. BCE)

Homer

(trans. by Richmond Lattimore)

*Composed in the ninth century BCE, Homer's epic tells of historical and legendary events dating back to the twelfth century BCE, an age when the Achaeans were the foremost tribe in the Mycenaean world. The epic recounts a brief period in the long Trojan War, focusing on the hero Achilleus who struggles to achieve **Arete** (excellence) as a warrior and as a human. He is aided and thwarted by external forces (gods and humans) and internal forces (his own psyche). His eventual success provides Homer's audience with a model of what it means to be Greek, what it means to be heroic, and what it means to be human.*

BOOK ONE: THE QUARREL OF ACHILLES AND AGAMEMNON

     Sing, the anger of Peleus' son Achilleus
and its devastation, which put pains thousandfold upon the Achaians,
hurled in their multitudes to the house of Hades strong souls
of heroes, but gave their bodies to be the delicate feasting
5   of dogs, of all birds, and the will of Zeus was accomplished
since that time when first there stood in division of conflict
Atreus' son the lord of men[1] and brilliant Achilleus.
     What god was it then set them together in bitter collision?
Zeus' son and Leto's, Apollo, who in anger at the king drove
10   the foul pestilence along the host, and the people perished,
since Atreus' son had dishonoured Chryses,[2] priest of Apollo,
when he came beside the fast ships of the Achaians to ransom
back his daughter, carrying gifts beyond count and holding
in his hands wound on a staff of gold the ribbons of Apollo
15   who strikes from afar, and supplicated all the Achaians, ·

---

[1]Agamemnon, King of Mykenai and brother of Menelaos, whose wife, Helen, was the cause of the Trojan War.

[2]Agamemnon had taken the priest Chryses' daughter, Chryseis, as his concubine, so Chryses invoked Apollo who brought a plague upon the Achaians.

but above all Atreus' two sons, the marshals of the people:
'Sons of Atreus and you other strong-greaved Achaians,
to you may the gods grant who have their homes on Olympos
Priam's city to be plundered and a fair homecoming thereafter,
20   but may you give me back my own daughter and take the ransom,
giving honour to Zeus' son who strikes from afar, Apollo.'
    Then all the rest of the Achaians cried out in favour
that the priest be respected and the shining ransom be taken;
yet this pleased not the heart of Atreus' son Agamemnon,
25   but harshly he drove him away with a strong order upon him:
'Never let me find you again, old sir, near our hollow
ships, neither lingering now nor coming again hereafter,
for fear your staff and the god's ribbons help you no longer.
The girl I will not give back; sooner will old age come upon her
30   in my own house, in Argos, far from her own land, going
up and down by the loom and being in my bed as my companion.
So go now, do not make me angry; so you will be safer.'
    So he spoke, and the old man in terror obeyed him
and went silently away beside the murmuring sea beach.
35   Over and over the old man prayed as he walked in solitude
to King Apollo, whom Leto of the lovely hair bore: 'Hear me,
lord of the silver bow who set your power about Chryse
and Killa the sacrosanct,[3] who are lord in strength over Tenedos,
Smintheus, if ever it pleased your heart that I built your temple,
40   if ever it pleased you that I burned all the rich thigh pieces
of bulls, of goats, then bring to pass this wish I pray for:
let your arrows make the Danaans pay for my tears shed.'
    So he spoke in prayer, and Phoibos Apollo heard him,
and strode down along the pinnacles of Olympos, angered
45   in his heart, carrying across his shoulders the bow and the hooded
quiver; and the shafts clashed on the shoulders of the god walking
angrily. He came as night comes down and knelt then
apart and opposite the ships and let go an arrow.
Terrible was the clash that rose from the bow of silver.
50   First he went after the mules and the circling hounds, then let go
a tearing arrow against the men themselves and struck them.
The corpse fires burned everywhere and did not stop burning.
    Nine days up and down the host ranged the god's arrows,
but on the tenth Achilleus called the people to assembly;
55   a thing put into his mind by the goddess of the white arms, Hera,
who had pity upon the Danaans when she saw them dying.
Now when they were all assembled in one place together,

---

[3]**Chryse and Killa the sacrosanct**: towns in Trojan territory, Chryse being the home of Chryses.

Achilleus of the swift feet stood up among them and spoke forth:
'Son of Atreus, I believe now that straggling backwards
60   we must make our way home if we can even escape death,
if fighting now must crush the Achaians and the plague likewise.
No, come, let us ask some holy man, some prophet,
even an interpreter of dreams, since a dream also
comes from Zeus, who can tell why Phoibos Apollo is so angry,
65   if for the sake of some vow, some hecatomb[4] he blames us,
if given the fragrant smoke of lambs, of he goats, somehow
he can be made willing to beat the bane aside from us.'
     He spoke thus and sat down again, and among them stood up
Kalchas, Thestor's son, far the best of the bird interpreters,
70   who knew all things that were, the things to come and the things past,
who guided into the land of Ilion the ships of the Achaians
through that seercraft of his own that Phoibos Apollo gave him.
He in kind intention toward all stood forth and addressed them:
'You have bidden me, Achilleus beloved of Zeus, to explain to
75   you this anger of Apollo the lord who strikes from afar. Then
I will speak; yet make me a promise and swear before me
readily by word and work of your hands to defend me,
since I believe I shall make a man angry who holds great kingship
over the men of Argos, and all the Achaians obey him.
80   For a king when he is angry with a man beneath him is too strong,
and suppose even for the day itself he swallow down his anger,
he still keeps bitterness that remains until its fulfilment
deep in his chest. Speak forth then, tell me if you will protect me.'
     Then in answer again spoke Achilleus of the swift feet:
85   'Speak, interpreting whatever you know, and fear nothing.
In the name of Apollo beloved of Zeus to whom you, Kalchas,
make your prayers when you interpret the gods' will to the Danaans,
no man so long as I am alive above earth and see daylight
shall lay the weight of his hands on you beside the hollow ships,
90   not one of all the Danaans, even if you mean Agamemnon,
who now claims to be far the greatest of all the Achaians.'
     At this the blameless seer took courage again and spoke forth:
'No, it is not for the sake of some vow or hecatomb he blames us,
but for the sake of his priest whom Agamemnon dishonoured
95   and would not give him back his daughter nor accept the ransom.
Therefore the archer sent griefs against us and will send them
still, nor sooner thrust back the shameful plague from the Danaans
until we give the glancing-eyed girl back to her father

---

[4]**hecatomb:** sacrifice of a hundred cattle or oxen.

without price, without ransom, and lead also a blessed hecatomb
100 to Chryse; thus we might propitiate and persuade him.'
   He spoke thus and sat down again, and among them stood up
Atreus' son the hero wide-ruling Agamemnon
raging, the heart within filled black to the brim with anger
from beneath, but his two eyes showed like fire in their blazing.
105 First of all he eyed Kalchas bitterly and spoke to him:
'Seer of evil: never yet have you told me a good thing.
Always the evil things are dear to your heart to prophesy,
but nothing excellent have you said nor ever accomplished.
Now once more you make divination to the Danaans, argue
110 forth your reason why he who strikes from afar afflicts them,
because I for the sake of the girl Chryseis would not take
the shining ransom; and indeed I wish greatly to have her
in my own house; since I like her better than Klytaimestra
my own wife, for in truth she is no way inferior,
115 neither in build nor stature nor wit, not in accomplishment.
Still I am willing to give her back, if such is the best way.
I myself desire that my people be safe, not perish.
Find me then some prize that shall be my own, lest I only
among the Argives[5] go without, since that were unfitting;
120 you are all witnesses to this thing, that my prize goes elsewhere.'
   Then in answer again spoke brilliant swift-footed Achilleus:
'Son of Atreus, most lordly, greediest for gain of all men,
how shall the great-hearted Achaians give you a prize now?
There is no great store of things lying about I know of.
125 But what we took from the cities by storm has been distributed;
it is unbecoming for the people to call back things once given.
No, for the present give the girl back to the god; we Achaians
thrice and four times over will repay you, if ever Zeus gives
into our hands the strong-walled citadel of Troy to be plundered.'
130   Then in answer again spoke powerful Agamemnon:
'Not that way, good fighter though you be, godlike Achilleus,
strive to cheat, for you will not deceive, you will not persuade me.
What do you want? To keep your own prize and have me sit here
lacking one? Are you ordering me to give this girl back?
135 Either the great-hearted Achaians shall give me a new prize
chosen according to my desire to atone for the girl lost,
or else if they will not give me one I myself shall take her,
your own prize, or that of Aias, or that of Odysseus,
going myself in person; and he whom I visit will be bitter.
140 Still, these are things we shall deliberate again hereafter.

---

[5]**Argives**: Achaians.

Come, now, we must haul a black ship down to the bright sea,
and assemble rowers enough for it, and put on board it
the hecatomb, and the girl herself, Chryseis of the fair cheeks,
and let there be one responsible man in charge of her,
145   either Aias or Idomeneus or brilliant Odysseus,
or you yourself, son of Peleus, most terrifying of all men,
to reconcile by accomplishing sacrifice the archer.'
        Then looking darkly at him Achilleus of the swift feet spoke:
'O wrapped in shamelessness, with your mind forever on profit,
150   how shall any one of the Achaians readily obey you
either to go on a journey or to fight men strongly in battle?
I for my part did not come here for the sake of the Trojan
spearmen to fight against them, since to me they have done nothing.
Never yet have they driven away my cattle or my horses,
155   never in Phthia where the soil is rich and men grow great did they
spoil my harvest, since indeed there is much that lies between us,
the shadowy mountains and the echoing sea; but for your sake,
o great shamelessness, we followed, to do you favour,
you with the dog's eyes, to win your honour and Menelaos'
160   from the Trojans. You forget all this or else you care nothing.
And now my prize you threaten in person to strip from me,
for whom I laboured much, the gift of the sons of the Achaians.
Never, when the Achaians sack some well-founded citadel
of the Trojans, do I have a prize that is equal to your prize.
165   Always the greater part of the painful fighting is the work of
my hands; but when the time comes to distribute the booty
yours is far the greater reward, and I with some small thing
yet dear to me go back to my ships when I am weary with fighting.
Now I am returning to Phthia, since it is much better
170   to go home again with my curved ships, and I am minded no longer
to stay here dishonoured and pile up your wealth and your luxury.'
        Then answered him in turn the lord of men Agamemnon:
'Run away by all means if your heart drives you. I will not
entreat you to stay here for my sake. There are others with me
175   who will do me honour, and above all Zeus of the counsels.
To me you are the most hateful of all the kings whom the gods love.
Forever quarrelling is dear to your heart, and wars and battles;
and if you are very strong indeed, that is a god's gift.
Go home then with your own ships and your own companions,
180   be king over the Myrmidons. I care nothing about you.
I take no account of your anger. But here is my threat to you.
Even as Phoibos Apollo is taking away my Chryseis.
I shall convey her back in my own ship, with my own
followers; but I shall take the fair-cheeked Briseis,

185 your prize, I myself going to your shelter, that you may learn well
how much greater I am than you, and another man may shrink back
from likening himself to me and contending against me.'
    So he spoke. And the anger came on Peleus' son, and within
his shaggy breast the heart was divided two ways, pondering
190 whether to draw from beside his thigh the sharp sword, driving
away all those who stood between and kill the son of Atreus,
or else to check the spleen within and keep down his anger.
Now as he weighed in mind and spirit these two courses
and was drawing from its scabbard the great sword, Athene descended
195 from the sky. For Hera the goddess of the white arms sent her,
who loved both men equally in her heart and cared for them.
The goddess standing behind Peleus' son caught him by the fair hair,
appearing to him only, for no man of the others saw her.
Achilleus in amazement turned about, and straightway
200 knew Pallas Athene and the terrible eyes shining.
He uttered winged words and addressed her: 'Why have you come now,
o child of Zeus of the aegis, once more? Is it that you may see
the outrageousness of the son of Atreus Agamemnon?
Yet will I tell you this thing, and I think it shall be accomplished.
205 By such acts of arrogance he may even lose his own life.'
    Then in answer the goddess grey-eyed Athene spoke to him:
'I have come down to stay your anger—but will you obey me?—
from the sky; and the goddess of the white arms Hera sent me,
who loves both of you equally in her heart and cares for you.
210 Come then, do not take your sword in your hand, keep clear of fighting,
though indeed with words you may abuse him, and it will be that way.
And this also will I tell you and it will be a thing accomplished.
Some day three times over such shining gifts shall be given you
by reason of this outrage. Hold your hand then, and obey us.'
215   Then in answer again spoke Achilleus of the swift feet:
'Goddess, it is necessary that I obey the word of you two,
angry though I am in my heart. So it will be better.
If any man obeys the gods, they listen to him also.'
    He spoke, and laid his heavy hand on the silver sword hilt
220 and thrust the great blade back into the scabbard nor disobeyed
the word of Athene. And she went back again to Olympos
to the house of Zeus of the aegis with the other divinities.
    But Peleus' son once again in words of derision
spoke to Atreides,[6] and did not yet let go of his anger:
225 'You wine sack, with a dog's eyes, with a deer's heart. Never
once have you taken courage in your heart to arm with your people

---

[6]**Atreides:** son of Atreus, Agamemnon

for battle, or go into ambuscade with the best of the Achaians.
No, for in such things you see death. Far better to your mind
is it, all along the widespread host of the Achaians
230   to take away the gifts of any man who speaks up against you.
King who feed on your people, since you rule nonentities;
otherwise, son of Atreus, this were your last outrage.
But I will tell you this and swear a great oath upon it:
in the name of this sceptre, which never again will bear leaf nor
235   branch, now that it has left behind the cut stump in the mountains,
nor shall it ever blossom again, since the bronze blade stripped
bark and leafage, and now at last the sons of the Achaians
carry it in their hands in state when they administer
the justice of Zeus. And this shall be a great oath before you:
240   some day longing for Achilleus will come to the sons of the Achaians,
all of them. Then stricken at heart though you be, you will be able
to do nothing, when in their numbers before man-slaughtering Hektor
they drop and die. And then you will eat out the heart within you
in sorrow, that you did no honour to the best of the Achaians.'
245   Thus spoke Peleus' son and dashed to the ground the sceptre
studded with golden nails, and sat down again. But Atreides
raged still on the other side, and between them Nestor
the fair-spoken rose up, the lucid speaker of Pylos,
from whose lips the streams of words ran sweeter than honey.
250   In his time two generations of mortal men had perished,
those who had grown up with him and they who had been born to
these in sacred Pylos, and he was king in the third age.
He in kind intention toward both stood forth and addressed them:
'Oh, for shame. Great sorrow comes on the land of Achaia.
255   Now might Priam and the sons of Priam in truth be happy,
and all the rest of the Trojans be visited in their hearts with gladness,
were they to hear all this wherein you two are quarrelling,
you, who surpass all Danaans in council, in fighting.
Yet be persuaded. Both of you are younger than I am.
260   Yes, and in my time I have dealt with better men than
you are, and never once did they disregard me. Never
yet have I seen nor shall see again such men as these were,
men like Peirithoös, and Dryas, shepherd of the people,
Kaineus and Exadios, godlike Polyphemos,
265   or Theseus, Aigeus' son, in the likeness of the immortals.
These were the strongest generation of earth-born mortals,
the strongest, and they fought against the strongest, the beast men
living within the mountains, and terribly they destroyed them.
I was of the company of these men, coming from Pylos,
270   a long way from a distant land, since they had summoned me.

And I fought single-handed, yet against such men no one
of the mortals now alive upon earth could do battle. And also
these listened to the counsels I gave and heeded my bidding.
Do you also obey, since to be persuaded is better.

275   You, great man that you are, yet do not take the girl away
but let her be, a prize as the sons of the Achaians gave her
first. Nor, son of Peleus, think to match your strength with
the king, since never equal with the rest is the portion of honour
of the sceptred king to whom Zeus gives magnificence. Even

280   though you are the stronger man, and the mother who bore you was immortal,
yet is this man greater who is lord over more than you rule.
Son of Atreus, give up your anger; even I entreat you
to give over your bitterness against Achilleus, he who
stands as a great bulwark of battle over all the Achaians.'

285   Then in answer again spoke powerful Agamemnon:
'Yes, old sir, all this you have said is fair and orderly.
Yet here is a man who wishes to be above all others,
who wishes to hold power over all, and to be lord of
all, and give them their orders, yet I think one will not obey him.

290   And if the everlasting gods have made him a spearman,
yet they have not given him the right to speak abusively.'
          Then looking at him darkly brilliant Achilleus answered him:
'So must I be called of no account and a coward
if I must carry out every order you may happen to give me.

295   Tell other men to do these things, but give me no more
commands, since I for my part have no intention to obey you.
And put away in your thoughts this other thing I tell you.
With my hands I will not fight for the girl's sake, neither
with you nor any other man, since you take her away who gave her.

300   But of all the other things that are mine beside my fast black
ship, you shall take nothing away against my pleasure.
Come, then, only try it, that these others may see also;
instantly your own black blood will stain my spearpoint.'
          So these two after battling in words of contention

305   stood up, and broke the assembly beside the ships of the Achaians.
Peleus' son went back to his balanced ships and his shelter
with Patroklos, Menoitios' son, and his own companions.
But the son of Atreus drew a fast ship down to the water
and allotted into it twenty rowers and put on board it

310   the hecatomb for the god and Chryseis of the fair cheeks
leading her by the hand. And in charge went crafty Odysseus.
          These then putting out went over the ways of the water
while Atreus' son told his people to wash off their defilement.
And they washed it away and threw the washings into the salt sea.

315 Then they accomplished perfect hecatombs to Apollo,
     of bulls and goats along the beach of the barren salt sea.
     The savour of the burning swept in circles up to the bright sky.
          Thus these were busy about the army. But Agamemnon
     did not give up his anger and the first threat he made to Achilleus,
320 but to Talthybios he gave his orders and Eurybates
     who were heralds and hard-working henchmen to him: 'Go now
     to the shelter of Peleus' son Achilleus, to bring back
     Briseis of the fair cheeks leading her by the hand. And if he
     will not give her, I must come in person to take her
325 with many men behind me, and it will be the worse for him.'
          He spoke and sent them forth with this strong order upon them.
     They went against their will beside the beach of the barren
     salt sea, and came to the shelters and the ships of the Myrmidons.
     The man himself they found beside his shelter and his black ship
330 sitting. And Achilleus took no joy at all when he saw them.
     These two terrified and in awe of the king stood waiting
     quietly, and did not speak a word at all nor question him.
     But he knew the whole matter in his own heart, and spoke first:
     'Welcome, heralds, messengers of Zeus and of mortals.
335 Draw near. You are not to blame in my sight, but Agamemnon
     who sent the two of you here for the sake of the girl Briseis.
     Go then, illustrious Patroklos, and bring the girl forth
     and give her to these to be taken away. Yet let them be witnesses
     in the sight of the blessed gods, in the sight of mortal
340 men, and of this cruel king, if ever hereafter
     there shall be need of me to beat back the shameful destruction
     from the rest. For surely in ruinous heart he makes sacrifice
     and has not wit enough to look behind and before him
     that the Achaians fighting beside their ships shall not perish.'
345   So he spoke, and Patroklos obeyed his beloved companion.
     He led forth from the hut Briseis of the fair cheeks and gave her
     to be taken away; and they walked back beside the ships of the Achaians,
     and the woman all unwilling went with them still. But Achilleus
     weeping went and sat in sorrow apart from his companions
350 beside the beach of the grey sea looking out on the infinite water.
     Many times stretching forth his hands he called on his mother:
     'Since, my mother, you bore me to be a man with a short life,
     therefore Zeus of the loud thunder on Olympos should grant me
     honour at least. But now he has given me not even a little.
355 Now the son of Atreus, powerful Agamemnon,
     has dishonoured me, since he has taken away my prize and keeps it.'
          So he spoke in tears and the lady his mother heard him
     as she sat in the depths of the sea at the side of her aged father,

and lightly she emerged like a mist from the grey water.
360 She came and sat beside him as he wept, and stroked him
with her hand and called him by name and spoke to him: 'Why then,
child, do you lament? What sorrow has come to your heart now?
Tell me, do not hide it in your mind, and thus we shall both know.'
Sighing heavily Achilleus of the swift feet answered her:
365 'You know; since you know why must I tell you all this?
We went against Thebe, the sacred city of Eëtion,
and the city we sacked, and carried everything back to this place,
and the sons of the Achaians made a fair distribution
and for Atreus' son they chose out Chryseis of the fair cheeks.
370 Then Chryses, priest of him who strikes from afar, Apollo,
came beside the fast ships of the bronze-armoured Achaians to ransom
back his daughter, carrying gifts beyond count and holding
in his hands wound on a staff of gold the ribbons of Apollo
who strikes from afar, and supplicated all the Achaians,
375 but above all Atreus' two sons, the marshals of the people.
Then all the rest of the Achaians cried out in favour
that the priest be respected and the shining ransom be taken;
yet this pleased not the heart of Atreus' son Agamemnon,
but harshly he sent him away with a strong order upon him.
380 The old man went back again in anger, but Apollo
listened to his prayer, since he was very dear to him, and let go
the wicked arrow against the Argives. And now the people
were dying one after another while the god's shafts ranged
everywhere along the wide host of the Achaians, till the seer
385 knowing well the truth interpreted the designs of the archer.
It was I first of all urged then the god's appeasement;
and the anger took hold of Atreus' son, and in speed standing
he uttered his threat against me, and now it is a thing accomplished.
For the girl the glancing-eyed Achaians are taking to Chryse
390 in a fast ship, also carrying to the king presents. But even
now the heralds went away from my shelter leading
Briseus' daughter, whom the sons of the Achaians gave me.
You then, if you have power to, protect your own son, going
to Olympos and supplicating Zeus, if ever before now
395 either by word you comforted Zeus' heart or by action.
Since it is many times in my father's halls I have heard you
making claims, when you said you only among the immortals
beat aside shameful destruction from Kronos' son the dark-misted,
that time when all the other Olympians sought to bind him,
400 Hera and Poseidon and Pallas Athene. Then you,
goddess, went and set him free from his shackles, summoning
in speed the creature of the hundred hands to tall Olympos,

that creature the gods name Briareus, but all men
Aigaios' son, but he is far greater in strength than his father.
405 He rejoicing in the glory of it sat down by Kronion,
and the rest of the blessed gods were frightened and gave up binding him.
Sit beside him and take his knees and remind him of these things
now, if perhaps he might be willing to help the Trojans,
and pin the Achaians back against the ships and the water,
410 dying, so that thus they may all have profit of their own king,
that Atreus' son wide-ruling Agamemnon may recognize
his madness, that he did no honour to the best of the Achaians.'
  Thetis answered him then letting the tears fall: 'Ah me,
my child. Your birth was bitterness. Why did I raise you?
415 If only you could sit by your ships untroubled, not weeping,
since indeed your lifetime is to be short, of no length.
Now it has befallen that your life must be brief and bitter
beyond all men's. To a bad destiny I bore you in my chambers.
But I will go to cloud-dark Olympos and ask this
420 thing of Zeus who delights in the thunder. Perhaps he will do it.
Do you therefore continuing to sit by your swift ships
be angry at the Achaians and stay away from all fighting.
For Zeus went to the blameless Aithiopians at the Ocean
yesterday to feast, and the rest of the gods went with him.
425 On the twelfth day he will be coming back to Olympos,
and then I will go for your sake to the house of Zeus, bronze-founded,
and take him by the knees and I think I can persuade him.'
  So speaking she went away from that place and left him
sorrowing in his heart for the sake of the fair-girdled woman
430 whom they were taking by force against his will. But Odysseus
meanwhile drew near to Chryse conveying the sacred hecatomb.
These when they were inside the many-hollowed harbour
took down and gathered together the sails and stowed them in the black ship,
let down mast by the forestays, and settled it into the mast crutch
435 easily, and rowed her in with oars to the mooring.
They threw over the anchor stones and made fast the stern cables
and themselves stepped out on to the break of the sea beach,
and led forth the hecatomb to the archer Apollo,
and Chryseis herself stepped forth from the sea-going vessel.
440 Odysseus of the many designs guided her to the altar
and left her in her father's arms and spoke a word to him:
'Chryses, I was sent here by the lord of men Agamemnon
to lead back your daughter and accomplish a sacred hecatomb
to Apollo on behalf of the Danaans, that we may propitiate
445 the lord who has heaped unhappiness and tears on the Argives.'

He spoke, and left her in his arms. And he received gladly
his beloved child. And the men arranged the sacred hecatomb
for the god in orderly fashion around the strong-founded altar.
Next they washed their hands and took up the scattering barley.
450   Standing among them with lifted arms Chryses prayed in a great voice:
'Hear me, lord of the silver bow, who set your power about
Chryse and Killa the sacrosanct, who are lord in strength over
Tenedos;[7] if once before you listened to my prayers
and did me honour and smote strongly the host of the Achaians,
455   so one more time bring to pass the wish that I pray for.
Beat aside at last the shameful plague from the Danaans.'
     So he spoke in prayer, and Phoibos Apollo heard him.
And when all had made prayer and flung down the scattering barley
first they drew back the victims' heads and slaughtered them and skinned them,
460   and cut away the meat from the thighs and wrapped them in fat,
making a double fold, and laid shreds of flesh upon them.
The old man burned these on a cleft stick and poured the gleaming
wine over, while the young men with forks in their hands stood about him.
But when they had burned the thigh pieces and tasted the vitals,
465   they cut all the remainder into pieces and spitted them
and roasted all carefully and took off the pieces.
Then after they had finished the work and got the feast ready
they feasted, nor was any man's hunger denied a fair portion.
But when they had put away their desire for eating and drinking,
470   the young men filled the mixing bowls with pure wine, passing
a portion to all, when they had offered drink in the goblets.
All day long they propitiated the god with singing,
chanting a splendid hymn to Apollo, these young Achaians,
singing to the one who works from afar, who listened in gladness.
475   Afterwards when the sun went down and darkness came onward
they lay down and slept beside the ship's stern cables.
But when the young Dawn showed again with her rosy fingers,
they put forth to sea toward the wide camp of the Achaians.
And Apollo who works from afar sent them a favouring stern wind.
480   They set up the mast again and spread on it the white sails,
and the wind blew into the middle of the sail, and at the cutwater
a blue wave rose and sang strongly as the ship went onward.
She ran swiftly cutting across the swell her pathway.
But when they had come back to the wide camp of the Achaians
485   they hauled the black ship up on the mainland, high up
on the sand, and underneath her they fixed the long props.
Afterwards they scattered to their own ships and their shelters.

---

[7]**Tenedos:** island off the coast of the Troad (Troy country).

But that other still sat in anger beside his swift ships,
Peleus' son divinely born, Achilleus of the swift feet.

490 Never now would he go to assemblies where men win glory,
never more into battle, but continued to waste his heart out
sitting there, though he longed always for the clamour and fighting.
But when the twelfth dawn after this day appeared, the gods who
live forever came back to Olympos all in a body

495 and Zeus led them; nor did Thetis forget the entreaties
of her son, but she emerged from the sea's waves early
in the morning and went up to the tall sky and Olympos.
She found Kronos' broad-browed son apart from the others
sitting upon the highest peak of rugged Olympos.

500 She came and sat beside him with her left hand embracing
his knees, but took him underneath the chin with her right hand
and spoke in supplication to lord Zeus son of Kronos:
'Father Zeus, if ever before in word or action
I did you favour among the immortals, now grant what I ask for.

505 Now give honour to my son short-lived beyond all other
mortals. Since even now the lord of men Agamemnon
dishonours him, who has taken away his prize and keeps it.
Zeus of the counsels, lord of Olympos, now do him honour.
So long put strength into the Trojans, until the Achaians

510 give my son his rights, and his honour is increased among them.'
She spoke thus. But Zeus who gathers the clouds made no answer
but sat in silence a long time. And Thetis, as she had taken
his knees, clung fast to them and urged once more her question:
'Bend your head and promise me to accomplish this thing,

515 or else refuse it, you have nothing to fear, that I may know
by how much I am the most dishonoured of all gods.'
Deeply disturbed Zeus who gathers the clouds answered her:
'This is a disastrous matter when you set me in conflict
with Hera, and she troubles me with recriminations.

520 Since even as things are, forever among the immortals
she is at me and speaks of how I help the Trojans in battle.
Even so, go back again now, go away, for fear she
see us. I will look to these things that they be accomplished.
See then, I will bend my head that you may believe me.

525 For this among the immortal gods is the mightiest witness
I can give, and nothing I do shall be vain nor revocable
nor a thing unfulfilled when I bend my head in assent to it.'
He spoke, the son of Kronos, and nodded his head with the dark brows,
and the immortally anointed hair of the great god

530 swept from his divine head, and all Olympos was shaken.

So these two who had made their plans separated, and Thetis
leapt down again from shining Olympos into the sea's depth,
but Zeus went back to his own house, and all the gods rose up
from their chairs to greet the coming of their father, not one had courage
535 to keep his place as the father advanced, but stood up to greet him.
Thus he took his place on the throne; yet Hera was not
ignorant, having seen how he had been plotting counsels
with Thetis the silver-footed, the daughter of the sea's ancient,
and at once she spoke revilingly to Zeus son of Kronos:
540 'Treacherous one, what god has been plotting counsels with you?
Always it is dear to your heart in my absence to think of
secret things and decide upon them. Never have you patience
frankly to speak forth to me the thing that you purpose.'
Then to her the father of gods and men made answer:
545 'Hera, do not go on hoping that you will hear all my
thoughts, since these will be too hard for you, though you are my wife.
Any thought that it is right for you to listen to, no one
neither man nor any immortal shall hear it before you.
But anything that apart from the rest of the gods I wish to
550 plan, do not always question each detail nor probe me.'
Then the goddess the ox-eyed lady Hera answered:
'Majesty, son of Kronos, what sort of thing have you spoken?
Truly too much in time past I have not questioned nor probed you,
but you are entirely free to think out whatever pleases you.
555 Now, though, I am terribly afraid you were won over
by Thetis the silver-footed, the daughter of the sea's ancient.
For early in the morning she sat beside you and took your
knees, and I think you bowed your head in assent to do honour
to Achilleus, and to destroy many beside the ships of the Achaians.'
560 Then in return Zeus who gathers the clouds made answer:
'Dear lady, I never escape you, you are always full of suspicion.
Yet thus you can accomplish nothing surely, but be more
distant from my heart than ever, and it will be the worse for you.
If what you say is true, then that is the way I wish it.
565 But go then, sit down in silence, and do as I tell you,
for fear all the gods, as many as are on Olympos, can do nothing
if I come close and lay my unconquerable hands upon you.'
He spoke, and the goddess the ox-eyed lady Hera was frightened
and went and sat down in silence wrenching her heart to obedience,
570 and all the Uranian gods in the house of Zeus were troubled.
Hephaistos the renowned smith rose up to speak among them,
to bring comfort to his beloved mother, Hera of the white arms:
'This will be a disastrous matter and not endurable
if you two are to quarrel thus for the sake of mortals

575 and bring brawling among the gods. There will be no pleasure
in the stately feast at all, since vile things will be uppermost.
And I entreat my mother, though she herself understands it,
to be ingratiating toward our father Zeus, that no longer
our father may scold her and break up the quiet of our feasting.
580 For if the Olympian who handles the lightning should be minded
to hurl us out of our places, he is far too strong for any.
Do you therefore approach him again with words made gentle,
and at once the Olympian will be gracious again to us.'
He spoke, and springing to his feet put a two-handled goblet
585 into his mother's hands and spoke again to her once more:
'Have patience, my mother, and endure it, though you be saddened,
for fear that, dear as you are, I see you before my own eyes
struck down, and then sorry though I be I shall not be able
to do anything. It is too hard to fight against the Olympian.
590 There was a time once before now I was minded to help you,
and he caught me by the foot and threw me from the magic threshold,
and all day long I dropped helpless, and about sunset
I landed in Lemnos, and there was not much life left in me.
After that fall it was the Sintian men who took care of me.'
595 He spoke, and the goddess of the white arms Hera smiled at him,
and smiling she accepted the goblet out of her son's hand.
Thereafter beginning from the left he poured drinks for the other
gods, dipping up from the mixing bowl the sweet nectar.
But among the blessed immortals uncontrollable laughter
600 went up as they saw Hephaistos bustling about the palace.
Thus thereafter the whole day long until the sun went under
they feasted, nor was anyone's hunger denied a fair portion,
nor denied the beautifully wrought lyre in the hands of Apollo
nor the antiphonal sweet sound of the Muses singing.
605 Afterwards when the light of the flaming sun went under
they went away each one to sleep in his home where
for each one the far-renowned strong-handed Hephaistos
had built a house by means of his craftsmanship and cunning.
Zeus the Olympian and lord of the lightning went to
610 his own bed, where always he lay when sweet sleep came on him.
Going up to the bed he slept and Hera of the gold throne beside him.

[*The war drags on and though Achilleus has withdrawn
from battle, the Achaians press hard on the Trojans so that their
leader, Hektor, son of Priam, returns to the city to propitiate the
gods.*]

BOOK SIX: HEKTOR RETURNS TO TROY

      Now as Hektor had come to the Skaian gates and the oak tree,
all the wives of the Trojans and their daughters came running about him
to ask after their sons, after their brothers and neighbours,
their husbands; and he told them to pray to the immortals,
5   all, in turn; but there were sorrows in store for many.
      Now he entered the wonderfully built palace of Priam.
This was fashioned with smooth-stone cloister walks, and within it
were embodied fifty sleeping chambers of smoothed stone
built so as to connect with each other; and within these slept
10   each beside his own wedded wife, the sons of Priam.
In the same inner court on the opposite side, to face these,
lay the twelve close smooth-stone sleeping chambers of his daughters
built so as to connect with each other; and within these slept,
each by his own modest wife, the lords of the daughters of Priam.
15   There there came to meet Hektor his bountiful mother[8]
with Laodike, the loveliest looking of all her daughters.
She clung to his hand and called him by name and spoke to him: 'Why then,
child, have you come here and left behind the bold battle?
Surely it is these accursed sons of the Achaians who wear you
20   out, as they fight close to the city, and the spirit stirred you
to return, and from the peak of the citadel lift your hands, praying
to Zeus. But stay while I bring you honey-sweet wine, to pour out
a libation to father Zeus and the other immortals
first, and afterwards if you will drink yourself, be strengthened.
25   In a tired man, wine will bring back his strength to its bigness,
in a man tired as you are tired, defending your neighbours.'
      Tall Hektor of the shining helm spoke to her answering:
'My honoured mother, lift not to me the kindly sweet wine,
for fear you stagger my strength and make me forget my courage;
30   and with hands unwashed I would take shame to pour the glittering
wine to Zeus; there is no means for a man to pray to the dark-misted
son of Kronos, with blood and muck all spattered upon him.
But go yourself to the temple of the spoiler Athene,
assembling the ladies of honour, and with things to be sacrificed,
35   and take a robe, which seems to you the largest and loveliest
in the great house, and that which is far your dearest possession.
Lay this along the knees of Athene the lovely haired. Also
promise to dedicate within the shrine twelve heifers,
yearlings, never broken, if only she will have pity
40   on the town of Troy, and the Trojan wives, and their innocent children,

---

[8]his bountiful mother: Hekabe

if she will hold back from sacred Ilion the son of Tydeus,[9]
that wild spear-fighter, the strong one who drives men to thoughts of terror.
So go yourself to the temple of the spoiler Athene,
while I go in search of Paris,[10] to call him, if he will listen
45 to anything I tell him. How I wish at this moment the earth might
open beneath him. The Olympian let him live, a great sorrow
to the Trojans, and high-hearted Priam, and all of his children.
If only I could see him gone down to the house of the Death God,
then I could say my heart had forgotten its joyless affliction.'
50   So he spoke, and she going into the great house called out
to her handmaidens, who assembled throughout the city the highborn
women; while she descended into the fragrant store-chamber.
There lay the elaborately wrought robes, the work of Sidonian
women, whom Alexandros himself, the godlike, had brought home
55 from the land of Sidon, crossing the wide sea, on that journey
when he brought back also gloriously descended Helen.
Hekabe lifted out one and took it as gift to Athene,
that which was the loveliest in design and the largest,
and shone like a star. It lay beneath the others. She went on
60 her way, and a throng of noble women hastened about her.
      When these had come to Athene's temple on the peak of the citadel,
Theano of the fair cheeks opened the door for them, daughter
of Kisseus, and wife of Antenor, breaker of horses,
she whom the Trojans had established to be Athene's priestess.
65 With a wailing cry all lifted up their hands to Athene,
and Theano of the fair cheeks taking up the robe laid it
along the knees of Athene the lovely haired, and praying
she supplicated the daughter of powerful Zeus: 'O lady,
Athene, our city's defender, shining among goddesses:
70 break the spear of Diomedes, and grant that the man be
hurled on his face in front of the Skaian gates; so may we
instantly dedicate within your shrine twelve heifers,
yearlings, never broken, if only you will have pity
on the town of Troy, and the Trojan wives, and their innocent children.'
75   She spoke in prayer, but Pallas Athene turned her head from her.
      So they made their prayer to the daughter of Zeus the powerful.
But Hektor went away to the house of Alexandros,[11]
a splendid place he had built himself, with the men who at that time
were the best men for craftsmanship in the generous Troad,

---

[9]**son of Tydeus:** Diomedes, a fierce Greek warrior
[10]**Paris:** Hektor's brother who won Helen, Menelaos' wife, by judging Aphrodite the most beautiful of the goddesses, and thereby initiating the war. (Hera and Athene were the losing contestants in the beauty contest and hence hated Paris and all Trojans.)
[11]**Alexandros:** alternate name for Paris

80   who had made him a sleeping room and a hall and a courtyard
near the houses of Hektor and Priam, on the peak of the citadel.
There entered Hektor beloved of Zeus, in his hand holding
the eleven-cubit-long spear, whose shaft was tipped with a shining
bronze spearhead, and a ring of gold was hooped to hold it.

85   He found the man in his chamber busy with his splendid armour,
the corselet and the shield, and turning in his hands the curved bow,
while Helen of Argos was sitting among her attendant women
directing the magnificent work done by her handmaidens.
    But Hektor saw him, and in words of shame he rebuked him:

90   'Strange man! It is not fair to keep in your heart this coldness.
The people are dying around the city and around the steep wall
as they fight hard; and it is for you that this war with its clamour
has flared up about our city. You yourself would fight with another
whom you saw anywhere hanging back from the hateful encounter.

95   Up then, to keep our town from burning at once in the hot fire.'
    Then in answer the godlike Alexandros spoke to him:
'Hektor, seeing you have scolded me rightly, not beyond measure,
therefore I will tell, and you in turn understand and listen.
It was not so much in coldness and bitter will toward the Trojans

100   that I sat in my room, but I wished to give myself over to sorrow.
But just now with soft words my wife was winning me over
and urging me into the fight, and that way seems to me also
the better one. Victory passes back and forth between men.
Come then, wait for me now while I put on my armour of battle,

105   or go, and I will follow, and I think I can overtake you.'
    He spoke, but Hektor of the shining helm gave him no answer,
but Helen spoke to him in words of endearment: 'Brother
by marriage to me, who am a nasty bitch evil-intriguing,
how I wish that on that day when my mother first bore me

110   the foul whirlwind of the storm had caught me away and swept me
to the mountain, or into the wash of the sea deep-thundering
where the waves would have swept me away before all these things had
        happened.
Yet since the gods had brought it about that these vile things must be,

115   I wish I had been the wife of a better man than this is,
one who knew modesty and all things of shame that men say.
But this man's heart is no steadfast thing, nor yet will it be so
ever hereafter; for that I think he shall take the consequence.
But come now, come in and rest on this chair, my brother,

120   since it is on your heart beyond all that the hard work has fallen
for the sake of dishonoured me and the blind act of Alexandros,
us two, on whom Zeus set a vile destiny, so that hereafter
we shall be made into things of song for the men of the future.'

Then tall Hektor of the shining helm answered her: 'Do not, Helen,
125   make me sit with you, though you love me. You will not persuade me.
Already my heart within is hastening me to defend
the Trojans, who when I am away long greatly to have me.
Rather rouse this man, and let himself also be swift to action
so he may overtake me while I am still in the city.
130   For I am going first to my own house, so I can visit
my own people, my beloved wife and my son, who is little,
since I do not know if ever again I shall come back this way,
or whether the gods will strike me down at the hands of the Achaians.'
So speaking Hektor of the shining helm departed
135   and in speed made his way to his own well-established dwelling,
but failed to find in the house Andromache of the white arms;
for she, with the child, and followed by one fair-robed attendant,
had taken her place on the tower in lamentation, and tearful.
When he saw no sign of his perfect wife within the house, Hektor
140   stopped in his way on the threshold and spoke among the handmaidens:
'Come then, tell me truthfully as you may, handmaidens:
where has Andromache of the white arms gone? Is she
with any of the sisters of her lord or the wives of his brothers?
Or has she gone to the house of Athene, where all the other
145   lovely-haired women of Troy propitiate the grim goddess?'
Then in turn the hard-working housekeeper gave him an answer:
'Hektor, since you have urged me to tell you the truth, she is not
with any of the sisters of her lord or the wives of his brothers,
nor has she gone to the house of Athene, where all the other
150   lovely-haired women of Troy propitiate the grim goddess,
but she has gone to the great bastion of Ilion, because she heard that
the Trojans were losing, and great grew the strength of the Achaians.
Therefore she has gone in speed to the wall, like a woman
gone mad, and a nurse attending her carries the baby.'
155   So the housekeeper spoke, and Hektor hastened from his home
backward by the way he had come through the well-laid streets. So
as he had come to the gates on his way through the great city,
the Skaian gates, whereby he would issue into the plain, there
at last his own generous wife came running to meet him,
160   Andromache, the daughter of high-hearted Eëtion;
Eëtion, who had dwelt underneath wooded Plakos,
in Thebe below Plakos, lord over the Kilikian people.
It was his daughter who was given to Hektor of the bronze helm.
She came to him there, and beside her went an attendant carrying
165   the boy in the fold of her bosom, a little child, only a baby,
Hektor's son, the admired, beautiful as a star shining,
whom Hektor called Skamandrios, but all of the others

Astyanax—lord of the city; since Hektor alone saved Ilion.
Hektor smiled in silence as he looked on his son, but she,
170   Andromache, stood close beside him, letting her tears fall,
and clung to his hand and called him by name and spoke to him: 'Dearest,
your own great strength will be your death, and you have no pity
on your little son, nor on me, ill-starred, who soon must be your widow;
for presently the Achaians, gathering together,
175   will set upon you and kill you; and for me it would be far better
to sink into the earth when I have lost you, for there is no other
consolation for me after you have gone to your destiny—
only grief; since I have no father, no honoured mother.
It was brilliant Achilleus who slew my father, Eëtion,
180   when he stormed the strong-founded citadel of the Kilikians,
Thebe of the towering gates. He killed Eëtion
but did not strip his armour, for his heart respected the dead man,
but burned the body in all its elaborate war-gear
and piled a grave mound over it, and the nymphs of the mountains,
185   daughters of Zeus of the aegis, planted elm trees about it.
And they who were my seven brothers in the great house all went
upon a single day down into the house of the death god,
for swift-footed brilliant Achilleus slaughtered all of them
as they were tending their white sheep and their lumbering oxen;
190   and when he had led my mother, who was queen under wooded Plakos,
here, along with all his other possessions, Achilleus
released her again, accepting ransom beyond count, but Artemis[12]
of the showering arrows struck her down in the halls of her father.
Hektor, thus you are father to me, and my honoured mother,
195   you are my brother, and you it is who are my young husband.
Please take pity upon me then, stay here on the rampart,
that you may not leave your child an orphan, your wife a widow,
but draw your people up by the fig tree, there where the city
is openest to attack, and where the wall may be mounted.
200   Three times their bravest came that way, and fought there to storm it
about the two Aiantes and renowned Idomeneus,
about the two Atreidai and the fighting son of Tydeus.
Either some man well skilled in prophetic arts had spoken,
or the very spirit within themselves had stirred them to the onslaught.'
205   Then tall Hektor of the shining helm answered her: 'All these
things are in my mind also, lady; yet I would feel deep shame
before the Trojans, and the Trojan women with trailing garments,
if like a coward I were to shrink aside from the fighting;
and the spirit will not let me, since I have learned to be valiant

---

[12]**Artemis:** sister of Apollo, goddess of the hunt and protectress of wildlife.

210   and to fight always among the foremost ranks of the Trojans,
winning for my own self great glory, and for my father.
For I know this thing well in my heart, and my mind knows it:
there will come a day when sacred Ilion shall perish,
and Priam, and the people of Priam of the strong ash spear.
215   But it is not so much the pain to come of the Trojans
that troubles me, not even of Priam the king nor Hekabe,
not the thought of my brothers who in their numbers and valour
shall drop in the dust under the hands of men who hate them,
as troubles me the thought of you, when some bronze-armoured
220   Achaian leads you off, taking away your day of liberty,
in tears; and in Argos you must work at the loom of another,
and carry water from the spring Messeis or Hypereia,
all unwilling, but strong will be the necessity upon you;
and some day seeing you shedding tears a man will say of you:
225   "This is the wife of Hektor, who was ever the bravest fighter
of the Trojans, breakers of horses, in the days when they fought about Ilion."
So will one speak of you; and for you it will be yet a fresh grief,
to be widowed of such a man who could fight off the day of your slavery.
But may I be dead and the piled earth hide me under before I
230   hear you crying and know by this that they drag you captive.'
So speaking glorious Hektor held out his arms to his baby,
who shrank back to his fair-girdled nurse's bosom
screaming, and frightened at the aspect of his own father,
terrified as he saw the bronze and the crest with its horse-hair,
235   nodding dreadfully, as he thought, from the peak of the helmet.
Then his beloved father laughed out, and his honoured mother,
and at once glorious Hektor lifted from his head the helmet
and laid it in all its shining upon the ground. Then taking
up his dear son he tossed him about in his arms, and kissed him,
240   and lifted his voice in prayer to Zeus and the other immortals:
'Zeus, and you other immortals, grant that this boy, who is my son,
may be as I am, pre-eminent among the Trojans,
great in strength, as am I, and rule strongly over Ilion;
and some day let them say of him: "He is better by far than his father,"
245   as he comes in from the fighting; and let him kill his enemy
and bring home the blooded spoils, and delight the heart of his mother.'
So speaking he set his child again in the arms of his beloved
wife, who took him back again to her fragrant bosom
smiling in her tears; and her husband saw, and took pity upon her,
250   and stroked her with his hand, and called her by name and spoke to her:
'Poor Andromache! Why does your heart sorrow so much for me?
No man is going to hurl me to Hades, unless it is fated,
but as for fate, I think that no man yet has escaped it

once it has taken its first form, neither brave man nor coward.

255   Go therefore back to our house, and take up your own work,
the loom and the distaff, and see to it that your handmaidens
ply their work also; but the men must see to the fighting,
all men who are the people of Ilion, but I beyond others.'
    So glorious Hektor spoke and again took up the helmet

260   with its crest of horse-hair, while his beloved wife went homeward,
turning to look back on the way, letting the live tears fall.
And as she came in speed into the well-settled household
of Hektor the slayer of men, she found numbers of handmaidens
within, and her coming stirred all of them into lamentation.

265   So they mourned in his house over Hektor while he was living
still, for they thought he would never again come back from the fighting
alive, escaping the Achaian hands and their violence.
    But Paris in turn did not linger long in his high house,
but when he had put on his glorious armour with bronze elaborate

270   he ran in the confidence of his quick feet through the city.
As when some stalled horse who has been corn-fed at the manger
breaking free of his rope gallops over the plain in thunder
to his accustomed bathing place in a sweet-running river
and in the pride of his strength holds high his head, and the mane floats

275   over his shoulders; sure of his glorious strength, the quick knees
carry him to the loved places and the pasture of horses;
so from uttermost Pergamos[13] came Paris, the son of
Priam, shining in all his armour of war as the sun shines,
laughing aloud, and his quick feet carried him; suddenly thereafter

280   he came on brilliant Hektor, his brother, where he yet lingered
before turning away from the place where he had talked with his lady.
It was Alexandros the godlike who first spoke to him:
'Brother, I fear that I have held back your haste, by being
slow on the way, not coming in time, as you commanded me.'

285   Then tall Hektor of the shining helm spoke to him in answer:
'Strange man! There is no way that one, giving judgment in fairness,
could dishonour your work in battle, since you are a strong man.
But of your own accord you hang back, unwilling. And my heart
is grieved in its thought, when I hear shameful things spoken about you

290   by the Trojans, who undergo hard fighting for your sake.
Let us go now; some day hereafter we will make all right
with the immortal gods in the sky, if Zeus ever grant it,
setting up to them in our houses the wine-bowl of liberty
after we have driven out of Troy the strong-greaved Achaians.'

---

[13]**Pergamos**: the citadel of Troy

[*The Trojans rally and cause much destruction to the Greeks who realize their great need for Achilleus to return to battle.*]

BOOK NINE: THE EMBASSY TO ACHILLEUS

So the Trojans held their night watches. Meanwhile immortal
Panic, companion of cold Terror, gripped the Achaians
as all their best were stricken with grief that passes endurance.
As two winds rise to shake the sea where the fish swarm, Boreas
5 and Zephyros, north wind and west, that blow from Thraceward,
suddenly descending, and the darkened water is gathered
to crests, and far across the salt water scatters the seaweed;
so the heart in the breast of each Achaian was troubled.
    And the son of Atreus, stricken at heart with the great sorrow,
10 went among his heralds the clear-spoken and told them
to summon calling by name each man into the assembly
but with no outcry, and he himself was at work with the foremost.
They took their seats in assembly, dispirited, and Agamemnon
stood up before them, shedding tears, like a spring dark-running
15 that down the face of a rock impassable drips its dim water.
So, groaning heavily, Agamemnon spoke to the Argives:
'Friends, who are leaders of the Argives and keep their counsel:
Zeus son of Kronos has caught me badly in bitter futility.
He is hard: who before this time promised me and consented
20 that I might sack strong-walled Ilion and sail homeward.
Now he has devised a vile deception and bids me go back
to Argos in dishonour having lost many of my people.
Such is the way it will be pleasing to Zeus, who is too strong,
who before now has broken the crests of many cities
25 and will break them again, since his power is beyond all others.
Come then, do as I say, let us all be won over; let us
run away with our ships to the beloved land of our fathers
since no longer now shall we capture Troy of the wide ways.'
    So he spoke, and all of them stayed stricken to silence.
30 For some time the sons of the Achaians said nothing in sorrow;
but at long last Diomedes of the great war cry addressed them:
'Son of Atreus: I will be first to fight with your folly,
as is my right, lord, in this assembly; then do not be angered.
I was the first of the Danaans whose valour you slighted
35 and said I was unwarlike and without courage. The young men
of the Argives know all these things, and the elders know it.
The son of devious-devising Kronos has given you
gifts in two ways: with the sceptre he gave you honour beyond all,
but he did not give you a heart, and of all power this is the greatest.

40 Sir, sir, can you really believe the sons of the Achaians
  are so unwarlike and so weak of their hearts as you call them?
  But if in truth your own heart is so set upon going,
  go. The way is there, and next to the water are standing
  your ships that came—so many of them!—with you from Mykenai,
45 and yet the rest of the flowing-haired Achaians will stay here
  until we have sacked the city of Troy; let even these also
  run away with their ships to the beloved land of their fathers,
  still we two, Sthenelos and I, will fight till we witness
  the end of Ilion; for it was with God that we made our way hither.'
50   So he spoke, and all the sons of the Achaians shouted
  acclaim for the word of Diomedes, breaker of horses.
  And now Nestor the horseman stood forth among them and spoke to them:
  'Son of Tydeus, beyond others you are strong in battle,
  and in counsel also are noblest among all men of your own age.
55 Not one man of all the Achaians will belittle your words nor
  speak against them. Yet you have not made complete your argument,
  since you are a young man still and could even be my own son
  and my youngest born of all; yet still you argue in wisdom
  with the Argive kings, since all you have spoken was spoken fairly.
60 But let me speak, since I can call myself older than you are,
  and go through the whole matter, since there is none who can dishonour
  the thing I say, not even powerful Agamemnon.
  Out of all brotherhood, outlawed, homeless shall be that man
  ·who longs for all the horror of fighting among his own people.
65 But now let us give way to the darkness of night, and let us
  make ready our evening meal; and let the guards severally
  take their stations by the ditch we have dug outside the ramparts.
  This I would enjoin upon our young men; but thereafter
  do you, son of Atreus, take command, since you are our kingliest.
70 Divide a feast among the princes; it befits you, it is not
  unbecoming. Our shelters are filled with wine that the Achaian
  ships carry day by day from Thrace across the wide water.
  All hospitality is for you; you are lord over many.
  When many assemble together follow him who advises
75 the best counsel, for in truth there is need for all the Achaians
  of good close counsel, since now close to our ships the enemy·
  burn their numerous fires. What man could be cheered to see this?
  Here is the night that will break our army, or else will preserve it.'
   So he spoke, and they listened hard to him, and obeyed him,
80 and the sentries went forth rapidly in their armour, gathering
  about Nestor's son Thrasymedes, shepherd of the people,

and about Askalaphos and Ialmenos, sons both of Ares,[14]
about Meriones and Aphareus and Deïpyros
and about the son of Kreion, Lykomedes the brilliant.
85   There were seven leaders of the sentinels, and with each one a hundred
fighting men followed gripping in their hands the long spears.
They took position in the space between the ditch and the rampart,
and there they kindled their fires and each made ready his supper.
    But the son of Atreus led the assembled lords of the Achaians
90   to his own shelter, and set before them the feast in abundance.
They put their hands to the good things that lay ready before them.
But when they had put away their desire for eating and drinking,
the aged man began to weave his counsel before them
first, Nestor, whose advice had shown best before this.
95   He in kind intention toward all stood forth and addressed them:
'Son of Atreus, most lordly and king of men, Agamemnon,
with you I will end, with you I will make my beginning, since you
are lord over many people, and Zeus has given into your hand
the sceptre and rights of judgment, to be king over the people.
100   It is yours therefore to speak a word, yours also to listen,
and grant the right to another also, when his spirit stirs him
to speak for our good. All shall be yours when you lead the way. Still
I will speak in the way it seems best to my mind, and no one
shall have in his mind any thought that is better than this one
105   that I have in my mind either now or long before now
ever since that day, illustrious, when you went from the shelter
of angered Achilleus, taking by force the girl Briseis
against the will of the rest of us, since I for my part
urged you strongly not to, but you, giving way to your proud heart's
110   anger, dishonoured a great man, one whom the immortals
honour, since you have taken his prize and keep it. But let us
even now think how we can make this good and persuade him
with words of supplication and with the gifts of friendship.'
    Then in turn the lord of men Agamemnon spoke to him:
115   'Aged sir, this was no lie when you spoke of my madness.
I was mad, I myself will not deny it. Worth many
fighters is that man whom Zeus in his heart loves, as now
he has honoured this man and beaten down the Achaian people.
But since I was mad, in the persuasion of my heart's evil,
120   I am willing to make all good, and give back gifts in abundance.
Before you all I will count off my gifts in their splendour:
seven unfired tripods; ten talents' weight of gold; twenty
shining cauldrons; and twelve horses, strong, race-competitors

---

[14]Ares: god of war

who have won prizes in the speed of their feet. That man would not be

125   poor in possessions, to whom were given all these have won me,

nor be unpossessed of dearly honoured gold, were he given

all the prizes these single-foot horses have won for me.

I will give him seven women of Lesbos, the work of whose hands is

blameless, whom when he himself captured strong-founded Lesbos

130   I chose, and who in their beauty surpassed the races of women.

I will give him these, and with them shall go the one I took from him,

the daughter of Briseus. And to all this I will swear a great oath

that I never entered into her bed and never lay with her

as is natural for human people, between men and women.

135   All these gifts shall be his at once; but again, if hereafter

the gods grant that we storm and sack the great city of Priam,

let him go to his ship and load it deep as he pleases

with gold and bronze, when we Achaians divide the war spoils,

and let him choose for himself twenty of the Trojan women

140   who are the loveliest of all after Helen of Argos.

And if we come back to Achaian Argos, pride of the tilled land,

he may be my son-in-law; I will honour him with Orestes

my growing son, who is brought up there in abundant luxury.

Since, as I have three daughters there in my strong-built castle,

145   Chrysothemis and Laodike and Iphianassa,

let him lead away the one of these that he likes, with no bride-price,

to the house of Peleus, and with the girl I will grant him as dowry

many gifts, such as no man ever gave with his daughter.

I will grant to him seven citadels, strongly settled:

150   Kardamyle, and Enope, and Hire of the grasses,

Pherai the sacrosanct, and Antheia deep in the meadows,

with Aipeia the lovely and Pedasos of the vineyards.

All these lie near the sea, at the bottom of sandy Pylos,

and men live among them rich in cattle and rich in sheepflocks,

155   who will honour him as if he were a god with gifts given

and fulfil his prospering decrees underneath his sceptre.

All this I will bring to pass for him, if he changes from his anger.

Let him give way. For Hades[15] gives not way, and is pitiless,

and therefore he among all the gods is most hateful to mortals.

160   And let him yield place to me, inasmuch as I am the kinglier

and inasmuch as I can call myself born the elder.'

       Thereupon the Gerenian horseman Nestor answered him:

'Son of Atreus, most lordly and king of men, Agamemnon,

none could scorn any longer these gifts you offer to Achilleus

165   the king. Come, let us choose and send some men, who in all speed

---

[15]**Hades:** the god of death and the underworld

will go to the shelter of Achilleus, the son of Peleus;
or come, the men on whom my eye falls, let these take the duty.
First of all let Phoinix,[16] beloved of Zeus, be their leader,
and after him take Aias the great, and brilliant Odysseus,
170 and of the heralds let Odios and Eurybates go with them.
Bring also water for their hands, and bid them keep words of good omen,
so we may pray to Zeus, son of Kronos, if he will have pity.'
  So he spoke, and the word he spoke was pleasing to all of them.
And the heralds brought water at once, and poured it over
175 their hands, and the young men filled the mixing-bowl with pure wine
and passed it to all, pouring first a libation in goblets.
Then when they had poured out wine, and drunk as much as their hearts wished,
they set out from the shelter of Atreus' son, Agamemnon.
And the Gerenian horseman Nestor gave them much instruction,
180 looking eagerly at each, and most of all at Odysseus,
to try hard, so that they might win over the blameless Peleion.[17]
  So these two walked along the strand of the sea deep-thundering
with many prayers to the holder and shaker of the earth,[18] that they
might readily persuade the great heart of Aiakides.[19]
185 Now they came beside the shelters and ships of the Myrmidons
and they found Achilleus delighting his heart in a lyre, clear-sounding,
splendid and carefully wrought, with a bridge of silver upon it,
which he won out of the spoils when he ruined Eëtion's city.
With this he was pleasuring his heart, and singing of men's fame,
190 as Patroklos was sitting over against him, alone, in silence,
watching Aiakides and the time he would leave off singing.
Now these two came forward, as brilliant Odysseus led them,
and stood in his presence. Achilleus rose to his feet in amazement
holding the lyre as it was, leaving the place where he was sitting.
195 In the same way Patroklos, when he saw the men come, stood up.
And in greeting Achilleus the swift of foot spoke to them:
'Welcome. You are my friends who have come, and greatly I need you,
who even to this my anger are dearest of all the Achaians.'
  So brilliant Achilleus spoke, and guided them forward,
200 and caused them to sit down on couches with purple coverlets
and at once called over to Patroklos who was not far from him:
'Son of Menoitios, set up a mixing-bowl that is bigger,
and mix us stronger drink, and make ready a cup for each man,
since these who have come beneath my roof are the men that I love best.'

---

[16]**Phoinix:** Achilleus' former tutor
[17]**Peleion:** Achilleus, who came from the Mount Pelion region
[18]**the holder and shaker of the earth:** Poseidon, god of the sea and earthquakes
[19]**Aiakides:** descendant of Aiakos, i.e., Achilleus

205   So he spoke, and Patroklos obeyed his beloved companion,
and tossed down a great chopping-block into the firelight,
and laid upon it the back of a sheep, and one of a fat goat,
with the chine of a fatted pig edged thick with lard, and for him
Automedon held the meats, and brilliant Achilleus carved them,

210   and cut it well into pieces and spitted them, as meanwhile
Menoitios' son, a man like a god, made the fire blaze greatly.
But when the fire had burned itself out, and the flames had died down,
he scattered the embers apart, and extended the spits across them
lifting them to the andirons, and sprinkled the meats with divine salt.

215   Then when he had roasted all, and spread the food on the platters,
Patroklos took the bread and set it out on a table
in fair baskets, while Achilleus served the meats. Thereafter
he himself sat over against the godlike Odysseus
against the further wall, and told his companion, Patroklos,

220   to sacrifice to the gods; and he threw the firstlings in the fire.
They put their hands to the good things that lay ready before them.
But when they had put aside their desire for eating and drinking,
Aias nodded to Phoinix, and brilliant Odysseus saw it,
and filled a cup with wine, and lifted it to Achilleus:

225   'Your health, Achilleus. You have no lack of your equal portion
either within the shelter of Atreus' son, Agamemnon,
nor here now in your own. We have good things in abundance
to feast on; here it is not the desirable feast we think of,
but a trouble all too great, beloved of Zeus, that we look on

230   and are afraid. There is doubt if we save our strong-benched vessels
or if they will be destroyed, unless you put on your war strength.
The Trojans in their pride, with their far-renowned companions,
have set up an encampment close by the ships and the rampart,
and lit many fires along their army, and think no longer

235   of being held, but rather to drive in upon the black ships.
And Zeus, son of Kronos, lightens upon their right hand, showing them
portents of good, while Hektor in the huge pride of his strength rages
irresistibly, reliant on Zeus, and gives way to no one
neither god nor man, but the strong fury has descended upon him.

240   He prays now that the divine Dawn will show most quickly,
since he threatens to shear the uttermost horns from the ship-sterns,
to light the ships themselves with ravening fire, and to cut down
the Achaians themselves as they stir from the smoke beside them.
All this I fear terribly in my heart, lest immortals

245   accomplish all these threats, and lest for us it be destiny
to die here in Troy, far away from horse-pasturing Argos.
Up, then! if you are minded, late though it be, to rescue
the afflicted sons of the Achaians from the Trojan onslaught.

It will be an affliction to you hereafter, there will be no remedy
250 found to heal the evil thing when it has been done. No, beforehand
take thought to beat the evil day aside from the Danaans.
Dear friend, surely thus your father Peleus advised you
that day when he sent you away to Agamemnon from Phthia:
"My child, for the matter of strength, Athene and Hera will give it
255 if it be their will, but be it yours to hold fast in your bosom
the anger of the proud heart, for consideration is better.
Keep from the bad complication of quarrel, and all the more for this
the Argives will honour you, both their younger men and their elders."
So the old man advised, but you have forgotten. Yet even now
260 stop, and give way from the anger that hurts the heart. Agamemnon
offers you worthy recompense if you change from your anger.
Come then, if you will, listen to me, while I count off for you
all the gifts in his shelter that Agamemnon has promised:
Seven unfired tripods; ten talents' weight of gold; twenty
265 shining cauldrons; and twelve horses, strong, race-competitors
who have won prizes in the speed of their feet. That man would not be
poor in possessions, to whom were given all these have won him,
nor be unpossessed of dearly honoured gold, were he given
all the prizes Agamemnon's horses won in their speed for him.
270 He will give you seven women of Lesbos, the work of whose hands
is blameless, whom when you yourself captured strong-founded Lesbos
he chose, and who in their beauty surpassed the races of women.
He will give you these, and with them shall go the one he took from you,
the daughter of Briseus. And to all this he will swear a great oath
275 that he never entered into her bed and never lay with her
as is natural for human people, between men and women.
All these gifts shall be yours at once; but again, if hereafter
the gods grant that we storm and sack the great city of Priam,
you may go to your ship and load it deep as you please with
280 gold and bronze, when we Achaians divide the war spoils,
and you may choose for yourself twenty of the Trojan women,
who are the loveliest of all after Helen of Argos.
And if we come back to Achaian Argos, pride of the tilled land,
you could be his son-in-law; he would honour you with Orestes,
285 his growing son, who is brought up there in abundant luxury.
Since, as he has three daughters there in his strong-built castle,
Chrysothemis and Laodike and Iphianassa,
you may lead away the one of these that you like, with no bride-price,
to the house of Peleus; and with the girl he will grant you as dowry
290 many gifts, such as no man ever gave with his daughter.
He will grant you seven citadels, strongly settled:
Kardamyle and Enope and Hire of the grasses,

Pherai the sacrosanct, and Antheia deep in the meadows,
with Aipeia the lovely, and Pedasos of the vineyards.
295 All these lie near the sea, at the bottom of sandy Pylos,
and men live among them rich in cattle and rich in sheepflocks,
who will honour you as if you were a god with gifts given
and fulfil your prospering decrees underneath your sceptre.
All this he will bring to pass for you, if you change from your anger.
300 But if the son of Atreus is too much hated in your heart,
himself and his gifts, at least take pity on all the other
Achaians, who are afflicted along the host, and will honour you
as a god. You may win very great glory among them.
For now you might kill Hektor, since he would come very close to you
305 with the wicked fury upon him, since he thinks there is not his equal
among the rest of the Danaans the ships carried hither.'
    Then in answer to him spoke Achilleus of the swift feet:
'Son of Laertes and seed of Zeus, resourceful Odysseus:
without consideration for you I must make my answer,
310 the way I think, and the way it will be accomplished, that you may not
come one after another, and sit by me, and speak softly.
For as I detest the doorways of Death, I detest that man, who
hides one thing in the depths of his heart, and speaks forth another.
But I will speak to you the way it seems best to me: neither
315 do I think the son of Atreus, Agamemnon, will persuade me,
nor the rest of the Danaans, since there was no gratitude given
for fighting incessantly forever against your enemies.
Fate is the same for the man who holds back, the same if he fights hard.
We are all held in a single honour, the brave with the weaklings.
320 A man dies still if he has done nothing, as one who has done much.
Nothing is won for me, now that my heart has gone through its afflictions
in forever setting my life on the hazard of battle.
For as to her unwinged young ones the mother bird brings back
morsels, wherever she can find them, but as for herself it is suffering,
325 such was I, as I lay through all the many nights unsleeping,
such as I wore through the bloody days of the fighting,
striving with warriors for the sake of these men's women.
But I say that I have stormed from my ships twelve cities
of men, and by land eleven more through the generous Troad.
330 From all these we took forth treasures, goodly and numerous,
and we would bring them back, and give them to Agamemnon,
Atreus' son; while he, waiting back beside the swift ships,
would take them, and distribute them little by little, and keep many.
All the other prizes of honour he gave the great men and the princes
335 are held fast by them, but from me alone of all the Achaians
he has taken and keeps the bride of my heart. Let him lie beside her

and be happy. Yet why must the Argives fight with the Trojans?
And why was it the son of Atreus assembled and led here
these people? Was it not for the sake of lovely-haired Helen?
340 Are the sons of Atreus alone among mortal men the ones
who love their wives? Since any who is a good man, and careful,
loves her who is his own and cares for her, even as I now
loved this one from my heart, though it was my spear that won her.
Now that he has deceived me and taken from my hands my prize of honour,
345 let him try me no more. I know him well. He will not persuade me.
Let him take counsel with you, Odysseus, and the rest of the princes
how to fight the ravening fire away from his vessels.
Indeed, there has been much hard work done even without me;
he has built himself a wall and driven a ditch about it,
350 making it great and wide, and fixed the sharp stakes inside it.
Yet even so he cannot hold the strength of manslaughtering
Hektor; and yet when I was fighting among the Achaians
Hektor would not drive his attack beyond the wall's shelter
but would come forth only so far as the Skaian gates and the oak tree.
355 There once he endured me alone, and barely escaped my onslaught.
But, now I am unwilling to fight against brilliant Hektor,
tomorrow, when I have sacrificed to Zeus and to all gods,
and loaded well my ships, and rowed out on to the salt water,
you will see, if you have a mind to it and if it concerns you,
360 my ships in the dawn at sea on the Hellespont where the fish swarm
and my men manning them with good will to row. If the glorious
shaker of the earth should grant us a favouring passage
on the third day thereafter we might raise generous Phthia.
I have many possessions there that I left behind when l came here
365 on this desperate venture, and from here there is more gold, and red bronze,
and fair-girdled women, and grey iron I will take back;
all that was allotted to me. But my prize: he who gave it,
powerful Agamemnon, son of Atreus, has taken it back again
outrageously. Go back and proclaim to him all that I tell you,
370 openly, so other Achaians may turn against him in anger
if he hopes yet one more time to swindle some other Danaan,
wrapped as he is forever in shamelessness; yet he would not,
bold as a dog though he be, dare look in my face any longer.
I will join with him in no counsel, and in no action.
375 He cheated me and he did me hurt. Let him not beguile me
with words again. This is enough for him. Let him of his own will
be damned, since Zeus of the counsels has taken his wits away from him.
I hate his gifts. I hold him light as the strip of a splinter.
Not if he gave me ten times as much, and twenty times over
380 as he possesses now, not if more should come to him from elsewhere,

or gave all that is brought in to Orchomenos, all that is brought in
to Thebes of Egypt, where the greatest possessions lie up in the houses,
Thebes of the hundred gates, where through each of the gates two hundred
fighting men come forth to war with horses and chariots;

385   not if he gave me gifts as many as the sand or the dust is,
not even so would Agamemnon have his way with my spirit
until he had made good to me all this heartrending insolence.
Nor will I marry a daughter of Atreus' son, Agamemnon,
not if she challenged Aphrodite the golden for loveliness,

390   not if she matched the work of her hands with grey-eyed Athene;
not even so will I marry her; let him pick some other Achaian,
one who is to his liking and is kinglier than I am.
For if the gods will keep me alive, and I win homeward,
Peleus himself will presently arrange a wife for me.

395   There are many Achaian girls in the land of Hellas and Phthia,
daughters of great men who hold strong places in guard. And of these
any one that I please I might make my beloved lady.
And the great desire in my heart drives me rather in that place
to take a wedded wife in marriage, the bride of my fancy,

400   to enjoy with her the possessions won by aged Peleus. For not
worth the value of my life are all the possessions they fable
were won for Ilion, that strong-founded citadel, in the old days
when there was peace, before the coming of the sons of the Achaians;
not all that the stone doorsill of the Archer holds fast within it,

405   of Phoibos Apollo in Pytho[20] of the rocks. Of possessions
cattle and fat sheep are things to be had for the lifting,
and tripods can be won, and the tawny high heads of horses,
but a man's life cannot come back again, it cannot be lifted
nor captured again by force, once it has crossed the teeth's barrier.

410   For my mother Thetis the goddess of the silver feet tells me
I carry two sorts of destiny toward the day of my death. Either,
if I stay here and fight beside the city of the Trojans,
my return home is gone, but my glory shall be everlasting;
but if I return home to the beloved land of my fathers,

415   the excellence of my glory is gone, but there will be a long life
left for me, and my end in death will not come to me quickly.
And this would be my counsel to others also, to sail back
home again, since no longer shall you find any term set
on the sheer city of Ilion, since Zeus of the wide brows has strongly

420   held his own hand over it, and its people are made bold.
    Do you go back therefore to the great men of the Achaians,
and take them this message, since such is the privilege of the princes:

---

[20]**Pytho**: the shrine of Apollo at Delphi

that they think out in their minds some other scheme that is better,
which might rescue their ships, and the people of the Achaians
425 who man the hollow ships, since this plan will not work for them
which they thought of by reason of my anger. Let Phoinix
remain here with us and sleep here, so that tomorrow
he may come with us in our ships to the beloved land of our fathers,
if he will; but I will never use force to hold him.'
430   So he spoke, and all of them stayed stricken to silence
in amazement at his words. He had spoken to them very strongly.
But at long last Phoinix the aged horseman spoke out
in a stormburst of tears, and fearing for the ships of the Achaians:
'If it is going home, glorious Achilleus, you ponder
435 in your heart, and are utterly unwilling to drive the obliterating
fire from the fast ships, since anger has descended on your spirit,
how then shall I, dear child, be left in this place behind you
all alone? Peleus the aged horseman sent me forth with you
on that day when he sent you from Phthia to Agamemnon
440 a mere child, who knew nothing yet of the joining of battle
nor of debate where men are made pre-eminent. Therefore
he sent me along with you to teach you of all these matters,
to make you a speaker of words and one who accomplished in action.
Therefore apart from you, dear child, I would not be willing
445 to be left behind, not were the god in person to promise
he would scale away my old age and make me a young man blossoming
as I was that time when I first left Hellas, the land of fair women,
running from the hatred of Ormenos' son Amyntor,
my father; who hated me for the sake of a fair-haired mistress.
450 For he made love to her himself, and dishonoured his own wife,
my mother; who was forever taking my knees and entreating me
to lie with this mistress instead so that she would hate the old man.
I was persuaded and did it; and my father when he heard of it straightway
called down his curses, and invoked against me the dreaded furies[21]
455 that I might never have any son born of my seed to dandle
on my knees; and the divinities, Zeus of the underworld[22]
and Persephone the honoured goddess, accomplished his curses.
Then I took it into my mind to cut him down with the sharp bronze,
but some one of the immortals checked my anger, reminding me
460 of rumour among the people and men's maledictions repeated,
that I might not be called a parricide among the Achaians.
But now no more could the heart in my breast be ruled entirely

---

[21]**furies**: goddesses aroused for crimes against kin when there is no one else to exact
vengeance, hence they represent a kind of justice or balance
[22]**Zeus of the underworld**: Hades; Persephone is his wife

to range still among these halls when my father was angered.
Rather it was the many kinsmen and cousins about me

465 who held me closed in the house, with supplications repeated,
and slaughtered fat sheep in their numbers, and shambling horn-curved
cattle, and numerous swine with the fat abundant upon them
were singed and stretched out across the flame of Hephaistos,
and much wine was drunk that was stored in the jars of the old man.

470 Nine nights they slept nightlong in their places beside me,
and they kept up an interchange of watches, and the fire was never
put out; one below the gate of the strong-closed courtyard,
and one in the ante-chamber before the doors of the bedroom.
But when the tenth night had come to me in its darkness,

475 then I broke the close-compacted doors of the chamber
and got away, and overleapt the fence of the courtyard
lightly, unnoticed by the guarding men and the women servants.
Then I fled far away through the wide spaces of Hellas
and came as far as generous Phthia, mother of sheepflocks,

480 and to lord Peleus, who accepted me with a good will
and gave me his love, even as a father loves his own son
who is a single child brought up among many possessions.
He made me a rich man, and granted me many people,
and I lived, lord over the Dolopes, in remotest Phthia,

485 and, godlike Achilleus, I made you all that you are now,
and loved you out of my heart, for you would not go with another
out to any feast, nor taste any food in your own halls
until I had set you on my knees, and cut little pieces
from the meat, and given you all you wished, and held the wine for you.

490 And many times you soaked the shirt that was on my body
with wine you would spit up in the troublesomeness of your childhood.
So I have suffered much through you, and have had much trouble,
thinking always how the gods would not bring to birth any children
of my own; so that it was you, godlike Achilleus, I made

495 my own child, so that some day you might keep hard affliction from me.
Then, Achilleus, beat down your great anger. It is not
yours to have a pitiless heart. The very immortals
can be moved; their virtue and honour and strength are greater than ours are,
and yet with sacrifices and offerings for endearment,

500 with libations and with savour men turn back even the immortals
in supplication, when any man does wrong and transgresses.
For there are also the spirits of Prayer, the daughters of great Zeus,
and they are lame of their feet, and wrinkled, and cast their eyes sidelong,
who toil on their way left far behind by the spirit of Ruin:

505 but she, Ruin, is strong and sound on her feet, and therefore
far outruns all Prayers, and wins into every country

to force men astray; and the Prayers follow as healers after her.
If a man venerates these daughters of Zeus as they draw near,
such a man they bring great advantage, and hear his entreaty;
510 but if a man shall deny them, and stubbornly with a harsh word
refuse, they go to Zeus, son of Kronos, in supplication
that Ruin may overtake this man, that he be hurt, and punished.
So, Achilleus: grant, you also, that Zeus' daughters be given
their honour, which, lordly though they be, curbs the will of others.
515 Since, were he not bringing gifts and naming still more hereafter,
Atreus' son; were he to remain still swollen with rancour,
even I would not bid you throw your anger aside, nor
defend the Argives, though they needed you sorely. But see now,
he offers you much straightway, and has promised you more hereafter;
520 he has sent the best men to you to supplicate you, choosing them
out of the Achaian host, those who to yourself are the dearest
of all the Argives. Do not you make vain their argument
nor their footsteps, though before this one could not blame your anger.
Thus it was in the old days also, the deeds that we hear of
525 from the great men, when the swelling anger descended upon them.
The heroes would take gifts; they would listen, and be persuaded.
For I remember this action of old, it is not a new thing,
and how it went; you are all my friends, I will tell it among you.
        The Kouretes and the steadfast Aitolians were fighting
530 and slaughtering one another about the city of Kalydon,
the Aitolians in lovely Kalydon's defence, the Kouretes
furious to storm and sack it in war. For Artemis,
she of the golden chair, had driven this evil upon them,
angered that Oineus had not given the pride of the orchards
535 to her, first fruits; the rest of the gods were given due sacrifice,
but alone to this daughter of great Zeus he had given nothing.
He had forgotten, or had not thought, in his hard delusion,
and in wrath at his whole mighty line the Lady of Arrows
sent upon them the fierce wild boar with the shining teeth, who
540 after the way of his kind did much evil to the orchards of Oineus.
For he ripped up whole tall trees from the ground and scattered them headlong
roots and all, even to the very flowers of the orchard.
The son of Oineus killed this boar, Meleagros, assembling
together many hunting men out of numerous cities
545 with their hounds; since the boar might not have been killed by a few men,
so huge was he, and had put many men on the sad fire for burning.
But the goddess again made a great stir of anger and crying
battle, over the head of the boar and the bristling boar's hide,
between Kouretes and the high-hearted Aitolians. So long
550 as Meleagros lover of battle stayed in the fighting

it went the worse for the Kouretes, and they could not even
hold their ground outside the wall, though they were so many.
But when the anger came upon Meleagros, such anger
as wells in the hearts of others also, though their minds are careful,
555   he, in the wrath of his heart against his own mother, Althaia,
lay apart with his wedded bride, Kleopatra the lovely,
daughter of sweet-stepping Marpessa, child of Euenos,
and Idas, who was the strongest of all men upon earth
in his time; for he even took up the bow to face the King's onset,
560   Phoibos Apollo, for the sake of the sweet-stepping maiden;
a girl her father and honoured mother had named in their palace
Alkyone, sea-bird, as a by-name, since for her sake
her mother with the sorrow-laden cry of a sea-bird
wept because far-reaching Phoibos Apollo had taken her;
565   with this Kleopatra he lay mulling his heart-sore anger,
raging by reason of his mother's curses, which she called down
from the gods upon him, in deep grief for the death of her brother,
and many times beating with her hands on the earth abundant
she called on Hades and on honoured Persephone, lying
570   at length along the ground, and the tears were wet on her bosom,
to give death to her son; and Erinys, the mist-walking,
she of the heart without pity, heard her out of the dark places.
Presently there was thunder about the gates, and the sound rose
of towers under assault, and the Aitolian elders
575   supplicated him, sending their noblest priests of the immortals,
to come forth and defend them; they offered him a great gift:
wherever might lie the richest ground in lovely Kalydon,
there they told him to choose out a piece of land, an entirely
good one, of fifty acres, the half of it to be vineyard
580   and the half of it unworked ploughland of the plain to be furrowed.
And the aged horseman Oineus again and again entreated him,
and took his place at the threshold of the high-vaulted chamber
and shook against the bolted doors, pleading with his own son.
And again and again his honoured mother and his sisters
585   entreated him, but he only refused the more; then his own friends
who were the most honoured and dearest of all entreated him;
but even so they could not persuade the heart within him
until, as the chamber was under close assault, the Kouretes
were mounting along the towers and set fire to the great city.
590   And then at last his wife, the fair-girdled bride, supplicated
Meleagros, in tears, and rehearsed in their numbers before him
all the sorrows that come to men when their city is taken:
they kill the men, and the fire leaves the city in ashes,
and strangers lead the children away and the deep-girdled women.

595 And the heart, as he listened to all this evil, was stirred within him,
     and he rose, and went, and closed his body in shining armour.
     So he gave way in his own heart, and drove back the day of evil
     from the Aitolians; yet these no longer would make good
     their many and gracious gifts; yet he drove back the evil from them.
600   Listen, then; do not have such a thought in your mind; let not
     the spirit within you turn you that way, dear friend. It would be worse
     to defend the ships after they are burning. No, with gifts promised
     go forth. The Achaians will honour you as they would an immortal.
     But if without gifts you go into the fighting where men perish,
605 your honour will no longer be as great, though you drive back the battle.'
         Then in answer to him spoke Achilleus of the swift feet:
     'Phoinix my father, aged, illustrious, such honour is a thing
     I need not. I think I am honoured already in Zeus' ordinance
     which will hold me here beside my curved ships as long as life's wind
610 stays in my breast, as long as my knees have their spring beneath me.
     And put away in your thoughts this other thing I tell you.
     Stop confusing my heart with lamentation and sorrow
     for the favour of great Atreides. It does not become you
     to love this man, for fear you turn hateful to me, who love you.
615 It should be your pride with me to hurt whoever shall hurt me.
     Be king equally with me; take half of my honour.
     These men will carry back the message; you stay here and sleep here
     in a soft bed, and we shall decide tomorrow, as dawn shows,
     whether to go back home again or else to remain here.'
620   He spoke, aloud, saying nothing, nodded with his brows to Patroklos
     to make up a neat bed for Phoinix, so the others might presently
     think of going home from his shelter. The son of Telamon,
     Aias the godlike, saw it, and now spoke his word among them:
     'Son of Laertes and seed of Zeus, resourceful Odysseus:
625 let us go. I think that nothing will he accomplished
     by argument on this errand; it is best to go back quickly
     and tell this story, though it is not good, to the Danaans
     who sit there waiting for us to come back, seeing that Achilleus
     has made savage the proud-hearted spirit within his body.
630 He is hard, and does not remember that friends' affection
     wherein we honoured him by the ships, far beyond all others.
     Pitiless. And yet a man takes from his brother's slayer
     the blood price, or the price for a child who was killed, and the guilty
     one, when he has largely repaid, stays still in the country,
635 and the injured man's heart is curbed, and his pride, and his anger
     when he has taken the price; but the gods put in your breast a spirit
     not to be placated, bad, for the sake of one single
     girl. Yet now we offer you seven, surpassingly lovely,

and much beside these. Now make gracious the spirit within you.
640 Respect your own house; see, we are under the same roof with you,
from the multitude of the Danaans, we who desire beyond all
others to have your honour and love, out of all the Achaians.'
    Then in answer to him spoke Achilleus of the swift feet:
'Son of Telamon, seed of Zeus, Aias, lord of the people:
645 all that you have said seems spoken after my own mind.
Yet still the heart in me swells up in anger, when I remember
the disgrace that he wrought upon me before the Argives,
the son of Atreus, as if I were some dishonoured vagabond.
Do you then go back to him, and take him this message:
650 that I shall not think again of the bloody fighting
until such time as the son of wise Priam, Hektor the brilliant,
comes all the way to the ships of the Myrmidons, and their shelters,
slaughtering the Argives, and shall darken with fire our vessels.
But around my own shelter, I think, and beside my black ship
655 Hektor will be held, though he be very hungry for battle.'
    He spoke, and they taking each a two-handled cup poured out
a libation, then went back to their ships, and Odysseus led them.
Now Patroklos gave the maids and his followers orders
to make up without delay a neat bed for Phoinix.
660 And these obeyed him and made up the bed as he had commanded,
laying fleeces on it, and a blanket, and a sheet of fine linen.
There the old man lay down and waited for the divine Dawn.
But Achilleus slept in the inward corner of the strong-built shelter,
and a woman lay beside him, one he had taken from Lesbos,
665 Phorbas' daughter, Diomede of the fair colouring.
In the other corner Patroklos went to bed; with him also
was a girl, Iphis the fair-girdled, whom brilliant Achilleus
gave him, when he took sheer Skyros, Enyeus' citadel.
    Now when these had come back to the shelters of Agamemnon,
670 the sons of the Achaians greeted them with their gold cups
uplifted, one after another, standing, and asked them questions.
And the first to question them was the lord of men, Agamemnon:
'Tell me, honoured Odysseus, great glory of the Achaians:
is he willing to fight the ravening fire away from our vessels,
675 or did he refuse, and does the anger still hold his proud heart?'
    Then long-suffering great Odysseus spoke to him in answer:
'Son of Atreus, most lordly, king of men, Agamemnon.
That man will not quench his anger, but still more than ever
is filled with rage. He refuses you and refuses your presents.
680 He tells you yourself to take counsel among the Argives
how to save your ships, and the people of the Achaians.
And he himself has threatened that tomorrow as dawn shows

he will drag down his strong-benched, oarswept ships to the water.
He said it would be his counsel to others also, to sail back
685   home again, since no longer will you find any term set
on the sheer city of Ilion, since Zeus of the wide brows has strongly
held his own hand over it, and its people are made bold.
So he spoke. There are these to attest it who went there with me
also, Aias, and the two heralds, both men of good counsel.
690   But aged Phoinix stayed there for the night, as Achilleus urged him,
so he might go home in the ships to the beloved land of his fathers
if Phoinix will; but he will never use force to persuade him.'
      So he spoke, and all of them stayed stricken to silence
in amazement at his words. He had spoken to them very strongly.
695   For a long time the sons of the Achaians said nothing, in sorrow,
but at long last Diomedes of the great war cry spoke to them:
'Son of Atreus, most lordly and king of men, Agamemnon,
I wish you had not supplicated the blameless son of Peleus
with innumerable gifts offered. He is a proud man without this,
700   and now you have driven him far deeper into his pride. Rather
we shall pay him no more attention, whether he comes in with us
or stays away. He will fight again, whenever the time comes
that the heart in his body urges him to, and the god drives him.
Come then, do as I say, and let us all be won over.
705   Go to sleep, now that the inward heart is made happy
with food and drink, for these are the strength and courage within us.
But when the lovely dawn shows forth with rose fingers, Atreides,
rapidly form before our ships both people and horses
stirring them on, and yourself be ready to fight in the foremost.'
710   So he spoke, and all the kings gave him their approval,
acclaiming the word of Diomedes, breaker of horses.
Then they poured a libation, and each man went to his shelter,
where they went to their beds and took the blessing of slumber.

    [*Things go badly for the Greeks until Patroklos dons Achilleus' armor, hoping to fool the Trojans. His plan has some success, but Hektor, aided by Apollo, slays Patroklos and strips his armor.*]

BOOK EIGHTEEN: THE SHIELD OF ACHILLEUS

    So these fought on in the likeness of blazing fire. Meanwhile,
Antilochos came, a swift-footed messenger, to Achilleus,
and found him sitting in front of the steep-homed ships, thinking
over in his heart of things which had now been accomplished.
5   Disturbed, Achilleus spoke to the spirit in his own great heart:

'Ah me, how is it that once again the flowing-haired Achaians
are driven out of the plain on their ships in fear and confusion?
May the gods not accomplish vile sorrows upon the heart in me
in the way my mother once made it clear to me, when she told me

10   how while I yet lived the bravest of all the Myrmidons
must leave the light of the sun beneath the hands of the Trojans.
Surely, then, the strong son of Menoitios[23] has perished.
Unhappy! and yet I told him, once he had beaten the fierce fire
off, to come back to the ships, not fight in strength against Hektor.'

15   Now as he was pondering this in his heart and his spirit,
meanwhile the son of stately Nestor was drawing near him
and wept warm tears, and gave Achilleus his sorrowful message:
'Ah me, son of valiant Peleus; you must hear from me
the ghastly message of a thing I wish never had happened.

20   Patroklos has fallen, and now they are fighting over his body
which is naked. Hektor of the shining helm has taken his armour.'
        He spoke, and the black cloud of sorrow closed on Achilleus.
In both hands he caught up the grimy dust, and poured it
over his head and face, and fouled his handsome countenance,

25   and the black ashes were scattered over his immortal tunic.
And he himself, mightily in his might, in the dust lay
at length, and took and tore at his hair with his hands, and defiled it.
And the handmaidens Achilleus and Patroklos had taken
captive, stricken at heart cried out aloud, and came running

30   out of doors about valiant Achilleus, and all of them
beat their breasts with their hands, and the limbs went slack in each of them.
On the other side Antilochos mourned with him, letting the tears fall,
and held the hands of Achilleus as he grieved in his proud heart,
fearing Achilleus might cut his throat with the iron. He cried out

35   terribly, aloud, and the lady his mother heard him
as she sat in the depths of the sea at the side of her aged father,
and she cried shrill in turn, and the goddesses gathered about her,
all who along the depth of the sea were daughters of Nereus.
For Glauke was there, Kymodoke and Thaleia,

40   Nesaie and Speio and Thoë, and ox-eyed Halia;
Kymothoë was there, Aktaia and Limnoreia,
Melite and Iaira, Amphithoë and Agauë,
Doto and Proto, Dynamene and Pherousa,
Dexamene and Amphinome and Kallianeira;

45   Doris and Panope and glorious Galateia,
Nemertes and Apseudes and Kallianassa;
Klymene was there, Ianeira and Ianassa,

---

[23]**son of Menoitios:** Patroklos

Maira and Oreithyia and lovely-haired Amatheia,
and the rest who along the depth of the sea were daughters of Nereus.

50   The silvery cave was filled with these, and together all of them
beat their breasts, and among them Thetis led out the threnody:
'Hear me, Nereids, my sisters; so you may all know
well all the sorrows that are in my heart, when you hear of them from me.
Ah me, my sorrow, the bitterness in this best of child-bearing,

55   since I gave birth to a son who was without fault and powerful,
conspicuous among heroes; and he shot up like a young tree,
and I nurtured him, like a tree grown in the pride of the orchard.
I sent him away with the curved ships into the land of Ilion
to fight with the Trojans; but I shall never again receive him

60   won home again to his country and into the house of Peleus.
Yet while I see him live and he looks on the sunlight, he has
sorrows, and though I go to him I can do nothing to help him.
Yet I shall go, to look on my dear son, and to listen
to the sorrow that has come to him as he stays back from the fighting.'

65   So she spoke, and left the cave, and the others together
went with her in tears, and about them the wave of the water
was broken. Now these, when they came to the generous Troad,
followed each other out on the sea-shore, where close together
the ships of the Myrmidons were hauled up about swift Achilleus.

70   There as he sighed heavily the lady his mother stood by him
and cried out shrill and aloud, and took her son's head in her arms, then
sorrowing for him she spoke to him in winged words: 'Why then,
child, do you lament? What sorrow has come to your heart now?
Speak out, do not hide it. These things are brought to accomplishment

75   through Zeus: in the way that you lifted your hands and prayed for,
that all the sons of the Achaians be pinned on their grounded vessels
by reason of your loss, and suffer things that are shameful.'
Then sighing heavily Achilleus of the swift feet answered her:
'My mother, all these things the Olympian brought to accomplishment.

80   But what pleasure is this to me, since my dear companion has perished,
Patroklos, whom I loved beyond all other companions,
as well as my own life. I have lost him, and Hektor, who killed him,
has stripped away that gigantic armour, a wonder to look on
and splendid, which the gods gave Peleus, a glorious present,

85   on that day they drove you to the marriage bed of a mortal.
I wish you had gone on living then with the other goddesses
of the sea, and that Peleus had married some mortal woman.
As it is, there must be on your heart a numberless sorrow
for your son's death, since you can never again receive him

90   won home again to his country; since the spirit within does not drive me
to go on living and be among men, except on condition

that Hektor first be beaten down under my spear, lose his life
and pay the price for stripping Patroklos, the son of Menoitios.'
    Then in turn Thetis spoke to him, letting the tears fall:
95   'Then I must lose you soon, my child, by what you are saying,
since it is decreed your death must come soon after Hektor's.'
    Then deeply disturbed Achilleus of the swift feet answered her:
'I must die soon, then; since I was not to stand by my companion
when he was killed. And now, far away from the land of his fathers,
100 he has perished, and lacked my fighting strength to defend him.
Now, since I am not going back to the beloved land of my fathers,
since I was no light of safety to Patroklos, nor to my other
companions, who in their numbers went down before glorious Hektor,
but sit here beside my ships, a useless weight on the good land,
105 I, who am such as no other of the bronze-armoured Achaians
in battle, though there are others also better in council—
why, I wish that strife would vanish away from among gods and mortals,
and gall, which makes a man grow angry for all his great mind,
that gall of anger that swarms like smoke inside of a man's heart
110 and becomes a thing sweeter to him by far than the dripping of honey.
So it was here that the lord of men Agamemnon angered me.
Still, we will let all this be a thing of the past, and for all our
sorrow beat down by force the anger deeply within us.
Now I shall go, to overtake that killer of a dear life,
115 Hektor; then I will accept my own death, at whatever
time Zeus wishes to bring it about, and the other immortals.
For not even the strength of Herakles fled away from destruction,
although he was dearest of all to lord Zeus, son of Kronos,
but his fate beat him under, and the wearisome anger of Hera.
120 So I likewise, if such is the fate which has been wrought for me,
shall lie still, when I am dead. Now I must win excellent glory,
and drive some one of the women of Troy, or some deep-girdled
Dardanian woman, lifting up to her soft cheeks both hands
to wipe away the close bursts of tears in her lamentation,
125 and learn that I stayed too long out of the fighting. Do not
hold me back from the fight, though you love me. You will not persuade me.'
    In turn the goddess Thetis of the silver feet answered him:
'Yes, it is true, my child, this is no cowardly action,
to beat aside sudden death from your afflicted companions.
130 Yet, see now, your splendid armour, glaring and brazen,
is held among the Trojans, and Hektor of the shining helmet
wears it on his own shoulders, and glories in it. Yet I think
he will not glory for long, since his death stands very close to him.
Therefore do not yet go into the grind of the war god,
135 not before with your own eyes you see me come back to you.

For I am coming to you at dawn and as the sun rises
bringing splendid armour to you from the lord Hephaistos.'
       So she spoke, and turned, and went away from her son,
and turning now to her sisters of the sea she spoke to them:
140   'Do you now go back into the wide fold of the water
to visit the ancient of the sea and the house of our father,
and tell him everything. I am going to tall Olympos
and to Hephaistos, the glorious smith, if he might be willing
to give me for my son renowned and radiant armour.'
145   She spoke, and they plunged back beneath the wave of the water,
while she the goddess Thetis of the silver feet went onward
to Olympos, to bring back to her son the glorious armour.
       So her feet carried her to Olympos; meanwhile the Achaians
with inhuman clamour before the attack of manslaughtering Hektor
150   fled until they were making for their own ships and the Hellespont;
nor could the strong-greaved Achaians have dragged the body
of Patroklos, henchman of Achilleus, from under the missiles,
for once again the men and the horses came over upon him,
and Hektor, Priam's son, who fought like a flame in his fury.
155   Three times from behind glorious Hektor caught him
by the feet, trying to drag him, and called aloud on the Trojans.
Three times the two Aiantes with their battle-fury upon them
beat him from the corpse, but he, steady in the confidence of his great strength,
kept making, now a rush into the crowd, or again at another time
160   stood fast, with his great cry, but gave not a bit of ground backward.
And as herdsmen who dwell in the fields are not able to frighten
a tawny lion in his great hunger away from a carcass,
so the two Aiantes, marshals of men, were not able
to scare Hektor, Priam's son, away from the body.
165   And now he would have dragged it away and won glory forever
had not swift wind-footed Iris come running from Olympos
with a message for Peleus' son to arm. She came secretly
from Zeus and the other gods, since it was Hera who sent her.
She came and stood close to him and addressed him in winged words:
170   'Rise up, son of Peleus, most terrifying of all men.
Defend Patroklos, for whose sake the terrible fighting
stands now in front of the ships. They are destroying each other;
the Achaians fight in defence over the fallen body
while the others, the Trojans, are rushing to drag the corpse off
175   to windy Ilion, and beyond all glorious Hektor
rages to haul it away, since the anger within him is urgent
to cut the head from the soft neck and set it on sharp stakes.
Up, then, lie here no longer; let shame come into your heart, lest

Patroklos become sport for the dogs of Troy to worry,
180   your shame, if the body goes from here with defilement upon it.'
      Then in turn Achilleus of the swift feet answered her:
'Divine Iris, what god sent you to me with a message?'
      Then in turn swift wind-footed Iris spoke to him:
'Hera sent me, the honoured wife of Zeus; but the son of
185   Kronos, who sits on high, does not know this, nor any other
immortal, of all those who dwell by the snows of Olympos.'
      Then in answer to her spoke Achilleus of the swift feet:
'How shall I go into the fighting? They have my armour.
And my beloved mother told me I must not be armoured,
190   not before with my own eyes I see her come back to me.
She promised she would bring magnificent arms from Hephaistos.
Nor do I know of another whose glorious armour I could wear
unless it were the great shield of Telamonian Aias.
But he himself wears it, I think, and goes in the foremost
195   of the spear-fight over the body of fallen Patroklos.'
      Then in turn swift wind-footed Iris spoke to him:
'Yes, we also know well how they hold your glorious armour.
But go to the ditch, and show yourself as you are to the Trojans,
if perhaps the Trojans might be frightened, and give way
200   from their attack, and the fighting sons of the Achaians get wind
again after hard work. There is little breathing space in the fighting.'
      So speaking Iris of the swift feet went away from him;
but Achilleus, the beloved of Zeus, rose up, and Athene
swept about his powerful shoulders the fluttering aegis;
205   and she, the divine among goddesses, about his head circled
a golden cloud, and kindled from it a flame far-shining.
As when a flare goes up into the high air from a city
from an island far away, with enemies fighting about it
who all day long are in the hateful division of Ares
210   fighting from their own city, but as the sun goes down signal
fires blaze out one after another, so that the glare goes
pulsing high for men of the neighbouring islands to see it,
in case they might come over in ships to beat off the enemy;
so from the head of Achilleus the blaze shot into the bright air.
215   He went from the wall and stood by the ditch, nor mixed with the other
Achaians, since he followed the close command of his mother.
There he stood, and shouted, and from her place Pallas Athene
gave cry, and drove an endless terror upon the Trojans.
As loud as comes the voice that is screamed out by a trumpet
220   by murderous attackers who beleaguer a city,
so then high and clear went up the voice of Aiakides.
But the Trojans, when they heard the brazen voice of Aiakides,

the heart was shaken in all, and the very floating-maned horses
turned their chariots about, since their hearts saw the coming afflictions.
225 The charioteers were dumbfounded as they saw the unwearied dangerous
fire that played above the head of great-hearted Peleion
blazing, and kindled by the goddess grey-eyed Athene.
Three times across the ditch brilliant Achilleus gave his great cry,
and three times the Trojans and their renowned companions were routed.
230 There at that time twelve of the best men among them perished
upon their own chariots and spears. Meanwhile the Achaians
gladly pulled Patroklos out from under the missiles
and set him upon a litter, and his own companions about him
stood mourning, and along with them swift-footed Achilleus
235 went, letting fall warm tears as he saw his steadfast companion
lying there on a carried litter and torn with the sharp bronze,
the man he had sent off before with horses and chariot
into the fighting; who never again came home to be welcomed.
      Now the lady Hera of the ox eyes drove the unwilling
240 weariless sun god to sink in the depth of the Ocean,
and the sun went down, and the brilliant Achaians gave over
their strong fighting, and the doubtful collision of battle.
      The Trojans on the other side moved from the strong encounter
in their turn, and unyoked their running horses from under the chariots,
245 and gathered into assembly before taking thought for their supper.
They stood on their feet in assembly, nor did any man have the patience
to sit down, but the terror was on them all, seeing that Achilleus
had appeared, after he had stayed so long from the difficult fighting.
First to speak among them was the careful Poulydamas,
250 Panthoös' son, who alone of them looked before and behind him.[24]
He was companion to Hektor, and born on the same night with him,
but he was better in words, the other with the spear far better.
He in kind intention toward all stood forth and addressed them:
'Now take careful thought, dear friends; for I myself urge you
255 to go back into the city and not wait for the divine dawn
in the plain beside the ships. We are too far from the wall now.
While this man was still angry with great Agamemnon,
for all that time the Achaians were easier men to fight with.
For I also used then to be one who was glad to sleep out
260 near their ships, and I hoped to capture the oarswept vessels.
But now I terribly dread the swift-footed son of Peleus.
So violent is the valour in him, he will not be willing
to stay here in the plain, where now Achaians and Trojans

---

[24]**Poulydamas/ . . . looked before and behind him**: a prophet who knew the past and future

from either side sunder between them the wrath of the war god.
265 With him, the fight will be for the sake of our city and women.
Let us go into the town; believe me; thus it will happen.
For this present, immortal night has stopped the swift-footed
son of Peleus, but if he catches us still in this place
tomorrow, and drives upon us in arms, a man will be well
270 aware of him, be glad to get back into sacred Ilion,
the man who escapes; there will be many Trojans the vultures
and dogs will feed on. But let such a word be out of my hearing!
If all of us will do as I say, though it hurts us to do it,
this night we will hold our strength in the market place, and the great walls
275 and the gateways, and the long, smooth-planed, close-joined gate timbers
that close to fit them shall defend our city. Then, early
in the morning, under dawn, we shall arm ourselves in our war gear
and take stations along the walls. The worse for him, if he endeavours
to come away from the ships and fight us here for our city.
280 Back he must go to his ships again, when he wears out the strong necks
of his horses, driving them at a gallop everywhere by the city.
His valour will not give him leave to burst in upon us
nor sack our town. Sooner the circling dogs will feed on him.'
      Then looking darkly at him Hektor of the shining helm spoke:
285 'Poulydamas, these things that you argue please me no longer
when you tell us to go back again and be cooped in our city.
Have you not all had your glut of being fenced in our outworks?
There was a time when mortal men would speak of the city
of Priam as a place with much gold and much bronze. But now
290 the lovely treasures that lay away in our houses have vanished,
and many possessions have been sold and gone into Phrygia
and into Maionia the lovely, when great Zeus was angry.
But now, when the son of devious-devising Kronos has given
me the winning of glory by the ships, to pin the Achaians
295 on the sea, why, fool, no longer show these thoughts to our people.
Not one of the Trojans will obey you. I shall not allow it.
Come, then, do as I say and let us all be persuaded.
Now, take your supper by positions along the encampment,
and do not forget your watch, and let every man be wakeful.
300 And if any Trojan is strongly concerned about his possessions,
let him gather them and give them to the people, to use them in common.
It is better for one of us to enjoy them than for the Achaians.
In the morning, under dawn, we shall arm ourselves in our war gear
and waken the bitter god of war by the hollow vessels.
305 If it is true that brilliant Achilleus is risen beside their
ships, then the worse for him if he tries it, since I for my part
will not run from him out of the sorrowful battle, but rather

stand fast, to see if he wins the great glory, or if I can win it.
The war god is impartial. Before now he has killed the killer.'
310   So spoke Hektor, and the Trojans thundered to hear him;
fools, since Pallas Athene had taken away the wits from them.
They gave their applause to Hektor in his counsel of evil,
but none to Poulydamas, who had spoken good sense before them.
They took their supper along the encampment. Meanwhile the Achaians
315   mourned all night in lamentation over Patroklos.
Peleus' son led the thronging chant of their lamentation,
and laid his manslaughtering hands over the chest of his dear friend
with outbursts of incessant grief. As some great bearded lion
when some man, a deer hunter, has stolen his cubs away from him
320   out of the close wood; the lion comes back too late, and is anguished,
and turns into many valleys quartering after the man's trail
on the chance of finding him, and taken with bitter anger;
so he, groaning heavily, spoke out to the Myrmidons:
'Ah me. It was an empty word I cast forth on that day
325   when in his halls I tried to comfort the hero Menoitios.
I told him I would bring back his son in glory to Opous
with Ilion sacked, and bringing his share of war spoils allotted.
But Zeus does not bring to accomplishment all thoughts in men's minds.
Thus it is destiny for us both to stain the same soil
330   here in Troy; since I shall never come home, and my father,
Peleus the aged rider, will not welcome me in his great house,
nor Thetis my mother, but in this place the earth will receive me.
But seeing that it is I, Patroklos, who follow you underground,
I will not bury you till I bring to this place the armour
335   and the head of Hektor, since he was your great-hearted murderer.
Before your burning pyre I shall behead twelve glorious
children of the Trojans, for my anger over your slaying.
Until then, you shall lie where you are in front of my curved ships
and beside you women of Troy and deep-girdled Dardanian women
340   shall sorrow for you night and day and shed tears for you, those whom
you and I worked hard to capture by force and the long spear
in days when we were storming the rich cities of mortals.'
        So speaking brilliant Achilleus gave orders to his companions
to set a great cauldron across the fire, so that with all speed
345   they could wash away the clotted blood from Patroklos.
They set up over the blaze of the fire a bath-water cauldron
and poured water into it and put logs underneath and kindled them.
The fire worked on the swell of the cauldron, and the water heated.
But when the water had come to a boil in the shining bronze, then
350   they washed the body and anointed it softly with olive oil
and stopped the gashes in his body with stored-up unguents

and laid him on a bed, and shrouded him in a thin sheet
from head to foot, and covered that over with a white mantle.
Then all night long, gathered about Achilleus of the swift feet,
355   the Myrmidons mourned for Patroklos and lamented over him.
But Zeus spoke to Hera, who was his wife and his sister:
'So you have acted, then, lady Hera of the ox eyes.
You have roused up Achilleus of the swift feet. It must be then
that the flowing-haired Achaians are born of your own generation.'
360   Then the goddess the ox-eyed lady Hera answered him:
'Majesty, son of Kronos, what sort of thing have you spoken?
Even one who is mortal will try to accomplish his purpose
for another, though he be a man and knows not such wisdom as we do.
As for me then, who claim I am highest of all the goddesses,
365   both ways, since I am eldest born and am called your consort,
yours, and you in turn are lord over all the immortals,
how could I not weave sorrows for the men of Troy, when I hate them?'
Now as these two were saying things like this to each other,
Thetis of the silver feet came to the house of Hephaistos,
370   imperishable, starry, and shining among the immortals,
built in bronze for himself by the god of the dragging footsteps.
She found him sweating as he turned here and there to his bellows
busily, since he was working on twenty tripods
which were to stand against the wall of his strong-founded dwelling.
375   And he had set golden wheels underneath the base of each one
so that of their own motion they could wheel into the immortal
gathering, and return to his house: a wonder to look at.
These so far finished, but the elaborate ear handles
were not yet on. He was forging these, and beating the chains out.
380   As he was at work on this in his craftsmanship and his cunning
meanwhile the goddess Thetis the silver-footed drew near him.
Charis of the shining veil saw her as she came forward,
she, the lovely goddess the renowned strong-armed one had married.
She came, and caught her hand and called her by name and spoke to her:
385   'Why is it, Thetis of the light robes, you have come to our house now?
We honour you and love you; but you have not come much before this.
But come in with me, so I may put entertainment before you.'
She spoke, and, shining among divinities, led the way forward
and made Thetis sit down in a chair that was wrought elaborately
390   and splendid with silver nails, and under it was a footstool.
She called to Hephaistos the renowned smith and spoke a word to him:
'Hephaistos, come this way; here is Thetis, who has need of you.'
Hearing her the renowned smith of the strong arms answered her:
'Then there is a goddess we honour and respect in our house.
395   She saved me when I suffered much at the time of my great fall

through the will of my own brazen-faced mother, who wanted
to hide me, for being lame. Then my soul would have taken much suffering
had not Eurynome and Thetis caught me and held me,
Eurynome, daughter of Ocean, whose stream bends back in a circle.
400   With them I worked nine years as a smith, and wrought many intricate
things; pins that bend back, curved clasps, cups, necklaces, working
there in the hollow of the cave, and the stream of Ocean around us
went on forever with its foam and its murmur. No other
among the gods or among mortal men knew about us
405   except Eurynome and Thetis. They knew, since they saved me.
Now she has come into our house; so I must by all means
do everything to give recompense to lovely-haired Thetis
for my life. Therefore set out before her fair entertainment
while I am putting away my bellows and all my instruments.'
410   He spoke, and took the huge blower off from the block of the anvil
limping; and yet his shrunken legs moved lightly beneath him.
He set the bellows away from the fire, and gathered and put away
all the tools with which he worked in a silver strongbox.
Then with a sponge he wiped clean his forehead, and both hands,
415   and his massive neck and hairy chest, and put on a tunic,
and took up a heavy stick in his hand, and went to the doorway
limping. And in support of their master moved his attendants.
These are golden, and in appearance like living young women.
There is intelligence in their hearts, and there is speech in them
420   and strength, and from the immortal gods they have learned how to do things.
These stirred nimbly in support of their master, and moving
near to where Thetis sat in her shining chair, Hephaistos
caught her by the hand and called her by name and spoke a word to her:
'Why is it, Thetis of the light robes, you have come to our house now?
425   We honour you and love you; but you have not come much before this.
Speak forth what is in your mind. My heart is urgent to do it
if I can, and if it is a thing that can be accomplished.'
        Then in turn Thetis answered him, letting the tears fall:
'Hephaistos, is there among all the goddesses on Olympos
430   one who in her heart has endured so many grim sorrows
as the griefs Zeus, son of Kronos, has given me beyond others?
Of all the other sisters of the sea he gave me to a mortal,
to Peleus, Aiakos' son, and I had to endure mortal marriage
though much against my will. And now he, broken by mournful
435   old age, lies away in his halls. Yet I have other troubles.
For since he has given me a son to bear and to raise up
conspicuous among heroes, and he shot up like a young tree,
I nurtured him, like a tree grown in the pride of the orchard.
I sent him away in the curved ships to the land of Ilion

440   to fight with the Trojans; but I shall never again receive him
won home again to his country and into the house of Peleus.
Yet while I see him live and he looks on the sunlight, he has
sorrows, and though I go to him I can do nothing to help him.
And the girl the sons of the Achaians chose out for his honour

445   powerful Agamemnon took her away again out of his hands.
For her his heart has been wasting in sorrow; but meanwhile the Trojans
pinned the Achaians against their grounded ships, and would not
let them win outside, and the elders of the Argives entreated
my son, and named the many glorious gifts they would give him.

450   But at that time he refused himself to fight the death from them;
nevertheless he put his own armour upon Patroklos
and sent him into the fighting, and gave many men to go with him.
All day they fought about the Skaian Gates, and on that day
they would have stormed the city, if only Phoibos Apollo

455   had not killed the fighting son of Menoitios there in the first ranks
after he had wrought much damage, and given the glory to Hektor.
Therefore now I come to your knees; so might you be willing
to give me for my short-lived son a shield and a helmet
and two beautiful greaves fitted with clasps for the ankles

460   and a corselet. What he had was lost with his steadfast companion
when the Trojans killed him. Now my son lies on the ground, heart sorrowing.
      Hearing her the renowned smith of the strong arms answered her:
'Do not fear. Let not these things be a thought in your mind.
And I wish that I could hide him away from death and its sorrow

465   at that time when his hard fate comes upon him, as surely
as there shall be fine armour for him, such as another
man out of many men shall wonder at, when he looks on it.'
      So he spoke, and left her there, and went to his bellows.
He turned these toward the fire and gave them their orders for working.

470   And the bellows, all twenty of them, blew on the crucibles,
from all directions blasting forth wind to blow the flames high
now as he hurried to be at this place and now at another,
wherever Hephaistos might wish them to blow, and the work went forward.
He cast on the fire bronze which is weariless, and tin with it

475   and valuable gold, and silver, and thereafter set forth
upon its standard the great anvil, and gripped in one hand
the ponderous hammer, while in the other he grasped the pincers.
      First of all he forged a shield that was huge and heavy,
elaborating it about, and threw around it a shining

480   triple rim that glittered, and the shield strap was cast of silver.
There were five folds composing the shield itself, and upon it
he elaborated many things in his skill and craftsmanship.

He made the earth upon it, and the sky, and the sea's water,
and the tireless sun, and the moon waxing into her fullness,
485 and on it all the constellations that festoon the heavens,
the Pleiades and the Hyades and the strength of Orion
and the Bear, whom men give also the name of the Wagon,[25]
who turns about in a fixed place and looks at Orion
and she alone is never plunged in the wash of the Ocean.
490 On it he wrought in all their beauty two cities of mortal
men. And there were marriages in one, and festivals.
They were leading the brides along the city from their maiden chambers
under the flaring of torches, and the loud bride song was arising.
The young men followed the circles of the dance, and among them
495 the flutes and lyres kept up their clamour as in the meantime
the women standing each at the door of her court admired them.
The people were assembled in the market place, where a quarrel
had arisen, and two men were disputing over the blood price
for a man who had been killed. One man promised full restitution
500 in a public statement, but the other refused and would accept nothing.
Both then made for an arbitrator, to have a decision;
and people were speaking up on either side, to help both men.
But the heralds kept the people in hand, as meanwhile the elders
were in session on benches of polished stone in the sacred circle
505 and held in their hands the staves of the heralds who lift their voices.
The two men rushed before these, and took turns speaking their cases,
and between them lay on the ground two talents of gold, to be given
to that judge who in this case spoke the straightest opinion.
But around the other city were lying two forces of armed men
510 shining in their war gear. For one side counsel was divided
whether to storm and sack, or share between both sides the property
and all the possessions the lovely citadel held hard within it.
But the city's people were not giving way, and armed for an ambush.
Their beloved wives and their little children stood on the rampart
515 to hold it, and with them the men with age upon them, but meanwhile
the others went out. And Ares led them, and Pallas Athene.
These were gold, both, and golden raiment upon them, and they were
beautiful and huge in their armour, being divinities,
and conspicuous from afar, but the people around them were smaller.
520 These, when they were come to the place that was set for their ambush,
in a river, where there was a watering place for all animals,
there they sat down in place shrouding themselves in the bright bronze.
But apart from these were sitting two men to watch for the rest of them
and waiting until they could see the sheep and the shambling cattle,

---

[25]**the Bear . . . the Wagon:** also called the Big Dipper

525   who appeared presently, and two herdsmen went along with them
       playing happily on pipes, and took no thought of the treachery.
       Those others saw them, and made a rush, and quickly thereafter
       cut off on both sides the herds of cattle and the beautiful
       flocks of shining sheep, and killed the shepherds upon them.
530   But the other army, as soon as they heard the uproar arising
       from the cattle, as they sat in their councils, suddenly mounted
       behind their light-foot horses, and went after, and soon overtook them.
       These stood their ground and fought a battle by the banks of the river,
       and they were making casts at each other with their spears bronze-headed;
535   and Hate was there with Confusion among them, and Death the destructive;
       she was holding a live man with a new wound, and another
       one unhurt, and dragged a dead man by the feet through the carnage.
       The clothing upon her shoulders showed strong red with the men's blood.
       All closed together like living men and fought with each other
540   and dragged away from each other the corpses of those who had fallen.
          He made upon it a soft field, the pride of the tilled land,
       wide and triple-ploughed, with many ploughmen upon it
       who wheeled their teams at the turn and drove them in either direction.
       And as these making their turn would reach the end-strip of the field,
545   a man would come up to them at this point and hand them a flagon
       of honey-sweet wine, and they would turn again to the furrows
       in their haste to come again to the end-strip of the deep field.
       The earth darkened behind them and looked like earth that has been ploughed
       though it was gold. Such was the wonder of the shield's forging.
550   He made on it the precinct of a king, where the labourers
       were reaping, with the sharp reaping hooks in their hands. Of the cut swathes
       some fell along the lines of reaping, one after another,
       while the sheaf-binders caught up others and tied them with bind-ropes.
       There were three sheaf-binders who stood by, and behind them
555   were children picking up the cut swathes, and filled their arms with them
       and carried and gave them always; and by them the king in silence
       and holding his staff stood near the line of the reapers, happily.
       And apart and under a tree the heralds made a feast ready
       and trimmed a great ox they had slaughtered. Meanwhile the women
560   scattered, for the workmen to eat, abundant white barley.
          He made on it a great vineyard heavy with clusters,
       lovely and in gold, but the grapes upon it were darkened
       and the vines themselves stood out through poles of silver. About them
       he made a field-ditch of dark metal, and drove all around this
565   a fence of tin; and there was only one path to the vineyard,
       and along it ran the grape-bearers for the vineyard's stripping.
       Young girls and young men, in all their light-hearted innocence,
       carried the kind, sweet fruit away in their woven baskets,

and in their midst a youth with a singing lyre played charmingly
570   upon it for them, and sang the beautiful song for Linos
in a light voice, and they followed him, and with singing and whistling
and light dance-steps of their feet kept time to the music.
    He made upon it a herd of horn-straight oxen. The cattle
were wrought of gold and of tin, and thronged in speed and with lowing
575   out of the dung of the farmyard to a pasturing place by a sounding
river, and beside the moving field of a reed bed.
The herdsmen were of gold who went along with the cattle,
four of them, and nine dogs shifting their feet followed them.
But among the foremost of the cattle two formidable lions
580   had caught hold of a bellowing bull, and he with loud lowings
was dragged away, as the dogs and the young men went in pursuit of him.
But the two lions, breaking open the hide of the great ox,
gulped the black blood and the inward guts, as meanwhile the herdsmen
were in the act of setting and urging the quick dogs on them.
585   But they, before they could get their teeth in, turned back from the lions,
but would come and take their stand very close, and bayed, and kept clear.
    And the renowned smith of the strong arms made on it a meadow
large and in a lovely valley for the glimmering sheepflocks,
with dwelling places upon it, and covered shelters, and sheepfolds.
590   And the renowned smith of the strong arms made elaborate on it
a dancing floor, like that which once in the wide spaces of Knosos
Daidalos built for Ariadne[26] of the lovely tresses.
And there were young men on it and young girls, sought for their beauty
with gifts of oxen, dancing, and holding hands at the wrist. These
595   wore, the maidens long light robes, but the men wore tunics
of finespun work and shining softly, touched with olive oil.
And the girls wore fair garlands on their heads, while the young men
carried golden knives that hung from sword-belts of silver.
At whiles on their understanding feet they would run very lightly,
600   as when a potter crouching makes trial of his wheel, holding
it close in his hands, to see if it will run smooth. At another
time they would form rows, and run, rows crossing each other.
And around the lovely chorus of dancers stood a great multitude
happily watching, while among the dancers two acrobats
605   led the measures of song and dance revolving among them.
    He made on it the great strength of the Ocean River
which ran around the uttermost rim of the shield's strong structure.
    Then after he had wrought this shield, which was huge and heavy,
he wrought for him a corselet brighter than fire in its shining,

---

[26]**Ariadne:** daughter of Minos, King of Krete; Minus had Daidalos construct the Labyrinth at Knosos to hide the Minotaur monster.

610 and wrought him a helmet, massive and fitting close to his temples,
lovely and intricate work, and laid a gold top-ridge along it,
and out of pliable tin wrought him leg-armour. Thereafter
when the renowned smith of the strong arms had finished the armour
he lifted it and laid it before the mother of Achilleus.
615 And she like a hawk came sweeping down from the snows of Olympos
and carried with her the shining armour, the gift of Hephaistos.

BOOK NINETEEN: ARMING FOR BATTLE

Now on the yellow-robed arose from the river of Ocean
to carry her light to men and to immortals. And Thetis
came to the ships and carried with her the gifts of Hephaistos.
She found her beloved son lying in the arms of Patroklos
5 crying shrill, and his companions in their numbers about him
mourned. She, shining among divinities, stood there beside them.
She clung to her son's hand and called him by name and spoke to him:
'My child, now, though we grieve for him, we must let this man lie
dead, in the way he first was killed through the gods' designing.
10 Accept rather from me the glorious arms of Hephaistos,
so splendid, and such as no man has ever worn on his shoulders.'
     The goddess spoke so, and set down the armour on the ground
before Achilleus, and all its elaboration clashed loudly.
Trembling took hold of all the Myrmidons. None had the courage
15 to look straight at it. They were afraid of it. Only Achilleus
looked, and as he looked the anger came harder upon him
and his eyes glittered terribly under his lids, like sunflare.
He was glad, holding in his hands the shining gifts of Hephaistos.
But when he had satisfied his heart with looking at the intricate
20 armour, he spoke to his mother and addressed her in winged words:
'My mother, the god has given me these weapons; they are such
as are the work of immortals. No mortal man could have made them.
Therefore now I shall arm myself in them. Yet I am sadly
afraid, during this time, for the warlike son of Menoitios
25 that flies might get into the wounds beaten by bronze in his body
and breed worms in them, and these make foul the body, seeing
that the life is killed in him, and that all his flesh may be rotted.'
     In turn the goddess Thetis the silver-footed answered him:
'My child, no longer let these things be a care in your mind.
30 I shall endeavour to drive from him the swarming and fierce things,
those flies, which feed upon the bodies of men who have perished;
and although he lie here till a year has gone to fulfilment,
still his body shall be as it was, or firmer than ever.
Go then and summon into assembly the fighting Achaians,

35   and unsay your anger against Agamemnon, shepherd of the people,
      and arm at once for the fighting, and put your war strength upon you.'
          She spoke so, and drove the strength of great courage into him;
      and meanwhile through the nostrils of Patroklos she distilled
      ambrosia and red nectar, so that his flesh might not spoil.
40   But he, brilliant Achilleus, walked along by the sea-shore
      crying his terrible cry, and stirred up the fighting Achaians.
      And even those who before had stayed where the ships were assembled,
      they who were helmsmen of the ships and handled the steering oar,
      they who were stewards among the ships and dispensers of rations,
45   even these came then to assembly, since now Achilleus
      had appeared, after staying so long from the sorrowful battle.
      And there were two who came limping among them, henchmen of Ares
      both, Tydeus' son the staunch in battle, and brilliant Odysseus,
      leaning on spears, since they had the pain of their wounds yet upon them,
50   and came and took their seats in the front rank of those assembled.
      And last of them came in the lord of men Agamemnon
      with a wound on him, seeing that Koön, the son of Antenor,
      had stabbed him with the bronze edge of the spear in the strong encounter.
      But now, when all the Achaians were in one body together,
55   Achilleus of the swift feet stood up before them and spoke to them:
      'Son of Atreus, was this after all the better way for
      both, for you and me, that we, for all our hearts' sorrow,
      quarrelled together for the sake of a girl in soul-perishing hatred?
      I wish Artemis had killed her beside the ships with an arrow
60   on that day when I destroyed Lyrnessos and took her.
      For thus not all these too many Achaians would have bitten
      the dust, by enemy hands, when I was away in my anger.
      This way was better for the Trojans and Hektor; yet I think
      the Achaians will too long remember this quarrel between us.
65   Still, we will let all this be a thing of the past, though it hurts us,
      and beat down by constraint the anger that rises inside us.
      Now I am making an end of my anger. It does not become me
      unrelentingly to rage on. Come, then! The more quickly
      drive on the flowing-haired Achaians into the fighting,
70   so that I may go up against the Trojans, and find out
      if they still wish to sleep out beside the ships. I think rather
      they will be glad to rest where they are, whoever among them
      gets away with his life from the fury of our spears' onset.'
          He spoke, and the strong-greaved Achaians were pleasured to hear him
75   and how the great-hearted son of Peleus unsaid his anger.
      Now among them spoke forth the lord of men Agamemnon
      from the place where he was sitting, and did not stand up among them:
      'Fighting men and friends, O Danaans, henchmen of Ares:

it is well to listen to the speaker, it is not becoming
80   to break in on him. This will be hard for him, though he be able.
How among the great murmur of people shall anyone listen
or speak either? A man, though he speak very clearly, is baffled.
I shall address the son of Peleus; yet all you other
Argives listen also, and give my word careful attention.
85   This is the word the Achaians have spoken often against me
and found fault with me in it, yet I am not responsible
but Zeus is, and Destiny, and Erinys the mist-walking
who in assembly caught my heart in the savage delusion
on that day I myself stripped from him the prize of Achilleus.
90   Yet what could I do? It is the god who accomplishes all things.
Delusion is the elder daughter of Zeus, the accursed
who deludes all; her feet are delicate and they step not
on the firm earth, but she walks the air above men's heads
and leads them astray. She has entangled others before me.
95   Yes, for once Zeus even was deluded, though men say
he is the highest one of gods and mortals. Yet Hera
who is female deluded even Zeus in her craftiness
on that day when in strong wall-circled Thebe Alkmene[27]
was at her time to bring forth the strength of Herakles. Therefore
100   Zeus spoke forth and made a vow before all the immortals:
"Hear me, all you gods and all you goddesses; hear me
while I speak forth what the heart within my breast urges.
This day Eileithyia of women's child-pains shall bring forth
a man to the light who, among the men sprung of the generation
105   of my blood, shall be lord over all those dwelling about him."
Then in guileful intention the lady Hera said to him:
"You will be a liar, not put fulfilment on what you have spoken.
Come, then, lord of Olympos, and swear before me a strong oath
that he shall be lord over all those dwelling about him
110   who this day shall fall between the feet of a woman,
that man who is born of the blood of your generation." So Hera
spoke. And Zeus was entirely unaware of her falsehood,
but swore a great oath, and therein lay all his deception.
But Hera in a flash of speed left the horn of Olympos
115   and rapidly came to Argos of Achaia, where she knew
was the mighty wife of Sthenelos, descended of Perseus.[28]
And she was carrying a son, and this was the seventh month for her,
but she brought him sooner into the light, and made him premature,
and stayed the childbirth of Alkmene, and held back the birth pangs.

---

[27]**Alkmene:** mortal woman impregnated by Zeus, mother of Herakles
[28]**Perseus:** son of Zeus

120   She went herself and spoke the message to Zeus, son of Kronos:
       "Father Zeus of the shining bolt, I will tell you a message
       for your heart. A great man is born, who will be lord over the Argives,
       Eurystheus, son of Sthenelos, of the seed of Perseus,
       your generation. It is not unfit that he should rule over
125   the Argives." She spoke, and the sharp sorrow struck at his deep heart.
       He caught by the shining hair of her head the goddess Delusion
       in the anger of his heart, and swore a strong oath, that never
       after this might Delusion, who deludes all, come back
       to Olympos and the starry sky. So speaking, he whirled her
130   about in his hand and slung her out of the starry heaven,
       and presently she came to men's establishments. But Zeus
       would forever grieve over her each time that he saw his dear son
       doing some shameful work of the tasks that Eurystheus set him.
       So I in my time, when tall Hektor of the shining helm
135   was forever destroying the Argives against the sterns of their vessels,
       could not forget Delusion, the way I was first deluded.
       But since I was deluded and Zeus took my wits away from me,
       I am willing to make all good and give back gifts in abundance.
       Rise up, then, to the fighting and rouse the rest of the people.
140   Here am I, to give you all those gifts, as many
       as brilliant Odysseus yesterday went to your shelter and promised.
       Or if you will, hold back, though you lean hard into the battle,
       while my followers take the gifts from my ship and bring them
       to you, so you may see what I give to comfort your spirit.'
145   Then in answer to him spoke Achilleus of the swift feet:
       'Son of Atreus, most lordly and king of men, Agamemnon,
       the gifts are yours to give if you wish, and as it is proper,
       or to keep with yourself. But now let us remember our joy in warcraft,
       immediately, for it is not fitting to stay here and waste time
150   nor delay, since there is still a big work to be done.
       So can a man see once more Achilleus among the front fighters
       with the bronze spear wrecking the Trojan battalions. Therefore
       let each of you remember this and fight his antagonist.'
            Then in answer to him spoke resourceful Odysseus
155   'Not that way, good fighter that you are, godlike Achilleus.
       Do not drive the sons of the Achaians on Ilion when they are hungry,
       to fight against the Trojans, since not short will be the time
       of battle, once the massed formations of men have encountered
       together, with the god inspiring fury in both sides.
160   Rather tell the men of Achaia here by their swift ships,
       to take food and wine, since these make fighting fury and warcraft.
       For a man will not have strength to fight his way forward all day
       long until the sun goes down if he is starved for food. Even

        though in his heart he be very passionate for the battle,
165   yet without his knowing it his limbs will go heavy, and hunger
        and thirst will catch up with him and comber his knees as he moves on.
        But when a man has been well filled with wine and with eating
        and then does battle all day long against the enemy,
        why, then the heart inside him is full of cheer, nor do his limbs
170   get weary, until all are ready to give over the fighting.
        Come then, tell your men to scatter and bid them get ready
        a meal; and as for the gifts, let the lord of men Agamemnon
        bring them to the middle of our assembly so all the Achaians
        can see them before their eyes, so your own heart may be pleasured.
175   And let him stand up before the Argives and swear an oath to you
        that he never entered into her bed and never lay with her[29]
        as is natural for people, my lord, between men and women.
        And by this let the spirit in your own heart be made gracious.
        After that in his own shelter let him appease you
180   with a generous meal, so you will lack nothing of what is due you.
        And you, son of Atreus, after this be more righteous to another
        man. For there is no fault when even one who is a king
        appeases a man, when the king was the first one to be angry.'
            Then in turn the lord of men Agamemnon answered him:
185   'Hearing what you have said, son of Laertes, I am pleased with you.
        Fairly have you gone through everything and explained it.
        And all this I am willing to swear to, and my heart urges me,
        and I will not be foresworn before the gods. Let Achilleus
        stay here the while, though he lean very hard toward the work of the war god,
190   and remain the rest of you all here assembled, until the gifts come
        back from my shelter and while we cut our oaths of fidelity.
        And for you yourself, Odysseus, I give you this errand, this order,
        that you choose out excellent young men of all the Achaians
        and bring the gifts back here from my ship, all that you promised
195   yesterday to Achilleus, and bring the women back also.
        And in the wide host of the Achaians let Talthybios make ready
        a boar for me, and dedicate it to Zeus and Helios.'
            Then in answer to him spoke Achilleus of the swift feet:
        'Son of Atreus, most lordly and king of men, Agamemnon,
200   at some other time rather you should busy yourself about these things,
        when there is some stopping point in the fighting, at some time
        when there is not so much fury inside of my heart. But now
        as things are they lie there torn whom the son of Priam
        Hektor has beaten down, since Zeus was giving him glory,
205   and then you urge a man to eating. No, but I would now

---

[29]**never lay with her:** Briseus, the war booty of Achilleus, taken by Agamemnon

drive forward the sons of the Achaians into the fighting
starving and unfed, and afterwards when the sun sets
make ready a great dinner, when we have paid off our defilement.
But before this, for me at least, neither drink nor food shall
210 go down my very throat, since my companion has perished
and lies inside my shelter torn about with the cutting
bronze, and turned against the forecourt while my companions
mourn about him. Food and drink mean nothing to my heart
but blood does, and slaughter, and the groaning of men in the hard work.'
215   Then in answer to him spoke resourceful Odysseus:
'Son of Peleus, Achilleus, far greatest of the Achaians,
you are stronger than I am and greater by not a little
with the spear, yet I in turn might overpass you in wisdom
by far, since I was born before you and have learned more things.
220 Therefore let your heart endure to listen to my words.
When there is battle men have suddenly their fill of it
when the bronze scatters on the ground the straw in most numbers
and the harvest is most thin, when Zeus has poised his balance,
Zeus, who is administrator to men in their fighting.
225   There is no way the Achaians can mourn a dead man by denying
the belly. Too many fall day by day, one upon another,
and how could anyone find breathing space from his labour?
No, but we must harden our hearts and bury the man who
dies, when we have wept over him on the day, and all those
230 who are left about from the hateful work of war must remember
food and drink, so that afterwards all the more strongly
we may fight on forever relentless against our enemies
with the weariless bronze put on about our bodies. Let one not
wait longing for any other summons to stir on the people.
235 This summons now shall be an evil on anyone left behind
by the ships of the Argives. Therefore let us drive on together
and wake the bitter war god on the Trojans, breakers of horses.'
     He spoke, and went away with the sons of glorious Nestor,
with Meges, the son of Phyleus, and Meriones, and Thoas,
240 and Lykomedes, the son of Kreion, and Melanippos. These went
on their way to the shelter of Atreus' son Agamemnon.
No sooner was the order given than the thing had been done.
They brought back seven tripods from the shelter, those Agamemnon
had promised, and twenty shining cauldrons, twelve horses. They brought back
245 immediately the seven women the work of whose hands was
blameless, and the eighth of them was Briseis of the fair cheeks.
Odysseus weighed out ten full talents of gold and led them
back, and the young men of the Achaians carried the other gifts.
They brought these into the midst of assembly, and Agamemnon

250   stood up, and Talthybios in voice like an immortal
stood beside the shepherd of the people with the boar in his hands.
Atreus' son laid hands upon his work-knife, and drew it
from where it hung ever beside the great sheath of his war sword,
and cut first hairs away from the boar, and lifting his hands up
255   to Zeus, prayed, while all the Argives stayed fast at their places
in silence and in order of station, and listened to their king.
He spoke before them in prayer gazing into the wide sky:
'Let Zeus first be my witness, highest of the gods and greatest,
and Earth, and Helios the Sun, and Furies, who underground
260   avenge dead men, when any man has sworn to a falsehood,
that I have never laid a hand on the girl Briseis
on pretext to go to bed with her, or for any other
reason, but she remained, not singled out, in my shelter.
If any of this is falsely sworn, may the gods give me many
265   griefs, all that they inflict on those who swear falsely before them.'
       So he spoke, and with pitiless bronze he cut the boar's throat.
Talthybios whirled the body about, and threw it in the great reach
of the grey sea, to feed the fishes. Meanwhile Achilleus
stood up among the battle-fond Achaians, and spoke to them:
270   'Father Zeus, great are the delusions with which you visit men.
Without you, the son of Atreus could never have stirred so
the heart inside my breast, nor taken the girl away from me
against my will, and be in helplessness. No, but Zeus somehow
wished that death should befall great numbers of the Achaians.
275   Go now and take your dinner, so we may draw on the battle.'
       So he spoke, and suddenly broke up the assembly.
Now these scattered away each man to his own ship. Meanwhile
the great-hearted Myrmidons disposed of the presents.
They went on their way carrying them to the ship of godlike Achilleus,
280   and stowed the gifts in the shelters, and let the women be settled,
while proud henchmen drove the horses into Achilleus' horse-herd.
       And now, in the likeness of golden Aphrodite, Briseis
when she saw Patroklos lying torn with sharp bronze, folding
him in her arms cried shrilly above him and with her hands tore
285   at her breasts and her soft throat and her beautiful forehead.
The woman like the immortals mourning for him spoke to him:
'Patroklos, far most pleasing to my heart in its sorrows,
I left you here alive when I went away from the shelter,
but now I come back, lord of the people, to find you have fallen.
290   So evil in my life takes over from evil forever.
The husband on whom my father and honoured mother bestowed me
I saw before my city lying torn with the sharp bronze,
and my three brothers, whom a single mother bore with me

and who were close to me, all went on one day to destruction.
295 And yet you would not let me, when swift Achilleus had cut down
my husband, and sacked the city of godlike Mynes, you would not
let me sorrow, but said you would make me godlike Achilleus'
wedded lawful wife, that you would take me back in the ships
to Phthia, and formalize my marriage among the Myrmidons.
300 Therefore I weep your death without ceasing. You were kind always.'
So she spoke, lamenting, and the women sorrowed around her
grieving openly for Patroklos, but for her own sorrows
each. But the lords of Achaia were gathered about Achilleus
beseeching him to eat, but he with a groan denied them:
305 'I beg of you, if any dear companion will listen
to me, stop urging me to satisfy the heart in me
with food and drink, since this strong sorrow has come upon me.
I will hold out till the sun goes down and endure, though it be hard.'
So he spoke, and caused the rest of the kings to scatter;
310 but the two sons of Atreus stayed with him, and brilliant Odysseus,
and Nestor, and Idomeneus, and the aged charioteer, Phoinix,
comforting him close in his sorrow, yet his heart would not
be comforted, till he went into the jaws of the bleeding battle.
Remembering Patroklos he sighed much for him, and spoke aloud:
315 'There was a time, ill fated, o dearest of all my companions,
when you yourself would set the desirable dinner before me
quickly and expertly, at the time the Achaians were urgent
to carry sorrowful war on the Trojans, breakers of horses.
But now you lie here torn before me, and my heart goes starved
320 for meat and drink, though they are here beside me, by reason
of longing for you. There is nothing worse than this I could suffer,
not even if I were to hear of the death of my father
who now, I think, in Phthia somewhere lets fall a soft tear
for bereavement of such a son, for me, who now in a strange land
325 make war upon the Trojans for the sake of accursed Helen;
or the death of my dear son, who is raised for my sake in Skyros
now, if godlike Neoptolemos is still one of the living.
Before now the spirit inside my breast was hopeful
that I alone should die far away from horse-pasturing Argos
330 here in Troy; I hoped you would win back again to Phthia
so that in a fast black ship you could take my son back
from Skyros to Phthia, and show him all my possessions,
my property, my serving men, my great high-roofed house.
For by this time I think that Peleus must altogether
335 have perished, or still keeps a little scant life in sorrow
for the hatefulness of old age and because he waits ever from me
the evil message, for the day he hears I have been killed.'

So he spoke, mourning, and the elders lamented around him
remembering each those he had left behind in his own halls.
340 The son of Kronos took pity on them as he watched them mourning
and immediately spoke in winged words to Athene:
'My child, have you utterly abandoned the man of your choice?
Is there no longer deep concern in your heart for Achilleus?
Now he has sat down before the steep horned ships and is mourning
345 for his own beloved companion, while all the others
have gone to take their dinner, but he is fasting and unfed.
Go then to him and distil nectar inside his chest, and delicate
ambrosia, so the weakness of hunger will not come upon him.'
     Speaking so, he stirred Athene, who was eager before this,
350 and she in the likeness of a wide-winged, thin-crying
hawk plummeted from the sky through the bright air. Now the Achaians
were arming at once along the encampment. She dropped the delicate
ambrosia and the nectar inside the breast of Achilleus
softly, so no sad weakness of hunger would come on his knees,
355 and she herself went back to the close house of her powerful
father, while they were scattering out away from the fast ships.
As when in their thickness the snowflakes of Zeus come fluttering
cold beneath the blast of the north wind born in the bright sky,
so now in their thickness the pride of the helms bright shining
360 were carried out from the ships, and shields massive in the middle
and the corselets strongly hollowed and the ash spears were worn forth.
The shining swept to the sky and all earth was laughing about them
under the glitter of bronze and beneath their feet stirred the thunder
of men, within whose midst brilliant Achilleus helmed him.
365 A clash went from the grinding of his teeth, and his eyes glowed
as if they were the stare of a fire, and the heart inside him
was entered with sorrow beyond endurance. Raging at the Trojans
he put on the gifts of the god, that Hephaistos wrought him with much toil.
     First he placed along his legs the fair greaves linked with
370 silver fastenings to hold the greaves at the ankles.
Afterward he girt on about his chest the corselet,
and across his shoulders slung the sword with the nails of silver,
a bronze sword, and caught up the great shield, huge and heavy
next, and from it the light glimmered far, as from the moon.
375 And as when from across water a light shines to mariners
from a blazing fire, when the fire is burning high in the mountains
in a desolate steading, as the mariners are carried unwilling
by storm winds over the fish-swarming sea, far away from their loved ones;
so the light from the fair elaborate shield of Achilleus
380 shot into the high air. And lifting the helm he set it
massive upon his head, and the helmet crested with horse-hair

shone like a star, the golden fringes were shaken about it
which Hephaistos had driven close along the horn of the helmet.
And brilliant Achilleus tried himself in his armour, to see
385   if it fitted close, and how his glorious limbs ran within it,
and the armour became as wings and upheld the shepherd of the people.
Next he pulled out from its standing place the spear of his father,
huge, heavy, thick, which no one else of all the Achaians
could handle, but Achilleus alone knew how to wield it,
390   the Pelian ash spear which Cheiron had brought to his father
from high on Pelion, to be death for fighters in battle.
Automedon and Alkimos, in charge of the horses,
yoked them, and put the fair breast straps about them, and forced the bits home
between their jaws, and pulled the reins back against the compacted
395   chariot seat, and one, Automedon, took up the shining
whip caught close in his hand and vaulted up to the chariot,
while behind him Achilleus helmed for battle took his stance
shining in all his armour like the sun when he crosses above us,
and cried in a terrible voice on the horses of his father:
400   'Xanthos, Balios, Bay and Dapple, famed sons of Podarge,
take care to bring in another way your charioteer back
to the company of the Danaans, when we give over fighting,
not leave him to lie fallen there, as you did to Patroklos.'
       Then from beneath the yoke the gleam-footed horse answered him,
405   Xanthos, and as he spoke bowed his head, so that all the mane
fell away from the pad and swept the ground by the cross-yoke;
the goddess of the white arms, Hera, had put a voice in him:
"We shall still keep you safe for this time, o hard Achilleus.
And yet the day of your death is near, but it is not we
410   who are to blame, but a great god and powerful Destiny.
For it was not because we were slow, because we were careless,
that the Trojans have taken the armour from the shoulders of Patroklos,
but it was that high god, the child of lovely-haired Leto,[30]
who killed him among the champions and gave the glory to Hektor.
415   But for us, we two could run with the blast of the west wind
who they say is the lightest of all things; yet still for you
there is destiny to be killed in force by a god and a mortal.'[31]
       When he had spoken so the Furies stopped the voice in him,
but deeply disturbed, Achilleus of the swift feet answered him:
420   'Xanthos, why do you prophesy my death? This is not for you.
I myself know well it is destined for me to die here

---

[30]**the child of lovely-haired Leto:** Apollo
[31]**a mortal:** Paris, with Apollo's aid, will slay Achilleus

far from my beloved father and mother. But for all that
I will not stop till the Trojans have had enough of my fighting.'
    He spoke, and shouting held on in the foremost his single-foot horses.

BOOK TWENTY-TWO: THE SLAYING OF HEKTOR

    So along the city the Trojans, who had run like fawns, dried
the sweat off from their bodies and drank and slaked their thirst, leaning
along the magnificent battlements. Meanwhile the Achaians
sloping their shields across their shoulders came close to the rampart.
5   But his deadly fate held Hektor shackled, so that he stood fast
in front of Ilion and the Skaian gates. Now Phoibos
Apollo spoke aloud to Peleion: 'Why, son of Peleus,
do you keep after me in the speed of your feet, being mortal
while I am an immortal god? Even yet you have not
10   seen that I am a god, but strain after me in your fury.
Now hard fighting with the Trojans whom you stampeded means nothing
to you. They are crowded in the city, but you bent away here.
You will never kill me. I am not one who is fated.'
    Deeply vexed Achilleus of the swift feet spoke to him:
15   'You have balked me, striker from afar, most malignant of all gods,
when you turned me here away from the rampart, else many Trojans
would have caught the soil in their teeth before they got back into Ilion.
Now you have robbed me of great glory, and rescued these people
lightly, since you have no retribution to fear hereafter.
20   Else I would punish you, if only the strength were in me.'
    He spoke, and stalked away against the city, with high thoughts
in mind, and in tearing speed, like a racehorse with his chariot
who runs lightly as he pulls the chariot over the flat land.
Such was the action of Achilleus in feet and quick knees.
25   The aged Priam was the first of all whose eyes saw him
as he swept across the flat land in full shining, like that star
which comes on in the autumn and whose conspicuous brightness
far outshines the stars that are numbered in the night's darkening,
the star they give the name of Orion's Dog,[32] which is brightest
30   among the stars, and yet is wrought as a sign of evil
and brings on the great fever for unfortunate mortals.
Such was the flare of the bronze that girt his chest in his running.
The old man groaned aloud and with both hands high uplifted
beat his head, and groaned amain, and spoke supplicating
35   his beloved son, who there still in front of the gateway
stood fast in determined fury to fight with Achilleus.

---

[32]**Orion's Dog:** the star Sirius, in the constellation Canis Major

The old man stretching his hands out called pitifully to him:
'Hektor, beloved child, do not wait the attack of this man
alone, away from the others. You might encounter your destiny
40   beaten down by Peleion, since he is far stronger than you are.
A hard man: I wish he were as beloved of the immortal
as loved by me. Soon he would lie dead, and the dogs and the vultures
would eat him, and bitter sorrow so be taken from my heart.
He has made me desolate of my sons, who were brave and many.
45   He killed them, or sold them away among the far-lying islands.
Even now there are two sons, Lykaon and Polydoros,
whom I cannot see among the Trojans pent up in the city,
sons Laothoë a princess among women bore to me.[33]
But if these are alive somewhere in the army, then I can
50   set them free for bronze and gold; it is there inside, since
Altes the aged and renowned gave much with his daughter.
But if they are dead already and gone down to the house of Hades,
it is sorrow to our hearts, who bore them, myself and their mother,
but to the rest of the people a sorrow that will be fleeting
55   beside their sorrow for you, if you go down before Achilleus.
Come then inside the wall, my child, so that you can rescue
the Trojans and the women of Troy, neither win the high glory
for Peleus' son, and yourself be robbed of your very life. Oh, take
pity on me, the unfortunate still alive, still sentient
60   but ill-starred, whom the father, Kronos' son, on the threshold of old age
will blast with hard fate, after I have looked upon evils
and seen my sons destroyed and my daughters dragged away captive
and the chambers of marriage wrecked and the innocent children taken
and dashed to the ground in the hatefulness of war, and the wives
65   of my sons dragged off by the accursed hands of the Achaians.
And myself last of all, my dogs in front of my doorway
will rip me raw, after some man with stroke of the sharp bronze
spear, or with spearcast, has torn the life out of my body;
those dogs I raised in my halls to be at my table, to guard my
70   gates, who will lap my blood in the savagery of their anger
and then lie down in my courts. For a young man all is decorous
when he is cut down in battle and torn with the sharp bronze, and lies there
dead, and though dead still all that shows about him is beautiful;
but when an old man is dead and down, and the dogs mutilate
75   the grey head and the grey beard and the parts that are secret,
this, for all sad mortality, is the sight most pitiful.'
      So the old man spoke, and in his hands seizing the grey hairs
tore them from his head, but could not move the spirit in Hektor.

---

[33]Priam boasted of having over 50 sons and fortunately had more than one wife.

And side by side with him his mother in tears was mourning
80   and laid the fold of her bosom bare and with one hand held out
a breast, and wept her tears for him and called to him in winged words:
'Hektor, my child, look upon these and obey, and take pity
on me; if ever I gave you the breast to quiet your sorrow.
Remember all these things, dear child, and from inside the wall
85   beat off this grim man. Do not go out as champion against him,
o hard one; for if he kills you I can no longer
mourn you on the death-bed, sweet branch, o child of my bearing,
nor can your generous wife mourn you, but a big way from us
beside the ships of the Argives the running dogs will feed on you.'
90   So these two in tears and with much supplication called out
to their dear son, but could not move the spirit in Hektor,
but he awaited Achilleus as he came on, gigantic.
But as a snake waits for a man by his hole, in the mountains,
glutted with evil poisons, and the fell venom has got inside him,
95   and coiled about the hole he stares malignant, so Hektor
would not give ground but kept unquenched the fury within him
and sloped his shining shield against the jut of the bastion.
Deeply troubled he spoke to his own great-hearted spirit:
'Ah me! If I go now inside the wall and the gateway,
100   Poulydamas will be first to put a reproach upon me,
since he tried to make me lead the Trojans inside the city
on that accursed night when brilliant Achilleus rose up,
and I would not obey him, but that would have been far better.
Now, since by my own recklessness I have ruined my people,
105   I feel shame before the Trojans and the Trojan women with trailing
robes, that someone who is less of a man than I will say of me:
"Hektor believed in his own strength and ruined his people."
Thus they will speak; and as for me, it would be much better
at that time, to go against Achilleus, and slay him, and come back,
110   or else be killed by him in glory in front of the city.
Or if again I set down my shield massive in the middle
and my ponderous helm, and lean my spear up against the rampart
and go out as I am to meet Achilleus the blameless
and promise to give back Helen, and with her all her possessions,
115   all those things that once in the hollow ships Alexandros
brought back to Troy, and these were the beginning of the quarrel;
to give these to Atreus' sons to take away, and for the Achaians
also to divide up all that is hidden within the city,
and take an oath thereafter for the Trojans in conclave
120   not to hide anything away, but distribute all of it,
as much as the lovely citadel keeps guarded within it;
yet still, why does the heart within me debate on these things?

I might go up to him, and he take no pity upon me
nor respect my position, but kill me naked so, as if I were
125   a woman, once I stripped my armour from me. There is no
way any more from a tree or a rock to talk to him gently
whispering like a young man and a young girl, in the way
a young man and a young maiden whisper together.
Better to bring on the fight with him as soon as it may be.
130   We shall see to which one the Olympian grants the glory.'
        So he pondered, waiting, but Achilleus was closing upon him
in the likeness of the lord of battles, the helm-shining warrior,
and shaking from above his shoulder the dangerous Pelian
ash spear, while the bronze that closed about him was shining
135   like the flare of blazing fire or the sun in its rising.
And the shivers took hold of Hektor when he saw him, and he could no longer
stand his ground there, but left the gates behind, and fled, frightened,
and Peleus' son went after him in the confidence of his quick feet.
As when a hawk in the mountains who moves lightest of things flying
140   makes his effortless swoop for a trembling dove, but she slips away
from beneath and flies and he shrill screaming close after her
plunges for her again and again, heart furious to take her;
so Achilleus went straight for him in fury, but Hektor
fled away under the Trojan wall and moved his knees rapidly.
145   They raced along by the watching point and the windy fig tree
always away from under the wall and along the wagon-way
and came to the two sweet-running well springs. There there are double
springs of water that jet up, the springs of whirling Skamandros.
One of these runs hot water and the steam on all sides
150   of it rises as if from a fire that was burning inside it.
But the other in the summer-time runs water that is like hail
or chill snow or ice that forms from water. Beside these
in this place, and close to them, are the washing-hollows
of stone, and magnificent, where the wives of the Trojans and their lovely
155   daughters washed the clothes to shining, in the old days
when there was peace, before the coming of the sons of the Achaians.
They ran beside these, one escaping, the other after him.
It was a great man who fled, but far better he who pursued him
rapidly, since here was no festal beast, no ox-hide
160   they strove for, for these are prizes that are given men for their running.
No, they ran for the life of Hektor, breaker of horses.
As when about the turnposts racing single-foot horses
run at full speed, when a great prize is laid up for their winning,
a tripod or a woman, in games for a man's funeral,
165   so these two swept whirling about the city of Priam
in the speed of their feet, while all the gods were looking upon them.

First to speak among them was the father of gods and mortals:
'Ah me, this is a man beloved whom now my eyes watch
being chased around the wall; my heart is mourning for Hektor
170   who has burned in my honour many thigh pieces of oxen
on the peaks of Ida with all her folds, or again on the uttermost
part of the citadel, but now the brilliant Achilleus
drives him in speed of his feet around the city of Priam.
Come then, you immortals, take thought and take counsel, whether
175   to rescue this man or whether to make him, for all his valour,
go down under the hands of Achilleus, the son of Peleus.'
      Then in answer the goddess grey-eyed Athene spoke to him:
'Father of the shining bolt, dark misted, what is this you said?
Do you wish to bring back a man who is mortal, one long since
180   doomed by his destiny, from ill-sounding death and release him?
Do it, then; but not all the rest of us gods shall approve you.'
      Then Zeus the gatherer of the clouds spoke to her in answer:
'Tritogeneia, dear daughter, do not lose heart; for I say this
not in outright anger, and my meaning toward you is kindly.
185   Act as your purpose would have you do, and hold back no longer.'
      So he spoke, and stirred on Athene, who was eager before this,
and she went in a flash of speed down the pinnacles of Olympos.
But swift Achilleus kept unremittingly after Hektor,
chasing him, as a dog in the mountains who has flushed from his covert
190   a deer's fawn follows him through the folding ways and the valleys,
and though the fawn crouched down under a bush and be hidden
he keeps running and noses him out until he comes on him;
so Hektor could not lose himself from swift-footed Peleion.
If ever he made a dash right on for the gates of Dardanos
195   to get quickly under the strong-built bastions, endeavouring
that they from above with missiles thrown might somehow defend him,
each time Achilleus would get in front and force him to turn back
into the plain, and himself kept his flying course next the city.
As in a dream a man is not able to follow one who runs
200   from him, nor can the runner escape, nor the other pursue him,
so he could not run him down in his speed, nor the other get clear.
How then could Hektor have escaped the death spirits, had not
Apollo, for this last and uttermost time, stood by him
close, and driven strength into him, and made his knees light?
205   But brilliant Achilleus kept shaking his head at his own people
and would not let them throw their bitter projectiles at Hektor
for fear the thrower might win the glory, and himself come second.
But when for the fourth time they had come around to the well springs
then the Father balanced his golden scales, and in them
210   he set two fateful portions of death, which lays men prostrate,

one for Achilleus, and one for Hektor, breaker of horses,
and balanced it by the middle; and Hektor's death-day was heavier
and dragged downward toward death, and Phoibos Apollo forsook him.
But the goddess grey-eyed Athene came now to Peleion

215 and stood close beside him and addressed him in winged words: 'Beloved
of Zeus, shining Achilleus, I am hopeful now that you and I
will take back great glory to the ships of the Achaians, after
we have killed Hektor, for all his slakeless fury for battle.
Now there is no way for him to get clear away from us,

220 not though Apollo who strikes from afar should be willing to undergo
much, and wallow before our father Zeus of the aegis.
Stand you here then and get your wind again, while I go
to this man and persuade him to stand up to you in combat.'
So spoke Athene, and he was glad at heart, and obeyed her,

225 and stopped, and stood leaning on his bronze-barbed ash spear. Meanwhile
Athene left him there, and caught up with brilliant Hektor,
and likened herself in form and weariless voice to Deïphobos.
She came now and stood close to him and addressed him in winged words:
'Dear brother, indeed swift-footed Achilleus is using you roughly

230 and chasing you on swift feet around the city of Priam.
Come on, then; let us stand fast against him and beat him back from us.'
Then tall Hektor of the shining helm answered her: 'Deïphobos,
before now you were dearest to me by far of my brothers,
of all those who were sons of Priam and Hekabe, and now

235 I am minded all the more within my heart to honour you,
you who dared for my sake, when your eyes saw me, to come forth
from the fortifications, while the others stand fast inside them.'
Then in turn the goddess grey-eyed Athene answered him:
'My brother, it is true our father and the lady our mother, taking

240 my knees in turn, and my companions about me, entreated
that I stay within, such was the terror upon all of them.
But the heart within me was worn away by hard sorrow for you.
But now let us go straight on and fight hard, let there be no sparing
of our spears, so that we can find out whether Achilleus

245 will kill us both and carry our bloody war spoils back
to the hollow ships, or will himself go down under your spear.'
So Athene spoke and led him on by beguilement.
Now as the two in their advance were come close together,
first of the two to speak was tall helm-glittering Hektor:

250 'Son of Peleus, I will no longer run from you, as before this
I fled three times around the great city of Priam, and dared not
stand to your onfall. But now my spirit in turn has driven me
to stand and face you. I must take you now, or I must be taken.
Come then, shall we swear before the gods? For these are the highest

255   who shall be witnesses and watch over our agreements.
       Brutal as you are I will not defile you, if Zeus grants
       to me that I can wear you out, and take the life from you.
       But after I have stripped your glorious armour, Achilleus,
       I will give your corpse back to the Achaians. Do you do likewise.'
260   Then looking darkly at him swift-footed Achilleus answered:
       'Hektor, argue me no agreements. I cannot forgive you.
       As there are no trustworthy oaths between men and lions,
       nor wolves and lambs have spirit that can be brought to agreement
       but forever these hold feelings of hate for each other,
265   so there can be no love between you and me, nor shall there be
       oaths between us, but one or the other must fall before then
       to glut with his blood Ares the god who fights under the shield's guard.
       Remember every valour of yours, for now the need comes
       hardest upon you to be a spearman and a bold warrior.
270   There shall be no more escape for you, but Pallas Athene
       will kill you soon by my spear. You will pay in a lump for all those
       sorrows of my companions you killed in your spear's fury.'
       So he spoke, and balanced the spear far shadowed, and threw it;
       but glorious Hektor kept his eyes on him, and avoided it,
275   for he dropped, watchful, to his knee, and the bronze spear flew over his shoulder
       and stuck in the ground, but Pallas Athene snatched it, and gave it
       back to Achilleus, unseen by Hektor shepherd of the people.
       But now Hektor spoke out to the blameless son of Peleus:
       'You missed; and it was not, o Achilleus like the immortals,
280   from Zeus that you knew my destiny; but you thought so; or rather
       you are someone clever in speech and spoke to swindle me,
       to make me afraid of you and forget my valour and war strength.
       You will not stick your spear in my back as I run away from you
       but drive it into my chest as I storm straight in against you;
285   if the god gives you that; and now look out for my brazen
       spear. I wish it might be taken full length in your body.
       And indeed the war would be a lighter thing for the Trojans
       if you were dead, seeing that you are their greatest affliction.'
       So he spoke, and balanced the spear far shadowed, and threw it,
290   and struck the middle of Peleïdes' shield, nor missed it,
       but the spear was driven far back from the shield, and Hektor was angered
       because his swift weapon had been loosed from his hand in a vain cast.
       He stood discouraged, and had no other ash spear; but lifting
       his voice he called aloud on Deïphobos of the pale shield,
295   and asked him for a long spear, but Deïphobos was not near him.
       And Hektor knew the truth inside his heart, and spoke aloud:
       'No use. Here at last the gods have summoned me deathward.
       I thought Deïphobos the hero was here close beside me,

but he is behind the wall and it was Athene cheating me,
300 and now evil death is close to me, and no longer far away,
and there is no way out. So it must long since have been pleasing
to Zeus, and Zeus' son who strikes from afar, this way; though before this
they defended me gladly. But now my death is upon me.
Let me at least not die without a struggle, inglorious,
305 but do some big thing first, that men to come shall know of it.'
So he spoke, and pulling out the sharp sword that was slung
at the hollow of his side, huge and heavy, and gathering
himself together, he made his swoop, like a high-flown eagle
who launches himself out of the murk of the clouds on the flat land
310 to catch away a tender lamb or a shivering hare; so
Hektor made his swoop, swinging his sharp sword, and Achilleus
charged, the heart within him loaded with savage fury.
In front of his chest the beautiful elaborate great shield
covered him, and with the glittering helm with four horns
315 he nodded; the lovely golden fringes were shaken about it
which Hephaistos had driven close along the horn of the helmet.
And as a star moves among stars in the night's darkening,
Hesper, who is the fairest star who stands in the sky, such
was the shining from the pointed spear Achilleus was shaking
320 in his right hand with evil intention toward brilliant Hektor.
He was eyeing Hektor's splendid body, to see where it might best
give way, but all the rest of the skin was held in the armour,
brazen and splendid, he stripped when he cut down the strength of Patroklos;
yet showed where the collar-bones hold the neck from the shoulders,
325 the throat, where death of the soul comes most swiftly; in this place
brilliant Achilleus drove the spear as he came on in fury,
and clean through the soft part of the neck the spearpoint was driven.
Yet the ash spear heavy with bronze did not sever the windpipe,
so that Hektor could still make exchange of words spoken.
330 But he dropped in the dust, and brilliant Achilleus vaunted above him:
'Hektor, surely you thought as you killed Patroklos you would be
safe, and since I was far away you thought nothing of me,
O fool, for an avenger was left, far greater than he was,
behind him and away by the hollow ships. And it was I;
335 and I have broken your strength; on you the dogs and the vultures
shall feed and foully rip you; the Achaians will bury Patroklos.'
In his weakness Hektor of the shining helm spoke to him:
'I entreat you, by your life, by your knees, by your parents,
do not let the dogs feed on me by the ships of the Achaians,
340 but take yourself the bronze and gold that are there in abundance,
those gifts that my father and the lady my mother will give you,

and give my body to be taken home again, so that the Trojans
and the wives of the Trojans may give me in death my rite of burning.'
     But looking darkly at him swift-footed Achilleus answered:
345   'No more entreating of me, you dog, by knees or parents.
I wish only that my spirit and fury would drive me
to hack your meat away and eat it raw for the things that
you have done to me. So there is no one who can hold the dogs off
from your head, not if they bring here and set before me ten times
350   and twenty times the ransom, and promise more in addition,
not if Priam son of Dardanos should offer to weigh out
your bulk in gold; not even so shall the lady your mother
who herself bore you lay you on the death-bed and mourn you:
no, but the dogs and the birds will have you all for their feasting.'
355   Then, dying, Hektor of the shining helmet spoke to him:
'I know you well as I look upon you, I know that I could not
persuade you, since indeed in your breast is a heart of iron.
Be careful now; for I might be made into the gods' curse
upon you, on that day when Paris and Phoibos Apollo
360   destroy you in the Skaian gates, for all your valour.'
     He spoke, and as he spoke the end of death closed in upon him,
and the soul fluttering free of the limbs went down into Death's house
mourning her destiny, leaving youth and manhood behind her.
Now though he was a dead man brilliant Achilleus spoke to him:
365   'Die: and I will take my own death at whatever time
Zeus and the rest of the immortals choose to accomplish it.'
     He spoke, and pulled the brazen spear from the body, and laid it
on one side, and stripped away from the shoulders the bloody
armour. And the other sons of the Achaians came running about him,
370   and gazed upon the stature and on the imposing beauty
of Hektor; and none stood beside him who did not stab him;
and thus they would speak one to another, each looking at his neighbour:
'See now, Hektor is much softer to handle than he was
when he set the ships ablaze with the burning firebrand.'
375   So as they stood beside him they would speak, and stab him.
But now, when he had despoiled the body, swift-footed brilliant
Achilleus stood among the Achaians and addressed them in winged words:
'Friends, who are leaders of the Argives and keep their counsel:
since the gods have granted me the killing of this man
380   who has done us much damage, such as not all the others together
have done, come, let us go in armour about the city
to see if we can find out what purpose is in the Trojans,
whether they will abandon their high city, now that this man
has fallen, or are minded to stay, though Hektor lives no longer.
385   Yet still, why does the heart within me debate on these things?

There is a dead man who lies by the ships, unwept, unburied:
Patroklos: and I will not forget him, never so long as
I remain among the living and my knees have their spring beneath me.
And though the dead forget the dead in the house of Hades,
390   even there I shall still remember my beloved companion.
But now, you young men of the Achaians, let us go back, singing
a victory song, to our hollow ships; and take this with us.
We have won ourselves enormous fame; we have killed the great Hektor
whom the Trojans glorified as if he were a god in their city.'
395   He spoke, and now thought of shameful treatment for glorious Hektor.
In both of his feet at the back he made holes by the tendons
in the space between ankle and heel, and drew thongs of ox-hide through them,
and fastened them to the chariot so as to let the head drag,
and mounted the chariot, and lifted the glorious armour inside it,
400   then whipped the horses to a run, and they winged their way unreluctant.
A cloud of dust rose where Hektor was dragged, his dark hair was falling
about him, and all that head that was once so handsome was tumbled
in the dust; since by this time Zeus had given him over
to his enemies, to be defiled in the land of his fathers.
405   So all his head was dragged in the dust; and now his mother
tore out her hair, and threw the shining veil far from her
and raised a great wail as she looked upon her son; and his father
beloved groaned pitifully, and all his people about him
were taken with wailing and lamentation all through the city.
410   It was most like what would have happened, if all lowering
Ilion had been burning top to bottom in fire.
His people could scarcely keep the old man in his impatience
from storming out of the Dardanian gates; he implored them
all, and wallowed in the muck before them calling on each man
415   and naming him by his name: 'Give way, dear friends,
and let me alone though you care for me, leave me to go out
from the city and make my way to the ships of the Achaians.
I must be suppliant to this man, who is harsh and violent,
and he might have respect for my age and take pity upon it
420   since I am old, and his father also is old, as I am,
Peleus, who begot and reared him to be an affliction
on the Trojans. He has given us most sorrow, beyond all others,
such is the number of my flowering sons he has cut down.
But for all of these I mourn not so much, in spite of my sorrow,
425   as for one, Hektor, and the sharp grief for him will carry me downward
into Death's house. I wish he had died in my arms, for that way
we two, I myself and his mother who bore him unhappy,
might so have glutted ourselves with weeping for him and mourning.'

So he spoke, in tears, and beside him mourned the citizens.
430 But for the women of Troy Hekabe led out the thronging
chant of sorrow: 'Child, I am wretched. What shall my life be
in my sorrows, now you are dead, who by day and in the night
were my glory in the town, and to all of the Trojans
and the women of Troy a blessing throughout their city. They adored you
435 as if you were a god, since in truth you were their high honour
while you lived. Now death and fate have closed in upon you.'
So she spoke in tears but the wife of Hektor had not yet
heard: for no sure messenger had come to her and told her
how her husband had held his ground there outside the gates;
440 but she was weaving a web in the inner room of the high house,
a red folding robe, and inworking elaborate figures.
She called out through the house to her lovely-haired handmaidens
to set a great cauldron over the fire, so that there would be
hot water for Hektor's bath as he came back out of the fighting;
445 poor innocent, nor knew how, far from waters for bathing,
Pallas Athene had cut him down at the hands of Achilleus.
She heard from the great bastion the noise of mourning and sorrow.
Her limbs spun, and the shuttle dropped from her hand to the ground. Then
she called aloud to her lovely-haired handmaidens: 'Come here.
450 Two of you come with me, so I can see what has happened.
I heard the voice of Hektor's honoured mother; within me
my own heart rising beats in my mouth, my limbs under me
are frozen. Surely some evil is near for the children of Priam.
May what I say come never close to my ear; yet dreadfully
455 I fear that great Achilleus might have cut off bold Hektor
alone, away from the city, and be driving him into the flat land,
might put an end to that bitter pride of courage, that always
was on him, since he would never stay back where the men were in numbers
but break far out in front, and give way in his fury to no man.'
460 So she spoke, and ran out of the house like a raving woman
with pulsing heart, and her two handmaidens went along with her.
But when she came to the bastion and where the men were gathered
she stopped, staring, on the wall; and she saw him
being dragged in front of the city, and the running horses
465 dragged him at random toward the hollow ships of the Achaians.
The darkness of night misted over the eyes of Andromache.
She fell backward, and gasped the life breath from her, and far off
threw from her head the shining gear that ordered her headdress,
the diadem and the cap, and the holding-band woven together,
470 and the circlet, which Aphrodite the golden once had given her
on that day when Hektor of the shining helmet led her forth
from the house of Eëtion, and gave numberless gifts to win her.

And about her stood thronging her husband's sisters and the wives of his brothers
and these, in her despair for death, held her up among them.
475 But she, when she breathed again and the life was gathered back into her,
lifted her voice among the women of Troy in mourning:
'Hektor, I grieve for you. You and I were born to a single
destiny, you in Troy in the house of Priam, and I
in Thebe, underneath the timbered mountain of Plakos
480 in the house of Eëtion, who cared for me when I was little,
ill-fated he, I ill-starred. I wish he had never begotten me.
Now you go down to the house of Death in the secret places
of the earth, and left me here behind in the sorrow of mourning,
a widow in your house, and the boy is only a baby
485 who was born to you and me, the unfortunate. You cannot help him,
Hektor, any more, since you are dead. Nor can he help you.
Though he escape the attack of the Achaians with all its sorrows,
yet all his days for your sake there will be hard work for him
and sorrows, for others will take his lands away from him. The day
490 of bereavement leaves a child with no agemates to befriend him.
He bows his head before every man, his cheeks are bewept, he
goes, needy, a boy among his father's companions,
and tugs at this man by the mantle, that man by the tunic,
and they pity him, and one gives him a tiny drink from a goblet,
495 enough to moisten his lips, not enough to moisten his palate.
But one whose parents are living beats him out of the banquet
hitting him with his fists and in words also abuses him:
"Get out, you! Your father is not dining among us."
And the boy goes away in tears to his widowed mother,
500 Astyanax, who in days before on the knees of his father
would eat only the marrow or the flesh of sheep that was fattest.
And when sleep would come upon him and he was done with his playing,
he would go to sleep in a bed, in the arms of his nurse, in a soft
bed, with his heart given all its fill of luxury.
505 Now, with his dear father gone, he has much to suffer:
he, whom the Trojans have called Astyanax, lord of the city,
since it was you alone who defended the gates and the long walls.
But now, beside the curving ships, far away from your parents,
the writhing worms will feed, when the dogs have had enough of you,
510 on your naked corpse, though in your house there is clothing laid up
that is fine-textured and pleasant, wrought by the hands of women.
But all of these I will burn up in the fire's blazing,
no use to you, since you will never be laid away in them;
but in your honour, from the men of Troy and the Trojan women.'
515   So she spoke, in tears; and the women joined in her mourning.

[*Funeral games celebrate the burial of Patroklos, though Achilleus' anger at Hektor remains unabated.*]

BOOK TWENTY-FOUR: THE MEETING OF PRIAM AND ACHILLEUS

And the games broke up, and the people scattered to go away, each man
to his fast-running ship, and the rest of them took thought of their dinner
and of sweet sleep and its enjoyment; only Achilleus
wept still as he remembered his beloved companion, nor did sleep
5   who subdues all come over him, but he tossed from one side to the other
in longing for Patroklos, for his manhood and his great strength
and all the actions he had seen to the end with him, and the hardships
he had suffered; the wars of men; hard crossing of the big waters.
Remembering all these things he let fall the swelling tears, lying
10   sometimes along his side, sometimes on his back, and now again
prone on his face; then he would stand upright, and pace turning
in distraction along the beach of the sea, nor did dawn rising
escape him as she brightened across the sea and the beaches.
Then, when he had yoked running horses under the chariot
15   he would fasten Hektor behind the chariot, so as to drag him,
and draw him three times around the tomb of Menoitios' fallen
son, then rest again in his shelter, and throw down the dead man
and leave him to lie sprawled on his face in the dust. But Apollo
had pity on him, though he was only a dead man, and guarded
20   the body from all ugliness, and hid all of it under the golden
aegis, so that it might not be torn when Achilleus dragged it.
So Achilleus in his standing fury outraged great Hektor.
The blessed gods as they looked upon him were filled with compassion
and kept urging clear-sighted Argeïphontes to steal the body.
25   There this was pleasing to all the others, but never to Hera
nor Poseidon, nor the girl of the grey eyes,[34] who kept still
their hatred for sacred Ilion as in the beginning,
and for Priam and his people, because of the delusion of Paris
who insulted the goddesses when they came to him in his courtyard
30   and favoured her who supplied the lust that led to disaster.
But now, as it was the twelfth dawn after the death of Hektor,
Phoibos Apollo spoke his word out among the immortals:
'You are hard, you gods, and destructive. Now did not Hektor
burn thigh pieces of oxen and unblemished goats in your honour?
35   Now you cannot bring yourselves to save him, though he is only
a corpse, for his wife to look upon, his child and his mother
and Priam his father, and his people, who presently thereafter

---

[34]**the girl of the grey eyes:** Athene

would burn his body in the fire and give him his rites of burial.
No, you gods; your desire is to help this cursed Achilleus

40   within whose breast there are no feelings of justice, nor can
his mind be bent, but his purposes are fierce, like a lion
who when he has given way to his own great strength and his haughty
spirit, goes among the flocks of men, to devour them.
So Achilleus has destroyed pity, and there is not in him

45   any shame; which does much harm to men but profits them also.
For a man must some day lose one who was even closer
than this; a brother from the same womb, or a son. And yet
he weeps for him, and sorrows for him, and then it is over,
for the Destinies put in mortal men the heart of endurance.

50   But this man, now he has torn the heart of life from great Hektor,
ties him to his horses and drags him around his beloved companion's
tomb; and nothing is gained thereby for his good, or his honour.
Great as he is, let him take care not to make us angry;
for see, he does dishonour to the dumb earth in his fury.'

55   Then bitterly Hera of the white arms answered him, saying:
'What you have said could be true, lord of the silver bow, only
if you give Hektor such pride of place as you give to Achilleus.
But Hektor was mortal, and suckled at the breast of a woman,
while Achilleus is the child of a goddess, one whom I myself

60   nourished and brought up and gave her as bride to her husband
Peleus, one dear to the hearts of the immortals, for you all
went, you gods, to the wedding; and you too feasted among them
and held your lyre, o friend of the evil, faithless forever.'

     In turn Zeus who gathers the clouds spoke to her in answer:

65   'Hera, be not utterly angry with the gods, for there shall not
be the same pride of place given both. Yet Hektor also
was loved by the gods, best of all the mortals in Ilion.
I loved him too. He never failed of gifts to my liking.
Never yet has my altar gone without fair sacrifice,

70   the smoke and the savour of it, since that is our portion of honour.
The stealing of him we will dismiss, for it is not possible
to take bold Hektor secretly from Achilleus, since always
his mother is near him night and day; but it would be better
if one of the gods would summon Thetis here to my presence

75   so that I can say a close word to her, and see that Achilleus
is given gifts by Priam and gives back the body of Hektor.'

     He spoke, and Iris storm-footed sprang away with the message,
and at a point between Samos and Imbros of the high cliffs
plunged in the dark water, and the sea crashed moaning about her.

80   She plummeted to the sea floor like a lead weight which, mounted
along the horn of an ox who ranges the fields, goes downward

and takes death with it to the raw-ravening fish. She found Thetis
inside the hollow of her cave, and gathered about her
sat the rest of the sea goddesses, and she in their midst
85 was mourning the death of her blameless son, who so soon was destined
to die in Troy of the rich soil, far from the land of his fathers.
Iris the swift-foot came close beside her and spoke to her:
'Rise, Thetis. Zeus whose purposes are infinite calls you.'
In turn Thetis the goddess, the silver-footed, answered her:
90 'What does he, the great god, want with me? I feel shamefast
to mingle with the immortals, and my heart is confused with sorrows.
But I will go. No word shall be in vain, if he says it.'
So she spoke, and shining among the divinities took up
her black veil, and there is no darker garment. She went
95 on her way, and in front of her rapid wind-footed Iris
guided her, and the wave of the water opened about them.
They stepped out on the dry land and swept to the sky. There they found
the son of Kronos of the wide brows, and gathered about him
sat all the rest of the gods, the blessed, who live forever.
100 She sat down beside Zeus father, and Athene made a place for her.
Hera put into her hand a beautiful golden goblet
and spoke to her to comfort her, and Thetis accepting drank from it.
The father of gods and men began the discourse among them:
'You have come to Olympos, divine Thetis, for all your sorrow,
105 with an unforgotten grief in your heart. I myself know this.
But even so I will tell you why I summoned you hither.
For nine days there has risen a quarrel among the immortals
over the body of Hektor, and Achilleus, stormer of cities.
They keep urging clear-sighted Argeïphontes to steal the body,
110 but I still put upon Achilleus the honour that he has, guarding
your reverence and your love for me into time afterwards. Go then
in all speed to the encampment and give to your son this message:
tell him that the gods frown upon him, that beyond all other
immortals I myself am angered that in his heart's madness
115 he holds Hektor beside the curved ships and did not give him
back. Perhaps in fear of me he will give back Hektor.
Then I will send Iris to Priam of the great heart, with an order
to ransom his dear son, going down to the ships of the Achaians
and bringing gifts to Achilleus which might soften his anger.'
120 He spoke and the goddess silver-foot Thetis did not disobey him
but descended in a flash of speed from the peaks of Olympos
and made her way to the shelter of her son, and there found him
in close lamentation, and his beloved companions about him
were busy at their work and made ready the morning meal, and there
125 stood a great fleecy sheep being sacrificed in the shelter.

His honoured mother came close to him and sat down beside him,
and stroked him with her hand and called him by name and spoke to him:
'My child, how long will you go on eating your heart out in sorrow
and lamentation, and remember neither your food nor going
130   to bed? It is a good thing even to lie with a woman
in love. For you will not be with me long, but already
death and powerful destiny stand closely above you.
But listen hard to me, for I come from Zeus with a message.
He says that the gods frown upon you, that beyond all other
135   immortals he himself is angered that in your heart's madness
you hold Hektor beside the curved ships and did not redeem him.
Come, then, give him up and accept ransom for the body.'
     Then in turn Achilleus of the swift feet answered her:
'So be it. He can bring the ransom and take off the body,
140   if the Olympian himself so urgently bids it.'
     So, where the ships were drawn together, the son and his mother
conversed at long length in winged words. But the son of Kronos
stirred Iris to go down to sacred Ilion, saying:
'Go forth, Iris the swift, leaving your place on Olympos,
145   and go to Priam of the great heart within Ilion, tell him
to ransom his dear son, going down to the ships of the Achaians
and bringing gifts to Achilleus which might soften his anger:
alone, let no other man of the Trojans go with him, but only
let one elder herald attend him, one who can manage
150   the mules and the easily running wagon, so he can carry
the dead man, whom great Achilleus slew, back to the city.
Let death not be a thought in his heart, let him have no fear;
such an escort shall I send to guide him, Argeïphontes
who shall lead him until he brings him to Achilleus. And after
155   he has brought him inside the shelter of Achilleus, neither
will the man himself kill him, but will hold back all the others,
for he is no witless man nor unwatchful, nor is he wicked,
but will in all kindness spare one who comes to him as a suppliant.'
     He spoke, and storm-footed Iris swept away with the message
160   and came to the house of Priam. There she found outcry and mourning.
The sons sitting around their father inside the courtyard
made their clothes sodden with their tears, and among them the old man
sat veiled, beaten into his mantle. Dung lay thick
on the head and neck of the aged man, for he had been rolling
165   in it, he had gathered and smeared it on with his hands. And his daughters
all up and down the house and the wives of his sons were mourning
as they remembered all those men in their numbers and valour
who lay dead, their lives perished at the hands of the Argives.
The messenger of Zeus stood beside Priam and spoke to him

170   in a small voice, and yet the shivers took hold of his body:
    'Take heart, Priam, son of Dardanos, do not be frightened.
    I come to you not eyeing you with evil intention
    but with the purpose of good toward you. I am a messenger
    of Zeus, who far away cares much for you and is pitiful.
175   The Olympian orders you to ransom Hektor the brilliant,
    to bring gifts to Achilleus which may soften his anger:
    alone, let no other man of the Trojans go with you, but only
    let one elder herald attend you, one who can manage
    the mules and the easily running wagon, so he can carry
180   the dead man, whom great Achilleus slew, back to the city.
    Let death not be a thought in your heart, you need have no fear,
    such an escort shall go with you to guide you, Argeïphontes
    who will lead you till he brings you to Achilleus. And after
    he has brought you inside the shelter of Achilleus, neither
185   will the man himself kill you but will hold back all the others;
    for he is no witless man nor unwatchful, nor is he wicked
    but will in all kindness spare one who comes to him as a suppliant.'
       So Iris the swift-footed spoke and went away from him.
    Thereupon he ordered his sons to make ready the easily rolling
190   mule wagon, and to fasten upon it the carrying basket.
    He himself went into the storeroom, which was fragrant
    and of cedar, and high-ceilinged, with many bright treasures inside it.
    He called out to Hekabe his wife, and said to her:
    'Dear wife, a messenger came to me from Zeus on Olympos,
195   that I must go to the ships of the Achaians and ransom my dear son,
    bringing gifts to Achilleus which may soften his anger.
    Come then, tell me. What does it seem best to your own mind
    for me to do? My heart, my strength are terribly urgent
    that I go there to the ships within the wide army of the Achaians.'
200   So he spoke, and his wife cried out aloud, and answered him:
    'Ah me, where has that wisdom gone for which you were famous
    in time before, among outlanders and those you rule over?
    How can you wish to go alone to the ships of the Achaians
    before the eyes of a man who has slaughtered in such numbers
205   such brave sons of yours? The heart in you is iron. For if
    he has you within his grasp and lays eyes upon you, that man
    who is savage and not to be trusted will not take pity upon you
    nor have respect for your rights. Let us sit apart in our palace
    now, and weep for Hektor, and the way at the first strong Destiny
210   spun with his life line when he was born, when I gave birth to him,
    that the dogs with their shifting feet should feed on him, far from his parents,
    gone down before a stronger man; I wish I could set teeth
    in the middle of his liver and eat it. That would be vengeance

for what he did to my son; for he slew him when he was no coward
215   but standing before the men of Troy and the deep-girdled women
of Troy, with no thought in his mind of flight or withdrawal.'
    In turn the aged Priam, the godlike, answered her saying:
'Do not hold me back when I would be going, neither yourself be
a bird of bad omen in my palace. You will not persuade me.
220   If it had been some other who ordered me, one of the mortals,
one of those who are soothsayers, or priests, or diviners,
I might have called it a lie and we might rather have rejected it.
But now, for I myself heard the god and looked straight upon her,
I am going, and this word shall not be in vain. If it is my destiny
225   to die there by the ships of the bronze-armoured Achaians,
then I wish that. Achilleus can slay me at once, with my own son
caught in my arms, once I have my fill of mourning above him.'
    He spoke, and lifted back the fair covering of his clothes-chest
and from inside took out twelve robes surpassingly lovely
230   and twelve mantles to be worn single, as many blankets,
as many great white cloaks, also the same number of tunics.
He weighed and carried out ten full talents of gold, and brought forth
two shining tripods, and four cauldrons, and brought out a goblet
of surpassing loveliness that the men of Thrace had given him
235   when he went to them with a message, but now the old man spared not
even this in his halls, so much was it his heart's desire
to ransom back his beloved son. But he drove off the Trojans
all from his cloister walks, scolding them with words of revilement:
'Get out, you failures, you disgraces. Have you not also
240   mourning of your own at home that you come to me with your sorrows?
Is it not enough that Zeus, son of Kronos, has given me sorrow
in losing the best of my sons? You also shall be aware of this
since you will be all the easier for the Achaians to slaughter
now he is dead. But, for myself, before my eyes look
245   upon this city as it is destroyed and its people are slaughtered,
my wish is to go sooner down to the house of the death god.'
    He spoke, and went after the men with a stick, and they fled outside
before the fury of the old man. He was scolding his children
and cursing Helenos, and Paris, Agathon the brilliant,
250   Pammon and Antiphonos, Polites of the great war cry,
Deïphobos and Hippothoös and proud Dios. There were nine
sons to whom now the old man gave orders and spoke to them roughly:
'Make haste, wicked children, my disgraces. I wish all of you
had been killed beside the running ships in the place of Hektor.
255   Ah me, for my evil destiny. I have had the noblest
of sons in Troy, but I say not one of them is left to me,
Mestor like a god and Troilos whose delight was in horses,

and Hektor, who was a god among men, for he did not seem like
one who was child of a mortal man, but of a god. All these
260   Ares has killed, and all that are left me are the disgraces,
the liars and the dancers, champions of the chorus, the plunderers
of their own people in their land of lambs and kids. Well then,
will you not get my wagon ready and be quick about it,
and put all these things on it, so we can get on with our journey?'
265   So he spoke, and they in terror at the old man's scolding
hauled out the easily running wagon for mules, a fine thing
new-fabricated, and fastened the carrying basket upon it.
They took away from its peg the mule yoke made of boxwood
with its massive knob, well fitted with guiding rings, and brought forth
270   the yoke lashing (together with the yoke itself) of nine cubits
and snugged it well into place upon the smooth-polished wagon-pole
at the foot of the beam, then slipped the ring over the peg, and lashed it
with three turns on either side to the knob, and afterwards
fastened it all in order and secured it under a hooked guard.
275   Then they carried out and piled into the smooth-polished mule wagon
all the unnumbered spoils to be given for the head of Hektor,
then yoked the powerful-footed mules who pulled in the harness
and whom the Mysians gave once as glorious presents to Priam;
but for Priam they led under the yoke those horses the old man
280   himself had kept, and cared for them at his polished manger.
Now in the high house the yoking was done for the herald
and Priam, men both with close counsels in their minds. And now came
Hekabe with sorrowful heart and stood close beside them
carrying in her right hand the kind, sweet wine in a golden
285   goblet, so that before they went they might pour a drink-offering.
She stood in front of the horses, called Priam by name and spoke to him:
'Here, pour a libation to Zeus father, and pray you may come back
home again from those who hate you, since it seems the spirit
within you drives you upon the ships, though I would not have it.
290   Make your prayer then to the dark-misted, the son of Kronos
on Ida, who looks out on all the Troad, and ask him
for a bird of omen, a rapid messenger, which to his own mind
is dearest of all birds and his strength is the biggest, one seen
on the right, so that once your eyes have rested upon him
295   you can trust in him and go to the ships of the fast-mounted Danaans.
But if Zeus of the wide brows will not grant you his own messenger,
then I, for one, would never urge you on nor advise you
to go to the Argive ships, for all your passion to do it.'
Then in answer to her again spoke Priam the godlike:
300   'My lady, I will not disregard this wherein you urge me.
It is well to lift hands to Zeus and ask if he will have mercy.'

The old man spoke, and told the housekeeper who attended them
to pour unstained water over his hands. She standing beside them
and serving them held the washing-bowl in her hands, and a pitcher.
305 He washed his hands and took the cup from his wife. He stood up
in the middle of the enclosure, and prayed, and poured the wine out
looking up into the sky, and gave utterance and spoke, saying:
'Father Zeus, watching over us from Ida, most high, most honoured:
grant that I come to Achilleus for love and pity; but send me
310 a bird of omen, a rapid messenger which to your own mind
is dearest of all birds and his strength is biggest, one seen
on the right, so that once my eyes have rested upon him
I may trust in him and go to the ships of the fast-mounted Danaans.'
So he spoke in prayer, and Zeus of the counsels heard him.
315 Straightway he sent down the most lordly of birds, an eagle,
the dark one, the marauder, called as well the black eagle.
And as big as is the build of the door to a towering chamber
in the house of a rich man, strongly fitted with bars, of such size
was the spread of his wings on either side. He swept through the city
320 appearing on the right hand, and the people looking upon him
were uplifted and the hearts made glad in the breasts of all of them.
Now in urgent haste the old man mounted into his chariot
and drove out through the forecourt and the thundering close. Before him
the mules hauled the wagon on its four wheels, Idaios
325 the sober-minded driving them, and behind him the horses
came on as the old man laid the lash upon them and urged them
rapidly through the town, and all his kinsmen were following
much lamenting, as if he went to his death. When the two men
had gone down through the city, and out, and come to the flat land,
330 the rest of them turned back to go to Ilion, the sons
and the sons-in-law. And Zeus of the wide brows failed not to notice
the two as they showed in the plain. He saw the old man and took pity
upon him, and spoke directly to his beloved son, Hermes:
'Hermes, for to you beyond all other gods it is dearest
335 to be man's companion, and you listen to whom you will, go now
on your way, and so guide Priam inside the hollow ships
of the Achaians, that no man shall see him, none be aware of him,
of the other Danaans, till he has come to the son of Peleus.'
He spoke, nor disobeyed him the courier, Argeïphontes.
340 Immediately he bound upon his feet the fair sandals
golden and immortal, that carried him over the water
as over the dry land of the main abreast of the wind's blast.
He caught up the staff, with which he mazes the eyes of those mortals
whose eyes he would maze, or wakes again the sleepers. Holding
345 this in his hands, strong Argeïphontes winged his way onward

until he came suddenly to Troy and the Hellespont, and there
walked on, and there took the likeness of a young man, a noble,
with beard new grown, which is the most graceful time of young manhood.
    Now when the two had driven past the great tomb of Ilos[35]
350   they stayed their mules and horses to water them in the river,
for by this time darkness had descended on the land; and the herald
made out Hermes, who was coming toward them at a short distance.
He lifted his voice and spoke aloud to Priam: 'Take thought,
son of Dardanos. Here is work for a mind that is careful.
355   I see a man; I think he will presently tear us to pieces.
Come then, let us run away with our horses, or if not, then
clasp his knees and entreat him to have mercy upon us.'
    So he spoke, and the old man's mind was confused, he was badly
frightened, and the hairs stood up all over his gnarled body
360   and he stood staring, but the kindly god himself coming closer
took the old man's hand, and spoke to him and asked him a question
'Where, my father, are you thus guiding your mules and horses
through the immortal night while other mortals are sleeping?
Have you no fear of the Achaians whose wind is fury,
365   who hate you, who are your enemies, are near? For if one
of these were to see you, how you are conveying so many
treasures through the swift black night, what then could you think of?
You are not young yourself, and he who attends you is aged
for beating off any man who might pick a quarrel with you.
370   But I will do you no harm myself, I will even keep off
another who would. You seem to me like a beloved father.'
    In answer to him again spoke aged Priam the godlike:
'Yes, in truth, dear child, all this is much as you tell me;
yet still there is some god who has held his hand above me,
375   who sent such a wayfarer as you to meet me, an omen
of good, for such you are by your form, your admired beauty
and the wisdom in your mind. Your parents are fortunate in you.'
    Then in turn answered him the courier Argeïphontes:
'Yes, old sir, all this that you said is fair and orderly.
380   But come, tell me this thing and recite it to me accurately.
Can it be you convey these treasures in all their numbers and beauty
to outland men, so that they can be still kept safe for you?
Or are all of you by now abandoning sacred Ilion
in fear, such a one was he who died, the best man among you,
385   your son; who was never wanting when you fought against the Achaians.'

---

[35]Ilos: Priam's grandfather

In answer to him again spoke aged Priam the godlike:
'But who are you, o best of men, and who are your parents?
Since you spoke of my ill-starred son's death, and with honour.'
Then in turn answered him the courier Argeïphontes:
390 'You try me out, aged sir. You ask me of glorious Hektor
whom many a time my eyes have seen in the fighting where men win
glory, as also on that time when he drove back the Argives
on their ships and kept killing them with the stroke of the sharp bronze,
and we stood by and wondered at him; for then Achilleus
395 would not let us fight by reason of his anger at Agamemnon.
For I am Achilleus' henchman, and the same strong-wrought vessel
brought us here; and I am a Myrmidon, and my father
is Polyktor; a man of substance, but aged, as you are.
He has six sons beside, and I am the seventh, and I shook
400 lots with the others, and it was my lot to come on this venture.
But now I have come to the plain away from the ships, for at daybreak
the glancing-eyed Achaians will do battle around the city.
They chafe from sitting here too long, nor have the Achaians'
kings the strength to hold them back as they break for the fighting.'
405 In answer to him again spoke aged Priam the godlike:
'If then you are henchman to Peleïd Achilleus,
come, tell me the entire truth, and whether my son lies
still beside the ships, or whether by now he has been hewn
limb from limb and thrown before the dogs by Achilleus.'
410 Then in turn answered him the courier Argeïphontes:
'Aged sir, neither have any dogs eaten him, nor have
the birds, but he lies yet beside the ship of Achilleus
at the shelters, and as he was; now here is the twelfth dawn
he has lain there, nor does his flesh decay, nor do worms feed
415 on him, they who devour men who have fallen in battle.
It is true, Achilleus drags him at random around his beloved
companion's tomb, as dawn on dawn appears, yet he cannot
mutilate him; you yourself can see when you go there
how fresh with dew he lies, and the blood is all washed from him,
420 nor is there any corruption, and all the wounds have been closed up
where he was struck, since many drove the bronze in his body.
So it is that the blessed immortals care for your son, though
he is nothing but a dead man; because in their hearts they loved him.'
He spoke, and the old man was made joyful and answered him, saying:
425 'My child, surely it is good to give the immortals
their due gifts; because my own son, if ever I had one,
never forgot in his halls the gods who live on Olympos.
Therefore they remembered him even in death's stage. Come, then,
accept at my hands this beautiful drinking-cup, and give me

430   protection for my body, and with the gods' grace be my escort
        until I make my way to the shelter of the son of Peleus.'
                In turn answered him the courier Argeïphontes:
        'You try me out, aged sir, for I am young, but you will not
        persuade me, telling me to accept your gifts when Achilleus
435   does not know. I fear him at heart and have too much reverence
        to rob him. Such a thing might be to my sorrow hereafter.
        But I would be your escort and take good care of you, even
        till I came to glorious Argos in a fast ship or following
        on foot, and none would fight you because he despised your escort.'
440   The kind god spoke, and sprang up behind the horses and into
        the chariot, and rapidly caught in his hands the lash and the guide reins,
        and breathed great strength into the mules and horses. Now after
        they had got to the fortifications about the ships, and the ditch, there
        were sentries, who had just begun to make ready their dinner,
445   but about these the courier Argeïphontes drifted
        sleep, on all, and quickly opened the gate, and shoved back
        the door-bars, and brought in Priam and the glorious gifts on the wagon.
        But when they had got to the shelter of Peleus' son: a towering
        shelter the Myrmidons had built for their king, hewing
450   the timbers of pine, and they made a roof of thatch above it
        shaggy with grass that they had gathered out of the meadows;
        and around it made a great courtyard for their king, with hedgepoles
        set close together; the gate was secured by a single door-piece
        of pine, and three Achaians could ram it home in its socket
455   and three could pull back and open the huge door-bar; three other
        Achaians, that is, but Achilleus all by himself could close it.
        At this time Hermes, the kind god, opened the gate for the old man
        and brought in the glorious gifts for Peleus' son, the swift-footed,
        and dismounted to the ground from behind the horses, and spoke forth:
460   'Aged sir, I who came to you am a god immortal,
        Hermes. My father sent me down to guide and go with you.
        But now I am going back again, and I will not go in
        before the eyes of Achilleus, for it would make others angry
        for an immortal god so to face mortal men with favour.
465   But go you in yourself and clasp the knees of Peleion
        and entreat him in the name of his father, the name of his mother
        of the lovely hair, and his child, and so move the spirit within him.'
                So Hermes spoke, and went away to the height of Olympos,
        but Priam vaulted down to the ground from behind the horses
470   and left Idaios where he was, for he stayed behind, holding
        in hand the horses and mules. The old man made straight for the dwelling
        where Achilleus the beloved of Zeus was sitting. He found him
        inside, and his companions were sitting apart, as two only,

Automedon the hero and Alkimos, scion of Ares,
475 were busy beside him. He had just now got through with his dinner,
with eating and drinking, and the table still stood by. Tall Priam
came in unseen by the other men and stood close beside him
and caught the knees of Achilleus in his arms, and kissed the hands
that were dangerous and manslaughtering and had killed so many
480 of his sons. As when dense disaster closes on one who has murdered
a man in his own land, and he comes to the country of others,
to a man of substance, and wonder seizes on those who behold him,
so Achilleus wondered as he looked on Priam, a godlike
man, and the rest of them wondered also, and looked at each other.
485 But now Priam spoke to him in the words of a suppliant:
'Achilleus like the gods, remember your father, one who
is of years like mine, and on the door-sill of sorrowful old age.
And they who dwell nearby encompass him and afflict him,
nor is there any to defend him against the wrath, the destruction.
490 Yet surely he, when he hears of you and that you are still living,
is gladdened within his heart and all his days he is hopeful
that he will see his beloved son come home from the Troad.
But for me, my destiny was evil. I have had the noblest
of sons in Troy, but I say not one of them is left to me.
495 Fifty were my sons, when the sons of the Achaians came here.
Nineteen were born to me from the womb of a single mother,
and other women bore the rest in my palace; and of these
violent Ares broke the strength in the knees of most of them,
but one was left me who guarded my city and people, that one
500 you killed a few days since as he fought in defence of his country,
Hektor; for whose sake I come now to the ships of the Achaians
to win him back from you, and I bring you gifts beyond number.
Honour then the gods, Achilleus, and take pity upon me
remembering your father, yet I am still more pitiful;
505 I have gone through what no other mortal on earth has gone through;
I put my lips to the hands of the man who has killed my children.'
        So he spoke, and stirred in the other a passion of grieving
for his own father. He took the old man's hand and pushed him
gently away, and the two remembered, as Priam sat huddled
510 at the feet of Achilleus and wept close for manslaughtering Hektor
and Achilleus wept now for his own father, now again
for Patroklos. The sound of their mourning moved in the house.
Then when great Achilleus had taken full satisfaction in sorrow
and the passion for it had gone from his mind and body, thereafter
515 he rose from his chair, and took the old man by the hand, and set him
on his feet again, in pity for the grey head and the grey beard,
and spoke to him and addressed him in winged words: 'Ah, unlucky,

surely you have had much evil to endure in your spirit.
How could you dare to come alone to the ships of the Achaians

520 and before my eyes, when I am one who have killed in such numbers
such brave sons of yours? The heart in you is iron. Come, then,
and sit down upon this chair, and you and I will even let
our sorrows lie still in the heart for all our grieving. There is not
any advantage to be won from grim lamentation.

525 Such is the way the gods spun life for unfortunate mortals,
that we live in unhappiness, but the gods themselves have no sorrows.
There are two urns that stand on the door-sill of Zeus. They are unlike
for the gifts they bestow: an urn of evils, an urn of blessings.
If Zeus who delights in thunder mingles these and bestows them

530 on man, he shifts, and moves now in evil, again in good fortune.
But when Zeus bestows from the urn of sorrows, he makes a failure
of man, and the evil hunger drives him over the shining
earth, and he wanders respected neither of gods nor mortals.
Such were the shining gifts given by the gods to Peleus

535 from his birth, who outshone all men beside for his riches
and pride of possession, and was lord over the Myrmidons. Thereto
the gods bestowed an immortal wife on him, who was mortal.
But even on him the god piled evil also. There was not
any generation of strong sons born to him in his great house

540 but a single all-untimely child he had, and I give him
no care as he grows old, since far from the land of my fathers
I sit here in Troy, and bring nothing but sorrow to you and your children.
And you, old sir, we are told you prospered once; for as much
as Lesbos, Makar's hold, confines to the north above it

545 and Phrygia from the north confines, and enormous Hellespont,
of these, old sir, you were lord once in your wealth and your children.
But now the Uranian gods brought us, an affliction upon you,
forever there is fighting about your city, and men killed.
But bear up, nor mourn endlessly in your heart, for there is not

550 anything to be gained from grief for your son; you will never
bring him back; sooner you must go through yet another sorrow.'
        In answer to him again spoke aged Priam the godlike:
'Do not, beloved of Zeus, make me sit on a chair while Hektor
lies yet forlorn among the shelters; rather with all speed

555 give him back, so my eyes may behold him, and accept the ransom
we bring you, which is great. You may have joy of it, and go back
to the land of your own fathers, since once you have permitted me
to go on living myself and continue to look on the sunlight.'
        Then looking darkly at him spoke swift-footed Achilleus:

560 'No longer stir me up, old sir. I myself am minded
to give Hektor back to you. A messenger came to me from Zeus,

my mother, she who bore me, the daughter of the sea's ancient.
I know you, Priam, in my heart, and it does not escape me
that some god led you to the running ships of the Achaians.

565   For no mortal would dare come to our encampment, not even
one strong in youth. He could not get by the pickets, he could not
lightly unbar the bolt that secures our gateway. Therefore
you must not further make my spirit move in my sorrows,
for fear, old sir, I might not let you alone in my shelter,

570   suppliant as you are; and be guilty before the god's orders.'
       He spoke, and the old man was frightened and did as he told him.
The son of Peleus bounded to the door of the house like a lion,
nor went alone, but the two henchmen followed attending,
the hero Automedon and Alkimos, those whom Achilleus

575   honoured beyond all companions after Patroklos dead. These two
now set free from under the yoke the mules and the horses,
and led inside the herald, the old king's crier, and gave him
a chair to sit in, then from the smooth-polished mule wagon
lifted out the innumerable spoils for the head of Hektor,

580   but left inside it two great cloaks and a finespun tunic
to shroud the corpse in when they carried him home. Then Achilleus
called out to his serving-maids to wash the body and anoint it
all over; but take it first aside, since otherwise Priam
might see his son and in the heart's sorrow not hold in his anger

585   at the sight, and the deep heart in Achilleus be shaken to anger;
that he might not kill Priam and be guilty before the god's orders.
Then when the serving-maids had washed the corpse and anointed it
with olive oil, they threw a fair great cloak and a tunic
about him, and Achilleus himself lifted him and laid him

590   on a litter, and his friends helped him lift it to the smooth-polished
mule wagon. He groaned then, and called by name on his beloved companion:
'Be not angry with me, Patroklos, if you discover,
though you be in the house of Hades, that I gave back great Hektor
to his loved father, for the ransom he gave me was not unworthy.

595   I will give you your share of the spoils, as much as is fitting.'
       So spoke great Achilleus and went back into the shelter
and sat down on the elaborate couch from which he had risen,
against the inward wall, and now spoke his word to Priam:
'Your son is given back to you, aged sir, as you asked it.

600   He lies on a bier. When dawn shows you yourself shall see him
as you take him away. Now you and I must remember our supper.
For even Niobe, she of the lovely tresses, remembered
to eat, whose twelve children were destroyed in her palace,
six daughters, and six sons in the pride of their youth, whom Apollo

605   killed with arrows from his silver bow, being angered

with Niobe, and shaft-showering Artemis killed the daughters;
because Niobe likened herself to Leto of the fair colouring
and said Leto had borne only two, she herself had borne many;
but the two, though they were only two, destroyed all those others.

610 Nine days long they lay in their blood, nor was there anyone
to bury them, for the son of Kronos made stones out of
the people; but on the tenth day the Uranian gods buried them.
But she remembered to eat when she was worn out with weeping.
And now somewhere among the rocks, in the lonely mountains,

615 in Sipylos, where they say is the resting place of the goddesses
who are nymphs, and dance beside the waters of Acheloios,
there, stone still, she broods on the sorrows that the gods gave her.
Come then, we also, aged magnificent sir, must remember
to eat, and afterwards you may take your beloved son back

620 to Ilion, and mourn for him; and he will be much lamented.'
        So spoke fleet Achilleus and sprang to his feet and slaughtered
a gleaming sheep, and his friends skinned it and butchered it fairly,
and cut up the meat expertly into small pieces, and spitted them,
and roasted all carefully and took off the pieces.

625 Automedon took the bread and set it out on the table
in fair baskets, while Achilleus served the meats. And thereon
they put their hands to the good things that lay ready before them.
But when they had put aside their desire for eating and drinking,
Priam, son of Dardanos, gazed upon Achilleus, wondering

630 at his size and beauty, for he seemed like an outright vision
of gods. Achilleus in turn gazed on Dardanian Priam
and wondered, as he saw his brave looks and listened to him talking.
But when they had taken their fill of gazing one on the other,
first of the two to speak was the aged man, Priam the godlike:

635 'Give me, beloved of Zeus, a place to sleep presently, so that
we may even go to bed and take the pleasure of sweet sleep.
For my eyes have not closed underneath my lids since that time
when my son lost his life beneath your hands, but always
I have been grieving and brooding over my numberless sorrows

640 and wallowed in the muck about my courtyard's enclosure.
Now I have tasted food again and have let the gleaming
wine go down my throat. Before, I had tasted nothing.'
        He spoke, and Achilleus ordered his serving-maids and companions
to make a bed in the porch's shelter and to lay upon it

645 fine underbedding of purple, and spread blankets above it
and fleecy robes to be an over-all covering. The maid-servants
went forth from the main house, and in their hands held torches,
and set to work, and presently had two beds made. Achilleus
of the swift feet now looked at Priam and said, sarcastic:

650 'Sleep outside, aged sir and good friend, for fear some Achaian
might come in here on a matter of counsel, since they keep coming
and sitting by me and making plans; as they are supposed to.
But if one of these come through the fleeting black night should notice you,
he would go straight and tell Agamemnon, shepherd of the people,
655 and there would be delay in the ransoming of the body.
But come, tell me this and count off for me exactly
how many days you intend for the burial of great Hektor.
Tell me, so I myself shall stay still and hold back the people.'
        In answer to him again spoke aged Priam the godlike:
660 'If you are willing that we accomplish a complete funeral
for great Hektor, this, Achilleus, is what you could do and give
me pleasure. For you know surely how we are penned in our city,
and wood is far to bring in from the hills, and the Trojans are frightened
badly. Nine days we would keep him in our palace and mourn him,
665 and bury him on the tenth day, and the people feast by him,
and on the eleventh day we would make the grave-barrow for him,
and on the twelfth day fight again; if so we must do.'
        Then in turn swift-footed brilliant Achilleus answered him:
'Then all this, aged Priam, shall be done as you ask it.
670 I will hold off our attack for as much time as you bid me.'
        So he spoke, and took the aged king by the right hand
at the wrist, so that his heart might have no fear. Then these two,
Priam and the herald who were both men of close counsel,
slept in the place outside the house, in the porch's shelter;
675 but Achilleus slept in the inward corner of the strong-built shelter,
and at his side lay Briseis of the fair colouring.
        Now the rest of the gods and men who were lords of chariots
slept nightlong, with the easy bondage of slumber upon them,
only sleep had not caught Hermes the kind god, who pondered
680 now in his heart the problem of how to escort King Priam
from the ships and not be seen by the devoted gate-wardens.
He stood above his head and spoke a word to him, saying:
'Aged sir, you can have no thought of evil from the way
you sleep still among your enemies now Achilleus has left you
685 unharmed. You have ransomed now your dear son and given much for him.
But the sons you left behind would give three times as much ransom
for you, who are alive, were Atreus' son Agamemnon
to recognize you, and all the other Achaians learn of you.'
        He spoke, and the old man was afraid, and wakened his herald,
690 and lightly Hermes harnessed for them the mules and the horses
and himself drove them through the encampment. And no man knew of them.
        But when they came to the crossing-place of the fair-running river,
of whirling Xanthos, a stream whose father was Zeus the immortal,

there Hermes left them and went away to the height of Olympos,
695 and dawn, she of the yellow robe, scattered over all earth,
and they drove their horses on to the city with lamentation
and clamour, while the mules drew the body. Nor was any other
aware of them at the first, no man, no fair-girdled woman,
only Kassandra, a girl like Aphrodite the golden,
700 who had gone up to the height of the Pergamos. She saw
her dear father standing in the chariot, his herald and crier
with him. She saw Hektor drawn by the mules on a litter.
She cried out then in sorrow and spoke to the entire city:
'Come, men of Troy and Trojan women; look upon Hektor
705 if ever before you were joyful when you saw him come back living
from battle; for he was a great joy to his city, and all his people.'
    She spoke, and there was no man left there in all the city
nor woman, but all were held in sorrow passing endurance.
They met Priam beside the gates as he brought the dead in.
710 First among them were Hektor's wife and his honoured mother
who tore their hair, and ran up beside the smooth-rolling wagon,
and touched his head. And the multitude, wailing, stood there about them.
And now and there in front of the gates they would have lamented
all day till the sun went down and let fall their tears for Hektor,
715 except that the old man spoke from the chariot to his people:
'Give me way to get through with my mules; then afterwards
you may sate yourselves with mourning, when I have him inside the palace.'
    So he spoke, and they stood apart and made way for the wagon.
And when they had brought him inside the renowned house, they laid him
720 then on a carved bed, and seated beside him the singers
who were to lead the melody in the dirge, and the singers
chanted the song of sorrow, and the women were mourning beside them.
Andromache of the white arms led the lamentation
of the women, and held in her arms the head of manslaughtering Hektor:
725 'My husband, you were lost young from life, and have left me
a widow in your house, and the boy is only a baby
who was born to you and me, the unhappy. I think he will never
come of age, for before then head to heel this city
will be sacked, for you, its defender, are gone, you who guarded
730 the city, and the grave wives, and the innocent children,
wives who before long must go away in the hollow ships,
and among them I shall also go, and you, my child, follow
where I go, and there do much hard work that is unworthy
of you, drudgery for a hard master; or else some Achaian
735 will take you by hand and hurl you from the tower into horrible

death,[36] in anger because Hektor once killed his brother,
or his father, or his son; there were so many Achaians
whose teeth bit the vast earth, beaten down by the hands of Hektor.
Your father was no merciful man in the horror of battle.
740   Therefore your people are grieving for you all through their city,
Hektor, and you left for your parents mourning and sorrow
beyond words, but for me passing all others is left the bitterness
and the pain, for you did not die in bed, and stretch your arms to me,
nor tell me some last intimate word that I could remember
745   always, all the nights and days of my weeping for you.'
        So she spoke in tears, and the women were mourning about her.
Now Hekabe led out the thronging chant of their sorrow:
'Hektor, of all my sons the dearest by far to my spirit;
while you still lived for me you were dear to the gods, and even
750   in the stage of death they cared about you still. There were others
of my sons whom at times swift-footed Achilleus captured,
and he would sell them as slaves far across the unresting salt water
into Samos, and Imbros, and Lemnos in the gloom of the mists. You,
when he had taken your life with the thin edge of the bronze sword,
755   he dragged again and again around his beloved companion's
tomb, Patroklos', whom you killed, but even so did not
bring him back to life. Now you lie in the palace, handsome
and fresh with dew, in the likeness of one whom he of the silver
bow, Apollo, has attacked and killed with his gentle arrows.'
760   So she spoke, in tears, and wakened the endless mourning.
Third and last Helen led the song of sorrow among them:
'Hektor, of all my lord's brothers dearest by far to my spirit:
my husband is Alexandros, like an immortal, who brought me
here to Troy; and I should have died before I came with him;
765   and here now is the twentieth year upon me since I came
from the place where I was, forsaking the land of my fathers. In this time
I have never heard a harsh saying from you, nor an insult.
No, but when another, one of my lord's brothers or sisters, a fair-robed
wife of some brother, would say a harsh word to me in the palace,
770   or my lord's mother—but his father was gentle always, a father
indeed—then you would speak and put them off and restrain them
by your own gentleness of heart and your gentle words. Therefore
I mourn for you in sorrow of heart and mourn myself also
and my ill luck. There was no other in all the wide Troad
775   who was kind to me, and my friend; all others shrank when they saw me.'

---

[36]**horrible/death:** this in fact will be the case as Euripedes dramatizes in the tragedy *Trojan Women*

So she spoke in tears, and the vast populace grieved with her.
Now Priam the aged king spoke forth his word to his people:
'Now, men of Troy, bring timber into the city, and let not
your hearts fear a close ambush of the Argives. Achilleus
780 promised me, as he sent me on my way from the black ships,
that none should do us injury until the twelfth dawn comes.'
He spoke, and they harnessed to the wagons their mules and their oxen
and presently were gathered in front of the city. Nine days
they spent bringing in an endless supply of timber. But when
785 the tenth dawn had shone forth with her light upon mortals,
they carried out bold Hektor, weeping, and set the body
aloft a towering pyre for burning. And set fire to it.
But when the young dawn showed again with her rosy fingers,
the people gathered around the pyre of illustrious Hektor.
790 But when all were gathered to one place and assembled together,
first with gleaming wine they put out the pyre that was burning,
all where the fury of the fire still was in force, and thereafter
the brothers and companions of Hektor gathered the white bones
up, mourning, as the tears swelled and ran down their cheeks. Then
795 they laid what they had gathered up in a golden casket
and wrapped this about with soft robes of purple, and presently
put it away in the hollow of the grave, and over it
piled huge stones laid close together. Lightly and quickly
they piled up the grave-barrow, and on all sides were set watchmen
800 for fear the strong-greaved Achaians might too soon set upon them.
They piled up the grave-barrow and went away, and thereafter
assembled in a fair gathering and held a glorious
feast within the house of Priam, king under God's hand.
Such was their burial of Hektor, breaker of horses.

3. THE ODYSSEY
(c. 8th c. BCE)

Homer

(trans. by Allan Mandelbaum)

The Odyssey, *the second of Homer's great epics, tells of the aftermath of the Trojan War when the victorious Greek tribes set sail for home. Odysseus, absent from his wife Penelope, son Telemachos, and Kingdom of Ithaca for the ten years of the war, has earned a reputation for skill as a clever strategist, while his wife and young son have been struggling to maintain the Kingdom. Odysseus's long and arduous journey home is thus but one of several heroic threads in the Homeric tapestry of what it means to be Greek, and what it means to be human.*

[See separate text.]

4. THE ORESTEIA
(458 BCE)

Aeschylus

(trans. by Richmond Lattimore)

Aeschylus was born in 525 BCE in Eleusis (near Athens) and fought in the Persian Wars at Marathon, Salamis, and Plataea before becoming the first great Greek tragedian. His Oresteia won the competition at the annual Festival of Dionysus in 458 BCE. The trilogy (three plays linked by a common theme) dramatizes the evolution of justice in Athens beginning with the tragic consequences of seeking justice by vengeance (Agamemnon, Libation Bearers), to the greater justice of trial by jury (Eumenides). Aeschylus thus proudly celebrates the triumph of rational decision making and democracy over brute force and tyranny.

AGAMEMNON

CHARACTERS

WATCHMAN
CLYTAEMESTRA
HERALD
AGAMEMNON
CASSANDRA
AEGISTHUS
CHORUS OF ARGIVE ELDERS
ATTENDANTS of CLYTAEMESTRA: of AGAMEMNON: BODYGUARD of
    AEGISTHUS (all silent parts)
TIME, directly after the fall of Troy

SCENE: Argos, before the palace of King AGAMEMNON. The WATCHMAN, who
    speaks the opening lines, is posted on the roof of the palace.
    CLYTAEMESTRA's entrances are made from a door in the center of the stage;
    all others, from the wings.

5   [*The* WATCHMAN, *alone.*]

       I ask the gods some respite from the weariness
       of this watchtime measured by years I lie awake
       elbowed upon the Atreidae's roof dogwise to mark
       the grand processionals of all the stars of night
10   burdened with winter and again with heat for men,
       dynasties in their shining blazoned on the air,
       these stars, upon their wane and when the rest arise.

       I wait; to read the meaning in that beacon light,
       a blaze of fire to carry out of Troy the rumor
15   and outcry of its capture; to such end a lady's
       male strength of heart in its high confidence ordains.
       Now as this bed stricken with night and drenched with dew
       I keep, nor ever with kind dreams for company:
       since fear in sleep's place stands forever at my head
20   against strong closure of my eyes, or any rest:
       I mince such medicine against sleep failed: I sing,
       only to weep again the pity of this house
       no longer, as once, administered in the grand way.
       Now let there be again redemption from distress,
25   the flare burning from the blackness in good augury.

       [*A light shows in the distance.*]

       Oh hail, blaze of the darkness, harbinger of day's
       shining, and of processionals and dance and choirs
       of multitudes in Argos for this day of grace.
30   Ahoy!
       I cry the news aloud to Agamemnon's queen,
       that she may rise up from her bed of state with speed
       to raise the rumor of gladness welcoming this beacon,
       and singing rise, if truly the citadel of Ilium
35   has fallen, as the shining of this flare proclaims.
       I also, I, will make my choral prelude, since
       my lord's dice cast aright are counted as my own,
       and mine the tripled sixes of this torchlit throw.

       May it only happen. May my king come home, and I
40   take up within this hand the hand I love. The rest
       I leave to silence; for an ox stands huge upon
       my tongue. The house itself, could it take voice, might speak

aloud and plain. I speak to those who understand,
but if they fail, I have forgotten everything.

45   [*Exit. The* CHORUS *enters, speaking.*]

Ten years since the great contestants
of Priam's right,
Menelaus and Agamemnon, my lord,
twin throned, twin sceptered, in twofold power
50   of kings from God, the Atreidae,
put forth from this shore
the thousand ships of the Argives,
the strength and the armies.
Their cry of war went shrill from the heart,
55   as eagles stricken in agony
for young perished, high from the nest
eddy and circle
to bend and sweep of the wings' stroke,
lost far below
60   the fledgelings, the nest, and the tendance.
Yet someone hears in the air, a god,
Apollo, Pan, or Zeus, the high
thin wail of these sky-guests, and drives
late to its mark
65   the Fury upon the transgressors.

So drives Zeus the great guest god
the Atreidae against Alexander:
for one woman's promiscuous sake
the struggling masses, legs tired,
70   knees grinding in dust,
spears broken in the onset.
Danaans and Trojans
they have it alike. It goes as it goes
now. The end will be destiny.
75   You cannot burn flesh or pour unguents,
not innocent cool tears,
that will soften the gods' stiff anger.

But we; dishonored, old in our bones,
cast off even then from the gathering horde,
80   stay here, to prop up
on staves the strength of a baby.
Since the young vigor that urges

inward to the heart
is frail as age, no warcraft yet perfect,
85   while beyond age, leaf
withered, man goes three footed
no stronger than a child is,
a dream that falters in daylight.

[CLYTAEMESTRA *enters quietly. The* CHORUS *continues to speak.*]

90   But you, lady,
daughter of Tyndareus, Clytaemestra, our queen:
What is there to be done? What new thing have you heard?
In persuasion of what
report do you order such sacrifice?
95   To all the gods of the city,
the high and the deep spirits,
to them of the sky and the market places,
the altars blaze with oblations.
The staggered flame goes sky high
100   one place, then another,
drugged by the simple soft
persuasion of sacred unguents,
the deep stored oil of the kings.
Of these things what can be told
105   openly, speak.
Be healer to this perplexity
that grows now into darkness of thought,
while again sweet hope shining from the flames
beats back the pitiless pondering
110   of sorrow that eats my heart.

I have mastery yet to chant the wonder at the wayside
given to kings. Still by God's grace there surges within me
singing magic
grown to my life and power,
115   how the wild bird portent
hurled forth the Achaeans'
twin-stemmed power single hearted,
lords of the youth of Hellas,
with spear and hand of strength
120   to the land of Teucrus.
Kings of birds to the kings of the ships,
one black, one blazed with silver,
clear seen by the royal house

on the right, the spear hand,
125   they lighted, watched by all
tore a hare, ripe, bursting with young unborn yet,
stayed from her last fleet running.
Sing sorrow, sorrow: but good win out in the end.

Then the grave seer of the host saw through to the hearts divided,
130   knew the fighting sons of Atreus feeding on the hare
with the host, their people.
Seeing beyond, he spoke:
"With time, this foray
shall stalk the castle of Priam.
135   Before then, under
the walls, Fate shall spoil
in violence the rich herds of the people.
Only let no doom of the gods darken
upon this huge iron forged to curb Troy—
140   from inward. Artemis the undefiled
is angered with pity
at the flying hounds of her father
eating the unborn young in the hare and the shivering mother.
She is sick at the eagles' feasting.
145   Sing sorrow, sorrow: but good win out in the end.

Lovely you are and kind
to the tender young of ravening lions.
For sucklings of all the savage
beasts that lurk in the lonely places you have sympathy.
150   Grant meaning to these appearances
good, yet not without evil.
Healer Apollo, I pray you
let her not with cross winds
bind the ships of the Danaans
155   to time-long anchorage
forcing a second sacrifice unholy, untasted,
working bitterness in the blood
and faith lost. For the terror returns like sickness to lurk in the house;
the secret anger remembers the child that shall be avenged."
160   Such, with great good things beside, rang out in the voice of Calchas,
these fatal signs from the birds by the way to the house of the princes,
wherewith in sympathy
sing sorrow, sorrow: but good win out in the end.

Zeus: whatever he may be, if this name
165   pleases him in invocation,
thus I call upon him.
I have pondered everything
yet I cannot find a way,
only Zeus, to cast this dead weight of ignorance
170   finally from out my brain.

He who in time long ago was great,
throbbing with gigantic strength,
shall be as if he never were, unspoken.
He who followed him has found
175   his master, and is gone.
Cry aloud without fear the victory of Zeus,
you will not have failed the truth:

Zeus, who guided men to think,
who has laid it down that wisdom
180   comes alone through suffering.
Still there drips in sleep against the heart
grief of memory; against
our pleasure we are temperate
From the gods who sit in grandeur
185   grace comes somehow violent.

On that day the elder king
of the Achaean ships, no more
strict against the prophet's word,
turned with the crosswinds of fortune,
190   when no ship sailed, no pail was full,
and the Achaean people sulked
fast against the shore at Aulis
facing Chalcis, where the tides ebb and surge:

and winds blew from the Strymon, bearing
195   sick idleness, ships tied fast, and hunger,
distraction of the mind, carelessness
for hull and cable;
with time's length bent to double measure
by delay crumbled the flower and pride
200   of Argos. Then against the bitter wind
the seer's voice clashed out
another medicine

more hateful yet, and spoke of Artemis, so that the kings
dashed their staves to the ground and could not hold their tears.

205   The elder lord spoke aloud before them:
"My fate is angry if I disobey these,
but angry if I slaughter
this child, the beauty of my house,
with maiden blood shed staining
210   these father's hands beside the altar.
What of these things goes now without disaster?
How shall I fail my ships
and lose my faith of battle?
For them to urge such sacrifice of innocent blood
215   angrily, for their wrath is great—it is right. May all be well yet."

But when necessity's yoke was put upon him
he changed, and from the heart the breath came bitter
and sacrilegious, utterly infidel,
to warp a will now to be stopped at nothing.
220   The sickening in men's minds, tough,
reckless in fresh cruelty brings daring. He endured then
to sacrifice his daughter
to stay the strength of war waged for a woman,
first offering for the ships' sake.

225   Her supplications and her cries of father
were nothing, nor the child's lamentation
to kings passioned for battle.
The father prayed, called to his men to lift her
with strength of hand swept in her robes aloft
230   and prone above the altar, as you might lift
a goat for sacrifice, with guards
against the lips' sweet edge, to check
the curse cried on the house of Atreus
by force of bit and speech drowned in strength.

235   Pouring then to the ground her saffron mantle
she struck the sacrificers with
the eyes' arrows of pity,
lovely as in a painted scene, and striving
to speak—as many times
240   at the kind festive table of her father
she had sung, and in the clear voice of a stainless maiden

with love had graced the song
of worship when the third cup was poured.

245　What happened next I saw not, neither speak it.
The crafts of Calchas fail not of outcome.
Justice so moves that those only learn
who suffer; and the future
you shall know when it has come; before then, forget it.
It is grief too soon given.
250　All will come clear in the next dawn's sunlight.
Let good fortune follow these things as
she who is here desires,
our Apian land's singlehearted protectress.

255　[*The* CHORUS *now turns toward* CLYTAEMESTRA, *and the
leader speaks to her.*]

I have come in reverence, Clytaemestra, of your power.
For when the man is gone and the throne void, his right
falls to the prince's lady, and honor must be given.
Is it some grace—or otherwise—that you have heard
260　to make you sacrifice at messages of good hope?
I should be glad to hear, but must not blame your silence.
CLYTAEMESTRA
As it was said of old, may the dawn child be born
to be an angel of blessing from the kindly night.
265　You shall know joy beyond all you ever hoped to hear.
The men of Argos have taken Priam's citadel.
CHORUS
What have you said? Your words escaped my unbelief.
CLYTAEMESTRA
270　The Achaeans are in Troy. Is that not clear enough?
CHORUS
This slow delight steals over me to bring forth tears.
CLYTAEMESTRA
Yes, for your eyes betray the loyal heart within.
275　CHORUS
Yet how can I be certain? Is there some evidence?
CLYTAEMESTRA
There is, there must be; unless a god has lied to me.
CHORUS
280　Is it dream visions, easy to believe, you credit?
CLYTAEMESTRA
I accept nothing from a brain that is dull with sleep.

CHORUS
    The charm, then, of some rumor, that made rich your hope?
285 CLYTAEMESTRA
    Am I some young girl, that you find my thoughts so silly?
CHORUS
    How long, then, is it since the citadel was stormed?
CLYTAEMESTRA
290   It is the night, the mother of this dawn I hailed.
CHORUS
    What kind of messenger could come in speed like this?
CLYTAEMESTRA
    Hephaestus, who cast forth the shining blaze from Ida.
295   And beacon after beacon picking up the flare
    carried it here; Ida to the Hermaean horn
    of Lemnos, where it shone above the isle, and next
    the sheer rock face of Zeus on Athos caught it up;
    and plunging skyward to arch the shoulders of the sea
300   the strength of the running flare in exultation,
    pine timbers flaming into gold, like the sunrise,
    brought the bright message to Macistus' sentinel cliffs,
    who, never slow nor in the carelessness of sleep
    caught up, sent on his relay in the courier chain,
305   and far across Euripus' streams the beacon flare
    carried to signal watchmen on Messapion.
    These took it again in turn, and heaping high a pile
    of silvery brush flamed it to throw the message on.
    And the flare sickened never, but grown stronger yet
310   outleapt the river valley of Asopus like
    the very moon for shining, to Cithaeron's scaur
    to waken the next station of the flaming post.
    These watchers, not contemptuous of the far-thrown blaze,
    kindled another beacon vaster than commanded.
315   The light leaned high above Gorgopis' staring marsh,
    and striking Aegyplanctus' mountain top, drove on
    yet one more relay, lest the flare die down in speed.
    Kindled once more with stintless heaping force, they send
    the beard of flame to hugeness, passing far beyond
320   the promontory that gazes on the Saronic strait
    and flaming far, until it plunged at last to strike
    the steep rock of Arachnus near at hand, our watchtower.
    And thence there fell upon this house of Atreus' sons
    the flare whose fathers mount to the Idaean beacon.
325   These are the changes on my torchlight messengers,
    one from another running out the laps assigned.

The first and the last sprinters have the victory.
By such proof and such symbol I announce to you
my lord at Troy has sent his messengers to me.

330 CHORUS

The gods, lady, shall have my prayers and thanks straightway.
And yet to hear your story till all wonder fades
would be my wish, could you but tell it once again.

CLYTAEMESTRA

335 The Achaeans have got Troy, upon this very day.
I think the city echoes with a clash of cries.
Pour vinegar and oil into the selfsame bowl,
you could not say they mix in friendship, but fight on.
Thus variant sound the voices of the conquerors

340 and conquered, from the opposition of their fates.
Trojans are stooping now to gather in their arms
their dead, husbands and brothers; children lean to clasp
the aged who begot them, crying upon the death
of those most dear, from lips that never will be free.

345 The Achaeans have their midnight work after the fighting
that sets them down to feed on all the city has,
ravenous, headlong, by no rank and file assigned,
but as each man has drawn his shaken lot by chance.
And in the Trojan houses that their spears have taken

350 they settle now, free of the open sky, the frosts
and dampness of the evening; without sentinels set
they sleep the sleep of happiness the whole night through.
And if they reverence the gods who hold the city
and all the holy temples of the captured land,

355 they, the despoilers, might not be despoiled in turn.
Let not their passion overwhelm them; let no lust
seize on these men to violate what they must not.
The run to safety and home is yet to make; they must turn
the pole, and run the backstretch of the double course.

360 Yet, though the host come home without offence to high
gods, even so the anger of these slaughtered men
may never sleep. Oh, let there be no fresh wrong done!

Such are the thoughts you hear from me, a woman merely.
Yet may the best win through, that none may fail to see.

365 Of all good things to wish this is my dearest choice.

CHORUS

My lady, no grave man could speak with better grace.
I have listened to the proofs of your tale, and I believe,
and go to make my glad thanksgivings to the gods.

370   This pleasure is not unworthy of the grief that gave it.
    O Zeus our lord and Night beloved,
    bestower of power and beauty,
    you slung above the bastions of Troy
    the binding net, that none, neither great
375   nor young, might outleap
    the gigantic toils
    of enslavement and final disaster.
    I gaze in awe on Zeus of the guests
    who wrung from Alexander such payment.
380   He bent the bow with slow care, that neither
    the shaft might hurdle the stars, nor fall
    spent to the earth, short driven.

    They have the stroke of Zeus to tell of.
    This thing is clear and you may trace it.
385   He acted as he had decreed. A man thought
    the gods deigned not to punish mortals
    who trampled down the delicacy of things
    inviolable. That man was wicked.
    The curse on great daring
390   shines clear; it wrings atonement
    from those high hearts that drive to evil,
    from houses blossoming to pride
    and peril. Let there be
    wealth without tears; enough for
395   the wise man who will ask no further.
    There is not any armor
    in gold against perdition
    for him who spurns the high altar
    of Justice down to the darkness.

400   Persuasion the persistent overwhelms him,
    she, strong daughter of designing Ruin.
    And every medicine is vain; the sin
    smolders not, but burns to evil beauty.
    As cheap bronze tortured
405   at the touchstone relapses
    to blackness and grime, so this man
    tested shows vain
    as a child that strives to catch the bird flying
    and wins shame that shall bring down his city.
410   No god will hear such a man's entreaty,
    but whoso turns to these ways

they strike him down in his wickedness.
This was Paris: he came
to the house of the sons of Atreus,
415   stole the woman away, and shamed
the guest's right of the board shared.

She left among her people the stir and clamor
of shields and of spearheads,
the ships to sail and the armor.
420   She took to Ilium her dowry, death.
She stepped forth lightly between the gates
daring beyond all daring. And the prophets
about the great house wept aloud and spoke:
"Alas, alas for the house and for the champions,
425   alas for the bed signed with their love together.
Here now is silence, scorned, unreproachful.
The agony of his loss is clear before us.
Longing for her who lies beyond the sea
he shall see a phantom queen in his household.
430   Her images in their beauty
are bitterness to her lord now
where in the emptiness of eyes
all passion has faded."

Shining in dreams the sorrowful
435   memories pass; they bring him
vain delight only.
It is vain, to dream and to see splendors,
and the image slipping from the arms' embrace
escapes, not to return again,
440   on wings drifting down the ways of sleep.

Such have the sorrows been in the house by the hearthside;
such have there been, and yet there are worse than these.
In all Hellas, for those who swarmed to the host
the heartbreaking misery
445   shows in the house of each.
Many are they who are touched at the heart by these things.
Those they sent forth they knew;
now, in place of the young men
urns and ashes are carried home
450   to the houses of the fighters.

The god of war, money changer of dead bodies,
held the balance of his spear in the fighting,
and from the corpse-fires at Ilium
sent to their dearest the dust
455   heavy and bitter with tears shed
packing smooth the urns with
ashes that once were men.
They praise them through their tears, how this man
knew well the craft of battle, how another
460   went down splendid in the slaughter:
and all for some strange woman.
Thus they mutter in secrecy,
and the slow anger creeps below their grief
at Atreus' sons and their quarrels.
465   There by the walls of Ilium
the young men in their beauty keep
graves deep in the alien soil
they hated and they conquered.

The citizens speak: their voice is dull with hatred.
470   The curse of the people must be paid for.
There lurks for me in the hooded night
terror of what may be told me.
The gods fail not to mark
those who have killed many.
475   The black Furies stalking the man
fortunate beyond all right
wrench back again the set of his life
and drop him to darkness. There among
the ciphers there is no more comfort
480   in power. And the vaunt of high glory
is bitterness; for God's thunderbolts
crash on the towering mountains.
Let me attain no envied wealth,
let me not plunder cities,
485   neither be taken in turn, and face
life in the power of another.

[*Various members of the* CHORUS, *speaking severally.*]

From the beacon's bright message
the fleet rumor runs
490   through the city. If this be real
who knows? Perhaps the gods have sent some lie to us.

Who of us is so childish or so reft of wit
that by the beacon's messages
his heart flamed must despond again
495   when the tale changes in the end?

It is like a woman indeed
to take the rapture before the fact has shown for true.

They believe too easily, are too quick to shift
from ground to ground; and swift indeed
500   the rumor voiced by a woman dies again.

Now we shall understand these torches and their shining,
the beacons, and the interchange of flame and flame.
They may be real; yet bright and dreamwise ecstasy
in light's appearance might have charmed our hearts awry.
505   I see a herald coming from the beach, his brows
shaded with sprigs of olive; and upon his feet
the dust, dry sister of the mire, makes plain to me
that he will find a voice, not merely kindle flame
from mountain timber, and make signals from the smoke,
510   but tell us outright, whether to be happy, or—
but I shrink back from naming the alternative.
That which appeared was good; may yet more good be given.

And any man who prays that different things befall
the city, may he reap the crime of his own heart.

515   [*The* HERALD *enters, and speaks.*]

Soil of my fathers, Argive earth I tread upon,
in daylight of the tenth year I have come back to you.
All my hopes broke but one, and this I have at last.
I never could have dared to dream that I might die
520   in Argos, and be buried in this beloved soil.
Hail to the Argive land and to its sunlight, hail
to its high sovereign, Zeus, and to the Pythian king.
May you no longer shower your arrows on our heads.
Beside Scamandrus you were grim; be satisfied
525   and turn to savior now and healer of our hurts,
my lord Apollo. Gods of the market place assembled,
I greet you all, and my own patron deity
Hermes, beloved herald, in whose right all heralds
are sacred; and you heroes that sent forth the host,

530   propitiously take back all that the spear has left.
     O great hall of the kings and house beloved; seats
     of sanctity; divinities that face the sun:
     if ever before, look now with kind and glowing eyes
     to greet our king in state after so long a time.
535   He comes, lord Agamemnon, bearing light in gloom
     to you, and to all that are assembled here.
     Salute him with good favor, as he well deserves,
     the man who has wrecked Ilium with the spade of Zeus
     vindictive, whereby all their plain has been laid waste.
540   Gone are their altars, the sacred places of the gods
     are gone, and scattered all the seed within the ground.
     With such a yoke as this gripped to the neck of Troy
     he comes, the king, Atreus' elder son, a man
     fortunate to be honored far above all men
545   alive; not Paris nor the city tied to him
     can boast he did more than was done him in return.
     Guilty of rape and theft, condemned, he lost the prize
     captured, and broke to sheer destruction all the house
     of his fathers, with the very ground whereon it stood.
550   Twice over the sons of Priam have atoned their sins.
     CHORUS
     Hail and be glad, herald of the Achaean host.
     HERALD
     I am happy; I no longer ask the gods for death.
555   CHORUS
     Did passion for your country so strip bare your heart?
     HERALD
     So that the tears broke in my eyes, for happiness.
     CHORUS
560   You were taken with that sickness, then, that brings delight.
     HERALD
     How? I cannot deal with such words until I understand.
     CHORUS
     Struck with desire of those who loved as much again.
565   HERALD
     You mean our country longed for us, as we for home?
     CHORUS
     So that I sighed, out of the darkness of my heart.
     HERALD
570   Whence came this black thought to afflict the mind with fear?
     CHORUS
     Long since it was my silence kept disaster off.

HERALD

But how? There were some you feared when the kings went away?

575 CHORUS

So much that as you said now, even death were grace.

HERALD

Well: the end has been good. And in the length of time
part of our fortune you could say held favorable,

580 but part we cursed again. And who, except the gods,
can live time through forever without any pain?
Were I to tell you of the hard work done, the nights
exposed, the cramped sea-quarters, the foul beds—what part
of day's disposal did we not cry out loud?

585 Ashore, the horror stayed with us and grew. We lay
against the ramparts of our enemies, and from
the sky, and from the ground, the meadow dews came out
to soak our clothes and fill our hair with lice. And if
I were to tell of winter time, when all birds died,

590 the snows of Ida past endurance she sent down,
or summer heat, when in the lazy noon the sea
fell level and asleep under a windless sky—
but why live such grief over again? That time is gone
for us, and gone for those who died. Never again

595 need they rise up, nor care again for anything.
Why must a live man count the numbers of the slain,
why grieve at fortune's wrath that fades to break once more?
I call a long farewell to all our unhappiness.
For us, survivors of the Argive armament,

600 the pleasure wins, pain casts no weight in the opposite scale.
And here, in this sun's shining, we can boast aloud,
whose fame has gone with wings across the land and sea:
"Upon a time the Argive host took Troy, and on
the houses of the gods who live in Hellas nailed

605 the spoils, to be the glory of days long ago."
And they who hear such things shall call this city blest
and the leaders of the host; and high the grace of God
shall be exalted, that did this. You have the story.

CHORUS

610 I must give way; your story shows that I was wrong.
Old men are always young enough to learn, with profit.
But Clytaemestra and her house must hear, above
others, this news that makes luxurious my life.

[CLYTAEMESTRA *comes forward and speaks.*]

-147-

615 I raised my cry of joy, and it was long ago
when the first beacon flare of message came by night
to speak of capture and of Ilium's overthrow.
But there was one who laughed at me, who said: "You trust
in beacons so, and you believe that Troy has fallen?
620 How like a woman, for the heart to lift so light."
Men spoke like that; they thought I wandered in my wits;
yet I made sacrifice, and in the womanish strain
voice after voice caught up the cry along the city
to echo in the temples of the gods and bless
625 and still the fragrant flame that melts the sacrifice.

Why should you tell me then the whole long tale at large
when from my lord himself I shall hear all the story?
But now, how best to speed my preparation to
receive my honored lord come home again—what else
630 is light more sweet for woman to behold than this,
to spread the gates before her husband home from war
and saved by God's hand?—take this message to the king:
Come, and with speed, back to the city that longs for him,
and may he find a wife within his house as true
635 as on the day he left her, watchdog of the house
gentle to him alone, fierce to his enemies,
and such a woman in all her ways as this, who has
not broken the seal upon her in the length of days.
With no man else have I known delight, nor any shame
640 of evil speech, more than I know how to temper bronze.

[CLYTAEMESTRA *goes to the back of the stage.*]

HERALD
A vaunt like this, so loaded as it is with truth,
it well becomes a highborn lady to proclaim.
645 CHORUS
Thus has she spoken to you, and well you understand,
words that impress interpreters whose thought is clear.
But tell me, herald; I would learn of Menelaus,
that power beloved in this land. Has he survived
650 also, and come with you back to his home again?
HERALD
I know no way to lie and make my tale so fair
that friends could reap joy of it for any length of time.

CHORUS

655   Is there no means to speak us fair, and yet tell the truth?
      It will not hide, when truth and good are torn asunder.

HERALD

      He is gone out of the sight of the Achaean host,
      vessel and man alike. I speak no falsehood there.

660 CHORUS

      Was it when he had put out from Ilium in your sight,
      or did a storm that struck you both whirl him away?

HERALD

      How like a master bowman you have hit the mark

665   and in your speech cut a long sorrow to brief stature.

CHORUS

      But then the rumor in the host that sailed beside,
      was it that he had perished, or might yet be living?

HERALD

670   No man knows. There is none could tell us that for sure
      except the Sun, from whom this earth has life and increase.

CHORUS

      How did this storm, by wrath of the divinities,
      strike on our multitude at sea? How did it end?

675 HERALD

      It is not well to stain the blessing of this day
      with speech of evil weight. Such gods are honored apart.
      And when the messenger of a shaken host, sad faced,
      brings to his city news it prayed never to hear,

680   this scores one wound upon the body of the people;
      and that from many houses many men are slain
      by the two-lashed whip dear to the War God's hand, this turns
      disaster double-bladed, bloodily made two.
      The messenger so freighted with a charge of tears

685   should make his song of triumph at the Furies' door.
      But, carrying the fair message of our hopes' salvation,
      come home to a glad city's hospitality,
      how shall I mix my gracious news with foul, and tell
      of the storm on the Achaeans by God's anger sent?

690   For they, of old the deepest enemies, sea and fire,
      made a conspiracy and gave the oath of hand
      to blast in ruin our unhappy Argive army.
      At night the sea began to rise in waves of death.
      Ship against ship the Thracian stormwind shattered us,

695   and gored and split, our vessels, swept in violence
      of storm and whirlwind, beaten by the breaking rain,
      drove on in darkness, spun by the wicked shepherd's hand.

But when the sun came up again to light the dawn,
we saw the Aegaean Sea blossoming with dead men,
700   the men of Achaea, and the wreckage of their ships.
For us, and for our ship, some god, no man, by guile
or by entreaty's force prevailing, laid his hand
upon the helm and brought us through with hull unscarred.
Life-giving fortune deigned to take our ship in charge
705   that neither riding in deep water she took the surf
nor drove to shoal and break upon some rocky shore.
But then, delivered from death at sea, in the pale day,
incredulous of our own luck, we shepherded
in our sad thoughts the fresh disaster of the fleet
710   so pitifully torn and shaken by the storm.
Now of these others, if there are any left alive
they speak of us as men who perished, must they not?
Even as we, who fear that they are gone. But may
it all come well in the end. For Menelaus: be sure
715   if any of them come back that he will be the first.
If he is still where some sun's gleam can track him down,
alive and open-eyed, by blessed hand of God
who willed that not yet should his seed be utterly gone,
there is some hope that he will still come home again.
720   You have heard all; and be sure, you have heard the truth.

[*The* HERALD *goes out.*]

CHORUS

Who is he that named you so
fatally in every way?
725   Could it be some mind unseen
in divination of your destiny
shaping to the lips that name
for the bride of spears and blood,
Helen, which is death? Appropriately
730   death of ships, death of men and cities
from the bower's soft curtained
and secluded luxury she sailed then,
driven on the giant west wind,
and armored men in their thousands came,
735   huntsmen down the oar blade's fading footprint
to struggle in blood with those
who by the banks of Simoeis
beached their hulls where the leaves break.

And on Ilium in truth
740   in the likeness of the name
the sure purpose of the Wrath drove
marriage with death: for the guest board
shamed, and Zeus kindly to strangers,
the vengeance wrought on those men
745   who graced in too loud voice the bride-song
fallen to their lot to sing,
the kinsmen and the brothers.
And changing its song's measure
the ancient city of Priam
750   chants in high strain of lamentation,
calling Paris him of the fatal marriage;
for it endured its life's end
in desolation and tears
and the piteous blood of its people.

755   Once a man fostered in his house
a lion cub, from the mother's milk
torn, craving the breast given.
In the first steps of its young life
mild, it played with children
760   and delighted the old.
Caught in the arm's cradle
they pampered it like a newborn child,
shining eyed and broken to the hand
to stay the stress of its hunger.

765   But it grew with time, and the lion
in the blood strain came out; it paid
grace to those who had fostered it
in blood and death for the sheep flocks,
a grim feast forbidden.
770   The house reeked with blood run
nor could its people beat down the bane,
the giant murderer's onslaught.
This thing they raised in their house was blessed
by God to be priest of destruction.

775   And that which first came to the city of Ilium,
call it a dream of calm
and the wind dying,
the loveliness and luxury of much gold,
the melting shafts of the eyes' glances,

780   the blossom that breaks the heart with longing.
But she turned in mid-step of her course to make
bitter the consummation,
whirling on Priam's people
to blight with her touch and nearness.
785   Zeus hospitable sent her,
a vengeance to make brides weep.

It has been made long since and grown old among men,
this saying: human wealth
grown to fulness of stature
790   breeds again nor dies without issue.
From high good fortune in the blood
blossoms the quenchless agony.
Far from others I hold my own
mind; only the act of evil
795   breeds others to follow,
young sins in its own likeness.
Houses clear in their right are given
children in all loveliness.

But Pride aging is made
800   in men's dark actions
ripe with the young pride
late or soon when the dawn of destiny
comes and birth is given
to the spirit none may fight nor beat down,
805   sinful Daring; and in those halls
the black visaged Disasters stamped
in the likeness of their fathers.

And Righteousness is a shining in
the smoke of mean houses.
810   Her blessing is on the just man.
From high halls starred with gold by reeking hands
she turns back
with eyes that glance away to the simple in heart,
spurning the strength of gold
815   stamped false with flattery.
And all things she steers to fulfilment.

[AGAMEMNON *enters in a chariot, with* CASSANDRA *beside him.
The* CHORUS *speaks to him.*]

Behold, my king: sacker of Troy's citadel,
820   own issue of Atreus.
How shall I hail you? How give honor
not crossing too high nor yet bending short
of this time's graces?
For many among men are they who set high
825   the show of honor, yet break justice.
If one be unhappy, all else are fain
to grieve with him: yet the teeth of sorrow
come nowise near to the heart's edge.
And in joy likewise they show joy's semblance,
830   and torture the face to the false smile.
Yet the good shepherd, who knows his flock,
the eyes of men cannot lie to him,
that with water of feigned
love seem to smile from the true heart.
835   But I: when you marshalled this armament
for Helen's sake, I will not hide it,
in ugly style you were written in my heart
for steering aslant the mind's course
to bring home by blood
840   sacrifice and dead men that wild spirit.
But now, in love drawn up from the deep heart,
not skimmed at the edge, we hail you.
You have won, your labor is made gladness.
Ask all men: you will learn in time
845   which of your citizens have been just
in the city's sway, which were reckless.

AGAMEMNON

To Argos first, and to the gods within the land,
I must give due greeting; they have worked with me to bring
850   me home; they helped me in the vengeance I have wrought
on Priam's city. Not from the lips of men the gods
heard justice, but in one firm cast they laid their votes
within the urn of blood that Ilium must die
and all her people; while above the opposite vase
855   the hand hovered and there was hope, but no vote fell.
The stormclouds of their ruin live; the ash that dies
upon them gushes still in smoke their pride of wealth.
For all this we must thank the gods with grace of much
high praise and memory, we who fenced within our toils
860   of wrath the city; and, because one woman strayed,
the beast of Argos broke them, the fierce young within
the horse, the armored people who marked out their leap

against the setting of the Pleiades. A wild
and bloody lion swarmed above the towers of Troy
865   to glut its hunger lapping at the blood of kings.

This to the gods, a prelude strung to length of words.
But, for the thought you spoke, I heard and I remember
and stand behind you. For I say that it is true.
In few men is it part of nature to respect
870   a friend's prosperity without begrudging him,
as envy's wicked poison settling to the heart
piles up the pain in one sick with unhappiness,
who, staggered under sufferings that are all his own,
winces again to the vision of a neighbor's bliss.
875   And I can speak, for I have seen, I know it well,
this mirror of companionship, this shadow's ghost,
these men who seemed my friends in all sincerity.
One man of them all, Odysseus, he who sailed unwilling,
once yoked to me carried his harness, nor went slack.
880   Dead though he be or living, I can say it still.

Now in the business of the city and the gods
we must ordain full conclave of all citizens
and take our counsel. We shall see what element
is strong, and plan that it shall keep its virtue still.
885   But that which must be healed—we must use medicine,
or burn, or amputate, with kind intention, take
all means at hand that might beat down corruption's pain.

So to the King's house and the home about the hearth
I take my way, with greeting to the gods within
890   who sent me forth, and who have brought me home once more.
My prize was conquest; may it never fail again.

[CLYTAEMESTRA *comes forward and speaks.*]

Grave gentlemen of Argolis assembled here,
I take no shame to speak aloud before you all
895   the love I bear my husband. In the lapse of time
modesty fades; it is human.

                                    What I tell you now
I learned not from another; this is my own sad life
all the long years this man was gone at Ilium.
900   It is evil and a thing of terror when a wife

sits in the house forlorn with no man by, and hears
rumors that like a fever die to break again,
and men come in with news of fear, and on their heels
another messenger, with worse news to cry aloud
905 here in this house. Had Agamemnon taken all
the wounds the tale whereof was carried home to me,
he had been cut full of gashes like a fishing net.
If he had died each time that rumor told his death,
he must have been some triple-bodied Geryon
910 back from the dead with threefold cloak of earth upon
his body, and killed once for every shape assumed.
Because such tales broke out forever on my rest,
many a time they cut me down and freed my throat
from the noose overslung where I had caught it fast.
915 And therefore is your son, in whom my love and yours
are sealed and pledged, not here to stand with us today,
Orestes. It were right; yet do not be amazed.
Strophius of Phocis, comrade in arms and faithful friend
to you, is keeping him. He spoke to me of peril
920 on two counts; of your danger under Ilium,
and here, of revolution and the clamorous people
who might cast down the council—since it lies in men's
nature to trample on the fighter already down.
Such my excuse to you, and without subterfuge.

925 For me: the rippling springs that were my tears have dried
utterly up, nor left one drop within. I keep
the pain upon my eyes where late at night I wept
over the beacons long ago set for your sake,
untended left forever. In the midst of dreams
930 the whisper that a gnat's thin wings could winnow broke
my sleep apart. I thought I saw you suffer wounds
more than the time that slept with me could ever hold.

Now all my suffering is past, with griefless heart
I hail this man, the watchdog of the fold and hall;
935 the stay that keeps the ship alive; the post to grip
groundward the towering roof; a father's single child;
land seen by sailors after all their hope was gone;
splendor of daybreak shining from the night of storm;
the running spring a parched wayfarer strays upon.
940 Oh, it is sweet to escape from all necessity!

Such is my greeting to him, that he well deserves.
Let none bear malice; for the harm that went before
I took, and it was great.
                              Now, my beloved one,
945 step from your chariot; yet let not your foot, my lord,
sacker of Ilium, touch the earth. My maidens there!
Why this delay? Your task has been appointed you,
to strew the ground before his feet with tapestries.
Let there spring up into the house he never hoped
950 to see, where Justice leads him in, a crimson path.

In all things else, my heart's unsleeping care shall act
with the gods' aid to set aright what fate ordained.

[CLYTAEMESTRA's *handmaidens spread a bright carpet between*
the chariot and the door.]

955 AGAMEMNON
Daughter of Leda, you who kept my house for me,
there is one way your welcome matched my absence well.
You strained it to great length. Yet properly to praise
me thus belongs by right to other lips, not yours.
960 And all this—do not try in woman's ways to make
me delicate, nor, as if I were some Asiatic
bow down to earth and with wide mouth cry out to me,
nor cross my path with jealousy by strewing the ground
with robes. Such state becomes the gods, and none beside.
965 I am a mortal, a man; I cannot trample upon
these tinted splendors without fear thrown in my path.
I tell you, as a man, not god, to reverence me.
Discordant is the murmur at such treading down
of lovely things; while God's most lordly gift to man
970 is decency of mind. Call that man only blest
who has in sweet tranquillity brought his life to close.
If I could only act as such, my hope is good.
CLYTAEMESTRA
Yet tell me this one thing, and do not cross my will.
975 AGAMEMNON
My will is mine. I shall not make it soft for you.
CLYTAEMESTRA
It was in fear surely that you vowed this course to God.
AGAMEMNON
980 No man has spoken knowing better what he said.

CLYTAEMESTRA

If Priam had won as you have, what would he have done?

AGAMEMNON

I well believe he might have walked on tapestries.

985   CLYTAEMESTRA

Be not ashamed before the bitterness of men.

AGAMEMNON

The people murmur, and their voice is great in strength.

CLYTAEMESTRA

990   Yet he who goes unenvied shall not be admired.

AGAMEMNON

Surely this lust for conflict is not womanlike?

CLYTAEMESTRA

Yet for the mighty even to give way is grace.

995   AGAMEMNON

Does such a victory as this mean so much to you?

CLYTAEMESTRA

Oh yield! The power is yours. Give way of your free will.

AGAMEMNON

1000   Since you must have it—here, let someone with all speed
take off these sandals, slaves for my feet to tread upon.
And as I crush these garments stained from the rich sea
let no god's eyes of hatred strike me from afar.
Great the extravagance, and great the shame I feel
1005   to spoil such treasure and such silver's worth of webs.

So much for all this. Take this stranger girl within
now, and be kind. The conqueror who uses softly
his power, is watched from far in the kind eyes of God,
and this slave's yoke is one no man will wear from choice.
1010   Gift of the host to me, and flower exquisite
from all my many treasures, she attends me here.

Now since my will was bent to listen to you in this
my feet crush purple as I pass within the hall.

CLYTAEMESTRA

1015   The sea is there, and who shall drain its yield? It breeds
precious as silver, ever of itself renewed,
the purple ooze wherein our garments shall be dipped.
And by God's grace this house keeps full sufficiency
of all. Poverty is a thing beyond its thought.
1020   I could have vowed to trample many splendors down
had such decree been ordained from the oracles
those days when all my study was to bring home your life.

For when the root lives yet the leaves will come again
to fence the house with shade against the Dog Star's heat,
1025 and now you have come home to keep your hearth and house
you bring with you the symbol of our winter's warmth;
but when Zeus ripens the green clusters into wine
there shall be coolness in the house upon those days
because the master ranges his own halls once more.

1030 Zeus, Zeus accomplisher, accomplish these my prayers.
Let your mind bring these things to pass. It is your will.

[AGAMEMNON *and* CLYTAEMESTRA *enter the house.*
CASSANDRA *remains in the chariot. The* CHORUS *speaks.*]

Why must this persistent fear
1035 beat its wings so ceaselessly
and so close against my mantic heart?
Why this strain unwanted, unrepaid, thus prophetic?
Nor can valor of good hope
seated near the chambered depth
1040 of the spirit cast it out
as dreams of dark fancy; and yet time
has buried in the mounding sand
the sea cables since that day
when against Ilium
1045 the army and the ships put to sea.

Yet I have seen with these eyes
Agamemnon home again.
Still the spirit sings, drawing deep
from within this unlyric threnody of the Fury.
1050 Hope is gone utterly,
the sweet strength is far away.
Surely this is not fantasy.
Surely it is real, this whirl of drifts
that spin the stricken heart.
1055 Still I pray; may all this
expectation fade as vanity
into unfulfilment, and not be.

Yet it is true: the high strength of men
knows no content with limitation. Sickness
1060 chambered beside it beats at the wall between.
Man's fate that sets a true

course yet may strike upon
the blind and sudden reefs of disaster.
But if before such time, fear
1065 throw overboard some precious thing
of the cargo, with deliberate cast,
not all the house, laboring
with weight of ruin, shall go down,
nor sink the hull deep within the sea.
1070 And great and affluent the gift of Zeus
in yield of ploughed acres year on year
makes void again sick starvation.

But when the black and mortal blood of man
has fallen to the ground before his feet, who then
1075 can sing spells to call it back again?
Did Zeus not warn us once
when he struck to impotence
that one who could in truth charm back the dead men?
Had the gods not so ordained
1080 that fate should stand against fate
to check any man's excess,
my heart now would have outrun speech
to break forth the water of its grief.
But this is so; I murmur deep in darkness
1085 sore at heart; my hope is gone now
ever again to unwind some crucial good
from the flames about my heart.

[CLYTAEMESTRA *comes out from the house again*
and speaks to CASSANDRA.]

1090 Cassandra, you may go within the house as well,
since Zeus in no unkindness has ordained that you
must share our lustral water, stand with the great throng
of slaves that flock to the altar of our household god.
Step from this chariot, then, and do not be so proud.
1095 And think—they say that long ago Alcmena's son
was sold in bondage and endured the bread of slaves.
But if constraint of fact forces you to such fate,
be glad indeed for masters ancient in their wealth.
They who have reaped success beyond their dreams of hope
1100 are savage above need and standard toward their slaves.
From us you shall have all you have the right to ask.

CHORUS
　　What she has spoken is for you, and clear enough.
　　Fenced in these fatal nets wherein you find yourself
1105　　you should obey her if you can; perhaps you can not.
CLYTAEMESTRA
　　Unless she uses speech incomprehensible,
　　barbarian, wild as the swallow's song, I speak
　　within her understanding, and she must obey.
1110 CHORUS
　　Go with her. What she bids is best in circumstance
　　that rings you now. Obey, and leave this carriage seat.
CLYTAEMESTRA
　　I have no leisure to stand outside the house and waste
1115　　time on this woman. At the central altarstone
　　the flocks are standing, ready for the sacrifice
　　we make to this glad day we never hoped to see.
　　You: if you are obeying my commands at all, be quick.
　　But if in ignorance you fail to comprehend,
1120　　speak not, but make with your barbarian hand some sign.
CHORUS
　　I think this stranger girl needs some interpreter
　　who understands. She is like some captive animal.
CLYTAEMESTRA
1125　　No, she is in the passion of her own wild thoughts.
　　Leaving her captured city she has come to us
　　untrained to take the curb, and will not understand
　　until her rage and strength have foamed away in blood.
　　I shall throw down no more commands for her contempt.

1130　　[CLYTAEMESTRA *goes back into the house.*]

CHORUS
　　I, though, shall not be angry, for I pity her.
　　Come down, poor creature, leave the empty car. Give way
　　to compulsion and take up the yoke that shall be yours.

1135　　[CASSANDRA *descends from the chariot and cries out loud.*]

　　Oh shame upon the earth!
　　Apollo, Apollo!
CHORUS
　　You cry on Loxias in agony? He is not
1140　　of those immortals the unhappy supplicate.

CASSANDRA

Oh shame upon the earth!

Apollo, Apollo!

CHORUS

1145 Now once again in bitter voice she calls upon

this god, who has not part in any lamentation.

CASSANDRA

Apollo, Apollo!

Lord of the ways, my ruin.

1150 You have undone me once again, and utterly.

CHORUS

I think she will be prophetic of her own disaster.

Even in the slave's heart the gift divine lives on.

CASSANDRA

1155 Apollo, Apollo!

Lord of the ways, my ruin.

Where have you led me now at last? What house is this?

CHORUS

The house of the Atreidae. If you understand

1160 not that, I can tell you; and so much at least is true.

CASSANDRA

No, but a house that God hates, guilty within

of kindred blood shed, torture of its own,

the shambles for men's butchery, the dripping floor.

1165 CHORUS

The stranger is keen scented like some hound upon

the trail of blood that leads her to discovered death.

CASSANDRA

Behold there the witnesses to my faith.

1170 The small children wail for their own death

and the flesh roasted that their father fed upon.

CHORUS

We had been told before of this prophetic fame

of yours: we want no prophets in this place at all.

1175 CASSANDRA

Ah, for shame, what can she purpose now?

What is this new and huge

stroke of atrocity she plans within the house

to beat down the beloved beyond hope of healing?

1180 Rescue is far away.

CHORUS

I can make nothing of these prophecies. The rest

I understood; the city is full of the sound of them.

CASSANDRA

1185   So cruel then, that you can do this thing?
The husband of your own bed
to bathe bright with water—how shall I speak the end?
This thing shall be done with speed. The hand gropes now, and the other
hand follows in turn.

1190 CHORUS

No, I am lost. After the darkness of her speech
I go bewildered in a mist of prophecies.

CASSANDRA

No, no, see there! What is that thing that shows?

1195   Is it some net of death?
Or is the trap the woman there, the murderess?
Let now the slakeless fury in the race
rear up to howl aloud over this monstrous death.

CHORUS

1200   Upon what demon in the house do you call, to raise
the cry of triumph? All your speech makes dark my hope.
And to the heart below trickles the pale drop
as in the hour of death
timed to our sunset and the mortal radiance.

1205   Ruin is near, and swift.

CASSANDRA

See there, see there! Keep from his mate the bull.
Caught in the folded web's
entanglement she pinions him and with the black horn

1210   strikes. And he crumples in the watered bath.
Guile, I tell you, and death there in the caldron wrought.

CHORUS

I am not proud in skill to guess at prophecies,
yet even I can see the evil in this thing.

1215   From divination what good ever has come to men?
Art, and multiplication of words
drifting through tangled evil bring
terror to them that hear.

CASSANDRA

1220   Alas, alas for the wretchedness of my ill-starred life.
This pain flooding the song of sorrow is mine alone.
Why have you brought me here in all unhappiness?
Why, why? Except to die with him? What else could be?

CHORUS

1225   You are possessed of God, mazed at heart
to sing your own death
song, the wild lyric as

in clamor for Itys, Itys over and over again
her long life of tears weeping forever grieves
1230   the brown nightingale.
CASSANDRA
Oh for the nightingale's pure song and a fate like hers.
With fashion of beating wings the gods clothed her about
and a sweet life gave her and without lamentation.
1235   But mine is the sheer edge of the tearing iron.
CHORUS
Whence come, beat upon beat, driven of God,
vain passions of tears?
Whence your cries, terrified, clashing in horror,
1240   in wrought melody and the singing speech?
Whence take you the marks to this path of prophecy
and speech of terror?
CASSANDRA
Oh marriage of Paris, death to the men beloved!
1245   Alas, Scamandrus, water my fathers drank.
There was a time I too at your springs
drank and grew strong. Ah me,
for now beside the deadly rivers, Cocytus
and Acheron, I must cry out my prophecies.
1250   CHORUS
What is this word, too clear, you have uttered now?
A child could understand.
And deep within goes the stroke of the dripping fang
as mortal pain at the trebled song of your agony
1255   shivers the heart to hear.
CASSANDRA
O sorrow, sorrow of my city dragged to uttermost death.
O sacrifices my father made at the wall.
Flocks of the pastured sheep slaughtered there.
1260   And no use at all
to save our city from its pain inflicted now.
And I too, with brain ablaze in fever, shall go down.
CHORUS
This follows the run of your song.
1265   Is it, in cruel force of weight,
some divinity kneeling upon you brings
the death song of your passionate suffering?
I can not see the end.
CASSANDRA
1270   No longer shall my prophecies like some young girl
new-married glance from under veils, but bright and strong

as winds blow into morning and the sun's uprise
shall wax along the swell like some great wave, to burst
at last upon the shining of this agony.
1275 Now I will tell you plainly and from no cryptic speech;
bear me then witness, running at my heels upon
the scent of these old brutal things done long ago.
There is a choir that sings as one, that shall not again
leave this house ever; the song thereof breaks harsh with menace.
1280 And drugged to double fury on the wine of men's
blood shed, there lurks forever here a drunken rout
of ingrown vengeful spirits never to be cast forth.
Hanging above the hall they chant their song of hate
and the old sin; and taking up the strain in turn
1285 spit curses on that man who spoiled his brother's bed.
Did I go wide, or hit, like a real archer? Am I
some swindling seer who hawks his lies from door to door?
Upon your oath, bear witness that I know by heart
the legend of ancient wickedness within this house.
1290 CHORUS
And how could an oath, though cast in rigid honesty,
do any good? And still we stand amazed at you,
reared in an alien city far beyond the sea,
how can you strike, as if you had been there, the truth.
1295 CASSANDRA
Apollo was the seer who set me to this work.
CHORUS
Struck with some passion for you, and himself a god?
CASSANDRA
1300 There was a time I blushed to speak about these things.
CHORUS
True; they who prosper take on airs of vanity.
CASSANDRA
Yes, then; he wrestled with me, and he breathed delight.
1305 CHORUS
Did you come to the getting of children then, as people do?
CASSANDRA
I promised that to Loxias, but I broke my word.
CHORUS
1310 Were you already ecstatic in the skills of God?
CASSANDRA
Yes; even then I read my city's destinies.
CHORUS
So Loxias' wrath did you no harm? How could that be?

1315   CASSANDRA
      For this my trespass, none believed me ever again.
      CHORUS
      But we do; all that you foretell seems true to us.
      CASSANDRA
1320   But this is evil, see!
      Now once again the pain of grim, true prophecy
      shivers my whirling brain in a storm of things foreseen.
      Look there, see what is hovering above the house,
      so small and young, imaged as in the shadow of dreams,
1325   like children almost, killed by those most dear to them,
      and their hands filled with their own flesh, as food to eat.
      I see them holding out the inward parts, the vitals,
      oh pitiful, that meat their father tasted of. . . .
      I tell you: There is one that plots vengeance for this,
1330   the strengthless lion rolling in his master's bed,
      who keeps, ah me, the house against his lord's return;
      my lord too, now that I wear the slave's yoke on my neck.
      King of the ships, who tore up Ilium by the roots,
      what does he know of this accursed bitch, who licks
1335   his hand, who fawns on him with lifted ears, who like
      a secret death shall strike the coward's stroke, nor fail?
      No, this is daring when the female shall strike down
      the male. What can I call her and be right? What beast
      of loathing? Viper double-fanged, or Scylla witch
1340   holed in the rocks and bane of men that range the sea;
      smoldering mother of death to smoke relentless hate
      on those most dear. How she stood up and howled aloud
      and unashamed, as at the breaking point of battle,
      in feigned gladness for his salvation from the sea!
1345   What does it matter now if men believe or no?
      What is to come will come. And soon you too will stand
      beside, to murmur in pity that my words were true.
      CHORUS
      Thyestes' feast upon the flesh of his own children
1350   I understand in terror at the thought, and fear
      is on me hearing truth and no tale fabricated.
      The rest: I heard it, but wander still far from the course.
      CASSANDRA
      I tell you, you shall look on Agamemnon dead.
1355   CHORUS
      Peace, peace, poor woman; put those bitter lips to sleep.
      CASSANDRA
      Useless; there is no god of healing in this story.

CHORUS

1360   Not if it must be; may it somehow fail to come.

CASSANDRA

    Prayers, yes; they do not pray; they plan to strike, and kill.

CHORUS

    What man is it who moves this beastly thing to be?

1365 CASSANDRA

    What man? You did mistake my divination then.

CHORUS

    It may be; I could not follow through the schemer's plan.

CASSANDRA

1370   Yet I know Greek; I think I know it far too well.

CHORUS

    And Pythian oracles are Greek, yet hard to read.

CASSANDRA

    Oh, flame and pain that sweeps me once again! My lord,

1375   Apollo, King of Light, the pain, aye me, the pain!

    This is the woman-lioness, who goes to bed

    with the wolf, when her proud lion ranges far away,

    and she will cut me down; as a wife mixing drugs

    she wills to shred the virtue of my punishment

1380   into her bowl of wrath as she makes sharp the blade

    against her man, death that he brought a mistress home.

    Why do I wear these mockeries upon my body,

    this staff of prophecy, these flowers at my throat?

    At least I will spoil you before I die. Out, down,

1385   break, damn you! This for all that you have done to me.

    Make someone else, not me, luxurious in disaster. . . .

    Lo now, this is Apollo who has stripped me here

    of my prophetic robes. He watched me all the time

    wearing this glory, mocked of all, my dearest ones

1390   who hated me with all their hearts, so vain, so wrong;

    called like some gypsy wandering from door to door

    beggar, corrupt, half-starved, and I endured it all.

    And now the seer has done with me, his prophetess,

    and led me into such a place as this, to die.

1395   Lost are my father's altars, but the block is there

    to reek with sacrificial blood, my own. We two

    must die, yet die not vengeless by the gods. For there

    shall come one to avenge us also, born to slay

    his mother, and to wreak death for his father's blood.

1400   Outlaw and wanderer, driven far from his own land,

    he will come back to cope these stones of inward hate.

    For this is a strong oath and sworn by the high gods,

that he shall cast men headlong for his father felled.
Why am I then so pitiful? Why must I weep?
1405 Since once I saw the citadel of Ilium
die as it died, and those who broke the city, doomed
by the gods, fare as they have fared accordingly,
I will go through with it. I too will take my fate.
I call as on the gates of death upon these gates
1410 to pray only for this thing, that the stroke be true,
and that with no convulsion, with a rush of blood
in painless death, I may close up these eyes, and rest.

CHORUS
O woman much enduring and so greatly wise,
1415 you have said much. But if this thing you know be true,
this death that comes upon you, how can you, serene,
walk to the altar like a driven ox of God?

CASSANDRA
Friends, there is no escape for any longer time.

1420 CHORUS
Yet longest left in time is to be honored still.

CASSANDRA
The day is here and now; I can not win by flight.

CHORUS
1425 Woman, be sure your heart is brave; you can take much.

CASSANDRA
None but the unhappy people ever hear such praise.

CHORUS
Yet there is a grace on mortals who so nobly die.

1430 CASSANDRA
Alas for you, father, and for your lordly sons.
Ah!

CHORUS
What now? What terror whirls you backward from the door?

1435 CASSANDRA
Foul, foul!

CHORUS
What foulness then, unless some horror in the mind?

CASSANDRA
1440 That room within reeks with blood like a slaughter house.

CHORUS
What then? Only these victims butchered at the hearth.

CASSANDRA
There is a breath about it like an open grave.

1445 CHORUS
This is no Syrian pride of frankincense you mean.

CASSANDRA
So. I am going in, and mourning as I go
my death and Agamemnon's. Let my life be done.
1450 Ah friends,
truly this is no wild bird fluttering at a bush,
nor vain my speech. Bear witness to me when I die,
when falls for me, a woman slain, another woman,
and when a man dies for this wickedly mated man.
1455 Here in my death I claim this stranger's grace of you.
CHORUS
Poor wretch, I pity you the fate you see so clear.
CASSANDRA
Yet once more will I speak, and not this time my own
1460 death's threnody. I call upon the Sun in prayer
against that ultimate shining when the avengers strike
these monsters down in blood, that they avenge as well
one simple slave who died, a small thing, lightly killed.

Alas, poor men, their destiny. When all goes well
1465 a shadow will overthrow it. If it be unkind
one stroke of a wet sponge wipes all the picture out;
and that is far the most unhappy thing of all.

[CASSANDRA *goes slowly into the house.*]

CHORUS
1470 High fortune is a thing slakeless
for mortals. There is no man who shall point
his finger to drive it back from the door
and speak the words: "Come no longer."
Now to this man the blessed ones have given
1475 Priam's city to be captured
and return in the gods' honor.
Must he give blood for generations gone,
die for those slain and in death pile up
more death to come for the blood shed,
1480 what mortal else who hears shall claim
he was born clear of the dark angel?

[AGAMEMNON, *inside the house.*]

Ah, I am struck a deadly blow and deep within!
CHORUS
1485 Silence: who cried out that he was stabbed to death within the house?

AGAMEMNON

    Ah me, again, they struck again. I am wounded twice.

CHORUS

    How the king cried out aloud to us! I believe the thing is done.

1490   Come, let us put our heads together, try to find some safe way out.

[*The members of the* CHORUS *go about distractedly, each one speaking in turn.*]

    Listen, let me tell you what I think is best to do.
    Let the herald call all citizens to rally here.

    No, better to burst in upon them now, at once,
1495   and take them with the blood still running from their blades.

    I am with this man and I cast my vote to him.
    Act now. This is the perilous and instant time.

    Anyone can see it, by these first steps they have taken,
    they purpose to be tyrants here upon our city.

1500   Yes, for we waste time, while they trample to the ground
    deliberation's honor, and their hands sleep not.

    I can not tell which counsel of yours to call my own.
    It is the man of action who can plan as well.

    I feel as he does; nor can I see how by words
1505   we shall set the dead man back upon his feet again.

    Do you mean, to drag our lives out long, that we must yield
    to the house shamed, and leadership of such as these?

    No, we can never endure that; better to be killed.
    Death is a softer thing by far than tyranny.

1510   Shall we, by no more proof than that he cried in pain,
    be sure, as by divination, that our lord is dead?

    Yes, we should know what is true before we break our rage.
    Here is sheer guessing and far different from sure knowledge.

    From all sides the voices multiply to make me choose
1515   this course; to learn first how it stands with Agamemnon.

[*The doors of the palace open, disclosing the bodies of* AGAMEMNON *and* CASSANDRA, *with* CLYTAEMESTRA *standing over them.*]

CLYTAEMESTRA

Much have I said before to serve necessity,
1520   but I will take no shame now to unsay it all.
How else could I, arming hate against hateful men
disguised in seeming tenderness, fence high the nets
of ruin beyond overleaping? Thus to me
the conflict born of ancient bitterness is not
1525   a thing new thought upon, but pondered deep in time.
I stand now where I struck him down. The thing is done.
Thus have I wrought, and I will not deny it now.
That he might not escape nor beat aside his death,
as fishermen cast their huge circling nets, I spread
1530   deadly abundance of rich robes, and caught him fast.
I struck him twice. In two great cries of agony
he buckled at the knees and fell. When he was down
I struck him the third blow, in thanks and reverence
to Zeus the lord of dead men underneath the ground.
1535   Thus he went down, and the life struggled out of him;
and as he died he spattered me with the dark red
and violent driven rain of bitter savored blood
to make me glad, as gardens stand among the showers
of God in glory at the birthtime of the buds.

1540   These being the facts, elders of Argos assembled here,
be glad, if it be your pleasure; but for me, I glory.
Were it religion to pour wine above the slain,
this man deserved, more than deserved, such sacrament.
He filled our cup with evil things unspeakable
1545   and now himself come home has drunk it to the dregs.

CHORUS

We stand here stunned. How can you speak this way, with mouth
so arrogant, to vaunt above your fallen lord?

CLYTAEMESTRA

1550   You try me out as if I were a woman and vain;
but my heart is not fluttered as I speak before you.
You know it. You can praise or blame me as you wish;
it is all one to me. That man is Agamemnon,
my husband; he is dead; the work of this right hand
1555   that struck in strength of righteousness. And that is that.

CHORUS

    Woman, what evil thing planted upon the earth
    or dragged from the running salt sea could you have tasted now
    to wear such brutality and walk in the people's hate?
1560   You have cast away, you have cut away. You shall go homeless now,
    crushed with men's bitterness.

CLYTAEMESTRA

    Now it is I you doom to be cast out from my city
    with men's hate heaped and curses roaring in my ears.
1565   Yet look upon this dead man; you would not cross him once
    when with no thought more than as if a beast had died,
    when his ranged pastures swarmed with the deep fleece of flocks,
    he slaughtered like a victim his own child, my pain
    grown into love, to charm away the winds of Thrace.
1570   Were you not bound to hunt him then clear of this soil
    for the guilt stained upon him? Yet you hear what I
    have done, and lo, you are a stern judge. But I say to you:
    go on and threaten me, but know that I am ready,
    if fairly you can beat me down beneath your hand,
1575   for you to rule; but if the god grant otherwise,
    you shall be taught—too late, for sure—to keep your place.

CHORUS

    Great your design, your speech is a clamor of pride.
    Swung to the red act drives the fury within your brain
1580   signed clear in the splash of blood over your eyes.
    Yet to come is stroke given for stroke
    vengeless, forlorn of friends.

CLYTAEMESTRA

    Now hear you this, the right behind my sacrament:
1585   By my child's Justice driven to fulfilment, by
    her Wrath and Fury, to whom I sacrificed this man,
    the hope that walks my chambers is not traced with fear
    while yet Aegisthus makes the fire shine on my hearth,
    my good friend, now as always, who shall be for us
1590   the shield of our defiance, no weak thing; while he,
    this other, is fallen, stained with this woman you behold,
    plaything of all the golden girls at Ilium;
    and here lies she, the captive of his spear, who saw
    wonders, who shared his bed, the wise in revelations
1595   and loving mistress, who yet knew the feel as well
    of the men's rowing benches. Their reward is not
    unworthy. He lies there; and she who swanlike cried
    aloud her lyric mortal lamentation out

is laid against his fond heart, and to me has given
1600   a delicate excitement to my bed's delight.
CHORUS
        O that in speed, without pain
        and the slow bed of sickness
        death could come to us now, death that forever
1605   carries sleep without ending, now that our lord is down,
        our shield, kindest of men,
        who for a woman's grace suffered so much,
        struck down at last by a woman.

        Alas, Helen, wild heart
1610   for the multitudes, for the thousand lives
        you killed under Troy's shadow,
        you alone, to shine in man's memory
        as blood flower never to be washed out. Surely a demon then
        of death walked in the house, men's agony.
1615 CLYTAEMESTRA
        No, be not so heavy, nor yet draw down
        in prayer death's ending,
        neither turn all wrath against Helen
        for men dead, that she alone killed
1620   all those Danaan lives, to work
        the grief that is past all healing.
CHORUS
        Divinity that kneel on this house and the two
        strains of the blood of Tantalus,
1625   in the hands and hearts of women you steer
        the strength tearing my heart.
        Standing above the corpse, obscene
        as some carrion crow she sings
        the crippled song and is proud.
1630 CLYTAEMESTRA
        Thus have you set the speech of your lips
        straight, calling by name
        the spirit thrice glutted that lives in this race.
        From him deep in the nerve is given
1635   the love and the blood drunk, that before
        the old wound dries, it bleeds again.
CHORUS
        Surely it is a huge
        and heavy spirit bending the house you cry;
1640   alas, the bitter glory
        of a doom that shall never be done with;

and all through Zeus, Zeus,
first cause, prime mover.
For what thing without Zeus is done among mortals?
1645   What here is without God's blessing?

O king, my king
how shall I weep for you?
What can I say out of my heart of pity?
Caught in this spider's web you lie,
1650   your life gasped out in indecent death,
struck prone to this shameful bed
by your lady's hand of treachery
and the stroke twin edged of the iron.

CLYTAEMESTRA
1655   Can you claim I have done this?
Speak of me never
more as the wife of Agamemnon.
In the shadow of this corpse's queen
the old stark avenger
1660   of Atreus for his revel of hate
struck down this man,
last blood for the slaughtered children.

CHORUS
What man shall testify
1665   your hands are clean of this murder?
How? How? Yet from his father's blood
might swarm some fiend to guide you.
The black ruin that shoulders
through the streaming blood of brothers
1670   strides at last where he shall win requital
for the children who were eaten.

O king, my king
how shall I weep for you?
What can I say out of my heart of pity?
1675   Caught in this spider's web you lie,
your life gasped out in indecent death,
struck prone to this shameful bed
by your lady's hand of treachery
and the stroke twin edged of the iron.

1680   CLYTAEMESTRA
No shame, I think, in the death given
this man. And did he not
first of all in this house wreak death

by treachery?
1685 The flower of this man's love and mine,
Iphigeneia of the tears
he dealt with even as he has suffered.
Let his speech in death's house be not loud.
With the sword he struck,
1690 with the sword he paid for his own act.
CHORUS
My thoughts are swept away and I go bewildered.
Where shall I turn the brain's
activity in speed when the house is falling?
1695 There is fear in the beat of the blood rain breaking
wall and tower. The drops come thicker.
Still fate grinds on yet more stones the blade
for more acts of terror.

Earth, my earth, why did you not fold me under
1700 before ever I saw this man lie dead
fenced by the tub in silver?
Who shall bury him? Who shall mourn him?
Shall you dare this who have killed
your lord? Make lamentation,
1705 render the graceless grace to his soul
for huge things done in wickedness?
Who over this great man's grave shall lay
the blessing of tears
worked soberly from a true heart?
1710 CLYTAEMESTRA
Not for you to speak of such tendance.
Through us he fell,
by us he died; we shall bury.
There will be no tears in this house for him.
1715 It must be Iphigeneia
his child, who else,
shall greet her father by the whirling stream
and the ferry of tears
to close him in her arms and kiss him.
1720 CHORUS
Here is anger for anger. Between them
who shall judge lightly?
The spoiler is robbed; he killed, he has paid.
The truth stands ever beside God's throne
1725 eternal: he who has wrought shall pay; that is law.

Then who shall tear the curse from their blood?
The seed is stiffened to ruin.

CLYTAEMESTRA

You see truth in the future

1730   at last. Yet I wish
to seal my oath with the Spirit
in the house: I will endure all things as they stand
now, hard though it be. Hereafter
let him go forth to make bleed with death

1735   and guilt the houses of others.
I will take some small
measure of our riches, and be content
that I swept from these halls
the murder, the sin, and the fury.

1740   [AEGISTHUS *enters, followed at a little distance by his armed bodyguard.*]

O splendor and exaltation of this day of doom!
Now I can say once more that the high gods look down
on mortal crimes to vindicate the right at last,
now that I see this man—sweet sight—before me here

1745   sprawled in the tangling nets of fury, to atone
the calculated evil of his father's hand.
For Atreus, this man's father, King of Argolis—
I tell you the clear story—drove my father forth,
Thyestes, his own brother, who had challenged him

1750   in his king's right—forth from his city and his home.
Yet sad Thyestes came again to supplicate
the hearth, and win some grace, in that he was not slain
nor soiled the doorstone of his fathers with blood spilled.
Not his own blood. But Atreus, this man's godless sire,

1755   angrily hospitable set a feast for him,
in seeming a glad day of fresh meat slain and good
cheer; then served my father his own children's flesh
to feed on. For he carved away the extremities,
hands, feet, and cut the flesh apart, and covered them

1760   served in a dish to my father at his table apart,
who with no thought for the featureless meal before him ate
that ghastly food whose curse works now before your eyes.
But when he knew the terrible thing that he had done,
he spat the dead meat from him with a cry, and reeled

1765   spurning the table back to heel with strength the curse:
"Thus crash in ruin all the seed of Pleisthenes."
Out of such acts you see this dead man stricken here,

and it was I, in my right, who wrought this murder, I
third born to my unhappy father, and with him
1770   driven, a helpless baby in arms, to banishment.
Yet I grew up, and justice brought me home again,
till from afar I laid my hands upon this man,
since it was I who pieced together the fell plot.
Now I can die in honor again, if die I must,
1775   having seen him caught in the cords of his just punishment.

CHORUS

Aegisthus, this strong vaunting in distress is vile,
You claim that you deliberately killed the king,
you, and you only, wrought the pity of this death.
1780   I tell you then: There shall be no escape, your head
shall face the stones of anger from the people's hands.

AEGISTHUS

So loud from you, stooped to the meanest rowing bench
with the ship's masters lordly on the deck above?
1785   You are old men; well, you shall learn how hard it is
at your age, to be taught how to behave yourselves.
But there are chains, there is starvation with its pain,
excellent teachers of good manners to old men,
wise surgeons and exemplars. Look! Can you not see it?
1790   Lash not at the goads for fear you hit them, and be hurt.

CHORUS

So then you, like a woman, waited the war out
here in the house, shaming the master's bed with lust,
and planned against the lord of war this treacherous death?

1795 AEGISTHUS

It is just such words as these will make you cry in pain.
Not yours the lips of Orpheus, no, quite otherwise,
whose voice of rapture dragged all creatures in his train.
You shall be dragged, for baby whimperings sobbed out
1800   in rage. Once broken, you will be easier to deal with.

CHORUS

How shall you be lord of the men of Argos, you
who planned the murder of this man, yet could not dare
to act it out, and cut him down with your own hand?

1805 AEGISTHUS

No, clearly the deception was the woman's part,
and I was suspect, that had hated him so long.
Still with his money I shall endeavor to control
the citizens. The mutinous man shall feel the yoke
1810   drag at his neck, no cornfed racing colt that runs

free traced; but hunger, grim companion of the dark
dungeon shall see him broken to the hand at last.

CHORUS

1815
But why, why then, you coward, could you not have slain
your man yourself? Why must it be his wife who killed,
to curse the country and the gods within the ground?
Oh, can Orestes live, be somewhere in sunlight still?
Shall fate grown gracious ever bring him back again
in strength of hand to overwhelm these murderers?

1820
AEGISTHUS

You shall learn then, since you stick to stubbornness of mouth and hand.
Up now from your cover, my henchmen: here is work for you to do.

CHORUS

Look, they come! Let every man clap fist upon his hilted sword.

1825
AEGISTHUS

I too am sword-handed against you; I am not afraid of death.

CHORUS

Death you said and death it shall be; we take up the word of fate.

CLYTAEMESTRA

1830
No, my dearest, dearest of all men, we have done enough. No more
violence. Here is a monstrous harvest and a bitter reaping time.
There is pain enough already. Let us not be bloody now.
Honored gentlemen of Argos, go to your homes now and give way
to the stress of fate and season. We could not do otherwise

1835
than we did. If this is the end of suffering, we can be content
broken as we are by the brute heel of angry destiny.
Thus a woman speaks among you. Shall men deign to understand?

AEGISTHUS

Yes, but think of these foolish lips that blossom into leering gibes,

1840
think of the taunts they spit against me daring destiny and power,
sober opinion lost in insults hurled against my majesty.

CHORUS

It was never the Argive way to grovel at a vile man's feet.

AEGISTHUS

1845
I shall not forget this; in the days to come I shall be there.

CHORUS

Nevermore, if God's hand guiding brings Orestes home again.

AEGISTHUS

Exiles feed on empty dreams of hope. I know it. I was one.

1850
CHORUS

Have your way, gorge and grow fat, soil justice, while the power is yours.

AEGISTHUS

You shall pay, make no mistake, for this misguided insolence.

CHORUS
1855   Crow and strut, brave cockerel by your hen; you have no threats to fear.
CLYTAEMESTRA
        These are howls of impotent rage; forget them, dearest; you and I
        have the power; we two shall bring good order to our house at least.

[*They enter the house. The doors close. All persons leave the stage.*]

THE LIBATION BEARERS

CHARACTERS

ORESTES, *son of* AGAMEMNON *and* CLYTAEMESTRA
PYLADES, *his friend*
ELECTRA, *his sister*
CHORUS, *of foreign serving-women*
A SERVANT (DOORKEEPER)
CLYTAEMESTRA, *now wife of* AEGISTHUS, *queen of Argos*
CILISSA, *the nurse*
AEGISTHUS, *now king of Argos*
A follower of AEGISTHUS
Various attendants of ORESTES, CLYTAEMESTRA, AEGISTHUS *(silent parts)*

SCENE: *Argos. The first part of the play takes place at the tomb of* AGAMEMNON:
        the last part before the door of CLYTAEMESTRA's *palace. No mechanical
        change of scene is necessary. The altar or tomb of* AGAMEMNON *should be
        well down stage. The door to the house should be in the center, back.*

5   [*Enter, as travelers,* ORESTES *and* PYLADES.]

ORESTES
        Hermes, lord of the dead, who watch over the powers
        of my fathers, be my savior and stand by my claim.
        Here is my own soil that I walk. I have come home;
10   and by this mounded gravebank I invoke my sire
        to hear, to listen.
        Here is a lock of hair for Inachus, who made
        me grow to manhood. Here a strand to mark my grief.
        I was not by, my father, to mourn for your death
15   nor stretched my hand out when they took your corpse away.

4. *Aeschylus*/The Oresteia (Libation Bearers)

[*The chorus, with* ELECTRA, *enter from the side.*]

But what can this mean that I see, this group that comes
of women veiled in dignities of black? At what
sudden occurrence can I guess? Is this some new
20   wound struck into our house? I think they bring these urns
to pour, in my father's honor, to appease the powers
below. Can I be right? Surely, I think I see
Electra, my own sister, walk in bitter show
of mourning. Zeus, Zeus, grant me vengeance for my father's
25   murder. Stand and fight beside me, of your grace.

Pylades, stand we out of their way. So may I learn
the meaning of these women; what their prayer would ask.
CHORUS
I came in haste out of the house
30   to carry libations, hurt by the hard stroke of hands.
My cheek shows bright, ripped in the bloody furrows
of nails gashing the skin.
This is my life: to feed the heart on hard-drawn breath.
And in my grief, with splitting weft
35   of ragtorn linen across my heart's
brave show of robes
came sound of my hands' strokes
in sorrows whence smiles are fled.

Terror, the dream diviner of
40   this house, belled clear, shuddered the skin, blew wrath
from sleep, a cry in night's obscure watches,
a voice of fear deep in the house,
dropping deadweight in women's inner chambers.
And they who read the dream meanings
45   and spoke under guarantee of God
told how under earth
dead men held a grudge still
and smoldered at their murderers.

On such grace without grace, evil's turning aside
50   (Earth, Earth, kind mother!)
bent, the godless woman
sends me forth. But terror
is on me for this word let fall.
What can wash off the blood once spilled upon the ground?
55   O hearth soaked in sorrow,

o wreckage of a fallen house.
Sunless and where men fear to walk
the mists huddle upon this house
where the high lords have perished.

60 The pride not to be warred with, fought with, not to be beaten down
of old, sounded in all men's
ears, in all hearts sounded,
has shrunk away. A man
goes in fear. High fortune,
65 this in man's eyes is god and more than god is this.
But, as a beam balances, so
sudden disasters wait, to strike
some in the brightness, some in gloom
of half dark in their elder time.
70 Desperate night holds others.

Through too much glut of blood drunk by our fostering ground
the vengeful gore is caked and hard, will not drain through.
The deep-run ruin carries away
the man of guilt. Swarming infection boils within.

75 For one who handles the bridal close, there is no cure.
All the world's waters running in a single drift
may try to wash blood from the hand
of the stained man; they only bring new blood guilt on.

But as for me: gods have forced on my city
80 resisted fate. From our fathers' houses
they led us here, to take the lot of slaves.
And mine it is to wrench my will, and consent
to their commands, right or wrong,
to beat down my edged hate.
85 And yet under veils I weep
the vanities that have killed
my lord; and freeze with sorrow in the secret heart.
ELECTRA
Attendant women, who order our house, since you
90 are with me in this supplication and escort
me here, be also my advisers in this rite.
What shall I say, as I pour out these outpourings
of sorrow? How say the good word, how make my prayer
to my father? Shall I say I bring it to the man
95 beloved, from a loving wife, and mean my mother? I

have not the daring to say this, nor know what else
to say, as I pour this liquid on my father's tomb.
Shall I say this sentence, regular in human use:
"Grant good return to those who send to you these flowers
100   of honor: gifts to match the . . . evil they have done."

Or, quiet and dishonored, as my father died
shall I pour out this offering for the ground to drink,
and go, like one who empties garbage out of doors,
and turn my eyes, and throw the vessel far away.

105   Dear friends, in this deliberation stay with me.
We hold a common hatred in this house. Do not
for fear of any, hide your thought inside your heart.
The day of destiny waits for the free man as well
as for the man enslaved beneath an alien hand.
110   If you know any better course than mine, tell me.
CHORUS
In reverence for your father's tomb as if it were
an altar, I will speak my heart's thought, as you ask.
ELECTRA
115   Tell me then, please, as you respect my father's grave.
CHORUS
Say words of grace for those of good will, as you pour.
ELECTRA
Whom of those closest to me can I call my friend?
120   CHORUS
Yourself first; all who hate Aegisthus after that.
ELECTRA
You mean these prayers shall be for you, and for myself?
CHORUS
125   You see it now; but it is you whose thought this is.
ELECTRA
Is there some other we should bring in on our side?
CHORUS
Remember Orestes, though he wanders far away.
130   ELECTRA
That was well spoken; you did well reminding me.
CHORUS
Remember, too, the murderers, and against them . . .
ELECTRA
135   What shall I say? Guide and instruct my ignorance.
CHORUS
Invoke the coming of some man, or more than man.

ELECTRA
> To come to judge them, or to give them punishment?

140 CHORUS
> Say simply: "one to kill them, for the life they took."

ELECTRA
> I can ask this, and not be wrong in the gods' eyes?

CHORUS
145
> May you not hurt your enemy, when he struck first?

ELECTRA
> Almighty herald of the world above, the world
> below: Hermes, lord of the dead, help me; announce
> my prayers to the charmed spirits underground, who watch
150
> over my father's house, that they may hear. Tell Earth
> herself, who brings all things to birth, who gives them strength,
> then gathers their big yield into herself at last.
> I myself pour these lustral waters to the dead,
> and speak, and call upon my father: Pity me;
155
> pity your own Orestes. How shall we be lords
> in our house? We have been sold, and go as wanderers
> because our mother bought herself, for us, a man,
> Aegisthus, he who helped her hand to cut you down.
> Now I am what a slave is, and Orestes lives
160
> outcast from his great properties, while they go proud
> in the high style and luxury of what you worked
> to win. By some good fortune let Orestes come
> back home. Such is my prayer, my father. Hear me; hear.
> And for myself, grant that I be more temperate
165
> of heart than my mother; that I act with purer hand.

> Such are my prayers for us; but for our enemies,
> father, I pray that your avenger come, that they
> who killed you shall be killed in turn, as they deserve.
> Between my prayer for good and prayer for good I set
170
> this prayer for evil; and I speak it against Them.
> For us, bring blessings up into the world. Let Earth
> and conquering Justice, and all gods beside, give aid.

> Such are my prayers; and over them I pour these drink
> offerings. Yours the strain now, yours to make them flower
175
> with mourning song, and incantation for the dead.

CHORUS
> Let the tear fall, that clashes as it dies
> as died our fallen lord;
> die on this mound that fences good from evil,

180   washing away the death stain accursed
of drink offerings shed. Hear me, oh hear, my lord,
majesty hear me from your dark heart; oh hear.
Let one come, in strength
of spear, some man at arms who will set free the house

185   holding the Scythian bow backbent in his hands,
a barbarous god of war spattering arrows
or closing to slash, with sword hilted fast to his hand.

ELECTRA
Father, the earth has drunk my offerings poured to you.

190   Something has happened here, my women. Help me now.

CHORUS
Speak, if you will. My heart is in a dance of fear.

ELECTRA
Someone has cut a strand of hair and laid it on

195   the tomb.

CHORUS
                   What man? Or was it some deep-waisted girl?

ELECTRA
There is a mark, which makes it plain for any to guess.

200   CHORUS
Explain, and let your youth instruct my elder age.

ELECTRA
No one could have cut off this strand, except myself.

CHORUS

205   Those others, whom it would have become, are full of hate.

ELECTRA
Yet here it is, and for appearance matches well . . .

CHORUS
With whose hair? Tell me. This is what I long to know. . . .

210   ELECTRA
With my own hair. It is almost exactly like.

CHORUS
Can it then be a secret gift from Orestes?

ELECTRA

215   It seems that it must be nobody's hair but his.

CHORUS
Did Orestes dare to come back here? How could this be?

ELECTRA
He sent this severed strand, to do my father grace.

220   CHORUS
It will not stop my tears if you are right. You mean
that he can never again set foot upon this land.

ELECTRA
>
> The bitter wash has surged upon my heart as well.
225   I am struck through, as by the cross-stab of a sword,
> and from my eyes the thirsty and unguarded drops
> burst in a storm of tears like winter rain, as I
> look on this strand of hair. How could I think some other
> man, some burgess, could ever go grand in hair like this?
230   *She* never could have cut it, she who murdered him
> and is my mother, but no mother in her heart
> which has assumed God's hate and hates her children. No.
> And yet, how can I say in open outright confidence
> this is a treasured token from the best beloved
235   of men to me, Orestes? Does hope fawn on me?
> Ah
> I wish it had the kind voice of a messenger
> so that my mind would not be torn in two, I not
> shaken, but it could tell me plain to throw this strand
240   away as vile, if it was cut from a hated head,
> or like a brother could have mourned with me, and been
> a treasured splendor for my father, and his grave.
>
> The gods know, and we call upon the gods; they know
> how we are spun in circles like seafarers, in
245   what storms. But if we are to win, and our ship live,
> from one small seed could burgeon an enormous tree.
>
> But see, here is another sign. Footprints are here.
> The feet that made them are alike, and look like mine.
> There are two sets of footprints: of the man who gave
250   his hair, and one who shared the road with him. I step
> where he has stepped, and heelmarks, and the space between
> his heel and toe are like the prints I make. Oh, this
> is torment, and my wits are going.

[ORESTES *comes from his place of concealment.*]

255 ORESTES
> Pray for what is to come, and tell the gods that they
> have brought your former prayers to pass. Pray for success.

ELECTRA
> Upon what ground? What have I won yet from the gods?

260 ORESTES
> You have come in sight of all you long since prayed to see.

ELECTRA

How did you know what man was subject of my prayer?

ORESTES

265   I know about Orestes, how he stirred your heart.

ELECTRA

Yes; but how am I given an answer to my prayers?

ORESTES

Look at me. Look for no one closer to you than I.

ELECTRA

270   Is this some net of treachery, friend, you catch me in?

ORESTES

Then I must be contriving plots against myself.

ELECTRA

275   It is your pleasure to laugh at my unhappiness.

ORESTES

I only mock my own then, if I laugh at you.

ELECTRA

Are you really Orestes? Can I call you by that name?

ORESTES

280   You see my actual self and are slow to learn. And yet
you saw this strand of hair I cut in sign of grief
and shuddered with excitement, for you thought you saw
me, and again when you were measuring my tracks.

285   Now lay the severed strand against where it was cut
and see how well your brother's hair matches my head.
Look at this piece of weaving, the work of your hand
with its blade strokes and figured design of beasts. No, no,
control yourself, and do not lose your head for joy.

290   I know those nearest to us hate us bitterly.

ELECTRA

O dearest, treasured darling of my father's house,
hope of the seed of our salvation, wept for, trust
your strength of hand, and win your father's house again.

295   O bright beloved presence, you bring back four lives
to me. To call you father is constraint of fact,
and all the love I could have borne my mother turns
your way, while she is loathed as she deserves; my love
for a pitilessly slaughtered sister turns to you.

300   And now you were my steadfast brother after all.
You alone bring me honor; but let Force, and Right,
and Zeus almighty, third with them, be on your side.

ORESTES

Zeus, Zeus, direct all that we try to do. Behold

305   the orphaned children of the eagle-father, now

that he has died entangled in the binding coils
of the deadly viper, and the young he left behind
are worn with hunger of starvation, not full grown
to bring their shelter slain food, as their father did.
310   I, with my sister, whom I name, Electra here,
stand in your sight, children whose father is lost. We both
are driven from the house that should be ours. If you
destroy these fledgelings of a father who gave you
sacrifice and high honor, from what hand like his
315   shall you be given the sacred feast which is your right?
Destroy the eagle's brood, and you have no more means
to send your signs to mortals for their strong belief;
nor, if the stump rot through on this baronial tree,
shall it sustain your altars on sacrificial days.
320   Safe keep it: from a little thing you can raise up
a house to grandeur, though it now seem overthrown,

CHORUS

    O children, silence! Saviors of your father's house,
be silent, children. Otherwise someone may hear
325   and for mere love of gossip carry news of all
you do, to those in power, to those I long to see
some day as corpses in the leaking pitch and flame.

ORESTES

    The big strength of Apollo's oracle will not
330   forsake me. For he charged me to win through this hazard,
with divination of much, and speech articulate,
the winters of disaster under the warm heart
were I to fail against my father's murderers;
told me to cut them down in their own fashion, turn
335   to the bull's fury in the loss of my estates.
He said that else I must myself pay penalty
with my own life, and suffer much sad punishment;
spoke of the angers that come out of the ground from those
beneath who turn against men; spoke of sicknesses,
340   ulcers that ride upon the flesh, and cling, and with
wild teeth eat away the natural tissue, how on this
disease shall grow in turn a leprous fur. He spoke
of other ways again by which the avengers might
attack, brought to fulfilment from my father's blood.
345   For the dark arrow of the dead men underground
from those within my blood who fell and turn to call
upon me; madness and empty terror in the night
on one who sees clear and whose eyes move in the dark,
must tear him loose and shake him until, with all his bulk

350   degraded by the bronze-loaded lash, he lose his city.
       And such as he can have no share in the communal bowl
       allowed them, no cup filled for friends to drink. The wrath
       of the father comes unseen on them to drive them back
       from altars. None can take them in nor shelter them.
355   Dishonored and unloved by all the man must die
       at last, shrunken and wasted away in painful death.

       Shall I not trust such oracles as this? Or if
       I do not trust them, here is work that must be done.
       Here numerous desires converge to drive me on:
360   the god's urgency and my father's passion, and
       with these the loss of my estates wears hard on me;
       the thought that these my citizens, most high renowned
       of men, who toppled Troy in show of courage, must
       go subject to this brace of women; since his heart
365   is female; or, if it be not, that soon will show.
CHORUS
       Almighty Destinies, by the will
       of Zeus let these things
       be done, in the turning of Justice.
370   For the word of hatred spoken, let hate
       be a word fulfilled. The spirit of Right
       cries out aloud and extracts atonement
       due: blood stroke for the stroke of blood
       shall be paid. Who acts, shall endure. So speaks
375   the voice of the age-old wisdom.
ORESTES
       Father, o my dread father, what thing
       can I say, can I accomplish
       from this far place where I stand, to mark
380   and reach you there in your chamber
       with light that will match your dark?
       Yet it is called an action
       of grace to mourn in style for the house,
       once great, of the sons of Atreus.
385 CHORUS
       Child, when the fire burns
       and tears with teeth at the dead man
       it can not wear out the heart of will.
       He shows his wrath in the after-
390   days. One dies, and is dirged.
       Light falls on the man who killed him.
       He is hunted down by the deathsong

for sires slain and for fathers,
disturbed, and stern, and enormous.

395 ELECTRA

Hear me, my father; hear in turn
all the tears of my sorrows.
Two children stand at your tomb to sing
the burden of your death chant.

400 Your grave is shelter to suppliants,
shelter to the outdriven.
What here is good; what escape from grief?
Can we outwrestle disaster?

CHORUS

405 Yet from such as this the god, if he will,
can work out strains that are fairer.
For dirges chanted over the grave
the winner's song in the lordly house;
bring home to new arms the beloved.

410 ORESTES

If only at Ilium,
father, and by some Lycian's hands
you had gone down at the spear's stroke,
you would have left high fame in your house,

415 in the going forth of your children
eyes' admiration;
founded the deep piled bank of earth
for grave by the doubled water
with light lift for your household;

420 CHORUS

loved then by those he loved
down there beneath the ground
who died as heroes, he would have held
state, and a lord's majesty,

425 vassal only to those most great,
the Kings of the under darkness.
For he was King on earth when he lived
over those whose hands held power of life
and death, and the staff of authority.

430 ELECTRA

No, but not under Troy's
ramparts, father, should you have died,
nor, with the rest of the spearstruck hordes
have found your grave by Scamandrus' crossing.

435 Sooner, his murderers
should have been killed, as he was,

by those they loved, and have found their death,
and men remote from this outrage
had heard the distant story.

440 CHORUS

Child, child, you are dreaming, since dreaming is a light
pastime, of fortune more golden than gold
or the Blessed Ones north of the North Wind.
But the stroke of the twofold lash is pounding

445 close, and powers gather under ground
to give aid. The hands of those who are lords
are unclean, and these are accursed.
Power grows on the side of the children.

ORESTES

450 This cry has come to your ear
like a deep driven arrow.
Zeus, Zeus, force up from below
ground the delayed destruction
on the hard heart and the daring

455 hand, for the right of our fathers.

CHORUS

May I claim right to close the deathsong
chanted in glory across
the man speared and the woman

460 dying. Why darken what deep within me forever
flitters? Long since against the heart's
stem a bitter wind has blown
thin anger and burdened hatred.

ELECTRA

465 May Zeus, from all shoulder's strength,
pound down his fist upon them,
ohay, smash their heads.
Let the land once more believe.
There has been wrong done. I ask for right.

470 Hear me, Earth. Hear me, grandeurs of Darkness.

CHORUS

It is but law that when the red drops have been spilled
upon the ground they cry aloud for fresh
blood. For the death act calls out on Fury

475 to bring out of those who were slain before
new ruin on ruin accomplished.

ORESTES

Hear me, you lordships of the world below.
Behold in assembled power, curses come from the dead,

480 behold the last of the sons of Atreus, foundering

lost, without future, cast
from house and right. O god, where shall we turn?
CHORUS
The heart jumped in me once again
485 to hear this unhappy prayer.
I was disconsolate then
and the deep heart within
darkened to hear you speak it.
But when strength came back hope lifted
490 me again, and the sorrow
was gone and the light was on me.
ELECTRA
Of what thing can we speak, and strike more close,
than of the sorrows they who bore us have given?
495 So let her fawn if she likes. It softens not.
For we are bloody like the wolf
and savage born from the savage mother.
CHORUS
I struck my breast in the stroke-style of the Arian,
500 the Cissian mourning woman,
and the hail-beat of the drifting fists was there to see
as the rising pace went in a pattern of blows
downward and upward until the crashing strokes
played on my hammered, my all-stricken head.
505 ELECTRA
O cruel, cruel
all daring mother, in cruel processional
with all his citizens gone,
with all sorrow for him forgotten
510 you dared bury your unbewept lord.
ORESTES
O all unworthy of him, that you tell me.
Shall she not pay for this dishonor
for all the immortals,
515 for all my own hands can do?
Let me but take her life and die for it.
CHORUS
Know then, they hobbled him beneath the armpits,
with his own hands. She wrought so, in his burial
520 to make his death a burden
beyond your strength to carry.
The mutilation of your father. Hear it.
ELECTRA
You tell of how my father was murdered. Meanwhile I

525   stood apart, dishonored, nothing worth,
         in the dark corner, as you would kennel a vicious dog,
         and burst in an outrush of tears, that came that day
         where smiles would not, and hid the streaming of my grief.
         Hear such, and carve the letters of it on your heart.

530   CHORUS
         Let words such as these
         drip deep in your ears, but on a quiet heart.
         So far all stands as it stands;
         what is to come, yourself burn to know.

535   You must be hard, give no ground, to win home.
     ORESTES
         I speak to you. Be with those you love, my father.
     ELECTRA
         And I, all in my tears, ask with him.

540   CHORUS
         We gather into murmurous revolt. Hear
         us, hear. Come back into the light.
         Be with us against those we hate.
     ORESTES

545   Warstrength shall collide with warstrength; right with right.
     ELECTRA
         O gods, be just in what you bring to pass.
     CHORUS
         My flesh crawls as I listen to them pray.

550   The day of doom has waited long.
         They call for it. It may come.

         O pain grown into the race
         and blood-dripping stroke
         and grinding cry of disaster,

555   moaning and impossible weight to bear.
         Sickness that fights all remedy.

         Here in the house there lies
         the cure for this, not to be brought
         from outside, never from others

560   but in themselves, through the fierce wreck and bloodshed.
         Here is a song sung to the gods beneath us.
         Hear then, you blessed ones under the ground,
         and answer these prayers with strength on our side,
         free gift for your children's conquest.

565   ORESTES
         Father, o King who died no kingly death, I ask

the gift of lordship at your hands, to rule your house.

ELECTRA

570   I too, my father, ask of you such grace as this:
to murder Aegisthus with strong hand, and then go free.

ORESTES

So shall your memory have the feasts that men honor
in custom. Otherwise when feasts are gay, and portions
burn for the earth, you shall be there, and none give heed.

575 ELECTRA

I too out of my own full dowership shall bring
libations for my bridal from my father's house.
Of all tombs, yours shall be the lordliest in my eyes.

ORESTES

580   O Earth, let my father emerge to watch me fight.

ELECTRA

Persephone, grant still the wonder of success.

ORESTES

Think of that bath, father, where you were stripped of life.

585 ELECTRA

Think of the casting net that they contrived for you.

ORESTES

They caught you like a beast in toils no bronzesmith made.

ELECTRA

590   Rather, hid you in shrouds that were thought out in shame.

ORESTES

Will you not waken, father, to these challenges?

ELECTRA

Will you not rear upright that best beloved head?

595 ORESTES

Send out your right to battle on the side of those
you love, or give us holds like those they caught you in.
For they threw you. Would you not see them thrown in turn?

ELECTRA

600   Hear one more cry, father, from me. It is my last.
Your nestlings huddle suppliant at your tomb: look forth
and pity them, female with the male strain alike.
Do not wipe out this seed of the Pelopidae.
So, though you died, you shall not yet be dead, for when
605   a man dies, children are the voice of his salvation
afterward. Like corks upon the net, these hold
the drenched and flaxen meshes, and they will not drown.
Hear us, then. Our complaints are for your sake, and if
you honor this our argument, you save yourself.

610 CHORUS

None can find fault with the length of this discourse you drew
out, to show honor to a grave and fate unwept
before. The rest is action. Since your heart is set
that way, now you must strike and prove your destiny.

615 ORESTES

So. But I am not wandering from my strict course
when I ask why she sent these libations, for what cause
she acknowledges, too late, a crime for which there is
no cure. Here was a wretched grace brought to a man

620 dead and unfeeling. This I fail to understand.
The offerings are too small for the act done. Pour out
all your possessions to atone one act of blood,
you waste your work, it is all useless, reason says.
Explain me this, for I would learn it, if you know.

625 CHORUS

I know, child, I was there. It was the dreams she had.
The godless woman had been shaken in the night
by floating terrors, when she sent these offerings.

ORESTES

630 Do you know the dream, too? Can you tell it to me right?

CHORUS

She told me herself. She dreamed she gave birth to a snake.

ORESTES

What is the end of the story then? What is the point?

635 CHORUS

She laid it swathed for sleep as if it were a child.

ORESTES

A little monster. Did it want some kind of food?

CHORUS

640 She herself, in the dream, gave it her breast to suck.

ORESTES

How was her nipple not torn by such a beastly thing?

CHORUS

It was. The creature drew in blood along with the milk.

645 ORESTES

No void dream this. It is the vision of a man.

CHORUS

She woke screaming out of her sleep, shaky with fear,
as torches kindled all about the house, out of

650 the blind dark that had been on them, to comfort the queen.
So now she sends these mourning offerings to be poured
and hopes they are medicinal for her disease.

ORESTES

655

But I pray to the earth and to my father's grave
that this dream is for me and that I will succeed.
See, I divine it, and it coheres all in one piece.
If this snake came out of the same place whence I came,
if she wrapped it in robes, as she wrapped me, and if
its jaws gaped wide around the breast that suckled me,

660

and if it stained the intimate milk with an outburst
of blood, so that for fright and pain she cried aloud,
it follows then, that as she nursed this hideous thing
of prophecy, she must be cruelly murdered. I
turn snake to kill her. This is what the dream portends.

665 CHORUS

I choose you my interpreter to read these dreams.
So may it happen. Now you must rehearse your side
in their parts. For some, this means the parts they must not play.

ORESTES

670

Simple to tell them. My sister here must go inside.
I charge her to keep secret what we have agreed,
so that, as they by treachery killed a man of high
degree, by treachery tangled in the self same net
they too shall die, in the way Loxias has ordained,

675

my lord Apollo, whose word was never false before.
Disguised as an outlander, for which I have all gear,
I shall go to the outer gates with Pylades
whom you see here. He is hereditary friend
and companion-in-arms of my house. We two shall both assume

680

the Parnassian dialect and imitate the way
they talk in Phocis. If none at the door will take us in
kindly, because the house is in a curse of ills,
we shall stay there, till anybody who goes by
the house will wonder why we are shut out, and say:

685

"why does Aegisthus keep the suppliant turned away
from his gates, if he is hereabouts and knows of this?"
But if I once cross the doorstone of the outer gates
and find my man seated upon my father's throne,
or if he comes down to confront me, and uplifts

690

his eyes to mine, then lets them drop again, be sure,
before he can say: "where does the stranger come from?" I
shall plunge my sword with lightning speed, and drop him dead.
Our Fury who is never starved for blood shall drink
for the third time a cupful of unwatered blood.

695   Electra, keep a careful eye on all within
       the house, so that our plans will hold together. You,
       women: I charge you, hold your tongues religiously.
       Be silent if you must, or speak in the way that will
       help us. And now I call upon the god who stands
700   close, to look on, and guide the actions of my sword.

[*Exeunt* ORESTES *and* PYLADES. *Exit separately,* ELECTRA.]

CHORUS
       Numberless, the earth breeds
       dangers, and the sober thought of fear.
705   The bending sea's arms swarm
       with bitter, savage beasts.
       Torches blossom to burn along
       the high space between ground and sky.
       Things fly, and things walk the earth.
710   Remember too
       the storm and wrath of the whirlwind.

       But who can recount all
       the high daring in the will
       of man, and in the stubborn hearts of women
715   the all-adventurous passions
       that couple with man's overthrow.
       The female force, the desperate
       love crams its resisted way
       on marriage and the dark embrace
720   of brute beasts, of mortal men.

       Let him, who goes not on flimsy wings
       of thought, learn from her,
       Althaea, Thestius'
       daughter: who maimed her child, and hard
725   of heart, in deliberate guile
       set fire to the bloody torch, her own son's
       agemate, that from the day he emerged
       from the mother's womb crying
       shared the measure of all his life
730   down to the marked death day.

       And in the legends there is one more, a girl
       of blood, figure of hate
       who, for the enemy's

735
sake killed one near in blood, seduced by the wrought
golden necklace from Crete,
wherewith Minos bribed her. She sundered
from Nisus his immortal hair
as he all unsuspecting
breathed in a tranquil sleep. Foul wretch,
740
Hermes of death has got her now.

Since I recall cruelties from quarrels long
ago, in vain, and married love turned to bitterness
a house would fend far away
by curse; the guile, treacheries of the woman's heart
745
against a lord armored in
power, a lord his enemies revered,
I prize the hearth not inflamed within the house,
the woman's right pushed not into daring.

Of all foul things legends tell the Lemnian
750
outranks, a vile wizard's charm, detestable
so that man names a hideous
crime "Lemnian" in memory of their wickedness.
When once the gods loathe a breed
of men they go outcast and forgotten.
755
No man respects what the gods have turned against.
What of these tales I gather has no meaning?

The sword edges near the lungs.
It stabs deep, bittersharp,
and right drives it. For that which had no right
760
lies not yet stamped into the ground, although
one in sin transgressed Zeus' majesty.

Right's anvil stands staunch on the ground
and the smith, Destiny, hammers out the sword.
Delayed in glory, pensive from
765
the murk, Vengeance brings home at last
a child, to wipe out the stain of blood shed long ago.

[*Enter* ORESTES *and* PYLADES.]

ORESTES
In there! Inside! Does anyone hear me knocking at
770
the gate? I will try again. Is anyone at home?

Try a third time. I ask for someone to come from the house,
if Aegisthus lets it welcome friendly visitors.
SERVANT [*inside*]
All right, I hear you. Where does the stranger come from, then?
775 ORESTES
Announce me to the masters of the house. It is
to them I come, and I have news for them to hear.
And be quick, for the darkening chariot of night
leans to its course; the hour for wayfarers to drop
780 anchor in some place that entertains all travelers.
Have someone of authority in the house come out,
the lady of the place or, more appropriately,
its lord, for then no delicacy in speaking blurs
the spoken word. A man takes courage and speaks out
785 to another man, and makes clear everything he means.

[*Enter* CLYTAEMESTRA.]

CLYTAEMESTRA
Friends, tell me only what you would have, and it is yours.
We have all comforts that go with a house like ours,
790 hot baths, and beds to charm away your weariness
with rest, and the regard of temperate eyes. But if
you have some higher business, more a matter of state,
that is the men's concern, and I will tell them of it.
ORESTES
795 I am a Daulian stranger out of Phocis. As
I traveled with my pack and my own following
making for Argos, where my feet are rested now,
I met a man I did not know, nor did he know
me, but he asked what way I took, and told me his.
800 It was a Phocian, Strophius; for he told me his name
and said: "Friend, since in any case you make for Argos,
remember carefully to tell Orestes' parents
that he is dead; please do not let it slip your mind.
Then, if his people decide to have him brought back home,
805 or bury him where he went to live, all outlander
forever, carry their requests again to me.
For as it is the bronze walls of an urn close in
the ashes of a man who has been deeply mourned."

So much I know, no more. But whether I now talk
810 with those who have authority and concern in this
I do not know. I think his father should be cold.

CLYTAEMESTRA
　　Ah me. You tell us how we are stormed from head to heel.
　　Oh curse upon our house, bitter antagonist,
815　　how far your eyes range. What was clean out of your way
　　your archery brings down with a distant deadly shot
　　to strip unhappy me of all I ever loved.
　　Even Orestes now! He was so well advised
　　to keep his foot clear of this swamp of death. But now
820　　set down as traitor the hope that was our healer once
　　and made us look for a bright revel in our house.

ORESTES
　　I could have wished, with hosts so prosperous as you,
　　to have made myself known by some more gracious news
825　　and so been entertained by you. For what is there
　　more kindly than the feeling between host and guest?
　　Yet it had been abuse of duty in my heart
　　had I not given so great a matter to his friends,
　　being so bound by promise and the stranger's rights.

830 CLYTAEMESTRA
　　You shall not find that your reception falls below
　　your worth, nor be any the less our friend for this.
　　Some other would have brought the news in any case.
　　But it is the hour for travelers who all day have trudged
835　　the long road, to be given the rest that they deserve.
　　Escort this gentleman with his companion and
　　his men, to where our masculine friends are made at home.
　　Look after them, in manner worthy of a house
　　like ours; you are responsible for their good care.
840　　Meanwhile, we shall communicate these matters to
　　the masters of the house, and with our numerous friends
　　deliberate the issues of this fatal news.

　　[*Exeunt all but the* CHORUS.]

CHORUS
845　　Handmaidens of this house, who help our cause,
　　how can our lips frame
　　some force that will show for Orestes?
　　O Lady Earth, Earth Queen, who now
　　ride mounded over the lord of ships
850　　where the King's corpse lies buried,
　　hear us, help us.
　　Now the time breaks for Persuasion in stealth
　　to go down to the pit, with Hermes of death

and the dark, to direct
855   trial by the sword's fierce edge.

I think our newcomer is at his deadly work;
I see Orestes' old nurse coming forth, in tears.

[*Enter* CILISSA.]

Now where away, Cilissa, through the castle gates,
860   with sorrow as your hireless fellow-wayfarer?
CILISSA
The woman who is our mistress told me to make haste
and summon Aegisthus for the strangers, "so that he
can come and hear, as man to man, in more detail
865   this news that they have brought." She put a sad face on
before the servants, to hide the smile inside her eyes
over this work that has been done so happily
for her—though on this house the curse is now complete
from the plain story that the stranger men have brought.
870   But as for that Aegisthus, oh, he will be pleased
enough to hear the story. Poor unhappy me,
all my long-standing mixture of misfortunes, hard
burden enough, here in this house of Atreus,
when it befell me made the heart ache in my breast.
875   But never yet did I have to bear a hurt like this.
I took the other troubles bravely as they came:
but now, darling Orestes! I wore out my life
for him. I took him from his mother, brought him up.
There were times when he screamed at night and woke me from
880   my rest; I had to do many hard tasks, and now
useless; a baby is like a beast, it does not think
but you have to nurse it, do you not, the way it wants.
For the child still in swaddling clothes can not tell us
if he is hungry or thirsty, if he needs to make
885   water. Children's young insides are a law to themselves.
I needed second sight for this, and many a time
I think I missed, and had to wash the baby's clothes.
The nurse and laundrywoman had a combined duty
and that was I. I was skilled in both handicrafts,
890   and so Orestes' father gave him to my charge.
And now, unhappy, I am told that he is dead
and go to take the story to that man who has
defiled our house; he will be glad to hear such news.

CHORUS

895   Did she say he should come back armed in any way?

CILISSA

    How, armed? Say it again. I do not understand.

CHORUS

    Was he to come with bodyguards, or by himself?

900 CILISSA

    She said to bring his followers, the men-at-arms.

CHORUS

    Now, if you hate our master, do not tell him that,

    but simply bid him come as quickly as he can

905   and cheerfully. In that way he will not take fright.

    It is the messenger who makes the bent word straight.

CILISSA

    But are you happy over what I have told you?

CHORUS

910   Perhaps: if Zeus might turn our evil wind to good.

CILISSA

    How so? Orestes, once hope of the house, is gone.

CHORUS

    Not yet. It would be a poor seer who saw it thus.

915 CILISSA

    What is this? Have you some news that has not been told?

CHORUS

    Go on and take your message, do as you were bid.

    The gods' concerns are what concern only the gods.

920 CILISSA

    I will go then and do all this as you have told

    me to. May all be for the best. So grant us god.

[*Exit* CILISSA.]

CHORUS

925   Now to my supplication, Zeus,

    father of Olympian gods,

    grant that those who struggle hard to see

    temperate things done in the house win their aim

    in full. All that I spoke

930   was spoken in right. Yours, Zeus, to protect.

    Zeus, Zeus, make him who is now

    in the house stand above those who

    hate. If you rear him to greatness,

    double and three times

935   and blithely he will repay you.

See the colt of this man whom you loved
harnessed to the chariot
of suffering. Set upon the race he runs
sure control. Make us not see him break
940   stride, but clean down the course
hold the strain of his striding speed.

You that, deep in the house
sway their secret pride of wealth,
hear us, gods of sympathy.
945   For things done in time past
wash out the blood in fair-spoken verdict.
Let the old murder in
the house breed no more.

And you, who keep, magnificent, the hallowed and huge
950   cavern, o grant that the man's house lift up its head
and look on the shining of daylight
and liberty with eyes made
glad with gazing out from the helm of darkness.

And with right may the son
955   of Maia lend his hand, strong to send
wind fair for action, if he will.
Much else lies secret he may show at need.
He speaks the markless word, by
night hoods darkness on the eyes
960   nor shows more plainly when the day is there.

Then at last we shall sing
for deliverance of the house
the woman's song that sets the wind
fair, no thin drawn and grief
965   struck wail, but this: "The ship sails fair."
My way, mine, the advantage piles here, with wreck
and ruin far from those I love.

Be not fear struck when your turn comes in the action
but with a great cry *Father*
970   when she cries *Child* to you
go on through with the innocent murder.

Yours to raise high within
your body the heart of Perseus
and for those under the ground you loved
975 and those yet above, exact
what their bitter passion may desire; make
disaster a thing of blood inside the house;
wipe out the man stained with murder.

[*Enter* AEGISTHUS.]

980 AEGISTHUS
It is not without summons that I come, but called
by messenger, with news that there are strangers here
arrived, telling a story that brings no delight:
the death of Orestes. For our house, already bitten
985 and poisoned, to take this new load upon itself
would be a thing of dripping fear and blood. Yet how
shall I pass upon these rumors? As the living truth?
For messages made out of women's terror leap
high in the upward air and empty die. Do *you*
990 know anything of this by which to clear my mind?
CHORUS
We heard, yes. But go on inside and hear it from
the strangers. Messengers are never quite so sure
as a man's questions answered by the men themselves.
995 AEGISTHUS
I wish to question, carefully, this messenger
and learn if he himself was by when the man died
or if he heard but some blind rumor and so speaks.
The mind has eyes, not to be easily deceived.

1000 [*Exit* AEGISTHUS.]

CHORUS
Zeus, Zeus, what shall I say, where make
a beginning of prayer for the gods' aid?
My will is good
1005 but how shall I speak to match my need?
The bloody edges of the knives that rip
man-flesh are moving to work. It will mean
utter and final ruin imposed
on Agamemnon's
1010 house: or our man will kindle a flame
and light of liberty, win the domain

and huge treasure again of his fathers.
Forlorn challenger, though blessed by god,
Orestes must come to grips with two,
1015   so wrestle. Yet may he throw them.

[*A cry is heard from inside the house.*]

Listen, it goes
but how? What has been done in the house?
Stand we aside until the work is done, for so
1020   we shall not seem to be accountable in this
foul business. For the fight is done, the issue drawn.

[*Enter a follower of* AEGISTHUS.]

FOLLOWER
O sorrow, all is sorrow for our stricken lord.
1025   Raise up again a triple cry of sorrow, for
Aegisthus lives no longer. Open there, open
quick as you may, and slide back the doorbars on the women's
gates. It will take the strength of a young arm, but not
to fight for one who is dead and done for. What use there?
1030   Ahoy!
My cry is to the deaf and I babble in vain
at sleepers to no purpose. Clytaemestra, where
is she, does what? Her neck is on the razor's edge
and ripe for lopping, as she did to others before.

1035   [*Enter* CLYTAEMESTRA.]

CLYTAEMESTRA
What is this, and why are you shouting in the house?
FOLLOWER
I tell you, he is alive and killing the dead.
1040   CLYTAEMESTRA
Ah, so. You speak in riddles, but I read the rhyme.
We have been won with the treachery by which we slew.
Bring me quick, somebody, an ax to kill a man

[*Exit* FOLLOWER.]

1045   and we shall see if we can beat him before we
go down—so far gone are we in this wretched fight.

[*Enter* ORESTES *and* PYLADES *with swords drawn.*]

ORESTES
You next: the other one in there has had enough.

1050 CLYTAEMESTRA
Beloved, strong Aegisthus, are you dead indeed?

ORESTES
You love your man, then? You shall lie in the same grave
with him, and never be unfaithful even in death.

1055 CLYTAEMESTRA
Hold, my son. Oh take pity, child, before this breast
where many a time, a drowsing baby, you would feed
and with soft gums sucked in the milk that made you strong.

ORESTES
1060 What shall I do, Pylades? Be shamed to kill my mother?

PYLADES
What then becomes thereafter of the oracles
declared by Loxias at Pytho? What of sworn oaths?
Count all men hateful to you rather than the gods.

1065 ORESTES
I judge that you win. Your advice is good.

[*To* CLYTAEMESTRA.]

Come here.
My purpose is to kill you over his body.
1070 You thought him bigger than my father while he lived.
Die then and sleep beside him, since he is the man
you love, and he you should have loved got only your hate.

CLYTAEMESTRA
I raised you when you were little. May I grow old with you?

1075 ORESTES
You killed my father. Would you make your home with me?

CLYTAEMESTRA
Destiny had some part in that, my child.

ORESTES
1080 Why then
destiny has so wrought that this shall be your death.

CLYTAEMESTRA
A mother has her curse, child. Are you not afraid?

ORESTES
1085 No. You bore me and threw me away, to a hard life.

CLYTAEMESTRA
I sent you to a friend's house. This was no throwing away.

ORESTES
I was born of a free father. You sold me.
1090 CLYTAEMESTRA
So? Where then is the price that I received for you?
ORESTES
I could say. It would be indecent to tell you.
CLYTAEMESTRA
1095 Or if you do, tell also your father's vanities.
ORESTES
Blame him not. He suffered while you were sitting here at home.
CLYTAEMESTRA
It hurts women to be kept from their men, my child.
1100 ORESTES
The man's hard work supports the women who sit at home.
CLYTAEMESTRA
I think, child, that you mean to kill your mother.
ORESTES
1105   No.
It will be you who kill yourself. It will not be I.
CLYTAEMESTRA
Take care. Your mother's curse, like dogs, will drag you down.
ORESTES
1110 How shall I escape my father's curse, if I fail here?
CLYTAEMESTRA
I feel like one who wastes live tears upon a tomb.
ORESTES
Yes, this is death, your wages for my father's fate.
1115 CLYTAEMESTRA
You are the snake I gave birth to, and gave the breast.
ORESTES
Indeed, the terror of your dreams saw things to come
clearly. You killed, and it was wrong. Now suffer wrong.

1120 [ORESTES *and* PYLADES *take* CLYTAEMESTRA *inside the house.*]

CHORUS
I have sorrow even for this pair in their twofold
downfall. But since Orestes had the hardiness
to end this chain of bloodlettings, here lies our choice,
1125 that the eyes' light in this house shall not utterly die.

Justice came at the last to Priam and all his sons
and it was heavy and hard,
but into the house of Agamemnon returned

the double lion, the double assault,
1130 and the Pythian-steered exile
drove home to the hilt
vengeance, moving strongly in guidance sent by the god.

Raise up the high cry o over our lordships' house
won free of distress, free of its fortunes wasted
1135 by two stained with murder,
free of its mournful luck.

He came back; his work lay in the secret attack
and it was stealthy and hard
but in the fighting his hand was steered by the very daughter
1140 of Zeus: Right we call her,
mortals who speak of her and name her well. Her wind
is fury and death visited upon those she hates.

All that Loxias, who on Parnassus holds
the huge, the deep cleft in the ground, shrilled aloud,
1145 by guile that is no guile
returns now to assault the wrong done and grown old.
Divinity keeps, we know not how, strength to resist
surrender to the wicked.
The power that holds the sky's majesty wins our worship.

1150 Light is here to behold.
The big bit that held our house is taken away.
Rise up, you halls, arise; for time grown too long
you lay tumbled along the ground.

Time brings all things to pass. Presently time shall cross
1155 the outgates of the house after the stain is driven
entire from the hearth
by ceremonies that wash clean and cast out the furies.
The dice of fortune shall be thrown once more, and lie
in a fair fall smiling
1160 up at the new indwellers come to live in the house.

[*The doors of the house open, to show* ORESTES *standing over the bodies of* CLYTAEMESTRA *and* AEGISTHUS. *His attendants display the robe in which* CLYTAEMESTRA *had entangled* AGAMEMNON *and which she displayed after his murder.*]

1165   ORESTES

Behold the twin tyrannies of our land, these two
who killed my father and who sacked my house. For a time
they sat upon their thrones and kept their pride of state,
and they are lovers still. So may you judge by what

1170   befell them, for as they were pledged their oath abides.
They swore together death for my unhappy sire
and swore to die together. Now they keep their oath.

Behold again, o audience of these evil things,
the engine against my wretched father they devised,

1175   the hands' entanglement, the hobbles for his feet.
Spread it out. Stand around me in a circle and
display this net that caught a man. So shall, not my
father, but that great father who sees all, the Sun,
look on my mother's sacrilegious handiwork

1180   and be a witness for me in my day of trial
how it was in all right that I achieved this death,
my mother's: for of Aegisthus' death I take no count:
he has his seducer's punishment, no more than law.

But she, who plotted this foul death against the man

1185   by whom she carried the weight of children underneath
her zone, burden once loved, shown hard and hateful now,
what does she seem to be? Some water snake, some viper
whose touch is rot even to him who felt no fang
strike, by that brutal and wrong daring in her heart.

1190   And this thing: what shall I call it and be right, in all
eloquence? Trap for an animal or winding sheet
for dead man? Or bath curtain? Since it is a net,
robe you could call it, to entangle a man's feet.
Some highwayman might own a thing like this, to catch

1195   the wayfarer and rob him of his money and
so make a living. With a treacherous thing like this
he could take many victims and go warm within.

May no such wife as she was come to live with me.
Sooner, let God destroy me, with no children born.

1200   CHORUS

Ah, but the pitiful work.
Dismal the death that was your ending.
He is left alive; pain flowers for him.

ORESTES

1205   Did she do it or did she not? My witness is
this great robe. It was thus she stained Aegisthus' sword.
Dip it and dip it again, the smear of blood conspires
with time to spoil the beauty of this precious thing.
Now I can praise him, now I can stand by to mourn

1210   and speak before this web that killed my father; yet
I grieve for the thing done, the death, and all our race.
I have won; but my victory is soiled, and has no pride.

CHORUS

There is no mortal man who shall turn

1215   unhurt his life's course to an end not marred.
There is trouble here. There is more to come.

ORESTES

I would have you know, I see not how this thing will end.
I am a charioteer whose course is wrenched outside

1220   the track, for I am beaten, my rebellious senses
bolt with me headlong and the fear against my heart
is ready for the singing and dance of wrath. But while
I hold some grip still on my wits, I say publicly
to my friends: I killed my mother not without some right.

1225   My father's murder stained her, and the gods' disgust.
As for the spells that charmed me to such daring, I
give you in chief the seer of Pytho, Loxias. He
declared I could do this and not be charged with wrong.
Of my evasion's punishment I will not speak:

1230   no archery could hit such height of agony.
And look upon me now, how I go armored in
leafed branch and garland on my way to the centrestone
and sanctuary, and Apollo's level place,
the shining of the fabulous fire that never dies,

1235   to escape this blood that is my own. Loxias ordained
that I should turn me to no other shrine than this.
To all men of Argos in time to come I say
they shall be witness, how these evil things were done.
I go, an outcast wanderer from this land, and leave

1240   behind, in life, in death, the name of what I did.

CHORUS

No, what you did was well done. Do not therefore bind
your mouth to foul speech. Keep no evil on your lips.
You liberated all the Argive city when

1245   you lopped the heads of these two snakes with one clean stroke.

ORESTES

No!

Women who serve this house, they come like gorgons, they
wear robes of black, and they are wreathed in a tangle

1250   of snakes. I can no longer stay.

CHORUS

Orestes, dearest to your father of all men
what fancies whirl you? Hold, do not give way to fear.

ORESTES

1255   These are no fancies of affliction. They are clear,
and real, and here; the bloodhounds of my mother's hate.

CHORUS

It is the blood still wet upon your hands, that makes
this shaken turbulence be thrown upon your sense.

1260   ORESTES

Ah, Lord Apollo, how they grow and multiply,
repulsive for the blood drops of their dripping eyes.

CHORUS

There is one way to make you clean: let Loxias

1265   touch you, and set you free from these disturbances.

ORESTES

You can not see them, but I see them. I am driven
from this place. I can stay here no longer.

[*Exit.*]

1270   CHORUS

Good luck go with you then, and may the god look on
you with favor and guard you in kind circumstance.

Here on this house of the kings the third
storm has broken, with wind

1275   from the inward race, and gone its course.
The children were eaten: there was the first
affliction, the curse of Thyestes.
Next came the royal death, when a man
and lord of Achaean armies went down

1280   killed in the bath. Third
is for the savior. He came. Shall I call
it that, or death? Where
is the end? Where shall the fury of fate
be stilled to sleep, be done with?

1285   [*Exeunt.*]

THE EUMENIDES

CHARACTERS

PRIESTESS OF APOLLO, *the* PYTHIA
APOLLO
HERMES *(silent)*
GHOST OF CLYTAEMESTRA
ORESTES
ATHENE
CHORUS OF EUMENIDES (FURIES)
SECOND CHORUS; *women of Athens*
JURYMEN, HERALD, CITIZENS OF ATHENS *(all silent parts)*

SCENE: *For the first part of the play the scene is Delphi, before the sanctuary of* PYTHIAN APOLLO. *The action of the rest of the play takes place at Athens, on the Acropolis before the temple of Athene. A simple change in the backdrop will indicate the shift.*

5 [*Enter, alone, the* PYTHIA.]

PYTHIA
    I give first place of honor in my prayer to her
    who of the gods first prophesied, the Earth; and next
10   to Themis, who succeeded to her mother's place
    of prophecy; so runs the legend; and in third
    succession, given by free consent, not won by force,
    another Titan daughter of Earth was seated here.
    This was Phoebe. She gave it as a birthday gift
15   to Phoebus, who is called still after Phoebe's name.
    And he, leaving the pond of Delos and the reef,
    grounded his ship at the roadstead of Pallas, then
    made his way to this land and a Parnassian home.
    Deep in respect for his degree Hephaestus' sons
20   conveyed him here, for these are builders of roads, and changed
    the wilderness to a land that was no wilderness.
    He came so, and the people highly honored him,
    with Delphus, lord and helmsman of the country. Zeus
    made his mind full with godship and prophetic craft
25   and placed him, fourth in a line of seers, upon this throne.
    So, Loxias is the spokesman of his father, Zeus.
        These are the gods I set in the proem of my prayer.

But Pallas-before-the-temple has her right in all
I say. I worship the nymphs where the Corycian rock
30   is hollowed inward, haunt of birds and paced by gods.
Bromius, whom I forget not, sways this place. From here
in divine form he led his Bacchanals in arms
to hunt down Pentheus like a hare in the deathtrap.
I call upon the springs of Pleistus, on the power
35   of Poseidon, and on final loftiest Zeus,
then go to sit in prophecy on the throne. May all
grant me that this of all my entrances shall be
the best by far. If there are any Hellenes here
let them draw lots, so enter, as the custom is.
40   My prophecy is only as the god may guide.

[*She enters the temple and almost immediately comes out again.*]

Things terrible to tell and for the eyes to see
terrible drove me out again from Loxias' house
so that I have no strength and cannot stand on springing
45   feet, but run with hands' help and my legs have no speed.
An old woman afraid is nothing: a child, no more.
    See, I am on my way to the wreath-hung recess
and on the centrestone I see a man with god's
defilement on him postured in the suppliant's seat
50   with blood dripping from his hands and from a new-drawn sword,
holding too a branch that had grown high on an olive
tree, decorously wrapped in a great tuft of wool,
and the fleece shone. So far, at least, I can speak clear.
    In front of this man slept a startling company
55   of women lying all upon the chairs. Or not
women, I think I call them rather gorgons, only
not gorgons either, since their shape is not the same.
I saw some creatures painted in a picture once,
who tore the food from Phineus, only these had no
60   wings, that could be seen; they are black and utterly
repulsive, and they snore with breath that drives one back.
From their eyes drips the foul ooze, and their dress is such
as is not right to wear in the presence of the gods'
statues, nor even into any human house.
65   I have never seen the tribe that owns this company
nor know what piece of earth can claim with pride it bore
such brood, and without hurt and tears for labor given.
    Now after this the master of the house must take
his own measures: Apollo Loxias, who is very strong

70   and heals by divination; reads portentous signs,
and so clears out the houses others hold as well.

[*Exit. The doors of the temple open and show* ORESTES *surrounded by the sleeping* FURIES, APOLLO *and* HERMES *beside him.*]

APOLLO

75   I will not give you up. Through to the end standing
your guardian, whether by your side or far away,
I shall not weaken toward your enemies. See now
how I have caught and overpowered these lewd creatures.
The repulsive maidens have been stilled to sleep, those gray

80   and aged children, they with whom no mortal man,
no god, nor even any beast, will have to do.
It was because of evil they were born, because
they hold the evil darkness of the Pit below
Earth, loathed alike by men and by the heavenly gods.

85   Nevertheless, run from them, never weaken. They
will track you down as you stride on across the long
land, and your driven feet forever pound the earth,
on across the main water and the circle-washed
cities. Be herdsman to this hard march. Never fail

90   until you come at last to Pallas' citadel.
Kneel there, and clasp the ancient idol in your arms,
and there we shall find those who will judge this case, and words
to say that will have magic in their figures. Thus
you will be rid of your afflictions, once for all.

95   For it was I who made you strike your mother down.

ORESTES

      My lord Apollo, you understand what it means to do
no wrong. Learn also what it is not to neglect.
None can mistrust your power to do good, if you will.

100 APOLLO

      Remember: the fear must not give you a beaten heart.
Hermes, you are my brother from a single sire.
Look after him, and as you are named the god who guides,
be such in strong fact. He is my suppliant. Shepherd him

105 with fortunate escort on his journeys among men.
The wanderer has rights which Zeus acknowledges.

[*Exit* APOLLO, *then* ORESTES *guided by* HERMES. *Enter the ghost of* CLYTAEMESTRA.]

CLYTAEMESTRA

110   You would sleep, then? And what use are you, if you sleep?
It is because of you I go dishonored thus
among the rest of the dead. Because of those I killed
my bad name among the perished suffers no eclipse
but I am driven in disgrace. I say to you
115   that I am charged with guilt most grave by these. And yet
I suffered too, horribly, and from those most dear,
yet none among the powers is angered for my sake
that I was slaughtered, and by matricidal hands.
Look at these gashes in my heart, think where they came
120   from. Eyes illuminate the sleeping brain,
but in the daylight man's future cannot be seen.
        Yet I have given you much to lap up, outpourings
without wine, sober propitiations, sacrificed
in secrecy of night and on a hearth of fire
125   for you, at an hour given to no other god.
Now I watch all these honors trampled into the ground,
and he is out and gone away like any fawn
so lightly, from the very middle of your nets,
sprung clear, and laughing merrily at you. Hear me.
130   It is my life depends upon this spoken plea.
Think then, o goddesses beneath the ground. For I,
the dream of Clytaemestra, call upon your name.

[*The* FURIES *stir in their sleep and whimper.*]

CLYTAEMESTRA

135   Oh, whimper, then, but your man has got away and gone
far. He has friends to help him, who are not like mine.

[*They whimper again.*]

CLYTAEMESTRA

    Too much sleep and no pity for my plight. I stand,
140   his mother, here, killed by Orestes. He is gone.

[*They moan in their sleep.*]

CLYTAEMESTRA

    You moan, you sleep. Get on your feet quickly, will you?
What have you yet got done, except to do evil?

145   [*They moan again.*]

CLYTAEMESTRA

Sleep and fatigue, two masterful conspirators,
have dimmed the deadly anger of the mother-snake.

[*The* CHORUS *start violently, then speak in their sleep.*]

150 CHORUS

Get him, get him, get him, get him. Make sure.

CLYTAEMESTRA

The beast you are after is a dream, but like the hound
whose thought of hunting has no lapse, you bay him on.
155   What are you about? Up, let not work's weariness
beat you, nor slacken with sleep so you forget my pain.
Scold your own heart and hurt it, as it well deserves,
for this is discipline's spur upon her own. Let go
upon this man the stormblasts of your bloodshot breath,
160   wither him in your wind, after him, hunt him down
once more, and shrivel him in your vitals' heat and flame.

[*The ghost disappears, and the* CHORUS *waken and, as they waken, speak severally.*]

CHORUS

165   Waken. You are awake, wake her, as I did you.
You dream still? On your feet and kick your sleep aside.
Let us see whether this morning-song means vanity.

[*Here they begin to howl.*]

Sisters, we have had wrong done us.
170   When I have undergone so much and all in vain.
Suffering, suffering, bitter, oh shame shame,
unendurable wrong.
The hunted beast has slipped clean from our nets and gone.
Sleep won me, and I lost my capture.

175   Shame, son of Zeus! Robber is all you are.
A young god, you have ridden down powers gray with age,
taken the suppliant, though a godless man, who hurt
the mother who gave him birth.
Yourself a god, you stole the matricide away.
180   Where in this act shall any man say there is right?

The accusation came upon me from my dreams,
and hit me, as with goad in the mid-grip of his fist
the charioteer strikes,
but deep, beneath lobe and heart.
185   The executioner's cutting whip is mine to feel
and the weight of pain is big, heavy to bear.

Such are the actions of the younger gods. These hold
by unconditional force, beyond all right, a throne
that runs reeking blood,
190   blood at the feet, blood at the head.
The very stone centre of earth here in our eyes horrible
with blood and curse stands plain to see.

Himself divine, he has spoiled his secret shrine's
hearth with the stain, driven and hallooed the action on.
195   He made man's way cross the place of the ways of god
and blighted age-old distributions of power.

He has wounded me, but he shall not get this man away.
Let him hide under the ground, he shall never go free.
Cursed suppliant, he shall feel against his head
200   another murderer rising out of the same seed.

[APOLLO *enters again from his sanctuary.*]

APOLLO

Get out, I tell you, go and leave this house. Away
in haste, from your presence set the mantic chamber free,
205   else you may feel the flash and bite of a flying snake
launched from the twisted thong of gold that spans my bow
to make you in your pain spew out the black and foaming
blood of men, vomit the clots sucked from their veins.
This house is no right place for such as you to cling
210   upon; but where, by judgment given, heads are lopped
and eyes gouged out, throats cut, and by the spoil of sex
the glory of young boys is defeated, where mutilation
lives, and stoning, and the long moan of tortured men
spiked underneath the spine and stuck on pales. Listen
215   to how the gods spit out the manner of that feast
your loves lean to. The whole cast of your shape is guide
to what you are, the like of whom should hole in the cave
of the blood-reeking lion, not in oracular
interiors, like mine nearby, wipe off your filth.

220   Out then, you flock of goats without a herdsman, since
no god has such affection as to tend this brood.
CHORUS
My lord Apollo, it is your turn to listen now.
Your own part in this is more than accessory.
225   You are the one who did it; all the guilt is yours.
APOLLO
So? How? Continue speaking, until I understand.
CHORUS
You gave this outlander the word to kill his mother.
230   APOLLO
The word to exact price for his father. What of that?
CHORUS
You then dared take him in, fresh from his bloodletting.
APOLLO
235   Yes, and I told him to take refuge in this house.
CHORUS
You are abusive then to those who sped him here?
APOLLO
Yes. It was not for you to come near this house;
240   CHORUS
                      and yet
we have our duty. It was to do what we have done.
APOLLO
An office? You? Sound forth your glorious privilege.
245   CHORUS
This: to drive matricides out of their houses.
APOLLO
                   Then
what if it be the woman and she kills her man?
250   CHORUS
Such murder would not be the shedding of kindred blood.
APOLLO
You have made into a thing of no account, no place,
the sworn faith of Zeus and of Hera, lady
255   of consummations, and Cypris by such argument
is thrown away, outlawed, and yet the sweetest things
in man's life come from her, for married love between
man and woman is bigger than oaths, guarded by right
of nature. If when such kill each other you relent
260   so as not to take vengeance nor eye them in wrath,
then I deny your manhunt of Orestes goes
with right. I see that one cause moves you to strong rage

but on the other clearly you are unmoved to act.
Pallas divine shall review the pleadings of this case.

265 CHORUS
Nothing will ever make me let that man go free.

APOLLO
Keep after him then, and make more trouble for yourselves.

CHORUS
270 Do not try to dock my privilege by argument.

APOLLO
I would not take your privilege if you gave it me.

CHORUS
No, for you are called great beside the throne of Zeus
275 already, but the motherblood drives me, and I go
to win my right upon this man and hunt him down.

APOLLO
But I shall give the suppliant help and rescue, for
if I willingly fail him who turns to me for aid,
280 his wrath, before gods and men, is a fearful thing.

[*They go out, separately. The scene is now Athens, on the Acropolis
before the temple and statue of* ATHENE. ORESTES *enters and takes
suppliant posture at the feet of the statue.*]

ORESTES
285 My lady Athene, it is at Loxias' behest
I come. Then take in of your grace the wanderer
who comes, no suppliant, not unwashed of hand, but one
blunted at last, and worn and battered on the outland
habitations and the beaten ways of men.
290 Crossing the dry land and the sea alike, keeping
the ordinances of Apollo's oracle
I come, goddess, before your statue and your house
to keep watch here and wait the issue of my trial.

[*The* CHORUS *enter severally, looking for* ORESTES.]

295 CHORUS
So. Here the man has left a clear trail behind; keep on,
keep on, as the unspeaking accuser tells us, by
whose sense, like hounds after a bleeding fawn, we trail
our quarry by the splash and drip of blood. And now
300 my lungs are blown with abundant and with wearisome
work, mankilling. My range has been the entire extent
of land, and, flown unwinged across the open water,

I am here, and give way to no ship in my pursuit.
Our man has gone to cover somewhere in this place.
305   The welcome smell of human blood has told me so.

Look again, look again,
search everywhere, let
not the matricide
steal away and escape.

310   [*They see* ORESTES.]

See there! He clings to defence
again, his arms winding the immortal goddess'
image, so tries to be quit out of our hands.
It shall not be. His mother's blood spilled on the ground
315   can not come back again.
It is all soaked and drained into the ground and gone.

You must give back for her blood from the living man
red blood of your body to suck, and from your own
I could feed, with bitter-swallowed drench,
320   turn your strength limp while yet you live and drag you down
where you must pay for the pain of the murdered mother,
and watch the rest of the mortals stained with violence
against god or guest
or hurt parents who were close and dear,
325   each with the pain upon him that his crime deserves.
Hades is great, Hades calls men to reckoning
there under the ground,
sees all, and cuts it deep in his recording mind.

ORESTES
330   I have been beaten and been taught, I understand
the many rules of absolution, where it is right
to speak and where be silent. In this action now
speech has been ordered by my teacher, who is wise.
The stain of blood dulls now and fades upon my hand.
335   My blot of matricide is being washed away.
When it was fresh still, at the hearth of the god, Phoebus,
this was absolved and driven out by sacrifice
of swine, and the list were long if I went back to tell
of all I met who were not hurt by being with me.
340   Time in his aging overtakes all things alike.
Now it is from pure mouth and with good auspices
I call upon Athene, queen of this land, to come

and rescue me. She, without work of her spear, shall win
myself and all my land and all the Argive host
345   to stand her staunch companion for the rest of time.
Whether now ranging somewhere in the Libyan land
beside her father's crossing and by Triton's run
of waters she sets upright or enshrouded foot
rescuing there her friends, or on the Phlegraean flat
350   like some bold man of armies sweeps with eyes the scene,
let her come! She is a god and hears me far away.
So may she set me free from what is at my back.
CHORUS
Neither Apollo nor Athene's strength must win
355   you free, save you from going down forgotten, without
knowing where joy lies anywhere inside your heart,
blood drained, chewed dry by the powers of death, a wraith, a shell.
You will not speak to answer, spew my challenge away?
You are consecrate to me and fattened for my feast,
360   and you shall feed me while you live, not cut down first
at the altar. Hear the spell I sing to bind you in.

Come then, link we our choral. Ours
to show forth the power
and terror of our music, declare
365   our rights of office, how we conspire
to steer men's lives.
We hold we are straight and just. If a man
can spread his hands and show they are clean,
no wrath of ours shall lurk for him.
370   Unscathed he walks through his life time.
But one like this man before us, with stained
hidden hands, and the guilt upon him,
shall find us beside him, as witnesses
of the truth, and we show clear in the end
375   to avenge the blood of the murdered.

Mother, o my mother night, who gave me
birth, to be a vengeance on the seeing
and the blind, hear me. For Leto's
youngling takes my right away,
380   stealing from my clutch the prey
that crouches, whose blood would wipe
at last the motherblood away.

Over the beast doomed to the fire
this is the chant, scatter of wits,
385   frenzy and fear, hurting the heart,
song of the Furies
binding brain and blighting blood
in its stringless melody.

This is the purpose that the all-involving
390   destiny spun, to be ours and to be shaken
never: when mortals assume outrage
of own hand in violence,
these we dog, till one goes
under earth. Nor does death
395   set them altogether free.

over the beast doomed to the fire
this is the chant, scatter of wits,
frenzy and fear, hurting the heart,
song of the Furies
400   binding brain and blighting blood
in its stringless melody.

When we were born such lots were assigned for our keeping.
So the immortals must hold hands off, nor is there
one who shall sit at our feasting.
405   For sheer white robes I have no right and no portion.

I have chosen overthrow
of houses, where the Battlegod
grown within strikes near and dear
down. So we swoop upon this man
410   here. He is strong, but we wear him down
for the blood that is still wet on him.

Here we stand in our haste to wrench from all others
these devisings, make the gods clear of our counsels
so that even appeal comes
415   not to them, since Zeus has ruled our blood dripping company
outcast, nor will deal with us.

I have chosen overthrow
of houses, where the Battlegod
grown within strikes near and dear
420   down. So we swoop upon this man

here. He is strong, but we wear him down
for the blood that is still wet on him.

Men's illusions in their pride under the sky melt
down, and are diminished into the ground, gone
425   before the onset of our black robes, pulsing
of our vindictive feet against them.

For with a long leap from high
above and dead drop of weight
I bring foot's force crashing down
430   to cut the legs from under even
the runner, and spill him to ruin.

He falls, and does not know in the daze of his folly.
Such in the dark of man is the mist of infection
that hovers, and moaning rumor tells how his house lies
435   under fog that glooms above.

For with a long leap from high
above, and dead drop of weight,
I bring foot's force crashing down
to cut the legs from under even
440   the runner, and spill him to ruin.

All holds. For we are strong and skilled;
we have authority; we hold
memory of evil; we are stern
nor can men's pleadings bend us. We
445   drive through our duties, spurned, outcast
from gods, driven apart to stand in light
not of the sun. So sheer with rock are ways
for those who see, as upon those whose eyes are lost.

Is there a man who does not fear
450   this, does not shrink to hear
how my place has been ordained,
granted and given by destiny
and god, absolute? Privilege
primeval yet is mine, nor am I without place
455   though it be underneath the ground
and in no sunlight and in gloom that I must stand.

[ATHENE enters, *in full armor.*]

ATHENE

    From far away I heard the outcry of your call.
460   It was beside Scamandrus. I was taking seisin
    of land, for there the Achaean lords of war and first
    fighters gave me large portion of all their spears
    had won, the land root and stock to be mine for all
    eternity, for the sons of Theseus a choice gift.
465   From there, sped on my weariless feet, I came, wingless
    but in the rush and speed of the aegis fold. And now
    I see upon this land a novel company·
    which, though it brings no terror to my eyes, brings still
    wonder. Who are you? I address you all alike,
470   both you, the stranger kneeling at my image here,
    and you, who are like no seed ever begotten, not
    seen ever by the gods as goddesses, nor yet
    stamped in the likenesses of any human form.
    But no. This is the place of the just. Its rights forbid
475   even the innocent to speak evil of his mates.

CHORUS

    Daughter of Zeus, you shall hear all compressed to brief
    measure. We are the gloomy children of the night.
    Curses they call us in our homes beneath the ground.

480 ATHENE

    I know your race, then, and the names by which you are called.

CHORUS

    You shall be told of our position presently.

ATHENE

485   I can know that, if one will give me a clear account.

CHORUS

    We drive from home those who have shed the blood of men.

ATHENE

    Where is the place, then, where the killer's flight shall end?

490 CHORUS

    A place where happiness is nevermore allowed.

ATHENE

    Is he one? Do you blast him to this kind of flight?

CHORUS

495   Yes. He murdered his mother by deliberate choice.

ATHENE

    By random force, or was it fear of someone's wrath?

CHORUS

    Where is the spur to justify man's matricide?

500 ATHENE

    Here are two sides, and only half the argument.

CHORUS
He is unwilling to give or to accept an oath.
ATHENE
505   You wish to be called righteous rather than act right.
CHORUS
No. How so? Out of the riches of your wit, explain.
ATHENE
I say, wrong must not win by technicalities.
510 CHORUS
Examine him then yourself. Decide it, and be fair.
ATHENE
You would turn over authority in this case to me?
CHORUS
515   By all means. Your father's degree, and yours, deserve as much.
ATHENE
Your turn, stranger. What will you say in answer? Speak,
tell me your country and your birth, what has befallen
you, then defend yourself against the anger of these;
520   if it was confidence in the right that made you sit
to keep this image near my hearth, a suppliant
in the tradition of Ixion, sacrosanct.
Give me an answer which is plain to understand.
ORESTES
525   Lady Athene, first I will take the difficult thought
away that lies in these last words you spoke. I am
no suppliant, nor was it because I had a stain
upon my hand that I sat at your image. I
will give you a strong proof that what I say is true.
530   It is the law that the man of the bloody hand must speak
no word until, by action of one who can cleanse,
blood from a young victim has washed his blood away.
Long since, at the homes of others, I have been absolved
thus, both by running waters and by victims slain.

535   I count this scruple now out of the way. Learn next
with no delay where I am from. I am of Argos
and it is to my honor that you ask the name
of my father, Agamemnon, lord of seafarers,
and your companion when you made the Trojan city
540   of Ilium no city any more. He died
without honor when he came home. It was my mother
of the dark heart, who entangled him in subtle gyves
and cut him down. The bath is witness to his death.
I was an exile in the time before this. I came back

545   and killed the woman who gave me birth. I plead guilty.
     My father was dear, and this was vengeance for his blood.
     Apollo shares responsibility for this.
     He counterspurred my heart and told me of pains to come
     if I should fail to act against the guilty ones.
550   This is my case. Decide if it be right or wrong.
     I am in your hands. Where my fate falls, I shall accept.

ATHENE
     The matter is too big for any mortal man
     who thinks he can judge it. Even I have not the right
555   to analyse cases of murder where wrath's edge
     is sharp, and all the more since you have come, and clung
     a clean and innocent suppliant, against my doors.
     You bring no harm to my city. I respect your rights.

     Yet these, too, have their work. We cannot brush them aside,
560   and if this action so runs that they fail to win,
     the venom of their resolution will return
     to infect the soil, and sicken all my land to death.
     Here is dilemma. Whether I let them stay or drive
     them off, it is a hard course and will hurt. Then, since
565   the burden of the case is here, and rests on me,
     I shall select judges of manslaughter, and swear
     them in, establish a court into all time to come.

     Litigants, call your witnesses, have ready your proofs
     as evidence under bond to keep this case secure.
570   I will pick the finest of my citizens, and come
     back. They shall swear to make no judgment that is not
     just, and make clear where in this action the truth lies.

     [*Exit.*]

CHORUS
575   Here is overthrow of all
     the young laws, if the claim
     of this matricide shall stand
     good, his crime be sustained.
     Should this be, every man will find a way
580   to act at his own caprice;
     over and over again in time
     to come, parents shall await
     the deathstroke at their children's hands.

We are the Angry Ones. But we
585 shall watch no more over works
of men, and so act. We shall
let loose indiscriminate death.
Man shall learn from man's lot, forejudge
the evils of his neighbor's case,
590 see respite and windfall in storm:
pathetic prophet who consoles
with strengthless cures, in vain.

Nevermore let one who feels
the stroke of accident, uplift
595 his voice and make outcry, thus:
"Oh Justice!
Throned powers of the Furies, help!"
Such might be the pitiful cry
of some father, of the stricken
600 mother, their appeal. Now
the House of Justice has collapsed.

There are times when fear is good.
It must keep its watchful place
at the heart's controls. There is
605 advantage
in the wisdom won from pain.
Should the city, should the man
rear a heart that nowhere goes
in fear, how shall such a one
610 any more respect the right?

Refuse the life of anarchy;
refuse the life devoted to
one master.
The in-between has the power
615 by God's grant always, though
his ordinances vary.
I will speak in defence
of reason: for the very child
of vanity is violence;
620 but out of health
in the heart issues the beloved
and the longed-for, prosperity.

All for all I say to you:
bow before the altar of right.
625 You shall not
eye advantage, and heel
it over with foot of force.

Vengeance will be upon you.
The all is bigger than you.
630 Let man see this and take
care, to mother and father,
and to the guest
in the gates welcomed, give all rights
that befall their position.

635 The man who does right, free-willed, without constraint
shall not lose happiness
nor be wiped out with all his generation.
But the transgressor, I tell you, the bold man
who brings in confusion of goods unrightly won,
640 at long last and perforce, when ship toils
under tempest must strike his sail
in the wreck of his rigging.

He calls on those who hear not, caught inside
the hard wrestle of water.
645 The spirit laughs at the hot hearted man,
the man who said "never to me," watches him
pinned in distress, unable to run free of the crests.
He had good luck in his life. Now
he smashes it on the reef of Right
650 and drowns, unwept and forgotten.

[ATHENE *re-enters, guiding twelve citizens chosen as jurors and
attended by a* HERALD. *Other citizens follow.*]

ATHENE
Herald, make proclamation and hold in the host
655 assembled. Let the stabbing voice of the Etruscan
trumpet, blown to the full with mortal wind, crash out
its high call to all the assembled populace
For in the filling of this senatorial ground
it is best for all the city to be silent and learn
660 the measures I have laid down into the rest of time.
So too these litigants, that their case be fairly tried.

[*Trumpet call. All take their places. Enter* APOLLO.]

CHORUS

My lord Apollo, rule within your own domain.

665   What in this matter has to do with you? Declare.

APOLLO

I come to testify. This man, by observed law,

came to me as suppliant, took his place by hearth and hall,

and it was I who cleaned him of the stain of blood.

670   I have also come to help him win his case. I bear

responsibility for his mother's murder.

[*To* ATHENE.]

                                   You

who know the rules, initiate the trial. Preside.

675   ATHENE [*to the* FURIES]

I declare the trial opened. Yours is the first word.

For it must justly be the pursuer who speaks first

and opens the case, and makes plain what the action is.

CHORUS

680   We are many, but we shall cut it short. You, then,

word against word answer our charges one by one.

Say first, did you kill your mother or did you not?

ORESTES

Yes, I killed her. There shall be no denial of that.

685   CHORUS

There are three falls in the match and one has gone to us.

ORESTES

So you say. But you have not even thrown your man.

CHORUS

690   So. Then how did you kill her? You are bound to say.

ORESTES

I do. With drawn sword in my hand I cut her throat.

CHORUS

By whose persuasion and advice did you do this?

695   ORESTES

By order of this god, here. So he testifies.

CHORUS

The Prophet guided you into this matricide?

ORESTES

700   Yes. I have never complained of this. I do not now.

CHORUS

When sentence seizes you, you will talk a different way.

ORESTES

    I have no fear. My father will aid me from the grave.

705 CHORUS

    Kill your mother, then put trust in a corpse! Trust on.

ORESTES

    Yes. She was dirtied twice over with disgrace.

CHORUS

710   Tell me how, and explain it to the judges here.

ORESTES

    She murdered her husband, and thereby my father too.

CHORUS

    Of this stain, death has set her free. But you still live.

715 ORESTES

    When she lived, why did you not descend and drive her out?

CHORUS

    The man she killed was not of blood congenital.

ORESTES

720   But am I then involved with my mother by blood-bond?

CHORUS

    Murderer, yes. How else could she have nursed you beneath
    her heart? Do you forswear your mother's intimate blood?

ORESTES

725   Yours to bear witness now, Apollo, and expound
    the case for me, if I was right to cut her down.
    I will not deny I did this thing, because I did
    do it. But was the bloodshed right or not? Decide
    and answer. As you answer, I shall state my case.

730 APOLLO

    To you, established by Athene in your power,
    I shall speak justly. I am a prophet, I shall not
    lie. Never, for man, woman, nor city, from my throne
    of prophecy have I spoken a word, except

735   that which Zeus, father of Olympians, might command.
    This is justice. Recognize then how great its strength.
    I tell you, follow our father's will. For not even
    the oath that binds you is more strong than Zeus is strong.

CHORUS

740   Then Zeus, as you say, authorized the oracle
    to this Orestes, stating he could wreak the death
    of his father on his mother, and it would have no force?

APOLLO

    It is not the same thing for a man of blood to die

745   honored with the king's staff given by the hand of god,
    and that by means of a woman, not with the far cast

of fierce arrows, as an Amazon might have done,
but in a way that you shall hear, o Pallas and you
who sit in state to judge this action by your vote.

750 He had come home from his campaigning. He had done
better than worse, in the eyes of a fair judge. She lay
in wait for him. It was the bath. When he was at
its edge, she hooded the robe on him, and in the blind
and complex toils tangled her man, and chopped him down.

755 There is the story of the death of a great man,
solemn in all men's sight, lord of the host of ships.
I have called the woman what she was, so that the people
whose duty it is to try this case may be inflamed.

CHORUS

760 Zeus, by your story, gives first place to the father's death.
Yet Zeus himself shackled elder Cronus, his own
father. Is this not contradiction? I testify,
judges, that this is being said in your hearing.

APOLLO

765 You foul animals, from whom the gods turn in disgust,
Zeus could undo shackles, such hurt can be made good,
and there is every kind of way to get out. But once
the dust has drained down all a man's blood, once the man
has died, there is no raising of him up again.

770 This is a thing for which my father never made
curative spells. All other states, without effort
of hard breath, he can completely rearrange.

CHORUS

See what it means to force acquittal of this man.

775 He has spilled his mother's blood upon the ground. Shall he
then be at home in Argos in his father's house?
What altars of the community shall he use? Is there
a brotherhood's lustration that will let him in?

APOLLO

780 I will tell you, and I will answer correctly. Watch.
The mother is no parent of that which is called
her child, but only nurse of the new-planted seed
that grows. The parent is he who mounts. A stranger she
preserves a stranger's seed, if no god interfere.

785 I will show you proof of what I have explained. There can
be a father without any mother. There she stands,
the living witness, daughter of Olympian Zeus,
she who was never fostered in the dark of the womb

yet such a child as no goddess could bring to birth.
790   In all else, Pallas, as I best may understand,
I shall make great your city and its populace.
So I have brought this man to sit beside the hearth
of your house, to be your true friend for the rest of time,
so you shall win him, goddess, to fight by your side,
795   and among men to come this shall stand a strong bond
that his and your own people's children shall be friends.

ATHENE
Shall I assume that enough has now been said, and tell
the judges to render what they believe a true verdict?

800 CHORUS
Every arrow we had has been shot now. We wait
on their decision, to see how the case has gone.

ATHENE
So then. How shall I act correctly in your eyes?

805 APOLLO
You have heard what you have heard, and as you cast your votes,
good friends, respect in your hearts the oath that you have sworn.

ATHENE
If it please you, men of Attica, hear my decree
810   now, on this first case of bloodletting I have judged.
For Aegeus' population, this forevermore
shall be the ground where justices deliberate.
Here is the Hill of Ares, here the Amazons
encamped and built their shelters when they came in arms
815   for spite of Theseus, here they piled their rival towers
to rise, new city, and dare his city long ago,
and slew their beasts for Ares. So this rock is named
from then the Hill of Ares. Here the reverence
of citizens, their fear and kindred do-no-wrong
820   shall hold by day and in the blessing of night alike
all while the people do not muddy their own laws
with foul infusions. But if bright water you stain
with mud, you nevermore will find it fit to drink.
No anarchy, no rule of a single master. Thus
825   I advise my citizens to govern and to grace,
and not to cast fear utterly from your city. What
man who fears nothing at all is ever righteous? Such
be your just terrors, and you may deserve and have
salvation for your citadel, your land's defence,
830   such as is nowhere else found among men, neither
among the Scythians, nor the land that Pelops held.
I establish this tribunal. It shall be untouched

by money-making, grave but quick to wrath, watchful
to protect those who sleep, a sentry on the land.

835 These words I have unreeled are for my citizens,
advice into the future. All must stand upright
now, take each man his ballot in his hand, think on
his oath, and make his judgment. For my word is said.
CHORUS
840 I give you counsel by no means to disregard
this company. We can be a weight to crush your land.
APOLLO
I speak too. I command you to fear, and not
make void the yield of oracles from Zeus and me.
845 CHORUS
You honor bloody actions where you have no right.
The oracles you give shall be no longer clean.
APOLLO
My father's purposes are twisted then. For he
850 was appealed to by Ixion, the first murderer.
CHORUS
Talk! But for my part, if I do not win the case,
I shall come back to this land and it will feel my weight.
APOLLO
855 Neither among the elder nor the younger gods
have you consideration. I shall win this suit.
CHORUS
Such was your action in the house of Pheres. Then
you beguiled the Fates to let mortals go free from death.
860 APOLLO
Is it not right to do well by the man who shows
you worship, and above all when he stands in need?
CHORUS
You won the ancient goddesses over with wine
865 and so destroyed the orders of an elder time.
APOLLO
You shall not win the issue of this suit, but shall
be made to void your poison to no enemy's hurt.
CHORUS
870 Since you, a young god, would ride down my elder age,
I must stay here and listen to how the trial goes,
being yet uncertain to loose my anger on the state.
ATHENE
It is my task to render final judgment here.
875 This is a ballot for Orestes I shall cast.

There is no mother anywhere who gave me birth,
and, but for marriage, I am always for the male
with all my heart, and strongly on my father's side.
So, in a case where the wife has killed her husband, lord
880 of the house, her death shall not mean most to me. And if
the other votes are even, then Orestes wins.
You of the jurymen who have this duty assigned,
shake out the ballots from the vessels, with all speed.
ORESTES
885 Phoebus Apollo, what will the decision be?
CHORUS
Darkness of night, our mother, are you here to watch?
ORESTES
This is the end for me. The noose, or else the light.
890 CHORUS
Here our destruction, or our high duties confirmed.
APOLLO
Shake out the votes accurately, Athenian friends.
Be careful as you pick them up. Make no mistake.
895 In the lapse of judgment great disaster comes. The cast
of a single ballot has restored a house entire.
ATHENE
The man before us has escaped the charge of blood.
The ballots are in equal number for each side.
900 ORESTES
Pallas Athene, you have kept my house alive.
When I had lost the land of my fathers you gave me
a place to live. Among the Hellenes they shall say:
"A man of Argos lives again in the estates
905 of his father, all by grace of Pallas Athene, and
Apollo, and with them the all-ordaining god
the Savior"—who remembers my father's death, who looked
upon my mother's advocates, and rescues me.
I shall go home now, but before I go I swear
910 to this your country and to this your multitude
of people into all the bigness of time to be,
that never man who holds the helm of my state shall come
against your country in the ordered strength of spears,
but though I lie then in my grave, I still shall wreak
915 helpless bad luck and misadventure upon all
who stride across the oath that I have sworn: their ways
disconsolate make, their crossings full of evil
augury, so they shall be sorry that they moved.
But while they keep the upright way, and hold in high

920   regard the city of Pallas, and align their spears
to fight beside her, I shall be their gracious spirit.
And so farewell, you and your city's populace.
May you outwrestle and overthrow all those who come
against you, to your safety and your spears' success.

925   [*Exit. Exit also* APOLLO.]

CHORUS
Gods of the younger generation, you have ridden down
the laws of the elder time, torn them out of my hands.
I, disinherited, suffering, heavy with anger
930   shall let loose on the land
the vindictive poison
dripping deadly out of my heart upon the ground;
this from itself shall breed
cancer, the leafless, the barren
935   to strike, for the right, their low lands
and drag its smear of mortal infection on the ground.
What shall I do? Afflicted
I am mocked by these people.
I have borne what can not
940   be borne. Great the sorrow and the dishonor upon
the sad daughters of night.
ATHENE
Listen to me. I would not have you be so grieved.
For you have not been beaten. This was the result
945   of a fair ballot which was even. You were not
dishonored, but the luminous evidence of Zeus
was there, and he who spoke the oracle was he
who ordered Orestes so to act and not be hurt.
Do not be angry any longer with this land
950   nor bring the bulk of your hatred down on it, do not
render it barren of fruit, nor spill the dripping rain
of death in fierce and jagged lines to eat the seeds.
In complete honesty I promise you a place
of your own, deep hidden under ground that is yours by right
955   where you shall sit on shining chairs beside the hearth
to accept devotions offered by your citizens.
CHORUS
Gods of the younger generation, you have ridden down
the laws of the elder time, torn them out of my hands.
960   I, disinherited, suffering, heavy with anger
shall let loose on the land

-233-

the vindictive poison
dripping deadly out of my heart upon the ground;
this from itself shall breed
965   cancer, the leafless, the barren
to strike, for the right, their low lands
and drag its smear of mortal infection on the ground.
What shall I do? Afflicted
I am mocked by these people.
970   I have borne what can not
be borne. Great the sorrow and the dishonor upon
the sad daughters of night.

ATHENE

No, not dishonored. You are goddesses. Do not
975   in too much anger make this place of mortal men
uninhabitable. I have Zeus behind me. Do
we need to speak of that? I am the only god
who know the keys to where his thunderbolts are locked.
We do not need such, do we? Be reasonable
980   and do not from a reckless mouth cast on the land
spells that will ruin every thing which might bear fruit.
No. Put to sleep the bitter strength in the black wave
and live with me and share my pride of worship. Here
is a big land, and from it you shall win first fruits
985   in offerings for children and the marriage rite
for always. Then you will say my argument was good.

CHORUS

That they could treat me so!
I, the mind of the past, to be driven under the ground
990   out cast, like dirt!
The wind I breathe is fury and utter hate.
Earth, ah, earth
what is this agony that crawls under my ribs?
Night, hear me, o Night,
995   mother. They have wiped me out
and the hard hands of the gods
and their treacheries have taken my old rights away.

ATHENE

I will bear your angers. You are elder born than I
1000   and in that you are wiser far than I. Yet still
Zeus gave me too intelligence not to be despised.
If you go away into some land of foreigners,
I warn you, you will come to love this country. Time
in his forward flood shall ever grow more dignified
1005   for the people of this city. And you, in your place

of eminence beside Erechtheus in his house
shall win from female and from male processionals
more than all lands of men beside could ever give.
Only in this place that I haunt do not inflict
1010   your bloody stimulus to twist the inward hearts
of young men, raging in a fury not of wine,
nor, as if plucking the heart from fighting cocks,
engraft among my citizens that spirit of war
that turns their battle fury inward on themselves.
1015   No, let our wars range outward hard against the man
who has fallen horribly in love with high renown.
No true fighter I call the bird that fights at home.
Such life I offer you, and it is yours to take.
Do good, receive good, and be honored as the good
1020   are honored. Share our country, the beloved of god.

CHORUS

That they could treat me so!
I, the mind of the past, to be driven under the ground
out cast, like dirt!
1025   The wind I breathe is fury and utter hate.
Earth, ah, earth
what is this agony that crawls under my ribs?
Night, hear me, o Night,
mother. They have wiped me out
1030   and the hard hands of the gods
and their treacheries have taken my old rights away.

ATHENE

I will not weary of telling you all the good things
I offer, so that you can never say that you,
1035   an elder god, were driven unfriended from the land
by me in my youth, and by my mortal citizens.
But if you hold Persuasion has her sacred place
of worship, in the sweet beguilement of my voice,
then you might stay with us. But if you wish to stay
1040   then it would not be justice to inflict your rage
upon this city, your resentment or bad luck
to armies. Yours the baron's portion in this land
if you will, in all justice, with full privilege.

CHORUS

1045   Lady Athene, what is this place you say is mine?

ATHENE

A place free of all grief and pain. Take it for yours.

CHORUS

If I do take it, shall I have some definite powers?

1050 ATHENE
No household shall be prosperous without your will.
CHORUS
You will do this? You will really let me be so strong?
ATHENE
1055 So we shall straighten the lives of all who worship us.
CHORUS
You guarantee such honor for the rest of time?
ATHENE
I have no need to promise what I can not do.
1060 CHORUS
I think you will have your way with me. My hate is going.
ATHENE
Stay here, then. You will win the hearts of others, too.
CHORUS
1065 I will put a spell upon the land. What shall it be?
ATHENE
Something that has no traffic with evil success.
Let it come out of the ground, out of the sea's water,
and from the high air make the waft of gentle gales
1070 wash over the country in full sunlight, and the seed
and stream of the soil's yield and of the grazing beasts
be strong and never fail our people as time goes,
and make the human seed be kept alive. Make more
the issue of those who worship more your ways, for as
1075 the gardener works in love, so love I best of all
the unblighted generation of these upright men.
All such is yours for granting. In the speech and show
and pride of battle, I myself shall not endure
this city's eclipse in the estimation of mankind.
1080 CHORUS
I accept this home at Athene's side.
I shall not forget the cause
of this city, which Zeus all powerful and Ares
rule, stronghold of divinities,
1085 glory of Hellene gods, their guarded altar.
So with forecast of good
I speak this prayer for them
that the sun's bright magnificence shall break out wave
on wave of all the happiness
1090 life can give, across their land.
ATHENE
Here are my actions. In all good will
toward these citizens I establish in power

spirits who are large, difficult to soften.
1095   To them is given the handling entire
of men's lives. That man
who has not felt the weight of their hands
takes the strokes of life, knows not whence, not why,
for crimes wreaked in past generations
1100   drag him before these powers. Loud his voice
but the silent doom
hates hard, and breaks him to dust.

CHORUS
Let there blow no wind that wrecks the trees.
1105   I pronounce words of grace.
Nor blaze of heat blind the blossoms of grown plants, nor
cross the circles of its right
place. Let no barren deadly sickness creep and kill.
Flocks fatten. Earth be kind
1110   to them, with double fold of fruit
in time appointed for its yielding. Secret child
of earth, her hidden wealth, bestow
blessing and surprise of gods.

ATHENE
1115   Strong guard of our city, hear you these
and what they portend? Fury is a high queen
of strength even among the immortal gods
and the undergods, and for humankind
their work is accomplished, absolute, clear:
1120   for some, singing; for some, life dimmed
in tears; theirs the disposition.

CHORUS
Death of manhood cut down
before its prime I forbid:
1125   girls' grace and glory find
men to live life with them.
Grant, you who have the power.
And o, steering spirits of law,
goddesses of destiny,
1130   sisters from my mother, hear;
in all houses implicate,
in all time heavy of hand
on whom your just arrest befalls,
august among goddesses, bestow.

1135 ATHENE
It is my glory to hear how these
generosities

are given my land. I admire the eyes
of Persuasion, who guided the speech of my mouth

1140 toward these, when they were reluctant and wild.
Zeus, who guides men's speech in councils, was too
strong; and my ambition
for good wins out in the whole issue.

CHORUS

1145 This my prayer: Civil War
fattening on men's ruin shall
not thunder in our city. Let
not the dry dust that drinks
the black blood of citizens

1150 through passion for revenge
and bloodshed for bloodshed
be given our state to prey upon.
Let them render grace for grace.
Let love be their common will;

1155 let them hate with single heart.
Much wrong in the world thereby is healed.

ATHENE

Are they taking thought to discover that road
where speech goes straight?

1160 In the terror upon the faces of these
I see great good for our citizens.
While with good will you hold in high honor
these spirits, their will shall be good, as you steer
your city, your land

1165 on an upright course clear through to the end.

CHORUS

Farewell, farewell. High destiny shall be yours
by right. Farewell, citizens
seated near the throne of Zeus,

1170 beloved by the maiden he loves,
civilized as years go by,
sheltered under Athene's wings,
grand even in her father's sight.

ATHENE

1175 Goddesses, farewell. Mine to lead, as these
attend us, to where
by the sacred light new chambers are given.
Go then. Sped by majestic sacrifice
from these, plunge beneath the ground. There hold

1180 off what might hurt the land; pour in
the city's advantage, success in the end.

You, children of Cranaus, you who keep
the citadel, guide these guests of the state.
For good things given,
1185   your hearts' desire be for good to return.

CHORUS

Farewell and again farewell, words spoken twice over,
all who by this citadel,
mortal men, spirits divine,
1190   hold the city of Pallas, grace
this my guestship in your land.
Life will give you no regrets.

ATHENE

Well said. I assent to all the burden of your prayers,
1195   and by the light of flaring torches now attend
your passage to the deep and subterranean hold,
as by us walk those women whose high privilege
it is to guard my image. Flower of all the land
of Theseus, let them issue now, grave companies,
1200   maidens, wives, elder women, in processional.
In the investiture of purple stained robes
dignify them, and let the torchlight go before
so that the kindly company of these within
our ground may shine in the future of strong men to come.

1205   CHORUS [*by the women who have been forming for processional*]

Home, home, o high, o aspiring
Daughters of Night, aged children, in blithe processional.
Bless them, all here, with silence.

In the primeval dark of earth-hollows
1210   held in high veneration with rights sacrificial
bless them, all people, with silence.

Gracious be, wish what the land wishes,
follow, grave goddesses, flushed in the flamesprung
torchlight gay on your journey.
1215   Singing all follow our footsteps.

There shall be peace forever between these people
of Pallas and their guests. Zeus the all seeing
met with Destiny to confirm it.
Singing all follow our footsteps.

1220   [*Exeunt omnes, in procession.*]

5. OEDIPUS REX
(431 BCE)

Sophocles

(trans. by Dudley Fitts and Robert Fitzgerald)

Sophocles (c. 496–406 BCE) was the most successful and prolific of ancient Greek dramatists. The tragedy of Oedipus Rex *(431 BCE) is the best known of his 123 plays (only seven are extant) and was cited as the model of drama by Aristotle in his* Poetics. *Thematically, it is the first part of an unofficial trilogy, along with* Oedipus at Colonus *(409 BCE) and* Antigone *(441 BCE), tracing the tragic fate of Oedipus and his heirs. Destined to slay his father and marry his mother, Oedipus attempts to elude the prophecies while unwittingly fulfilling them. His tragedy raises questions of fate, free will and human responsibility, and demonstrates heroic honesty and endurance.*

CHARACTERS

OEDIPUS
A PRIEST
CREON
TEIRESIAS
IOCASTÊ
MESSENGER
SHEPHERD OF LAÏOS
SECOND MESSENGER
CHORUS OF THEBAN ELDERS

[SCENE: *Before the palace of* OEDIPUS, *King of Thebes. A central door and two lateral doors open onto a platform which runs the length of the façade. On the platform, right and left, are altars; and three steps lead down into the "orchestra," or chorus-ground. At the beginning of the action these steps are crowded by Suppliants who have brought branches and chaplets of olive leaves and who lie in various attitudes of despair.* OEDIPUS *enters.*]

PROLOGUE

OEDIPUS: My children, generations of the living
    In the line of Kadmos,[1] nursed at his ancient hearth:
    Why have you strewn yourselves before these altars
    In supplication, with your boughs and garlands?
5   The breath of incense rises from the city
    With a sound of prayer and lamentation.
                           Children,
    I would not have you speak through messengers,
    And therefore I have come myself to hear you—
10   I, Oedipus, who bear the famous name.
    (To a priest.) You, there, since you are eldest in the company,
    Speak for them all, tell me what preys upon you,
    Whether you come in dread, or crave some blessing:
    Tell me, and never doubt that I will help you
15   In every way I can; I should be heartless
    Were I not moved to find you suppliant here.
PRIEST: Great Oedipus, O powerful King of Thebes!
    You see how all the ages of our people
    Cling to your altar steps: here are boys
20   Who can barely stand alone, and here are priests
    By weight of age, as I am a priest of God,
    And young men chosen from those yet unmarried;
    As for the others, all that multitude,
    They wait with olive chaplets in the squares,
25   At the two shrines of Pallas,[2] and where Apollo[3]
    Speaks in the glowing embers.
                      Your own eyes
    Must tell you: Thebes is in her extremity
    And cannot lift her head from the surge of death.
30   A rust consumes the buds and fruits of the earth;
    The herds are sick; children die unborn,
    And labor is vain. The god of plague and pyre
    Raids like detestable lightning through the city,
    And all the house of Kadmos is laid waste,
35   All emptied, and all darkened: Death alone
    Battens upon the misery of Thebes.
    You are not one of the immortal gods, we know;
    Yet we have come to you to make our prayer
    As to the man of all men best in adversity

---

[1] **Kadmos** mythical founder of Thebes
[2] **Pallas** Athena, goddess of wisdom, protectress of Athens
[3] **Apollo** god of fight and healing

40   And wisest in the ways of God. You saved us
      From the Sphinx,[4] that flinty singer, and the tribute
      We paid to her so long; yet you were never
      Better informed than we, nor could we teach you:
      It was some god breathed in you to set us free.

45   Therefore, O mighty King, we turn to you:
      Find us our safety, find us a remedy,
      Whether by counsel of the gods or the men.
      A king of wisdom tested in the past
      Can act in a time of troubles, and act well.
50   Noblest of men, restore
      Life to your city! Think how all men call you
      Liberator for your triumph long ago;
      Ah, when your years of kingship are remembered,
      Let them not say *We rose, but later fell*—
55   Keep the State from going down in the storm!
      Once, years ago, with happy augury,
      You brought us fortune; be the same again!
      No man questions your power to rule the land:
      But rule over men, not over a dead city!
60   Ships are only hulls, citadels are nothing,
      When no life moves in the empty passageways.
OEDIPUS: Poor children! You may be sure I know
      All that you longed for in your coming here.
      I know that you are deathly sick; and yet,
65   Sick as you are, not one is as sick as I.
      Each of you suffers in himself alone
      His anguish, not another's; but my spirit
      Groans for the city, for myself, for you.

      I was not sleeping, you are not waking me.
70   No, I have been in tears for a long while
      And in my restless thought walked many ways.
      In all my search, I found one helpful course,
      And that I have taken: I have sent Creon,
      Son of Menoikeus, brother of the Queen,
75   To Delphi, Apollo's place of revelation,
      To learn there, if he can,

---

[4] **Sphinx** a monster (body of a lion, wings of a bird, face of a woman) who asked the riddle "What goes on four legs in the morning, two at noon, and three in the evening?" and who killed those who could not answer. When Oedipus responded correctly that man crawls on all foyers in infancy, walks upright its maturity, and uses a staff in old age, the Sphinx destroyed herself.

What act or pledge of mine may save the city.
I have counted the days, and now, this very day,
I am troubled, for he has overstayed his time.
80   What is he doing? He has been gone too long.
Yet whenever he comes back, I should do ill
To scant whatever hint the god may give.
PRIEST: It is a timely promise. At this instant
They tell me Creon is here.
85   OEDIPUS: O Lord Apollo!
May his news be fair as his face is radiant!
PRIEST: It could not be otherwise: he is crowned with bay,
The chaplet is thick with berries.
OEDIPUS: We shall soon know;
90   He is near enough to hear us now.

[*Enter* CREON.]
                                        O Prince:
Brother: son of Menoikeus:
What answer do you bring us from the god?
CREON: It is favorable. I can tell you, great afflictions
95   Will turn out well, if they are taken well.
OEDIPUS: What was the oracle? These vague words
Leave me still hanging between hope and fear.
CREON: Is it your pleasure to hear me with all these
Gathered around us? I am prepared to speak,
100   But should we not go in?
OEDIPUS: Let them all hear it.
It is for them I suffer, more than myself.
CREON: Then I will tell you what I heard at Delphi.

In plain words
105   The god commands us to expel from the land of Thebes
An old defilement that it seems we shelter.
It is a deathly thing, beyond expiation.
We must not let it feed up on us longer.
OEDIPUS: What defilement? How shall we rid ourselves of it?
110   CREON: By exile or death, blood for blood. It was
Murder that brought the plague-wind on the city.
OEDIPUS: Murder of whom? Surely the god has named him?
CREON: My lord: long ago Laïos was our king,
Before you came to govern us.
115   OEDIPUS: I know;
I learned of him from others; I never saw him.

CREON: He was murdered; and Apollo commands us now
    To take revenge upon whoever killed him.
OEDIPUS: Upon whom? Where are they? Where shall we find a clue
120   To solve that crime, after so many years?
CREON: Here in this land, he said.

                                If we make enquiry,
    We may touch things that otherwise escape us.
OEDIPUS: Tell me: Was Laïos murdered in his house,
125   Or in the fields, or in some foreign country?
CREON: He said he planned to make a pilgrimage.
    He did not come home again.
OEDIPUS: And was there no one,
    No witness, no companion, to tell what happened?
130 CREON: They were all killed but one, and he got away
    So frightened that he could remember one thing only.
OEDIPUS: What was that one thing? One may be the key
    To everything, if we resolve to use it.
CREON: He said that a band of highwaymen attacked them,
135   Outnumbered them, and overwhelmed the King.
OEDIPUS: Strange, that a highwayman should be so daring—
    Unless some faction here bribed him to do it.
CREON: We thought of that. But after Laïos' death
    New troubles arose and we had no avenger.
140 OEDIPUS: What troubles could prevent your hunting down the killers?
CREON: The riddling Sphinx's song
    Made us deaf to all mysteries but her own.
OEDIPUS: Then once more I must bring what is dark to light.
    It is most fitting that Apollo shows,
145   As you do, this compunction for the dead.
    You shall see how I stand by you, as I should,
    To avenge the city and the city's god,
    And not as though it were for some distant friend,
    But for my own sake, to be rid of evil.
150   Whoever killed King Laïos might—who knows?—
    Decide at any moment to kill me as well.
    By avenging the murdered king I protect myself.
    Come, then, my children: leave the altar steps,
    Lift up your olive boughs!
155   One of you go
    And summon the people of Kadmos to gather here.
    I will do all that I can; you may tell them that.

[*Exit a Page.*]

    So, with the help of God,
    We shall be saved—or else indeed we are lost.
160   PRIEST: Let us rise, children. It was for this we came,
    And now the King has promised it himself
    Phoibos[5] has sent us an oracle; may he descend
    Himself to save us and cave out the plague.

[*Exeunt* OEDIPUS *and* CREON *into the palace by the central door. The* PRIEST *and the Suppliants disperse right and left. After a short pause the* CHORUS *enters the orchestra.*]

PÁRODOS

STROPHE 1

    CHORUS: What is God singing in his profound
165   Delphi of gold and shadow?
    What oracle for Thebes, the sunwhipped city?
    Fear unjoints me, the roots of my heart tremble.
    Now I remember, O Healer, your power, and wonder;
    Will you send doom like a sudden cloud, or weave it
170   Like nightfall of the past?
    Speak, speak to us, issue of holy sound:
    Dearest to our expectancy: be tender!

ANTISTROPHE 1

    Let me pray to Athenê, the immortal daughter of Zeus,
    And to Artemis her sister
175   Who keeps her famous throne in the market ring,
    And to Apollo, bowman at the far butts of heaven—

    O gods, descend! Like three streams leap against
    The fires of our grief, the fires of darkness;
    Be swift to bring us rest!

180   As in the old time from the brilliant house
    Of air you stepped to save us, come again!

---

[5] **Phoibos** Phoebus Apollo, the sun god

STROPHE 2

Now our afflictions have no end,
Now all our stricken host lies down
And no man fights off death with his mind;
185   The noble plowland bears no grain,
And groaning mothers cannot bear—
See, how our lives like birds take wing,
Like sparks that fly when a fire soars,
To the shore of the god of evening.

ANTISTROPHE 2

190   The plague burns on, it is pitiless
Though pallid children laden with death
Lie unwept in the stony ways,
And old gray women by every path
Flock to the strand about the altars

195   There to strike their breasts and cry
Worship of Phoibos in wailing prayers:
Be kind, God's golden child!

STROPHE 3

There are no swords in this attack by fire,
No shields, but we are ringed with cries.
200   Send the besieger plunging from our homes
Into the vast sea-room of the Atlantic
Or into the waves that form eastward of Thrace—
For the day ravages what the night spares—

Destroy our enemy, lord of the thunder!
205   Let him be riven by lightning from heaven!

ANTISTROPHE 3

Phoibos Apollo, stretch the sun's bowstring,
That golden cord, until it sing for us,
Flashing arrows in heaven!
                Artemis, Huntress,
210   Race with flaring lights upon our mountains!

O scarlet god, O golden-banded brow,
O Theban Bacchus[6] in a storm of Maenads,[7]

[*Enter* OEDIPUS, *center.*]

Whirl upon Death, that all the Undying hate!
Come with blinding cressets, come in joy!

SCENE I

215   OEDIPUS: Is this your prayer? It may be answered. Come,
         Listen to me, act as the crisis demands,
         And you shall have relief from all these evils.
         Until now I was a stranger to this tale,
         As I had been a stranger to the crime.
220   Could I track down the murderer without a clue?
         But now, friends,
         As one who became a citizen after the murder,
         I make this proclamation to all Thebans:
         If any man knows by whose hand Laïos, son of Labdakos,
225   Met his death, I direct that man to tell me everything,
         No matter what he fears for having so long withheld it.
         Let it stand as promised that no further trouble
         Will come to him, but he may leave the land in safety.

         Moreover: If anyone knows the murderer to be foreign,
230   Let him not keep silent: he shall have his reward from me.
         However, if he does conceal it; if any man
         Fearing for his friend or for himself disobeys this edict,
         Hear what I propose to do:

         I solemnly forbid the people of this country,
235   Where power and throne are mine, ever to receive that man
         Or speak to him, no matter who he is, or let him
         Join in sacrifice, lustration, or in prayer.
         I decree that he be driven from every house,

         Being, as he is, corruption itself to us: the Delphic
240   Voice of Zeus has pronounced this revelation.
         Thus I associate myself with the oracle
         And take the side of the murdered king.

---

[6] **Bacchos** Dionysos, god of wine, thus scarlet-faced
[7] **Maenads** Dionysos's female attendants

As for the criminal, I pray to God—
Whether it be a lurking thief, or one of a number—
245   I pray that that man's life be consumed in evil and wretchedness.
And as for me, this curse applies no less
If it should turn out that the culprit is my guest here,
Sharing my hearth.
               You have heard the penalty.
250   I lay it on you now to attend to this
For my sake, for Apollo's, for the sick
Sterile city that heaven has abandoned.
Suppose the oracle had given you no command:
Should this defilement go uncleansed for ever?
255   You should have found the murderer: your king,
A noble king, had been destroyed!
               Now I,
Having the power that he held before me,
Having his bed, begetting children there
260   Upon his wife, as he would have, had he lived—
Their son would have been my children's brother,
If Laïos had had luck in fatherhood!
(But surely ill luck rushed upon his reign)—
I say I take the son's part, just as though
265   I were his son, to press the fight for him
And see it won! I'll find the hand that brought
Death to Labdakos' and Polydoros' child,
Heir of Kadmos' and Agenor's line.
And as for those who fail me,
270   May the gods deny them the fruit of the earth,
Fruit of the womb, and may they rot utterly!
Let them be wretched as we are wretched, and worse!

For you, for loyal Thebans, and for all
Who find my actions right, I pray the favor
275   Of justice, and of all the immortal gods.
CHORAGOS:[8] Since I am under oath, my lord, I swear
I did not do the murder, I cannot name
The murderer. Might not the oracle
That has ordained the search tell where to find him?
280   OEDIPUS: An honest question. But no man in the world
Can make the gods do more than the gods will.
CHORAGOS: There is one last expedient—

---

[8] **Choragos** leader of the Chorus

OEDIPUS: Tell me what it is.
 Though it seem slight, you must not hold it back.
285 CHORAGOS: A lord clairvoyant to the lord Apollo,
  As we all know, is the skilled Teiresias.
  One might learn much about this from him, Oedipus.
 OEDIPUS: I am not wasting time:
  Creon spoke of this, and I have sent for him—
290 Twice, in fact; it is strange that he is not here.
 CHORAGOS: The other matter—that old report—seems useless.
 OEDIPUS: Tell me. I am interested in all reports.
 CHORAGOS: The King was said to have been killed by highwaymen.
 OEDIPUS: I know. But we have no witnesses to that.
295 CHORAGOS: If the killer can feel a particle of dread,
  Your curse will bring him out of hiding!
 OEDIPUS: No.
  The man who dared that act will fear no curse.

[*Enter the blind seer* TEIRESIAS, *led by a Page.*]

 CHORAGOS: But there is one man who may detect the criminal.
300 This is Teiresias, this is the holy prophet
  In whom, alone of all men, truth was born.
 OEDIPUS: Teiresias: seer: student of mysteries,
  Of all that's taught and all that no man tells,
  Secrets of Heaven and secrets of the earth:
305 Blind though you are, you know the city lies
  Sick with plague; and from this plague, my lord,
  We find that you alone can guard or save us.
  Possibly you did not hear the messengers?
  Apollo, when we sent to him,
310 Sent us back word that this great pestilence
  Would lift, but only if we established clearly
  The identity of those who murdered Laïos.
  They must be killed or exiled.
          Can you use
315 Birdflight or any art of divination
  To purify yourself, and Thebes, and me
  From this contagion? We are in your hands.
  There is no fairer duty
  Than that of helping others in distress.
320 TEIRESIAS: How dreadful knowledge of the truth can be
  When there's no help in truth! I knew this well,
  But did not act on it: else I should not have come.
 OEDIPUS: What is troubling you? Why are your eyes so cold?

TEIRESIAS: Let me go home. Bear your own fate, and I'll
325   Bear mine. It is better so: trust what I say.
OEDIPUS: What you say is ungracious and unhelpful
        To your native country. Do not refuse to speak.
TEIRESIAS: When it comes to speech, your own is neither temperate
        Nor opportune. I wish to be more prudent.
330   OEDIPUS: In God's name, we all beg you—
TEIRESIAS: You are all ignorant.
        No; I will never tell you what I know.
        Now it is my misery; then, it would be yours.
OEDIPUS: What! You do know something, and will not tell us?
335   You would betray us all and wreck the State?
TEIRESIAS: I do not intend to torture myself, or you.
        Why persist in asking? You will not persuade me.
OEDIPUS: What a wicked man you are! You'd try a stone's
        Patience! Out with it! Have you no feeling at all?
340   TEIRESIAS: You call me unfeeling. If you could only see
        The nature of your feelings . . .
OEDIPUS: Why,
        Who would not feel as I do? Who could endure
        Your arrogance toward the city?
345   TEIRESIAS: What does it matter!
        Whether I speak or not, it is bound to come
OEDIPUS: Then, if "it" is bound to come, you are bound to tell me.
TEIRESIAS: No, I will not go on. Rage as you please.
OEDIPUS: Rage? Why not!
350   And I'll tell you what I think:
        You planned it, you had it done, you all but
        Killed him with your own hands: if you had eyes,
        I'd say the crime was yours, and yours alone.
TEIRESIAS: So? I charge you, then,
355   Abide by the proclamation you have made.
        From this day forth
        Never speak again to these men or to me;
        You yourself are the pollution of this country.
OEDIPUS: You dare say that! Can you possibly think you have
360   Some way of going free, after such insolence?
TEIRESIAS: I have gone free. It is the truth sustains me.
OEDIPUS: Who taught you shamelessness? It was not your craft.
TEIRESIAS: You did. You made me speak. I did not want to.
OEDIPUS: Speak what? Let me hear it again more clearly.
365   TEIRESIAS: Was it not clear before? Are you tempting me?
OEDIPUS: I did not understand it. Say it again.
TEIRESIAS: I say that you are the murderer whom you seek.

OEDIPUS: Now twice you have spat out infamy. You'll pay for it!

TEIRESIAS: Would you care for more? Do you wish to be really angry?

370 OEDIPUS: Say what you will. Whatever you say is worthless.

TEIRESIAS: I say you live in hideous shame with those
    Most dear to you. You cannot see the evil.

OEDIPUS: It seems you can go on mouthing like this for ever.

TEIRESIAS: I can, if there is power in truth.

375 OEDIPUS: There is:
    But not for you, not for you,
    You sightless, witless, senseless, mad old man!

TEIRESIAS: You are the madman. There is no one here
    Who will not curse you soon, as you curse me.

380 OEDIPUS: You child of endless night! You cannot hurt me
    Or any other man who sees the sun.

TEIRESIAS: True: it is not from me your fate will come.
    That lies within Apollo's competence,
    As it is his concern.

385 OEDIPUS: Tell me:
    Are you speaking for Creon, or for yourself?

TEIRESIAS: Creon is no threat. You weave your own doom.

OEDIPUS: Wealth, power, craft of statesmanship!
    · Kingly position, everywhere admired!

390   What savage envy is stored up against these,
    If Creon, whom I trusted, Creon my friend,
    For this great office which the city once
    Put in my hands unsought—if for this power
    Creon desires in secret to destroy me!

395   He has brought this decrepit fortune-teller, this
    Collector of dirty pennies, this prophet fraud—
    Why, he is no more clairvoyant than I am!
                          Tell us:
    Has your mystic mummery ever approached the truth?

400   When that hellcat the Sphinx was performing here,
    What help were you to these people?
    Her magic was not for the first man who came along:
    It demanded a real exorcist. Your birds—
    What good were they? or the gods, for the matter of that?

405   But I came by,
    Oedipus, the simple man, who knows nothing—
    I thought it out for myself, no birds helped me!
    And this is the man you think you can destroy,
    That you may be close to Creon, when he's king!

410   Well, you and your friend Creon, it seems to me,

Will suffer most. If you were not an old man,
You would have paid already for your plot.
CHORAGOS: We cannot see that his words or yours
Have spoken except in anger, Oedipus,

415   And of anger we have no need. How can God's will
Be accomplished best? That is what most concerns us.
TEIRESIAS: You are a king. But where argument's concerned
I am your man, as much a king as you.
I am not your servant, but Apollo's.

420   I have no need of Creon to speak for me.

Listen to me. You mock my blindness, do you?
But I say that you, with both your eyes, are blind:
You cannot see the wretchedness of your life,
Not in whose house you live, no, nor with whom.

425   Who are your father and mother? Can you tell me?
You do not even know the blind wrongs
That you have done them, on earth and in the world below.
But the double lash of your parents' curse will whip you
Out of this land some day, with only night

430   Upon your precious eyes.
Your cries then—where will they not be heard?
What fastness of Kithairon⁹ will not echo them?
And that bridal-descant of yours—you'll know it then,
The song they sang when you came here to Thebes

435   And found your misguided berthing.
All this, and more, that you cannot guess at now,
Will bring you to yourself among your children.
Be angry, then. Curse Creon. Curse my words.
I tell you, no man that walks upon the earth

440   Shall be rooted out more horribly than you.
OEDIPUS: Am I to bear this from him?—Damnation
Take you! Out of this place! Out of my sight!
TEIRESIAS: I would not have come at all if you had not asked me.
OEDIPUS: Could I have told that you'd talk nonsense, that

445   You'd come here to make a fool of yourself, and of me?
TEIRESIAS: A fool? Your parents thought me sane enough.
OEDIPUS: My parents again!—Wait: who were my parents?
TEIRESIAS: This day will give you a father, and break your heart.
OEDIPUS: Your infantile riddles! Your damned abracadabra!

450   TEIRESIAS: You were a great man once at solving riddles.
OEDIPUS: Mock me with that if you like; you will find it true.

---

⁹ **fastness of Kithairon** stronghold in a mountain near Thebes

TEIRESIAS: It was true enough. It brought about your ruin.

OEDIPUS: But if it saved this town.

TEIRESIAS *(to the Page):* Boy, give me your hand.

455 OEDIPUS: Yes, boy; lead him away.

—While you are here

We can do nothing. Go; leave us in peace.

TEIRESIAS: I will go when I have said what I have to say.

How can you hurt me? And I tell you again:

460 The man you have been looking for all this time,

The damned man, the murderer of Laïos,

That man is in Thebes. To your mind he is foreignborn,

But it will soon be shown that he is a Theban,

A revelation that will fail to please.

465 A blind man,

Who has his eyes now; a penniless man, who is rich now;

And he will go tapping the strange earth with his staff;

To the children with whom he lives now he will be

Brother and father—the very same; to her

470 Who bore him, son and husband—the very same

Who came to his father's bed, wet with his father's blood.

Enough. Go think that over.

If later you find error in what I have said,

You may say that I have no skill in prophecy.

[*Exit* TEIRESIAS, *led by his Page.* OEDIPUS *goes into the palace.*]

ODE I

STROPHE 1

475 CHORUS: The Delphic stone of prophecies

Remembers ancient regicide

And a still bloody hand.

That killer's hour of flight has come.

He must be stronger than riderless

480 Coursers of untiring wind,

For the son of Zeus[10] armed with his father's thunder

Leaps in lightning after him;

And the Furies[11] follow him, the sad Furies.

---

[10] **son of Zeus** Apollo

[11] **Furies** avenging deities

ANTISTROPHE 1

485

Holy Parnossos' peak of snow
Flashes and blinds that secret man,
That all shall hunt him down:
Though he may roam the forest shade
Like a bull gone wild from pasture
To rage through glooms of stone.

490

Doom comes down on him; flight will not avail him;
For the world's heart calls him desolate,
And the immortal Furies follow, for ever follow.

STROPHE 2

But now a wilder thing is heard
From the old man skilled at hearing Fate in the wingbeat of a bird.

495

Bewildered as a blown bird, my soul hovers and cannot find
Foothold in this debate, or any reason or rest of mind.
But no man ever brought—none can bring
Proof of strife between Thebes' royal house,
Labdakos' line,[12] and the son of Polybos;[13]

500

And never until now has any man brought word
Of Laïos' dark death staining Oedipus the King.

ANTISTROPHE 2

Divine Zeus and Apollo hold
Perfect intelligence alone of all tales ever told;
And well though this diviner works, he works in his own night;

505

No man can judge that rough unknown or trust in second sight,
For wisdom changes hands among the wise.
Shall I believe my great lord criminal,
At a raging word that a blind old man let fall?
I saw him, when the carrion woman faced him of old,

510

Prove his heroic mind! These evil words are lies.

SCENE II

CREON: Men of Thebes:
   I am told that heavy accusations
   Have been brought against me by King Oedipus.
   I am not the kind of man to bear this tamely.

---

[12] **Labdakos' line** family of Laïos
[13] **son of Polybos** Oedipus (so the Chorus believes)

515   If in these present difficulties
      He holds me accountable for any harm to him
      Through anything I have said or done—why, then,
      I do not value life in this dishonor.
      It is not as though this rumor touched upon
520   Some private indiscretion. The matter is grave.
      The fact is that I am being called disloyal
      To the State, to my fellow citizens, to my friends.
CHORAGOS: He may have spoken in anger, not from his mind.
CREON: But did you hear him say I was the one
525   Who seduced the old prophet into lying?
CHORAGOS: The thing was said; I do not know how seriously.
CREON: But you were watching him! Were his eyes steady?
      Did he look like a man in his right mind?
CHORAGOS: I do not know.
530   I cannot judge the behavior of great men.
      But here is the King himself

[*Enter* OEDIPUS.]

OEDIPUS: So you dared come back.
      Why? How brazen of you to come to my house,
      You murderer!
535   Do you think I do not know
      That you plotted to kill me, plotted to steal my throne?
      Tell me, in God's name: am I coward, a fool,
      That you should dream you could accomplish this?
      A fool who could not see your slippery game?
540   A coward, not to fight back when I saw it?
      You are the fool, Creon, are you not? hoping
      Without support or friends to get a throne?
      Thrones may be won or bought: you could do neither.
CREON: Now listen to me. You have talked; let me talk, too.
545   You cannot judge unless you know the facts.
OEDIPUS: You speak well: there is one fact; but I find it hard
      To learn from the deadliest enemy I have.
CREON: That above all I must dispute with you.
OEDIPUS: That above all I will not hear you deny.
550 CREON: If you think there is anything good in being stubborn
      Against all reason, then I say you are wrong.
OEDIPUS: If you think a man can sin against his own kind
      And not be punished for it, I say you are mad.
CREON: I agree. But tell me: what have I done to you?
555 OEDIPUS: You advised me to send for that wizard, did you not?

CREON: I did. I should do it again.

OEDIPUS: Very well. Now tell me:
       How long has it been since Laïos—

CREON: What of Laïos?

560   OEDIPUS: Since he vanished in that onset by the road?

CREON: It was long ago, a long time.

OEDIPUS: And this prophet,
       Was he practicing here then?

CREON: He was; and with honor, as now.

565   OEDIPUS: Did he speak of me at that time?

CREON: He never did;
       At least, not when I was present.

OEDIPUS: But . . . the enquiry?
       I suppose you held one?

570   CREON: We did, but we learned nothing.

OEDIPUS: Why did the prophet not speak against me then?

CREON: I do not know; and I am the kind of man
       Who holds his tongue when he has no facts to go on.

OEDIPUS: There's one fact that you know, and you could tell it.

575   CREON: What fact is that? If I know it, you shall have it.

OEDIPUS: If he were not involved with you, he could not say
       That it was I who murdered Laïos.

CREON: If he says that, you are the one that knows it!—
       But now it is my turn to question you.

580   OEDIPUS: Put your questions. I am no murderer.

CREON: First, then: You married my sister?

OEDIPUS: I married your sister.

CREON: And you rule the kingdom equally with her?

OEDIPUS: Everything that she wants she has from me.

585   CREON: And I am the third, equal to both of you?

OEDIPUS: That is why I call you a bad friend.

CREON: No. Reason it out, as I have done.
       Think of this first. Would any sane man prefer
       Power, with all a king's anxieties,

590   To that same power and the grace of sleep?
       Certainly not I.
       I have never longed for the king's power—only his rights.
       Would any wise man differ from me in this?
       As matters stand, I have my way in everything

595   With your consent, and no responsibilities.
       If I were king, I should be a slave to policy.
       How could I desire a scepter more
       Than what is now mine—untroubled influence?
       No, I have not gone mad: I need no honors.

600 Except those with the perquisites I have now.
I am welcome everywhere; every man salutes me,
And those who want your favor seek my ear,
Since I know how to manage what they ask.
Should I exchange this ease for that anxiety?
605 Besides, no sober mind is treasonable.
I hate anarchy
And never would deal with any man who likes it.

Test what I have said. Go to the priestess
At Delphi, ask if I quoted her correctly.
610 And as for this other thing: if I am found
Guilty of treason with Teiresias,
Then sentence me to death! You have my word
It is a sentence I should cast my vote for—
But not without evidence!
615   You do wrong
When you take good men for bad, bad men for good.
A true friend thrown aside—why, life itself
Is not more precious!
                   In time you will know this well:
620 For time, and time alone, will show the just man,
Though scoundrels are discovered in a day.
CHORAGOS: This is well said, and a prudent man would ponder it.
Judgments too quickly formed are dangerous.
OEDIPUS: But is he not quick in his duplicity?
625 And shall I not be quick to parry him?
Would you have me stand still, hold my peace, and let
This man win everything, through my inaction?
CREON: And you want—what is it, then? To banish me?
OEDIPUS: No, not exile. It is your death I want,
630 So that all the world may see what treason means.
CREON: You will persist, then? You will not believe me?
OEDIPUS: How can I believe you?
CREON: Then you are a fool.
OEDIPUS: To save myself?
635 CREON: In justice, think of me.
OEDIPUS: You are evil incarnate.
CREON: But suppose that you are wrong?
OEDIPUS: Still I must rule.
CREON: But not if you rule badly.
640 OEDIPUS: O city, city!
CREON: It is my city, too!

CHORAGOS: Now, my lords, be still. I see the Queen,
    Iocastê, coming from her palace chambers;
    And it is time she came, for the sake of you both.
645   This dreadful quarrel can be resolved through her.

[*Enter* IOCASTÊ.]

IOCASTÊ: Poor foolish men, what wicked din is this?
    With Thebes sick to death, is it not shameful
    That you should rake some private quarrel up?
650   (*To* OEDIPUS.) Come into the house.
                      — And you, Creon, go now:
    Let us have no more of this tumult over nothing.
CREON: Nothing? No, sister: what your husband plans for me
    Is one of two great evils: exile or death.
655 OEDIPUS: He is right.
                  Why, woman, I have caught him squarely
    Plotting against my life.
CREON: No! Let me die
    Accurst if ever I have wished you harm!
660 IOCASTÊ: Ah, believe it, Oedipus!
    In the name of the gods, respect this oath of his
    For my sake, for the sake of these people here!

STROPHE 1

CHORAGOS: Open your mind to her, my lord. Be ruled by her, I beg you!
OEDIPUS: What would you have me do?
665 CHORAGOS: Respect Creon's word. He has never spoken like a fool,
    And now he has sworn an oath.
OEDIPUS: You know what you ask?
CHORAGOS: I do.
OEDIPUS: Speak on, then.
670 CHORAGOS: A friend so sworn should not be baited so,
    In blind malice, and without final proof.
OEDIPUS: You are aware, I hope, that what you say
    Means death for me, or exile at the least.

STROPHE 2

CHORAGOS: No, I swear by Helios,[14] first in Heaven!
675   May I die friendless and accurst,
    The worst of deaths, if ever I meant that!
        It is the withering fields

---

[14] Helios sun god

That hurt my sick heart:
Must we bear all these ills,
680   And now your bad blood as well?
OEDIPUS: Then let him go. And let me die, if I must,
    Or be driven by him in shame from the land of Thebes.
    It is your unhappiness, and not his talk,
    That touches me.
685   As for him—
    Wherever he is, I will hate him as long as I live.
CREON: Ugly in yielding, as you were ugly in rage!
    Natures like yours chiefly torment themselves.
OEDIPUS: Can you not go? Can you not leave me?
690 CREON: I can.
    You do not know me; but the city knows me,
    And in its eyes I am just, if not in yours.

[*Exit* CREON.]

ANTISTROPHE 1

CHORAGOS: Lady Iocastê, did you not ask the King to go to his chambers?
IOCASTÊ: First tell me what has happened.
695 CHORAGOS: There was suspicion without evidence; yet it rankled
    As even false charges will.
IOCASTÊ: On both sides?
CHORAGOS: On both.
IOCASTÊ: But what was said?
700 CHORAGOS: Oh let it rest, let it be done with!
    Have we not suffered enough?
OEDIPUS: You see to what your decency has brought you:
    You have made difficulties where my heart saw none.

ANTISTROPHE 2

CHORAGOS: Oedipus, it is not once only I have told you—
705   You must know I should count myself unwise
    To the point of madness, should I now forsake you—
      You, under whose hand,
        In the storm of another time,
      Our dear land sailed out free,
710   But now stand fast at the helm!
IOCASTÊ: In God's name, Oedipus, inform your wife as well:
    Why are you so set in this hard anger?

OEDIPUS: I will tell you, for none of these men deserves
    My confidence as you do. It is Creon's work,
715   His treachery, his plotting against me.
IOCASTÊ: Go on, if you can make this clear to me.
OEDIPUS: He charges me with the murder of Laïos.
IOCASTÊ: Has he some knowledge? Or does he speak from hearsay?
OEDIPUS: He would not commit himself to such a charge,
720   But he has brought in that damnable soothsayer
    To tell his story.
IOCASTÊ: Set your mind at rest.
    If it is a question of soothsayers, I tell you
    That you will find no man whose craft gives knowledge
725   Of the unknowable.
                    Here is my proof.

    An oracle was reported to Laïos once
    (I will not say from Phoibos himself, but from
    His appointed ministers, at any rate)
730   That his doom would be death at the hands of his own son—
    His son, born of his flesh and of mine!

    Now, you remember the story: Laïos was killed
    By marauding strangers where three highways meet;
    But his child had not been three days in this world
735   Before the King had pierced the baby's ankles
    And left him to die on a lonely mountainside.

    Thus, Apollo never caused that child
    To kill his father, and it was not Laïos fate
    To die at the hands of his son, as he had feared.
740   This is what prophets and prophecies are worth!
    Have no dread of them.
                  It is God himself
    Who can show us what he wills, in his own way.
OEDIPUS: How strange a shadowy memory crossed my mind,
745   Just now while you were speaking; it chilled my heart.
IOCASTÊ: What do you mean? What memory do you speak of?
OEDIPUS: If I understand you, Laïos was killed
    At a place where three roads meet.
IOCASTÊ: So it was said;
750   We have no later story.
OEDIPUS: Where did it happen?
IOCASTÊ: Phokis, it is called: at a place where the Theban Way
    Divides into the roads towards Delphi and Daulia.

OEDIPUS: When?

755   IOCASTÊ: We had the news not long before you came
And proved the right to your succession here.

OEDIPUS: Ah, what net has God been weaving for me?

IOCASTÊ: Oedipus! Why does this trouble you?

OEDIPUS: Do not ask me yet.

760   First, tell me how Laïos looked, and tell me
How old he was.

IOCASTÊ: He was tall, his hair just touched
With white, his form was not unlike your own.

OEDIPUS: I think that I myself may be accurst

765   By my own ignorant edict.

IOCASTÊ: You speak strangely.
It makes me tremble to look at you, my King.

OEDIPUS: I am not sure that the blind man cannot see.
But I should know better if you were to tell me—

770   IOCASTÊ: Anything—though I dread to hear you ask it.

OEDIPUS: Was the King lightly escorted, or did he ride
With a large company, as a ruler should?

IOCASTÊ: There were five men with him in all: one was a herald;
And a single chariot, which he was driving.

775   OEDIPUS: Alas, that makes it plain enough!

                        But who—
Who told you how it happened?

IOCASTÊ: A household servant,
The only one to escape.

780   OEDIPUS: And is he still
A servant of ours?

IOCASTÊ: No, for when he came back at last
And found you enthroned in the place of the dead king,
He came to me, touched my hand with his, and begged

785   That I would send him away to the frontier district
Where only the shepherds go—
As far away from the city as I could send him.
I granted his prayer; for although the man was a slave,
He had earned more than this favor at my hands.

790   OEDIPUS: Can he be called back quickly?

IOCASTÊ: Easily.
But why?

OEDIPUS: I have taken too much upon myself
Without enquiry, therefore I wish to consult him.

795   IOCASTÊ: Then he shall come.

                  But am I not one also
To whom you might confide these fears of yours!

OEDIPUS: That is your right; it will not be denied you,
    Now least of all; for I have reached a pitch
800   Of wild foreboding. Is there anyone
    To whom I should sooner speak?
    Polybos of Corinth is my father.
    My mother is a Dorian: Meropê.
    I grew up chief among the men of Corinth
805   Until a strange thing happened—
    Not worth my passion, it may be, but strange.

    At a feast, a drunken man maundering in his cups
    Cries out that I am not my father's son!

    I contained myself that night, though I felt anger
810   And a sinking heart. The next day I visited
    My father and mother, and questioned them. They stormed,
    Calling it all the slanderous rant of a fool;
    And this relieved me. Yet the suspicion
    Remained always aching in my mind;
815   I knew there was talk; I could not rest;
    And finally, saying nothing to my parents,
    I went to the shrine at Delphi.
    The god dismissed my question without reply:
    He spoke of other things.
820   Some were clear,
    Full of wretchedness, dreadful, unbearable:
    As, that I should lie with my own mother, breed
    Children from whom all men would turn their eyes;
    And that I should be my father's murderer.
825   I heard all this, and fled. And from that day
    Corinth to me was only in the stars
    Descending in that quarter of the sky,
    As I wandered farther and farther on my way
    To a land where I should never see the evil
830   Sung by the oracle. And I came to this country
    Where, so you say, King Laïos was killed.
    I will tell you all that happened there, my lady.

    There were three highways
    Coming together at a place I passed;
835   And there a herald came towards me, and a chariot
    Drawn by horses, with a man such as you describe
    Seated in it. The groom leading the horses
    Forced me off the road at his lord's command;

But as this charioteer lurched over toward me
840   I struck him in my rage. The old man saw me
And brought his double goad down upon my head
As I came abreast.

               He was paid back, and more!
Swinging my club in this right hand I knocked him
845   Out of his car, and he rolled on the ground.

                           I killed him.

I killed them all.
Now if that stranger and Laïos were—kin,
Where is a man more miserable than I?
850   More hated by the gods? Citizen and alien alike
Must never shelter me or speak to me—
I must be shunned by all.

                   And I myself
Pronounced this malediction upon myself!

855   Think of it: I have touched you with these hands,
These hands that killed your husband. What defilement!

Am I all evil, then? It must be so,
Since l must flee from Thebes, yet never again
See my own countrymen, my own country,
860   For fear of joining my mother in marriage
And killing Polybos, my father.

                   Ah,
If I was created so, born to this fate,
Who could deny the savagery of God?

865   O holy majesty of heavenly powers!
May I never see that day! Never!
Rather let me vanish from the race of men
Than know the abomination destined me!
CHORAGOS: We too, my lord, have felt dismay at this.
870   But there is hope: you have yet to hear the shepherd.
OEDIPUS: Indeed, I fear no other hope is left me.
IOCASTÊ: What do you hope from him when he comes?
OEDIPUS: This much:
If his account of the murder tallies with yours,
875   Then I am cleared.
IOCASTÊ: What was it that I said
Of such importance?
OEDIPUS: Why, "marauders," you said,
Killed the King, according to this man's story.

880   If he maintains that still, if there were several,
Clearly the guilt is not mine: I was alone.
But if he says one man, singlehanded, did it,
Then the evidence all points to me.
IOCASTÊ: You may be sure that he said there were several;
885   And can he call back that story now? He cannot.
The whole city heard it as plainly as I.
But suppose he alters some detail of it:
He cannot ever show that Laïos' death
Fulfilled the oracle: for Apollo said
890   My child was doomed to kill him; and my child—
Poor baby!—it was my child that died first.

No. From now on, where oracles are concerned,
I would not waste a second thought on any.
OEDIPUS: You may be right.
895   But come: let someone go
For the shepherd at once. This matter must be settled.
IOCASTÊ: I will send for him.
I would not wish to cross you in anything,
And surely not in this.—Let us go in.

[*Exeunt into the palace.*]

ODE II

STROPHE 1

900   CHORUS: Let me be reverent in the ways of right,
Lowly the paths I journey on;
Let all my words and actions keep
The laws of the pure universe
From highest Heaven handed down.
905   For Heaven is their bright nurse,
Those generations of the realms of light;
Ah, never of mortal kind were they begot,
Nor are they slaves of memory, lost in sleep:
Their Father is greater than Time, and ages not.

ANTISTROPHE 1

910   The tyrant is a child of Pride
Who drinks from his great sickening cup
Recklessness and vanity,

Until from his high crest headlong
He plummets to the dust of hope.
915　　That strong man is not strong.
But let no fair ambition be denied;
May God protect the wrestler for the State
In government, in comely policy,
Who will fear God, and on His ordinance wait.

STROPHE 2

920　　Haughtiness and the high hand of disdain
Tempt and outrage God's holy law;
And any mortal who dares hold
No immortal Power in awe
Will be caught up in a net of pain:
925　　The price for which his levity is sold.
Let each man take due earnings, then,
And keep his hands from holy things.
And from blasphemy stand apart—
Else the crackling blast of heaven
930　　Blows on his head, and on his desperate heart;
Though fools will honor impious men,
In their cities no tragic poet sings.

ANTISTROPHE 2

Shall we lose faith in Delphi's obscurities,
We who have heard the world's core
935　　Discredited, and the sacred wood
Of Zeus at Elis praised no more?
The deeds and the strange prophecies
Must make a pattern yet to be understood.
Zeus, if indeed you are lord of all,
940　　Throned in light over night and day,
Mirror this in your endless mind:
Our masters call the oracle
Words on the wind, and the Delphic vision blind!
Their hearts no longer know Apollo,
945　　And reverence for the gods has died away.

SCENE III

[*Enter* IOCASTÊ.]

IOCASTÊ: Princes of Thebes, it has occurred to me
    To visit the altars of the gods, bearing
    These branches as a suppliant, and this incense.
    Our King is not himself: his noble soul
950   Is overwrought with fantasies of dread,
    Else he would consider
    The new prophecies in the light of the old.
    He will listen to any voice that speaks disaster,
    And my advice goes for nothing.

[*She approaches the altar, right.*]

955   To you, then, Apollo,
    Lycean lord, since you are nearest, I turn in prayer.
    Receive these offerings, and grant us deliverance
    From defilement. Our hearts are heavy with fear
    When we see our leader distracted, as helpless sailors
960   Are terrified by the confusion of their helmsman.

[*Enter* MESSENGER.]

MESSENGER: Friends, no doubt you can direct me:
    Where shall I find the house of Oedipus.
    Or, better still, where is the King himself?
CHORAGOS: It is this very place, stranger; he is inside.
965   This is his wife and mother of his children.
MESSENGER: I wish her happiness in a happy house,
    Blest in all the fulfillment of her marriage.
IOCASTÊ: I wish as much for you: your courtesy
    Deserves a like good fortune. But now, tell me:
970   Why have you come? What have you to say to us?
MESSENGER: Good news, my lady, for your house and your husband.
IOCASTÊ: What news? Who sent you here?
MESSENGER: I am from Corinth.
    The news I bring ought to mean joy for you,
975   Though it may be you will find some grief in it.
IOCASTÊ: What is it? How can it touch us in both ways?
MESSENGER: The people of Corinth, they say,
    Intend to call Oedipus to be their king.
IOCASTÊ: But old Polybos—is he not reigning still?
980   MESSENGER: No. Death holds him in his sepulchre.

IOCASTÊ: What are you saying? Polybos is dead?

MESSENGER: If I am not telling the truth, may I die myself.

IOCASTÊ *(to a Maidservant):* Go in, go quickly; tell this to your master.

      O riddlers of God's will, where are you now!

985   This was the man whom Oedipus, long ago,

      Feared so, fled so, in dread of destroying him—

      But it was another fate by which he died.

[*Enter OEDIPUS, center.*]

OEDIPUS: Dearest Iocastê, why have you sent for me?

IOCASTÊ: Listen to what this man says, and then tell me

990   What has become of the solemn prophecies.

OEDIPUS: Who is this man? What is his news for me?

IOCASTÊ: He has come from Corinth to announce your father's death!

OEDIPUS: Is it true, stranger? Tell me in your own words.

MESSENGER: I cannot say it more clearly: the King is dead.

995 OEDIPUS: Was it by treason? Or by an attack of illness?

MESSENGER: A little thing brings old men to their rest.

OEDIPUS: It was sickness, then?

MESSENGER: Yes, and his many years.

OEDIPUS: Ah!

1000   Why should a man respect the Pythian hearth,[15] or

      Give heed to the birds that jangle above his head?

      They prophesied that I should kill Polybos,

      Kill my own father; but he is dead and buried,

      And I am here—I never touched him, never,

1005   Unless he died in grief for my departure,

      And thus, in a sense, through me. No, Polybos

      Has packed the oracles off with him underground.

      They are empty words.

IOCASTÊ: Had I not told you so?

1010 OEDIPUS: You had; it was my faint heart that betrayed me.

IOCASTÊ: From now on never think of those things again.

OEDIPUS: And yet—must I not fear my mother's bed?

IOCASTÊ: Why should anyone in this world be afraid,

      Since Fate rules us and nothing can be foreseen?

1015   A man should live only for the present day.

      Have no more fear of sleeping with your mother.

      How many men, in dreams, have lain with their mothers!

      No reasonable man is troubled by such things.

---

[15] **Pythian hearth** Delphi (also called Pytho because a great snake had lived there), where Apollo spoke through a priestess

OEDIPUS: That is true; only—

1020   If only my mother were not still alive!
          But she is alive. I cannot help my dread.
IOCASTÊ: Yet this news of your father's death is wonderful.
OEDIPUS: Wonderful. But I fear the living woman.
MESSENGER: Tell me, who is this woman that you fear?

1025   OEDIPUS: It is Meropê, man; the wife of King Polybos.
MESSENGER: Meropê? Why should you be afraid of her?
OEDIPUS: An oracle of the gods, a dreadful saying.
MESSENGER: Can you tell me about it or are you sworn to silence?
OEDIPUS: I can tell you, and I will.

1030   Apollo said through his prophet that I was the man
          Who should marry his own mother, shed his father's blood
          With his own hands. And so, for all these years
          I have kept clear of Corinth, and no harm has come—
          Though it would have been sweet to see my parents again.

1035   MESSENGER: And is this the fear that drove you out of Corinth?
OEDIPUS: Would you have me kill my father?
MESSENGER: As for that
          You must be reassured by the news I gave you.
OEDIPUS: If you could reassure me, I would reward you.

1040   MESSENGER: I had that in mind, I will confess: I thought
          I could count on you when you returned to Corinth.
OEDIPUS: No: I will never go near my parents again.
MESSENGER: Ah, son, you still do not know what you are doing—
OEDIPUS: What do you mean? In the name of God tell me!

1045   MESSENGER:—If these are your reasons for not going home—
OEDIPUS: I tell you, I fear the oracle may come true.
MESSENGER: And guilt may come upon you through your parents?
OEDIPUS: That is the dread that is always in my heart.
MESSENGER: Can you not see that all your fears are groundless?

1050   OEDIPUS: How can you say that? They are my parents, surely?
MESSENGER: Polybos was not your father.
OEDIPUS: Not my father?
MESSENGER: No more your father than the man speaking to you.
OEDIPUS: But you are nothing to me!

1055   MESSENGER: Neither was he.
OEDIPUS: Then why did he call me son?
MESSENGER: I will tell you:
          Long ago he had you from my hands, as a gift.
OEDIPUS: Then how could he love me so, if I was not his?

1060   MESSENGER: He had no children, and his heart turned to you.
OEDIPUS: What of you? Did you buy me?
          Did you find me by chance?

MESSENGER: I came upon you in the crooked pass of Kithairon.
OEDIPUS: And what were you doing there?
1065   MESSENGER: Tending my flocks.
OEDIPUS: A wandering shepherd?
MESSENGER: But your savior, son, that day.
OEDIPUS: From what did you save me?
MESSENGER: Your ankles should tell you that.
1070   OEDIPUS: Ah, stranger, why do you speak of that childhood pain?
MESSENGER: I cut the bonds that tied your ankles together.
OEDIPUS: I have had the mark as long as I can remember.
MESSENGER: That was why you were given the name you bear.[16]
OEDIPUS: God! Was it my father or my mother who did it?
1075   Tell me!
MESSENGER: I do not know. The man who gave you to me
      Can tell you better than I.
OEDIPUS: It was not you that found me, but another?
MESSENGER: It was another shepherd gave you to me.
1080   OEDIPUS: Who was he? Can you tell me who he was?
MESSENGER: I think he was said to be one of Laïos' people.
OEDIPUS: You mean the Laïos who was king here years ago?
MESSENGER: Yes; King Laïos; and the man was one of his herdsmen.
OEDIPUS: Is he still alive? Can I see him?
1085   MESSENGER: These men here
      Know best about such things.
OEDIPUS: Does anyone here
      Know this shepherd that he is talking about?
      Have you seen him in the fields, or in the town?
1090   If you have, tell me. It is time things were made plain.
CHORAGOS: I think the man he means is that same shepherd
      You have already asked to see. Iocastê perhaps
      Could tell you something.
OEDIPUS: Do you know anything
1095   About him, Lady? Is he the man we have summoned?
      Is that the man this shepherd means?
IOCASTÊ: Why think of him?
      Forget this herdsman. Forget it all.
      This talk is a waste of time.
1100   OEDIPUS: How can you say that.
      When the clues to my true birth are in my hands?
IOCASTÊ: For God's love, let us have no more questioning!
      Is your life nothing to you?
      My own is pain enough for me to bear.

---

[16] **name you bear** "Oedipus" means "swollen-foot"

1105 OEDIPUS: You need not worry. Suppose my mother a slave,
　　　　And born of slaves: no baseness can touch you.
　　IOCASTÊ: Listen to me, I beg you: do not do this thing!
　　OEDIPUS: I will not listen; the truth must be made known.
　　IOCASTÊ: Everything that I say is for your own good!
1110 OEDIPUS: 　　　　　　　　　　　　　　My own good
　　　　Snaps my patience, then: I want none of it.
　　IOCASTÊ: You are fatally wrong! May you never learn who you are!
　　OEDIPUS: Go, one of you, and bring the shepherd here.
　　　　Let us leave this woman to brag of her royal name.
1115 IOCASTÊ: Ah, miserable!
　　　　That is the only word I have for you now.
　　　　That is the only word I can ever have.

[*Exit into the palace.*]

　　CHORAGOS: Why has she left us, Oedipus? Why has she gone
　　　　In such a passion of sorrow? I fear this silence:
1120 　　　Something dreadful may come of it.
　　OEDIPUS: 　　　　　　　　　　　Let it come!
　　　　However base my birth, I must know about it.
　　　　The Queen, like a woman, is perhaps ashamed
　　　　To think of my low origin. But I
1125 　　Am a child of luck; I cannot be dishonored.
　　　　Luck is my mother; the passing months, my brothers,
　　　　Have seen me rich and poor.
　　　　　　　　　　　　　If this is so,
　　　　How could I wish that I were someone else?
1130 　　How could I not be glad to know my birth?

ODE III

STROPHE

　　CHORUS: If ever the coming time were known
　　　　To my heart's pondering,
　　　　Kithairon, now by Heaven I see the torches
　　　　At the festival of the next full moon,
1135 　　And see the dance, and hear the choir sing
　　　　A grace to your gentle shade:
　　　　Mountain where Oedipus was found,
　　　　O mountain guard of a noble race!
　　　　May the god who heals us lend his aid,
1140 　　And let that glory come to pass
　　　　For our king's cradling-ground.

ANTISTROPHE

Of the nymphs that flower beyond the years.
Who bore you, royal child,
To Pan of the hills or the timberline Apollo,
1145   Cold in delight where the upland clears.
Or Hermês for whom Kyllenê's[17] heights are piled?
Or flushed as evening cloud,
Great Dionysos, roamer of mountains,
He—was it he who found you there,
1150   And caught you up in his own proud
Arms from the sweet god-ravisher
Who laughed by the Muses' fountains?

SCENE IV

OEDIPUS: Sirs: though I do not know the man,
    I think I see him coming, this shepherd we want:
1155   He is old, like our friend here, and the men
    Bringing him seem to be servants of my house.
    But you can tell, if you have ever seen him.

[*Enter SHEPHERD escorted by servants.*]

CHORAGOS: I know him, he was Laïos' man. You can trust him.
OEDIPUS: Tell me first, you from Corinth: is this the shepherd
1160   We were discussing?
MESSENGER: This is the very man.
OEDIPUS (*to Shepherd*): Come here. No, look at me. You must answer
    Everything I ask.—You belonged to Laïos?
SHEPHERD: Yes: born his slave, brought up in his house.
1165 OEDIPUS: Tell me: what kind of work did you do for him?
SHEPHERD: I was a shepherd of his, most of my life.
OEDIPUS: Where mainly did you go for pasturage?
SHEPHERD: Sometimes Kithairon, sometimes the hills near-by.
OEDIPUS: Do you remember ever seeing this man out there?
1170 SHEPHERD: What would he be doing there? This man?
OEDIPUS: This man standing here. Have you ever seen him before?
SHEPHERD: No. At least, not to my recollection.
MESSENGER: And that is not strange, my lord. But I'll refresh
    His memory: he must remember when we two
1175   Spent three whole seasons together, March to September,

---

[17] **Hermês . . . Kyllenê's** Hermês, messenger of the gods, was said to have been born on Mt. Kyllenê.

On Kithairon or thereabouts. He had two flocks;
I had one. Each autumn I'd drive mine home
And he would go back with his to Laïos' sheepfold.—
Is this not true, just as I have described it?

1180 SHEPHERD: True, yes; but it was all so long ago.
MESSENGER: Well, then: do you remember, back in those days
    That you gave me a baby boy to bring up as my own?
SHEPHERD: What if I did? What are you trying to say?
MESSENGER: King Oedipus was once that little child.

1185 SHEPHERD: Damn you, hold your tongue!
OEDIPUS: No more of that!
    It is your tongue needs watching, not this man's.
SHEPHERD: My King, my Master, what is it I have done wrong?
OEDIPUS: You have not answered his question about the boy.

1190 SHEPHERD: He does not know . . . He is only making trouble . . .
OEDIPUS: Come, speak plainly, or it will go hard with you.
SHEPHERD: In God's name, do not torture an old man!
OEDIPUS: Come here, one of you; bind his arms behind him.
SHEPHERD: Unhappy king! What more do you wish to learn?

1195 OEDIPUS: Did you give this man the child he speaks of?
SHEPHERD: I did.
    And I would to God I had died that very day.
OEDIPUS: You will die now unless you speak the truth.
SHEPHERD: Yet if I speak the truth, I am worse than dead.

1200 OEDIPUS: Very well; since you insist upon delaying—
SHEPHERD: No! I have told you already that I gave him the boy.
OEDIPUS: Where did you get him? From your house?
    From somewhere else?
SHEPHERD: Not from mine, no. A man gave him to me.

1205 OEDIPUS: Is that man here? Do you know whose slave he was?
SHEPHERD: For God's love, my King, do not ask me any more!
OEDIPUS: You are a dead man if I have to ask you again.
SHEPHERD: Then . . . Then the child was from the palace of Laïos.
OEDIPUS: A slave child? or a child of his own line?

1210 SHEPHERD: Ah, I am on the brink of dreadful speech!
OEDIPUS: And I of dreadful hearing. Yet I must hear.
SHEPHERD: If you must be told, then . . .
                      They said it was Laïos' child,
    But it is your wife who can tell you about that.

1215 OEDIPUS: My wife!—Did she give it to you?
SHEPHERD: My lord, she did.
OEDIPUS: Do you know why?
SHEPHERD: I was told to get rid of it.
OEDIPUS: An unspeakable mother!

1220   SHEPHERD: There had been prophecies . . .
          OEDIPUS: Tell me.
          SHEPHERD: It was said that the boy would kill his own father.
          OEDIPUS: Then why did you give him over to this old man?
          SHEPHERD: I pitied the baby, my King,
1225   And I thought that this man would take him far away
          To his own country.
                      He saved him—but for what a fate!
          For if you are what this man says you are,
          No man living is more wretched than Oedipus.
1230   OEDIPUS: Ah God!
                It was true!
                     All the prophecies!
                          — Now,
          O Light, may I look on you for the last time!
1235   I, Oedipus,
          Oedipus, damned in his birth, in his marriage damned,
          Damned in the blood he shed with his own hand!

          [*He rushes into the palace.*]

ODE IV

STROPHE 1

CHORUS: Alas for the seed of men.

          What measure shall l give these generations
1240   That breathe on the void and are void
          And exist and do not exist?

          Who bears more weight of joy
          Than mass of sunlight shifting in images,
          Or who shall make his thought stay on
1245   That down time drifts away?

          Your splendor is all fallen.

          O naked brow of wrath and tears,
          O change of Oedipus!
          I who saw your days call no man blest—
1250   Your great days like ghósts góne.

ANTISTROPHE 1

That mind was a strong bow.
Deep, how deep you drew it then, hard archer,
At a dim fearful range,
And brought dear glory down!

1255   You overcame the stranger—
The virgin with her hooking lion claws—
And though death sang, stood like a tower
To make pale Thebes take heart.
Fortress against our sorrow!

1260   Divine king, giver of laws,
Majestic Oedipus!
No prince in Thebes had ever such renown,
No prince won such grace of power.

STROPHE 2

And now of all men ever known
1265   Most pitiful is this man's story:
His fortunes are most changed, his state
Fallen to a low slave's
Ground under bitter fate.

O Oedipus, most royal one!
1270   The great door that expelled you to the light
Gave it night—ah, gave night to your glory:
As to the father, to the fathering son.

All understood too late.

How could that queen whom Laïos won,
1275   The garden that he harrowed at his height,
Be silent when that act was done?

ANTISTROPHE 2

But all eyes fail before time's eye,
All actions come to justice there.
Though never willed, though far down the deep past,
1280   Your bed, your dread sirings,
Are brought to book at last.
Child by Laïos doomed to die,
Then doomed to lose that fortunate little death,

Would God you never took breath in this air
1285   That with my wailing lips I take to cry:

For I weep the world's outcast.

I was blind, and now I can tell why:
Asleep, for you had given ease of breath
To Thebes, while the false years went by.

1290   **EXODOS**

[*Enter, from the palace,* SECOND MESSENGER.]

SECOND MESSENGER: Elders of Thebes, most honored in this land,
What horrors are yours to see and hear, what weight
Of sorrow to be endured, if, true to your birth,
1295   You venerate the line of Labdakos!
I think neither Istros nor Phasis, those great rivers,
Could purify this place of the corruption
It shelters now, or soon must bring to light—
Evil not done unconsciously, but willed.

1300   The greatest griefs are those we cause ourselves.
CHORAGOS: Surely, friend, we have grief enough already;
What new sorrow do you mean?
SECOND MESSENGER: The Queen is dead.
CHORAGOS: Iocastê? Dead? But at whose hand?
1305   SECOND MESSENGER: Her own.
The full horror of what happened you cannot know,
For you did not see it; but I, who did, will tell you
As clearly as I can how she met her death.

When she had left us,
1310   In passionate silence, passing through the court,
She ran to her apartment in the house,
Her hair clutched by the fingers of both hands.
She closed the doors behind her; then, by that bed
Where long ago the fatal son was conceived—
1315   That son who should bring about his father's death—
We heard her call upon Laïos, dead so many years,
And heard her wail for the double fruit of her marriage,
A husband by her husband, children by her child.

Exactly how she died I do not know:
1320   For Oedipus burst in moaning and would not let us
Keep vigil to the end: it was by him
As he stormed about the room that our eyes were caught.
From one to another of us he went, begging a sword,
Cursing the wife who was not his wife, the mother
1325   Whose womb had carried his own children and himself.
I do not know: it was none of us aided him,
But surely one of the gods was in control!
For with a dreadful cry
He hurled his weight, as though wrenched out of himself,
1330   At the twin doors: the bolts gave, and he rushed in.
And there we saw her hanging, her body swaying
From the cruel cord she had noosed about her neck.
A great sob broke from him heartbreaking to hear,
As he loosed the rope and lowered her to the ground.

1335   I would blot out from my mind what happened next!
For the King ripped from her gown the golden brooches
That were her ornament, and raised them, and plunged them down
Straight into his own eyeballs, crying, "No more,
No more shall you look on the misery about me,
1340   The horrors of my own doing! Too long you have known
The faces of those whom I should never have seen,
Too long been blind to those for whom I was searching!
From this hour, go in darkness!" And as he spoke,
He struck at his eyes—not once, but many times;
1345   And the blood spattered his beard,
Bursting from his ruined sockets like red hail.
So from the unhappiness of two this evil has sprung,
A curse on the man and woman alike. The old
Happiness of the house of Labdakos
1350   Was happiness enough: where is it today?
It is all wailing and ruin, disgrace, death—all
The misery of mankind that has a name—
And it is wholly and for ever theirs.
CHORAGOS: Is he in agony still? Is there no rest for him?
1355 SECOND MESSENGER: He is calling for someone to lead him to the gates
So that all the children of Kadmos may look upon
His father's murderer, his mother's—no,
I cannot say it!
                And then he will leave Thebes,
1360   Self-exiled, in order that the curse
Which he himself pronounced may depart from the house.

He is weak, and there is none to lead him,
So terrible is his suffering.
                                    But you will see:
1365   Look, the doors are opening: in a moment
        You will see a thing that would crush a heart of stone.

[*The central door is opened;* OEDIPUS, *blinded, is led in.*]

CHORAGOS: Dreadful indeed for men to see.
        Never have my own eyes
        Looked on a sight so full of fear.
1370   Oedipus!
        What madness came upon you, what daemon[18]
        Leaped on your life with heavier
        Punishment than a mortal man can bear?
        No: I cannot even
1375   Look at you, poor ruined one.
        And I would speak, question, ponder,
        If I were able. No.
        You make me shudder.
OEDIPUS: God. God.
1380   Is there a sorrow greater?
        Where shall I find harbor in this world?
        My voice is hurled far on a dark wind.
        What has God done to me?
CHORAGOS: Too terrible to think of, or to see.

STROPHE 1

1385   OEDIPUS: O cloud of night,
        Never to be turned away: night coming on,
        I cannot tell how: night like a shroud!
        My fair winds brought me here.
                                    Oh God. Again
1390   The pain of the spikes where I had sight,
        The flooding pain
        Of memory, never to be gouged out.
CHORAGOS: This is not strange.
        You suffer it all twice over, remorse in pain,
1395   Pain in remorse.

---

[18] **daemon** a spirit, not necessarily evil

ANTISTROPHE 1

OEDIPUS: Ah dear friend
    Are you faithful even yet, you alone?
    Are you still standing near me, will you stay here,
    Patient, to care for the blind?
1400   The blind man!
    Yet even blind I know who it is attends me,
    By the voice's tone—
    Though my new darkness hide the comforter.
CHORAGOS: Oh fearful act!
1405   What god was it drove you to rake black
    Night across your eyes?

STROPHE 2

OEDIPUS: Apollo. Apollo. Dear
1410   Children, the god was Apollo.
    He brought my sick, sick fate upon me.
    But the blinding hand was my own!
    How could I bear to see
    When all my sight was horror everywhere?
1415 CHORAGOS: Everywhere; that is true.
OEDIPUS: And now what is left?
    Images? Love? A greeting even,
    Sweet to the senses? Is there anything?
    Ah, no, friends: lead me away.
1420   Lead me away from Thebes.
                          Lead the great wreck
    And hell of Oedipus, whom the gods hate.
CHORAGOS: Your fate is clear, you are not blind to that.
    Would God you had never found it out!

ANTISTROPHE 2

1425 OEDIPUS: Death take the man who unbound
    My feet on that hillside
    And delivered me from death to life! What life?
    If only I had died,
    This weight of monstrous doom
1430   Could not have dragged me and my darlings down.
CHORAGOS: I would have wished the same.
OEDIPUS: Oh never to have come here
    With my father's blood upon me! Never
    To have been the man they call his mother's husband!

1435   Oh accurst! O child of evil,
      To have entered that wretched bed—
                              The selfsame one!
      More primal than sin itself, this fell to me.
      CHORAGOS: I do not know how I can answer you.
1440   You were better dead than alive and blind.
      OEDIPUS: Do not counsel me any more. This punishment
      That I have laid upon myself is just.
      If I had eyes,
      I do not know how I could bear the sight
1445   Of my father, when I came to the house of Death,
      Or my mother: for I have sinned against them both
      So vilely that I could not make my peace
      By strangling my own life.
                      Or do you think my children,
1450   Born as they were born, would be sweet to my eyes?
      Ah never, never! Nor this town with its high walls,
      Nor the holy images of the gods.
                     For I,
      Thrice miserable—Oedipus, noblest of all the line
1455   Of Kadmos, have condemned myself to enjoy
      These things no more, by my own malediction
      Expelling that man whom the gods declared
      To be a defilement in the house of Laïos.
      After exposing the rankness of my own guilt,
1460   How could I look men frankly in the eyes?
      No, I swear it,
      If I could have stifled my hearing at its source,
      I would have done it and made all this body
      A tight cell of misery, blank to light and sound:
1465   So I should have been safe in a dark agony
      Beyond all recollection.
                    Ah Kithairon!
      Why did you shelter me? When I was cast upon you,
      Why did I not die? Then I should never
1470   Have shown the world my execrable birth.

      Ah Polybos! Corinth, city that I believed
      The ancient seat of my ancestors: how fair
      I seemed, your child! And all the while this evil
      Was cancerous within me!
1475   For I am sick
      In my daily life, sick in my origin.

O three roads, dark ravine, woodland and way
Where three roads met: you, drinking my father's blood,
My own blood, spilled by my own hand: can you remember
1480   The unspeakable things I did there, and the things
I went on from there to do?

                O marriage, marriage!
The act that engendered me, and again the act
Performed by the son in the same bed—
1485   Ah, the net
Of incest, mingling fathers, brothers, sons,
With brides, wives, mothers: the last evil
That can be known by men: no tongue can say
How evil!
1490   No. For the love of God, conceal me
Somewhere far from Thebes; or kill me; or hurl me
Into the sea, away from men's eyes for ever.
Come, lead me. You need not fear to touch me.
Of all men, I alone can bear this guilt.

[*Enter* CREON.]

1495   CHORAGOS: We are not the ones to decide; but Creon here
        May fitly judge of what you ask. He only
        Is left to protect the city in your place.
    OEDIPUS: Alas, how can I speak to him? What right have I
        To beg his courtesy whom I have deeply wronged?
1500   CREON: I have not come to mock you, Oedipus,
        Or to reproach you, either.
        (*To Attendants.*)   —You, standing there:
        If you have lost all respect for man's dignity,
        At least respect the flame of Lord Helios:
1505   Do not allow this pollution to show itself
        Openly here, an affront to the earth
        And Heaven's rain and the light of day. No, take him
        Into the house as quickly as you can.
        For it is proper
1510   That only the close kindred see his grief.
    OEDIPUS: I pray you in God's name, since your courtesy
        Ignores my dark expectation, visiting
        With mercy this man of all men most execrable:
        Give me what I ask—for your good, not for mine.
1515   CREON: And what is it that you would have me do?
    OEDIPUS: Drive me out of this country as quickly as may be
        To a place where no human voice can ever greet me.

CREON: I should have done that before now—only,
    God's will had not been wholly revealed to me.
1520 OEDIPUS: But his command is plain: the parricide
    Must be destroyed. I am that evil man.
CREON: That is the sense of it, yes; but as things are,
    We had best discover clearly what is to be done.
OEDIPUS: You would learn more about a man like me?
1525 CREON: You are ready now to listen to the god.
OEDIPUS: I will listen. But it is to you
    That I must turn for help. I beg you, hear me.

The woman in there—
    Give her whatever funeral you think proper:
1530 She is your sister.
              — But let me go, Creon!
Let me purge my father's Thebes of the pollution
Of my living here, and go out to the wild hills,
To Kithairon, that has won such fame with me,
1535 The tomb my mother and father appointed for me,
And let me die there, as they willed I should.
And yet I know
Death will not ever come to me through sickness
Or in any natural way: I have been preserved
1540 For some unthinkable fate. But let that be.
As for my sons, you need not care for them.
They are men, they will find some way to live.
But my poor daughters, who have shared my table,
Who never before have been parted from their father—
1545 Take care of them, Creon; do this for me.
And will you let me touch them with my hands
A last time, and let us weep together?
Be kind, my lord,
Great prince, be kind!
1550   Could I but touch them,
They would be mine again, as when I had my eyes.

[*Enter* ANTIGONÊ *and* ISMENÊ, *attended.*]

Ah, God!
Is it my dearest children I hear weeping?
Has Creon pitied me and sent my daughters?
1555 CREON: Yes, Oedipus: I knew that they were dear to you
    In the old days, and know you must love them still.

OEDIPUS: May God bless you for this—and be a friendlier
Guardian to you than he has been to me!

1560   Children, where are you?
    Come quickly to my hands: they are your brother's—
    Hands that have brought your father's once clear eyes
    To this way of seeing—
                  Ah dearest ones,
1565   I had neither sight nor knowledge then, your father
    By the woman who was the source of his life!
    And I weep for you—having no strength to see you—
    I weep for you when I think of the bitterness
    That men will visit upon you all your lives.
1570   What homes, what festivals can you attend
    Without being forced to depart again in tears?
    And when you come to marriageable age,
    Where is the man, my daughters, who would dare
    Risk the bane that lies on all my children?
1575   Is there any evil wanting? Your father killed
    His father; sowed the womb of her who bore him;
    Engendered you at the fount of his own existence!
    That is what they will say of you.
                   Then, whom
1580   Can you ever marry? There are no bridegrooms for you,
    And your lives must wither away in sterile dreaming.
    O Creon, son of Menoikeus!
    You are the only father my daughters have,
    Since we, their parents, are both of us gone for ever.
1585   They are your own blood: you will not let them
    Fall into beggary and loneliness;
    You will keep them from the miseries that are mine!
    Take pity on them; see, they are only children,
    Friendless except for you. Promise me this,
1590   Great Prince, and give me your hand in token of it.

[CREON *clasps his right hand.*]

Children:
I could say much, if you could understand me,
But as it is, I have only this prayer for you:
Live where you can, be as happy as you can—
1595   Happier, please God, than God has made your father!
CREON: Enough. You have wept enough. Now go within.
OEDIPUS: I must; but it is hard.

CREON: Time eases all things.
OEDIPUS: But you must promise—
1600   CREON: Say what you desire.
OEDIPUS: Send me from Thebes!
CREON: God grant that I may!
OEDIPUS: But since God hates me . . .
CREON: No, he will grant your wish.
1605   OEDIPUS: You promise?
CREON: I cannot speak beyond my knowledge.
OEDIPUS: Then lead me in.
CREON: Come now, and leave your children.
OEDIPUS: No! Do not take them from me!
1610   CREON: Think no longer
        That you are in command here, but rather think
        How, when you were, you served your own destruction.

        [*Exeunt into the house all but the* C H O R U S; *the*
        CHORAGOS *chants directly to the audience.*]

CHORAGOS: Men of Thebes: look upon Oedipus.
        This is the king who solved the famous riddle
1615   And towered up, most powerful of men.
        No mortal eyes but looked on him with envy,
        Yet in the end ruin swept over him.
        Let every man in mankind's frailty
        Consider his last day; and let none
1620   Presume on his good fortune until he find
        Life, at his death, a memory without pain.

6. *ANTIGONÊ*
(441 BCE)

Sophocles

(trans. by Dudley Fitts and Robert Fitzgerald)

As in Oedipus Rex, *the first part of Sophocles's unofficial trilogy,* Antigonê *(441 BCE) raises the issues of human control, intellectual honesty, and responsibility. The challenge is posed by Creon, King of Thebes, who decrees a law forbidding the burial of Polyneicês, Oedipus's son and a traitor to Thebes. Antigonê and Ismene, sisters of Polyneicês, choose different courses of action with regard to their sacred and filial obligation to bury their brother: Ismene to obey the law of the King, and Antigonê to obey the gods, defy Creon, and suffer the consequences. Her death in turn unleashes the deaths of Creon's son and wife and at last brings Creon to wisdom.*

CHARACTERS

ANTIGONÊ
ISMENÊ
EURYDICÊ
CREON
HAIMON
TEIRESIAS
A SENTRY
A MESSENGER
CHORUS

[SCENE: Before the palace of Creon, King of Thebes. A central double door and two lateral doors. A platform extends the length of the façade, and from this platform three steps lead down into the "orchestra," or chorus-ground.]

[TIME: Dawn of the day after the repulse of the Argive army from the assault on Thebes.]

PROLOGUE

[*Antigonê and Ismenê enter from the central door of the palace.*]

ANTIGONÊ: Ismenê, dear sister,
    You would think that we had already suffered enough
5   For the curse on Oedipus.[1]
    I cannot imagine any grief
    That you and I have not gone through. And now—
    Have they told you of the new decree of our King Creon?
ISMENÊ: I have heard nothing: I know
10   That two sisters lost two brothers, a double death
    In a single hour; and I know that the Argive army
    Fled in the night; but beyond this, nothing.
ANTIGONÊ: I thought so. And that is why I wanted you
    To come out here with me. There is something we must do.
15 ISMENÊ: Why do you speak so strangely?
ANTIGONÊ: Listen, Ismenê:
    Creon buried our brother Eteoclês
    With military honors, gave him a soldier's funeral,
    And it was right that he should; but Polyneicês,
20   Who fought as bravely and died as miserably,—
    They say that Creon has sworn
    No one shall bury him, no one mourn for him,
    But his body must lie in the fields, a sweet treasure
    For carrion birds to find as they search for food.
25   That is what they say, and our good Creon is coming here
    To announce it publicly; and the penalty—
    Stoning to death in the public square!
                       There it is,
    And now you can prove what you are:
30   A true sister, or a traitor to your family.
ISMENÊ: Antigonê, you are mad! What could I possibly do?
ANTIGONÊ: You must decide whether you will help me or not.
ISMENÊ: I do not understand you. Help you in what?
ANTIGONÊ: Ismenê, I am going to bury him. Will you come?
35 ISMENÊ: Bury him! You have just said the new law forbids it.
ANTIGONÊ: He is my brother. And he is your brother, too.

---

[1] **Oedipus** once King of Thebes, was the father of Antigonê and Ismenê, and of their brothers Polyneicês and Eteoclês. Oedipus unwittingly killed his father, Laïos, and married his own mother, Iocastê. When he learned what he had done, he blinded himself and left Thebes. Eteoclês and Polyneicês quarreled. Polyneicês was driven out but returned to assault Thebes. In the battle each brother killed the other; Creon became king and ordered that Polyneicês be left to rot unburied on the battlefield as a traitor.

ISMENÊ: But think of the danger! Think what Creon will do!

ANTIGONÊ: Creon is not strong enough to stand in my way.

ISMENÊ: Ah sister!

40   Oedipus died, everyone hating him
          For what his own search brought to light, his eyes
          Ripped out by his own hand; and Iocastê died,
          His mother and wife at once: she twisted the cords
          That strangled her life; and our two brothers died,
45   Each killed by the other's sword. And we are left:
          But oh, Antigonê,
          Think how much more terrible than these
          Our own death would be if we should go against Creon
          And do what he has forbidden! We are only women,
50   We cannot fight with men, Antigonê!
          The law is strong, we must give in to the law
          In this thing, and in worse. I beg the Dead
          To forgive me, but I am helpless: I must yield
          To those in authority. And I think it is dangerous business
55   To be always meddling.

ANTIGONÊ: If that is what you think,
          I should not want you, even if you asked to come.
          You have made your choice, you can be what you want to be.
          But I will bury him; and if I must die,
60   I say that this crime is holy: I shall lie down
          With him in death, and I shall be as dear
          To him as he to me.

                                   It is the dead,
          Not the living, who make the longest demands:
65   We die for ever . . .

                                   You may do as you like,
          Since apparently the laws of the gods mean nothing to you.

ISMENÊ: They mean a great deal to me; but I have no strength
          To break laws that were made for the public good.

70   ANTIGONÊ: That must be your excuse, I suppose. But as for me,
          I will bury the brother I love.

ISMENÊ: Antigonê,
          I am so afraid for you!

ANTIGONÊ: You need not be:
75   You have yourself to consider, after all.

ISMENÊ: But no one must hear of this, you must tell no one!
          I will keep it a secret, I promise!

ANTIGONÊ: O tell it! Tell everyone!
          Think how they'll hate you when it all comes out
80   If they learn that you knew about it all the time!

ISMENÊ: So fiery! You should be cold with fear.

ANTIGONÊ: Perhaps. But I am doing only what I must.

ISMENÊ: But can you do it? I say that you cannot.

ANTIGONÊ: Very well: when my strength gives out,

85   I shall do no more.

ISMENÊ: Impossible things should not be tried at all.

ANTIGONÊ: Go away, Ismenê:

    I shall be hating you soon, and the dead will too,

    For your words are hateful. Leave me my foolish plan:

90   I am not afraid of the danger; if it means death.

    It will not be the worst of deaths—death without honor.

ISMENÊ: Go then, if you feel that you must.

    You are unwise,

    But a loyal friend indeed to those who love you.

95   [*Exit into the palace. Antigonê goes off, left. Enter the Chorus.*]

PÁRODOS

STROPHE 1

CHORUS: Now the long blade of the sun, lying

    Level east to west, touches with glory

    Thebes of the Seven Gates. Open, unlidded

100   Eye of golden day! O marching light

    Across the eddy and rush of Dircê's stream,[2]

    Striking the white shields of the enemy

    Thrown headlong backward from the blaze of morning!

CHORAGOS:[3] Polyneicês their commander

105   Roused them with windy phrases,

    He the wild eagle screaming

    Insults above our land,

    His wings their shields of snow,

    His crest their marshalled helms.

ANTISTROPHE 1

110 CHORUS: Against our seven gates in a yawning ring

    The famished spears came onward in the night;

    But before his jaws were sated with our blood,

---

[2] **Dircê's stream** a stream west of Thebes

[3] **Choragos** leader of the Chorus

Or pine fire took the garland of our towers,
He was thrown back; and as he fumed, great Thebes—
115 No tender victim for his noisy power—
Rose like a dragon behind him, shouting war.
CHORAGOS: For God[4] hates utterly
The bray of bragging tongues;
And when he beheld their smiling,
120 Their swagger of golden helms,
The frown of his thunder blasted
Their first man from our walls.

STROPHE 2

CHORUS: We heard his shout of triumph high in the air
Turn to a scream; far out in a flaming arc
125 He fell with his windy torch, and the earth struck him.
And others storming in fury no less than his
Found shock of death in the dusty joy of battle.
CHORAGOS: Seven captains at seven gates
Yielded their clanging arms to the god
130 That bends the battle-line and breaks it.
These two only, brothers in blood,
Face to face in matchless rage,
Mirroring each the other's death,
Clashed in long combat.

ANTISTROPHE 2

135 CHORUS: But now in the beautiful morning of victory
Let Thebes of the many chariots sing for joy!
With hearts for dancing we'll take leave of war:
Our temples shall be sweet with hymns of praise,
And the long nights shall echo with our chorus.

SCENE I

140 CHORAGOS: But now at last our new King is coming:
Creon of Thebes, Menoikeus' son.
In this auspicious dawn of his rein
What are the new complexities
That shifting Fate has woven for him?

---

[4]**God** Zeus, the chief of the Olympian deities. (The translators consistently use the term "God" which should not be misunderstood as monotheism.)

145   What is his counsel? Why has he summoned
      The old men to hear him?

      [*Enter Creon from the palace, center. He addresses the Chorus from the top step.*]

      CREON: Gentlemen: I have the honor to inform you that our Ship of State, which
150   recent storms have threatened to destroy, has come safely to harbor at last,
      guided by the merciful wisdom of Heaven. I have summoned you here this
      morning because I know that I can depend upon you: your devotion to King
      Laïos was absolute; you never hesitated in your duty to our late ruler
      Oedipus; and when Oedipus died, your loyalty was transferred to his
155   children. Unfortunately, as you know, his two sons, the princes Eteoclês and
      Polyneicês, have killed each other in battle; and I, as the next in blood, have
      succeeded to the full power of the throne.
          I am aware, of course, that no Ruler can expect complete loyalty from his
      subjects until he has been tested in office. Nevertheless, I say to you at the
160   very outset that I have nothing but contempt for the kind of Governor who is
      afraid, for whatever reason, to follow the course that he knows is best for the
      State; and as for the man who sets private friendship above the public
      welfare,—I have no use for him, either. I call God to witness that if I saw my
      country headed for ruin, I should not be afraid to speak out plainly; and I
165   need hardly remind you that I would never have any dealings with an enemy
      of the people. No one values friendship more highly than I; but we must
      remember that friends made at the risk of wrecking our Ship are not real
      friends at all.
          These are my principles, at any rate, and that is why I have made the
170   following decision concerning the sons of Oedipus: Eteoclês, who died as a
      man should die, fighting for his country, is to be buried with full military
      honors, with all the ceremony that is usual when the greatest heroes die; but
      his brother Polyneicês, who broke his exile to come back with fire and sword
      against his native city and the shrines of his fathers' gods, whose one idea
175   was to spill the blood of his blood and sell his own people into slavery—
      Polyneicês, I say, is to have no burial: no man is to touch him or say the least
      prayer for him; he shall lie on the plain, unburied; and the birds and the
      scavenging dogs can do with him whatever they like.
          This is my command, and you can see the wisdom behind it. As long as I
180   am King, no traitor is going to be honored with the loyal man. But whoever
      shows by word and deed that he is on the side of the State,—he shall have my
      respect while he is living and my reverence when he is dead.
      CHORAGOS: If that is your will, Creon son of Menoikeus,
      You have the right to enforce it: we are yours.
185   CREON: That is my will. Take care that you do your part.
      CHORAGOS: We are old men: let the younger ones carry it out.

CREON: I do not mean that: the sentries have been appointed.
CHORAGOS: Then what is it that you would have us do?
CREON: You will give no support to whoever breaks this law.
190   CHORAGOS: Only a crazy man is in love with death!
CREON: And death it is; yet money talks, and the wisest
       Have sometimes been known to count a few coins too many.

[*Enter Sentry from left.*]

SENTRY: I'll not say that I'm out of breath from running, King, because every time
195   I stopped to think about what I have to tell you, I felt like going back. And all
       the time a voice kept saying, "You fool, don't you know you're walking
       straight into trouble?"; and then another voice: "Yes but if you let somebody
       else get the news to Creon first, it will be even worse than that for you!" But
       good sense won out, at least I hope it was good sense, and here I am with a
200   story that makes no sense at all; but I'll tell it anyhow, because, as they say,
       what's going to happen's going to happen and—
CREON: Come to the point. What have you to say?
SENTRY: I did not do it. I did not see who did it. You must not punish me for what
       someone else has done.
205   CREON: A comprehensive defense! More effective, perhaps.
       If I knew its purpose. Come: what is it?
SENTRY: A dreadful thing . . . I don't know how to put it—
CREON: Out with it!
SENTRY: Well, then;
210   The dead man—
               Polyneicês—

[*Pause. The Sentry is overcome, fumbles for words. Creon waits impassively.*]

                out there—
215   someone,—
New dust on the slimy flesh!

[*Pause. No sign from Creon.*]

Someone has given it burial that way, and
Gone . . .

220   [*Long pause. Creon finally speaks with deadly control.*]

CREON: And the man who dared do this?

SENTRY: I swear I
          Do not know! You must believe me!
                                                    Listen:
225   The ground was dry, not a sign of digging, no,
          Not a wheeltrack in the dust, no trace of anyone.
          It was when they relieved us this morning: and one of them,
          The corporal, pointed to it.
                                        There it was,
230   The strangest—
                          Look:
          The body, just mounded over with light dust: you see?
          Not buried really, but as if they'd covered it
          Just enough for the ghost's peace. And no sign
235   Of dogs or any wild animal that had been there.

          And then what a scene there was! Every man of us
          Accusing the other: we all proved the other man did it,
          We all had proof that we could not have done it.
          We were ready to take hot iron in our hands,
240   Walk through fire, swear by all the gods,
          It was not I!
          I do not know who it was, but it was not I!

          [*Creon's rage has been mounting steadily, but the Sentry is
          too intent upon his story to notice it.*]

245   And then, when this came to nothing, someone said
          A thing that silenced us and made us stare
          Down at the ground: you had to be told the news,
          And one of us had to do it! We threw the dice,
          And the bad luck fell to me. So here I am,
250   No happier to be here than you are to have me:
          Nobody likes the man who brings bad news.
CHORAGOS: I have been wondering, King: can it be that the gods have done this?
CREON (*furiously*): Stop!
          Must you doddering wrecks
255   Go out of your heads entirely? "The gods"!
          Intolerable!
          The gods favor this corpse? Why? How had he served them?
          Tried to loot their temples, burn their images,
          Yes, and the whole State, and its laws with it!
260   Is it your senile opinion that the gods love to honor bad men?
          A pious thought!—

                        No, from the very beginning
            There have been those who have whispered together,
            Stiff-necked anarchists, putting their heads together,
265   Scheming against me in alleys. These are the men,
            And they have bribed my own guard to do this thing.
            (*Sententiously.*) Money!
            There's nothing in the world so demoralizing as money.
            Down go your cities,
270   Homes gone, men gone, honest hearts corrupted,
            Crookedness of all kinds, and all for money!
            (*To Sentry.*)   But you—!
            I swear by God and by the throne of God,
            The man who has done this thing shall pay for it!
275   Find that man, bring him here to me, or your death
            Will be the least of your problems: I'll string you up
            Alive, and there will be certain ways to make you
            Discover your employer before you die;
            And the process may teach you a lesson you seem to have missed:
280   The dearest profit is sometimes all too dear:
            That depends on the source. Do you understand me?
            A fortune won is often misfortune.
      SENTRY: King, may I speak?
      CREON: Your very voice distresses me.
285   SENTRY: Are you sure that it is my voice, and not your conscience?
      CREON: By God, he wants to analyze me now!
      SENTRY: It is not what I say, but what has been done, that hurts you.
      CREON: You talk too much.
      SENTRY: Maybe; but I've done nothing.
290   CREON: Sold your soul for some silver: that's all you've done.
      SENTRY: How dreadful it is when the right judge judges wrong!
      CREON: Your figures of speech
            May entertain you now; but unless you bring me the man,
            You will get little profit from them in the end.

295   [*Exit Creon into the palace.*]

      SENTRY: "Bring me the man"—!
            I'd like nothing better than bringing him the man!
            But bring him or not, you have seen the last of me here.
            At any rate, I am safe!

300   [*Exit Sentry.*]

ODE I

STROPHE 1

CHORUS: Numberless are the world's wonders, but none
More wonderful than man; the stormgray sea
Yields to his prows, the huge crests bear him high:
Earth, holy and inexhaustible, is graven
305   With shining furrows where his plows have gone
Year after year, the timeless labor of stallions.

ANTISTROPHE I

The lightboned birds and beasts that cling to cover,
The lithe fish lighting their reaches of dim water,
All are taken, tamed in the net of his mind;
310   The lion on the hill, the wild horse windy-maned,
Resign to him; and his blunt yoke has broken
The sultry shoulders of the mountain bull.

STROPHE 2

Words also, and thought as rapid as air,
He fashions to his good use; statecraft is his,
315   And his the skill that deflects the arrows of snow,
The spears of winter rain: from every wind
He has made himself secure—from all but one:
In the late wind of death he cannot stand.

ANTISTROPHE 2

O clear intelligence, force beyond all measure!
320   O fate of man, working both good and evil!
When the laws are kept, how proudly his city stands!
When the laws are broken, what of his city then?
Never may the anárchic man find rest at my hearth,
Never be it said that my thoughts are his thoughts.

SCENE II

325   [*Reenter Sentry leading Antigonê.*]

CHORAGOS: What does this mean? Surely this captive woman
Is the Princess, Antigonê. Why should she be taken?
SENTRY: Here is the one who did it! We caught her
In the very act of burying him.—Where is Creon?

330   CHORAGOS: Just coming from the house:

         [*Enter Creon, center.*]

     CREON: What has happened?
         Why have you come back so soon?
     SENTRY (*expansively*):   O King,
335   A man should never be too sure of anything:
         I would have sworn
         That you'd not see me here again: your anger
         Frightened me so, and the things you threatened me with;
         But how could I tell then
340   That I'd be able to solve the case so soon?
         No dice-throwing this time: I was only too glad to come!
         Here is this woman. She is the guilty one:
         We found her trying to bury him.
         Take her, then; question her; judge her as you will.
345   I am through with the whole thing now, and glad of it.
     CREON: But this is Antigonê! Why have you brought her here?
     SENTRY: She was burying him, I tell you!
     CREON [*severely*]:   Is this the truth?
     SENTRY: I saw her with my own eyes. Can I say more?
350   CREON: The details: come, tell me quickly!
     SENTRY: It was like this:
         After those terrible threats of yours, King,
         We went back and brushed the dust away from the body.
         The flesh was soft by now, and stinking,
355   So we sat on a hill to windward and kept guard.
         No napping this time! We kept each other awake.
         But nothing happened until the white round sun
         Whirled in the center of the round sky over us:
         Then, suddenly,
360   A storm of dust roared up from the earth, and the sky
         Went out, the plain vanished with all its trees
         In the stinging dark. We closed our eyes and endured it.
         The whirlwind lasted a long time, but it passed;
         And then we looked, and there was Antigonê!
365   I have seen
         A mother bird come back to a stripped nest, heard
         Her crying bitterly a broken note or two
         For the young ones stolen. Just so, when this girl
         Found the bare corpse, and all her love's work wasted,
370   She wept, and cried on heaven to damn the hands
         That had done this thing.

And then she brought more dust

And sprinkled wine three times for her brother's ghost.
We ran and took her at once. She was not afraid,
375   Not even when we charged her with what she had done.
She denied nothing.

And this was a comfort to me,

And some uneasiness: for it is a good thing
To escape from death, but it is no great pleasure
380   To bring death to a friend.

Yet I always say

There is nothing so comfortable as your own safe skin!
CREON (*slowly, dangerously*): And you, Antigonê,
You with your head hanging,—do you confess this thing?
385   ANTIGONÊ: I do. I deny nothing.
CREON (*to Sentry*):   You may go.

[*Exit Sentry.*]

(*To Antigonê.*) Tell me, tell me briefly:
Had you heard my proclamation touching this matter?
390   ANTIGONÊ: It was public. Could I help hearing it?
CREON: And yet you dared defy the law.
ANTIGONÊ: I dared.
It was not God's proclamation. That final Justice
That rules the world below makes no such laws.

395   Your edict, King, was strong,
But all your strength is weakness itself against
The immortal unrecorded laws of God.
They are not merely now: they were, and shall be,
Operative for ever, beyond man utterly.

400   I knew I must die, even without your decree:
I am only mortal. And if I must die
Now, before it is my time to die,
Surely this is no hardship: can anyone
Living, as I live, with evil all about me,
405   Think Death less than a friend? This death of mine
Is of no importance; but if I had left my brother
Lying in death unburied, I should have suffered.
Now I do not.

You smile at me. Ah Creon,

410   Think me a fool, if you like; but it may well be
That a fool convicts me of folly.

CHORAGOS: Like father, like daughter: both headstrong, deaf to reason!
    She has never learned to yield:
CREON: She has much to learn.
415   The inflexible heart breaks first, the toughest iron
    Cracks first, and the wildest horses bend their necks
    At the pull of the smallest curb.
                           Pride? In a slave?
    This girl is guilty of a double insolence,
420   Breaking the given laws and boasting of it.
    Who is the man here,
    She or I, if this crime goes unpunished?
    Sister's child, or more than sister's child.
    Or closer yet in blood—she and her sister
425   Win bitter death for this!
    (*To Servants.*)   Go, some of you,
    Arrest Ismenê. I accuse her equally.
    Bring her: you will find her sniffling in the house there.

    Her mind's a traitor: crimes kept in the dark
430   Cry for light, and the guardian brain shudders;
    But how much worse than this
    Is brazen boasting of barefaced anarchy!
ANTIGONÊ: Creon, what more do you want than my death?
CREON: Nothing.
435   That gives me everything.
ANTIGONÊ: Then I beg you: kill me.
    This talking is a great weariness: your words
    Are distasteful to me, and I am sure that mine
    Seem so to you. And yet they should not seem so:
440   I should have praise and honor for what I have done.
    All these men here would praise me
    Were their lips not frozen shut with fear of you.
    (*Bitterly.*) Ah the good fortune of kings,
    Licensed to say and do whatever they please!
445 CREON: You are alone here in that opinion.
ANTIGONÊ: No, they are with me. But they keep their tongues in leash.
CREON: Maybe. But you are guilty, and they are not.
ANTIGONÊ: There is no guilt in reverence for the dead.
CREON: But Eteoclês—was he not your brother too?
450 ANTIGONÊ: My brother too.
CREON: And you insult his memory?
ANTIGONÊ (*softly*): The dead man would not say that I insult it.
CREON: He would: for you honor a traitor as much as him.
ANTIGONÊ: His own brother, traitor or not, and equal in blood.

455 CREON: He made war on his country. Eteoclês defended it.
ANTIGONÊ: Nevertheless, there are honors due all the dead.
CREON: But not the same for the wicked as for the just.
ANTIGONÊ: Ah Creon, Creon,
Which of us can say what the gods hold wicked?
460 CREON: An enemy is an enemy, even dead.
ANTIGONÊ: It is my nature to join in love, not hate.
CREON (*finally losing patience*): Go join them then; if you must have your love,
Find it in hell!
CHORAGOS: But see, Ismenê comes:

465 [*Enter Ismenê, guarded.*]

Those tears are sisterly, the cloud
That shadows her eyes rains down gentle sorrow.
CREON You too, Ismenê,
Snake in my ordered house, sucking my blood
470 Stealthily—and all the time I never knew
That these two sisters were aiming at my throne!

Ismenê,
Do you confess your share in this crime, or deny it?
Answer me.
475 ISMENÊ: Yes, if she will let me say so. I am guilty.
ANTIGONÊ (*coldly*): No, Ismenê. You have no right to say so.
You would not help me, and I will not have you help me.
ISMENÊ: But now I know what you meant; and I am here
To join you, to take my share of punishment.
480 ANTIGONÊ: The dead man and the gods who rule the dead
Know whose act this was. Words are not friends.
ISMENÊ: Do you refuse me, Antigonê? I want to die with you:
I too have a duty that I must discharge to the dead.
ANTIGONÊ: You shall not lessen my death by sharing it.
485 ISMENÊ: What do I care for life when you are dead?
ANTIGONÊ: Ask Creon. You're always hanging on his opinions.
ISMENÊ: You are laughing at me. Why, Antigonê?
ANTIGONÊ: It's a joyless laughter, Ismenê.
ISMENÊ: But can I do nothing?
490 ANTIGONÊ: Yes. Save yourself. I shall not envy you.
There are those who will praise you; I shall have honor, too.
ISMENÊ: But we are equally guilty!
ANTIGONÊ: No more, Ismenê.
You are alive, but I belong to Death.

495 CREON (*to the Chorus*): Gentlemen, I beg you to observe these girls:
    One has just now lost her mind; the other,
    It seems, has never had a mind at all.
  ISMENÊ: Grief teaches the steadiest minds to waver, King.
  CREON: Yours certainly did, when you assumed guilt with the guilty!
500 ISMENÊ: But how could I go on living without her?
  CREON: You are.
    She is already dead.
  ISMENÊ: But your own son's bride!
  CREON: There are places enough for him to push his plow.
505   I want no wicked women for my sons!
  ISMENÊ: O dearest Haimon, how your father wrongs you!
  CREON: I've had enough of your childish talk of marriage!
  CHORAGOS: Do you really intend to steal this girl from your son?
  CREON: No; Death will do that for me.
510 CHORAGOS: Then she must die?
  CREON (*ironically*): You dazzle me.
           —But enough of this talk!
  (*To Guards.*) You, there, take them away and guard them well:
  For they are but women, and even brave men run
515 When they see Death coming.

  [*Exeunt Ismenê, Antigonê, and Guards.*]

ODE II

STROPHE 1

CHORUS: Fortunate is the man who has never tasted God's vengeance!
  Where once the anger of heaven has struck, that house is shaken
  For ever: damnation rises behind each child
520 Like a wave cresting out of the black northeast,
  When the long darkness under sea roars up
  And bursts drumming death upon the windwhipped sand.

ANTISTROPHE 1

I have seen this gathering sorrow from time long past
  Loom upon Oedipus' children: generation from generation
525 Takes the compulsive rage of the enemy god.
  So lately this last flower of Oedipus' line
  Drank the sunlight! but now a passionate word
  And a handful of dust have closed up all its beauty.

What mortal arrogance
530   Transcends the wrath of Zeus?
Sleep cannot lull him nor the effortless long months
Of the timeless gods: but he is young for ever,
And his house is the shining day of high Olympos.
        All that is and shall be,
535   And all the past, is his.
No pride on earth is free of the curse of heaven.

The straying dreams of men
        May bring them ghosts of joy:
But as they drowse, the waking embers burn them;
540   Or they walk with fixed eyes, as blind men walk.
But the ancient wisdom speaks for our own time:
        Fate works most for woe
        With Folly's fairest show.
Man's little pleasure is the spring of sorrow.

SCENE III

545   CHORAGOS: But here is Haimon, King, the last of all your sons.
        Is it grief for Antigonê that brings him here,
        And bitterness at being robbed of his bride?

        [*Enter Haimon.*]

        CREON: We shall soon see, and no need of diviners.
550   —Son,
        You have heard my final judgment on that girl:
        Have you come here hating me, or have you come
        With deference and with love, whatever I do?
    HAIMON: I am your son, father. You are my guide.
555   You make things clear for me, and I obey you.
        No marriage means more to me than your continuing wisdom.
    CREON: Good. That is the way to behave: subordinate
        Everything else, my son, to your father's will.
        This is what a man prays for, that he may get
560   Sons attentive and dutiful in his house,
        Each one hating his father's enemies,
        Honoring his father's friends. But if his sons
        Fail him, if they turn out unprofitably,

What has he fathered but trouble for himself
565 And amusement for the malicious?
                                    So you are right
Not to lose your head over this woman.
Your pleasure with her would soon grow cold, Haimon
And then you'd have a hellcat in bed and elsewhere.
570 Let her find her husband in Hell!
Of all the people in this city, only she
Has had contempt for my law and broken it.

Do you want me to show myself weak before the people?
Or to break my sworn word? No, and I will not.
575 The woman dies.
I suppose she'll plead "family ties." Well, let her.
If I permit my own family to rebel,
How shall I earn the world's obedience?
Show me the man who keeps his house in hand,
580 He's fit for public authority.
                                    I'll have no dealings
With lawbreakers, critics of the government:
Whoever is chosen to govern should be obeyed—
Must be obeyed, in all things, great and small,
585 Just and unjust! O Haimon,
The man who knows how to obey, and that man only,
Knows how to give commands when the time comes.
You can depend on him, no matter how fast
The spears come: he's a good soldier, he'll stick it out.

590 Anarchy, anarchy! Show me a greater evil!
This is why cities tumble and the great houses rain down,
This is what scatters armies!
No, no: good lives are made so by discipline.
We keep the laws then, and the lawmakers,
595 And no woman shall seduce us. If we must lose,
Let's lose to a man, at least! Is a woman stronger than we?
CHORAGOS: Unless time has rusted my wits,
What you say, King, is said with point and dignity.
HAIMON (*boyishly earnest*): Father:
600 Reason is God's crowning gift to man, and you are right
To warn me against losing mine. I cannot say—
I hope that I shall never want to say!—that you
Have reasoned badly. Yet there are other men
Who can reason, too; and their opinions might be helpful.
605 You are not in a position to know everything

That people say or do, or what they feel:
Your temper terrifies—everyone
Will tell you only what you like to hear.
But I, at any rate, can listen; and I have heard them
610   Muttering and whispering in the dark about this girl.
They say no woman has ever, so unreasonably,
Died so shameful a death for a generous act:
"She covered her brother's body. Is this indecent?
She kept him from dogs and vultures. Is this a crime?
615   Death?—She should have all the honor that we can give her!"

This is the way they talk out there in the city.

You must believe me:
Nothing is closer to me than your happiness.
What could be closer? Must not any son
620   Value his father's fortune as his father does his?
I beg you, do not be unchangeable:
Do not believe that you alone can be right.
The man who thinks that,
The man who maintains that only he has the power
625   To reason correctly, the gift to speak, the soul—
A man like that, when you know him, turns out empty.

It is not reason never to yield to reason!

In flood time you can see how some trees bend,
And because they bend, even their twigs are safe,
630   While stubborn trees are torn up, roots and all.
And the same thing happens in sailing:
Make your sheet fast, never slacken,—and over you go,
Head over heels and under: and there's your voyage.
Forget you are angry! Let yourself be moved!
635   I know I am young; but please let me say this:
The ideal condition
Would be, I admit, that men should be right by instinct;
But since we are all too likely to go astray,
The reasonable thing is to learn from those who can teach.
640 CHORAGOS: You will do well to listen to him, King,
If what he says is sensible. And you, Haimon,
Must listen to your father.—Both speak well.
CREON: You consider it right for a man of my years and experience
To go to school to a boy?
645 HAIMON: It is not right

If I am wrong. But if I am young, and right,
What does my age matter?
CREON: You think it right to stand up for an anarchist?
HAIMON: Not at all. I pay no respect to criminals.
650 CREON: Then she is not a criminal?
HAIMON: The City would deny it, to a man.
CREON: And the City proposes to teach me how to rule?
HAIMON: Ah. Who is it that's talking like a boy now?
CREON: My voice is the one voice giving orders in this City!
655 HAIMON: It is no City if it takes orders from one voice.
CREON: The State is the King!
HAIMON: Yes, if the State is a desert.

[*Pause.*]

CREON: This boy, it seems, has sold out to a woman.
660 HAIMON: If you are a woman: my concern is only for you.
CREON: So? Your "concern"! In a public brawl with your father!
HAIMON: How about you, in a public brawl with justice?
CREON: With justice, when all that I do is within my rights?
HAIMON: You have no right to trample on God's right.
665 CREON (*completely out of control*): Fool, adolescent fool! Taken in by a woman!
HAIMON: You'd never see me taken in by anything vile.
CREON: Every word you say is for her!
HAIMON (*quietly, darkly*):   And for you.
And for me. And for the gods under the earth.
670 CREON: You'll never marry her while she lives.
HAIMON: Then she must die.—But her death will cause another.
CREON: Another?
Have you lost your senses? Is this an open threat?
HAIMON: There is no threat in speaking to emptiness.
675 CREON: I swear you'll regret this superior tone of yours!
You are the empty one!
HAIMON: If you were not my father,
I'd say you were perverse.
CREON: You girlstruck fool, don't play at words with me!
680 HAIMON: I am sorry. You prefer silence.
CREON: Now, by God—!
I swear, by all the gods in heaven above us,
You'll watch it, I swear you shall!
(*To the Servants.*) Bring her out!
685 Bring the woman out! Let her die before his eyes!
Here, this instant, with her bridegroom beside her!

HAIMON: Not here, no; she will not die here, King.
    And you will never see my face again.
    Go on raving as long as you've a friend to endure you.

690   [*Exit Haimon.*]

CHORAGOS: Gone, gone.
    Creon, a young man in a rage is dangerous!
CREON: Let him do, or dream to do, more than a man can.
    He shall not save these girls from death.
695 CHORAGOS: These girls?
    You have sentenced them both?
CREON: No, you are right.
    I will not kill the one whose hands are clean.
CHORAGOS: But Antigonê?
700 CREON (*somberly*):   I will carry her far away
    Out there in the wilderness, and lock her
    Living in a vault of stone. She shall have food,
    As the custom is, to absolve the State of her death.
    And there let her pray to the gods of hell:
705   They are her only gods:
    Perhaps they will show her an escape from death,
    Or she may learn,
            though late,
    That piety shown the dead is pity in vain.

710   [*Exit Creon.*]

ODE III

STROPHE

CHORUS: Love, unconquerable
    Waster of rich men, keeper
    Of warm lights and all-night vigil
    In the soft face of a girl:
715   Sea-wanderer, forest-visitor!
    Even the pure Immortals cannot escape you,
    And mortal man, in his one day's dusk,
    Trembles before your glory.

ANTISTROPHE

    Surely you swerve upon ruin
720   The just man's consenting heart,

As here you have made bright anger
Stake between father and son—
And none has conquered but Love!
A girl's glánce wórking the will of heaven:
725   Pleasure to her alone who mocks us,
Merciless Aphroditê.[5]

SCENE IV

CHORAGOS (*as Antigonê enters guarded*): But I can no longer stand in awe of
         this,
Nor, seeing what I see, keep back my tears.
730   Here is Antigonê, passing to that chamber
Where all find sleep at last.

STROPHE 1

ANTIGONÊ: Look upon me, friends, and pity me
Turning back at the night's edge to say
Good-by to the sun that shines for me no longer;
735   Now sleepy Death
Summons me down to Acheron,[6] that cold shore:
There is no bridesong there, nor any music.
CHORUS: Yet not unpraised, not without a kind of honor,
You walk at last into the underworld;
740   Untouched by sickness, broken by no sword.
What woman has ever found your way to death?

ANTISTROPHE 1

ANTIGONÊ: How often I have heard the story of Niobê,[7]
Tantalos' wretched daughter, how the stone
Clung fast about her, ivy-close: and they say
745   The rain falls endlessly
And sifting soft snow; her tears are never done.
I feel the loneliness of her death in mine.
CHORUS: But she was born of heaven, and you
Are woman, woman-born. If her death is yours,

---

[5] **Aphroditê** goddess of love

[6] **Acheron** a river of the underworld, which was ruled by Hades

[7] **Niobê** Niobê boasted of her numerous children, provoking Leto, the mother of Apollo, to destroy them. Niobê wept profusely, and finally was turned into a stone on Mount Sipylus, whose streams are her tears.

750   A mortal woman's, is this not for you
         Glory in our world and in the world beyond?

STROPHE 2

ANTIGONÊ: You laugh at me. Ah, friends, friends,
         Can you not wait until I am dead? O Thebes,
         O men many-charioted, in love with Fortune,
755   Dear springs of Dircê, sacred Theban grove,
         Be witnesses for me, denied all pity,
         Unjustly judged! and think a word of love
         For her whose path turns
         Under dark earth, where there are no more tears.
760   CHORUS: You have passed beyond human daring and come at last
         Into a place of stone where Justice sits.
         I cannot tell
         What shape of your father's guilt appears in this.

ANTISTROPHE 2

ANTIGONÊ: You have touched it at last: that bridal bed
765   Unspeakable, horror of son and mother mingling:
         Their crime, infection of all our family!
         O Oedipus, father and brother!
         Your marriage strikes from the grave to murder mine.
         I have been a stranger here in my own land:
770   All my life
         The blasphemy of my birth has followed me.
         CHORUS: Reverence is a virtue, but strength
         Lives in established law: that must prevail.
         You have made your choice,
775   Your death is the doing of your conscious hand.

EPODE

ANTIGONÊ: Then let me go, since all your words are bitter,
         And the very light of the sun is cold to me.
         Lead me to my vigil, where I must have
         Neither love nor lamentation; no song, but silence.

780   [*Creon interrupts impatiently.*]

CREON: If dirges and planned lamentations could put off death,
         Men would be singing for ever.
         (*To the Servants.*)   Take her, go!

You know your orders: take her to the vault
785   And leave her alone there. And if she lives or dies,
That's her affair, not ours: our hands are clean.
ANTIGONÊ: O tomb, vaulted bride-bed in eternal rock,
Soon I shall be with my own again
Where Persephonê[8] welcomes the thin ghosts underground:
790   And I shall see my father again, and you, mother,
And dearest Polyneicês—
                        dearest indeed
To me, since it was my hand
That washed him clean and poured the ritual wine:
795   And my reward is death before my time!

And yet, as men's hearts know, I have done no wrong,
I have not sinned before God. Or if I have,
I shall know the truth in death. But if the guilt
Lies upon Creon who judged me, then, I pray,
800   May his punishment equal my own.
CHORAGOS: O passionate heart,
Unyielding, tormented still by the same winds!
CREON: Her guards shall have good cause to regret their delaying.
ANTIGONÊ: Ah! That voice is like the voice of death!
805   CREON: I can give you no reason to think you are mistaken.
ANTIGONÊ: Thebes, and you my fathers' gods,
And rulers of Thebes, you see me now, the last
Unhappy daughter of a line of kings,
Your kings, led away to death. You will remember
810   What things I suffer, and at what men's hands,
Because I would not transgress the laws of heaven.
(*To the Guards, simply.*) Come: let us wait no longer.

[*Exit Antigonê, left, guarded.*]

ODE IV

STROPHE 1

CHORUS: All Danaê's beauty was locked away
815   In a brazen cell where the sunlight could not come:
A small room still as any grave, enclosed her.
Yet she was a princess too,
And Zeus in a rain of gold poured love upon her.
O child, child,

---

[8] **Persephone** queen of the underworld

820 No power in wealth or war
Or tough sea-blackened ships
Can prevail against untiring Destiny!

ANTISTROPHE 1

And Dryas' son[9] also, that furious king,
Bore the god's prisoning anger for his pride:
825 Scaled up by Dionysos in deaf stone,
His madness died among echoes.
So at the last he learned what dreadful power
His tongue had mocked:
For he had profaned the revels,
830 And fired the wrath of the nine
Implacable Sisters[10] that love the sound of the flute.

STROPHE 2

And old men tell a half-remembered tale
Of horror where a dark ledge splits the sea
And a double surf beats on the gráy shóres:
835 How a king's new woman,[11] sick
With hatred for the queen he had imprisoned,
Ripped out his two sons' eyes with her bloody hands
While grinning Arês[12] watched the shuttle plunge
Four times: four blind wounds crying for revenge,

ANTISTROPHE 2

840 Crying, tears and blood mingled.—Piteously born,
Those sons whose mother was of heavenly birth!
Her father was the god of the North Wind
And she was cradled by gales,
She raced with young colts on the glittering hills
845 And walked untrammeled in the open light:
But in her marriage deathless Fate found means
To build a tomb like yours for all her joy.

---

[9] **Dryas' son** Lycurgus, King of Thrace

[10] **Sisters** the Muses

[11] **king's new woman** Eidothea second wife of King Phineus, blinded her stepsons. Their mother, Cleopatra, had been imprisoned in a cave. Phineus was the son of a king, and Cleopatra, his first wife, was the daughter of Boreas, the North Wind, but this illustrious ancestry could not protect his sons from violence and darkness.

[12] **Arês** god of war

SCENE V

[*Enter blind Teiresias, led by a boy. The opening speeches of Teiresias should be in singsong contrast to the realistic lines of Creon.*]

850

TEIRESIAS: This is the way the blind man comes, Princes, Princes,
    Lock-step, two heads lit by the eyes of one.
CREON: What new thing have you to tell us, old Teiresias?
TEIRESIAS: I have much to tell you: listen to the prophet, Creon.

855

CREON: I am not aware that I have ever failed to listen.
TEIRESIAS: Then you have done wisely, King, and ruled well.
CREON: I admit my debt to you. But what have you to say?
TEIRESIAS: This, Creon: you stand once more on the edge of fate.
CREON: What do you mean? Your words are a kind of dread.

860

TEIRESIAS: Listen, Creon:
    I was sitting in my chair of augury, at the place
    Where the birds gather about me. They were all a-chatter,
    As is their habit, when suddenly I heard
    A strange note in their jangling, a scream, a

865

    Whirring fury; I knew that they were fighting,
    Tearing each other, dying
    In a whirlwind of wings clashing. And I was afraid.
    I began the rites of burnt-offering at the altar,
    But Hephaistos[13] failed me: instead of bright flame,

870

    There was only the sputtering slime of the fat thigh-flesh
    Melting: the entrails dissolved in gray smoke,
    The bare bone burst from the welter. And no blaze!

    This was a sign from heaven. My boy described it,
    Seeing for me as I see for others.

875

    I tell you, Creon, you yourself have brought
    This new calamity upon us. Our hearths and altars
    Are stained with the corruption of dogs and carrion birds
    That glut themselves on the corpse of Oedipus' son.
    The gods are deaf when we pray to them, their fire

880

    Recoils from our offering, their birds of omen
    Have no cry of comfort, for they are gorged
    With the thick blood of the dead.
                O my son,
    These are no trifles! Think: all men make mistakes,

---

[13] **Hephaistos** god of fire and blacksmith for the gods

885 But a good man yields when he knows his course is wrong,
And repairs the evil. The only crime is pride.
Give in to the dead man, then: do not fight with a corpse—
What glory is it to kill a man who is dead?
Think, I beg you:
890 It is for your own good that I speak as I do.
You should be able to yield for your own good.
CREON: It seems that prophets have made me their especial province.
All my life long
I have been a kind of butt for the dull arrows
895 Of doddering fortune-tellers!
                         No, Teiresias:
If your birds—if the great eagles of God himself
Should carry him stinking bit by bit to heaven,
I would not yield. I am not afraid of pollution:
900 No man can defile the gods.
                         Do what you will,
Go into business, make money, speculate
In India gold or that synthetic gold from Sardis,
Get rich otherwise than by my consent to bury him.
905 Teiresias, it is a sorry thing when a wise man
Sells his wisdom, lets out his words for hire!
TEIRESIAS: Ah Creon! Is there no man left in the world—
CREON: To do what?—Come, let's have the aphorism!
TEIRESIAS: No man who knows that wisdom outweighs any wealth?
910 CREON: As surely as bribes are baser than any baseness.
TEIRESIAS: You are sick, Creon! You are deathly sick!
CREON: As you say: it is not my place to challenge a prophet.
TEIRESIAS: Yet you have said my prophecy is for sale.
CREON: The generation of prophets has always loved gold.
915 TEIRESIAS: The generation of kings has always loved brass.
CREON: You forget yourself! You are speaking to your King.
TEIRESIAS: I know it. You are a king because of me.
CREON: You have a certain skill; but you have sold out.
TEIRESIAS: King, you will drive me to words that—
920 CREON: Say them, say them!
Only remember: I will not pay you for them.
TEIRESIAS: No, you will find them too costly.
CREON: No doubt. Speak:
Whatever you say, you will not change my will.
925 TEIRESIAS: Then take this, and take it to heart!
The time is not far off when you shall pay back
Corpse for corpse, flesh of your own flesh.
You have thrust the child of this world into living night,

You have kept from the gods below the child that is theirs:
930   The one in a grave before her death, the other,
Dead, denied the grave. This is your crime:
And the Furies and the dark gods of Hell
Are swift with terrible punishment for you.

Do you want to buy me now, Creon?

935   Not many days,
And your house will be full of men and women weeping,
And curses will be hurled at you from far
Cities grieving for sons unburied, left to rot
Before the walls of Thebes.

940   These are my arrows, Creon: they are all for you.

(*To Boy.*) But come, child: lead me home.
Let him waste his fine anger upon younger men.
Maybe he will learn at last
To control a wiser tongue in a better head.

945   [*Exit Teiresias.*]

CHORAGOS: The old man has gone, King, but his words
     Remain to plague us. I am old, too,
     But I cannot remember that he was ever false.
CREON: That is true. . . . It troubles me.
950   Oh it is hard to give in! but it is worse
     To risk everything for stubborn pride.
CHORAGOS: Creon: take my advice.
CREON: What shall I do?
CHORAGOS: Go quickly: free Antigonê from her vault
955   And build a tomb for the body of Polyneicês.
CREON: You would have me do this!
CHORAGOS: Creon, yes!
     And it must be done at once: God moves
     Swiftly to cancel the folly of stubborn men.
960 CREON: It is hard to deny the heart! But I
     Will do it: I will not fight with destiny.
CHORAGOS: You must go yourself, you cannot leave it to others.
CREON: I will go.
            —Bring axes, servants: Come with me to the tomb.
965   I buried her, I
Will set her free.

Oh quickly! My mind misgives—
The laws of the gods are mighty, and a man must serve them
To the last day of his life!

970 [*Exit Creon.*]

PAEAN[14]

STROPHE 1

CHORAGOS: God of many names
CHORUS: O Iacchos

                                                            son
        of Kadmeian Sémelê
975   O born of the Thunder!
        Guardian of the West
                          Regent
        of Eleusis' plain
                          O Prince of maenad Thebes
980   and the Dragon Field by rippling Ismenós:[15]

ANTISTROPHE 1

CHORAGOS: God of many names
CHORUS: The flame of torches
        flares on our hills
                          the nymphs of Iacchos
985   dance at the spring of Castalia:[16]
        from the vine-close mountain
                          come ah come in ivy:
        Evohé evohé! sings through the streets of Thebes

STROPHE 2

CHORAGOS: God of many names
990 CHORUS: Iacchos of Thebes
        heavenly Child
                          of Sémelê bride of the Thunderer!
        The shadow of plague is upon us:

---

[14] **Paean** a hymn (here dedicated to Iacchos, also called Dionysos. His father was Zeus, his mother was Sémelê, daughter of Kadmos. Iacchos's worshipers were the Maenads, whose cry was "*Evohé evohé*").

[15] **Ismenós** a river east of Thebes. From a dragon's teeth, sown near the river, there sprang men who became the ancestors of the Theban nobility.

[16] **Castalia** a spring on Mount Parnasos

come

995   with clement feet

oh come from Parnasos

down the long slopes

across the lamenting water

ANTISTROPHE 2

CHORAGOS: Iô Fire! Chorister of the throbbing stars!
1000   O purest among the voices of the night!
        Thou son of God, blaze for us!
    CHORUS: Come with choric rapture of circling Maenads
        Who cry *Iô Iacche!*
            God of many names!

EXODOS

1005   [*Enter Messenger from left.*]

    MESSENGER: Men of the line of Kadmos,[17] you who live
        Near Amphion's citadel,[18]
                    I cannot say
    Of any condition of human life "This is fixed.
1010   This is clearly good, or bad." Fate raises up,
    And Fate casts down the happy and unhappy alike:
    No man can foretell his Fate.
                        Take the case of Creon:
    Creon was happy once, as I count happiness:
1015   Victorious in battle, sole governor of the land,
    Fortunate father of children nobly born.
    And now it has all gone from him! Who can say
    That a man is still alive when his life's joy fails?
    He is a walking dead man. Grant him rich,
1020   Let him live like a king in his great house:
    If his pleasure is gone, I would not give
    So much as the shadow of smoke for all he owns.
    CHORAGOS: Your words hint at sorrow: what is your news for us?
    MESSENGER: They are dead. The living are guilty of their death.
1025   CHORAGOS: Who is guilty? Who is dead? Speak!

---

[17] **Kadmos** who sowed the dragon's teeth, was founder of Thebes.

[18] **Amphion's citadel** Amphion played so sweetly on his lyre that he charmed stones to form a wall around Thebes.

MESSENGER: Haimon.
    Haimon is dead, and the hand that killed him
    Is his own hand.
CHORAGOS: His father's? or his own?
1030   MESSENGER: His own, driven mad by the murder his father had done.
CHORAGOS: Teiresias, Teiresias, how clearly you saw it all!
MESSENGER: This is my news: you must draw what conclusions you can from it.
CHORAGOS: But look: Eurydicê, our Queen:
    Has she overheard us?

1035   [*Enter Eurydicê from the palace, center.*]

EURYDICÊ: I have heard something, friends:
    As I was unlocking the gate of Pallas'[19] shrine,
    For I needed her help today, I heard a voice
    Telling of some new sorrow. And I fainted
1040   There at the temple with all my maidens about me.
    But speak again: whatever it is, I can bear it:
    Grief and I are no strangers.
MESSENGER: Dearest Lady,
    I will tell you plainly all that I have seen.
1045   I shall not try to comfort you: what is the use,
    Since comfort could lie only in what is not true?
    The truth is always best.
                    I went with Creon
    To the outer plain where Polyneicês was lying,
1050   No friend to pity him, his body shredded by dogs.
    We made our prayers in that place to Hecatê
    And Pluto,[20] that they would be merciful. And we bathed
    The corpse with holy water, and we brought
    Fresh-broken branches to burn what was left of it,
1055   And upon the urn we heaped up a towering barrow
    Of the earth of his own land.
                    When we were done, we ran
    To the vault where Antigonê lay on her couch of stone.
    One of the servants had gone ahead,
1060   And while he was yet far off he heard a voice
    Grieving within the chamber, and he came back
    And told Creon. And as the King went closer,
    The air was full of wailing, the words lost,

---

[19] **Pallas** Pallas Athene, goddess of wisdom
[20] **Hecatê/And Pluto** Hecatê and Pluto (also known as Hades) were deities of the underworld.

And he begged us to make all haste. "Am I a prophet?"
1065   He said, weeping, "And must I walk this road,
The saddest of all that I have gone before?
My son's voice calls me on. Oh quickly, quickly!
Look through the crevice there, and tell me
If it is Haimon, or some deception of the gods!"

1070   We obeyed; and in the cavern's farthest corner
We saw her lying:
She had made a noose of her fine linen veil
And hanged herself. Haimon lay beside her,
His arms about her waist, lamenting her,
1075   His love lost under ground, crying out
That his father had stolen her away from him.
When Creon saw him the tears rushed to his eyes
And he called to him: "What have you done, child? Speak to me.
What are you thinking that makes your eyes so strange?
1080   O my son, my son, I come to you on my knees!"
But Haimon spat in his face. He said not a word,
Staring—
            And suddenly drew his sword
And lunged. Creon shrank back, the blade missed; and the boy
1085   Desperate against himself, drove it half its length
Into his own side, and fell. And as he died
He gathered Antigonê close in his arms again,
Choking, his blood bright red on her white cheek.
And now he lies dead with the dead, and she is his
1090   At last, his bride in the house of the dead.

[*Exit Eurydicê into the palace.*]

CHORAGOS: She has left us without a word. What can this mean?
MESSENGER: It troubles me, too; yet she knows what is best,
Her grief is too great for public lamentation,
1095   And doubtless she has gone to her chamber to weep
For her dead son, leading her maidens in his dirge.

[*Pause.*]

CHORAGOS: It may be so: but I fear this deep silence.
MESSENGER: I will see what she is doing. I will go in.

1100   [*Exit Messenger into the palace.*]

[*Enter Creon with attendants, bearing Haimon's body.*]

CHORAGOS: But here is the king himself: oh look at him,
    Bearing his own damnation in his arms.
CREON: Nothing you say can touch me any more.
1105   My own blind heart has brought me
    From darkness to final darkness. Here you see
    The father murdering, the murdered son—
    And all my civic wisdom!

    Haimon my son, so young, so young to die,
1110   I was the fool, not you; and you died for me.
CHORAGOS: That is the truth; but you were late in learning it.
CREON: This truth is hard to bear. Surely a god
    Has crushed me beneath the hugest weight of heaven,
    And driven me headlong a barbaric way
1115   To trample out the thing I held most dear.
    The pains that men will take to come to pain!

[*Enter Messenger from the palace.*]

MESSENGER: The burden you carry in your hands is heavy,
1120   But it is not all: you will find more in your house.
CREON: What burden worse than this shall I find there?
MESSENGER: The Queen is dead.
CREON: O port of death, deaf world,
    Is there no pity for me? And you, Angel of evil,
1125   I was dead, and your words are death again.
    Is it true, boy? Can it be true?
    Is my wife dead? Has death bred death?
MESSENGER: You can see for yourself.

[*The doors are opened and the body of Eurydicê is disclosed
1130   within.*]

CREON: Oh pity!
    All true, all true, and more than I can bear!
    O my wife, my son!
MESSENGER: She stood before the altar, and her heart
1135   Welcomed the knife her own hand guided,
    And a great cry burst from her lips for Megareus[21] dead,
    And for Haimon dead, her sons; and her last breath

---

[21] **Megareus,** brother of Haimon, had died in the assault on Thebes.

Was a curse for their father, the murderer of her sons.

And she fell, and the dark flowed in through her closing eyes.

1140 CREON: O God, I am sick with fear.

Are there no swords here? Has no one a blow for me?

MESSENGER: Her curse is upon you for the deaths of both.

CREON: It is right that it should be. I alone am guilty.

I know it, and I say it. Lead me in,

1145 Quickly, friends.

I have neither life nor substance. Lead me in.

CHORAGOS: You are right, if there can be right in so much wrong.

The briefest way is best in a world of sorrow.

CREON: Let it come,

1150 Let death come quickly, and be kind to me.

I would not ever see the sun again.

CHORAGOS: All that will come when it will; but we, meanwhile,

Have much to do. Leave the future to itself.

CREON: All my heart was in that prayer!

1155 CHORAGOS: Then do not pray any more: the sky is deaf.

CREON: Lead me away. I have been rash and foolish.

I have killed my son and my wife.

I look for comfort; my comfort lies here dead.

Whatever my hands have touched has come to nothing.

1160 Fate has brought all my pride to a thought of dust.

[*As Creon is being led into the house, the Choragos advances and speaks directly to the audience.*]

CHORAGOS: There is no happiness where there is no wisdom;

No wisdom but in submission to the gods.

1165 Big words are always punished,

And proud men in old age learn to be wise.

7. MEDEA
(431 BCE)

Euripides

(trans. by Rex Warner)

    Euripides (480–405 BCE) was the least appreciated of the great tragedians in his day, probably because of the bleak outlook he projects. Medea, produced in 431 BCE, reflects the contemporary loss of faith in rationality, as both Medea and Athens embark on irrational, destructive paths in killing "their children." The reversal of traditional gender roles and enigmatic intrusion of the gods who condone the wickedness suggests cosmic disorder that spells the demise of the Golden Age of Greece.

MEDEA, *princess of Colchis and wife of Jason*
JASON, *son of Aeson, king of Iolcos*
Two CHILDREN *of Medea and Jason*
KREON, *king of Corinth*
AIGEUS, *king of Athens*
NURSE *to Medea*
TUTOR *to Medea's children*
MESSENGER
CHORUS OF CORINTHIAN WOMEN

[Scene—*In front of* MEDEA's *house in Corinth. Enter from the house* MEDEA's *nurse.*]

NURSE: How I wish the Argo[1] never had reached the land
    Of Colchis, skimming through the blue Symplegades,
    Nor ever had fallen in the glades of Pelion[2]
    The smitten fir-tree to furnish oars for the hands

---

[1] The ship in which Jason and his companions sailed on the quest for the Golden Fleece.

[2] A mountain in northern Greece near Iolcos, the place from which Jason sailed. The Symplegades were clashing rocks that crushed ships endeavoring to pass between them. They were supposed to be located at the Hellespont, the passage between the Mediterranean and Black seas.

5   Of heroes who in Pelias'[3] name attempted
The Golden Fleece! For then my mistress Medea[4]
Would not have sailed for the towers of the land of Iolcos,
Her heart on fire with passionate love for Jason;
Nor would she have persuaded the daughters of Pelias
10   To kill their father,[5] and now be living here
In Corinth[6] with her husband and children. She gave
Pleasure to the people of her land of exile,
And she herself helped Jason in every way.
This is indeed the greatest salvation of all,—
15   For the wife not to stand apart from the husband.
But now there's hatred everywhere. Love is diseased.
For, deserting his own children and my mistress,
Jason has taken a royal wife to his bed,
The daughter of the ruler of this land, Kreon.
20   And poor Medea is slighted, and cries aloud on the
Vows they made to each other, the right hands clasped
In eternal promise. She calls upon the gods to witness
What sort of return Jason has made to her love.
She lies without food and gives herself up to suffering,
25   Wasting away every moment of the day in tears.
So it has gone since she knew herself slighted by him.
Not stirring an eye, not moving her face from the ground,
No more than either a rock or a surging sea water
She listens when she is given friendly advice.
30   Except that sometimes she twists back her white neck and
Moans to herself, calling out on her father's name,
And her land, and her home betrayed when she came away with
A man who now is determined to dishonor her.
Poor creature, she has discovered by her sufferings
35   What it means to one not to have lost one's own country.
She has turned from the children and does not like to see them.
I am afraid she may think of some dreadful thing,
For her heart is violent. She will never put up with
The treatment she is getting. I know and fear her

---

[3] He seized the kingdom of Iolcos, expelling Aeson, Jason's father. When Jason came to claim his rights, Pelias sent him to get the Golden Fleece.

[4] Daughter of the king of Colchis who fell in love with Jason and helped him take the Golden Fleece away from her own country.

[5] After Jason and Medea returned to Iolcos, Medea (who had a reputation as a sorceress) persuaded Pelias' daughters to cut Pelias up and boil the pieces, which would restore him to youth. The experiment was, of course, unsuccessful, and Pelias' son banished Jason and Medea from the kingdom.

[6] On the isthmus between the Peloponnese and Attica, where they took refuge. In Euripides' time it was a wealthy trading city, a commercial rival of Athens.

40   Lest she may sharpen a sword and thrust to the heart,
Stealing into the palace where the bed is made,
Or even kill the king and the new-wedded groom,
And thus bring a greater misfortune on herself.
She's a strange woman. I know it won't be easy

45   To make an enemy of her and come off best.
But here the children come. They have finished playing.
They have no thought at all of their mother's trouble.
Indeed it is not usual for the young to grieve.

       [*Enter from the right of the slave who is the* TUTOR *to*

50   MEDEA's *two small* CHILDREN. *The* CHILDREN *follow*
him.]

TUTOR: You old retainer of my mistress's household,
       Why are you standing here all alone in front of the
       Gates and moaning to yourself over your misfortune?

55   Medea could not wish you to leave her alone.
NURSE: Old man, and guardian of the children of Jason,
       If one is a good servant, it's a terrible thing
       When one's master's luck is out; it goes to one's heart.
       So I myself have got into such a state of grief

60   That a longing stole over me to come outside here
       And tell the earth and air of my mistress's sorrows.
TUTOR: Has the poor lady not yet given up her crying?
NURSE: Given up? She's at the start, not halfway through her tears.
TUTOR: Poor fool,—if I may call my mistress such a name,—

65   How ignorant she is of trouble more to come.
NURSE: What do you mean, old man? You needn't fear to speak.
TUTOR: Nothing. I take back the words which I used just now.
NURSE: Don't, by your beard, hide this from me, your fellow-servant.
       If need be, I'll keep quiet about what you tell me.

70   TUTOR: I heard a person saying, while I myself seemed
       Not to be paying attention, when I was at the place
       Where the old draught-players[7] sit, by the holy fountain,
       That Kreon, ruler of the land, intends to drive
       These children and their mother in exile from Corinth.

75   But whether what he said is really true or not
       I do not know. I pray that it may not be true.
NURSE: And will Jason put up with it that his children
       Should suffer so, though he's no friend to their mother?
TUTOR: Old ties give place to new ones. As for Jason, he

---

[7] Checker players.

80 No longer has a feeling for this house of ours.
NURSE: It's black indeed for us, when we add new to old
 Sorrows before even the present sky cleared.
TUTOR: But you be silent, and keep all this to yourself.
 It is not the right time to tell our mistress of it.
85 NURSE: Do you hear, children, what a father he is to you?
 I wish he were dead,—but no, he is still my master.
 Yet certainly he has proved unkind to his dear ones.
TUTOR: What's strange in that? Have you only just discovered
 That everyone loves himself more than his neighbor?
90 Some have good reason, others get something out of it.
 So Jason neglects his children for the new bride.
NURSE: Go indoors, children. That will be the best thing.
 And you, keep them to themselves as much as possible.
 Don't bring them near their mother in her angry mood.
95 For I've seen her already blazing her eyes at them
 As though she meant some mischief and I am sure that
 She'll not stop raging until she has struck at someone.
 May it be an enemy and not a friend she hurts!

[MEDEA *is heard inside the house.*]

100 MEDEA: Ah, wretch! Ah, lost in my sufferings,
 I wish, I wish I might die.
NURSE: What did I say, dear children? Your mother
 Frets her heart and frets it to anger.
 Run away quickly into the house,
105 And keep well out of her sight.
 Don't go anywhere near, but be careful
 Of the wildness and bitter nature
 Of that proud mind.
 Go now! Run quickly indoors.
110 It is clear that she soon will put lightning
 In that cloud of her cries that is rising
 With a passion increasing. Oh, what will she do,
 Proud-hearted and not to be checked on her course,
 A soul bitten into with wrong?

115 [*The* TUTOR *takes the* CHILDREN *into the house.*]

MEDEA: Ah, I have suffered
 What should be wept for bitterly. I hate you,
 Children of a hateful mother. I curse you
 And your father. Let the whole house crash.

120 NURSE: Ah, I pity you, you poor creature.
How can your children share in their father's
Wickedness? Why do you hate them? Oh children,
How much I fear that something may happen!
Great people's tempers are terrible, always
125 Having their own way, seldom checked,
Dangerous they shift from mood to mood.
How much better to have been accustomed
To live on equal terms with one's neighbors.
I would like to be safe and grow old in a
130 Humble way. What is moderate sounds best,
Also in practice *is* best for everyone.
Greatness brings no profit to people.
God indeed, when in anger, brings
Greater ruin to great men's houses.

135 [*Enter, on the right, a* CHORUS OF CORINTHIAN
WOMEN. *They have come to inquire about* MEDEA *and to
attempt to console her.*]

CHORUS: I heard the voice, I heard the cry
Of Colchis' wretched daughter.
140 Tell me, mother, is she not yet
At rest? Within the double gates
Of the court I hear her cry. I am sorry
For the sorrow of this home. O, say, what has happened?
NURSE: There is no home. It's over and done with.
145 Her husband holds fast to his royal wedding,
While she, my mistress, cries out her eyes
There in her room, and takes no warmth from
Any word of any friend.
MEDEA: Oh, I wish
150 That lightning from heaven would split my head open.
Oh, what use have I for life?
I would find my release in death
And leave hateful existence behind me.
CHORUS: O God and Earth and Heaven!
155 Did you hear what a cry was that
Which the sad wife sings?
Poor foolish one, why should you long
For that appalling rest?
The final end of death comes fast.
160 No need to pray for that.
Suppose your man gives honor

To another woman's bed.
It often happens. Don't be hurt.
God will be your friend in this.

165   You must not waste away
Grieving too much for him who shared your bed.
MEDEA: Great Themis, lady Artemis,[8] behold
The things I suffer, though I made him promise,
My hateful husband. I pray that I may see him,

170   Him and his bride and all their palace shattered
For the wrong they dare to do me without cause.
Oh, my father! Oh, my country! In what dishonor
I left you, killing my own brother for it.[9]
NURSE: Do you hear what she says, and how she cries

175   On Themis, the goddess of Promises, and on Zeus,
Whom we believe to be the Keeper of Oaths?
Of this I am sure, that no small thing
Will appease my mistress's anger.
CHORUS: Will she come into our presence?

180   Will she listen when we are speaking
To the words we say?
I wish she might relax her rage
And temper of her heart.
My willingness to help will never

185   Be wanting to my friends.
But go inside and bring her
Out of the house to us,
And speak kindly to her: hurry,
Before she wrongs her own.

190   This passion of hers moves to something great.
NURSE: I will, but I doubt if I'll manage
To win my mistress over.
But still I'll attempt it to please you.
Such a look she will flash on her servants

195   If any comes near with a message,
Like a lioness guarding her cubs.
It is right, I think, to consider
Both stupid and lacking in foresight
Those poets of old who wrote songs

200   For revels and dinners and banquets,
Pleasant sounds for men living at ease;
But none of them all has discovered

---

[8] The protector of women in pain and distress. Themis, a Titan, was justice personified.
[9] Medea killed him to delay the pursuit when she escaped with Jason.

How to put an end with their singing
Or musical instruments grief,
205   Bitter grief, from which death and disaster
Cheat the hopes of a house. Yet how good
If music could cure men of this! But why raise
To no purpose the voice at a banquet? For *there* is
Already abundance of pleasure for men
210   With a joy of its own.

[*The* NURSE *goes into the house.*]

CHORUS: I heard a shriek that is laden with sorrow.
Shrilling out her hard grief she cries out
Upon him who betrayed both her bed and her marriage.
215   Wronged, she calls on the gods,
On the justice of Zeus, the oath sworn,
Which brought her away
To the opposite shore of the Greeks
Through the gloomy salt straits to the gateway
220   Of the salty unlimited sea.

[MEDEA, *attended by servants, comes out of the house.*]

MEDEA: Women of Corinth, I have come outside to you
Lest you should be indignant with me; for I know
That many people are overproud, some when alone,
225   And others when in company. And those who live
Quietly, as I do, get a bad reputation.
For a just judgement is not evident in the eyes
When a man at first sight hates another, before
Learning his character, being in no way injured;
230   And a foreigner[10] especially must adapt himself.
I'd not approve of even a fellow-countryman
Who by pride and want of manners offends his neighbors.
But on me this thing has fallen so unexpectedly,
It has broken my heart. I am finished. I let go
235   All my life's joy. My friends, I only want to die.
It was everything to me to think well of one man,
And he, my own husband, has turned out wholly vile.
Of all things which are living and can form a judgment

---

[10] Foreign residents were encouraged to come to Athens but were rarely admitted to the rights of full citizenship, which was a jealously regarded privilege.

We women are the most unfortunate creatures.[11]

240   Firstly, with an excess of wealth it is required
For us to buy a husband and take for our bodies
A master; for not to take one is even worse.
And now the question is serious whether we take
A good or bad one; for there is no easy escape

245   For a woman, nor can she say no to her marriage.
She arrives among new modes of behavior and manners,
And needs prophetic power, unless she has learnt at home,
How best to manage him who shares the bed with her.
And if we work out all this well and carefully,

250   And the husband lives with us and lightly bears his yoke,
Then life is enviable. If not, I'd rather die.
A man, when he's tired of the company of his home,
Goes out of the house and puts an end to his boredom
And turns to a friend or companion of his own age.

255   But we are forced to keep our eyes on one alone.
What they say of us is that we have a peaceful time
Living at home, while they do the fighting in war.
How wrong they are! I would very much rather stand
Three times in front of battle than bear one child.

260   Yet what applies to me does not apply to you.
You have a country. Your family home is here.
You enjoy life and the company of your friends.
But I am deserted, a refugee, thought nothing of
By my husband,—something he won in a foreign land.

265   I have no mother or brother, nor any relation
With whom I can take refuge in this sea of woe.
This much then is the service I would beg from you:
If I can find the means or devise any scheme
To pay my husband back for what he has done to me,—

270   Him and his father-in-law and the girl who married him,—
Just to keep silent. For in other ways a woman
Is full of fear, defenseless, dreads the sight of cold
Steel; but, when once she is wronged in the matter of love,
No other soul can hold so many thoughts of blood.

275   CHORUS: This I will promise. You are in the right, Medea,
In paying your husband back. I am not surprised at you
For being sad. But look! I see our king Kreon
Approaching. He will tell us of some new plan.

---

[11] Athenian rights and institutions were made for men; the women had few privileges and almost no legal rights. Lines 240–241 refer to the dowry that had to be provided for the bride.

[*Enter, from the right,* KREON, *with attendants.*]

280 KREON: You, with that angry look, so set against your husband,
Medea, I order you to leave my territories
An exile, and take along with you your two children,
And not to waste time doing it. It is my decree,
And I will see it done. I will not return home
285 Until you are cast from the boundaries of my land.
MEDEA: Oh, this is the end for me. I am utterly lost.
Now I am in the full force of the storm of hate
And have no harbor from ruin to reach easily.
Yet still, in spite of it all, I'll ask the question:
290 What is your reason, Kreon, for banishing me?
KREON: I am afraid of you,—why should I dissemble it?—
Afraid that you may injure my daughter mortally.
Many things accumulate to support my feeling.
You are a clever woman, versed in evil arts,
295 And are angry at having lost your husband's love.
I hear that you are threatening, so they tell me,
To do something against my daughter and Jason
And me, too. I shall take my precautions first.
I tell you, I prefer to earn your hatred now
300 Than to be soft-hearted and afterwards regret it.
MEDEA: This is not the first time, Kreon. Often previously
Through being considered clever I have suffered much.
A person of sense ought never to have his children
Brought up to be more clever than the average.
305 For, apart from cleverness bringing them no profit,
It will make them objects of envy and ill-will.
If you put new ideas before the eyes of fools
They'll think you foolish and worthless into the bargain;
And if you are thought superior to those who have
310 Some reputation for learning, you will become hated.
I have some knowledge myself of how this happens;
For being clever, I find that some will envy me,
Others object to me. Yet all my cleverness
Is not so much. Well, then, are you frightened, Kreon,
315 That I should harm you? There is no need. It is not
My way to transgress the authority of a king.
How have you injured me? You gave your daughter away
To the man you wanted. O, certainly I hate
My husband, but you, I think, have acted wisely;
320 Nor do I grudge it you that your affairs go well.
May the marriage be a lucky one! Only let me

Live in this land. For even though I have been wronged,
I will not raise my voice, but submit to my betters.
KREON: What you say sounds gentle enough. Still in my heart
325   I greatly dread that you are plotting some evil,
And therefore I trust you even less than before.
A sharp-tempered woman, or for that matter a man,
Is easier to deal with than the clever type
Who holds her tongue. No. You must go. No need for more
330   Speeches. The thing is fixed. By no manner of means
Shall you, an enemy of mine, stay in my country.
MEDEA: I beg you. By your knees, by your new-wedded girl.
KREON: Your words are wasted. You will never persuade me.
MEDEA: Will you drive me out, and give no heed to my prayers?
335   KREON: I will, for I love my family more than you.
MEDEA: O my country! How bitterly now I remember you!
KREON: I love my country too,—next after my children.
MEDEA: O what an evil to men is passionate love!
KREON: That would depend on the luck that goes along with it.
340   MEDEA: O God, do not forget who is the cause of this!
KREON: Go. It is no use. Spare me the pain of forcing you.
MEDEA: I am spared no pain. I lack no pain to be spared me.
KREON: Then you'll be removed by force by one of my men.
MEDEA: No, Kreon, not that! But do listen, I beg you.
345   KREON: Woman, you seem to want to create a disturbance.
MEDEA: I *will* go into exile. *This* is not what I beg for.
KREON: Why then this violence and clinging to my hand?
MEDEA: Allow me to remain here just for this one day,
So I may consider where to live in my exile,
350   And look for support for my children, since their father
Chooses to make no kind of provision for them.
Have pity on them! You have children of your own.
It is natural for you to look kindly on them.
For myself I do not mind if I go into exile.
355   It is the children being in trouble that I mind.
KREON: There is nothing tyrannical about my nature,
And by showing mercy I have often been the loser.
Even now I know that I am making a mistake.
All the same you shall have your will. But this I tell you,
360   That if the light of heaven tomorrow shall see you,
You and your children in the confines of my land,
You die. This word I have spoken is firmly fixed.
But now, if you must stay, stay for this day alone.
For in it you can do none of the things I fear.

365   [*Exit* KREON *with his attendants.*]

CHORUS: Oh, unfortunate one! Oh, cruel!
     Where will you turn? Who will help you?
     What house or what land to preserve you
     From ill can you find?
370   Medea, a god had thrown suffering
     Upon you in waves of despair.
MEDEA: Things have gone badly every way. No doubt of that.
     But not these things this far, and don't imagine so.
     There are still trials to come for the new-wedded pair,
375   And for their relations pain that will mean something.
     Do you think that I would ever have fawned on that man
     Unless I had some end to gain or profit in it?
     I would not even have spoken or touched him with my hands.
     But he has got to such a pitch of foolishness
380   That, though he could have made nothing of all my plans
     By exiling me, he has given me this one day
     To stay here, and in this I will make dead bodies
     Of three of my enemies,—father, the girl and my husband.
     I have many ways of death which I might suit to them,
385   And do not know, friends, which one to take in hand;
     Whether to set fire underneath their bridal mansion,
     Or sharpen a sword and thrust it to the heart,
     Stealing into the palace where the bed is made.
     There is just one obstacle to this. If I am caught
390   Breaking into the house and scheming against it,
     I shall die, and give my enemies cause for laughter.
     It is best to go by the straight road, the one in which
     I am most skilled, and make away with them by poison.
     So be it then.
395   And now suppose them dead. What town will receive me?
     What friend will offer me a refuge in his land,
     Or the guarantee of his house and save my own life?
     There is none. So I must wait a little time yet,
     And if some sure defense should then appear for me,
400   In craft and silence I will set about this murder.
     But if my fate should drive me on without help,
     Even though death is certain, I will take the sword
     Myself and kill, and steadfastly advance to crime.
     It shall not be,—I swear it by her, my mistress,
405   Whom most I honor and have chosen as partner,

Hecate,[12] who dwells in the recesses of my hearth,—
That any man shall be glad to have injured me.
Bitter I will make their marriage for them and mournful,
Bitter the alliance and the driving me out of the land.
410 Ah, come, Medea, in your plotting and scheming
Leave nothing untried of all those things which you know.
Go forward to the dreadful act. The test has come
For resolution. You see how you are treated. Never
Shall you be mocked by Jason's Corinthian wedding,
415 Whose father was noble, whose grandfather Helios.[13]
You have the skill. What is more, you were born a woman,
And women, though most helpless in doing good deeds,
Are of every evil the cleverest of contrivers.
CHORUS: Flow backward to your sources, sacred rivers,
420 And let the world's great order be reversed.
It is the thoughts of *men* that are deceitful,
Their pledges that are loose.
Story shall now turn my condition to a fair one,
Women are paid their due.
425 No more shall evil-sounding fame be theirs.

Cease now, you muses of the ancient singers,
To tell the tale of my unfaithfulness;
For not on us did Phoebus,[14] lord of music,
Bestow the lyre's divine
430 Power, for otherwise I should have sung an answer
To the other sex. Long time
Has much to tell of us, and much of them.

You sailed away from your father's home,
With a heart on fire you passed
435 The double rocks of the sea.
And now in a foreign country
You have lost your rest in a widowed bed,
And are driven forth, a refugee
In dishonor from the land.

440 Good faith has gone, and no more remains
In great Greece a sense of shame.
It has flown away to the sky.

---

[12] The patron of witchcraft, sometimes identified with Artemis.
[13] The sun, father of Medea's father, Aeëtes.
[14] Apollo.

No father's house for a haven
Is at hand for you now, and another queen
445 Of your bed has dispossessed you and
Is mistress of your home.

[*Enter* JASON, *with attendants.*]

JASON: This is not the first occasion that I have noticed
How hopeless it is to deal with a stubborn temper.
450 For, with reasonable submission to our ruler's will,
You might have lived in this land and kept your home.
As it is you are going to be exiled for your loose speaking.
Not that I mind myself. You are free to continue
Telling everyone that Jason is a worthless man.
455 But as to your talk about the king, consider
Yourself most lucky that exile is your punishment.
I, for my part, have always tried to calm down
The anger of the king, and wished you to remain.
But you will not give up your folly, continually
460 Speaking ill of him, and so you are going to be banished.
All the same, and in spite of your conduct, I'll not desert
My friends, but have come to make some provision for you,
So that you and the children may not be penniless
Or in need of anything in exile. Certainly
465 Exile brings many troubles with it. And even
If you hate me, I cannot think badly of you.
MEDEA: O coward in every way,—that is what I call you,
With bitterest reproach for your lack of manliness,
You have come, you, my worst enemy, have come to me!
470 It is not an example of over-confidence
Or of boldness thus to look your friends in the face,
Friends you have injured,—no, it is the worst of all
Human diseases, shamelessness. But you did well
To come for I can speak ill of you and lighten
475 My heart, and you will suffer while you are listening.
And first I will begin from what happened first.
I saved your life, and every Greek knows I saved it
Who was a ship-mate of yours aboard the Argo,
When you were sent to control the bulls that breathed fire
480 And yoke them, and when you would sow that deadly field.
Also that snake, who encircled with his many folds

The Golden Fleece and guarded it and never slept,[15]
I killed, and so gave you the safety of the light.
And I myself betrayed my father and my home,

485   And came with you to Pelias' land of Iolcos.
And then, showing more willingness to help than wisdom,
I killed him, Pelias, with a most dreadful death
At his own daughters' hands, and took away your fear.
This is how I behaved to you, you wretched man,

490   And you forsook me, took another bride to bed
Though you had children; for, if that had not been,
You would have had an excuse for another wedding.
Faith in your word has gone. Indeed I cannot tell
Whether you think the gods whose names you swore by then

495   Have ceased to rule and that new standards are set up,
Since you must know you have broken your word to me.
O my right hand, and the knees which you often clasped
In supplication, how senselessly I am treated
By this bad man, and how my hopes have missed their mark!

500   Come, I will share my thoughts as though you were a friend,—
You! Can I think that you would ever treat me well?
But I will do it, and these questions will make you
Appear the baser. Where am I to go? To my father's?
Him I betrayed and his land when I came with you.

505   To Pelias' wretched daughters? What a fine welcome
They would prepare for me who murdered their father!
For this is my position,—hated by my friends
At home, I have, in kindness to you, made enemies
Of others whom there was no need to have injured.

510   And how happy among Greek women you have made me
On your side for all this! A distinguished husband
I have,—for breaking promises. When in misery
I am cast out of the land and go into exile,
Quite without friends and all alone with my children,

515   That will be a fine shame for the new-wedded groom,
For his children to wander as beggars and she who saved him.
O God, you have given to mortals a sure method
Of telling the gold that is pure from the counterfeit;
Why is there no mark engraved upon men's bodies,

520   By which we could know the true ones from the false ones?

---

[15] These lines refer to ordeals through which Jason had to pass to win the fleece and in which Medea helped him. He had to yoke a team of fire-breathing bulls, then sow a field that immediately sprouted armed warriors, and then deal with the snake that guarded the fleece.

CHORUS: It is a strange form of anger, difficult to cure
  When two friends turn upon each other in hatred.
JASON: As for me, it seems I must be no bad speaker.
  But, like a man who has a good grip of the tiller,
525 Reef up his sail, and so run away from under
  This mouthing tempest, woman, of your bitter tongue.
  Since you insist on building up your kindness to me,
  My view is that Cypris[16] was alone responsible
  Of men and gods for the preserving of my life.
530 You are clever enough,—but really I need not enter
  Into the story of how it was love's inescapable
  Power that compelled you to keep my person safe.
  On this I will not go into too much detail.
  In so far as you helped me, you did well enough.
535 But on this question of saving me, I can prove
  You have certainly got from me more than you gave.
  Firstly, instead of living among barbarians,
  You inhabit a Greek land and understand our ways,
  How to live by law instead of the sweet will of force.
540 And all the Greeks considered you a clever woman.
  You were honored for it; while, if you were living at
  The ends of the earth, nobody would have heard you.
  For my part, rather than stores of gold in my house
  Or power to sing even sweeter songs than Orpheus,
545 I'd choose the fate that made me a distinguished man.
  There is my reply to your story of my labors.
  Remember it was you who started the argument.
  Next for your attack on my wedding with the princess:
  Here I will prove that, first, it was a clever move,
550 Secondly, a wise one, and, finally, that I made it
  In your best interests and the children's. Please keep calm.
  When I arrived here from the land of Iolcos,
  Involved, as I was, in every kind of difficulty,
  What luckier chance could I have come across than this,
555 An exile to marry the daughter of the king?
  It was not,—the point that seems to upset you—that I
  Grew tired of your bed and felt the need of a new bride;
  Nor with any wish to outdo your number of children,
  We have enough already. I am quite content.
560 But,—this was the main reason—that we might live well,
  And not be short of anything. I know that all
  A man's friends leave him stone-cold if he becomes poor.

---

[16] Aphrodite, goddess of love.

Also that I might bring my children up worthy
Of my position, and, by producing more of them

565 To be brothers of yours, we would draw the families
Together and all be happy. You need no children.
And it pays me to do good to those I have now
By having others. Do you think this is a bad plan?
You wouldn't if the love question hadn't upset you.

570 But you women have got into such a state of mind
That, if your life at night is good, you think you have
Everything; but, if in that quarter things go wrong,
You will consider your best and truest interests
Most hateful. It would have been better far for men

575 To have got their children in some other way, and women
Not to have existed. Then life would have been good.
CHORUS: Jason, though you have made this speech of yours look well,
Still I think, even though others do not agree,
You have betrayed your wife and are acting badly.

580 MEDEA: Surely in many ways I hold different views
From others, for I think that the plausible speaker
Who is a villain deserves the greatest punishment.
Confident in his tongue's power to adorn evil,
He stops at nothing. Yet he is not really wise.

585 As in your case. There is no need to put on the airs
Of a clever speaker, for one word will lay you flat.
If you were not a coward, you would not have married
Behind my back, but discussed it with me first.
JASON: And you, no doubt, would have furthered the proposal,

590 If I had told you of it, you who even now
Are incapable of controlling your bitter temper.
MEDEA: It was not that. No, you thought it was not respectable
As you got on in years to have a foreign wife.
JASON: Make sure of this: it was not because of a woman

595 I made the royal alliance in which I now live,
But, as I said before, I wished to preserve you
And breed a royal progeny to be brothers
To the children I have now, a sure defense to us.
MEDEA: Let me have no happy fortune that brings pain with it,

600 Or prosperity which is upsetting to the mind!
JASON: Change your ideas of what you want, and show more sense.
Do not consider painful what is good for you,
Nor, when you are lucky, think yourself unfortunate.
MEDEA: You can insult me. You have somewhere to turn to.

605 But I shall go from this land into exile, friendless.
JASON: It was what you chose yourself. Don't blame others for it.

MEDEA: And how did I choose it? Did I betray my husband?
JASON: You called down wicked curses on the king's family.
MEDEA: A curse, that is what I am become to your house too.
610 JASON: I do not propose to go into all the rest of it;
But, if you wish for the children or for yourself
In exile to have some of my money to help you,
Say so, for I am prepared to give with open hand,
Or to provide you with introductions to my friends
615 Who will treat you well. You are a fool if you do not
Accept this. Cease your anger and you will profit.
MEDEA: I shall never accept the favors of friends of yours,
Nor take a thing from you, so you need not offer it.
There is no benefit in the gifts of a bad man.
620 JASON: Then, in any case, I call the gods to witness that
I wish to help you and the children in every way,
But you refuse what is good for you. Obstinately
You push away your friends. You are sure to suffer for it.
MEDEA: Go! No doubt you hanker for your virginal bride,
625 And are guilty of lingering too long out of her house.
Enjoy your wedding. But perhaps,—with the help of God—
You will make the kind of marriage that you will regret.

[JASON *goes out with attendants.*]

CHORUS: When love is in excess
630 It brings a man no honor
Nor any worthiness.
But if in moderation Cypris comes,
There is no other power at all so gracious.
O goddess, never on me let loose the unerring
635 Shaft of your bow in the poison of desire.

Let my heart be wise.
It is the gods' best gift.
On me let mighty Cypris
Inflict no wordy wars or restless anger
640 To urge my passion to a different love.
But with discernment may she guide women's weddings,
Honoring most what is peaceful in the bed.

O country and home,
Never, never may I be without you,
645 Living the hopeless life,
Hard to pass through and painful,

Most pitiable of all.
Let death first lay me low and death
Free me from this daylight.
650   There is no sorrow above
The loss of a native land.

I have seen it myself,
Do not tell of a secondhand story.
Neither city nor friend
655   Pitied you when you suffered
The worst of sufferings.
O let him die ungraced whose heart
Will not reward his friends,
Who cannot open an honest mind
660   No friend will he be of mine.

[*Enter* AIGEUS, *king of Athens, and old friend of* MEDEA.]

AIGEUS: Medea, greeting! This is best introduction
Of which men know for conversation between friends.
MEDEA: Greeting to you too, Aigeus, son of King Pandion,
665   Where have you come from to visit this country's soil?
AIGEUS: I have just left the ancient oracle of Phoebus.
MEDEA: And why did you go to earth's prophetic center?
AIGEUS: I went to inquire how children might be born to me.
MEDEA: Is it so? Your life still up to this point childless?
670   AIGEUS: Yes. But the fate of some power we have no children.
MEDEA: Have you no wife, or is there none to share your bed?
AIGEUS: There is. Yes, I am joined to my wife in marriage.
MEDEA: And what did Phoebus say to you about children?
AIGEUS: Words too wise for a mere man to guess their meaning.
675   MEDEA: Is it proper for me to be told the God's reply?
AIGEUS: It is. For sure what is needed is cleverness.
MEDEA: Then what was his message? Tell me, if I may hear,
AIGEUS: I am not to loosen the hanging foot of the wine-skin[17] ...
MEDEA: Until you have done something, or reached some country?
680   AIGEUS: Until I return again to my hearth and house.
MEDEA: And for what purpose have you journeyed to this land?
AIGEUS: There is a man called Pittheus, king of Troezen.[18]
MEDEA: A son of Pelops, they say, a most righteous man.

---

[17] Cryptic; probably not to have intercourse.

[18] In the Peloponnese. Pittheus was Aigeus' father-in-law. Corinth was on the way from Delphi to Troezen.

AIGEUS: With him I wish to discuss the reply of the god.
685   MEDEA: Yes. He is wise and experienced in such matters.
AIGEUS: And to me also the dearest of all my spear-friends.[19]
MEDEA: Well, I hope you have good luck, and achieve your will.
AIGEUS: But why this downcast eye of yours, and this pale cheek?
MEDEA: O Aigeus, my husband has been the worst of all to me.
690   AIGEUS: What do you mean? Say clearly what has caused this grief.
MEDEA: Jason wrongs me, though I have never injured him.
AIGEUS: What has he done? Tell me about it in clearer words.
MEDEA: He has taken a wife to his house, supplanting me.
AIGEUS: Surely he would not dare to do a thing like that.
695   MEDEA: Be sure he has. Once dear, I now am slighted by him.
AIGEUS: Did he fall in love? Or is he tired of your love?
MEDEA: He was greatly in love, this traitor to his friends.
AIGEUS: Then let him go, if, as you say, he is so bad.
MEDEA: A passionate love,—for an alliance with the king.
700   AIGEUS: And who gave him his wife? Tell me the rest of it.
MEDEA: It was Kreon, he who rules this land of Corinth.
AIGEUS: Indeed, Medea, your grief was understandable.
MEDEA: I am ruined. And there is more to come: I am banished.
AIGEUS: Banished? By whom? Here you tell me of a new wrong.
705   MEDEA: Kreon drives me an exile from the land of Corinth.
AIGEUS: Does Jason consent? I cannot approve of this.
MEDEA: He pretends not to, but he will put up with it.
    Ah, Aigeus, I beg and beseech you, by your beard
    And by your knees I am making myself your suppliant,
710   Have pity on me, have pity on your poor friend,
    And do not let me go into exile desolate,
    But receive me in your land and at your very hearth.
    So may your love, with God's help, lead to the bearing
    Of children, and so may you yourself die happy.
715   You do not know what a chance you have come on here.
    I will end your childlessness, and I will make you able
    To beget children. The drugs I know can do this.
AIGEUS: For many reasons, woman, I am anxious to do
    This favor for you. First, for the sake of the gods,
720   And then for the birth of children which you promise,
    For in that respect I am entirely at my wits' end.
    But this is my position: if you reach my land,
    I, being in my rights, will try to befriend you.
    But this much I must warn you of beforehand:
725   I shall not agree to take you out of this country;

---

[19] Allies in war, companions in fighting.

But if you by yourself can reach my house, then you
Shall stay there safely. To none will I give you up.
But from this land you must make your escape yourself,
For I do not wish to incur blame from my friends.

730 MEDEA: It shall be so. But, if I might have a pledge from you
For this, then I would have from you all I desire.

AIGEUS: Do you not trust me? What is it rankles with you?

MEDEA: I trust you, yes. But the house of Pelias hates me,
And so does Kreon. If you are bound by this oath,

735 When they try to drag me from your land, you will not
Abandon me; but if our pact is only words,
With no oath to the gods, you will be lightly armed,
Unable to resist their summons. I am weak,
While they have wealth to help them and a royal house.

740 AIGEUS: You show much foresight for such negotiations.
Well, if you will have it so, I will not refuse.
For, both on my side this will be the safest way
To have some excuse to put forward to your enemies,
And for you it is more certain. You may name the gods.

745 MEDEA: Swear by the plain of Earth, and Helios, father
Of my father, and name together all the gods . . .

AIGEUS: That I will act or not act in what way? Speak.

MEDEA: That you yourself will never cast me from your land,
Nor, if any of my enemies should demand me,

750 Will you, in your life, willingly hand me over.

AIGEUS: I swear by the Earth, by the holy light of Helios,
By all the gods, I will abide by this you say.

MEDEA: Enough. And, if you fail, what shall happen to you?

AIGEUS: What comes to those who have no regard for heaven.

755 MEDEA: Go on your way. Farewell. For I am satisfied,
And I will reach your city as soon as I can,
Having done the deed I have to do and gained my end.

[AIGEUS *goes out.*]

CHORUS: May Hermes, god of travelers,
760 Escort you, Aigeus, to your home!
And may you have the things you wish
So eagerly; for you
Appear to me to be a generous man.

MEDEA: God, and God's daughter, justice, and light of Helios!
765 Now, friends, has come the time of my triumph over
My enemies, and now my foot is on the road.
Now I am confident they will pay the penalty.

For this man, Aigeus, has been like a harbor to me
In all my plans just where I was most distressed.
770 To him I can fasten the cable of my safety
When I have reached the town and fortress of Pallas.[20]
And now I shall tell to you the whole of my plan.
Listen to these words that are not spoken idly.
I shall send one of my servants to find Jason
775 And request him to come once more into my sight.
And when he comes, the words I'll say will be soft ones.
I'll say that I agree with him, that I approve
Thy royal wedding he has made, betraying me.
I'll say it was profitable, an excellent idea.
780 But I shall beg that my children may remain here:
Not that I would leave in a country that hates me
Children of mine to feel their enemies' insults,
But that by a trick I may kill the king's daughter.
For I will send the children with gifts in their hands
785 To carry to the bride, so as not to be banished,—
A finely woven dress and a golden diadem.
And if she takes them and wears them upon her skin
She and all who touch the girl will die in agony;
Such a poison will I lay upon the gifts I send.
790 But there, however, I must leave that account paid.
I weep to think of what a deed I have to do
Next after that; for I shall kill my own children.
My children, there is none who can give them safety.
And when I have ruined the whole of Jason's house,
795 I shall leave the land and flee from the murder of my
Dear children, and I shall have done a dreadful deed.
For it is not bearable to be mocked by enemies.
So it must happen. What a profit have I in life?
I have no land, no home, no refuge from my pain.
800 My mistake was made the time I left behind me
My father's house, and trusted the words of a Greek,
Who, with heaven's help, will pay me the price for that.
For those children he had from me he will never
See alive again, nor will he on his new bride
805 Beget another child, for she is to be forced
To die a most terrible death by these my poisons.
Let no one think me a weak one, feeble-spirited,
A stay-at-home, but rather just the opposite,

---

[20]Athens, city of Pallas Athene.

One who can hurt my enemies and help my friends;
810   For the lives of such persons are most remembered.
CHORUS: Since you have shared the knowledge of your plan with us,
          I both wish to help you and support the normal
          Ways of mankind, and tell you not to do this thing.
MEDEA: I can do no other thing. It is understandable
815   For you to speak thus. You have not suffered as I have.
CHORUS: But can you have the heart to kill your flesh and blood?
MEDEA: Yes, for this is the best way to wound my husband.
CHORUS: And you too. Of women you will be most unhappy.
MEDEA: So it must be. No compromise is possible.

820   [*She turns to the* NURSE.]

          Go, you, at once, and tell Jason to come to me.
          You I employ on all affairs of greatest trust.
          Say nothing of these decisions which I have made,
          If you love your mistress, if you were born a woman.
825 CHORUS: From of old the children of Erechtheus[21] are
          Splendid, the sons of blessed gods. They dwell
          In Athens' holy and unconquered land,[22]
          Where famous Wisdom feeds them and they pass gaily
          Always through that most brilliant air where once, they say,
830   That golden Harmony gave birth to the nine
          Pure Muses of Pieria.[23]

          And beside the sweet flow of Cephisos' stream,
          Where Cypris[24] sailed, they say, to draw the water,
          And mild soft breezes breathed along her path,
835   And on her hair were flung the sweet-smelling garlands
          Of flowers of roses by the Lovers, the companions
          Of Wisdom, her escort, the helpers of men
          In every kind of excellence.

---

[21] An early king of Athens, a son of Hephaestus.

[22] It was the Athenians' boast that their descent from the original settlers was uninterrupted by an invasion. There is a topical reference here, for the play was produced in 431 B.C., in a time of imminent war.

[23] A fountain in Boeotia where the Muses were supposed to live. The sentence means that the fortunate balance (*Harmony*) of the elements and the genius of the people produced the cultivation of the arts (*the nine Pure Muses*).

[24] The goddess of love and, therefore, of the principle of fertility. Cephisos is an Athenian river.

How then can these holy rivers
840   Or this holy land love you,
Or the city find you a home,
You, who will kill your children,
You, not pure with the rest?
O think of the blow at your children
845   And think of the blood that you shed.
O, over and over I beg you,
By your knees I beg you do not
Be the murderess of your babes!
O where will you find the courage
850   Or the skill of hand and heart,
When you set yourself to attempt
A deed so dreadful to do?
How, when you look upon them,
Can you tearlessly hold the decision
855   For murder? You will not be able,
When your children fall down and implore you,
You will not be able to dip
Steadfast your hand in their blood.

[*Enter* JASON *with attendants.*]

860   JASON: I have come at your request. Indeed, although you are
Bitter against me, this you shall have: I will listen
To what new thing you want, woman, to get from me.
MEDEA: Jason, I beg you to be forgiving towards me
For what I said. It is natural for you to bear with
865   My temper, since we have had much love together.
I have talked with myself about this and I have
Reproached myself. "Fool" I said, "why am I so mad?
Why am I set against those who have planned wisely?
Why make myself as enemy of the authorities
870   And of my husband, who does the best thing for me
By marrying royalty and having children who
Will be as brothers to my own? What is wrong with me?
Let me give up anger, for the gods are kind to me.
Have I not children, and do I not know that we
875   In exile from our country must be short of friends?"
When I considered this I saw that I had shown
Great lack of sense, and that my anger was foolish.
Now I agree with you. I think that you are wise
In having this other wife as well as me, and I
880   Was mad. I should have helped you in these plans of yours,

Have joined in the wedding, stood by the marriage bed,
Have taken pleasure in attendance on your bride.
But we women are what we are,—perhaps a little
Worthless; and you men must not be like us in this,
885   Nor be foolish in return when we are foolish.
Now I give in, and admit that then I was wrong.
I have come to a better understanding now.

[*She turns towards the house.*]

Children, come here, my children, come outdoors to us!
890   Welcome your father with me, and say goodbye to him,
And with your mother, who just now was his enemy,
Join again in making friends with him who loves us.

[*Enter the* CHILDREN, *attended by the* TUTOR.]

We have made peace, and all our anger is over.
895   Take hold of his right hand,—O God, I am thinking
Of something which may happen in the secret future.
O children, will you just so, after a long life
Hold out your loving arms at the grave? O children,
How ready to cry I am, how full of foreboding!
900   I am ending at last this quarrel with your father,
And, look, my soft eyes have suddenly filled with tears.
CHORUS: And the pale tears have started also in my eyes.
O may the trouble not grow worse than now it is!
JASON: I approve of what you say. And I cannot blame you
905   Even for what you said before. It is natural
For a woman to be wild with her husband when he
Goes in for secret love. But now your mind has turned
To better reasoning. In the end you have come to
The right decision, like the clever woman you are.
910   And of you, children, your father is taking care.
He has made, with God's help, ample provision for you.
For I think that a time will come when you will be
The leading people in Corinth with your brothers.
You must grow up. As to the future, your father
915   And those of the gods who love him will deal with that.
I want to see you, when you have become young men,
Healthy and strong, better men than my enemies.
Medea, why are your eyes all wet with pale tears?
Why is your cheek so white and turned away from me?
920   Are not these words of mine pleasing for you to hear?

MEDEA: It is nothing. I was thinking about these children.
JASON: You must be cheerful. I shall look after them well.
MEDEA: I will be. It is not that I distrust your words,
    But a woman is a frail thing, prone to crying.
925 JASON: But why then should you grieve so much for these children?
MEDEA: I am their mother. When you prayed that they might live
    I felt unhappy to think that these things will be.
    But come, I have said something of the things I meant
    To say to you, and now I will tell you the rest.
930   Since it is the king's will to banish me from here,—
    And for me too I know that this is the best thing,
    Not to be in your way by living here or in
    The king's way, since they think me ill-disposed to them,—
    I then am going into exile from this land;
935   But do you, so that you may have the care of them,
    Beg Kreon that the children may not be banished.
JASON: I doubt if I'll succeed, but still I'll attempt it.
MEDEA: Then you must tell your wife to beg from her father
    That the children may be reprieved from banishment.
940 JASON: I will, and with her I shall certainly succeed.
MEDEA: If she is like the rest of us women, you will.
    And I too will take a hand with you in the business,
    For I will send her some gifts which are far fairer,
    I am sure of it, than those which now are in fashion,
945   A finely-woven dress and a golden diadem,
    And the children shall present them. Quick, let one of you
    Servants bring here to me that beautiful dress.

[*One of her attendants goes into the house.*]

    She will be happy not in one way, but in a hundred,
950   Having so fine a man as you to share her bed,
    And with this beautiful dress which Helios of old,
    My father's father, bestowed on his descendants.

[*Enter attendant carrying the poisoned dress and diadem.*]

    There, children, take these wedding presents in your hands.
955   Take them to the royal princess, the happy bride,
    And give them to her. She will not think little of them.
JASON: No, don't be foolish, and empty your hands of these.
    Do you think the palace is short of dresses to wear?
    Do you think there is no gold there? Keep them, don't give them

960   Away. If my wife considers me of any value,
                 She will think more of me than money, I am sure of it.
          MEDEA: No, let me have my way. They say the gods themselves
                 Are moved by gifts, and gold does more with men than words.
                 Hers is the luck, her fortune that which god blesses;
965   She is young and a princess; but for my children's reprieve
                 I would give my very life, and not gold only.
                 Go children, go together to that rich palace,
                 Be suppliants to the new wife of your father,
                 My lady, beg her not to let you be banished.
970   And give her the dress,—for this is of great importance,
                 That she should take the gift into her hand from yours.
                 Go, quick as you can. And bring your mother good news
                 By your success of those things which she longs to gain.

                 [JASON *goes out with his attendants, followed by the*
975   TUTOR *and the* CHILDREN *carrying the poisoned gifts.*]

          CHORUS: Now there is no hope left for the children's lives.
                 Now there is none. They are walking already to murder.
                 The bride, poor bride, will accept the curse of the gold,
                 Will accept the bright diadem.
980   Around her yellow hair she will set that dress
                 Of death with her own hands.
                 The grace and the perfume and glow of the golden robe
                 Will charm her to put them upon her and wear the wreath,
                 And now her wedding will be with the dead below,
985   Into such a trap she will fall,
                 Poor thing, into such a fate of death and never
                 Escape from under that curse.
                 You too, O wretched bridegroom, making your match with kings,
                 You do not see that you bring
990   Destruction on your children and on her,
                 Your wife, a fearful death.
                 Poor soul, what a fall is yours!

                 In your grief too I weep, mother of little children,
                 You who will murder your own,
995   In vengeance for the loss of married love
                 Which Jason has betrayed
                 As he lives with another wife.

                 [*Enter the* TUTOR *with the* CHILDREN.]

TUTOR: Mistress, I tell you that these children are reprieved,
1000   And the royal bride has been pleased to take in her hands
     Your gifts. In that quarter the children are secure.
     But come,
     Why do you stand confused when you are fortunate?
     Why have you turned round with your cheek away from me?
1005   Are not these words of mine pleasing for you to hear?
MEDEA: Oh! I am lost!
TUTOR: That word is not in harmony with my tidings.
MEDEA: I am lost, I am lost!
TUTOR: Am I in ignorance telling you
1010   Of some disaster, and not the good news I thought?
MEDEA: You have told what you have told. I do not blame you.
TUTOR: Why then this downcast eye, and this weeping of tears?
MEDEA: Oh, I am forced to weep, old man. The gods and I,
     I in a kind of madness have contrived all this.
1015 TUTOR: Courage! You too will be brought home by your children.
MEDEA: Ah, before that happens I shall bring others home.
TUTOR: Others before you have been parted from their children.
     Mortals must bear in resignation their ill luck.
MEDEA: That is what I shall do. But go inside the house,
1020   And do for the children your usual daily work.

     [*The* TUTOR *goes into the house.* MEDEA *turns to her* CHILDREN.]

O children, O my children, you have a city,
     You have a home, and you can leave me behind you,
1025   And without your mother you may live there for ever.
     But I am going in exile to another land
     Before I have seen you happy and taken pleasure in you,
     Before I have dressed your brides and made your marriage beds
     And held up the torch at the ceremony of wedding.
1030   Oh, what a wretch I am in this my self-willed thought!
     What was the purpose, children, for which I reared you?
     For all my travail and wearing myself away?
     They were sterile, those pains I had in my bearing of you.
     O surely once the hopes in you I had, poor me,
1035   Were high ones: you would look after me in old age,
     And when I died would deck me well with your own hands;
     A thing which all would have done. O but now it is gone,
     That lovely thought. For, once I am left without you,
     Sad will be the life I'll lead and sorrowful for me.
1040   And you will never see your mother again with

Your dear eyes, gone to another mode of living.
Why, children, do you look upon me with your eyes?
Why do you smile so sweetly that last smile of all?
Oh, Oh, what can I do? My spirit has gone from me,
1045   Friends, when I saw that bright look in the children's eyes.
I cannot bear to do it. I renounce my plans
I had before. I'll take my children away from
This land. Why should I hurt their father with the pain
They feel, and suffer twice as much of pain myself?
1050   No, no, I will not do it. I renounce my plans.
Ah, what is wrong with me? Do I want to let go
My enemies unhurt and be laughed at for it?
I must face this thing. Oh, but what a weak woman
Even to admit to my mind these soft arguments.
1055   Children, go into the house. And he whom law forbids
To stand in the attendance at my sacrifices,
Let him see to it. I shall not mar my handiwork.
Oh! Oh!
Do not, O my heart, you must not do these things!
1060   Poor heart, let them go, have pity upon the children.
If they live with you in Athens they will cheer you.
No! By Hell's avenging furies it shall not be,—
This shall never be, that I should suffer my children
To be the prey of my enemies' insolence.
1065   Every way is it fixed. The bride will not escape.
No, the diadem is now upon her head, and she,
The royal princess, is dying in the dress, I know it.
But,—for it is the most dreadful of roads for me
To tread, and them I shall send on a more dreadful still—
1070   I wish to speak to the children.

[*She calls the* CHILDREN *to her.*]

                        Come, children give
Me your hands, give your mother your hands to kiss them.
O the dear hands, and O how dear are these lips to me,
1075   And the generous eyes and the bearing of my children!
I wish you happiness, but not here in this world.
What is here you father took. O how good to hold you!
How delicate the skin, how sweet the breath of children!
Go, go! I am no longer able, no longer
1080   To look upon you. I am overcome by sorrow.

[*The* CHILDREN *go into the house.*]

I know indeed what evil I intend to do,
But stronger than all my afterthoughts is my fury,
Fury that brings upon mortals the greatest evils.

1085   *[She goes out to the right, towards the royal palace.]*

CHORUS: Often before
I have gone through more subtle reasons,
And have come upon questionings greater
Than a woman should strive to search out.
1090   But we too have a goddess to help us
And accompany us into wisdom.
Not all of us. Still you will find
Among many women a few,
And our sex is not without learning.
1095   This I say, that those you have never
Had children, who know nothing of it,
In happiness have the advantage
Over those who are parents.
The childless, who never discover
1100   Whether children turn out as a good thing
Or as something to cause pain, are spared
Many troubles in lacking this knowledge.
And those who have in their homes
The sweet presence of children, I see that their lives
1105   Are all wasted away by their worries.
First they must think how to bring them up well and
How to leave them something to live on.
And then after this whether all their toil
Is for those who will turn out good or bad,
1110   Is still an unanswered question.
And of one more trouble, the last of all,
That is common to mortals I tell.
For suppose you have found them enough for their living,
Suppose that the children have grown into youth
1115   And have turned out good, still, if God so wills it,
Death will away with your children's bodies,
And carry them off into Hades.
What is our profit, then, that for the sake of
Children the gods should pile upon mortals
1120   After all else
This most terrible grief of all?

[Enter MEDEA, from the spectators' right.]

MEDEA: Friends, I can tell you that for long I have waited
    For the event. I stare towards the place from where
1125   The news will come. And now, see one of Jason's servants
    Is on his way here, and that labored breath of his
    Shows he has tidings for us, and evil tidings.

[*Enter, also from the right, the* MESSENGER.]

MESSENGER: Medea, you who have done such a dreadful thing,
1130   So outrageous, run for your life, take what you can,
    A ship to bear you hence or chariot on land.
MEDEA: And what is the reason deserves such flight as this?
MESSENGER: She is dead, only just now, they royal princess,
    And Kreon dead too, her father, by your poisons.
1135 MEDEA: The finest words you have spoken. Now and hereafter
    I shall count you among my benefactors and friends.
MESSENGER: What! Are you right in the mind? Are you not mad,
    Woman? The house of the king is outraged by you.
    Do you enjoy it? Not afraid of such doings?
1140 MEDEA: To what you say I on my side have something too
    To say in answer. Do not be in a hurry, friend,
    But speak. How did they die? You will delight me twice
    As much again if you say they died in agony.
MESSENGER: When those two children, born of you, had entered in,
1145   Their father with them, and passed into the bride's house,
    We were pleased, we slaves who were distressed by your wrongs.
    All through the house we were talking of but one thing,
    How you and your husband had made up your quarrel.
    Some kissed the children's hands and some their yellow hair,
1150   And I myself was so full of my joy that I
    Followed the children into the women's quarters.
    Our mistress, whom we honor now instead of you,
    Before she noticed that your two children were there,
    Was keeping her eye fixed eagerly on Jason.
1155   Afterwards however she covered up her eyes,
    Her cheek paled and she turned herself away from him,
    So disgusted was she at the children's coming there.
    But your husband tried to end the girl's bad temper,
    And said "You must not look unkindly on your friends.
1160   Cease to be angry. Turn your head to me again.
    Have as your friends the same ones as your husband has.
    And take these gifts, and beg your father to reprieve
    These children from their exile. Do it for my sake."
    She, when she saw the dress, could not restrain herself.

1165	She agreed with all her husband said, and before
	He and the children had gone far from the palace,
	She took the gorgeous robe and dressed herself in it,
	And put the golden crown around her curly locks,
	And arranged the set of the hair in a shining mirror,
1170	And smiled at the lifeless image of herself in it.
	Then she rose from her chair and walked about the room,
	With her gleaming feet stepping most soft and delicate,
	All overjoyed with the present. Often and often
	She would stretch her foot out straight and look along it.
1175	But after that it was a fearful thing to see.
	The color of her face changed, and she staggered back,
	She ran, and her legs trembled, and she only just
	Managed to reach a chair without falling flat down.
	An aged woman servant who, I take it, thought
1180	This was some seizure of Pan[25] or another god,
	Cried out "God bless us," but that was before she saw
	The white foam breaking from her lips and her rolling
	The pupils of her eyes and her face all bloodless.
	Then she raised a different cry from that "God bless us,"
1185	A huge shriek, and the women ran, one to the king,
	One to the newly wedded husband to tell him
	What had happened to his bride; and with frequent sound
	The whole of the palace rang as they went running.
	One walking quickly round the course of a race-track
1190	Would now have turned the bend and be close to the goal,
	When she, poor girl, opened her shut and speechless eye,
	And with a terrible groan she came to herself.
	For a two-fold pain was moving up against her.
	The wreath of gold that was resting around her head
1195	Let forth a fearful stream of all-devouring fire,
	And the finely-woven dress your children gave to her,
	Was fastening on the unhappy girl's fine flesh.
	She leapt up from the chair, and all on fire she ran,
	Shaking her hair now this way and now that, trying
1200	To hurl the diadem away; but fixedly
	The gold preserved its grip, and, when she shook her hair,
	Then more and twice as fiercely the fire blazed out.
	Till, beaten by her fate, she fell down to the ground,
	Hard to be recognized except by a parent.
1205	Neither the setting of her eyes was plain to see,

---

[25] As the god of wild nature he was supposed to be the source of the sudden, apparently causeless terror that solitude in wild surroundings may produce and hence of all kinds of sudden madness (compare the English word *panic*).

Nor the shapeliness of her face. From the top of
Her head there oozed out blood and fire mixed together.
Like the drops on pine-bark, so the flesh from her bones
Dropped away, torn by the hidden fang of the poison.
1210   It was a fearful sight; and terror held us all
From touching the corpse. We had learned from what had happened.
But her wretched father, knowing nothing of the event,
Came suddenly to the house, and fell upon the corpse,
And at once cried out and folded his arms about her,
1215   And kissed her and spoke to her, saying, "O my poor child,
What heavenly power has so shamefully destroyed you?
And who has set me here like an ancient sepulchre,
Deprived of you? O let me die with you, my child!"
And when he had made an end of his wailing and crying,
1220   Then the old man wished to raise himself to his feet;
But, as the ivy clings to the twigs of the laurel,
So he stuck to the fine dress, and he struggled fearfully.
For he was trying to lift himself to his knee,
And she was pulling him down, and when he tugged hard
1225   He would be ripping his aged flesh from his bones.
At last his life was quenched and the unhappy man
Gave up the ghost, no longer could he hold up his head.
There they lie close, the daughter and the old father,
Dead bodies, an event he prayed for in his tears.
1230   As for your interests, I will say nothing of them,
For you will find your own escape from punishment.
Our human life I think and have thought a shadow,
And I do not fear to say that those who are held
Wise amongst men and who search the reasons of things
1235   Are those who bring the most sorrow on themselves.
For of mortals there is no one who is happy.
If wealth flows in upon one, one may be perhaps
Luckier than one's neighbor, but still not happy.

     [*Exit.*]

1240   CHORUS: Heaven, it seems, on this day has fastened many
Evils on Jason, and Jason has deserved them.
Poor girl, the daughter of Kreon, how I pity you
And your misfortunes, you who have gone quite away
To the house of Hades because of marrying Jason.
1245   MEDEA: Women, my task is fixed: as quickly as I may
To kill my children, and start away from this land,
And not, by wasting time, to suffer my children

To be slain by another hand less kindly to them.
Force every way will have it they must die, and since
1250 This must be so, then I, their mother, shall kill them.
O arm yourself in steel, my heart! Do not hang back
From doing this fearful and necessary wrong.
O come, my hand, poor wretched hand, and take the sword,
Take it, step forward to this bitter starting point,
1255 And do not be a coward, do not think of them,
How sweet they are, and how you are their mother. Just for
This one short day be forgetful of your children,
Afterwards weep; for even though you will kill them,
They were very dear,—O, I am an unhappy woman!

1260 [*With a cry she rushes into the house.*]

CHORUS: O Earth, and the far shining
Ray of the sun, look down, look down upon
This poor lost woman, look, before she raises
The hand of murder against her flesh and blood.
1265 Yours was the golden birth from which
She sprang, and now I fear divine
Blood may be shed by men.
O heavenly light, hold back her hand,
Check her, and drive from out the house
1270 The bloody Fury raised by fiends of Hell.

Vain waste, your care of children;
Was it in vain you bore the babes you loved,
After you passed the inhospitable strait
Between the dark blue rocks, Symplegades?
1275 O wretched one, how has it come,
This heavy anger on your heart,
The cruel bloody mind?
For God from mortals asks a stern
Price for the stain of kindred blood
1280 In like disaster falling on their homes.

[*A cry from one of the* CHILDREN *is heard.*]

CHORUS: Do you hear the cry, do you hear the children's cry?
O you hard heart, O woman fated for evil!
ONE OF THE CHILDREN: [*From within.*]
1285 What can I do and how escape my mother's hands?

ONE OF THE CHILDREN: [*From within.*] O my dear brother, I cannot tell.
    We are lost.
CHORUS: Shall I enter the house? O surely I should
    Defend the children from murder.
1290   A CHILD: [*From within.*]
    O help us, in God's name, for now we need your help.
    Now, now we are close to it. We are trapped by the sword.
CHORUS: O your heart must have been made of rock or steel,
    You who can kill
1295   With your own hand the fruit of your own womb.
    Of one alone I have heard, one woman alone
    Of those of old who laid her hands on her children,
    Ino, sent mad by heaven when the wife of Zeus
    Drove her out from her home and made her wander;
1300   And because of the wicked shedding of blood
    Of her own children she threw
    Herself, poor wretch, into the sea and stepped away
    Over the sea-cliff to die with her two children.
    What horror more can be? O women's love,
1305   So full of trouble,
    How many evils have you caused already!

    [*Enter* JASON, *with attendants.*]

JASON: You women, standing close in front of this dwelling,
    Is she, Medea, she who did this dreadful deed,
1310   Still in the house, or has she run away in flight?
    For she will have to hide herself beneath the earth,
    Or raise herself on wings into the height of air,
    If she wishes to escape the royal vengeance.
    Does she imagine that, having killed our rulers,
1315   She will herself escape uninjured from this house?
    But I am thinking not so much of her as for
    The children,—her the king's friends will make to suffer
    For what she did. So I have come to save the lives
    Of my boys, in case the royal house should harm them
1320   While taking vengeance for their mother's wicked deed.
CHORUS: O Jason, if you but knew how deeply you are
    Involved in sorrow, you would not have spoken so.
JASON: What is it? That she is planning to kill me also?
CHORUS: Your children are dead, and by their own mother's hand.
1325   JASON: What! This is it? O woman, you have destroyed me.
CHORUS: You must make up your mind your children are no more.
JASON: Where did she kill them? Was it here or in the house?

CHORUS: Open the gates and there you will see them murdered.
JASON: Quick as you can unlock the doors, men, and undo
1330   The fastenings and let me see this double evil,
          My children dead and her,—O her I will repay.

[*His attendants rush to the door.* MEDEA *appears above the
house in a chariot drawn by dragons. She has the dead bodies
of the* CHILDREN *with her.*]

1335 MEDEA: Why do you batter these gates and try to unbar them,
          Seeking the corpses and for me who did the deed?
          You may cease your trouble, and, if you have need of me,
          Speak, if you wish. You will never touch me with your hand,
          Such a chariot has Helios, my father's father,
1340   Given me to defend me from my enemies.
      JASON: You hateful thing, you woman most utterly loathed
          By the gods and me and by all the race of mankind,
          You who have had the heart to raise a sword against
          Our children, you, their mother, and left me childless,—
1345   You have done this, and do you still look at the sun
          And at the earth, after these most fearful doings?
          I wish you dead. Now I see it plain, though at that time
          I did not, when I took you from your foreign home
          And brought you to a Greek house, you, an evil thing,
1350   A traitress to your father and your native land.
          The gods hurled the avenging curse of yours on me.
          For your own brother you slew at your own hearthside,
          And then came aboard that beautiful ship, the Argo.
          And that was your beginning. When you were married
1355   To me, your husband, and had borne children to me,
          For the sake of pleasure in the bed you killed them.
          There is no Greek woman who would have dared such deeds,
          Out of the all those whom I passed over and chose you
          To marry instead, a bitter destructive match,
1360   A monster not a woman, having a nature
          Wilder than that of Scylla[26] in the Tuscan sea.
          Ah! no, not if I had ten thousand words of shame
          Could I sting you. You are naturally so brazen.
          Go, worker in evil, stained with your children's blood.
1365   For me remains to cry aloud upon my fate,
          Who will get no pleasure from my newly-wedded love,

---

26 A monster located in the straits between Italy and Sicily, who snatched sailors off
passing ships and devoured them.

And the boys whom I begot and brought up, never
Shall I speak to them alive. Oh, my life is over!
MEDEA: Long would be the answer which I might have made to
1370   These words of yours, if Zeus the father did not know
How I have treated you and what you did to me.
No, it was not to be that you should scorn my love,
And pleasantly live your life through, laughing at me;
Nor would the princess, nor he who offered to match,
1375   Kreon, drive me away without paying for it.
So now you may call me a monster, if you wish,
Or Scylla housed in the caves of the Tuscan sea
I too, as I had to, have taken hold of your heart.
JASON: You feel the pain yourself. You share in my sorrow.
1380   MEDEA: Yes, and my grief is gain when you cannot mock it.
JASON: O children, what a wicked mother she was to you!
MEDEA: They died from a disease they caught from their father.
JASON: I tell you it was not my hand that destroyed them.
MEDEA: But it was your insolence, and your virgin wedding.
1385   JASON: And just for the sake of that you chose to kill them.
MEDEA: Is love so small a pain, do you think, for a woman?
JASON: For a wise one, certainly. But you are wholly evil.
MEDEA: The children are dead. I say this to make you suffer.
JASON: The children, I think, will bring down curses on you.
1390   MEDEA: The gods know who was the author of this sorrow.
JASON: Yes, the gods know indeed, they know your loathsome heart.
MEDEA: Hate me. But I tire of your barking bitterness.
JASON: And I of yours. It is easier to leave you.
MEDEA: How then? What shall I do? I long to leave you too.
1395   JASON: Give me the bodies to bury and to mourn them.
MEDEA: No, that I will not. I will bury them myself,
Bearing them to Hera's temple on the promontory;
So that no enemy may evilly treat them
By tearing up their grave. In this land of Corinth
1400   I shall establish a holy feast and sacrifice[27]
Each year for ever to atone for the blood guilt.
And I myself go to the land of Erechtheus
To dwell in Aigeus' house, the son of Pandion.
While you, as is right, will die without distinction,
1405   Struck on the head by a piece of the Argo's timber,
And you will have seen the bitter end of my love.
JASON: May a Fury for the children's sake destroy you,
And justice, requitor of blood.

---

[27] Some such ceremony was still performed at Corinth in Euripides' time.

MEDEA: What heavenly power lends an ear
1410   To a breaker of oaths, a deceiver?
JASON: O, I hate you, murderess of children.
MEDEA: Go to your palace. Bury your bride.
JASON: I go, with two children to mourn for.
MEDEA: Not yet do you feel it. Wait for the future.
1415 JASON: Oh, children I loved!
MEDEA: I loved them, you did not.
JASON: You loved them, and killed them.
MEDEA: To make you feel pain
JASON: Oh, wretch that I am, how I long
1420   To kiss the dear lips of my children!
MEDEA: Now you would speak to them, now you would kiss them.
      Then you rejected them.
JASON: Let me, I beg you,
      Touch my boys' delicate flesh.
1425 MEDEA: I will not. Your words are all wasted.
JASON: O god, do you hear it, this persecution,
      These my sufferings from this hateful
      Woman, this monster, murderess of children?
      Still what I can do that I will do:
1430   I will lament and cry upon heaven,
      Calling the gods to bear me witness
      How you have killed my boys and prevent me from
      Touching their bodies or giving them burial.
      I wish I had never begot them to see them
1435   Afterwards slaughtered by you.
CHORUS: Zeus in Olympus is the overseer
      Of many doings. Many things the gods
      Achieve beyond our judgment. What we thought
      Is not confirmed and what we thought not god
1440   Contrives. And so it happens in this story.

8. TROJAN WOMEN
(415 BCE)

Euripides

(trans. by Paul Roche)

Euripides (480–405 BCE) earned a reputation as pessimist among his contemporaries, though his view proved to be realistic as Athenian power and prestige declined. His tragedy, Trojan Women, was produced in 415 BCE, when Athenian injustices in Melos and Syracuse made the enslavement of women all too realistic. The present and projected suffering of the women of fallen Troy is given highly stylized and ritualistic treatment to suggest a larger view of disorder extending beyond the human to the cosmic sphere.

CHARACTERS

POSEIDON, *god of the sea*
PALLAS ATHENA, *protectress of Athens*
HECUBA, *widow of Priam, king of Troy*
CHORUS, *of captured Trojan women*
TALTHYBIUS, *Greek officer and herald*
CASSANDRA, *daughter of Hecuba and Priam, a prophetess*
ANDROMACHE, *widow of Hector son of Priam*
MENELAUS, *king of Sparta and husband of Helen*
HELEN, *wife of Menelaus and cause of the Trojan War*
ASTYANAX, *a small boy, the son of Hector and Andromache*
GREEK SOLDIERS
ATTENDANTS

TIME AND SETTING

It is midmorning in the Greek camp on the plains of Troy. In the distance smoke still rises from the fallen city. A huddle of women awaiting their sentence of slavery and prostitution are grouped around the prostrate figure of Hecuba near a few disheveled tents. Poseidon strides into view. He is cloaked in a greenish mantle and his swarthy bearded face is turned towards Troy. He holds in his hands a trident.

PROLOGUE

POSEIDON: From the salt sea depths of the Aegean
    where the lacy feet of the Nereids weave and dance,
    I, Poseidon, come.
  Never have I lost my fondness
5   for this Phrygian city of Troy.
  No, not since the day that Phoebus and I
    with line and plummet threw up around her
    a stone girdle of towers.
  But look at her now
10   smoldering and wrecked by the Argive spear.
  It was Epeius the Phocian from Parnassus
    who with the help of Pallas built the wooden horse,
    crammed it with men, and thrust this load of ruin
    into the walled city.
15 It will be known hereafter
    as the Wooden Horse—pregnant with spears.

  The groves are now a desert,
    the sanctuaries of the gods spattered with blood.
  On the altar steps of Zeus the Protector
20   Priam lies dead—dead where he fell.
  The opulence of Phrygia,
    all its gold and all its plunder,
    are being loaded on to the Achaean ships
    as they lie in wait for a favorable breeze
25   to carry home those Greeks who yearn to see their wives and children,
    after a decade of useless seasons
    since they brought an army here to sack this city.

  As for me,
    I too have been overwhelmed:
30   overruled by those two goddesses in harness:
    Hera, patroness of Argos, and Athena,
    who together have set out to break this Phrygian town.
  So I must say farewell to famous Ilium,[1]
    farewell to all my shrines there . . .
35   for when grim doom lays its clutches on a city,
    all piety sickens too and devotion to the gods.

  Loud are the wailings on the banks of the Scamander

---

[1]Ilium: an alternate name for Troy. (Homer's *Iliad* title means the "story of Troy.")

of the many captive women being allotted to their masters.
Some go to the men of Arcady, some to men of Thessaly,
40   others to the scions of Theseus, the Athenian princes.
Inside the tents here are the rest of the Trojan women
    who have not yet been assigned: they are waiting
    to be picked by the chief men of the army.
Among them is the daughter of Tyndareus,
45   rightly deemed a prisoner: Helen of Sparta.

[POSEIDON *turns his gaze towards the prostrate* HECUBA]

If you want to see misery at its worst,
    look at the creature lying there, poor Hecuba,
    weeping a plethora of tears for a plethora of disasters.
Her daughter Polyxena was murdered secretly
50   and died bravely on Achilles' tomb, unhappy child.
Priam is no more; her children gone:
    all except Cassandra,[2] still a virgin and discarded by Apollo
    to rave her prophecies.
Agamemnon means to flout all decency and the god's decision
55   and drag her in the dark to bed.

[*Turning again towards the ruins of Troy*]

And now goodbye to my once so blessed city
    pinnacled in stone.
You would be standing yet
    if Zeus's daughter Pallas had not marked you out for ruin.

60   [*The goddess* PALLAS ATHENA *appears. Dressed like a soldier and wearing
the famous aegis—a breastplate with a Gorgon's head entwined with snakes—
she holds a shield and spear, looming over the landscape*]

FIRST EPISODE

ATHENA: [*approaching* POSEIDON]
    Will you permit me to address you
65   and call a halt to our ancient quarrel:
    you my father's closest kin and a mighty deity,
    so awed among the gods?
POSEIDON: I will. Ties of kinship, my lady Athena,

---

[2]Cassandra was beloved by Apollo who gave her the gift of prophecy; when she spurned his love, though he could not renege the gift, he stipulated that her prophecies would never be believed.

> work no small magic on the heart.

70 ATHENA: Thank you for your graciousness . . . And now, my lord
> there is something that you and I must plan together.

POSEIDON: About some message from the gods—
> Zeus perhaps, or some other deity?

ATHENA: No, about Troy—where we are standing now.

75 I need your help in a matter that affects us both.

POSEIDON: What! are you jettisoning your former hate,
> moved to pity now that Troy is flames and ash?

ATHENA: First things first. Will you join with me
> and help me carry out a plan?

80 POSEIDON: Of course! Once I'm told what it is.
> Are you helping the Achaeans or the Phrygians?

ATHENA: I want to make the Trojans whom I hated happy,
> and the homecoming of the Achaeans a disaster.

POSEIDON: How you shift from mood to mood,

85 plunging from hatred to excess of love!

ATHENA: So you haven't heard how my temples and I have been dishonored?

POSEIDON: I have: How Ajax hauled Cassandra from your sanctuary.

ATHENA: And the Achaeans have not done or said a thing.

POSEIDON: Although it was through your power that they took Ilium.

90 ATHENA: That is why I want to punish them.

POSEIDON: I am ready and willing. What do you propose?

ATHENA: I want you to wreck their passage home.

POSEIDON: What, before they start, on land, or out on the salt sea main?

ATHENA: After they've embarked from Troy for home.

95 Zeus will pelt them with rain and hail.
> Black tearing winds will blot out the sky,
> and to me he said he would give his thunderbolts and lightning
> to smash the Achaeans and set their ships on fire.

You for your part

100 must make the Aegean roar with mountainous surf and swirling currents.
> Choke the inlets of Euboea with bodies.
> Let the Achaeans in future learn
> to respect my shrines and reverence the other gods.

POSEIDON: It shall be done. This favor needs few words

105 I'll whip up the Aegean to a spume.
> The shores of Myconus,
> the reefs of Delos, Scyros, Lemnos,
> the capes of Caphareus
> shall be strewn with the washed-up bodies of the drowned.

* * *

-357-

110   Go now to Olympus,
         get from your father's hands the thunderbolts
         and watch for the moment when the Argive fleet casts off.

[ATHENA *takes her leave*]

     He is a fool that man who does not stop at sacking cities
115   but lays temples waste and tombs—
         those sanctuaries of the dead.

[POSEIDON *retires as* HECUBA *stirs. Half rising from where she is lying, she leans on one elbow. She is dressed in the pathetic rags of a once regal gown*]

LYRIC MONOLOGUE

STROPHE I

HECUBA: Lift up your head from the ground, you stricken one:
120   This is not Troy nor Troy's royal family.
         Change with the spirit of change, the changeable.
         Sail with the current, drift with the tide.
         Do not point your prow straight into the billows.
         Aiai! Aiai!
125   Why should I not lament in my misery,
         With country and spouse and children gone?
         How all the pomp of ancestry dwindles!
         How little did it ever amount to!

ANTISTROPHE I

         To be still or not to be still is the question:
130   Whether or not to cry out in regret—
         Stretched as I am on a rack of calamity,
         My limbs and my back heavy with weariness?
         Oh my head, my temples, oh my sides!
         Oh to toss and give rest to my spine!
135   To rock in a rhythm to the song of my tears!
         Such is the music of sorrowful souls.
         Such is the chant and the jangled tune
         Of ruin and doom, where there is no dance.

[HECUBA *struggles to her feet*]

STROPHE II

140   You prows of ships so neatly forging
         With flaying oars across the purple

Seas from the sheltering harbors of Hellas
With piping challenge of flute and fife,
You made fast your Egyptian hawsers
145   In the bay of Troy—how sad! sad!—
When you came here to retrieve
That cursed woman, Menelaus' bride:
That disgrace to her brother Castor,
Shame to the whole of Sparta, that
150   Murderess of Priam—father
Of fifty sons—who leaves me here,
The wretched Hecuba, collapsed
In utter dereliction . . . Oh!

[*She moves to a rock and sits*]

ANTISTROPHE II

155   What a sorry place to sit
Throned near Agamemnon's tents!
I who am to be transported:
Slave, old woman, gray head cropped
By sorrow . . . Come then, woebegone widows
160   Of Trojan heroes armed in bronze
And you husbandless virgins, weep
For smoldering Ilium. I, screeching
Like a mother bird for her young,
Intone for you a song most different
165   From the song I used to sing, when beating
Time with my foot as I leant on Priam's
Scepter and led the choir in worship
And dance to the strains of Phrygian music.

[*Out of the tents there emerges a band of women—unkempt, haggard, in rags—*
170   *who are some of the older captive Trojans, and form* CHORUS 1. *They press*
around HECUBA, *concerned and lost*]

CHORAL DIALOGUE

STROPHE I

LEADER: Hecuba, why this bawling? why this baying?
What is the news? These hovels are ringing
With your howls of anguish, and here inside
175   The Trojan women about to be slaves .

Tremble in terror.
HECUBA: My poor child, down by the ships
    The oarsmen are already preparing to row.
LEADER: Don't tell me! . . . Oh . . . then does it mean
180   It's time to say goodbye to my native land?
HECUBA: I am not sure, but suspect the worst.
LEADER: The worst? Ah, the worst!
    Come out of the tents, you women of Troy.
    Come and hear your horrible future:
185   The men of Argos are setting sail.
HECUBA: No, no! do not bring out
    My wandering, possessed Cassandra—
    To be the butt of Argive jeers.
    Do not heap grief upon grief.
190   Troy, my stricken Troy, is over:
    All are lost—living and dead.

[*A second group of women, younger, straggles from the tents, as pathetic in garb and demeanor as the first. They are* CHORUS 2]

ANTISTROPHE I

LEADER: Trembling I've crept from these tents, Agamemnon's,
195   To attend you, my queen. Is it death that they plan
    For miserable me, or are the mariners
    Manning their ships, getting ready to row?
HECUBA: My child, since dawn I've been waiting and watching,
    My sleepless heart numb with foreboding.
200 LEADER: Has any message come from the Greeks
    Turning me into a miserable slave?
HECUBA: No, but the lots are about to be drawn.
LEADER: Oh no! . . . Who will it be that gets me?
    Shall I be taken to Argos or Phthia,
205   Or to some islet far from Troy
    Where I shall be desolate?
HECUBA: I know! I know! . . . And as for me,
    Whose miserable slave am I to be?
    And where? Where shall this old woman
210   Be a drudge, a futile drone, the image
    Of a corpse and a ghastly uselessness . . .
    Perhaps as porter at a gate,
    Or a children's nurse—I who once
    Was the honored queen of Troy.

215 [*At this point the two* CHORUSES *unite. The members speaking severally survey with apprehension, curiosity, and sometimes almost with enthusiasm the possible places they may be taken to*]

STROPHE II

CHORUS 1 AND 2

1: Aiai! Aiai! Heartbreaking
   Are your lamentations . . .
220 2: Never again shall I work my shuttle
   Nimbly on a Trojan loom.
3: For the last time I look on the graves
   Of my parents . . . Oh, for the last time!
4: There's worse for me, much worse:
225   Forced to lie in the bed of a Greek—
   The greatest nightmare of them all.
5: Or a female slave fetching water
   From Pirene's sacred spring in Corinth.
6: For me, I hope it's glorious Athens . . .
230   Never never Sparta, Helen's
   Damnable home, where I'd have to
   Look on Menelaus as master—
7: That pillager of Troy!

ANTISTROPHE II

8: There's lovely Thessaly, land of Peneus
235   At the foot of Mount Olympus, rich
   Beyond all dreams—so I've heard—
   Fertile and fruitful in abundance.
9: Let me go there, my second choice
   After glorious, holy Athens
240 10: What about Etna, the domain
   Of Hephaestus, and Sicily
   The mother of mountains, which looks across
   To Phoenicia: famous I am told
   For its faraway crown of challenging peaks.
245 11: And opposites if you sail away
   Over the Sea of Ionia, a place
   The pretty river Crathis waters,
12: Which turns your hair a flaming gold
   And nourishes a land of vigorous men.
250 LEADER: But here comes an officer of the Greek army.

He must have news: he's in such a hurry.
What will it be? What will he tell us?
We're slaves already of the Dorian Greeks.

255   [TALTHYBIUS *marches briskly towards* HECUBA. *He is a man in the prime of life and wears the dashing uniform of the Greek army: short kilt, body-hugging tunic, heavy sandals laced up the bare calves, a flowing crimson cloak, and plumed helmet. In spite of his downright manner it becomes obvious that he is embarrassed by his mission and would like to get it over as quickly as possible.*]

SECOND EPISODE

260   TALTHYBIUS: Hecuba, madam, you are aware that . . .
       I've made . . . have made . . . several . . . er, trips before
       as a staff officer of the, er, Achaean army.
       So I'm known to you already, my lady . . .
       I'm Talthybius and I've come with official news.
265   HECUBA: [*dropping, trancelike, into verse*]
       Here it comes, dear women of Troy,
       What I have so long been dreading.
       TALTHYBIUS: You've all been allotted. Was that your dread?
       HECUBA: So, to a town in Thessaly?
270   Phthia perhaps, or is it to Thebes?
       TALTHYBIUS: You are all personally assigned, each to a man.
       HECUBA: [*with bitter sarcasm*] Personally assigned!
       To whom? Who are the lucky ones
       Among us ladies of Troy?
275   TALTHYBIUS: I can tell you. But ask one at a time, not all at once.
       HECUBA: Very well. My poor Cassandra,
       Tell me who got *her*.
       TALTHYBIUS: Very specially chosen . . . King Agamemnon got her.
       HECUBA: What? A slave for his Spartan wife?
280   No no no!
       TALTHYBIUS: Not that, but concubine: secret concubine.
       HECUBA: N . . . o? A consecrated virgin
       of Apollo, who won the right
       From the god with hair of gold
285   To remain unwed forever.
       TALTHYBIUS: He's shot through with lust for the maiden prophetess.
       HECUBA: O my daughter, throw away
       Those temple keys, cast off
       Those chaplets and those vestiges
290   Of your sanctified profession.
       TALTHYBIUS: So it goes for nothing to share the bed of a king?

HECUBA: [*after a long pause*] And my youngest child
      You wrenched from me—
      Where is she?

295 TALTHYBIUS: You mean Polyxena . . . who else?

HECUBA: Yes, her. Who drew *her*?

TALTHYBIUS: [*hedging*] She's been assigned to serve at the tomb of Achilles.

HECUBA: Great heavens! Have I borne a child
      To be lackey at a tomb? What curious
300   New law or ritual, my friend,
      Among the Greeks is this?

TALTHYBIUS: Her life has reached completion. She is free from cares.

HECUBA: [*reluctant to probe further*]
      And unfortunate Andromache, my stalwart Hector's wife
305   —what fate has she?

TALTHYBIUS: She? The son of Achilles got her. A real prize.

HECUBA: And me? Whose servant am I—this ancient carcass
      who has to use the third leg of a stick to walk?

TALTHYBIUS: Odysseus king of Ithaca drew you as his slave.

310 HECUBA: [*lapsing into verse again*] Ee . . . h!
      Batter that cropped pate of mine,
      Claw my nails through my cheeks . . .
      O . . . h!
      The lot I've drawn makes me slave
315   To that loathsome perfidious beast,
      That enemy of every right,
      A monster who knows no law:
      A twister with a double tongue
      Who lies and breaks his promises
320   And turns all friendship into hate.
      Cry for me, you daughters of Troy.
      This finishes me; it's total ruin:
      The worst, unluckiest lot of all.

LEADER: Your fate, my queen, now you know; but what of mine?
325   Who is to be my master? . . . In what part of Greece?

TALTHYBIUS: [*turning to the women of the* CHORUS]
      Enough!
    Go at once and bring Cassandra out.
    I must hand her over to the commander in chief,
330   then conduct the other captive women
      to the men to whom they've been allotted.

[*He stops short, seeing one of the tents all lit up*]

Hey, hey! What's going on in there?

All that blazing light!
335 Are the Trojan females burning down their nest
    with them inside just to avoid the trip to Argos?
My word! free spirits like these
    don't easily adjust to their misfortunes.
Open up in there! Open up!
340 Dying may be all right for you but not for the Greeks,
    and I'd be blamed.
HECUBA: No, it's not what you think, there is no fire:
    only my manic child Cassandra.
    Here she comes on the double.

345 [CASSANDRA *comes tumbling out of a tent in a kind of dance, holding aloft a*
flaming torch. She is dressed like a priestess in a flowing white alb, but it is
crumpled and dirty. Her face is smudged and her hair wild. Her head is
crammed with wilted sprigs of laurel and streamers of white wool. She
imagines she is about to be married to Agamemnon and that Hymen himself, the
350 *god of marriage, is in the temple ready to celebrate the wedding*]

LYRIC APOSTROPHE

[*In the following two strophes, Euripides lays the ground for a stunning irony.*
That which in the confused mists of impassioned euphoria on the part of
CASSANDRA *looks like an excited anticipation of her union with*
AGAMEMNON *is contradicted in the ensuing dialogue by a most sinister*
355 *threat: nothing less than the murder of* AGAMEMNON *aired the destruction of*
the house of Atreus]

STROPHE

CASSANDRA: Lift it up, let me parade this holy light.
    Look at it! Look at it
    Flooding this wedding shrine!
360   O Lord Hymeneus
    Bridegroom blest!
    And blessed am I about to be matched
    With a king in Argos, yes, Hymen, you nuptial god,
    While you my mother do nothing but moan and weep
365   For my dead father and dearest fatherland.
    So I must for myself for my own wedding
    Lift up aloft the flaming torch
    Flashing and flaring
    In your honor O Hymen,
370   In your honor O Hecate,
    With all the rubrics of light for a virgin's wedding.

ANTISTROPHE

Lift up your foot in the air and on with the dance.
    Hurray! Hurrah!
    Just like the glorious times
375   Of my father. The choir
    Is blessed. O Phoebus,
    Inside the temple festooned with laurel
    You yourself lead it to honor your priestess. Yes Hymen,
    Hymen hymeneal! . . . O mother take part in the singing,
380   Take part in the dance; swing out, swing in.
    To please me measure your footsteps with mine
    And shout out the nuptial song for the bride.
    Shout out her joy
    With relays of hymns.
385   Sing, you maidens of Troy
    For the spouse that destiny brings to my bed.

THIRD EPISODE

[*While* CASSANDRA, *flourishing her torch, continues to fling herself around in her manic dance, the* CHORUS LEADER *approaches* HECUBA *with concern*]

390   LEADER: Queen, can you not restrain your wild daughter
    before she prances her way into the Argive camp?

[HECUBA, *at a loss, throws up her arms in a bitter appeal to Hephaestus, god of fire*]

395   HECUBA: Hephaestus, you who light up the nuptials of mortals with torches,
    how cruel of you to parody with flame
    all the hopes I had so long ago!

[*Advancing on* CASSANDRA]

O my poor child,
400   never did I think you'd celebrate your marriage
    amid the spears and lances of the Argives.
Give me that light.
    In your hectic gyrations you cannot hold it straight.
    Our sufferings have not made you sensible:
405   you are the same as you always were.

[HECUBA *gently takes the torch from* CASSANDRA *and hands it to one of the* Trojan women]

Take these torches, dear women,
410   and let your response to these bridal overtures be tears.
CASSANDRA: Mother, crown me in triumph,
          Congratulate me in my royal match.
      Escort me to it
          and if you detect a lack of zeal, give me a push.
415   For by Loxias I swear
          I shall be a far more lethal bride
          than famous Agamemnon king of the Greeks
          ever bargained for.
      I shall kill him
420   and in my turn devastate his house
          and so avenge my brothers and my father.
      But let me not dwell on atrocities,³
          or chant of the ax that will sever my neck
          and the necks of others;
425   nor of the matricidal struggles
          that my marriage will engender
          nor of the annihilation of the house of Atreus.

      Let me talk instead
          of how our city is more fortunate than the Greeks'.
430   Possessed I may be
          but I shall rise above my frenzy.
      For the sake of a single woman and a single passion
          the Greeks have thrown away thousands of lives.
      Their oh-so-intelligent commander in chief
435   lost what he loved most
          for something he loved least.
      Yes, he gave up for his brother
          the jewel of his hearth, his own daughter,⁴
          all for a woman who was nowise dragged away
440   but went of her own free will.
      By the banks of the Scamander their armies died
          in battles for which neither their own borders

---

³ The chain of atrocities that Cassandra will only hint at comprises Clytemnestra's adultery with Aegisthus, leading to her murder of her husband, Agamemnon, and of Cassandra; the murder of Clytemnestra by her son, Orestes; and the subsequent madness of Orestes, the story of which is told in Aeschylus' *Oresteia.*

⁴ Iphigenia, whom Agamemnon sacrificed at Aulis to solicit favorable winds for the Greek armada to sail to Troy.

nor their towering cities were at stake.
And those the war god Ares took
445   never saw their children, never were enfolded
       in their shrouds by wifely hands
There they lie in an alien soil;
       while back at home were more miseries still:
       wives dying as widows,
450   lonely old men in houses without sons—
       sons they'd reared for nothing—
       over whose graves no one will come to sprinkle a little earth
       and the blood of sacrifice.
What a lovely panegyric for their whole campaign!
455   And best leave unsaid the ignominies at home:
       I'm not one to chant and celebrate obscenities.[5]
The Trojans on the other hand
       reaped the richest reward of all,
       to die for their native land.
460   And those that fell to the spear
       were carried home by loving hands,
       cradled in the caressing earth of their fathers
       and tended in their obsequies by pious hands.
Moreover, those Trojans who did not die in battle
465   lived at home with their wives and children:
       a happiness denied the Greeks.
As to the loss of Hector, listen and remember:
       he died the greatest of men;
       a thing made possible only by the coming of the Greeks.
470   Had they stayed at home,
       all that glory would be hidden.
And Paris:
       had he not wedded the daughter of Zeus,[6]

Of course, any man of sense shrinks from war,
475   but should war come, a brave man's death
       is a country's crowning pride—
       as a coward is its shame.
So, Mother, there is no need
       to feel sorry either for your country or my match,
480   for by this mating of mine

---

[5] Cassandra is thinking of the sexual scandals taking place in Argos, headed by the queen herself. During the ten years of war, wives and daughters would be an easy prey to crops of unenlisted young men growing up since the war began.

[6] **Daughter of Zeus:** Helen, whose mother, Leda, was visited by Zeus in the form of a swan.

those that you and I hate most
    I shall dispatch.

LEADER: It is all very well to laugh off your family's miseries,
    but everything you blithely chant you'll see is fiction[7]

485 TALTHYBIUS:

[*who has been listening amazed and with considerable irritation*]

Were it not for the fact that Apollo has frenzied away your reason,
    you'd not get off scot free for sending off my generals
    with such a blast of nonsense.

490 [*After a pause*]

It amazes me how the great and supposedly intelligent
    are not one whit superior to nonentities.
Look at the way this monarch of united Greece,
    the precious son of Atreus,
495   has fallen for this crazy girl!
Plain man that I am,
    I'd never let her near my bed.

[*Turning back to* CASSANDRA]

As for you,
500   because you are mentally deranged
    I'll consign to the breeze your insults to us Greeks
    and your overblown eulogy of Troy.
Come on, then, follow me to the ships—
    you, oh, so lovely bride of our commander.

505 [*Turning to* HECUBA]

And you,
    as soon as Odysseus, Laertes' son, summons you,
    be ready to follow.
At least you'll be a good woman's[8] slave,
510   as say all who went to Troy.

---

[7] Cassandra, for having refused the sexual overtures of Apollo, was fated by him always to prophesy the truth but never to be believed.

[8] *good woman's:* i.e., Penelope's, she being Odysseus' wife.

CASSANDRA:

[*With a dismissive and derisive glance at* TALTHYBIUS]

What a lackey!
How do such creatures manage to usurp
515   all the kudos of staff officers,
        universally hated as they are
        and mere pawns of kings and states?
So, you tell me that my mother
        will reach Odysseus' home?
520   What then becomes of Apollo's prophecy,
        made clear to me, which flatly says she dies right here?
        Of which the circumstances are too monstrous to mention.

And Odysseus, miserable man,
        he has no idea of the trials in store for him.
525   All my sufferings and all of Troy's
        are golden in comparison.
Heap ten years on these past ten
        before ever he reaches his native land—alone.
He will see the rock haunts and the clamping gorge
530   of the terrible Charybdis,
        and the mountain-lowering Cyclops who devours human flesh,
        and Circe on the Ligurian shores
        who turns men into swine.
He will suffer shipwreck on the briny deep,
535   and the craving for the lotus flower;
        see the sun god's sacred cattle
        whose butchered carcasses cry out in words
        that send Odysseus into panic.
To cut the saga short:
540   he shall go down into Hades
        and survive the marshes of the dead
        only to find at home a thousand sorrows.

But why should I go on about Odysseus' afflictions?
        Let me be brief.
545   Hades is where I hurry, to join my groom.
        Black will be the darkest night not day when he is buried.
Yes, you so seeming great commander of the Greeks.
Me? My naked body shall be tossed
        down the gullies where the winter torrents gush,
550   near to where my buried bridegroom lies,

there to be food for beasts of the wild
    I priestess of Apollo.

[CASSANDRA *begins to tear at her clothes and the various insignia of her office*]

555   Off with you, wreaths of my beloved god[9]
        talismans of ecstasy, farewell:
        I turn my back on the festivals at which I shone.
    Yes, off with you, I flense you from my skin,
        I a virgin still;
560   let the breezes waft them to you—you my prophet king.[10]

[*Turning to* TALTHYBIUS]

Where is the commander's ship? Where do I embark?
Watch for the wind, don't wait to swell the sails
    bearing me away, me one of the three
565   Furies . . . Mother, goodbye—you must not cry.
Darling land of my birth, farewell, and you my brothers
    under the earth, and you my father who gave us life,
        you'll not be waiting long for me.
Down to the dead I go victorious,
570   ruining the house of Atreus that ruined us.

[*At a sign from* TALTHYBIUS, *two guards roughly take hold of* CASSANDRA *and march her away.* HECUBA *faints. There is a stunned silence. At length the* CHORUS LEADER *turns to the rest of the women*]

LEADER: You ladies-in-waiting to old Hecuba,
575   do you not see how your queen has fallen to the ground—
Speechless, are you not going to raise her up?
Or will you just leave her lying there?
HECUBA: [*lifting her head*] No, let me lie where I have fallen
    Such kindness, dear girls, would not be kind.
580   Let me be submerged
        beneath all I have suffered and have still to suffer.
And you gods,
    how useless to expect any help from you!
And yet, and yet, to call upon the gods is salutary
585   when any of us runs headlong into trouble.

---

[9] **my beloved god:** Apollo.
[10] **my prophet King:** also Apollo.

Let me simply tell myself how happy once I was,
    though the contrast will be pitiable.

[*She raises herself on one arm*]

I was a queen and married a king;
590   became mother of princely sons:
          no mere ciphers but Phrygians most magnificent.
No woman of Troy or Greece or any foreign part
          could boast of mothering such sons as these;
          yet these I saw laid low by Grecian spears,
595   and at my dead sons' graves I sheared my hair
And Priam the sire of these, I witnessed—
          with my own eyes and not from some report—
          being butchered on his own hearth, and Troy sacked,
I saw my virgin daughters,
600   bred for bridegrooms of the highest rank,
          torn from my arms and all their breeding thrown to foreigners.

Last and worst of all my woes
          is being removed to Greece—an old slave woman.
What chores will they put me to,
605   an old crone like me?
Portress and keeper of keys? I who gave birth to Hector!
Baker of bread? The bare ground the prop
          for this old bony back that lay once in a royal bed?
And the clothes of this scarecrow? . . .
610   Tattered rags to match a tattered frame—
          fit symbols of my fall from bliss.

Yes, wretched me!
          For one sex-driven drive of one single woman
          what have I not suffered and have still to suffer?
615 Then Cassandra, my poor child,
          ecstatic medium of the gods,
          what a sorry end to your sacred virginhood!
And you, Polyxena, unhappy girl, where are you now?
Of all the children that I bore,
620   not a son, not a daughter is left to help me—
          me this most wretched woman.
So why bother to lift me up?
What good is there?
Just guide my footsteps that once proudly trod in Troy
625   to some mattress of straw and pillow of stone.

There let me flop with my face to the floor
    and waste away in tears.
Of all those seeming to succeed
    count no one happy till he is dead.

630   [*Two of the* TROJAN WOMEN—*former ladies-in-waiting to the queen—take* HECUBA *by the hand and escort her to a straw palliasse among the tents, where she lies down. The* CHORUS *chants ironically of the joy manifested in Troy when the citizens dragged the fatal Wooden Horse, its belly pregnant with armed Greeks, into the center of the city*]

FIRST CHORAL ODE

STROPHE

635   Utter this song, O Muse of Troy,
        A new song, a dirge of tears
        To dedicate to Ilium:
        Telling of how that four-footed thing-
        On-wheels of the Greeks ushered in
640   Our ruin and turned
        Us into slaves when the Achaeans
        Left that horse outside our gates
        Caparisoned in gold without,
        Clattering with spears within;
645   And all the citizens of Troy
        Gathering on the rocks outside
        Shouted: "Wheel the wooden idol in:
        A sacred gift to Zeus's daughter.
        It spells the end of all our woes."
650   What girls or ancients did not stream
        Out of their houses? All of them
        Singing with joy as they welcomed in
            This deadly ambushed gin.
        All the populace of Troy
655   Ran to the gates to gaze upon
        This ingenious Grecian thing
        Cut from mountain pine wherein
        Lurked the dread Dardanian doom:
        A gift to her,
660   The immortal maid . . . With ropes they hauled
        It like a black vessel launched
        To the temple home of Pallas where
        The very pavement soon would run

With Trojan blood. The happy task
665   Was hardly done when night came down
And all was dark. The air thrilled
With Libyan flute and Trojan song,
And the fluttering feet of dancing girls
Singing their joy; whilst everywhere
670   Torches blazed, and the houses too
Were all lit up—till blackness came
And the fires died down.

EPODE

LEADER: And on the very same night I
675   Myself was singing among the choirs
In front of the temple of Artemis
(Maid of the mountains, Zeus's daughter)
When suddenly the citadel
And all the city rang with shrieks.
680   Fragile infants clung with terror
To their mother's skirts as the god of war
Ares burst from his ambushed lair;
And Pallas thus achieved her end.
Around the altars then began
685   The butchering of Phrygians.
And on their solitary beds the girls
Cut off their hair: a fillip for
The Greek young men but mourning for
The land of Troy.

690   [*A four-wheeled cart drawn by a mule and conducted by Greek soldiers rattles into view over the stony ground. In the cart, sitting on top of a heap of captured Trojan spoil, is* ANDROMACHE *clutching her son* ASTYANAX. *Prominent in the pile is Hector's enormous shield.* HECUBA *slowly rises*]

LEADER: Hecuba, look, here comes Andromache
695   Carried in a strange-looking wagon.
Clutched to her apprehensive heart
Is Astyanax Hector's son—
Dear little fellow . . . Where will they take you,
Bereft wife sitting on top
700   Of a wagonload of Hector's armor
And plunder from Troy, which Achilles' son
Will hang up in the temples of Phthia
When he returns from Ilium?

LYRIC DIALOGUE

STROPHE I

705 ANDROMACHE: Our Greek masters are taking me away.
   HECUBA: Aiai! Aiai!
   ANDROMACHE: What good is weeping for me . . .
   HECUBA: Aiai! Aiai!
   ANDROMACHE: . . . and this stark ordeal?
710 HECUBA: O Zeus!
   ANDROMACHE: And all my crushing sorrow!
   HECUBA: My poor children!
   ANDROMACHE: Once so long ago.

ANTISTROPHE I

   HECUBA: Troy is gone.
715   All joy is gone from me . . .
   ANDROMACHE: Tragedy.
   HECUBA: All gone my noble brood.
   ANDROMACHE: Cruel, so cruel.
   HECUBA: For me terribly cruel.
720 ANDROMACHE: Horrible.
   HECUBA: I know, it is the end . . .
   ANDROMACHE: . . . of my city.
   HECUBA: . . . in smoke and burning.

STROPHE II

   ANDROMACHE: Husband of mine, oh could you come to me.
725 HECUBA: You summon my son from Hades, stricken girl.
   ANDROMACHE: Come to the help of your wife.

ANTISTROPHE II

   HECUBA: And you, martyr of the Achaeans . . .
   ANDROMACHE: Father
      Of my lord: venerable old Priam.
730 HECUBA: In Hades let me slumber.

STROPHE III

   ANDROMACHE: An infinite desire.
   HECUBA: Deep as my agony.

ANDROMACHE: A city sacked.

HECUBA: Pain lying on pain in layers.

735 ANDROMACHE: All caused by the gods' antipathy when your son
Was snatched from death.[11] And lusting after an odious woman
He crumbled the towers of Troy . . . Blood all over the floors
Of Pallas' temple; bodies strewn for vultures' picking.
So did he bend Troy under slavery's yoke.

ANTISTROPHE III

740 HECUBA: My sad beloved land!

ANDROMACHE: I weep on leaving you.

HECUBA: You see the pitiful end.

ANDROMACHE: The home where I gave birth.

HECUBA: Children, you have left your mother in a derelict city

745 Resounding with dirges, lamentations and tears.
What a surfeit of wailing! Surfeit of suffering!
Cry, cry and cry again for our lost homes.
Death at least lets go of tears, cancels sorrows.

[*End of Lyric Dialogue*]

FOURTH EPISODE

750 LEADER: Mother of Hector, who with his spear
slew so many Argives once, do you see what is happening?

HECUBA: I see the scheme of the gods: to raise to the skies the worthless
and dash to the ground the exalted.

ANDROMACHE: Yes, I with my son are captive stock:

755 highbirth to slave—what a reversal!

HECUBA: Fate is remorseless. Just moments ago
Cassandra was torn from me and is gone.

ANDROMACHE: Terrible! Terrible!
Like a second Ajax a second time

760 assaulting your child; but there is more.

HECUBA: I know. Without stint and measureless
one disaster hurries on another.

ANDROMACHE: Your daughter Polyxena is dead:
butchered on Achilles' tomb to appease his corpse.

765 HECUBA: No! No!
So that is what Talthybius meant.
His riddle now is deadly clear.

---

[11] Paris as a baby was exposed on Mount Ida but saved by shepherds.

ANDROMACHE: I myself saw her and I left this cart
  to cover her corpse and to bewail her.
770 HECUBA: I cry for you, my child, and your heinous slaughter.
  Yes I cry for your appalling death.
ANDROMACHE: She is dead, she is gone,
  but her death is happier than is life for me.
HECUBA: No, my child: sight and daylight are not death.
775 One is a nothingness, the other has hope.
ANDROMACHE: Mother, mother, listen, there is a greater truth—
  if I can only touch your heart with it.
  Never to have been born I count as death,
  a death superior to a life of bitterness.
780 In death there is no pain, no awareness of struggle;
  but one who falls from happiness to tragedy
  is riven with regret and memories of blessedness.
  In death it is as if Polyxena had never known the light
  and nothing of her trials.
785 But I who aimed at happiness
  hardly had attained it when it went.
  All that a woman can contrive through a balanced life
  I worked at under Hector's roof.
  Even if a woman has no other mark against her,
790 one single flaw will bring her to notoriety,
  which is, not keeping to the house.
  So that was my priority:
  to put such urges from me and stay at home.
  I never allowed the frilly gossip of women
795 to infiltrate my house,
  and kept to the steady counsels of my heart,
  with quiet tongue and eyes serene before my spouse.
  I knew when to rule my husband
  and when to let him win:
800 a virtue the Achaeans came to know of
  and it proved my downfall,
  for when I was captured the son of Achilles[12] claimed me for his own,
  so I shall be a slave in the house of my husband's murderers.

  And now if I put away the image of my darling Hector
805 and open my heart to a new man
  it will seem like disloyalty to the dead,
  but if I turn from this new lord
  I'll only earn his hate.

---

[12] **son of Achilles:** Neoptolemus, who was the slayer of Priam.

Yet they say that a single night in bed
810   suffices to end a woman's aversion to a man.
I, however, feel nothing but disgust
     for the woman who forgets her former man
     and beds down with a second.
Why, even a dray-mare
815   separated from the horse she pulls with
     shows repugnance for another partner in the yoke,
     and this in a mere animal of a lower order
     without speech or reason,
     whereas you, my dearest Hector, were my perfect mate:
820   noble, intelligent, rich, brave—a man great in every way.
You took me chaste from my father's house
     and you were the first to enter my bed.
But now you are no more
     and I am about to board a ship for Greece,
825   a prisoner of war and a subservient slave.

[*Turning to* HECUBA]

So I ask you:
     isn't your loss of Polyxena, whom you mourn,
     less harrowing than mine?
830 For me, not even those vestiges of hope common to mankind are left,
     and I do not deceive myself
     with the delusion, sweet though it be,
     of anything being right again.
LEADER: You face the same pain that I must face
835   and your lament gives lessons to my own.
HECUBA: Never have I been on board a ship
     but from all accounts and pictures that I've seen
     I know what it is like.
If a merely moderate storm is looming
840   the sailors bestir themselves in all directions.
One is at the helm, another grappling with sails
     another bailing water.
But if the full fury of the ocean is unleashed
     they resign themselves to fate and run with the sea.
845   So with me:
     I am dumb before the surge of all my sorrows
     and without a word succumb,
     powerless to withstand
     the tide of misery the gods sweep over me.
850 And so, my dearest daughter,

let us commit Hector to his destiny.
No tears from you will bring him back.
To your new master show respect,
    with that winning way of yours that charms a man.
855   If you do this you'll spread joy among your friends
        and render Troy a mighty service
        by bringing up this son of my son
        whose issue may one day rebuild Ilium
        and make our city rise again.

860   [*Glancing across the barren plain*]

But now we'll have to talk of something else,
    for whom do I see approaching but the Achaean errand boy,
    coming with a set of new injunctions.

[TALTHYBIUS *with an escort of guards marches in. His features register*
865   *embarrassment and reluctance as he walks across to* ANDROMACHE, *who has*
left the cart and stands near HECUBA, *holding* ASTYANAX *by the hand*]

TALTHYBIUS: Lady wife of Hector, once hero of the Phrygians,
    I beg you not to hate me. I'm no willing messenger
    of the decision the Achaeans and the Argives have made.
870   ANDROMACHE: What is this? What prelude to a new disaster?
TALTHYBIUS: The boy here . . . they have decreed . . . Oh how am I to say it? . . .
ANDROMACHE: Not, I hope, That he and I will be given to different masters?
TALTHYBIUS: No . . . No Greek will ever be his master.
ANDROMACHE: You mean he is to be left in Phrygia?
875   TALTHYBIUS: How do I break this to you? . . . It is awful.
ANDROMACHE: Thank you for demurring . . . unless you have good news.
TALTHYBIUS: Your son's to be killed. Now you know.
ANDROMACHE: No no no! This is worse than making me a whore.
TALTHYBIUS: The vote went with Odysseus in the Panhellenic council to . . .
880   ANDROMACHE: Aiai, aiai . . . this outmeasures every outrage.
TALTHYBIUS: . . . to not let grow up the son of such a famous father.
ANDROMACHE: Oh, would that his own children could suffer this decree!
TALTHYBIUS: He must be flung from the battlements of Troy.

[ANDROMACHE *throws her arms around* ASTYANAX *as if to protect him*]

885   Come, let it happen.
        You'll find that wiser in the end.
Let go of him.
Bear this agony with dignity.

You are powerless. Do not imagine that you're strong.
890 There's no help anywhere.
Consider: your husband and your city are no more
you yourself are held in bondage.
We are quite capable of dealing with a single woman.
Do not go looking for a fight.
895 Do not make a raving spectacle of yourself.
I do not want you upsetting the Achaeans.
That would anger the military
and the boy may not get a burial or proper obsequies.[13]
Keep quiet. Let things take their course,
900 then at least you will not leave your boy unburied
and you'll find the Greeks will treat you better.
ANDROMACHE: [*gathering* ASTYANAX *to her*]
My most precious, my most beloved boy,
you must say goodbye to your desolate mother:
905 our enemies want you dead;
your gallant father is your ruin,
as he was for others the salvation.
Yes, your father's valor spells your death knell now.
My own marriage, my night of honeymoon,
910 my very coming into Hector's home,
were not for this: not for bringing into the world
a babe for Greeks to butcher but to conceive a king—
a king for Asia and prosperity.

Poor child, are you crying?
915 What good to cling to me, to clutch my skirts
like a little bird cowering under its mother's wings?
There is no Hector
to rise up from the earth with his glorious spear
and deliver you;
920 no kinsman of your father, no strong men of Troy.
You must plunge from the heights in a piteous leap
and most hideously dash your breath away.

[*Folding him to her*]

My tender seedling, your mother's dearest baby,
925 the sweet smell of your skin swaddled at my breast,
and all for nothing.

---

[13] One must bear in mind how essential the Greeks regarded burial. The mere ritual of sprinkling earth on a corpse was a kind of sacrament ensuring the deceased a better life in the next world. (See Sophocles' *Antigonê*.)

The labor pains, the enduring care—all for nothing.
Kiss your mother now for the last time.
    Smother yourself in her.
930   Put your arms round me and hug me tight.
Press your lips to mine.

[*She turns fiercely towards* TALTHYBIUS *and his escort of soldiers*]

You barbarians! what un-Greek cruelties can you invent?
Must you kill a child—wholly innocent?
935   And you, Helen, daughter of Tyndareus,
    Zeus was never your father.
Let me tell you who your many fathers were:
    Destruction first, then Hate, Bloody Murder, Death,
    and whatever refuse spawns itself on earth.
940   Zeus your father? Don't tell me that!
    You born curse to uncountable Achaeans
    and to all the world besides.
Death take your lovely eyes
    that have ransacked the famous plains of Troy.

945   [*She prises* ASTYANAX *from her and pushes him towards* TALTHYBIUS,
turning away her gaze]

Go on, take him. Carry him away.
Hurl him to his death if that's what you want.
Feast on his broken flesh . . .
950   the gods are out to destroy us
        and I cannot shield from death one little child.

Now make a parcel of my wretched carcass and toss it in the hold.
    Today's my wedding day—the day I lost my child.
LEADER: Troy, unhappy Troy, where so many thousands of young men were lost
955   all for one woman's sake, one wanton lust!
TALTHYBIUS:

[*Advancing on* ASTYANAX]

Come, boy, now that you've left your sad mother's arms,
    you must climb the battlements that ring your ancestral towers.
960   There it has been voted that you end your life.

[ASTYANAX *turns and rushing back to his mother clings to her.* TALTHYBIUS, *his face grim with reluctance, strides forward and drags the screaming boy from his mother, then hands the struggling boy to a soldier*]

Take hold of him.

965   This kind of order needs a brute, someone merciless,
         much more heartless than I can be.

[*As the screams of* ASTYANAX *recede in the distance,* ANDROMACHE *is dragged back to the cart and* TALTHYBIUS, *rounding up his escort, marches away with the cart.* HECUBA, *swaying on her feet, stares in the direction of*
970   ASTYANAX]

HECUBA: Goodbye my child, son of my pitiable son,
         So cruelly torn from your mother and me.
         How can I bear it not to be able
         To do a thing for you. All I can offer
975   Is tearing my hair, beating my breasts.
         That is all I can do . . . Farewell
         My child. Farewell my city. Nothing,
         No agony for us is missing.
         Could anything make it more complete.

980   [HECUBA *collapses*]

SECOND CHORAL ODE

[*Beginning with a brief eulogy of Athens, the women of the* CHORUS *survey in a litany of contrasts legendary history and chant of a mythological attack on Troy in the past, setting it against the present sack of the city. Then, in an ironic reversal, of what the power of love has done to Ilium, they cite the example of*
985   *two beautiful Trojan boys who were abducted: Ganymede, the cupbearer, whom—suggests Euripides—Zeus wafted on high for highly dubious purposes, and Tithonus, with whom Aurora fell in love and whom she carried away in a four-horse chariot*]

STROPHE I

CHORUS: Telamon, monarch of Salamis,
990   island buzzing with bees,
         You set up your home on that sea-fingered
         isle that faces the hills
         Where Athena first planted the glaucous
         cuttings of olive—the crowning

995 Glory of shimmering Athens.
       Then you coupled your valor
With Heracles, son of Alcmena,
       the archer. So you departed,
Alas, you departed to sack
1000   our city of Ilium: Ilium
Even then our beloved
       country such ages ago,
When you came to these shores from Hellas.

ANTISTROPHE I

In a rage for the loss of his horses[14]
1005   Heracles came with Greece's
Flower of manhood over
       the ocean and anchored their ships
In the lovely bay of Simoïs
       and fastened their sterns with hawsers.
1010 With his infallible bow then
       he went to kill Laomedon.
With rubicund fire he tumbled
       the walls that Apollo with chisel
And plumb had erected so straightly.
1015   The land of Troy he demolished.
So this is the second occasion
       that Troy has been stricken. Yes, twice
That its blood-spattered walls have fallen.

STROPHE II

In vain, in vain with your golden
1020   cups do you prettily amble,
You Ganymede, to fill the
       goblets of Zeus—such an honor—
While the country that gave you birth
       is eaten up by fire,
1025 And the shores of the sea are raucous
       with cries like the screams of a seagull
Over her fledglings in danger.
       Oh the howling and wailing for children,
For husbands, for elderly mothers.

---

[14] In return for saving Hesione, daughter of Laomedon, king of Troy, from a monster, Heracles was to be given a team of horses. However, after Heracles had rescued Hesione, Laomedon reneged on his promise. Hence Heracles' rage against Troy.

1030   No more are the baths that refreshed you,
No more the gymnasiums and racetracks;
        yet you by the throne of Zeus
Serenely pose with the beauty
        of your young face while the javelins
1035 Of Hellas are crumbling
        the empire of Priam.

Antistrophe II

Love, O Love, long ago
        you came to Dardanus' palace
Having inflamed with passion
1040   the gods themselves in heaven.
Those were the days when you lifted
        Troy to the skies with divine
Bondings (I shall not refer
        to Zeus's disgraceful intentions).
1045 Yet today is the day that Dawn,
        white-winged solace of mortals,
Saw Pergamum in shambles;
        yet a son of this very soil,
Tithonus, was her husband,
1050   bred children in her bed,
Till a four-starred golden chariot
        carried him to heaven.
He was the hope of Troy,
        which the gods no longer love.

1055 [MENELAUS, *with a detachment of soldiers behind him, strides into camp. He is a man in his middle forties, complete in military uniform—sword, cape, plumed helmet, heavily strapped sandals—and is obviously pleased with his appearance*]

FIFTH EPISODE

MENELAUS: What a lovely sunny day
1060   to get my hands on my wife again—that Helen!
Yes, after so many trials
        I Menelaus am here at last with the Greek army behind me.
My coming to Troy was not as you might think
        because of a woman but because of a man:
1065   that treacherous creature who was a guest in my house
        and snatched my wife away.

Well, thanks to the gods,
    that man has had his punishment:
    he with his country has collapsed under the Grecian spear.
1070   As to that Spartan slut, my former wife
    (and I cannot bring myself to speak her name),[15]
    I am here to drag her back.
She's with the rest of the prisoners in the barracks,
    lumped together with them as a Trojan woman.
1075   My brave allies, who have gone through hell to get her back,
    have given her to me to kill,
    or if I do not kill her to bring her home to Argos.
I have decided not to settle the fate of Helen here in Troy,
    so our mariners will take her with me across the main to Greece.
1080   There I'll give her over to be killed
    by those who are crying to avenge their loved ones at Troy.

[*Summoning two of his soldiers*]

Go men, probe the barracks and fetch her here.
Drag her by the hair, the whore,
1085   and when the right wind blows
    we'll carry her to Greece.

[*As the soldiers depart,* HECUBA, *who has been listening, rises from her couch. She spreads out her hands in prayer*]

HECUBA: O thou, the fundament of our universe
1090   with your throne on earth—
    thou whoever thou art, beyond our comprehension, Zeus,
    be thou a law of nature or invention of mankind—
    thee I invoke.
MENELAUS: Meaning precisely what? . . . That's an odd prayer to make!
1095   HECUBA: [*ignoring his obtuseness*]
    I approve, Menelaus, of your killing your wife,
    but don't let her near you or she'll entangle you again.
She rivets men's eyes, she topples cities, she burns down houses,
    she casts such spells.
1100   We know her well,
    you and I and all her other victims.

---

[15] He has already spoken her name once (1060) and is to do so again (line 877 in the Greek). This is no slip on the part of Euripides the master ironist but a subtle hint of Menelaus' peculiar "thickness." Line numbers refer to the Greek text in the Loeb Classics edition.

[The two soldiers reappear, pulling HELEN *along with a rope. Despite the fact that she has suffered the same herding together and indignities as the other captive women, she has contrived to make the most of her appearance and is still*
1105   *stunningly beautiful]*

    HELEN: Menelaus, if you want to frighten me, this is a good beginning
       I've been dragged from the tents by your minions here.
       Of course I'm not surprised you probably hate me,
           all the same, I'd like to ask:
1110   what decision have you come to, you and the Greeks,
       about my life?
    MENELAUS: Nothing is settled,
          except that the entire army has given you to me to kill
          because of all the trouble you have caused.
1115   HELEN: Am I not at least to have the chance of showing
          that if I die I die unjustly?
    MENELAUS: I came here to kill you, not to argue.
    HECUBA: Give her a hearing, Menelaus:
          at least *that* before she dies.
1120   But allow me to state the case against her.
          You have no idea of the havoc she has caused in Troy.
       My indictment, every item in it,
          without the slightest room for doubt,
          will call for her death.
1125   MENELAUS: A waste of breath!
          But if she must, let her speak.
       It's for your sake, Hecuba, not hers—
          I hope she knows—that I grant this favor.
    HELEN: *[turning to face* MENELAUS]
1130   Whether my arguments seem good or bad to you,
          your response undoubtedly will be antagonistic.
       Nonetheless,
          knowing the kind of charges you will level at me
          I shall rebut them point by point as if we were debating.
1135   In the first place,

    [throwing an icy glance at HECUBA]

          this woman here who gave birth to Paris
          is the one who gave birth to all our troubles.
       The second cause of the ruin of Troy,
1140   and my ruin too,
          was old Priam, who failed to kill the newborn brat,
          even though he had been warned in dreams

that a firebrand, the future Alexander,[16]
would burn down Troy.

1145   Listen to what happened next.
           Alexander becomes the judge in the beauty contest of three goddesses.

        Pallas Athena promised him conquest of Greece
           at the head of a Phrygian army.
        Hera promised that if Paris made her win
1150   she would give him the whole kingdom of Asia
           and the farthest frontiers of Europe.
        But Aphrodite
           expatiating on the marvels of my body
           promised him exactly that
1155   if *she* came out on top in the contest of goddesses.

        Now consider the results:
           the blessings heaped on Greece are incalculable;[17]
           you are not slaves of a foreign power,
           you have not been ousted in battle
1160   nor crushed beneath some imperial tyranny.
        But I, I benefactor of Greece, have been ruined,
           sold for my beauty
           and am being punished instead of being crowned with garlands.

        That is not the point, you'll counter.
1165   Why did you elope from home?
        Why? Because of *him*—
           call him Paris or Alexander or what you will—
           the spellbinding son of this Hecuba.
        He came here with no mean goddess in his wake,
1170   while you, Menelaus, my husband you
           criminally left him in your palace,
           took off from home and sailed away to Crete.

        Well, I won't ask what prompted you
           but I'll ask myself: was I quite mad
1175   to abandon fatherland and home
           and go chasing after this foreign man?
        Ask Aphrodite. Punish her.

---

[16] **Alexander:** Paris.

[17] Helen means that if Pallas Athena had won the contest, Paris would have been given Greece, which would have been conquered by Troy. If Hera had won, Greece would have come under the suzerainty of a European empire.

Be mightier than Zeus, who may be master of the gods
but not of her.
1180   So I should be let off untouched.

All right, you'll say,
  but what about when Alexander died and passed to Hades
  and divine interference in my life had stopped?
Shouldn't I have fled from his house to the Argive ships?
1185   That is exactly what I tried to do.
I have witnesses: the sentries at the gates,
  the watchtower patrols.
Ask them how many times they caught me
  trying to slither down the battlements on ropes.
1190   But my new husband, the lately deceased Deïphobus,[18]
  kept me prisoner as his wife despite the Trojans.

So, my husband
  by what right can you with any justice kill me
  when I was impelled to marry Paris
1195   and when I've brought such benefits to Greece?
Instead of crowning me in triumph,
  you plunge me into the cruelest slavery. Why?
If your aim is to outdo the gods
  it is the silliest of pretensions.
1200   LEADER: Queen, stand by your children and your country,
  explode the specious pleading from this harlot's lips . . .
  Oh, she is formidable!
HECUBA: First let me defend the goddesses
  and undo the lies of her slanderous tongue.
1205   Never would Hera have been so completely brainless
  as to sell Argos to foreigners,
  or Pallas the Virgin to let Athens become a slave of Troy.
When they had their beauty contest on Mount Ida,
  they went in a flirtatious spirit, a spirit of play.
1210   Why should the goddess Hera set her heart on a beauty prize?
To win a husband preferable to Zeus?
  And was Athena simply panting for a spouse among the gods,
  she who'd wheedled from her father the promise
  of perpetual virginity—
1215   So great was her horror of getting married?
Do not try to camouflage your flagrancy

---

[18] *Deïphobus:* Son of Priam and Hecuba, who married Helen after raping her.

by imputing such idiocy to gods.
Nobody with sense believes you.

* * *

As to Aphrodite,
1220   you tell us that she came to Menelaus' palace with my son.
Don't make us laugh! . . .
        as if she couldn't transport you and your whole town of
        Amyclae to Ilium while remaining blissfully in heaven
My son enjoyed good looks beyond compare.
1225   It was your itch for him that you revamped into "Aphrodite."
When men make fools of themselves it's always "Aphrodite":
        the very name of the goddess spells mindless slavering.
So when you saw my son in his exotic garb,
        dripping in gold,
1230   you were stunned and lost your head.
There was nothing like it in dull old Argos.
Quitting Sparta for our Phrygian town
        you imagined rivers of gold that you would wallow in.
The palace of Menelaus could not contain
1235   your impudent drive for luxury;
        yet my son, you say, had to drag you away by force . . . Really!
Who in Sparta saw this happening?
How loud did you cry out?
The young man Castor was there, his twin brother too,
1240   not yet caught up among the stars.

And so you arrive at Troy,
        the Argives hot on your tracks,
        and the murderous clash of arms begins.
Each time there was news of a win for Menelaus,
1245   you'd praise him to the skies to annoy my son
        and prove how superior Menelaus was—in bed.
Each time the Trojans gained the upper hand,
        what was Menelaus? Nothing!
In this way, however fortune veered
1250   and with no regard to morals,
        you were always on the winning side.

Now you talk of ropes around your body
        and slithering down the walls,
        altogether loath to stay in Troy.
1255   Did anyone ever find you putting a noose around your neck
        or sharpening a dagger—
        as any decent woman would have done, pining for her husband?

How many times did I not remonstrate with you and say:
  "Listen, my girl—just go!
1260 My sons can always find other women.
  I'll help you to slip away to where their navy is
  and so stop this senseless war between Greece and us."

But no, this wasn't to your taste.
You luxuriated in Alexander's palace.
1265 You basked in the obsequiousness of us Orientals.
It was a big thing for you;
  and all the time you had the gall to deck yourself out
  and parade in broad day by your husband's side—
  you, you disreputable trollop!
1270 Not insolence but humility should have been your mood
You should have come cringing with shaven head,
  dressed in rags and trembling with compunction
  for all your shameless past.

[*Turning to* MENELAUS]

1275 The crux of my indictment, Menelaus, is:
  cap Greece's triumph with a crown of glory.
Set a precedent by law:
  death to every wife unfaithful to her spouse.
LEADER: Menelaus, be worthy of your ancestors and your house:
1280 punish your wife. Do not let Greece label you as soft
  when you've shown yourself so gallant in the field.
MENELAUS: I agree wholeheartedly with you
  that of her own free will she left my house for the bed of a foreign man
  and that blaming Aphrodite is a ruse.

1285 [*Turning to* HELEN]

Go, get ready to be stoned.
In a single instant expiate the years of Achaean suffering.
Let death be your lesson for disgracing me.
HELEN: [*throwing herself at his feet*]
1290 I clasp your knees and beg you:
  don't stamp me with a crime that came from heaven.
Forgive me, do not kill me.
HECUBA: [*with a sharp glance at* MENELAUS]
  Do not betray your allies whom she's slaughtered.
1295 Do not, I beg you, for them and their children's sake.
MENELAUS: That's enough, old woman . . . She means nothing to me.

[*Turning to his guards*]

Men, take her to the galleys. This is a command.
Prepare her for the crossing.

1300 [*The guards seize* HELEN *to lead her away*]

HECUBA: Make sure her galley is not the same as yours.
MENELAUS: Why? Has she put on weight? Ha ha!
HECUBA: Once a lover, forever vulnerable.
MENELAUS: That depends on the loved one's depth of love.
1305 However, you have a point. Let it be as you wish.
She shall not board the same ship as I.
Once in Argos this disgraceful woman
shall come to the disgraceful end she merits
and give a lesson to all wives in chastity . . .
1310 No easy matter, certainly,
but her death will go some way
to strike a little fear into wanton hearts
be they even more depraved than hers.

[*As* HELEN, *led by the guards, passes* MENELAUS, *she meets his gaze and*
1315 *notes the sweat breaking out on his forehead. She throws him a smile that seems*
to say: "Wait till we get to the ships and the long passage home. Oh yes, you are
vulnerable still!" MENELAUS *turns on his heel, followed by his guards.*
HECUBA, *overcome with grief, apprehension and exhaustion, sinks back on her*
palliasse. The women of the CHORUS *chant a lament to Zeus for having*
1320 *forsaken Ilium, listing the various sacred rituals that will never again take place*
in Troy. They then think of their dead husbands lying somewhere still
unburied, and of their children destined to live as orphans in unknown Greek
cities. Finally, they express a wish that a storm will strike MENELAUS' *ship*
and that the still dangerous HELEN *will never reach Argos*]

THIRD CHORAL ODE

STROPHE I

1325 CHORUS: Gone, done, never again
Will wafted fragrance arise
From the altars of Ilium.
Zeus, you've given them away
To the Greeks: the savory flames,
1330 The rising fumes of myrrh,
Pergamum the holy,

And Ida—oh, the glens
Of Ida with their ivy
Trickling beside the icy
1335   Torrents, and the peaks
Catching the early sun:
Bright purlieus of the divine.

ANTISTROPHE I

Gone too, beholden to you,
The sacrifices, choirs, psalms,
1340   Hymns of praise. And now no more
The celebrations in the dark
Of feasts at night for the gods.
Gone are the gilded effigies
In wood, the twelve-mooned cakes
1345   Offered under the Phrygian moon.
I wonder, my lord, I wonder
If you give a single thought
From your celestial throne
To the leaping flames and the lights
1350   Of my city burning still.

STROPHE II

Dearest, my husband, now dead,
Unwashed, unburied, you roam
In the realms of Hades while I
On the wings of a fast-moving ship must fly
1355   Over the waves to the plain
Of Argos where horses graze
And the people live behind walls
Which the hefty Cyclops raised
Soaring into the sky . . .
1360   Children throng the gates,
They wail and cry.
A young girl is shouting:
"Mother, I'm alone and the Greeks are taking me
Far from the sight of you:
1365   Away in a melancholy ship
Thrashing the waves with its oars
Towards Salamis the sacred
Or to Corinth on its isthmus
Standing between two seas:

1370   The strong portals of Pelops.

ANTISTROPHE **II**

         When the galley of Menelaus
         Is half across the main
         May Zeus's Aegean lightning
         Zigzagging from his holy hands blaze down
1375   Onto the bridge of his ship
         As he carries me away
         From Ilium in tears
         For slavery in Greece:
         Right at the hour when girls
1380   Hold up their golden mirrors
         Like Helen daughter of Zeus.
         Never let him see
         The land of his fathers, Laconia, not
         Even his hearth, his bedroom, the streets
1385   Of Pitana, nor the bronze
         Gates of Athena's temple
         For he has forgiven
         The marriage that brought such shame
         On noble Greece; such sorrows
1390   To the banks of Simoïs—Troy.
    LEADER: Horrible! Horrible! Blow upon blow
         On a blighted land . . . and now what's coming
         To the desolate wives of the heroes of Troy?
         I see Astyanax, whom the Greeks have thrown
1395   From the heights of the battlements and have slain.

[TALTHYBIUS *and his men arrive carrying the torn body of* ASTYANAX *on Hector's enormous shield.* HECUBA *rises as they approach her.* TALTHYBIUS, *crestfallen and dejected, tries to distract* HECUBA *from the horror of the scene by babbling about preparations to depart*]

SIXTH EPISODE

1400 TALTHYBIUS: Hecuba, one ship remains, its oars at the ready
         to ply for the shores of Phthia
         with the rest of the booty of Achilles' son.
      Neoptolemus himself has put to sea already,
         having heard a dismal report
1405   that his grandfather, Peleus
         has been driven from the land by Acastus son of Pelias.

For which reason he has left at once,
>   taking with him Andromache, torn from her country in tears
>   as she bade farewell to Hector's tomb . . . I too broke down.

1410 She begged Neoptolemus to give this poor son of Hector
>   hurled from the walls, a grave and have him laid out
>   on Hector's enormous shield—
>   the shield of bronze that protected his flanks
>   and filled the Achaeans with terror.

1415 She asked him not to take the body to the house of Pelius[19]
>   nor to her own—the dead boy's mother's—
>   new forced bridal abode in Argos:
>   it would be too much for her to see her mangled son.

Instead of a stone or cedar coffin
1420 >   she wants her child buried here beneath this shield.

He is to be laid in your arms
>   for you to enshroud his body as best you can with what you have left,
>   and covered in flowers.

Her master was in such a hurry.
1425 >   she could not herself bury her boy.

The rest of us,
>   as soon as you have dressed the corpse,
>   shall heap a mound for him and crown it with a spear.

Please perform this task as quickly as you can.
1430 One labor I have spared you:
>   when I passed the banks of Scamander River
>   I bathed the body and washed the wounds.

Now I shall go and dig his grave,
>   so when your work and mine is quickly done
1435 >   we can make all speed for home.

[*At a sign from* HECUBA *two of her women advance and take the shield from* TALTHYBIUS. *On it lies the pathetic little frame of* ASTYANAX, *curled up as if asleep. Although hideously bruised, his body has been washed clean and the golden curls of the young princeling lie around his ashen face. As*
1440 TALTHYBIUS *turns gently away and joins his escort of soldiers,* HECUBA *beckons the two women*]

HECUBA: Set the shield down on the ground—Hector's shield:
>   the great arc of it a heartrending sight,
>   no joy for me to see.

1445 [*She turns fiercely on the groups of Greek soldiers who are never far away*]

---

[19] house of Pelius: in Sparta.

Oh, you spear-mongering Greeks,
    if only your intelligence could match your prowess.
This was mindless murder—murder unmentionable.
What did you fear in this little child?
1450   That he would raise up fallen Troy? . . .
So all your bravery of old was sham.
Our city taken, Phrygia in rubbles,
    all Hector's triumphs and thousands of strong arms
    powerless to avert our ruin,
1455   and you are terrified of one little boy.
What blind panic! I despise you.

[*Glancing down at the dead body*]

My sweet baby,
    how untimely death has taken you!
1460   Had you only fallen in blooming manhood
        fighting for your city,
    or tasted the joys of wedlock and that royalty that makes us gods,
        that at least would have been some blessing—
        if indeed there can be any blessing here.
1465   The pleasures that you caught a glimpse of,
        enough to know their worth, are snatched from you,
        and your happiness of home is lost, forgotten.

[*Cradling his head*]

My stricken child,
1470   how ironically your own ancestral walls,
        Apollo's handiwork, have carded out your curls:
        those curls your mother used to stroke and kiss,
        which now are pierced by splintered blood-leached bone.
Nothing can describe the horror of it,
1475   And your hands, so like your father's,
        out of joint and limp!
Your dear lips,
        that sent forth so many childish sallies—silent now.
Bounding on to my bed you used to cry:
1480   "Grandmother, I'll chop off a big curl for you
        and bring a crowd of my pals to your burial
        to send you my love and last farewell."
It has not happened so.
It is not you but I, your grandmother,
1485   an old cityless, childless crone

that has to bury your torn body.
Wasted, lost forever,
    all those cuddles, all that care,
    all that watching while you slept.
1490   What frame of words is possible for your tomb?
Here lies a guileless babe
Killed by the Greeks who were afraid.
An epitaph to disgrace all Greece.
And now you possess nothing of your father's heritage
1495   except this shield of bronze—and for your tomb.

[*Running her hands along the rim*]

Sweet shield that guarded Hector's brawny arm,
    you have lost your valiant keeper.
Lovely the imprint of his flesh
1500   on the sling of your handle still.
Lovely the sweat marks on the sweep of your rim:
    the sweat that in the heat of battle ran from his face
    and dripped from his leaning chin.

[*Clapping her hands to summon her women*]

1505   Come, my women,
    fetch whatever trappings you can find from what remains to us
    to enshroud this most tragic dead.
Fate has shorn us of all finery
    but you shall have from me all I have.

1510   [*After a pause*]

What a fool that mortal is
    who rests complacent in prosperity!
Fortune is the prey of whims
    and like a maniac turns somersaults.
1515   No man for long escapes her jolts.
LEADER: Madam, from the Phrygian remnants left to us
    your women are bringing you some trappings for the dead.

[*The women come dragging a heavy basket from one of the tents. In it are disclosed a hodgepodge of items flung there in their last minutes of freedom:*
1520   *clothes, baubles, jewelry. As* HECUBA *and her handmaids sort through these, the dressing of* ASTYANAX'S *body begins*]

HECUBA: Dear child, among your fellows,
      no victory in horsemanship or archery was yours
      (pursuits admired in Phrygia, but modestly),
1525   And yet, I, the mother of your father,
        wrap you in this finery:
        all that is left of your inheritance:
        ripped from you by that she-devil Helen,
        as she has ripped from you your life
1530   and from top to bottom wrecked your home.
LEADER: These words break my heart, yes, break it,
      for this child born to be a city's mighty king.

[HECUBA, *reaching down into the basket, pulls out a magnificent tunic*]

HECUBA: This is the raiment you would have worn on your wedding day,
1535   with the noblest princess of Asia as your bride.
      It is of Phrygian workmanship the most gorgeous.
      And you, beloved shield of Hector,
        victorious mother of a thousand trophies,
        here is a wreath for you.

1540   [HECUBA *festoons the shield with a garland of wildflowers which her women found growing on the plain*]

      Without being dead you died with this dead body.
      Much more honored should you be
        than the armor of Odysseus—that corrupt and devious man.
1545 LEADER: Aiai, aiai! . . . a bitter hole . . . ready to receive you, child.
      Mother, cry.
HECUBA: Aiai! Aiai!
LEADER: Let us chant a dirge for the dead.
HECUBA: For tragedy.
1550 LEADER: Overwhelming tragedy for you.
HECUBA:

[*stooping over the body of* ASTYANAX]

      Let me be the one to bandage up your wounds . . .
        a useless doctor, one who cannot cure.
1555   Your father among the dead must do the rest.
LEADER: Batter your heads, oh, batter them.
      Clench your fists into clubs . . . O . . . h!
HECUBA: Listen, dear daughters . . .

[HECUBA *breaks off and gazes into the distance as if having a revelation*]

1560   LEADER: What is it, Hecuba? . . . Open your heart
        to us your ever faithful friends.
  HECUBA: Just that it is clear now
        the gods have singled me out for suffering
        and Troy for hate—above all other cities.
1565   In vain have we slaughtered our hecatombs, and the divine reply
        is to bury us under the earth, heap it on us, pack it down.
    It is as if we were to be smothered from view:
        unsung by the Muses, uncharted, unrecorded
        in ages to come.

1570   [*She beckons to two of the women to take* ASTYANAX *from her and lay him on
Hector's shield*]

    Come, lift the dead onto his sad tomb.
    Whatever is necessary has been done.
    Not that the rituals of funerals, in my opinion,
1575   have any interest for the dead.
    They are performed to satisfy the living.

    [*At a sign from* TALTHYBIUS *two soldiers come forward and take up the
shield with the limp body of* ASTYANAX *upon it and carry it to the grave
which* TALTHYBIUS *has had dug.* HECUBA *stares after them with a look of*
1580   *blankness and hopelessness*]

  LEADER:

    [*calling out after the cortege*]

    An agonized mother having to watch
        Her brightest hopes of life put out.
1585   Once it was thought how grand to be
        Engendered from a noble race,
        But a horrible death has ended that.

    [*In the distance along the battlements of Troy, soldiers are seen scurrying about
with lighted torches*]

1590   On the heights of Ilium what do I see?
        A waving of arms and firebrands:
        Some new disaster threatens Troy.

[TALTHYBIUS *hurries in leading a detachment of soldiers, all carrying firebrands*]

1595 TALTHYBIUS: Orders are for the officers in charge of firing the city of Priam
    to proceed at once with the incendiary flares
    and burn down Ilium, down to the ground.
  Then at last with hearts at ease we can sail for home.
  Meanwhile—to accomplish two commands in one—
1600   you daughters of Troy, as soon as you hear
    from the officers' camp the trumpets blare,
    get yourselves to the ships. It is the signal to leave
  And you, old woman, laden with sorrows, follow these men.
  They come from Odysseus to fetch you:
1605   your lot is to be his slave, far from your fatherland.
HECUBA: Yes, laden with sorrows!
    And now to cap it all as I say goodbye,
    my city is given up to flames.
  Very well then, start walking, you poor old feet,
1610   make one last effort to salute your broken town.

[*She takes a few steps and then stands with her arms open as if embracing the last of burning Troy*]

  O Troy, great city,
    once breath of grandeur on the barbarian scene,
1615   how fast your glory is extinct!
  They burn you down, and we,
    we are being herded off as slaves.
  O you gods . . .
    but why bother to invoke the gods?
1620   In the past they never heard my prayers.
  So, hurry, hurry into the flames.
  Let my glory be
    to die in the bonfire of my home.

[*As HECUBA begins to totter towards the flames, TALTHYBIUS signals to a*
1625 *group of guards*]

TALTHYBIUS: The poor creature is possessed, crazed by sorrow
    Go, retrieve her. Don't hesitate.
    She is Odysseus' prize.
    We must put her in his hands.

1630   [*The soldiers approach her, but she halts. Then she utters a long, ritual animal howl*]

LYRIC DIALOGUE

HECUBA: Ottototototoi.

        Cronos' son, lord of Phrygia,[20]

        Father of our race, do you see

1635   The perpetrations they have done,

        Done to the seed of Dardanus?

FULL CHORUS: He sees, but our glorious city

        Is a city no longer. There is no Troy.

HECUBA: Ottototototoi.

1640   The roofs of the citadel and the town,

        The crests of the ramparts—all aflame.

CHORUS: Up like smoke into the sky

        Our country vanishes in fire,

        Obliterated by the war.

1645   The lance has raged through all the halls.

[HECUBA *throws herself on her knees and beats the ground with her fists— ritual gesture whereby one summoned the dead from the bowels of the earth*]

HECUBA: Earth that has fed my children!

CHORUS: Eee . . . h! Eee . . . h!

1650 HECUBA: Hearken, my children, answer the call of a mother.

CHORUS: Your cries are summoning the dead.

HECUBA: They are—my withered limbs stretched on the ground.

        My two fists batter the earth.

[*The women of the* CHORUS *throw themselves down and imitate the behavior of*

1655 HECUBA]

CHORUS: We as well kneel on the earth

        And call on our husbands who are dead.

HECUBA: We are driven off, herded away . . .

CHORUS: How your cries rend the heart!

1660 HECUBA: . . . away to become household slaves.

CHORUS: Far far away!

HECUBA: Priam, my Priam, without a tomb,

        Dying too without a friend

        You do not see my misery.

---

[20] Cronos' son, lord of Phrygia: Zeus.

1665   CHORUS: Black was the veil that shadowed his eyes:
                Unholy the murder of a holy man.

           [HECUBA *and the rest of the women rise from the ground and with their arms flung wide address the burning city*]

           HECUBA: Farewell you courts of the gods, my beloved town!
1670   CHORUS: A . . . h!
           HECUBA: Demolished by deadly spear and flame.
           CHORUS: Soon to be rubble and a nameless land.
           HECUBA: Smoke and ash rise in the air.
                The place of my palace is blotted out.
1675   CHORUS: Yes, a land without a name.
                Little by little all is gone.
                Troy doomed does not exist.

           [*They hear a tremendous crash*]
           HECUBA: Listen, did you hear—realize . . .
1680   CHORUS: It is the collapse of the citadel.
           HECUBA: Gone. Everything is gone.
           CHORUS: A wave of ruin spreads through the ruins.

           [*Several long blasts on the trumpet echo over the plain*]

           HECUBA: [*gathering herself together*]
1685   Shake your silly shaking legs,
                Hecuba, begin your walk
                Towards your new life as slave.
           CHORUS: Sad, stricken Troy, farewell.
                We too must walk away
1690   To the Greek armada and set sail.

           [*As Troy continues to burn,* TALTHYBIUS *and his guards marshal the* WOMEN OF TROY *and lead them off.* HECUBA *stands for a moment with bent head and her back to the city. Then she slowly begins to follow, but her footsteps get slower and slower till at last she sinks to the ground with her eyes riveted*
1695   *on the burning city. Several of the* WOMEN *run back to help her, but when they reach her she is dead. Euripides does not include this scenario, but with* CASSANDRA's *prophecy (and she is never wrong)* HECUBA's *death at Troy is foretold*]

9. LYSISTRATA
(411 BCE)

Aristophanes

(trans. by Whitney A. Oates and C. T. Murphy)

Aristophanes (c. 445–c. 380 BCE) is the model of Greek comedic drama, as thirteen of his works are the only comedies extant. Though the comedic form shares many features with tragedy, the subject matter is not myth but characters and situations with contemporary reference, invented for burlesque and parody. Lysistrata offers a fresh solution to ending the Peloponnesian Wars which had been going on for twenty years without resolution. The heroine, whose name means "she who disbands armies," comes up with a plan to achieve peace: a sex strike against the war, by the women from all Hellas. Despite the comic stereotyping of the sexes, Aristophanes presents a serious theme urging his fellow Greeks to return to rational living.

CHARACTERS IN THE PLAY

LYSISTRATA
CALONICE   *Athenian women*
MYRRHINE
LAMPITO, *a Spartan woman*
LEADER *of the Chorus of Old Men*
CHORUS *of Old Men*
LEADER *of the Chorus of Old Women*
CHORUS *of Old Women*
ATHENIAN MAGISTRATE
THREE ATHENIAN WOMEN
CINESIAS, *an Athenian, husband of Myrrhine*
SPARTAN HERALD
SPARTAN AMBASSADORS
ATHENIAN AMBASSADORS
TWO ATHENIAN CITIZENS
CHORUS *of Athenians*
CHORUS *of Spartans*

SCENE: In Athens, beneath the Acropolis. In the center of the stage is the Propylaea, or gate-way to the Acropolis; to one side is a small grotto, sacred to Pan. The Orchestra represents a slope leading up to the gate-way.

It is early in the morning. LYSISTRATA is pacing impatiently up and down.

LYSISTRATA. If they'd been summoned to worship the God of Wine, or Pan, or to visit the Queen of Love, why, you couldn't have pushed your way through the streets for all the timbrels. But now there's not a single woman here—except my neighbor; here she comes.

5   [*Enter* CALONICE.]

Good day to you, Calonice.

CALONICE. And to you, Lysistrata. [*Noticing* LYSISTRATA's *impatient air*] But what ails you? Don't scowl, my dear; it's not becoming to you to knit your brows like that.

10   LYSISTRATA. [*Sadly*] Ah, Calonice, my heart aches; I'm so annoyed at us women. For among men we have a reputation for sly trickery—

CALONICE. And rightly too, on my word!

LYSISTRATA. —but when they were told to meet here to consider a matter of no small importance, they lie abed and don't come.

15   CALONICE. Oh, they'll come all right, my dear. It's not easy for a woman to get out, you know. One is working on her husband, another is getting up the maid, another has to put the baby to bed, or wash and feed it.

LYSISTRATA. But after all, there are other matters more important than all that.

CALONICE. My dear Lysistrata, just what is this matter you've summoned us

20   women to consider? What's up? Something big?

LYSISTRATA. Very big.

CALONICE. [*Interested*] Is it stout, too?

LYSISTRATA. [*Smiling*] Yes indeed—both big and stout.

CALONICE. What? And the women still haven't come?

25   LYSISTRATA. It's not what you suppose; they'd have come soon enough for *that*. But I've worked up something, and for many a sleepless night I've turned it this way and that.

CALONICE. [*In mock disappointment*] Oh, I guess it's pretty fine and slender, if you've turned it this way and that.

30   LYSISTRATA. So fine that the safety of the whole of Greece lies in us women.

CALONICE. In us women? It depends on a very slender reed then.

LYSISTRATA. Our country's fortunes are in our hands; and whether the Spartans shall perish—

CALONICE. Good! Let them perish, by all means.

35   LYSISTRATA. —and the Boeotians shall be completely annihilated.

CALONICE. Not completely! Please spare the eels.[1]

LYSISTRATA. As for Athens, I won't use any such unpleasant words. But you understand what I mean. But if the women will meet here—the Spartans, the Boeotians, and we Athenians—then all together we will save Greece.

40 CALONICE. But what could women do that's clever or distinguished? We just sit around all dolled up in silk robes, looking pretty in our sheer gowns and evening slippers.

LYSISTRATA. These are just the things I hope will save us: these silk robes, perfumes, evening slippers, rouge, and our chiffon blouses.

45 CALONICE. How so?

LYSISTRATA. So never a man alive will lift a spear against the foe—

CALONICE. I'll get a silk gown at once.

LYSISTRATA. —or take up his shield—

CALONICE. I'll put on my sheerest gown!

50 LYSISTRATA. —or sword.

CALONICE. I'll buy a pair of evening slippers.

LYSISTRATA. Well then, shouldn't the women have come?

CALONICE. Come? Why, they should have *flown* here.

LYSISTRATA. Well, my dear, just watch: they'll act in true Athenian fashion—

55 everything too late! And now there's not a woman here from the shore or from Salamis.

CALONICE. They're coming. I'm sure; at daybreak they were laying—to their oars to cross the straits.

LYSISTRATA. And those I expected would be the first to come—the women of

60 Acharnae—they haven't arrived.

CALONICE. Yet the wife of Theagenes means to come: she consulted Hecate[2] about it. [*Seeing a group of women approaching*] But look! Here come a few. And there are some more over here. Hurrah! Where do they come from?

LYSISTRATA. From Anagyra.

65 CALONICE. Yes indeed! We've raised up quite a stink from Anagyra anyway.

[*Enter* MYRRHINE *in haste, followed by several other women.*]

MYRRHINE. [*Breathlessly*] Have we come in time, Lysistrata? What do you say? Why so quiet?

LYSISTRATA. I can't say much for you, Myrrhine, coming at this hour on such

70 important business.

MYRRHINE. Why, I had trouble finding my girdle in the dark. But if it's so important, we're here now; tell us.

LYSISTRATA. No. Let's wait a little for the women from Boeotia and the Peloponnesus.

---

[1] **eels**: a favorite delicacy from Boeotian waters.
[2] **Hecate**: Greek goddess of the Underworld.

75   MYRRHINE. That's a much better suggestion. Look! Here comes Lampito now.

[*Enter* LAMPITO *with two other women.*]

LYSISTRATA. Greetings, my dear Spartan friend. How pretty you look, my dear. What a smooth complexion and well-developed figure! You could throttle an ox.

80   LAMPITO. Faith, yes, I think I could. I take exercises and kick my heels against my bum. [*She demonstrates with a few steps of the Spartan "bottom-kicking" dance.*]

LYSISTRATA. And what splendid breasts you have.

LAMPITO. La! You handle me like a prize steer.

LYSISTRATA. And who is this young lady with you?

85   LAMPITO. Faith, she's an Ambassadress from Boeotia.

LYSISTRATA. Oh yes, a Boeotian, and blooming like a garden too.

CALONICE. [*Lifting up her skirt*] My word! How neatly her garden's weeded!

LYSISTRATA. And who is the other girl?

LAMPITO. Oh, she's a Corinthian swell.

90   MYRRHINE. [*After a rapid examination*] Yes indeed. She swells very nicely [*Pointing*] here and here.

LAMPITO. Who has gathered together this company of women?

LYSISTRATA. I have.

LAMPITO. Speak up, then. What do you want?

95   MYRRHINE. Yes, my dear, tell us what this important matter is.

LYSISTRATA. Very well, I'll tell you. But before I speak, let me ask you a little question.

MYRRHINE. Anything you like.

LYSISTRATA. [*Earnestly*] Tell me: don't you yearn for the fathers of your

100   children, who are away at the wars? I know you all have husbands abroad.

CALONICE. Why, yes; mercy me! my husband's been away for five months in Thrace keeping guard on—Eucrates.

MYRRHINE. And mine for seven whole months in Pylus.

LAMPITO. And mine, as soon as ever he returns from the fray, readjusts his shield

105   and flies out of the house again.

LYSISTRATA. And as for lovers, there's not even a ghost of one left. Since the Milesians revolted from us, I've not even seen an eight-inch dingus to be a leather consolation for us widows. Are you willing, if I can find a way, to help me end the war?

110   MYRRHINE. Goodness, yes! I'd do it, even if I had to pawn my dress and—get drunk on the spot!

CALONICE. And I, even if I had to let myself be split in two like a flounder.

LAMPITO. I'd climb up Mt. Taygetus if I could catch a glimpse of peace.

LYSISTRATA. I'll tell you, then, in plain and simple words. My friends, if we are

115   going to force our men to make peace, we must do without—

MYRRHINE Without what? Tell us.

LYSISTRATA. Will you do it?

MYRRHINE. We'll do it, if it kills us.

LYSISTRATA. Well, then we must do without sex altogether.

120   [*General consternation*] Why do you turn away? Where go you? Why turn so pale? Why those tears? Will you do it or not? What means this hesitation?

MYRRHINE. I won't do it! Let the war go on.

CALONICE. Nor I! Let the war go on.

LYSISTRATA. So, my little flounder? Didn't you say jus t now you'd split

125   yourself in half?

CALONICE. Anything else you like. I'm willing, even if I have to walk through fire. Anything rather than sex. There's nothing like it, my dear.

LYSISTRATA. [*To* MYRRHINE] What about you?

MYRRHINE. [*Sullenly*] I'm willing to walk through fire, too.

130 LYSISTRATA. Oh vile and cursed breed! No wonder they make tragedies about us: we're naught but "love-affairs and bassinets." But you, my dear Spartan friend, if you alone are with me, our enterprise might yet succeed. Will you vote with me?

LAMPITO. 'Tis cruel hard, by my faith, for a woman to sleep alone without her

135   nooky; but for all that, we certainly do need peace.

LYSISTRATA. O my dearest friend! You're the only real woman here.

CALONICE. [*Wavering*] Well, if we do refrain from—[*Shuddering*] what you say (God forbid!), would that bring peace?

LYSISTRATA. My goodness, yes! If we sit at home all rouged and powdered,

140   dressed in our sheerest gowns, and neatly depilated, our men will get excited and want to take us; but if you don't come to them and keep away, they'll soon make a truce.

LAMPITO. Aye; Menelaus caught sight of Helen's naked breast and dropped his sword, they say.

145 CALONICE. What if the men give us up?

LYSISTRATA. "Flay a skinned dog," as Pherecrates says.

CALONICE. Rubbish! These make-shifts are no good. But suppose they grab us and drag us into the bedroom?

LYSISTRATA. Hold on to the door.

150 CALONICE. And if they beat us?

LYSISTRATA. Give in with a bad grace. There's no pleasure in it for them when they have to use violence. And you must torment them in every possible way. They'll give up soon enough; a man gets no joy if he doesn't get along with his wife.

155 MYRRHINE. If this is your opinion, we agree.

LAMPITO. As for our own men, we can persuade them to make a just and fair peace; but what about the Athenian rabble? Who will persuade them not to start any more monkey-shines?

LYSISTRATA. Don't worry. We guarantee to convince them.

160   LAMPITO. Not while their ships are rigged so well and they have that mighty treasure in the temple of Athene.

LYSISTRATA. We've taken good care for that too: we shall seize the Acropolis today. The older women have orders to do this, and while we are making our arrangements, they are to pretend to make a sacrifice and occupy the

165   Acropolis.

LAMPITO. All will be well then. That's a very fine idea.

LYSISTRATA. Let's ratify this, Lampito, with the most solemn oath.

LAMPITO. Tell us what oath we shall swear.

LYSISTRATA. Well said. Where's our Policewoman? [*To a Scythian slave*] What

170   are you gaping at? Set a shield upside-down here in front of me, and give me the sacred meats.

CALONICE. Lysistrata, what sort of an oath are we to take?

LYSISTRATA. What oath? I'm going to slaughter a sheep over the shield as they do in Aschylus.

175   CALONICE. Don't, Lysistrata! No oaths about peace over a shield.

LYSISTRATA. What shall the oath be, then?

CALONICE. How about getting a white horse somewhere and cutting out its entrails for the sacrifice?

LYSISTRATA. White horse indeed!

180   CALONICE. Well then, how shall we swear?

MYRRHINE. I'll tell you: let's place a large black bowl upside-down and then slaughter—a flask of Thasian wine. And then let's swear not to pour in a single drop of water.

LAMPITO. Lord! How I like that oath!

185   LYSISTRATA. Someone bring out a bowl and a flask.

[*A slave brings the utensils for the sacrifice.*]

CALONICE. Look, my friends! What a big jar! Here's a cup that 'twould give me joy to handle. [*She picks up the bowl.*]

LYSISTRATA. Set it down and put your hands on our victim.

190   [*As CALONICE places her hands on the flask*] O Lady of Persuasion and dear Loving Cup, graciously vouchsafe to receive this sacrifice from us women. [*She pours the wine into the bowl.*]

CALONICE. The blood has a good colour and spurts out nicely.

LAMPITO. Faith, it has a pleasant smell, too.

195   MYRRHINE. Oh, let me be the first to swear, ladies!

CALONICE. No, by our Lady! Not unless you're allotted the first turn.

LYSISTRATA. Place all your hands on the cup, and one of you repeat on behalf of all what I say. Then all will swear and ratify the oath. *I will suffer no man, be he husband or lover,*

200   CALONICE. *I will suffer no man, be he husband or lover,*

LYSISTRATA. *To approach me all hot and horny.* [*As CALONICE hesitates*] Say it!

CALONICE. [Slowly and painfully] *To approach me all hot and horny. O Lysistrata, I feel so weak in the knees!*

LYSISTRATA. *I will remain at home unmated,*

205 CALONICE. *I will remain at home unmated,*

LYSISTRATA. *Wearing my sheerest gown and carefully adorned,*

CALONICE. *Wearing my sheerest gown and carefully adorned,*

LYSISTRATA. *That my husband may burn with desire for me.*

CALONICE. *That my husband may burn with desire for me,*

210 LYSISTRATA. *And if he takes me by force against my will,*

CALONICE. *And if he takes me by force against my will,*

LYSISTRATA. *I shall do it badly and keep from moving.*

CALONICE. *I shall do it badly and keep from moving.*

LYSISTRATA. *I will not stretch my slippers toward the ceiling,*

215 CALONICE. *I will not stretch my slippers toward the ceiling,*

LYSISTRATA. *Nor will I take the posture of the lioness on the knifehandle.*

CALONICE. *Nor will I take the posture of the lioness on the knifehandle.*

LYSISTRATA. *If I keep this oath, may I be permitted to drink from this cup,*

CALONICE. *If I keep this oath, may I be permitted to drink from this cup,*

220 LYSISTRATA. *But if I break it, may the cup be filled with water.*

CALONICE. *But if I break it, may the cup be filled with water.*

LYSISTRATA. Do you all swear to this?

ALL. I do, so help me!

LYSISTRATA. Come then, I'll just consummate this offering.

225 [*She takes a long drink from the cup.*]

CALONICE. [*Snatching the cup away*] Shares, my dear! Let's drink to our continued friendship. [*A shout is heard from off-stage.*]

LAMPITO. What's that shouting?

LYSISTRATA. That's what I was telling you: the women have just seized the
230 Acropolis. Now, Lampito, go home and arrange matters in Sparta; and leave these two ladies here as hostages. We'll enter the Acropolis to join our friends and help them lock the gates.

CALONICE. Don't you suppose the men will come to attack us?

LYSISTRATA. Don't worry about them. Neither threats nor fire will suffice to
235 open the gates, except on the terms we've stated.

CALONICE. I should say not! Else we'd belie our reputation as unmanageable pests.

[LAMPITO *leaves the stage. The other women retire and enter the Acropolis through the Propylaea.*]

240 [*Enter the* CHORUS OF OLD MEN, *carrying fire-pots and a load of heavy sticks.*]

LEADER OF MEN. Onward, Draces, step by step, though your shoulder's aching.

Cursèd logs of olive-wood, what a load you're making!

FIRST SEMI-CHORUS OF OLD MEN. [*Singing*]

245 Aye, many surprises await a man who lives to a ripe old age;
  For who could suppose, Strymodorus my lad, that the women
   we've nourished (alas!),
   Who sat at home to vex our days,
   Would seize the holy image here
250   And occupy this sacred shrine,
   With bolts and bars, with fell design,
   To lock the Propylaea?

LEADER OF MEN. Come with speed, Philourgus, come! to the temple hast'ning.
  There we'll heap these logs about in a circle round them,
255 And whoever has conspired, raising this rebellion,
  Shall be roasted, scorched, and burnt, all without exception,
  Doomed by one unanimous vote—but first the wife of Lycon.

SECOND SEMI-CHORUS. [*Singing*]

  No, no! by Demeter,[3] while I'm alive, no woman shall mock at me.
260 Not even the Spartan Cleomenes, our citadel first to seize,
   Got off Unscathed; for all his pride
   And haughty Spartan arrogance,
   He left his arms and sneaked away,
   Stripped to his shirt, unkempt, unshav'd,
265   With six years' filth still on him.

LEADER OF MEN. I besieged that hero bold, sleeping at my station,
  Marshalled at these holy gates sixteen deep against him.
  Shall I not these cursèd pests punish for their daring,
  Burning these Euripides-and-God-detested women?
270 Aye! or else may Marathon overturn my trophy.

FIRST SEMI-CHORUS. [*Singing*]

  There remains of my road
   Just this brow of the hill;
   There I speed on my way.
275 Drag the logs up the hill, though we're got no ass to help.
   (God! my shoulder's bruised and sore!)
   Onward still must we go
   Blow the fire! Don't let it go out
   Now we're near the end of our road.

280 ALL. [*Blowing on the fire-pots*]

  Whew! Whew! Drat the smoke!

SECOND SEMI-CHORUS. [*Singing*]

  Lord, what smoke rushing forth
   From the pot, like a dog

---

[3]**Demeter:** Greek earth goddess, Zeus's sister.

285   Running mad, bites my eyes!
       This must be Lemnos[4]-fire. What a sharp and stinging smoke!
             Rushing onward to the shrine
             Aid the gods. Once for all
             Show your mettle, Laches my boy!
290   To the rescue hastening all!
   ALL. [*Blowing on the fire-pots*] Whew! Whew! Drat the smoke!

     [*The chorus has now reached the edge of the Orchestra nearest the stage, in front of the Propylaea. They begin laying their logs and fire-pots on the ground.*]

295   LEADER OF MEN. Thank heaven, this fire is still alive. Now let's first put down these logs here and place our torches in the pots to catch; then let's make a rush for the gates with a battering-ram. If the women don't unbar the gate at our summons, we'll have to smoke them out.
          Let me put down my load. Ouch! That hurts! [*To the audience*] Would any of
300   the generals in Samos[5] like to lend a hand with this log? [*Throwing down a log*] Well, *that* won't break my back any more, at any rate. [*Turning to his fire-pot*] Your job, my little pot, is to keep those coals alive and furnish me shortly with a red-hot torch.
          O mistress Victory, be my ally and grant me to rout these audacious women in
305   the Acropolis.

     [*While the men are busy with their logs and fires, the* CHORUS OF OLD WOMEN *enters, carrying pitchers of water.*]

   LEADER OF WOMEN. What's this I see? Smoke and flames? Is that a fire ablazing?
310   Let's rush upon them. Hurry up! They'll find us women ready.
   FIRST SEMI-CHORUS OF OLD WOMEN. [*Singing*]
             With wingèd foot onward I fly,
             Ere the flames consume Neodice;
             Lest Critylla be overwhelmed
315   By a lawless, accurst herd of old men.
         I shudder with fear. Am I too late to aid them?
         At break of the day filled we our jars with water
  Fresh from the spring, pushing our way straight through the crowds.
         Oh, what a din!
320   Mid crockery crashing, jostled by slave-girls,
          Sped we to save them, aiding our neighbors,

---

[4]**Lemnos-fire:** Lemnos was a volcanic island in the Aegean Sea.
[5]**Samos:** the headquarters of the Athenian fleet.

Bearing this water to put out the flames.

SECOND SEMI-CHORUS OF OLD WOMEN. [*Singing*]

325 　　　　Such news I've heard: doddering fools
　　　　Come with logs, like furnace-attendants,
　　　　Loaded down with three hundred pounds,
　　　Breathing many a vain, blustering threat,
　　　That all these abhorred sluts will be burnt to charcoal.
　　　O goddess, I pray never may they be kindled;
330 Grant them to save Greece and our men; madness and war help them to end.
　　With this as our purpose, golden-plumed Maiden,
　　Guardian of Athens, seized we thy precinct.
　　Be my ally, Warrior-maiden,
　　'Gainst these old men, bearing water with me.

335 [*The women have now reached their position in the Orchestra, and their* LEADER *advances toward the* LEADER OF THE MEN.]

LEADER OF WOMEN. Hold on there! What's this, you utter scoundrels? No decent, God-fearing citizens would act like this.

LEADER OF MEN. Oho! Here's something unexpected: a swarm of women have
340 　　come out to attack us.

LEADER OF WOMEN. What, do we frighten you? Surely you don't think we're too many for you. And yet there are ten thousand times more of us whom you haven't even seen.

LEADER OF MEN. What say, Phaedria? Shall we let these women wag their
345 　　tongues? Shan't we take our sticks and break them over their backs?

LEADER OF WOMEN. Let's set our pitchers on the ground; then if anyone lays a hand on us, they won't get in our way.

LEADER OF MEN. By God! If someone gave them two or three smacks on the jaw, like Bupalus, they wouldn't talk so much!

350 LEADER OF WOMEN. Go on, hit me, somebody! Here's my jaw! But no other bitch will bite a piece out of you before me.

LEADER OF MEN. Silence! or I'll knock out your—senility!

LEADER OF WOMEN. Just lay one finger on Stratyllis, I dare you!

LEADER OF MEN. Suppose I dust you off with this fist? What will you do?

355 LEADER OF WOMEN. I'll tear the living guts out of you with my teeth.

LEADER OF MEN. No poet is more clever than Euripides: "There is no beast so shameless as a woman. "

LEADER OF WOMEN. Let's pick up our jars of water, Rhodippe.

LEADER OF MEN. Why have you come here with water, you detestable slut?

360 LEADER OF WOMEN. And why have you come with fire, you funeral vault? To cremate yourself?

LEADER OF MEN. To light a fire and singe your friends.

LEADER OF WOMEN. And I've brought water to put out your fire.

LEADER OF MEN. What? You'll put out my fire?

365 LEADER OF WOMEN. Just try and see!

LEADER OF MEN. I wonder: shall I scorch you with this torch of mine?

LEADER OF WOMEN. If you've got any soap, I'll give you a bath.

LEADER OF MEN. Give *me* a bath, you stinking hag?

LEADER OF WOMEN. Yes—a bridal bath!

370 LEADER OF MEN. Just listen to her! What crust!

LEADER OF WOMEN. Well, I'm a free citizen.

LEADER OF MEN. I'll put an end to your bawling. [*The men pick up their torches.*]

LEADER OF WOMEN. You'll never do jury-duty again. [*The women pick up their*

375 *pitchers.*]

LEADER OF MEN. Singe her hair for her!

LEADER OF WOMEN. Do your duty, water! [*The women empty their pitchers on the men.*]

LEADER OF MEN. Ow! Ow! For heaven's sake!

380 LEADER OF WOMEN. Is it too hot?

LEADER OF MEN. What do you mean "hot"? Stop! What are you doing?

LEADER OF WOMEN. I'm watering you, so you'll be fresh and green.

LEADER OF MEN. But I'm all withered up with shaking.

LEADER OF WOMEN. Well, you've got a fire; why don't you dry yourself?

385 [*Enter an Athenian MAGISTRATE, accompanied by four Scythian policemen.*]

MAGISTRATE. Have these wanton women flared up again with their timbrels and their continual worship of Sabazius? Is this another Adonis-dirge upon the roof-tops—which we heard not long ago in the Assembly? That confounded Demostratus was urging us to sail to Sicily, and the whirling

390 women shouted, "Woe for Adonis!"[6] And then Demostratus said we'd best enroll the infantry from Zacynthus, and a tipsy woman on the roof shrieked, "Beat your breasts for Adonis!" And that vile and filthy lunatic forced his measure through. Such license do our women take.

395 LEADER OF MEN. What if you heard of the insolence of these women here? Besides their other violent acts, they threw water all over us, and we have to shake out our clothes just as if we'd leaked in them.

MAGISTRATE. And rightly, too, by God! For we ourselves lead the women astray and teach them to play the wanton; from these roots such notions

400 blossom forth. A man goes into the jeweler's shop and says, "About that necklace you made for my wife, goldsmith: last night, while she was dancing, the fastening-bolt slipped out of the hole. I have to sail over to Salamis today;

---

[6]The women worshipping Adonis, a god associated with death, were thought to put a hex on the Sicilian expedition.

405 if you're free, do come around tonight and fit in a new bolt for her." Another goes to the shoe-maker, a strapping young fellow with manly parts, and says, "See here, cobbler, the sandal-strap chafes my wife's little—toe; it's so tender. Come around during the siesta and stretch it a little, so she'll be more comfortable." Now we see the results of such treatment: here I'm a special Councillor and need money to procure oars for the galleys; and I'm locked out of the Treasury by these women.

410 But this is no time to stand around. Bring up crow-bars there! I'll put an end to their insolence. [*To one of the policemen*] What are you gaping at, you wretch? What are you staring at? Got an eye out for a tavern, eh? Set your crow-bars here to the gates and force them open. [*Retiring to safe distance*] I'll help from over here.

415 [*The gates are thrown open and* LYSISTRATA *comes out followed by several other women.*]

LYSISTRATA. Don't force the gates; I'm coming out of my own accord. We don't need crow-bars here; what we need is good sound common-sense.
MAGISTRATE. Is that so, you strumpet? Where's my policeman? Officer, arrest
420 her and tie her arms behind her back.
LYSISTRATA. By Artemis,[7] if he lays a finger on me, he'll pay for it, even if he is a public servant.

[*The policeman retires in terror.*]

MAGISTRATE. You there, are you afraid? Seize her round the waist—and you,
425 too. Tie her up, both of you!
FIRST WOMAN. [*As the second policeman approaches* LYSISTRATA] By Pandrosus,[8] if you but touch her with your hand, I'll kick the stuffings out of you.

[*The second policeman retires in terror.*]

430 MAGISTRATE. Just listen to that: "kick the stuffings out." Where's another policeman? Tie *her* up first, for her chatter.
SECOND WOMAN. By the Goddess of the Light, if you lay the tip of your finger on her, you'll soon need a doctor.

[*The third policeman retires in terror.*]

---

[7]**Artemis:** goddess of the hunt, childbirth, and the moon ("Phoebe").
[8]**Pandrosus:** a legendary Greek princess.

435   MAGISTRATE. What's this? Where's my policeman? Seize *her* too. I'll soon stop
        your sallies.
        THIRD WOMAN. By the Goddess to Tauros, if you go near her, I'll tear out your
        hair until it shrieks with pain.

        [*The fourth policeman retires in terror.*]

440   MAGISTRATE. Oh, damn it all! I've run out of policemen. But women must never
        defeat us. Officers, let's charge them all together. Close up your ranks!

        [*The policemen rally for a mass attack.*]

        LYSISTRATA. By heaven, you'll soon find out that we have four companies of
        warrior-women, all fully equipped within!
445   MAGISTRATE. [*Advancing*] Twist their arms off, men!
        LYSISTRATA. [*Shouting*] To the rescue, my valiant women!
            O sellers-of-barley-green-stuffs-and-eggs,
            O sellers-of-garlic, ye keepers-of-taverns, and vendors-of-bread,
               Grapple! Smite! Smash!
450   Won't you heap filth on them? Give them a tongue-lashing!

        [*The women beat off the policemen.*]

        Halt! Withdraw! No looting on the field.
        MAGISTRATE. Damn it! My police-force has put up a very poor show.
        LYSISTRATA. What did you expect? Did you think you were attacking slaves?
455   Didn't you know that women are filled with passion?
        MAGISTRATE. Aye, passion enough—for a good strong drink!
        LEADER OF MEN. O chief and leader of this land, why spend your words in
        vain?
        Don't argue with these shameless beasts. You know not how we've fared:
460   A soapless bath they've given us; our clothes are soundly soaked.
        LEADER OF WOMEN. Poor fool! You never should attack or strike a peaceful
        girl.
            But if you do, your eyes must swell. For I am quite content
            To sit unmoved, like modest maids, in peace and cause no pain;
465   But let a man stir up my hive, he'll find me like a wasp.
        CHORUS OF MEN. [*Singing*]
            O God, whatever shall we do with creatures like Womankind?
            This can't be endured by any man alive. Question them!
               Let us try to find out what this means.
470   To what end have they seized on this shrine,
               This steep and rugged, high and holy,
                 Undefiled Acropolis?

LEADER OF MEN. Come, put your questions; don't give in, and probe her every statement.

475   For base and shameful it would be to leave this plot untested.

MAGISTRATE. Well then, first of all I wish to ask her this: for what purpose have you barred us from the Acropolis?

LYSISTRATA. To keep the treasure safe, so you won't make war on account of it.

MAGISTRATE. What? Do we make war on account of the treasure?

480 LYSISTRATA. Yes, and you cause all our other troubles for it, too. Peisander[9] and those greedy office-seekers keep things stirred up so they can find occasions to steal. Now let them do what they like: they'll never again make off with any of this money.

MAGISTRATE. What will you do?

485 LYSISTRATA. What a question! We'll administer it ourselves.

MAGISTRATE. *You* will administer the treasure?

LYSISTRATA. What's so strange in that? Don't we administer the household money for you?

MAGISTRATE. That's different.

490 LYSISTRATA. How is it different?

MAGISTRATE. We've got to make war with this money.

LYSISTRATA. But that's the very first thing: you mustn't make war.

MAGISTRATE. How else can we be saved?

LYSISTRATA. We'll save you.

495 MAGISTRATE. *You*?

LYSISTRATA. Yes, we!

MAGISTRATE. God forbid!

LYSISTRATA. We'll save you, whether you want it or not.

MAGISTRATE. Oh! This is terrible!

500 LYSISTRATA. You don't like it, but we're going to do it none the less.

MAGISTRATE. Good God! it's illegal!

LYSISTRATA. We *will* save you, my little man!

MAGISTRATE. Suppose I don't want you to?

LYSISTRATA. That's all the more reason.

505 MAGISTRATE. What business have you with war and peace?

LYSISTRATA. I'll explain.

MAGISTRATE. [*Shaking his fist*] Speak up, or you'll smart for it.

LYSISTRATA. Just listen, and try to keep your hands still.

MAGISTRATE. I can't. I'm so mad I can't stop them.

510 FIRST WOMAN. Then you'll be the one to smart for it.

MAGISTRATE. Croak to yourself, old hag! [*To* LYSISTRATA] Now then, speak up.

LYSISTRATA. Very well. Formerly we endured the war for a good long time with our usual restraint, no matter what you men did. You wouldn't let us say

---

[9]Peisander: a corrupt politician who urged war.

515   "boo," although nothing you did suited us. But we watched you well, and though we stayed at home we'd often hear of some terribly stupid measure you'd proposed. Then, though grieving at heart, we'd smile sweetly and say, "What was passed in the Assembly today about writing on the treaty-stone?" "What's that to you?" my husband would say. "Hold your tongue!"

520   And I held my tongue.

FIRST WOMAN. But I wouldn't have—not I!

MAGISTRATE. You'd have been soundly smacked, if you hadn't kept still.

LYSISTRATA. So I kept still at home. Then we'd hear of some plan still worse than the first; we'd say, "Husband, how could you pass such a stupid

525   proposal?" He'd scowl at me and say, "If you don't mind your spinning, your head will be sore for weeks. *War shall be the concern of Men.*"

MAGISTRATE. And he was right, upon my word!

LYSISTRATA. Why right, you confounded fool, when your proposals were so stupid and we weren't allowed to make suggestions?

530   "There's not a *man* left in the country," says one. "No, not one," says another. Therefore all we women have decided in council to make a common effort to save Greece. How long should we have waited? Now, if you're willing to listen to our excellent proposals and keep silence for us in your turn, we still may save you.

535 MAGISTRATE. We men keep silence for you? That's terrible; I won't endure it!

LYSISTRATA. Silence!

MAGISTRATE. Silence for *you*, you wench, when you're wearing a snood? I'd rather die!

LYSISTRATA. Well, if that's all that bothers you—here! take my snood and tie it

540   round your head. [*During the following words the women dress up the* MAGISTRATE *in women's garments.*] And *now* keep quiet! Here, take this spinning-basket, too, and card your wool with robes tucked up, munching on beans. *War shall be the concern of Women!*

LEADER OF WOMEN. Arise and leave your pitchers, girls; no time is this to

545   falter.

We too must aid our loyal friends; our turn has come for action.

CHORUS OF WOMEN. [*Singing*]

I'll never tire of aiding them with song and dance; never may
Faintness keep my legs from moving to and fro endlessly.

550   For I yearn to do all for my friends;
They have charm, they have wit, they have grace,
With courage, brains, and best of virtues—
Patriotic sapience.

LEADER OF WOMEN. Come, child of manliest ancient dames, offspring of

555   stinging nettles,

Advance with rage unsoftened; for fair breezes speed you onward.

LYSISTRATA. If only sweet Eros and the Cyprian Queen of Love[10] shed charm over our breasts and limbs and inspire our men with amorous longing and priapic spasms, I think we may soon be called Peacemakers among the Greeks.

560 MAGISTRATE. What will you do?

LYSISTRATA. First of all, we'll stop those fellows who run madly about the Marketplace in arms.

FIRST WOMAN. Indeed we shall, by the Queen of Paphos.[11]

LYSISTRATA. For now they roam about the market, amid the pots and greenstuffs,
565 armed to the teeth like Corybantes.

MAGISTRATE. That's what manly fellows ought to do!

LYSISTRATA. But it's so silly: a chap with a Gorgon-emblazoned shield buying pickled herring.

FIRST WOMAN. Why, just the other day I saw one of those long-haired dandies
570 who command our cavalry ride up on horseback and pour into his bronze helmet the egg-broth he'd bought from an old dame. And there was a Thracian slinger too, shaking his lance like Tereus; he'd scared the life out of the poor fig-peddler and was gulping down all her ripest fruit.

MAGISTRATE. How can you stop all the confusion in the various states and
575 bring them together?

LYSISTRATA. Very easily.

MAGISTRATE. Tell me how.

LYSISTRATA. Just like a ball of wool, when it's confused and snarled: we take it thus, and draw out a thread here and a thread there with our spindles; thus
580 we'll unsnarl this war, if no one prevents us, and draw together the various states with embassies here and embassies there.

MAGISTRATE. Do you suppose you can stop this dreadful business with balls of wool and spindles, you nit-wits?

LYSISTRATA. Why, if *you* had any wits, you'd manage all affairs of state like our
585 wool-working.

MAGISTRATE. How so?

LYSISTRATA. First you ought to treat the city as we do when we wash the dirt out of a fleece: stretch it out and pluck and thrash out of the city all those prickly scoundrels; aye, and card out those who conspire and stick together
590 to gain office, pulling off their heads. Then card the wool, all of it, into one fair basket of goodwill, mingling in the aliens residing here, any loyal foreigners, and anyone who's in debt to the Treasury; and consider that all our colonies lie scattered round about like remnants; from all of these collect the wool and gather it together here, wind up a great ball, and then weave a
595 good stout cloak for the democracy.

MAGISTRATE. Dreadful! Talking about thrashing and winding balls of wool, when you haven't the slightest share in the war!

---

[10]**Cyprian Queen of Love**: i.e., Aphrodite.

[11]**Queen of Paphos**: i.e., Aphrodite.

LYSISTRATA. Why, you dirty scoundrel, we bear more than twice as much as you. First, we bear children and send off our sons as soldiers.

600 MAGISTRATE. Hush! Let bygones be bygones!

LYSISTRATA. Then, when we ought to be happy and enjoy our youth, we sleep alone because of your expeditions abroad. But never mind us married women: I grieve most for the maids who grow old at home unwed.

MAGISTRATE. Don't men grow old, too?

605 LYSISTRATA. For heaven's sake! That's not the same thing. When a man comes home, no matter how grey he is, he soon finds a girl to marry. But woman's bloom is short and fleeting; if she doesn't grasp her chance, no man is willing to marry her and she sits at home a prey to every fortune-teller.

MAGISTRATE. [*Coarsely*] But if a man can still get it up—

610 LYSISTRATA. See here, you: what's the matter? Aren't you dead yet? There's plenty of room for you. Buy yourself a shroud and I'll bake you a honey-cake. [*Handing him a copper coin for his passage across the Styx*] Here's your fare! Now get yourself a wreath.

615 [*During the following dialogue the women dress up the* MAGISTRATE *as a corpse.*]

FIRST WOMAN. Here, take these fillets.

SECOND WOMAN. Here, take this wreath.

LYSISTRATA. What do you want? What's lacking? Get moving; off to the ferry! Charon[12] is calling you; don't keep him from sailing.

620 MAGISTRATE. Am I to endure these insults? By God! I'm going straight to the magistrates to show them how I've been treated.

LYSISTRATA. Are you grumbling that you haven't been properly laid out? Well, the day after tomorrow we'll send around all the usual offerings early in the morning.

625 [*The* MAGISTRATE *goes out still wearing his funeral decorations.* LYSISTRATA *and the women retire into the Acropolis.*]

LEADER OF MEN. Wake, ye sons of freedom, wake! 'Tis no time for sleeping. Up and at them, like a man! Let us strip for action.

[*The* CHORUS OF MEN *remove their outer cloaks.*]

630 CHORUS OF MEN. [*Singing*]
Surely there is something here greater than infects the eye;
For without a doubt I smell Hippias'[13] tyranny.

---

[12]**Charon:** the ferryman of the river Styx in the Underworld.
[13]**Hippias:** the last tyrant of Athens (510 BCE).

Dreadful fear assails me lest certain hands of Spartan men,
Meeting here with Cleisthenes, have inspired through treachery
635   All these god-detested women secretly to seize
Athens' treasure in the temple, and to stop that pay
     Whence I live at my ease.
     LEADER OF MEN. Now isn't it terrible for them to advise the state and chatter
     about shields, being mere women?
640   And they think to reconcile us with the Spartans—men who hold nothing
     sacred any more than hungry wolves. Surely this is a web of deceit, my
     friends, to conceal an attempt at tyranny. But they'll never lord it over me; I'll
     be on my guard and from now on,
          "The blade I bear   A myrtle spray shall wear."
645   I'll occupy the market under arms and stand next to Aristogeiton.[14]
          Thus I'll stand beside him. [*He strikes the pose of the famous statue of the
     tyrannicides, with one arm raised.*] And here's my chance to take this accurst
     old hag and—[*Striking the* LEADER OF WOMEN] smack her on the jaw!
     LEADER OF WOMEN. You'll go home in such a state your Ma won't recognize
650   you!
     Ladies all, upon the ground let us place these garments.

[*The* CHORUS OF WOMEN *remove their outer garments.*]

CHORUS OF WOMEN. [*Singing*]
     Citizens of Athens, hear useful words for the state.
655   Rightly; for it nurtured me in my youth royally.
     As a child of seven years carried I the sacred box;
     Then I was a Miller-maid, grinding at Athene's shrine;
     Next I wore the saffron robe and played Brauronia's Bear;
     And I walked as Basket-bearer, wearing chains of figs,
660   As a sweet maiden fair.
     LEADER OF WOMEN. Therefore, am I not bound to give good advice to the city?
          Don't take it ill that I was born a woman, if I contribute something better
     than our present troubles. I pay my share; for I contribute MEN. But you
     miserable old fools contribute nothing, and after squandering our ancestral
665   treasure, the fruit of the Persian Wars, you make no contribution in return.
     And now, all on account of you, we're facing ruin.
          What, muttering, are you? If you annoy me, I'll take this hard, rough
     slipper and—[*Striking the* LEADER OF MEN] smack you on the jaw!
     CHORUS OF MEN. [*Singing*]
670   This is outright insolence! Things go from bad to worse.
     If you're men with any guts, prepare to meet the foe.
     Let us strip our tunics off! We need the smell of male

---

[14]Aristogeiton: a hero for assassinating the brother of the tyrant Hippias.

Vigor. And we cannot fight all swaddled up in clothes.

[*They strip off their tunics.*]

675   Come then, my comrades, on to the battle, ye who once to
         Leipsydrion came;
     Then ye were MEN. Now call back your youthful vigor.
         With light, wingèd footstep advance,
     Shaking old age from your frame.

680 LEADER OF MEN. If any of us give these wenches the slightest hold, they'll stop
at nothing: Such is their cunning.
     They will even build ships and sail against us, like Artemisia.[15] Or if
they turn to mounting, I count our Knights as done for: a woman's such a
tricky jockey when she gets astraddle, with a good firm seat for trotting. Just

685 look at those Amazons[16] that Micon painted, fighting on horseback against
men!
     But we must throw them all in the pillory—[*Seizing and choking the*
LEADER OF WOMEN] grabbing hold of yonder neck!

CHORUS OF WOMEN. [*Singing*]
690   'Ware my anger! Like a boar 'twill rush upon you men.
     Soon you'll bawl aloud for help, you'll be so soundly trimmed!
     Come, my friends, let's strip with speed, and lay aside these robes;
     Catch the scent of women's rage. Attack with tooth and nail!

[*They strip off their tunics.*]

695   Now then, come near me, you miserable man! you'll never eat garlic or black
beans again.
     And if you utter a single hard word, in rage I will "nurse" you as once
     The beetle requited her foe.

LEADER OF WOMEN. For you don't worry me; no, not so long as my Lampito
700   lives and our Theban friend, the noble Ismenia.
     You can't do anything, not even if you pass a dozen—decrees! You
miserable fool, all our neighbours hate you. Why, just the other day when I
was holding a festival for Hecate, I invited as playmate from our neighbours
the Boeotians a charming, well-bred Copaic—eel. But they refused to send me

705 one on account of your decrees.
     And you'll never stop passing decrees until I grab your foot and—
     [*Tripping up the* LEADER OF MEN] toss you down and break your neck!

---

[15]**Artemisia:** an Asian queen who had commanded a fleet against the Greeks in the
Persian Wars.
[16]**Amazons:** women warriors who cut off one breast in order to be skilled archers.

[*Here an interval of five days is supposed to elapse.* LYSISTRATA *comes out from the Acropolis.*]

710 LEADER OF WOMEN. [*Dramatically*] Empress of this great emprise and undertaking,

Why come you forth, I pray, with frowning brow?

LYSISTRATA. Ah, these cursèd women! Their deeds and female notions make me pace up and down in utter despair.

715 LEADER OF WOMEN. Ah, what sayest thou?

LYSISTRATA. The truth, alas! the truth.

LEADER OF WOMEN. What dreadful tale hast thou to tell thy friends?

LYSISTRATA. 'Tis shame to speak, and not to speak is hard.

LEADER OF WOMEN. Hide not from me whatever woes we suffer.

720 LYSISTRATA. Well then, to put it briefly, we want—laying!

LEADER OF WOMEN. O Zeus, Zeus!

LYSISTRATA. Why call on Zeus? That's the way things are. I can no longer keep them away from the men, and they're all deserting. I caught one wriggling through a hole near the grotto of Pan, another sliding down a rope, another

725 deserting her post; and yesterday I found one getting on a sparrow's back to fly off to Orsilochus, and had to pull her back by the hair. They're digging up all sorts of excuses to get home. Look, here comes one of them now. [*A woman comes hastily out of the Acropolis.*] Here you! Where are you off to in such a hurry?

730 FIRST WOMAN. I want to go home. My very best wool is being devoured by moths.

LYSISTRATA. Moths? Nonsense! Go back inside.

FIRST WOMAN. I'll come right back; I swear it. I just want to lay it out on the bed.

735 LYSISTRATA. Well, you won't lay it out, and you won't go home, either.

FIRST WOMAN. Shall I let my wool be ruined?

LYSISTRATA. If necessary, yes. [*Another woman comes out.*]

SECOND WOMAN. Oh dear! Oh dear! My precious flax! I left it at home all unpeeled.

740 LYSISTRATA. Here's another one, going home for her "flax." Come back here!

SECOND WOMAN. But I just want to work it up a little and then I'll be right back.

LYSISTRATA. No indeed! If you start this, all the other women will want to do the same. [*A third woman comes out.*]

745 THIRD WOMAN. O Eilithyia, goddess of travail, stop my labor till I come to a lawful spot!

LYSISTRATA. What's this nonsense?

THIRD WOMAN. I'm going to have a baby—right now!

LYSISTRATA. But you weren't even pregnant yesterday.

750   THIRD WOMAN. Well, I am today. O Lysistrata, do send me home to see a midwife, right away.

LYSISTRATA. What are you talking about? [*Putting her hand on her stomach*] What's this hard lump here?

THIRD WOMAN. A little boy.

755   LYSISTRATA. My goodness, what have you got there? It seems hollow; I'll just find out. [*Pulling aside her robe*] Why, you silly goose, you've got Athene's sacred helmet there. And you said you were having a baby!

THIRD WOMAN. Well, I *am* having one, I swear!

LYSISTRATA. Then what's this helmet for?

760   THIRD WOMAN. If the baby starts coming while I'm still in the Acropolis, I'll creep into this like a pigeon and give birth to it there.

LYSISTRATA. Stuff and nonsense! It's plain enough what you're up to. You just wait here for the christening of this—helmet.

THIRD WOMAN. But I can't sleep in the Acropolis since I saw the sacred snake.

765   FIRST WOMAN. And I'm dying for lack of sleep: the hooting of the owls keeps me awake.

LYSISTRATA. Enough of these shams, you wretched creatures. You want your husbands, I suppose. Well, don't you think they want us? I'm sure they're spending miserable nights. Hold out, my friends, and endure for just a little

770   while. There's an oracle that we shall conquer, if we don't split up. [*Producing a roll of paper*] Here it is.

FIRST WOMAN. Tell us what it says.

LYSISTRATA. Listen.

"When in the length of time the Swallows shall gather together,

775   Fleeing the Hoopoe's amorous flight and the Cockatoo shunning,

Then shall your woes be ended and Zeus who thunders in heaven

Set what's below on top—"

FIRST WOMAN. What? Are we going to be on top?

LYSISTRATA. "But if the Swallows rebel and flutter away from the temple,

780   Never a bird in the world shall seem more wanton and worthless."

FIRST WOMAN. That's clear enough, upon my word!

LYSISTRATA. By all that's holy, let's not give up the struggle now.

Let's go back inside. It would be a shame, my dear friends, to disobey the oracle.

785   [*The women all retire to the Acropolis again.*]

CHORUS OF MEN. [*Singing*]
     I have a tale to tell,
     Which I know full well.
       It was told me
790   In the nursery.

Once there was a likely lad,
>Melanion they name him;
The thought of marriage made him mad,
>For which I cannot blame him.

795 So off he went to mountains fair;
>(No women to unbraid him!)
A mighty hunter of the hare,
>He had a dog to aid him.

He never came back home to see
800 >Detested women's faces.
He showed a shrewd mentality.
>With him I'd fain change places!

ONE OF THE MEN. [*To one of the women*] Come here, old dame, give me a kiss.
WOMAN. You'll ne'er eat garlic, if you dare!
805 MAN. I want to kick you—just like this!
WOMAN. Oh, there's a leg with bushy hair!
MAN. Myronides and Phormio[17]
>Were hairy—and they thrashed the foe.
CHORUS OF WOMEN. [*Singing*]
810 >I have another tale,
>With which to assail
>>Your contention
>>'Bout Melanion.

Once upon a time a man
815 >Named Timon left our city,
To live in some deserted land.
>(We thought him rather witty.)

He dwelt alone amidst the thorn;
>In solitude he brooded.
820 From some grim Fury he was born:
>Such hatred he exuded.

He cursed you men, as scoundrels through
>And through, till life he ended.
He couldn't stand the sight of YOU!
825 >But women he befriended.

---

[17]**Myronides and Phormio:** Athenian generals.

WOMAN. [*To one of the men*] I'll smash your face in, if you like.

MAN. Oh no, please don't! You frighten me.

WOMAN. I'll lift my foot—and thus I'll strike.

MAN. Aha! Look there! What's that I see?

830   WOMAN. Whate'er you see, you cannot say
     That I'm not neatly trimmed today.

[LYSISTRATA *appears on* the wall of the Acropolis]

LYSISTRATA. Hello! Hello! Girls, come here quick!

[*Several women appear beside her.*]

835   WOMAN. What is it? Why are you calling?

LYSISTRATA. I see a man coming: he's in a dreadful state. He's mad with passion.
     O Queen of Cyprus, Cythera, and Paphos, just keep on this way!

WOMAN. Where is the fellow?

LYSISTRATA. There, beside the shrine of Demeter.

840   WOMAN. Oh yes, so he is. Who is he?

LYSISTRATA. Let's see. Do any of you know him?

MYRRHINE. Yes indeed. That's my husband, Cinesias.

LYSISTRATA. It's up to you, now: roast him, rack him, fool him, love him—and
     leave him! Do everything, except what our oath forbids.

845   MYRRHINE. Don't worry; I'll do it.

LYSISTRATA. I'll stay here to tease him and warm him up a bit. Off with you.

[*The other women retire from the wall. Enter* CINESIAS *followed by a slave carrying a baby.* CINESIAS *is obviously in great pain and distress.*]

CINESIAS. [*Groaning*] Oh-h! Oh-h-h! This is killing me! O God, what tortures I'm
850   suffering!

LYSISTRATA. [*From the wall*] Who's that within our lines?

CINESIAS. Me.

LYSISTRATA. A *man?*

CINESIAS. [*Pointing*] A *man*, indeed!

855   LYSISTRATA. Well, go away!

CINESIAS. Who are you to send me away?

LYSISTRATA. The captain of the guard.

CINESIAS. Oh, for heaven's sake, call out Myrrhine for me.

LYSISTRATA. Call Myrrhine? Nonsense! Who are you?

860   CINESIAS. Her husband, Cinesias of Paionidai.

LYSISTRATA. [*Appearing much impressed*] Oh, greetings, friend. Your name is
     not without honor here among us. Your wife is always talking about you, and

whenever she takes an egg or all apple, she says, "Here's to my dear Cinesias!"

865 CINESIAS. [*Quivering with excitement*] Oh, ye gods in heaven!

LYSISTRATA. Indeed she does! And whenever our conversations turn to men, your wife immediately says, "All others are mere rubbish compared with Cinesias."

CINESIAS. [*Groaning*] Oh! Do call her for me.

870 LYSISTRATA. Why should I? What will you give me?

CINESIAS. Whatever you want. All I have is yours—and you see what I've got.

LYSISTRATA. Well then, I'll go down and call her. [*She descends.*]

CINESIAS. And hurry up! I've had no joy of life ever since she left home. When I go in the house, I feel awful: everything seems so empty and I can't enjoy my

875 dinner. I'm in such a state all the time!

MYRRHINE. [*From behind the wall*] I do love him so. But he won't let me love him. No, no! Don't ask me to see him!

CINESIAS. O my darling, O Myrrhine honey, why do you do this to me? [MYRRHINE *appears on the wall.*] Come down here!

880 MYRRHINE. No, I won't come down.

CINESIAS. *Don't want you?* I'm in agony!

MYRRHINE. No; you don't want me.

CINESIAS. *Don't want you?* I'm in agony!

MYRRHINE. I'm going now.

885 CINESIAS. Please don't! At least, listen to your baby. [*To the baby*] Here you, call your mamma! [*Pinching the baby*]

BABY. Ma-ma! Ma-ma! Ma-ma!

CINESIAS. [*To* MYRRHINE] What's the matter with you? Have you no pity for your child, who hasn't been washed or fed for five whole days?

890 MYRRHINE. Oh, poor child; your father pays no attention to you.

CINESIAS. Come down then, you heartless wretch, for the baby's sake.

MYRRHINE. Oh, what it is to be a mother! I've got to come down, I suppose. [*She leaves the wall and shortly reappears at the gate.*]

CINESIAS. [*To himself*] She seems much younger, and she has such a sweet look

895 about her. Oh, the way she teases me! And her pretty, provoking ways make me burn with longing.

MYRRHINE. [*Coming out of the gate and taking the baby*] O my sweet little angel. Naughty papa! Here, let Mummy kiss you, Mamma's little sweetheart! [*She fondles the baby lovingly*]

900 CINESIAS. [*In despair*] You heartless creature, why do you do this? Why follow these other women and make both of us suffer so? [*He tries to embrace her.*]

MYRRHINE. Don't touch me!

CINESIAS. You're letting all our things at home go to wrack and ruin.

MYRRHINE. I don't care.

905 CINESIAS. You don't care that your wool is being plucked to pieces by the chickens?

MYRRHINE. Not in the least.

CINESIAS. And you haven't celebrated the rites of Aphrodite for ever so long. Won't you come home?

910 MYRRHINE. Not on your life, unless you men make a truce and stop the war.

CINESIAS. Well then, if that pleases you, we'll do it.

MYRRHINE. Well then, if that pleases *you*, I'll come home—afterwards! Right now I'm on oath not to.

CINESIAS. Then just lie down here with me for a moment.

915 MYRRHINE. No—[*In a teasing voice*] and yet, I won't say I don't love you.

CINESIAS. You love me? Oh, do lie down here, Myrrhine dear!

MYRRHINE. What, you silly fool! in front of the baby?

CINESIAS. [*Hastily thrusting the baby at the slave*] Of course not. Here—home! Take him Manes! [*The slave goes off with the baby.*] See, the baby's out of the

920 way. Now won't you lie down?

MYRRHINE. But where, my dear?

CINESIAS. Where? The grotto of Pan's a lovely spot.

MYRRHINE. How could I purify myself before returning to the shrine?

CINESIAS. Easily: just wash here in the Clepsydra.[18]

925 MYRRHINE. And then, shall I go back on my oath?

CINESIAS. On my head be it! Don't worry about the oath.

MYRRHINE. All right, then. just let me bring out a bed.

CINESIAS. No, don't. The ground's all right.

MYRRHINE. Heavens, no! Bad as you are, I won't let you lie on the bare ground.

930 [*She goes into the Acropolis.*]

CINESIAS. Why, she really loves me; it's plain to see.

MYRRHINE. [*Returning with a bed*] There! Now hurry up and lie down. I'll just slip off this dress. But—let's see: oh yes, I must fetch a mattress.

CINESIAS. Nonsense! No mattress for me.

935 MYRRHINE. Yes indeed! It's not nice on the bare springs.

CINESIAS. Give me a kiss.

MYRRHINE. [*Giving him a hasty kiss*] There! [*She goes.*]

CINESIAS. [*In mingled distress and delight*] Oh-h! Hurry back!

MYRRHINE. [*Returning with a mattress*] Here's the mattress; lie down on it. I'm

940 taking my things off now—but—let's see: you have no pillow.

CINESIAS. I don't *want* a pillow!

MYRRHINE. But I do. [*She goes.*]

CINESIAS. Cheated again, just like Heracles and his dinner!

MYRRHINE. [*Returning with a pillow*] Here, lift your head. [*To herself wondering*

945 *how else to tease him*] Is that all?

CINESIAS. Surely that's all! Do come here, precious!

MYRRHINE. I'm taking off my girdle. But remember: don't go back on your promise about the truce.

---

[18]Clepsydra: a rivulet on the Acropolis.

CINESIAS. Hope to die, if I do.
950 MYRRHINE. You don't have a blanket.
CINESIAS. [*Shouting in exasperation*] *I don't want one!* I want to—
MYRRHINE. Sh-h! There, there, I'll be back in a minute. [*She goes.*]
CINESIAS. She'll be the death of me with these bed-clothes.
MYRRHINE. [*Returning with a blanket*] Here, get up.
955 CINESIAS. I've got *this* up!
MYRRHINE. Would you like some perfume?
CINESIAS. Good heavens, no! I won't have it!
MYRRHINE. Yes, you shall, whether you want it or not. [*She goes.*]
CINESIAS. O lord! Confound all perfumes anyway!
960 MYRRHINE. [*Returning with a flask*] Stretch out your hand and put some on.
CINESIAS. [*Suspiciously*] By God, I don't much like this perfume. It smells of shilly-shallying, and has no scent of the marriage-bed.
MYRRHINE. Oh dear! This is Rhodian perfume I've brought.
CINESIAS. It's quite all right dear. Never mind.
965 MYRRHINE. Don't be silly! [*She goes out with the flask.*]
CINESIAS. Damn the man who first concocted perfumes!
MYRRHINE. [*Returning with another flask*] Here, try this flask.
CINESIAS. I've got another one all ready for you. Come, you wretch, lie down and stop bringing me things.
970 MYRRHINE. All right; I'm taking off my shoes. But, my dear, see that you vote for peace.
CINESIAS. [*Absently*] I'll consider it. [MYRRHINE *runs away to the Acropolis.*] I'm ruined! The wretch has skinned me and run away! [*Chanting, in tragic style*] Alas! Alas! Deceived, deserted by this fairest of women, whom shall I—
975 lay? Ah, my poor little child, how shall I nurture thee? Where's Cynalopex?[19] I needs must hire a nurse!
LEADER OF MEN. [*Chanting*] Ah, wretched man, in dreadful wise beguiled, bewrayed, thy soul is sore distressed. I pity thee, alas! alas! What soul, what loins, what liver could stand this strain? How firm and unyielding he stands,
980 with naught to aid him of a morning.
CINESIAS. O lord! O Zeus! What tortures I endure!
LEADER OF MEN. This is the way she's treated you, that vile and cursèd wanton.
LEADER OF WOMEN. Nay, not vile and cursèd, but sweet and dear.
985 LEADER OF MEN. Sweet, you say? Nay, hateful, hateful!
CINESIAS. Hateful indeed! O Zeus, Zeus!
Seize her and snatch her away,
Like a handful of dust, in a mighty,
Fiery tempest! Whirl her aloft, then let her drop
990 Down to the earth, with a crash, as she falls—

---

[19]Cynalopex: a local pimp and brothel owner.

On the point of this waiting
Thingummybob! [*He goes out.*]

[*Enter a Spartan* HERALD, *in an obvious state of excitement, which he is doing his best to conceal.*]

995 HERALD. Where can I find the Senate or the Prytanes?[20] I've got an important message.

[*The Athenian* MAGISTRATE *enters.*]

MAGISTRATE. Say there, are you a man or Priapus?[21]
HERALD. [*In annoyance*] I'm a herald, you lout! I've come from Sparta about the
1000 truce.
MAGISTRATE. Is that a spear you've got under your cloak?
HERALD. No, of course not!
MAGISTRATE. Why do you twist and turn so? Why hold your cloak in front of you? Did you rupture yourself on the trip?
1005 HERALD. By gum, the fellow's an old fool.
MAGISTRATE. [*Pointing*] Why, you dirty rascal, you're all excited.
HERALD. Not at all. Stop this tom-foolery.
MAGISTRATE. Well, what's that I see?
HERALD. A Spartan message-staff.
1010 MAGISTRATE. Oh, certainly! That's just the kind of message-staff I've got. But tell me the honest truth: How are things going in Sparta?
HERALD. All the land of Sparta is up in arms—and our allies are up, too. We need Pellene.[22]
MAGISTRATE. What brought this trouble on you? A sudden Panic?
1015 HERALD. No, Lampito started it and then all the other women in Sparta with one account chased their husbands out of their beds.
MAGISTRATE. How do you feel?
HERALD. Terrible. We walk around the city bent over like men lighting matches in a wind. For our women won't let us touch them until we all agree and make
1020 peace throughout Greece.
MAGISTRATE. This is a general conspiracy of the women; I see it now. Well, hurry back and tell the Spartans to send ambassadors here with full powers to arrange a truce. And I'll go tell the Council to choose ambassadors from here; I've got a little something here that will soon persuade them!
1025 HERALD. I'll fly there; for you've made an excellent suggestion.

---

[20]Prytanes: Senate Executive Committee.
[21]Priapus: a fertility god endowed with a huge phallus.
[22]Pellene: a famous Athenian prostitute.

[*The* HERALD *and the* MAGISTRATE *depart on opposite sides of the stage.*]

LEADER OF MEN. No beast or fire is harder than womankind to tame. Nor is the
    spotted leopard so devoid of shame.

LEADER OF WOMEN. Knowing this, you dare provoke us to attack? I'd be your
1030   steady friend, if you'd but take us back.

LEADER OF MEN. I'll never cease my hatred keen of womankind.

LEADER OF WOMEN. Just as you will. But now just let me help you find
    That cloak you threw aside. You look so silly there
    Without your clothes. Here, put it on and don't go bare.

1035 LEADER OF MEN. That's very kind, and shows you're not entirely bad. But I
    threw off my things when I was good and mad.

LEADER OF WOMEN. At last you seem a man, and won't be mocked, my lad.
    If you'd been nice to me, I'd take this little gnat
    That's in your eye and pluck it out for you, like that.

1040 LEADER OF MEN. So that's what's bothered me and bit my eye so long!
    Please dig it out for me. I own that I've been wrong.

LEADER OF WOMEN. I'll do so, though you've been a most ill-natured brat.
    Ye gods! See here! A huge and monstrous little gnat!

LEADER OF MEN. Oh, how that helps! For it was digging wells in me.
1045   And now it's out, my tears can roll down hard and free.

LEADER OF WOMEN. Here, let me wipe them off, although you're such a knave
    And kiss me.

LEADER OF MEN. No!

LEADER OF WOMEN. Whate'er you say, a kiss I'll have. [*She kisses him.*]

1050 LEADER OF MEN. Oh, confound these women! They've a coaxing way about
    them.
    He was wise and never spoke a truer word, who said,
    "We can't live with women, but we cannot live without them."
    Now I'll make a truce with you. We'll fight no more: instead,
1055   I will not injure you if you do me no wrong.
    And now let's join our ranks and then begin a song.

COMBINED CHORUS. [*Singing*]
    Athenians, we're not prepared,
    To say a single ugly word
1060   About our fellow-citizens.
  Quite the contrary: we desire but to say and to do
  Naught but good. Quite enough are the ills now on hand.

    Men and women, be advised:
     If anyone requires
1065   Money—minae two or three—
     We've got what he desires.

> My purse is yours, on easy terms:
>> When Peace shall reappear,
> Whate'er you've borrowed will be due.
>> So speak up without fear.

1070

> You needn't pay me back, you see,
>> If you call get a cent from me!

> We're about to entertain
>> Some foreign gentlemen;
> We've soup and tender, fresh-killed pork.
>> Come round to dine at ten.

1075

> Come early; wash and dress with care,
>> And bring the children, too.
> Then step right in, no "by your leave."
>> We'll be expecting you.

1080

> Walk in as if you owned the place.
> You'll find the door—shut in your face!

[*Enter a group of Spartan Ambassadors; they are in the same desperate condition as the Herald in the previous scene.*]

1085   LEADER OF CHORUS. Here come the envoys from Sparta, sprouting long beards and looking for all the world as if they were carrying pig-pens in front of them.

       Greetings, gentlemen of Sparta. Tell me, in what state have you come?

   SPARTAN. Why waste words? You can plainly see what state we're come in!

1090   LEADER OF CHORUS. Wow! You're in a pretty high-strung condition, and it seems to be getting worse.

   SPARTAN. It's indescribable. Won't someone please arrange a peace for us—in any way you like.

   LEADER OF CHORUS. Here come our own, native ambassadors, crouching like

1095   wrestlers and holding their clothes in front of them; this seems an athletic kind of malady.

[*Enter several Athenian Ambassadors.*]

   ATHENIAN. Can anyone tell us where Lysistrata is? You see our condition.

   LEADER OF CHORUS. Here's another case of the same complaint. Tell me, are the

1100   attacks worse in the morning?

   ATHENIAN. No, we're always afflicted this way. If someone doesn't soon arrange this truce, you'd better not let me get my hands on—Cleisthenes!

LEADER OF CHORUS. If you're smart, you'll arrange your cloaks so none of the fellows who smashed the Hermae[23] can see you.

1105 SPARTAN. Right you are; a very good suggestion.

ATHENIAN. Greetings, Spartan. We've suffered dreadful things.

SPARTAN. My dear fellow, we'd have suffered still worse if one of those fellows had seen us in this condition.

ATHENIAN. Well, gentlemen, We must get down to business. What's your errand
1110 here?

SPARTAN. We're ambassadors about peace.

ATHENIAN. Excellent; so are we. Only Lysistrata can arrange things for us; shall we summon her?

SPARTAN. Aye, and Lysistratus too, if you like.

1115 LEADER OF CHORUS. No need to summon her, it seems. She's coming out of her own accord.

[*Enter* LYSISTRATA *accompanied by a statue of a nude female figure, which represents Reconciliation.*]

Hail, noblest of women; now must thou be
1120 A judge shrewd and subtle, mild and severe,
e sweet yet majestic: all manners employ.
The leaders of Hellas, caught by thy love-charms
Have come to thy judgment, their charges submitting.

LYSISTRATA. This is no difficult task, if one catch them still in amorous passion,
1125 before they've resorted to each other. But I'll soon find out. Where's Reconciliation? Go, first bring the Spartans here, and don't seize them rudely and violently, as our tactless husbands used to do, but as befits a woman, like an old, familiar friend; if they won't give you their hands, take them however you can. Then go fetch these Athenians here, taking hold of whatever they
1130 offer you. Now then, men of Sparta, stand here beside me, and you Athenians on the other side, and listen to my words.

I am a woman, it is true, but I have a mind; I'm not badly off in native wit, and by listening to my father and my elders, I've had a decent schooling.

Now I intend to give you a scolding which you both deserve. With one
1135 common font you worship at the same altars, just like brothers, at Olympia, at Thermopylae, at Delphi—how many more might I name, if time permitted;— and the Barbarians stand by waiting with their armies; yet you are destroying the men and towns of Greece.

ATHENIAN. Oh, this tension is killing me!

1140 LYSISTRATA. And now, men of Sparta,—to turn to you—don't you remember how the Spartan Pericleidas came here once as a suppliant, and sitting at our

---

[23]**Hermae:** small phallic statues of Hermes that were smashed in protest when the Athenians set off on the expedition to Sicily.

altar, all pale with fear in his crimson cloak, begged us for an army? For all
Messene had attacked you and the god sent an earthquake too? Then Cimon
went forth with four thousand hoplites and saved all Lacedaemon. Such was
1145 the aid you received from Athens, and now you lay waste the country which
once treated you so well.

ATHENIAN. [*Hotly*] They're in the wrong, Lysistrata, upon my word, they are!

SPARTAN. [*Absently, looking at the statue of Reconciliation*] We're in the wrong.
What hips! How lovely they are!

1150 LYSISTRATA. Don't think I'm going to let you Athenians off. Don't you remember
how the Spartans came in arms when you were wearing the rough, sheepskin
cloak of slaves and slew the host of Thessalians, the comrades and allies of
Hippias? Fighting with you on that day, alone of all the Greeks, they set you
free and instead of a sheepskin gave your folk a handsome robe to wear.

1155 SPARTAN. [*Looking at* LYSISTRATA] I've never seen a more distinguished
woman.

ATHENIAN. [*Looking at Reconciliation*] I've never seen a more voluptuous body!

LYSISTRATA. Why then, with these many noble deeds to think of, do you fight
each other? Why don't you stop this villainy? Why not make peace? Tell me,
1160 what prevents it?

SPARTAN. [*Waving vaguely at Reconciliation*] We're willing, if you're willing to
give up your position on yonder flank.

LYSISTRATA. What position, my good man?

SPARTAN. Pylus; we've been panting for it for ever so long.

1165 ATHENIAN. No, by God! You shan't have it!

LYSISTRATA. Let them have it, my friend.

ATHENIAN. Then, what shall we have to rouse things up?

LYSISTRATA. Ask for another place in exchange.

ATHENIAN. Well, let's see: first of all [*Pointing to various parts of
1170 Reconciliation's anatomy*] give us Echinus here, this Maliac Inlet in back there,
and these two Megarian legs.

SPARTAN. No, by heavens! You can't have *everything*, you crazy fool!

LYSISTRATA. Let it go. Don't fight over a pair of legs.

ATHENIAN. [*Taking off his cloak*] I think I'll strip and do a little planting now.

1175 SPARTAN. [*Following suit*] And I'll just do a little fertilizing, by gosh!

LYSISTRATA. Wait until the truce is concluded. Now if you've decided on this
course, hold a conference and discuss the matter with your allies.

ATHENIAN. Allies? Don't be ridiculous! They're in the same state we are. Won't
all our allies want the same thing we do—to jump in bed with their women?

1180 SPARTAN. Ours will, I know.

ATHENIAN. Especially the Carystians,[24] by God!

LYSISTRATA. Very well. Now purify yourselves, that your wives may feast and
entertain you in the Acropolis; we've provisions by the basketful. Exchange

---

[24]Carystians: Athenian allies who had a reputation for being hedonists.

1185   your oaths and pledges there, and then each of you may take his wife and go home.

    ATHENIAN. Let's go at once.

    SPARTAN. Come on, where you will.

    ATHENIAN. For God's sake, let's hurry!

[*They all go into the Acropolis.*]

1190   CHORUS. [*Singing.*]

        Whate'er I have of coverlets
           And robes of varied hue
        And golden trinkets,—without stint
           I offer them to you.

1195   Take what you will and bear it home,
           Your children to delight,
        Or if your girl's a Basket-maid;
           Just choose whate'er's in sight.

        There's naught within so well secured
1200   You cannot break the seal
        And bear it off; just help yourselves;
           No hesitation feel.

        But you'll see nothing, though you try,
           Unless you've sharper eyes than I!

1205   If anyone needs bread to feed
           A growing family,
        I've lots of wheat and full-grown loaves;
           So just apply to me.

        Let every poor man who desires
1210   Come round and bring a sack
        To fetch the grain; my slave is there
           To load it on his back.

        But don't come near my door, I say.
        Beware the dog, and stay away!

1215   [*An* ATHENIAN *enters carrying a torch; he knocks at the gate.*]

    ATHENIAN. Open the door! [*To the* CHORUS, *which is clustered around the gate*]
    Make way, won't you! What are you hanging around for? Want me to singe

you with this torch? [*To himself*] No; it's a stale trick, I won't do it! [*To the audience*] Still, if I've got to do it to please *you*, I suppose I'll have to take the
1220   trouble.

[*A* SECOND ATHENIAN *comes out of the gate.*]

SECOND ATHENIAN. And I'll help you.
FIRST ATHENIAN. [*Waving his torch at the* CHORUS] Get out! Go bawl your heads off! Move on there, so the Spartans can leave in peace when the
1225   banquet's over.

[*They brandish their torches until the* CHORUS *leaves the Orchestra.*]

SECOND ATHENIAN. I've never seen such a pleasant banquet: the Spartans are charming fellows, indeed they are! And we Athenians are very witty in our cups.
1230   FIRST ATHENIAN. Naturally: for when we're sober we're never at our best. If the Athenians would listen to me, we'd always get a little tipsy on our embassies. As things are now, we go to Sparta when we're sober and look around to stir up trouble. And then we don't hear what they say—and as for what they *don't* say, we have all sorts of suspicions. And then we bring back
1235   varying reports about the mission. But this time everything is pleasant; even if a man should sing the Telamon-song when he ought to sing "Cleitagoras," we'd praise him and swear it was excellent.

[*The two* CHORUSES *return, as a* CHORUS OF ATHENIANS *and a* CHORUS OF SPARTANS.]

1240   Here they come back again. Go to the devil, you scoundrels!
SECOND ATHENIAN. Get out, I say! They're coming out from the feast.

[*Enter the Spartan and Athenian envoys, followed by* LYSISTRATA *and all the women.*]

SPARTAN. [*To one of his fellow-envoys*] My good fellow, take up your pipes; I
1245   want to do a fancy two-step and sing a jolly song for the Athenians.
ATHENIAN. Yes, do take your pipes, by all means. I'd love to see you dance.
SPARTAN. [*Singing and dancing with the* CHORUS OF SPARTANS]

      These youths inspire
    To song and dance, O Memory;
1250   Stir up my Muse, to tell how we
    And Athens' men, in our galleys clashing
    At Artemisium, 'gainst foemen dashing

In godlike ire,
Conquered the Persian and set Greece free.

1255   Leonidas
Led on his valiant warriors
Whetting their teeth like angry boars.
Abundant foam on their lips was flow'ring,
A stream of sweat from their limbs was show'ring.
1260   The Persian was
Numberless as the sand on the shores.

O Huntress who slayest the beasts in the glade,
O Virgin divine, hither come to our truce,
Unite us in bonds which all time will not loose.
1265   Grant us to find in this treaty, we pray,
An unfailing source of true friendship today,
And all of our days, helping us to refrain
From weaseling tricks which bring war in their train.
      Then hither, come hither! O huntress maid.

1270 LYSISTRATA. Come then, since all is fairly done, men of Sparta, lead away your
wives, and you, Athenians, take yours. Let every man stand beside his wife,
and every wife beside her man, and then, to celebrate our fortune, let's dance.
And in the future, let's take care to avoid these misunderstandings.
CHORUS OF ATHENIANS. [*Singing and dancing*]
1275   Lead on the dances, your graces revealing.
Call Artemis hither, call Artemis' twin,
Leader of dances, Apollo the Healing,
Kindly God—hither! let's summon him in!

Nysian Bacchus call,
1280 Who with his Maenads, his eyes flashing fire,
     Dances, and last of all
Zeus of the thunderbolt flaming, the Sire.
     And Hera in majesty,
     Queen of prosperity.

1285   Come, ye Powers who dwell above
     Unforgetting, our witnesses be
Of Peace with bonds of harmonious love—

The Peace which Cypris has wrought for me.
     Alleluia! Io Paean!
1290   Leap in joy—hurrah! hurrah!

'Tis victory—hurrah! hurrah!
Euoi! Euoi! Euai! Euai!

LYSISTRATA. [*To the Spartans*] Come now, sing a new song to cap ours.
CHORUS OF SPARTANS. [*Singing and dancing*]
1295   Leaving Taygetus fair and renown'd,
Muse of Laconia, hither come:
Amyclae's god in hymns resound,
Athene of the Brazen Home,
And Castor and Pollux, Tyndareus' sons,
1300   Who sport where Eurotas murmuring runs.

On with the dance! Heia! Ho!
All leaping along,
Mantles a-swinging as we go!
Of Sparta our song.
1305   There the holy chorus ever gladdens,
There the beat of stamping feet,
As our winsome fillies, lovely maidens,
Dance, beside Eurotas' banks a-skipping,—
Nimbly go to and fro
1310   Hast'ning, leaping feet in measures tripping,
Like the Bacchae's revels, hair a-streaming.
Leda's child, divine and mild,
Leads the holy dance, her fair face beaming.
On with the dance! as your hand
1315   Presses the hair
Streaming away unconfined.
Leap in the air
Light as the deer; footsteps resound
Aiding our dance, beating the ground.
1320   Praise Athene, Maid divine, unrivalled in her might,
Dweller in the Brazen Home, unconquered in the fight.

[*All go out singing and dancing.*]

10. THE PELOPONNESIAN WARS (SELECTIONS)
(c. 400 BCE)

Thucydides

(trans. by Richard Crawley)

Thucydides (c. 460–c. 400 BCE) was a participant in the war he recounts, though much of the writing took place when he was in exile and the history was not completed. As an historian, Thucydides aimed at exactness and objectivity even as he recreated dialogue and speeches, and provided analysis of contemporary events which was often critical of Athenian action. Thus his account offers both insight into the historical moment and insight into the behavior of mankind.

BOOK II, CHAPTER 6: PERICLES'S FUNERAL ORATION, 431 BCE [For an illustrated guide to the Funeral Oration, see http://nimbus.temple.edu/~siegel/texts/pericles/pericles.htm]

In the same winter the Athenians gave a funeral at the public cost to those who had first fallen in this war. It was a custom of their ancestors, and the manner of it is as follows. Three days before the ceremony, the bones of the dead are laid out in a tent which has been erected; and their friends bring to their
5   relatives such offerings as they please. In the funeral procession cypress coffins are borne in cars, one for each tribe; the bones of the deceased being placed in the coffin of their tribe. Among these is carried one empty bier decked for the missing, that is, for those whose bodies could not be recovered. Any citizen or stranger who pleases, joins in the procession: and the female relatives are there to wail at
10   the burial. The dead are laid in the public sepulchre in the Beautiful suburb of the city, in which those who fall in war are always buried; with the exception of those slain at Marathon, who for their singular and extraordinary valour were interred on the spot where they fell. After the bodies have been laid in the earth, a man chosen by the state, of approved wisdom and eminent reputation, pronounces
15   over them an appropriate panegyric; after which all retire. Such is the manner of the burying; and throughout the whole of the war, whenever the occasion arose, the established custom was observed. Meanwhile these were the first that had fallen, and Pericles, son of Xanthippus, was chosen to pronounce their eulogium. When the proper time arrived, he advanced from the sepulchre to an elevated
20   platform in order to be heard by as many of the crowd as possible, and spoke as follows:

"Most of my predecessors in this place have commended him who made this speech part of the law, telling us that it is well that it should be delivered at the burial of those who fall in battle. For myself, I should have thought that the worth which had displayed itself in deeds would be sufficiently rewarded by honours also shown by deeds; such as you now see in this funeral prepared at the people's cost. And I could have wished that the reputations of many brave men were not to be imperilled in the mouth of a single individual, to stand or fall according as he spoke well or ill. For it is hard to speak properly upon a subject where it is even difficult to convince your hearers that you are speaking the truth. On the one hand, the friend who is familiar with every fact of the story may think that some point has not been set forth with that fullness which he wishes and knows it to deserve; on the other, he who is a stranger to the matter may be led by envy to suspect exaggeration if he hears anything above his own nature. For men can endure to hear others praised only so long as they can severally persuade themselves of their own ability to equal the actions recounted: when this point is passed, envy comes in and with it incredulity. However, since our ancestors have stamped this custom with their approval, it becomes my duty to obey the law and to try to satisfy your several wishes and opinions as best I may.

"I shall begin with our ancestors: it is both just and proper that they should have the honour of the first mention on an occasion like the present. They dwelt in the country without break in the succession from generation to generation, and handed it down free to the present time by their valour. And if our more remote ancestors deserve praise, much more do our own fathers, who added to their inheritance the empire which we now possess, and spared no pains to be able to leave their acquisitions to us of the present generation. Lastly, there are few parts of our dominions that have not been augmented by those of us here, who are still more or less in the vigour of life; while the mother country has been furnished by us with everything that can enable her to depend on her own resources whether for war or for peace. That part of our history which tells of the military achievements which gave us our several possessions, or of the ready valour with which either we or our fathers stemmed the tide of Hellenic or foreign aggression, is a theme too familiar to my hearers for me to dilate on, and I shall therefore pass it by. But what was the road by which we reached our position, what the form of government under which our greatness grew, what the national habits out of which it sprang; these are questions which I may try to solve before I proceed to my panegyric upon these men; since I think this to be a subject upon which on the present occasion a speaker may properly dwell, and to which the whole assemblage, whether citizens or foreigners, may listen with advantage.

"Our constitution does not copy the laws of neighbouring states; we are rather a pattern to others than imitators ourselves. Its administration favours the many instead of the few; this is why it is called a democracy. If we look to the laws, they afford equal justice to all in their private differences; if no social standing, advancement in public life falls to reputation for capacity, class considerations not being allowed to interfere with merit; nor again does poverty

bar the way, if a man is able to serve the state, he is not hindered by the obscurity of his condition. The freedom which we enjoy in our government extends also to our ordinary life. There, far from exercising a jealous surveillance over each other, we do not feel called upon to be angry with our neighbour for doing what
70　he likes, or even to indulge in those injurious looks which cannot fail to be offensive, although they inflict no positive penalty. But all this ease in our private relations does not make us lawless as citizens. Against this fear is our chief safeguard, teaching us to obey the magistrates and the laws, particularly such as regard the protection of the injured, whether they are actually on the statute book,
75　or belong to that code which, although unwritten, yet cannot be broken without acknowledged disgrace.

　　"Further, we provide plenty of means for the mind to refresh itself from business. We celebrate games and sacrifices all the year round, and the elegance of our private establishments forms a daily source of pleasure and helps to banish
80　the spleen; while the magnitude of our city draws the produce of the world into our harbour, so that to the Athenian the fruits of other countries are as familiar a luxury as those of his own.

　　"If we turn to our military policy, there also we differ from our antagonists. We throw open our city to the world, and never by alien acts exclude foreigners
85　from any opportunity of learning or observing, although the eyes of an enemy may occasionally profit by our liberality; trusting less in system and policy than to the native spirit of our citizens; while in education, where our rivals from their very cradles by a painful discipline seek after manliness, at Athens we live exactly as we please, and yet are just as ready to encounter every legitimate danger. In proof
90　of this it may be noticed that the Lacedaemonians do not invade our country alone, but bring with them all their confederates; while we Athenians advance unsupported into the territory of a neighbour, and fighting upon a foreign soil usually vanquish with ease men who are defending their homes. Our united force was never yet encountered by any enemy, because we have at once to attend to our
95　marine and to dispatch our citizens by land upon a hundred different services; so that, wherever they engage with some such fraction of our strength, a success against a detachment is magnified into a victory over the nation, and a defeat into a reverse suffered at the hands of our entire people. And yet if with habits not of labour but of ease, and courage not of art but of nature, we are still willing to
100　encounter danger, we have the double advantage of escaping the experience of hardships in anticipation and of facing them in the hour of need as fearlessly as those who are never free from them.

　　"Nor are these the only points in which our city is worthy of admiration. We cultivate refinement without extravagance and knowledge without effeminacy;
105　wealth we employ more for use than for show, and place the real disgrace of poverty not in owning to the fact but in declining the struggle against it. Our public men have, besides politics, their private affairs to attend to, and our ordinary citizens, though occupied with the pursuits of industry, are still fair judges of public matters; for, unlike any other nation, regarding him who takes no

110 part in these duties not as unambitious but as useless, we Athenians are able to judge at all events if we cannot originate, and, instead of looking on discussion as a stumbling-block in the way of action, we think it an indispensable preliminary to any wise action at all. Again, in our enterprises we present the singular spectacle of daring and deliberation, each carried to its highest point, and both

115 united in the same persons; although usually decision is the fruit of ignorance, hesitation of reflection. But the palm of courage will surely be adjudged most justly to those, who best know the difference between hardship and pleasure and yet are never tempted to shrink from danger. In generosity we are equally singular, acquiring our friends by conferring, not by receiving, favours. Yet, of course, the

120 doer of the favour is the firmer friend of the two, in order by continued kindness to keep the recipient in his debt; while the debtor feels less keenly from the very consciousness that the return he makes will be a payment, not a free gift. And it is only the Athenians, who, fearless of consequences, confer their benefits not from calculations of expediency, but in the confidence of liberality.

125 "In short, I say that as a city we are the school of Hellas, while I doubt if the world can produce a man who, where he has only himself to depend upon, is equal to so many emergencies, and graced by so happy a versatility, as the Athenian. And that this is no mere boast thrown out for the occasion, but plain matter of fact, the power of the state acquired by these habits proves. For Athens alone of

130 her contemporaries is found when tested to be greater than her reputation, and alone gives no occasion to her assailants to blush at the antagonist by whom they have been worsted, or to her subjects to question her title by merit to rule. Rather, the admiration of the present and succeeding ages will be ours, since we have not left our power without witness, but have shown it by mighty proofs; and far from

135 needing a Homer for our panegyrist, or other of his craft whose verses might charm for the moment only for the impression which they gave to melt at the touch of fact, we have forced every sea and land to be the highway of our daring, and everywhere, whether for evil or for good, have left imperishable monuments behind us. Such is the Athens for which these men, in the assertion of their resolve

140 not to lose her, nobly fought and died; and well may every one of their survivors be ready to suffer in her cause.

"Indeed if I have dwelt at some length upon the character of our country, it has been to show that our stake in the struggle is not the same as theirs who have no such blessings to lose, and also that the panegyric of the men over whom I am

145 now speaking might be by definite proofs established. That panegyric is now in a great measure complete; for the Athens that I have celebrated is only what the heroism of these and their like have made her, men whose fame, unlike that of most Hellenes, will be found to be only commensurate with their deserts. And if a test of worth be wanted, it is to be found in their closing scene, and this not only in cases

150 in which it set the final seal upon their merit, but also in those in which it gave the first intimation of their having any. For there is justice in the claim that steadfastness in his country's battles should be as a cloak to cover a man's other imperfections; since the good action has blotted out the bad, and his merit as a

155 citizen more than outweighed his demerits as an individual. But none of these
allowed either wealth with its prospect of future enjoyment to unnerve his spirit,
or poverty with its hope of a day of freedom and riches to tempt him to shrink from
danger. No, holding that vengeance upon their enemies was more to be desired than
any personal blessings, and reckoning this to be the most glorious of hazards, they
joyfully determined to accept the risk, to make sure of their vengeance, and to let

160 their wishes wait; and while committing to hope the uncertainty of final success,
in the business before them they thought fit to act boldly and trust in themselves.
Thus choosing to die resisting, rather than to live submitting, they fled only from
dishonour, but met danger face to face, and after one brief moment, while at the
summit of their fortune, escaped, not from their fear, but from their glory.

165 "So died these men as became Athenians. You, their survivors, must determine
to have as unfaltering a resolution in the field, though you may pray that it may
have a happier issue. And not contented with ideas derived only from words of
the advantages which are bound up with the defence of your country, though these
would furnish a valuable text to a speaker even before an audience so alive to

170 them as the present, you must yourselves realize the power of Athens, and feed
your eyes upon her from day to day, till love of her fills your hearts; and then,
when all her greatness shall break upon you, you must reflect that it was by
courage, sense of duty, and a keen feeling of honour in action that men were
enabled to win all this, and that no personal failure in an enterprise could make

175 them consent to deprive their country of their valour, but they laid it at her feet as
the most glorious contribution that they could offer. For this offering of their lives
made in common by them all they each of them individually received that renown
which never grows old, and for a sepulchre, not so much that in which their bones
have been deposited, but that noblest of shrines wherein their glory is laid up to

180 be eternally remembered upon every occasion on which deed or story shall call for
its commemoration. For heroes have the whole earth for their tomb; and in lands
far from their own, where the column with its epitaph declares it, there is
enshrined in every breast a record unwritten with no tablet to preserve it, except
that of the heart. These take as your model and, judging happiness to be the fruit of

185 freedom and freedom of valour, never decline the dangers of war. For it is not the
miserable that would most justly be unsparing of their lives; these have nothing to
hope for: it is rather they to whom continued life may bring reverses as yet
unknown, and to whom a fall, if it came, would be most tremendous in its
consequences. And surely, to a man of spirit, the degradation of cowardice must be

190 immeasurably more grievous than the unfelt death which strikes him in the midst of
his strength and patriotism!

"Comfort, therefore, not condolence, is what I have to offer to the parents of
the dead who may be here. Numberless are the chances to which, as they know, the
life of man is subject; but fortunate indeed are they who draw for their lot a death

195 so glorious as that which has caused your mourning, and to whom life has been so
exactly measured as to terminate in the happiness in which it has been passed.
Still I know that this is a hard saying, especially when those are in question of

whom you will constantly be reminded by seeing in the homes of others blessings of which once you also boasted: for grief is felt not so much for the want of what we have never known, as for the loss of that to which we have been long accustomed. Yet you who are still of an age to beget children must bear up in the hope of having others in their stead; not only will they help you to forget those whom you have lost, but will be to the state at once a reinforcement and a security; for never can a fair or just policy be expected of the citizen who does not, like his fellows, bring to the decision the interests and apprehensions of a father. While those of you who have passed your prime must congratulate yourselves with the thought that the best part of your life was fortunate, and that the brief span that remains will be cheered by the fame of the departed. For it is only the love of honour that never grows old; and honour it is, not gain, as some would have it, that rejoices the heart of age and helplessness.

"Turning to the sons or brothers of the dead, I see an arduous struggle before you. When a man is gone, all are wont to praise him, and should your merit be ever so transcendent, you will still find it difficult not merely to overtake, but even to approach their renown. The living have envy to contend with, while those who are no longer in our path are honoured with a goodwill into which rivalry does not enter. On the other hand, if I must say anything on the subject of female excellence to those of you who will now be in widowhood, it will be all comprised in this brief exhortation. Great will be your glory in not falling short of your natural character; and greatest will be hers who is least talked of among the men, whether for good or for bad.

"My task is now finished. I have performed it to the best of my ability, and in word, at least, the requirements of the law are now satisfied. If deeds be in question, those who are here interred have received part of their honours already, and for the rest, their children will be brought up till manhood at the public expense: the state thus offers a valuable prize, as the garland of victory in this race of valour, for the reward both of those who have fallen and their survivors. And where the rewards for merit are greatest, there are found the best citizens.

"And now that you have brought to a close your lamentations for your relatives, you may depart."

BOOK V, CHAPTER 17: THE MELIAN DIALOGUE, 415 BCE

The next summer Alcibiades sailed with twenty ships to Argos and seized the suspected persons still left of the Lacedaemonian faction to the number of three hundred, whom the Athenians forthwith lodged in the neighbouring islands of their empire. The Athenians also made an expedition against the isle of Melos with thirty ships of their own, six Chian, and two Lesbian vessels, sixteen hundred heavy infantry, three hundred archers, and twenty mounted archers from Athens, and about fifteen hundred heavy infantry from the allies and the islanders. The Melians are a colony of Lacedaemon that would not submit to the Athenians like the other islanders, and at first remained neutral and took no part

240 in the struggle, but afterwards upon the Athenians using violence and plundering their territory, assumed an attitude of open hostility. Cleomedes, son of Lycomedes, and Tisias, son of Tisimachus, the generals, encamping in their territory with the above armament, before doing any harm to their land, sent envoys to negotiate. These the Melians did not bring before the people, but bade them state the object of their mission to the magistrates and the few; upon which

245 the Athenian envoys spoke as follows:

Athenians. Since the negotiations are not to go on before the people, in order that we may not be able to speak straight on without interruption, and deceive the ears of the multitude by seductive arguments which would pass without refutation (for we know that this is the meaning of our being brought before the few), what if

250 you who sit there were to pursue a method more cautious still? Make no set speech yourselves, but take us up at whatever you do not like, and settle that before going any farther. And first tell us if this proposition of ours suits you.

The Melian commissioners answered:

Melians. To the fairness of quietly instructing each other as you propose

255 there is nothing to object; but your military preparations are too far advanced to agree with what you say, as we see you are come to be judges in your own cause, and that all we can reasonably expect from this negotiation is war, if we prove to have right on our side and refuse to submit, and in the contrary case, slavery.

Athenians. If you have met to reason about presentiments of the future, or for

260 anything else than to consult for the safety of your state upon the facts that you see before you, we will give over; otherwise we will go on.

Melians. It is natural and excusable for men in our position to turn more ways than one both in thought and utterance. However, the question in this conference is, as you say, the safety of our country; and the discussion, if you

265 please, can proceed in the way which you propose.

Athenians. For ourselves, we shall not trouble you with specious pretences—either of how we have a right to our empire because we overthrew the Mede, or are now attacking you because of wrong that you have done us—and make a long speech which would not be believed; and in return we hope that you, instead of

270 thinking to influence us by saying that you did not join the Lacedaemonians, although their colonists, or that you have done us no wrong, will aim at what is feasible, holding in view the real sentiments of us both; since you know as well as we do that right, as the world goes, is only in question between equals in power, while the strong do what they can and the weak suffer what they must.

275 Melians. As we think, at any rate, it is expedient—we speak as we are obliged, since you enjoin us to let right alone and talk only of interest—that you should not destroy what is our common protection, the privilege of being allowed in danger to invoke what is fair and right, and even to profit by arguments not strictly valid if they can be got to pass current. And you are as much interested in

280 this as any, as your fall would be a signal for the heaviest vengeance and an example for the world to meditate upon.

285 Athenians. The end of our empire, if end it should, does not frighten us: a rival empire like Lacedaemon, even if Lacedaemon was our real antagonist, is not so terrible to the vanquished as subjects who by themselves attack and overpower their rulers. This, however, is a risk that we are content to take. We will now proceed to show you that we are come here in the interest of our empire, and that we shall say what we are now going to say, for the preservation of your country; as we would fain exercise that empire over you without trouble, and see you preserved for the good of us both.

290 Melians. And how, pray, could it turn out as good for us to serve as for you to rule?

Athenians. Because you would have the advantage of submitting before suffering the worst, and we should gain by not destroying you.

295 Melians. So that you would not consent to our being neutral, friends instead of enemies, but allies of neither side.

Athenians. No; for your hostility cannot so much hurt us as your friendship will be an argument to our subjects of our weakness, and your enmity of our power.

300 Melians. Is that your subjects' idea of equity, to put those who have nothing to do with you in the same category with peoples that are most of them your own colonists, and some conquered rebels?

Athenians. As far as right goes they think one has as much of it as the other, and that if any maintain their independence it is because they are strong, and that if we do not molest them it is because we are afraid; so that besides extending our 305 empire we should gain in security by your subjection; the fact that you are islanders and weaker than others rendering it all the more important that you should not succeed in baffling the masters of the sea.

Melians. But do you consider that there is no security in the policy which we indicate? For here again if you debar us from talking about justice and invite us to 310 obey your interest, we also must explain ours, and try to persuade you, if the two happen to coincide. How can you avoid making enemies of all existing neutrals who shall look at case from it that one day or another you will attack them? And what is this but to make greater the enemies that you have already, and to force others to become so who would otherwise have never thought of it?

315 Athenians. Why, the fact is that continentals generally give us but little alarm; the liberty which they enjoy will long prevent their taking precautions against us; it is rather islanders like yourselves, outside our empire, and subjects smarting under the yoke, who would be the most likely to take a rash step and lead themselves and us into obvious danger.

320 Melians. Well then, if you risk so much to retain your empire, and your subjects to get rid of it, it were surely great baseness and cowardice in us who are still free not to try everything that can be tried, before submitting to your yoke.

Athenians. Not if you are well advised, the contest not being an equal one, with honour as the prize and shame as the penalty, but a question of self- 325 preservation and of not resisting those who are far stronger than you are.

Melians. But we know that the fortune of war is sometimes more impartial than the disproportion of numbers might lead one to suppose; to submit is to give ourselves over to despair, while action still preserves for us a hope that we may stand erect.

330 Athenians. Hope, danger's comforter, may be indulged in by those who have abundant resources, if not without loss at all events without ruin; but its nature is to be extravagant, and those who go so far as to put their all upon the venture see it in its true colours only when they are ruined; but so long as the discovery would enable them to guard against it, it is never found wanting. Let not this be

335 the case with you, who are weak and hang on a single turn of the scale; nor be like the vulgar, who, abandoning such security as human means may still afford, when visible hopes fail them in extremity, turn to invisible, to prophecies and oracles, and other such inventions that delude men with hopes to their destruction.

Melians. You may be sure that we are as well aware as you of the difficulty

340 of contending against your power and fortune, unless the terms be equal. But we trust that the gods may grant us fortune as good as yours, since we are just men fighting against unjust, and that what we want in power will be made up by the alliance of the Lacedaemonians, who are bound, if only for very shame, to come to the aid of their kindred. Our confidence, therefore, after all is not so utterly

345 irrational.

Athenians. When you speak of the favour of the gods, we may as fairly hope for that as yourselves; neither our pretensions nor our conduct being in any way contrary to what men believe of the gods, or practise among themselves. Of the gods we believe, and of men we know, that by a necessary law of their nature they

350 rule wherever they can. And it is not as if we were the first to make this law, or to act upon it when made: we found it existing before us, and shall leave it to exist for ever after us; all we do is to make use of it, knowing that you and everybody else, having the same power as we have, would do the same as we do. Thus, as far as the gods are concerned, we have no fear and no reason to fear that we shall be

355 at a disadvantage. But when we come to your notion about the Lacedaemonians, which leads you to believe that shame will make them help you, here we bless your simplicity but do not envy your folly. The Lacedaemonians, when their own interests or their country's laws are in question, are the worthiest men alive; of their conduct towards others much might be said, but no clearer idea of it could be

360 given than by shortly saying that of all the men we know they are most conspicuous in considering what is agreeable honourable, and what is expedient just. Such a way of thinking does not promise much for the safety which you now unreasonably count upon.

Melians. But it is for this very reason that we now trust to their respect for

365 expediency to prevent them from betraying the Melians, their colonists, and thereby losing the confidence of their friends in Hellas and helping their enemies.

Athenians. Then you do not adopt the view that expediency goes with security, while justice and honour cannot be followed without danger; and danger the Lacedaemonians generally court as little as possible.

370   Melians. But we believe that they would be more likely to face even danger for our sake, and with more confidence than for others, as our nearness to Peloponnese makes it easier for them to act, and our common blood ensures our fidelity.

    Athenians. Yes, but what an intending ally trusts to is not the goodwill of
375 those who ask his aid, but a decided superiority of power for action; and the Lacedaemonians look to this even more than others. At least, such is their distrust of their home resources that it is only with numerous allies that they attack a neighbour; now is it likely that while we are masters of the sea they will cross over to an island?

380   Melians. But they would have others to send. The Cretan Sea is a wide one, and it is more difficult for those who command it to intercept others, than for those who wish to elude them to do so safely. And should the Lacedaemonians miscarry in this, they would fall upon your land, and upon those left of your allies whom Brasidas did not reach; and instead of places which are not yours, you will have
385 to fight for your own country and your own confederacy.

    Athenians. Some diversion of the kind you speak of you may one day experience, only to learn, as others have done, that the Athenians never once yet withdrew from a siege for fear of any. But we are struck by the fact that, after saying you would consult for the safety of your country, in all this discussion you
390 have mentioned nothing which men might trust in and think to be saved by. Your strongest arguments depend upon hope and the future, and your actual resources are too scanty, as compared with those arrayed against you, for you to come out victorious. You will therefore show great blindness of judgment, unless, after allowing us to retire, you can find some counsel more prudent than this. You will
395 surely not be caught by that idea of disgrace, which in dangers that are disgraceful, and at the same time too plain to be mistaken, proves so fatal to mankind; since in too many cases the very men that have their eyes perfectly open to what they are rushing into, let the thing called disgrace, by the mere influence of a seductive name, lead them on to a point at which they become so enslaved by the
400 phrase as in fact to fall willfully into hopeless disaster, and incur disgrace more disgraceful as the companion of error, than when it comes as the result of misfortune. This, if you are well advised, you will guard against; and you will not think it dishonourable to submit to the greatest city in Hellas, when it makes you the moderate offer of becoming its tributary ally, without ceasing to enjoy the
405 country that belongs to you; nor when you have the choice given you between war and security, will you be so blinded as to choose the worse. And it is certain that those who do not yield to their equals, who keep terms with their superiors, and are moderate towards their inferiors, on the whole succeed best. Think over the matter, therefore, after our withdrawal, and reflect once and again that it is for
410 your country that you are consulting, that you have not more than one, and that upon this one deliberation depends its prosperity or ruin.

    The Athenians now withdrew from the conference; and the Melians, left to themselves, came to a decision corresponding with what they had maintained in

415 the discussion, and answered: "Our resolution, Athenians, is the same as it was at first. We will not in a moment deprive of freedom a city that has been inhabited these seven hundred years; but we put our trust in the fortune by which the gods have preserved it until now, and in the help of men, that is, of the Lacedaemonians; and so we will try and save ourselves. Meanwhile we invite you to allow us to be friends to you and foes to neither party, and to retire from our country after

420 making such a treaty as shall seem fit to us both."

Such was the answer of the Melians. The Athenians now departing from the conference said: "Well, you alone, as it seems to us, judging from these resolutions, regard what is future as more certain than what is before your eyes, and what is out of sight, in your eagerness, as already coming to pass; and as you have staked

425 most on, and trusted most in, the Lacedaemonians, your fortune, and your hopes, so will you be most completely deceived."

The Athenian envoys now returned to the army; and the Melians showing no signs of yielding, the generals at once betook themselves to hostilities, and drew a line of circumvolution round the Melians, dividing the work among the different

430 states. Subsequently the Athenians returned with most of their army, leaving behind them a certain number of their own citizens and of the allies to keep guard by land and sea. The force thus left stayed on and besieged the place.

About the same time the Argives invaded the territory of Phlius and lost eighty men cut off in an ambush by the Phliasians and Argive exiles. Meanwhile

435 the Athenians at Pylos took so much plunder from the Lacedaemonians that the latter, although they still refrained from breaking off the treaty and going to war with Athens, yet proclaimed that any of their people that chose might plunder the Athenians. The Corinthians also commenced hostilities with the Athenians for private quarrels of their own; but the rest of the Peloponnesians stayed quiet.

440 Meanwhile the Melians attacked by night and took the part of the Athenian lines over against the market, and killed some of the men, and brought in corn and all else that they could find useful to them, and so returned and kept quiet, while the Athenians took measures to keep better guard in future.

Summer was now over. The next winter the Lacedaemonians intended to

445 invade the Argive territory, but arriving at the frontier found the sacrifices for crossing unfavourable, and went back again. This intention of theirs gave the Argives suspicions of certain of their fellow citizens, some of whom they arrested; others, however, escaped them. About the same time the Melians again took another part of the Athenian lines which were but feebly garrisoned.

450 Reinforcements afterwards arriving from Athens in consequence, under the command of Philocrates, son of Demeas, the siege was now pressed vigorously; and some treachery taking place inside, the Melians surrendered at discretion to the Athenians, who put to death all the grown men whom they took, and sold the women and children for slaves, and subsequently sent out five hundred colonists

455 and inhabited the place themselves.

11. THE APOLOGY

Plato
(c. 427 BCE–348 BCE)

(trans. by Benjamin Jowett)

Plato became acquainted with Socrates in 407 BCE and remained his disciple until Socrates was put to death in 399 BCE. During Socrates's life (b. 469 BCE), he was known as "the gadfly" of Athens for his challenge to stock responses and clichés. His wisdom, beginning with his recognition that he, unlike his opponents, knew when he knew nothing, is recorded in the works of Plato which give Socrates the principal role. In the Apology *monologue, Socrates defends his life work at his trial.*

THE APOLOGY

[For an illustrated guide to *The Apology,* see http://nimbus.temple.edu/~jsiegel/texts/Plato/Socrates.htm]

How you, O Athenians, have been affected by my accusers, I cannot tell; but I know that they almost made me forget who I was—so persuasively did they speak; and yet they have hardly uttered a word of truth. But of the many falsehoods told by them, there was one which quite amazed me;—I mean when they said that you
5   should be upon your guard and not allow yourselves to be deceived by the force of my eloquence. To say this, when they were certain to be detected as soon as I opened my lips and proved myself to be anything but a great speaker, did indeed appear to me most shameless—unless by the force of eloquence they mean the force of truth; for in such is their meaning, I admit that I am eloquent. But in how
10   different a way from theirs! Well, as I was saying, they have scarcely spoken the truth at all; but from me you shall hear the whole truth: not, however, delivered after their manner in a set oration duly ornamented with words and phrases. No, by heaven! but I shall use the words and arguments which occur to me at the moment; for I am confident in the justice of my cause (Or, I am certain that I am right
15   in taking this course.): at my time of life I ought not to be appearing before you, O men of Athens, in the character of a juvenile orator—let no one expect it of me. And I must beg of you to grant me a favour:—If I defend myself in my accustomed

20

manner, and you hear me using the words which I have been in the habit of using in the agora, at the tables of the money-changers, or anywhere else, I would ask you not to be surprised, and not to interrupt me on this account. For I am more than seventy years of age, and appearing now for the first time in a court of law, I am quite a stranger to the language of the place; and therefore I would have you regard me as if I were really a stranger, whom you would excuse if he spoke in his native tongue, and after the fashion of his country:—Am I making an unfair

25

request of you? Never mind the manner, which may or may not be good; but think only of the truth of my words, and give heed to that: let the speaker speak truly and the judge decide justly.

And first, I have to reply to the older charges and to my first accusers, and then I will go on to the later ones. For of old I have had many accusers, who have

30

accused me falsely to you during many years; and I am more afraid of them than of Anytus[1] and his associates, who are dangerous, too, in their own way. But far more dangerous are the others, who began when you were children, and took possession of your minds with their falsehoods, telling of one Socrates, a wise man, who speculated about the heaven above, and searched into the earth beneath,

35

and made the worse appear the better cause. The disseminators of this tale are the accusers whom I dread; for their hearers are apt to fancy that such enquirers do not believe in the existence of the gods. And they are many, and their charges against me are of ancient date, and they were made by them in the days when you were more impressible than you are now—in childhood, or it may have been in

40

youth—and the cause when heard went by default, for there was none to answer. And hardest of all, I do not know and cannot tell the names of my accusers; unless in the chance case of a Comic poet.[2] All who from envy and malice have persuaded you—some of them having first convinced themselves—all this class of men are most difficult to deal with; for I cannot have them up here, and cross-examine them,

45

and therefore I must simply fight with shadows in my own defence, and argue when there is no one who answers. I will ask you then to assume with me, as I was saying, that my opponents are of two kinds; one recent, the other ancient: and I hope that you will see the propriety of my answering the latter first, for these accusations you heard long before the others, and much oftener.

50

Well, then, I must make my defence, and endeavour to clear away in a short time, a slander which has lasted a long time. May I succeed, if to succeed be for my good and yours, or likely to avail me in my cause! The task is not an easy one; I quite understand the nature of it. And so leaving the event with God, in obedience to the law I will now make my defence.

55

I will begin at the beginning, and ask what is the accusation which has given rise to the slander of me, and in fact has encouraged Meletus to proof this charge against me. Well, what do the slanderers say? They shall be my prosecutors, and I will sum up their words in an affidavit:

---

[1]One of Socrates' accusers, along with Meletus and Lycon.
[2]Aristophanes made jokes of Socrates in several of his comedies.

"Socrates is an evil-doer, and a curious person, who searches into things
60   under the earth and in heaven, and he makes the worse appear the better cause;
and he teaches the aforesaid doctrines to others." Such is the nature of the
accusation: it is just what you have yourselves seen in the comedy of Aristophanes
(*Clouds*), who has introduced a man whom he calls Socrates, going about and
saying that he walks in air, and talking a deal of nonsense concerning matters of
65   which I do not pretend to know either much or little—not that I mean to speak
disparagingly of any one who is a student of natural philosophy. I should be very
sorry if Meletus could bring so grave a charge against me. But the simple truth is,
O Athenians, that I have nothing to do with physical speculations. Very many of
those here present are witnesses to the truth of this, and to them I appeal. Speak
70   then, you who have heard me, and tell your neighbours whether any of you have
ever known me hold forth in few words or in many upon such matters . . . You hear
their answer. And from what they say of this part of the charge you will be able to
judge of the truth of the rest.

As little foundation is there for the report that I am a teacher, and take money;
75   this accusation has no more truth in it than the other. Although, if a man were
really able to instruct mankind, to receive money for giving instruction would, in
my opinion, be an honour to him. There is Gorgias of Leontium, and Prodicus of
Ceos, and Hippias of Elis, who go the round of the cities, and are able to persuade
the young men to leave their own citizens by whom they might be taught for
80   nothing, and come to them whom they not only pay, but are thankful if they may be
allowed to pay them. There is at this time a Parian philosopher residing in Athens,
of whom I have heard; and I came to hear of him in this way:—I came across a man
who has spent a world of money on the Sophists, Callias, the son of Hipponicus,
and knowing that he had sons, I asked him: "Callias," I said, "if your two sons
85   were foals or calves, there would be no difficulty in finding some one to put over
them; we should hire a trainer of horses, or a farmer probably, who would
improve and perfect them in their own proper virtue and excellence; but as they
are human beings, whom are you thinking of placing over them? Is there any one
who understands human and political virtue? You must have thought about the
90   matter, for you have sons; is there any one?" "There is," he said. "Who is he?"
said I; "and of what country? and what does he charge?" "Evenus the Parian," he
replied; "he is the man, and his charge is five minae." Happy is Evenus, I said to
myself, if he really has this wisdom, and teaches at such a moderate charge. Had I
the same, I should have been very proud and conceited; but the truth is that I have
95   no knowledge of the kind.

I dare say, Athenians, that some one among you will reply, "Yes, Socrates, but
what is the origin of these accusations which are brought against you; there must
have been something strange which you have been doing? All these rumours and
this talk about you would never have arisen if you had been like other men: tell us,
100   then, what is the cause of them, for we should be sorry to judge hastily of you."
Now I regard this as a fair challenge, and I will endeavour to explain to you the
reason why I am called wise and have such an evil fame. Please to attend then.

And although some of you may think that I am joking, I declare that I will tell you the entire truth. Men of Athens, this reputation of mine has come of a certain sort

105 of wisdom which I possess. If you ask me what kind of wisdom, I reply, wisdom such as may perhaps be attained by man, for to that extent I am inclined to believe that I am wise; whereas the persons of whom I was speaking have a superhuman wisdom which I may fail to describe, because I have it not myself; and he who says that I have, speaks falsely, and is taking away my character. And here, O men of

110 Athens, I must beg you not to interrupt me, even if I seem to say something extravagant. For the word which I will speak is not mine. I will refer you to a witness who is worthy of credit; that witness shall be the God of Delphi—he will tell you about my wisdom, if I have any, and of what sort it is. You must have known Chaerephon; he was early a friend of mine, and also a friend of yours, for

115 he shared in the recent exile of the people, and returned with you. Well, Chaerephon, as you know, was very impetuous in all his doings, and he went to Delphi and boldly asked the oracle to tell him whether—as I was saying, I must beg you not to interrupt—he asked the oracle to tell him whether anyone was wiser than I was, and the Pythian prophetess answered, that there was no man

120 wiser. Chaerephon is dead himself; but his brother, who is in court, will confirm the truth of what I am saying.

Why do I mention this? Because I am going to explain to you why I have such an evil name. When I heard the answer, I said to myself, What can the god mean? and what is the interpretation of his riddle? for I know that I have no wisdom,

125 small or great. What then can he mean when he says that I am the wisest of men? And yet he is a god, and cannot lie; that would be against his nature. After long consideration, I thought of a method of trying the question. I reflected that if I could only find a man wiser than myself, then I might go to the god with a refutation in my hand. I should say to him, "Here is a man who is wiser than I am;

130 but you said that I was the wisest." Accordingly I went to one who had the reputation of wisdom, and observed him—his name I need not mention; he was a politician whom I selected for examination—and the result was as follows: When I began to talk with him, I could not help thinking that he was not really wise, although he was thought wise by many, and still wiser by himself; and thereupon I

135 tried to explain to him that he thought himself wise, but was not really wise; and the consequence was that he hated me, and his enmity was shared by several who were present and heard me. So I left him, saying to myself, as I went away: Well, although I do not suppose that either of us knows anything really beautiful and good, I am better off than he is,—for he knows nothing, and thinks that he knows; I

140 neither know nor think that I know. In this latter particular, then, I seem to have slightly the advantage of him. Then I went to another who had still higher pretensions to wisdom, and my conclusion was exactly the same. Whereupon I made another enemy of him, and of many others besides him.

Then I went to one man after another, being not unconscious of the enmity

145 which I provoked, and I lamented and feared this: but necessity was laid upon me,—the word of God, I thought, ought to be considered first. And I said to myself,

Go I must to all who appear to know, and find out the meaning of the oracle. And I swear to you, Athenians, by the dog I swear! for I must tell you the truth—the result of my mission was just this: I found that the men most in repute were all but the most foolish; and that others less esteemed were really wiser and better. I will tell you the tale of my wanderings and of the "Herculean" labours, as I may call them, which I endured only to find at last the oracle irrefutable. After the politicians, I went to the poets; tragic, dithyrambic, and all sorts. And there, I said to myself, you will be instantly detected; now you will find out that you are more ignorant than they are. Accordingly, I took them some of the most elaborate passages in their own writings, and asked what was the meaning of them— thinking that they would teach me something. Will you believe me? I am almost ashamed to confess the truth, but I must say that there is hardly a person present who would not have talked better about their poetry than they did themselves. Then I knew that not by wisdom do poets write poetry, but by a sort of genius and inspiration; they are like diviners or soothsayers who also say many fine things, but do not understand the meaning of them. The poets appeared to me to be much in the same case; and I further observed that upon the strength of their poetry they believed themselves to be the wisest of men in other things in which they were not wise. So I departed, conceiving myself to be superior to them for the same reason that I was superior to the politicians.

At last I went to the artisans. I was conscious that I knew nothing at all, as I may say, and I was sure that they knew many fine things; and here I was not mistaken, for they did know many things of which I was ignorant, and in this they certainly were wiser than I was. But I observed that even the good artisans fell into the same error as the poets;—because they were good workmen they thought that they also knew all sorts of high matters, and this defect in them overshadowed their wisdom; and therefore I asked myself on behalf of the oracle, whether I would like to be as I was, neither having their knowledge nor their ignorance, or like them in both; and I made answer to myself and to the oracle that I was better off as I was.

This inquisition has led to my having many enemies of the worst and most dangerous kind, and has given occasion also to many calumnies. And I am called wise, for my hearers always imagine that I myself possess the wisdom which I find wanting in others: but the truth is, O men of Athens, that God only is wise; and by his answer he intends to show that the wisdom of men is worth little or nothing; he is not speaking of Socrates, he is only using my name by way of illustration, as if he said, He, O men, is the wisest, who, like Socrates, knows that his wisdom is in truth worth nothing. And so I go about the world, obedient to the god, and search and make enquiry into the wisdom of any one, whether citizen or stranger, who appears to be wise; and if he is not wise, then in vindication of the oracle I show him that he is not wise; and my occupation quite absorbs me, and I have no time to give either to any public matter of interest or to any concern of my own, but I am in utter poverty by reason of my devotion to the god.

190　　　There is another thing:—young men of the richer classes, who have not much to do, come about me of their own accord; they like to hear the pretenders examined, and they often imitate me, and proceed to examine others; there are plenty of persons, as they quickly discover, who think that they know something, but really know little or nothing; and then those who are examined by them

195　　　instead of being angry with themselves are angry with me:

　　　This confounded Socrates, they say; this villainous misleader of youth!—and then if somebody asks them, Why, what evil does he practise or teach? they do not know, and cannot tell; but in order that they may not appear to be at a loss, they repeat the ready-made charges which are used against all philosophers about

200　　　teaching things up in the clouds and under the earth, and having no gods, and making the worse appear the better cause; for they do not like to confess that their pretence of knowledge has been detected—which is the truth; and as they are numerous and ambitious and energetic, and are drawn up in battle array and have persuasive tongues, they have filled your ears with their loud and inveterate

205　　　calumnies. And this is the reason why my three accusers, Meletus and Anytus and Lycon, have set upon me; Meletus, who has a quarrel with me on behalf of the poets; Anytus, on behalf of the craftsmen and politicians; Lycon, on behalf of the rhetoricians: and as I said at the beginning, I cannot expect to get rid of such a mass of calumny all in a moment. And this, O men of Athens, is the truth and the

210　　　whole truth; I have concealed nothing, I have dissembled nothing. And yet, I know that my plainness of speech makes them hate me, and what is their hatred but a proof that I am speaking the truth?—Hence has arisen the prejudice against me; and this is the reason of it, as you will find out either in this or in any future enquiry.

215　　　I have said enough in my defence against the first class of my accusers; I turn to the second class. They are headed by Meletus, that good man and true lover of his country, as he calls himself. Against these, too, I must try to make a defence:— Let their affidavit be read: it contains something of this kind: It says that Socrates is a doer of evil, who corrupts the youth; and who does not believe in the gods of

220　　　the state, but has other new divinities of his own. Such is the charge; and now let us examine the particular counts. He says that I am a doer of evil, and corrupt the youth; but I say, O men of Athens, that Meletus is a doer of evil, in that he pretends to be in earnest when he is only in jest, and is so eager to bring men to trial from a pretended zeal and interest about matters in which he really never had the

225　　　smallest interest. And the truth of this I will endeavour to prove to you.

　　　Come hither, Meletus, and let me ask a question of you. You think a great deal about the improvement of youth?

MELETUS: Yes, I do.

SOCRATES: Tell the judges, then, who is their improver; for you must know, as

230　　　you have taken the pains to discover their corrupter, and are citing and accusing me before them. Speak, then, and tell the judges who their improver is.—Observe, Meletus, that you are silent, and have nothing to say. But is not

this rather disgraceful, and a very considerable proof of what I was saying, that you have no interest in the matter? Speak up, friend, and tell us who their
235   improver is.

MELETUS: The laws.

SOCRATES: But that, my good sir, is not my meaning. I want to know who the person is, who, in the first place, knows the laws.

MELETUS: The judges, Socrates, who are present in court.

240 SOCRATES: What, do you mean to say, Meletus, that they are able to instruct and improve youth?

MELETUS: Certainly they are.

SOCRATES: What, all of them, or some only and not others?

MELETUS: All of them.

245 SOCRATES: By the goddess Here, that is good news! There are plenty of improvers, then. And what do you say of the audience,—do they improve them?

MELETUS: Yes, they do.

SOCRATES: And the senators?

250 MELETUS: Yes, the senators improve them.

SOCRATES: But perhaps the members of the assembly corrupt them?—or do they too improve them?

MELETUS: They improve them.

SOCRATES: Then every Athenian improves and elevates them; all with the
255   exception of myself; and I alone am their corrupter? Is that what you affirm?

MELETUS: That is what I stoutly affirm.

SOCRATES: I am very unfortunate if you are right. But suppose I ask you a question: How about horses? Does one man do them harm and all the world good? Is not the exact opposite the truth? One man is able to do them good, or
260   at least not many;—the trainer of horses, that is to say, does them good, and others who have to do with them rather injure them? Is not that true, Meletus, of horses, or of any other animals? Most assuredly it is; whether you and Anytus say yes or no. Happy indeed would be the condition of youth if they had one corrupter only, and all the rest of the world were their improvers.
265   But you, Meletus, have sufficiently shown that you never had a thought about the young: your carelessness is seen in your not caring about the very things which you bring against me.

    And now, Meletus, I will ask you another question—by Zeus I will: Which is better, to live among bad citizens, or among good ones? Answer,
270   friend, I say; the question is one which may be easily answered. Do not the good do their neighbours good, and the bad do them evil?

MELETUS: Certainly.

SOCRATES: And is there anyone who would rather be injured than benefited by those who live with him? Answer, my good friend, the law requires you to
275   answer—does any one like to be injured?

MELETUS: Certainly not.

SOCRATES: And when you accuse me of corrupting and deteriorating the youth, do you allege that I corrupt them intentionally or unintentionally?

MELETUS: Intentionally, I say.

280 SOCRATES: But you have just admitted that the good do their neighbours good, and the evil do them evil. Now, is that a truth which your superior wisdom has recognized thus early in life, and am I, at my age, in such darkness and ignorance as not to know that if a man with whom I have to live is corrupted by me, I am very likely to be harmed by him; and yet I corrupt him, and

285 intentionally, too—so you say, although neither I nor any other human being is ever likely to be convinced by you. But either I do not corrupt them, or I corrupt them unintentionally; and on either view of the case you lie. If my offence is unintentional, the law has no cognizance of unintentional offences: you ought to have taken me privately, and warned and admonished me; for if I

290 had been better advised, I should have left off doing what I only did unintentionally—no doubt I should; but you would have nothing to say to me and refused to teach me. And now you bring me up in this court, which is a place not of instruction, but of punishment.

It will be very clear to you, Athenians, as I was saying, that Meletus has

295 no care at all, great or small, about the matter. But still I should like to know, Meletus, in what I am affirmed to corrupt the young. I suppose you mean, as I infer from your indictment, that I teach them not to acknowledge the gods which the state acknowledges, but some other new divinities or spiritual agencies in their stead. These are the lessons by which I corrupt the youth, as

300 you say.

MELETUS: Yes, that I say emphatically.

SOCRATES: Then, by the gods, Meletus, of whom we are speaking, tell me and the court, in somewhat plainer terms, what you mean! for I do not as yet understand whether you affirm that I teach other men to acknowledge some

305 gods, and therefore that I do believe in gods, and am not an entire atheist— this you do not lay to my charge,—but only you say that they are not the same gods which the city recognizes—the charge is that they are different gods. Or, do you mean that I am an atheist simply, and a teacher of atheism?

MELETUS: I mean the latter—that you are a complete atheist.

310 SOCRATES: What an extraordinary statement! Why do you think so, Meletus? Do you mean that I do not believe in the godhead of the sun or moon, like other men?

MELETUS: I assure you, judges, that he does not: for he says that the sun is stone, and the moon earth.

315 SOCRATES: Friend Meletus, you think that you are accusing Anaxagoras: and you have but a bad opinion of the judges, if you fancy them illiterate to such a degree as not to know that these doctrines are found in the books of Anaxagoras the Clazomenian, which are full of them. And so, forsooth, the youth are said to be taught them by Socrates, when there are not unfrequently

320   exhibitions of them at the theatre[3]; and they might pay their money, and laugh at Socrates if he pretends to father these extraordinary views. And so, Meletus, you really think that I do not believe in any god?

MELETUS: I swear by Zeus that you believe absolutely in none at all.

SOCRATES: Nobody will believe you, Meletus, and I am pretty sure that you do

325   not believe yourself. I cannot help thinking, men of Athens, that Meletus is reckless and impudent, and that he has written this indictment in a spirit of mere wantonness and youthful bravado. Has he not compounded a riddle, thinking to try me? He said to himself:—I shall see whether the wise Socrates will discover my facetious contradiction, or whether I shall be able to deceive

330   him and the rest of them. For he certainly does appear to me to contradict himself in the indictment as much as if he said that Socrates is guilty of not believing in the gods, and yet of believing in them—but this is not like a person who is in earnest.

       I should like you, O men of Athens, to join me in examining what I

335   conceive to be his inconsistency; and do you, Meletus, answer. And I must remind the audience of my request that they would not make a disturbance if I speak in my accustomed manner:

       Did ever man, Meletus, believe in the existence of human things, and not of human beings? . . . I wish, men of Athens, that he would answer, and not be

340   always trying to get up an interruption. Did ever any man believe in horsemanship, and not in horses? or in flute-playing, and not in flute-players? No, my friend; I will answer to you and to the court, as you refuse to answer for yourself. There is no man who ever did. But now please to answer the next question: Can a man believe in spiritual and divine agencies, and not

345   in spirits or demigods?

MELETUS: He cannot.

SOCRATES: How lucky I am to have extracted that answer, by the assistance of the court! But then you swear in the indictment that I teach and believe in divine or spiritual agencies (new or old, no matter for that); at any rate, I

350   believe in spiritual agencies,—so you say and swear in the affidavit; and yet if I believe in divine beings, how can I help believing in spirits or demigods;— must I not? To be sure I must; and therefore I may assume that your silence gives consent. Now what are spirits or demigods? Are they not either gods or the sons of gods?

355 MELETUS: Certainly they are.

SOCRATES: But this is what I call the facetious riddle invented by you: the demigods or spirits are gods, and you say first that I do not believe in gods, and then again that I do believe in gods; that is, if I believe in demigods. For if the demigods are the illegitimate sons of gods, whether by the nymphs or by

360   any other mothers, of whom they are said to be the sons—what human being

---

[3]Probably in allusion to Aristophanes who caricatured, and to Euripides who borrowed the notions of Anaxagoras, as well as to other dramatic poets.

will ever believe that there are no gods if they are the sons of gods? You might as well affirm the existence of mules, and deny that of horses and asses. Such nonsense, Meletus, could only have been intended by you to make trial of me. You have put this into the indictment because you had nothing real of which
365 to accuse me. But no one who has a particle of understanding will ever be convinced by you that the same men can believe in divine and superhuman things, and yet not believe that there are gods and demigods and heroes.

I have said enough in answer to the charge of Meletus: any elaborate defence is unnecessary, but I know only too well how many are the enmities which I have
370 incurred, and this is what will be my destruction if I am destroyed;—not Meletus, nor yet Anytus, but the envy and detraction of the world, which has been the death of many good men, and will probably be the death of many more; there is no danger of my being the last of them.

Some one will say: And are you not ashamed, Socrates, of a course of life
375 which is likely to bring you to an untimely end? To him I may fairly answer: There you are mistaken: a man who is good for anything ought not to calculate the chance of living or dying; he ought only to consider whether in doing anything he is doing right or wrong—acting the part of a good man or of a bad. Whereas, upon your view, the heroes who fell at Troy were not good for much, and the son of
380 Thetis above all, who altogether despised danger in comparison with disgrace; and when he was so eager to slay Hector, his goddess mother said to him, that if he avenged his companion Patroclus, and slew Hector, he would die himself—"Fate," she said, in these or the like words, "waits for you next after Hector;" he, receiving this warning, utterly despised danger and death, and instead of fearing
385 them, feared rather to live in dishonour, and not to avenge his friend. "Let me die forthwith," he replies, "and be avenged of my enemy, rather than abide here by the beaked ships, a laughing-stock and a burden of the earth." Had Achilles any thought of death and danger? For wherever a man's place is, whether the place which he has chosen or that in which he has been placed by a commander, there he
390 ought to remain in the hour of danger; he should not think of death or of anything but of disgrace. And this, O men of Athens, is a true saying.

Strange, indeed, would be my conduct, O men of Athens, if I who, when I was ordered by the generals whom you chose to command me at Potidaea and Amphipolis and Delium, remained where they placed me, like any other man, facing
395 death—if now, when, as I conceive and imagine, God orders me to fulfil the philosopher's mission of searching into myself and other men, I were to desert my post through fear of death, or any other fear; that would indeed be strange, and I might justly be arraigned in court for denying the existence of the gods, if I disobeyed the oracle because I was afraid of death, fancying that I was wise when
400 I was not wise. For the fear of death is indeed the pretence of wisdom, and not real wisdom, being a pretence of knowing the unknown; and no one knows whether death, which men in their fear apprehend to be the greatest evil, may not be the greatest good. Is not this ignorance of a disgraceful sort, the ignorance which is the

conceit that a man knows what he does not know? And in this respect only I believe myself to differ from men in general, and may perhaps claim to be wiser than they are:—that whereas I know but little of the world below, I do not suppose that I know: but I do know that injustice and disobedience to a better, whether God or man, is evil and dishonourable, and I will never fear or avoid a possible good rather than a certain evil. And therefore if you let me go now, and are not convinced by Anytus, who said that since I had been prosecuted I must be put to death; (or if not that I ought never to have been prosecuted at all); and that if I escape now, your sons will all be utterly ruined by listening to my words—if you say to me, Socrates, this time we will not mind Anytus, and you shall be let off, but upon one condition, that you are not to enquire and speculate in this way any more, and that if you are caught doing so again you shall die;—if this was the condition on which you let me go, I should reply: Men of Athens, I honour and love you; but I shall obey God rather than you, and while I have life and strength I shall never cease from the practice and teaching of philosophy, exhorting any one whom I meet and saying to him after my manner: You, my friend,—a citizen of the great and mighty and wise city of Athens,—are you not ashamed of heaping up the greatest amount of money and honour and reputation, and caring so little about wisdom and truth and the greatest improvement of the soul, which you never regard or heed at all? And if the person with whom I am arguing, says: Yes, but I do care; then I do not leave him or let him go at once; but I proceed to interrogate and examine and cross-examine him, and if I think that he has no virtue in him, but only says that he has, I reproach him with undervaluing the greater, and overvaluing the less. And I shall repeat the same words to every one whom I meet, young and old, citizen and alien, but especially to the citizens, inasmuch as they are my brethren. For know that this is the command of God; and I believe that no greater good has ever happened in the state than my service to the God. For I do nothing but go about persuading you all, old and young alike, not to take thought for your persons or your properties, but first and chiefly to care about the greatest improvement of the soul. I tell you that virtue is not given by money, but that from virtue comes money and every other good of man, public as well as private. This is my teaching, and if this is the doctrine which corrupts the youth, I am a mischievous person. But if any one says that this is not my teaching, he is speaking an untruth. Wherefore, O men of Athens, I say to you, do as Anytus bids or not as Anytus bids, and either acquit me or not; but whichever you do, understand that I shall never alter my ways, not even if I have to die many times.

Men of Athens, do not interrupt, but hear me; there was an understanding between us that you should hear me to the end: I have something more to say, at which you may be inclined to cry out; but I believe that to hear me will be good for you, and therefore I beg that you will not cry out. I would have you know, that if you kill such a one as I am, you will injure yourselves more than you will injure me. Nothing will injure me, not Meletus nor yet Anytus—they cannot, for a bad man is not permitted to injure a better than himself. I do not deny that Anytus may, perhaps, kill him, or drive him into exile, or deprive him of civil rights; and he may imagine, and others may imagine, that he is inflicting a great injury upon him: but there I do not agree. For the evil of doing as he is doing—the evil of unjustly taking away the life of another—is greater far.

450

And now, Athenians, I am not going to argue for my own sake, as you may think, but for yours, that you may not sin against the God by condemning me, who am his gift to you. For if you kill me you will not easily find a successor to me, who, if I may use such a ludicrous figure of speech, am a sort of gadfly, given to the state by God; and the state is a great and noble steed who is tardy in his motions owing to his very size, and requires to be stirred into life. I am that gadfly which God has attached to the state, and all day long and in all places am always fastening upon you, arousing and persuading and reproaching you. You will not easily find another like me, and therefore I would advise you to spare me. I dare say that you may feel out of temper (like a person who is suddenly awakened from sleep), and you think that you might easily strike me dead as Anytus advises, and then you would sleep on for the remainder of your lives, unless God in his care of you sent you another gadfly. When I say that I am given to you by God, the proof of my mission is this:—if I had been like other men, I should not have neglected all my own concerns or patiently seen the neglect of them during all these years, and have been doing yours, coming to you individually like a father or elder brother, exhorting you to regard virtue; such conduct, I say, would be unlike human nature. If I had gained anything, or if my exhortations had been paid, there would have been some sense in my doing so; but now, as you will perceive, not even the impudence of my accusers dares to say that I have ever exacted or sought pay of any one; of that they have no witness. And I have a sufficient witness to the truth of what I say—my poverty.

455

460

465

470

Some one may wonder why I go about in private giving advice and busying myself with the concerns of others, but do not venture to come forward in public and advise the state. I will tell you why. You have heard me speak at sundry times and in divers places of an oracle or sign which comes to me, and is the divinity which Meletus ridicules in the indictment. This sign, which is a kind of voice, first began to come to me when I was a child; it always forbids but never commands me to do anything which I am going to do. This is what deters me from being a politician. And rightly, as I think. For I am certain, O men of Athens, that if I had engaged in politics, I should have perished long ago, and done no good either to you or to myself. And do not be offended at my telling you the truth: for the truth is, that no man who goes to war with you or any other multitude, honestly striving against the many lawless and unrighteous deeds which are done in a state, will save his life; he who will fight for the right, if he would live even for a brief space, must have a private station and not a public one.

475

480

485

I can give you convincing evidence of what I say, not words only, but what you value far more—actions. Let me relate to you a passage of my own life which will prove to you that I should never have yielded to injustice from any fear of death, and that "as I should have refused to yield" I must have died at once. I will tell you a tale of the courts, not very interesting perhaps, but nevertheless true.

490

The only office of state which I ever held, O men of Athens, was that of senator: the tribe Antiochis, which is my tribe, had the presidency at the trial of the generals who had not taken up the bodies of the slain after the battle of Arginusae;

495 and you proposed to try them in a body, contrary to law, as you all thought afterwards; but at the time I was the only one of the Prytanes who was opposed to the illegality, and I gave my vote against you; and when the orators threatened to impeach and arrest me, and you called and shouted, I made up my mind that I would run the risk, having law and justice with me, rather than take part in your

500 injustice because I feared imprisonment and death. This happened in the days of the democracy. But when the oligarchy of the Thirty was in power, they sent for me and four others into the rotunda, and bade us bring Leon the Salaminian from Salamis, as they wanted to put him to death. This was a specimen of the sort of commands which they were always giving with the view of implicating as many as

505 possible in their crimes; and then I showed, not in word only but in deed, that, if I may be allowed to use such an expression, I cared not a straw for death, and that my great and only care was lest I should do an unrighteous or unholy thing. For the strong arm of that oppressive power did not frighten me into doing wrong; and when we came out of the rotunda the other four went to Salamis and fetched Leon,

510 but I went quietly home. For which I might have lost my life, had not the power of the Thirty shortly afterwards come to an end. And many will witness to my words.

Now do you really imagine that I could have survived all these years, if I had led a public life, supposing that like a good man I had always maintained the right

515 and had made justice, as I ought, the first thing? No indeed, men of Athens, neither I nor any other man. But I have been always the same in all my actions, public as well as private, and never have I yielded any base compliance to those who are slanderously termed my disciples, or to any other. Not that I have any regular disciples. But if any one likes to come and hear me while I am pursuing my mission,

520 whether he be young or old, he is not excluded. Nor do I converse only with those who pay; but any one, whether he be rich or poor, may ask and answer me and listen to my words; and whether he turns out to be a bad man or a good one, neither result can be justly imputed to me; for I never taught or professed to teach him anything. And if any one says that he has ever learned or heard anything from

525 me in private which all the world has not heard, let me tell you that he is lying.

But I shall be asked, Why do people delight in continually conversing with you? I have told you already, Athenians, the whole truth about this matter: they like to hear the cross-examination of the pretenders to wisdom; there is amusement in it. Now this duty of cross-examining other men has been imposed upon me by

530 God; and has been signified to me by oracles, visions, and in every way in which the will of divine power was ever intimated to any one. This is true, O Athenians, or, if not true, would be soon refuted. If I am or have been corrupting the youth, those of them who are now grown up and have become sensible that I gave them bad advice in the days of their youth should come forward as accusers, and take

535 their revenge; or if they do not like to come themselves, some of their relatives,

fathers, brothers, or other kinsmen, should say what evil their families have suffered at my hands. Now is their time. Many of them I see in the court. There is Crito, who is of the same age and of the same deme with myself, and there is Critobulus his son, whom I also see. Then again there is Lysanias of Sphettus,

540   who is the father of Aeschines—he is present; and also there is Antiphon of Cephisus, who is the father of Epigenes; and there are the brothers of several who have associated with me. There is Nicostratus the son of Theosdotides, and the brother of Theodotus (now Theodotus himself is dead, and therefore he, at any rate, will not seek to stop him); and there is Paralus the son of Demodocus, who

545   had a brother Theages; and Adeimantus the son of Ariston, whose brother Plato is present; and Aeantodorus, who is the brother of Apollodorus, whom I also see. I might mention a great many others, some of whom Meletus should have produced as witnesses in the course of his speech; and let him still produce them, if he has forgotten—I will make way for him. And let him say, if he has any testimony of the

550   sort which he can produce. Nay, Athenians, the very opposite is the truth. For all these are ready to witness on behalf of the corrupter, of the injurer of their kindred, as Meletus and Anytus call me; not the corrupted youth only—there might have been a motive for that—but their uncorrupted elder relatives. Why should they too support me with their testimony? Why, indeed, except for the sake of truth

555   and justice, and because they know that I am speaking the truth, and that Meletus is a liar.

     Well, Athenians, this and the like of this is all the defence which I have to offer. Yet a word more. Perhaps there may be some one who is offended at me, when he calls to mind how he himself on a similar, or even a less serious occasion,

560   prayed and entreated the judges with many tears, and how he produced his children in court, which was a moving spectacle, together with a host of relations and friends; whereas I, who am probably in danger of my life, will do none of these things. The contrast may occur to his mind, and he may be set against me, and vote in anger because he is displeased at me on this account. Now if there be such a

565   person among you,—mind, I do not say that there is,—to him I may fairly reply: My friend, I am a man, and like other men, a creature of flesh and blood, and not "of wood or stone," as Homer says; and I have a family, yes, and sons, O Athenians, three in number, one almost a man, and two others who are still young; and yet I will not bring any of them hither in order to petition you for an acquittal. And

570   why not? Not from any self-assertion or want of respect for you. Whether I am or am not afraid of death is another question, of which I will not now speak. But, having regard to public opinion, I feel that such conduct would be discreditable to myself, and to you, and to the whole state. One who has reached my years, and who has a name for wisdom, ought not to demean himself. Whether this opinion of

575   me be deserved or not, at any rate the world has decided that Socrates is in some way superior to other men. And if those among you who are said to be superior in wisdom and courage, and any other virtue, demean themselves in this way, how shameful is their conduct! I have seen men of reputation, when they have been condemned, behaving in the strangest manner: they seemed to fancy that they were

580   going to suffer something dreadful if they died, and that they could be immortal if
you only allowed them to live; and I think that such are a dishonour to the state,
and that any stranger coming in would have said of them that the most eminent men
of Athens, to whom the Athenians themselves give honour and command, are no
better than women. And I say that these things ought not to be done by those of us

585   who have a reputation; and if they are done, you ought not to permit them; you
ought rather to show that you are far more disposed to condemn the man who gets
up a doleful scene and makes the city ridiculous, than him who holds his peace.

But, setting aside the question of public opinion, there seems to be something
wrong in asking a favour of a judge, and thus procuring an acquittal, instead of

590   informing and convincing him. For his duty is, not to make a present of justice, but
to give judgment; and he has sworn that he will judge according to the laws, and
not according to his own good pleasure; and we ought not to encourage you, nor
should you allow yourselves to be encouraged, in this habit of perjury—there can
be no piety in that. Do not then require me to do what I consider dishonourable

595   and impious and wrong, especially now, when I am being tried for impiety on the
indictment of Meletus. For if, O men of Athens, by force of persuasion and entreaty
I could overpower your oaths, then I should be teaching you to believe that there
are no gods, and in defending should simply convict myself of the charge of not
believing in them. But that is not so—far otherwise. For I do believe that there are

600   gods, and in a sense higher than that in which any of my accusers believe in them.
And to you and to God I commit my cause, to be determined by you as is best for
you and me.

[The Court deems Socrates guilty by a vote of 281–220; Socrates is then
allowed to propose his own penalty.]

605   There are many reasons why I am not grieved, O men of Athens, at the vote of
condemnation. I expected it, and am only surprised that the votes are so nearly
equal; for I had thought that the majority against me would have been far larger;
but now, had thirty votes gone over to the other side, I should have been acquitted.
And I may say, I think, that I have escaped Meletus. I may say more; for without

610   the assistance of Anytus and Lycon, any one may see that he would not have had a
fifth part of the votes, as the law requires, in which case he would have incurred a
fine of a thousand drachmae.

And so he proposes death as the penalty. And what shall I propose on my
part, O men of Athens? Clearly that which is my due. And what is my due? What

615   return shall be made to the man who has never had the wit to be idle during his
whole life; but has been careless of what the many care for—wealth, and family
interests, and military offices, and speaking in the assembly, and magistracies, and
plots, and parties. Reflecting that I was really too honest a man to be a politician
and live, I did not go where I could do no good to you or to myself; but where I

620   could do the greatest good privately to every one of you, thither I went, and sought
to persuade every man among you that he must look to himself, and seek virtue and
wisdom before he looks to his private interests, and look to the state before he

looks to the interests of the state; and that this should be the order which he observes in all his actions. What shall be done to such a one? Doubtless some

625 good thing, O men of Athens, if he has his reward; and the good should be of a kind suitable to him. What would be a reward suitable to a poor man who is your benefactor, and who desires leisure that he may instruct you? There can be no reward so fitting as maintenance in the Prytaneum,[4] O men of Athens, a reward which he deserves far more than the citizen who has won the prize at Olympia in

630 the horse or chariot race, whether the chariots were drawn by two horses or by many. For I am in want, and he has enough; and he only gives you the appearance of happiness, and I give you the reality. And if I am to estimate the penalty fairly, I should say that maintenance in the Prytaneum is the just return.

Perhaps you think that I am braving you in what I am saying now, as in what

635 I said before about the tears and prayers. But this is not so. I speak rather because I am convinced that I never intentionally wronged any one, although I cannot convince you—the time has been too short; if there were a law at Athens, as there is in other cities, that a capital cause should not be decided in one day, then I believe that I should have convinced you. But I cannot in a moment refute great

640 slanders; and, as I am convinced that I never wronged another, I will assuredly not wrong myself. I will not say of myself that I deserve any evil, or propose any penalty. Why should I? because I am afraid of the penalty of death which Meletus proposes? When I do not know whether death is a good or an evil, why should I propose a penalty which would certainly be an evil? Shall I say imprisonment?

645 And why should I live in prison, and be the slave of the magistrates of the year— of the Eleven? Or shall the penalty be a fine, and imprisonment until the fine is paid? There is the same objection. I should have to lie in prison, for money I have none, and cannot pay. And if I say exile (and this may possibly be the penalty which you will affix), I must indeed be blinded by the love of life, if I am so

650 irrational as to expect that when you, who are my own citizens, cannot endure my discourses and words, and have found them so grievous and odious that you will have no more of them, others are likely to endure me. No indeed, men of Athens, that is not very likely. And what a life should I lead, at my age, wandering from city to city, ever changing my place of exile, and always being driven out! For I am

655 quite sure that wherever I go, there, as here, the young men will flock to me; and if I drive them away, their elders will drive me out at their request; and if I let them come, their fathers and friends will drive me out for their sakes.

Some one will say: Yes, Socrates, but cannot you hold your tongue, and then you may go into a foreign city, and no one will interfere with you? Now I have

660 great difficulty in making you understand my answer to this. For if I tell you that to do as you say would be a disobedience to the God, and therefore that I cannot hold my tongue, you will not believe that I am serious; and if I say again that daily to discourse about virtue, and of those other things about which you hear me

---

[4]A place on the Acropolis where Olympic winners and other benefactors of Athens were honored.

665 examining myself and others, is the greatest good of man, and that the unexamined life is not worth living, you are still less likely to believe me. Yet I say what is true, although a thing of which it is hard for me to persuade you. Also, I have never been accustomed to think that I deserve to suffer any harm. Had I money I might have estimated the offence at what I was able to pay, and not have been much the worse. But I have none, and therefore I must ask you to proportion the

670 fine to my means. Well, perhaps I could afford a mina, and therefore I propose that penalty: Plato, Crito, Critobulus, and Apollodorus, my friends here, bid me say thirty minae, and they will be the sureties. Let thirty minae be the penalty; for which sum they will be ample security to you.

[The Court votes for the death penalty.]

675 Not much time will be gained, O Athenians, in return for the evil name which you will get from the detractors of the city, who will say that you killed Socrates, a wise man; for they will call me wise, even although I am not wise, when they want to reproach you. If you had waited a little while, your desire would have been fulfilled in the course of nature. For I am far advanced in years, as you may

680 perceive, and not far from death. I am speaking now not to all of you, but only to those who have condemned me to death. And I have another thing to say to them: you think that I was convicted because I had no words of the sort which would have procured my acquittal—I mean, if I had thought fit to leave nothing undone or unsaid. Not so; the deficiency which led to my conviction was not of words—

685 certainly not. But I had not the boldness or impudence or inclination to address you as you would have liked me to do, weeping and wailing and lamenting, and saying and doing many things which you have been accustomed to hear from others, and which, as I maintain, are unworthy of me. I thought at the time that I ought not to do anything common or mean when in danger: nor do I now repent of

690 the style of my defence; I would rather die having spoken after my manner, than speak in your manner and live. For neither in war nor yet at law ought I or any man to use every way of escaping death. Often in battle there can be no doubt that if a man will throw away his arms, and fall on his knees before his pursuers, he may escape death; and in other dangers there are other ways of escaping death, if a

695 man is willing to say and do anything. The difficulty, my friends, is not to avoid death, but to avoid unrighteousness; for that runs faster than death. I am old and move slowly, and the slower runner has overtaken me, and my accusers are keen and quick, and the faster runner, who is unrighteousness, has overtaken them. And now I depart hence condemned by you to suffer the penalty of death,—they too go

700 their ways condemned by the truth to suffer the penalty of villainy and wrong; and I must abide by my award—let them abide by theirs. I suppose that these things may be regarded as fated,—and I think that they are well.

And now, O men who have condemned me, I would fain prophesy to you; for I am about to die, and in the hour of death men are gifted with prophetic power. And

705 I prophesy to you who are my murderers, that immediately after my departure punishment far heavier than you have inflicted on me will surely await you. Me

you have killed because you wanted to escape the accuser, and not to give an account of your lives. But that will not be as you suppose: far otherwise. For I say that there will be more accusers of you than there are now; accusers whom

710 hitherto I have restrained: and as they are younger they will be more inconsiderate with you, and you will be more offended at them. If you think that by killing men you can prevent some one from censuring your evil lives, you are mistaken; that is not a way of escape which is either possible or honourable; the easiest and the noblest way is not to be disabling others, but to be improving

715 yourselves. This is the prophecy which I utter before my departure to the judges who have condemned me.

Friends, who would have acquitted me, I would like also to talk with you about the thing which has come to pass, while the magistrates are busy, and before I go to the place at which I must die. Stay then a little, for we may as well talk with

720 one another while there is time. You are my friends, and I should like to show you the meaning of this event which has happened to me. O my judges—for you I may truly call judges—I should like to tell you of a wonderful circumstance. Hitherto the divine faculty of which the internal oracle is the source has constantly been in the habit of opposing me even about trifles, if I was going to make a slip or error in

725 any matter; and now as you see there has come upon me that which may be thought, and is generally believed to be, the last and worst evil. But the oracle made no sign of opposition, either when I was leaving my house in the morning, or when I was on my way to the court, or while I was speaking, at anything which I was going to say; and yet I have often been stopped in the middle of a speech, but now in nothing

730 I either said or did touching the matter in hand has the oracle opposed me. What do I take to be the explanation of this silence? I will tell you. It is an intimation that what has happened to me is a good, and that those of us who think that death is an evil are in error. For the customary sign would surely have opposed me had I been going to evil and not to good.

735 Let us reflect in another way, and we shall see that there is great reason to hope that death is a good; for one of two things—either death is a state of nothingness and utter unconsciousness, or, as men say, there is a change and migration of the soul from this world to another. Now if you suppose that there is no consciousness, but a sleep like the sleep of him who is undisturbed even by

740 dreams, death will be an unspeakable gain. For if a person were to select the night in which his sleep was undisturbed even by dreams, and were to compare with this the other days and nights of his life, and then were to tell us how many days and nights he had passed in the course of his life better and more pleasantly than this one, I think that any man, I will not say a private man, but even the great king

745 will not find many such days or nights, when compared with the others. Now if death be of such a nature, I say that to die is gain; for eternity is then only a single night. But if death is the journey to another place, and there, as men say, all the dead abide, what good, O my friends and judges, can be greater than this? If indeed when the pilgrim arrives in the world below, he is delivered from the professors of

750 justice in this world, and finds the true judges who are said to give judgment there,

Minos and Rhadamanthus and Aeacus and Triptolemus, and other sons of God who were righteous in their own life, that pilgrimage will be worth making. What would not a man give if he might converse with Orpheus and Musaeus and Hesiod and Homer? Nay, if this be true, let me die again and again. I myself, too, shall have

755   a wonderful interest in there meeting and conversing with Palamedes, and Ajax the son of Telamon, and any other ancient hero who has suffered death through an unjust judgment; and there will be no small pleasure, as I think, in comparing my own sufferings with theirs. Above all, I shall then be able to continue my search into true and false knowledge; as in this world, so also in the next; and I shall find

760   out who is wise, and who pretends to be wise, and is not. What would not a man give, O judges, to be able to examine the leader of the great Trojan expedition; or Odysseus or Sisyphus, or numberless others, men and women too! What infinite delight would there be in conversing with them and asking them questions! In another world they do not put a man to death for asking questions: assuredly not.

765   For besides being happier than we are, they will be immortal, if what is said is true.

      Wherefore, O judges, be of good cheer about death, and know of a certainty, that no evil can happen to a good man, either in life or after death. He and his are not neglected by the gods; nor has my own approaching end happened by mere

770   chance. But I see clearly that the time had arrived when it was better for me to die and be released from trouble; wherefore the oracle gave no sign. For which reason, also, I am not angry with my condemners, or with my accusers; they have done me no harm, although they did not mean to do me any good; and for this I may gently blame them.

775   Still I have a favour to ask of them. When my sons are grown up, I would ask you, O my friends, to punish them; and I would have you trouble them, as I have troubled you, if they seem to care about riches, or anything, more than about virtue; or if they pretend to be something when they are really nothing,—then reprove them, as I have reproved you, for not caring about that for which they

780   ought to care, and thinking that they are something when they are really nothing. And if you do this, both I and my sons will have received justice at your hands.

      The hour of departure has arrived, and we go our ways—I to die, and you to live. Which is better God only knows.

12. THE REPUBLIC (SELECTIONS)

Plato
(c. 427 BCE–348 BCE)

(trans. by Benjamin Jowett)

Plato's most famous work, The Republic, *is a lengthy dialogue on the issue of justice: what it is, and how it can be achieved. Through the Socratic method of questioning, it demonstrates what justice is not (Ring of Gyges), the difficulty of achieving it (Divided Line, Allegory of the Cave), from whence justice is derived, and the immortality of the soul (Myth of Er). The dialogue reveals that justice is a harmony of parts, each part doing its appropriate task. For the person, justice ('happiness') is achieved when the rational faculty properly governs the spirited and appetitive faculties; for the state ('Man Writ Large'), the Philosopher King ('rational') governs as the Guardians ('spirited') defend and the Producers ('appetitive') supply the goods, each fulfilling its function, and the whole achieving justice.*

BOOK II: THE RING OF GYGES

. . . but to my mind the nature of justice and injustice have not yet been made clear. Setting aside their rewards and results, I want to know what they are in themselves, and how they inwardly work in the soul. If you, please, then, I will revive the argument of Thrasymachus. And first I will speak of the nature and
5   origin of justice according to the common view of them. Secondly, I will show that all men who practise justice do so against their will, of necessity, but not as a good. And thirdly, I will argue that there is reason in this view, for the life of the unjust is after all better far than the life of the just—if what they say is true, Socrates, since I myself am not of their opinion. But still I acknowledge that I am
10   perplexed when I hear the voices of Thrasymachus and myriads of others dinning in my ears; and, on the other hand, I have never yet heard the superiority of justice to injustice maintained by any one in a satisfactory way. I want to hear justice praised in respect of itself; then I shall be satisfied, and you are the person from whom I think that I am most likely to hear this; and therefore I will praise the
15   unjust life to the utmost of my power, and my manner of speaking will indicate the manner in which I desire to hear you too praising justice and censuring injustice. Will you say whether you approve of my proposal?

Indeed I do; nor can I imagine any theme about which a man of sense would oftener wish to converse.

20   I am delighted, he replied, to hear you say so, and shall begin by speaking, as I proposed, of the nature and origin of justice. They say that to do injustice is, by nature, good; to suffer injustice, evil; but that the evil is greater than the good. And so when men have both done and suffered injustice and have had experience of both, not being able to avoid the one and obtain the other, they think that they had

25   better agree among themselves to have neither; hence there arise laws and mutual covenants; and that which is ordained by law is termed by them lawful and just. This they affirm to be the origin and nature of justice;—it is a mean or compromise, between the best of all, which is to do injustice and not be punished, and the worst of all, which is to suffer injustice without the power of retaliation; and justice,

30   being at a middle point between the two, is tolerated not as a good, but as the lesser evil, and honoured by reason of the inability of men to do injustice. For no man who is worthy to be called a man would ever submit to such an agreement if he were able to resist; he would be mad if he did. Such is the received account, Socrates, of the nature and origin of justice.

35   Now that those who practise justice do so involuntarily and because they have not the power to be unjust will best appear if we imagine something of this kind: having given both to the just and the unjust power to do what they will, let us watch and see whither desire will lead them; then we shall discover in the very act the just and unjust man to be proceeding along the same road, following their

40   interest, which all natures deem to be their good, and are only diverted into the path of justice by the force of law. The liberty which we are supposing may be most completely given to them in the form of such a power as is said to have been possessed by Gyges, the ancestor of Croesus the Lydian. According to the tradition, Gyges was a shepherd in the service of the king of Lydia; there was a

45   great storm, and an earthquake made an opening in the earth at the place where he was feeding his flock. Amazed at the sight, he descended into the opening, where, among other marvels, he beheld a hollow brazen horse, having doors, at which he stooping and looking in saw a dead body of stature, as appeared to him, more than human, and having nothing on but a gold ring; this he took from the finger of the

50   dead and reascended. Now the shepherds met together, according to custom, that they might send their monthly report about the flocks to the king; into their assembly he came having the ring on his finger, and as he was sitting among them he chanced to turn the collet of the ring inside his hand, when instantly he became invisible to the rest of the company and they began to speak of him as if he were no

55   longer present. He was astonished at this, and again touching the ring he turned the collet outwards and reappeared; he made several trials of the ring, and always with the same result—when he turned the collet inwards he became invisible, when outwards he reappeared. Whereupon he contrived to be chosen one of the messengers who were sent to the court; whereas soon as he arrived he seduced the

60   queen, and with her help conspired against the king and slew him, and took the kingdom. Suppose now that there were two such magic rings, and the just put on

one of them and the unjust the other; no man can be imagined to be of such an iron nature that he would stand fast in justice. No man would keep his hands off what was not his own when he could safely take what he liked out of the market, or go
65   into houses and lie with any one at his pleasure, or kill or release from prison whom he would, and in all respects be like a God among men. Then the actions of the just would be as the actions of the unjust; they would both come at last to the same point. And this we may truly affirm to be a great proof that a man is just, not willingly or because he thinks that justice is any good to him individually, but of
70   necessity, for wherever any one thinks that he can safely be unjust, there he is unjust. For all men believe in their hearts that injustice is far more profitable to the individual than justice, and he who argues as I have been supposing, will say that they are right. If you could imagine any one obtaining this power of becoming invisible, and never doing any wrong or touching what was another's, he would
75   be thought by the lookers-on to be a most wretched idiot, although they would praise him to one another's faces, and keep up appearances with one another from a fear that they too might suffer injustice. Enough of this.

    Now, if we are to form a real judgment of the life of the just and unjust, we must isolate them; there is no other way; and how is the isolation to be effected? I
80   answer: Let the unjust man be entirely unjust, and the just man entirely just; nothing is to be taken away from either of them, and both are to be perfectly furnished for the work of their respective lives. First, let the unjust be like other distinguished masters of craft; like the skillful pilot or physician, who knows intuitively his own powers and keeps within their limits, and who, if he fails at
85   any point, is able to recover himself. So let the unjust make his unjust attempts in the right way, and lie hidden if he means to be great in his injustice (he who is found out is nobody): for the highest reach of injustice is, to be deemed just when you are not. Therefore I say that in the perfectly unjust man we must assume the most perfect injustice; there is to be no deduction, but we must allow him, while
90   doing the most unjust acts, to have acquired the greatest reputation for justice. If he have taken a false step he must be able to recover himself; he must be one who can speak with effect, if any of his deeds come to light, and who can force his way where force is required by his courage and strength, and command of money and friends. And at his side let us place the just man in his nobleness and simplicity,
95   wishing, as Aeschylus says, to be and not to seem good. There must be no seeming, for if he seem to be just he will be honoured and rewarded, and then we shall not know whether he is just for the sake of justice or for the sake of honours and rewards; therefore, let him be clothed in justice only, and have no other covering; and he must be imagined in a state of life the opposite of the former. Let him be the
100   best of men, and let him be thought the worst; then he will have been put to the proof; and we shall see whether he will be affected by the fear of infamy and its consequences. And let him continue thus to the hour of death; being just and seeming to be unjust. When both have reached the uttermost extreme, the one of justice and the other of injustice, let judgment be given which of them is the happier
105   of the two.

Heavens! my dear Glaucon, I said, how energetically you polish them up for the decision, first one and then the other, as if they were two statues. I do my best, he said. And now that we know what they are like there is no difficulty in tracing out the sort of life which awaits either of them. This I will proceed to describe; but as you may think the description a little too coarse, I ask you to suppose, Socrates, that the words which follow are not mine.—Let me put them into the mouths of the eulogists of injustice: They will tell you that the just man who is thought unjust will be scourged, racked, bound—will have his eyes burnt out; and, at last, after suffering every kind of evil, he will be impaled: Then he will understand that he ought to seem only, and not to be, just; the words of Aeschylus may be more truly spoken of the unjust than of the just. For the unjust is pursuing a reality; he does not live with a view to appearances—he wants to be really unjust and not to seem only:—

"His mind has a soil deep and fertile,
        Out of which spring his prudent counsels."

In the first place, he is thought just, and therefore bears rule in the city; he can marry whom he will, and give in marriage to whom he will; also he can trade and deal where he likes, and always to his own advantage, because he has no misgivings about injustice; and at every contest, whether in public or private, he gets the better of his antagonists, and gains at their expense, and is rich, and out of his gains he can benefit his friends, and harm his enemies; moreover, he can offer sacrifices, and dedicate gifts to the gods abundantly and magnificently, and can honour the gods or any man whom he wants to honour in a far better style than the just, and therefore he is likely to be dearer than they are to the gods. And thus, Socrates, gods and men are said to unite in making the life of the unjust better than the life of the just.

I was going to say something in answer to Glaucon, when Adeimantus, his brother, interposed: Socrates, he said, you do not suppose that there is nothing more to be urged?

Why, what else is there? I answered.

The strongest point of all has not been even mentioned, he replied. Well, then, according to the proverb,

"Let brother help brother"

—if he fails in any part do you assist him; although I must confess that Glaucon has already said quite enough to lay me in the dust, and take from me the power of helping justice.

Nonsense, he replied. But let me add something more: There is another side to Glaucon's argument about the praise and censure of justice and injustice, which is equally required in order to bring out what I believe to be his meaning. Parents and tutors are always telling their sons and their wards that they are to be just;

but why? not for the sake of justice, but for the sake of character and reputation; in the hope of obtaining for him who is reputed just some of those offices, marriages, and the like which Glaucon has enumerated among the advantages accruing to the unjust from the reputation of justice. More, however, is made of
150   appearances by this class of persons than by the others; for they throw in the good opinion of the gods, and will tell you of a shower of benefits which the heavens, as they say, rain upon the pious; and this accords with the testimony of the noble Hesiod and Homer, the first of whom says, that the gods make the oaks of the just—

"To bear acorns at their summit, and bees in the middle;
155   And the sheep are bowed down with the weight of their fleeces,"

and many other blessings of a like kind are provided for them. And Homer has a very similar strain; for he speaks of one whose fame is—

"As the fame of some blameless king who, like a god,
Maintains justice; to whom the black earth brings forth
160   Wheat and barley, whose trees are bowed with fruit,
And his sheep never fail to bear, and the sea gives him fish."

Still grander are the gifts of heaven which Musaeus and his son vouchsafe to the just; they take them down into the world below, where they have the saints lying on couches at a feast, everlastingly drunk, crowned with garlands; their idea
165   seems to be that an immortality of drunkenness is the highest meed of virtue. Some extend their rewards yet further; the posterity, as they say, of the faithful and just shall survive to the third and fourth generation. This is the style in which they praise justice. But about the wicked there is another strain; they bury them in a slough in Hades, and make them carry water in a sieve; also while they are yet
170   living they bring them to infamy, and inflict upon them the punishments which Glaucon described as the portion of the just who are reputed to be unjust; nothing else does their invention supply. Such is their manner of praising the one and censuring the other.

Once more, Socrates, I will ask you to consider another way of speaking
175   about justice and injustice, which is not confined to the poets, but is found in prose writers. The universal voice of mankind is always declaring that justice and virtue are honourable, but grievous and toilsome; and that the pleasures of vice and injustice are easy of attainment, and are only censured by law and opinion. They say also that honesty is for the most part less profitable than dishonesty;
180   and they are quite ready to call wicked men happy, and to honour them both in public and private when they are rich or in any other way influential, while they despise and overlook those who may be weak and poor, even though acknowledging them to be better than the others. But most extraordinary of all is their mode of speaking about virtue and the gods: they say that the gods apportion
185   calamity and misery to many good men, and good and happiness to the wicked.

And mendicant prophets go to rich men's doors and persuade them that they have a power committed to them by the gods of making an atonement for a man's own or his ancestor's sins by sacrifices or charms, with rejoicings and feasts; and they promise to harm an enemy, whether just or unjust, at a small cost; with magic arts
190   and incantations binding heaven, as they say, to execute their will. And the poets are the authorities to whom they appeal, now smoothing the path of vice with the words of Hesiod:—

> "Vice may be had in abundance without trouble; the way is smooth
> and her dwelling-place is near. But before virtue the gods have set toil,"

195   and a tedious and uphill road: then citing Homer as a witness that the gods may be influenced by men; for he also says:—

> "The gods, too, may be turned from their purpose; and men pray to them
> and avert their wrath by sacrifices and soothing entreaties, and by libations
> and the odour of fat, when they have sinned and transgressed."

200   And they produce a host of books written by Musaeus and Orpheus, who were children of the Moon and the Muses—that is what they say—according to which they perform their ritual, and persuade not only individuals, but whole cities, that expiations and atonements for sin may be made by sacrifices and amusements which fill a vacant hour, and are equally at the service of the living and the dead;
205   the latter sort they call mysteries, and they redeem us from the pains of hell, but if we neglect them no one knows what awaits us.

    He proceeded: And now when the young hear all this said about virtue and vice, and the way in which gods and men regard them, how are their minds likely to be affected, my dear Socrates,—those of them, I mean, who are quickwitted, and,
210   like bees on the wing, light on every flower, and from all that they hear are prone to draw conclusions as to what manner of persons they should be and in what way they should walk if they would make the best of life? Probably the youth will say to himself in the words of Pindar—

> "Can I by justice or by crooked ways of deceit ascend a loftier tower which
215   may
> be a fortress to me all my days?"

    For what men say is that, if I am really just and am not also thought just profit there is none, but the pain and loss on the other hand are unmistakeable. But if, though unjust, I acquire the reputation of justice, a heavenly life is promised to me.
220   Since then, as philosophers prove, appearance tyrannizes over truth and is lord of happiness, to appearance I must devote myself. I will describe around me a picture and shadow of virtue to be the vestibule and exterior of my house; behind I will trail the subtle and crafty fox, as Archilochus, greatest of sages, recommends. But I

225   hear some one exclaiming that the concealment of wickedness is often difficult; to which I answer, Nothing great is easy. Nevertheless, the argument indicates this, if we would be happy, to be the path along which we should proceed. With a view to concealment we will establish secret brotherhoods and political clubs. And there are professors of rhetoric who teach the art of persuading courts and assemblies; and so, partly by persuasion and partly by force, I shall make

230   unlawful gains and not be punished. Still I hear a voice saying that the gods cannot be deceived, neither can they be compelled. But what if there are no gods? or, suppose them to have no care of human things—why in either case should we mind about concealment? And even if there are gods, and they do care about us, yet we know of them only from tradition and the genealogies of the poets; and these

235   are the very persons who say that they may be influenced and turned by

"sacrifices and soothing entreaties and by offerings."

Let us be consistent then, and believe both or neither. If the poets speak truly, why then we had better be unjust, and offer of the fruits of injustice; for if we are just, although we may escape the vengeance of heaven, we shall lose the gains of

240   injustice; but, if we are unjust, we shall keep the gains, and by our sinning and praying, and praying and sinning, the gods will be propitiated, and we shall not be punished.

"But there is a world below in which either we or our posterity will suffer for our unjust deeds."

245   Yes, my friend, will be the reflection, but there are mysteries and atoning deities, and these have great power. That is what mighty cities declare; and the children of the gods, who were their poets and prophets, bear a like testimony.

      On what principle, then, shall we any longer choose justice rather than the worst injustice? when, if we only unite the latter with a deceitful regard to

250   appearances, we shall fare to our mind both with gods and men, in life and after death, as the most numerous and the highest authorities tell us. Knowing all this, Socrates, how can a man who has any superiority of mind or person or rank or wealth, be willing to honour justice; or indeed to refrain from laughing when he hears justice praised? And even if there should be some one who is able to

255   disprove the truth of my words, and who is satisfied that justice is best, still he is not angry with the unjust, but is very ready to forgive them, because he also knows that men are not just of their own free will; unless, peradventure, there be some one whom the divinity within him may have inspired with a hatred of injustice, or who has attained knowledge of the truth—but no other man. He only blames

260   injustice who, owing to cowardice or age or some weakness, has not the power of being unjust. And this is proved by the fact that when he obtains the power, he immediately becomes unjust as far as he can be. The cause of all this, Socrates, was indicated by us at the beginning of the argument, when my brother and I told you

265 how astonished we were to find that of all the professing panegyrists of justice— beginning with the ancient heroes of whom any memorial has been preserved to us, and ending with the men of our own time—no one has ever blamed injustice or praised justice except with a view to the glories, honours, and benefits which flow from them. No one has ever adequately described either in verse or prose the true essential nature of either of them abiding in the soul, and invisible to any human

270 or divine eye; or shown that of all the things of a man's soul which he has within him, justice is the greatest good, and injustice the greatest evil. Had this been the universal strain, had you sought to persuade us of this from our youth upwards, we should not have been on the watch to keep one another from doing wrong, but every one would have been his own watchman, because afraid, if he did wrong, of

275 harbouring in himself the greatest of evils. I dare say that Thrasymachus and others would seriously hold the language which I have been merely repeating, and words even stronger than these about justice and injustice, grossly, as I conceive, perverting their true nature. But I speak in this vehement manner, as I must frankly confess to you, because I want to hear from you the opposite side; and I would ask

280 you to show not only the superiority which justice has over injustice, but what effect they have on the possessor of them which makes the one to be a good and the other an evil to him. And please, as Glaucon requested of you, to exclude reputations; for unless you take away from each of them his true reputation and add on the false, we shall say that you do not praise justice, but the appearance of

285 it; we shall think that you are only exhorting us to keep injustice dark, and that you really agree with Thrasymachus in thinking that justice is another's good and the interest of the stronger, and that injustice is a man's own profit and interest, though injurious to the weaker. Now as you have admitted that justice is one of that highest class of goods which are desired indeed for their results, but in a far

290 greater degree for their own sakes—like sight or hearing or knowledge or health, or any other real and natural and not merely conventional good—I would ask you in your praise of justice to regard one point only: I mean the essential good and evil which justice and injustice work in the possessors of them. Let others praise justice and censure injustice, magnifying the rewards and honours of the one and

295 abusing the other; that is a manner of arguing which, coming from them, I am ready to tolerate, but from you who have spent your whole life in the consideration of this question, unless I hear the contrary from your own lips, I expect something better. And therefore, I say, not only prove to us that justice is better than injustice, but show what they either of them do to the possessor of them, which makes the

300 one to be a good and the other an evil, whether seen or unseen by gods and men.

BOOK VI: THE DIVIDED LINE

You have to imagine, then, that there are two ruling powers, and that one of them is set over the intellectual world, the other over the visible. I do not say heaven, lest you should fancy that I am playing upon the name. May I suppose that you have this distinction of the visible and intelligible fixed in your mind?

305   I have.

Now take a line which has been cut into two unequal parts, and divide each of them again in the same proportion, and suppose the two main divisions to answer, one to the visible and the other to the intelligible, and then compare the subdivisions in respect of their clearness and want of clearness, and you will find

310   that the first section in the sphere of the visible consists of images. And by images I mean, in the first place, shadows, and in the second place, reflections in water and in solid, smooth and polished bodies and the like: Do you understand?

Yes, I understand.

Imagine, now, the other section, of which this is only the resemblance, to

315   include the animals which we see, and everything that grows or is made.

Very good.

Would you not admit that both the sections of this division have different degrees of truth, and that the copy is to the original as the sphere of opinion is to the sphere of knowledge?

320   Most undoubtedly.

Next proceed to consider the manner in which the sphere of the intellectual is to be divided.

In what manner?

Thus:—There are two subdivisions, in the lower of which the soul uses the

325   figures given by the former division as images; the enquiry can only be hypothetical, and instead of going upwards to a principle descends to the other end; in the higher of the two, the soul passes out of hypotheses, and goes up to a principle which is above hypotheses, making no use of images as in the former case, but proceeding only in and through the ideas themselves.

330   I do not quite understand your meaning, he said.

Then I will try again; you will understand me better when I have made some preliminary remarks. You are aware that students of geometry, arithmetic, and the kindred sciences assume the odd and the even and the figures and three kinds of angles and the like in their several branches of science; these are their hypotheses,

335   which they and every body are supposed to know, and therefore they do not deign to give any account of them either to themselves or others; but they begin with them, and go on until they arrive at last, and in a consistent manner, at their conclusion?

Yes, he said, I know.

340   And do you not know also that although they make use of the visible forms and reason about them, they are thinking not of these, but of the ideals which they resemble; not of the figures which they draw, but of the absolute square and the absolute diameter, and so on—the forms which they draw or make, and which have shadows and reflections in water of their own, are converted by them into

345   images, but they are really seeking to behold the things themselves, which can only be seen with the eye of the mind?

That is true.

And of this kind I spoke as the intelligible, although in the search after it the soul is compelled to use hypotheses; not ascending to a first principle, because she is unable to rise above the region of hypothesis, but employing the objects of which the shadows below are resemblances in their turn as images, they having in relation to the shadows and reflections of them a greater distinctness, and therefore a higher value.

I understand, he said, that you are speaking of the province of geometry and the sister arts.

And when I speak of the other division of the intelligible, you will understand me to speak of that other sort of knowledge which reason herself attains by the power of dialectic, using the hypotheses not as first principles, but only as hypotheses—that is to say, as steps and points of departure into a world which is above hypotheses, in order that she may soar beyond them to the first principle of the whole; and clinging to this and then to that which depends on this, by successive steps she descends again without the aid of any sensible object, from ideas, through ideas, and in ideas she ends.

I understand you, he replied; not perfectly, for you seem to me to be describing a task which is really tremendous; but, at any rate, I understand you to say that knowledge and being, which the science of dialectic contemplates, are clearer than the notions of the arts, as they are termed, which proceed from hypotheses only: these are also contemplated by the understanding, and not by the senses: yet, because they start from hypotheses and do not ascend to a principle, those who contemplate them appear to you not to exercise the higher reason upon them, although when a first principle is added to them they are cognizable by the higher reason. And the habit which is concerned with geometry and the cognate sciences I suppose that you would term understanding and not reason, as being intermediate between opinion and reason.

You have quite conceived my meaning, I said; and now, corresponding to these four divisions, let there be four faculties in the soul—reason answering to the highest, understanding to the second, faith (or conviction) to the third, and perception of shadows to the last—and let there be a scale of them, and let us suppose that the several faculties have clearness in the same degree that their objects have truth.

I understand, he replied, and give my assent, and accept your arrangement.

BOOK VII: THE ALLEGORY OF THE CAVE

And now, I said, let me show in a figure how far our nature is enlightened or unenlightened:—Behold! human beings living in an underground den, which has a mouth open towards the light and reaching all along the den; here they have been from their childhood, and have their legs and necks chained so that they cannot move, and can only see before them, being prevented by the chains from turning round their heads. Above and behind them a fire is blazing at a distance, and between the fire and the prisoners there is a raised way; and you will see, if you

390   look, a low wall built along the way, like the screen which marionette players have in front of them, over which they show the puppets.

    I see.

    And do you see, I said, men passing along the wall carrying all sorts of vessels, and statues and figures of animals made of wood and stone and various materials, which appear over the wall? Some of them are talking, others silent.

395   You have shown me a strange image, and they are strange prisoners.

    Like ourselves, I replied; and they see only their own shadows, or the shadows of one another, which the fire throws on the opposite wall of the cave?

    True, he said; how could they see anything but the shadows if they were never allowed to move their heads?

400   And of the objects which are being carried in like manner they would only see the shadows?

    Yes, he said.

    And if they were able to converse with one another, would they not suppose that they were naming what was actually before them?

405   Very true.

    And suppose further that the prison had an echo which came from the other side, would they not be sure to fancy when one of the passers-by spoke that the voice which they heard came from the passing shadow?

    No question, he replied.

410   To them, I said, the truth would be literally nothing but the shadows of the images.

    That is certain.

    And now look again, and see what will naturally follow if the prisoners are released and disabused of their error. At first, when any of them is liberated and

415   compelled suddenly to stand up and turn his neck round and walk and look towards the light, he will suffer sharp pains; the glare will distress him, and he will be unable to see the realities of which in his former state he had seen the shadows; and then conceive some one saying to him, that what he saw before was an illusion, but that now, when he is approaching nearer to being and his eye is

420   turned towards more real existence, he has a clearer vision,—what will be his reply? And you may further imagine that his instructor is pointing to the objects as they pass and requiring him to name them,—will he not be perplexed? Will he not fancy that the shadows which he formerly saw are truer than the objects which are now shown to him?

425   Far truer.

    And if he is compelled to look straight at the light, will he not have a pain in his eyes which will make him turn away to take refuge in the objects of vision which he can see, and which he will conceive to be in reality clearer than the things which are now being shown to him?

430   True, he said.

    And suppose once more, that he is reluctantly dragged up a steep and rugged ascent, and held fast until he is forced into the presence of the sun himself, is he not likely to be pained and irritated? When he approaches the light his eyes will be dazzled, and he will not be able to see anything at all of what are now called

435   realities.

Not all in a moment, he said.

He will require to grow accustomed to the sight of the upper world. And first he will see the shadows best, next the reflections of men and other objects in the water, and then the objects themselves; then he will gaze upon the light of the moon

440   and the stars and the spangled heaven; and he will see the sky and the stars by night better than the sun or the light of the sun by day?

Certainly.

Last of all he will be able to see the sun, and not mere reflections of him in the water, but he will see him in his own proper place, and not in another; and he will

445   contemplate him as he is.

Certainly.

He will then proceed to argue that this is he who gives the season and the years, and is the guardian of all that is in the visible world, and in a certain way the cause of all things which he and his fellows have been accustomed to behold?

450   Clearly, he said, he would first see the sun and then reason about him.

And when he remembered his old habitation, and the wisdom of the den and his fellow-prisoners, do you not suppose that he would felicitate himself on the change, and pity them?

Certainly, he would.

455   And if they were in the habit of conferring honours among themselves on those who were quickest to observe the passing shadows and to remark which of them went before, and which followed after, and which were together; and who were therefore best able to draw conclusions as to the future, do you think that he would care for such honours and glories, or envy the possessors of them? Would

460   he not say with Homer,

"Better to be the poor servant of a poor master,"

and to endure anything, rather than think as they do and live after their manner?

Yes, he said, I think that he would rather suffer anything than entertain these false notions and live in this miserable manner.

465   Imagine once more, I said, such a one coming suddenly out of the sun to be replaced in his old situation; would he not be certain to have his eyes full of darkness?

To be sure, he said.

And if there were a contest, and he had to compete in measuring the shadows

470   with the prisoners who had never moved out of the den, while his sight was still weak, and before his eyes had become steady (and the time which would be needed to acquire this new habit of sight might be very considerable), would he not be ridiculous? Men would say of him that up he went and down he came without his eyes; and that it was better not even to think of ascending; and if any one tried to

475 loose another and lead him up to the light, let them only catch the offender, and
they would put him to death.

No question, he said.

This entire allegory, I said, you may now append, dear Glaucon, to the
previous argument; the prison house is the world of sight, the light of the fire is the
480 sun, and you will not misapprehend me if you interpret the journey upwards to be
the ascent of the soul into the intellectual world according to my poor belief,
which, at your desire, I have expressed—whether rightly or wrongly God knows.
But, whether true or false, my opinion is that in the world of knowledge the idea
of good appears last of all, and is seen only with an effort; and, when seen, is also
485 inferred to be the universal author of all things beautiful and right, parent of light
and of the lord of light in this visible world, and the immediate source of reason
and truth in the intellectual; and that this is the power upon which he who would
act rationally either in public or private life must have his eye fixed.

I agree, he said, as far as I am able to understand you.

490 Moreover, I said, you must not wonder that those who attain to this beatific
vision are unwilling to descend to human affairs; for their souls are ever
hastening into the upper world where they desire to dwell; which desire of theirs
is very natural, if our allegory may be trusted.

Yes, very natural.

495 And is there anything surprising in one who passes from divine
contemplations to the evil state of man, misbehaving himself in a ridiculous
manner; if, while his eyes are blinking and before he has become accustomed to the
surrounding darkness, he is compelled to fight in courts of law, or in other places,
about the images or the shadows of images of justice, and is endeavouring to meet
500 the conceptions of those who have never yet seen absolute justice?

Anything but surprising, he replied.

Any one who has common sense will remember that the bewilderments of the
eyes are of two kinds, and arise from two causes, either from coming out of the
light or from going into the light, which is true of the mind's eye, quite as much as
505 of the bodily eye; and he who remembers this when he sees any one whose vision
is perplexed and weak, will not be too ready to laugh; he will first ask whether
that soul of man has come out of the brighter life, and is unable to see because
unaccustomed to the dark, or having turned from darkness to the day is dazzled by
excess of light. And he will count the one happy in his condition and state of being,
510 and he will pity the other; or, if he has a mind to laugh at the soul which comes
from below into the light, there will be more reason in this than in the laugh which
greets him who returns from above out of the light into the den.

That, he said, is a very just distinction.

But then, if I am right, certain professors of education must be wrong when
515 they say that they can put a knowledge into the soul which was not there before,
like sight into blind eyes.

They undoubtedly say this, he replied.

Whereas, our argument shows that the power and capacity of learning exists in the soul already; and that just as the eye was unable to turn from darkness to
520   light without the whole body, so too the instrument of knowledge can only by the movement of the whole soul be turned from the world of becoming into that of being, and learn by degrees to endure the sight of being, and of the brightest and best of being, or in other words, of the good.

Very true.

525   And must there not be some art which will effect conversion in the easiest and quickest manner; not implanting the faculty of sight, for that exists already, but has been turned in the wrong direction, and is looking away from the truth?

Yes, he said, such an art may be presumed.

And whereas the other so-called virtues of the soul seem to be akin to bodily
530   qualities, for even when they are not originally innate they can be implanted later by habit and exercise, the virtue of wisdom more than anything else contains a divine element which always remains, and by this conversion is rendered useful and profitable; or, on the other hand, hurtful and useless. Did you never observe the narrow intelligence flashing from the keen eye of a clever rogue—how eager he
535   is, how clearly his paltry soul sees the way to his end; he is the reverse of blind, but his keen eye-sight is forced into the service of evil, and he is mischievous in proportion to his cleverness?

Very true, he said.

But what if there had been a circumcision of such natures in the days of their
540   youth; and they had been severed from those sensual pleasures, such as eating and drinking, which, like leaden weights, were attached to them at their birth, and which drag them down and turn the vision of their souls upon the things that are below—if, I say, they had been released from these impediments and turned in the opposite direction, the very same faculty in them would have seen the truth as
545   keenly as they see what their eyes are turned to now.

Very likely.

Yes, I said; and there is another thing which is likely, or rather a necessary inference from what has preceded, that neither the uneducated and uninformed of the truth, nor yet those who never make an end of their education, will be able
550   ministers of State; not the former, because they have no single aim of duty which is the rule of all their actions, private as well as public; nor the latter, because they will not act at all except upon compulsion, fancying that they are already dwelling apart in the islands of the blest.

Very true, he replied.

555   Then, I said, the business of us who are the founders of the State will be to compel the best minds to attain that knowledge which we have already shown to be the greatest of all—they must continue to ascend until they arrive at the good; but when they have ascended and seen enough we must not allow them to do as they do now.

560   What do you mean?

I mean that they remain in the upper world: but this must not be allowed; they must be made to descend again among the prisoners in the den, and partake of their labours and honours, whether they are worth having or not.

565 But is not this unjust? he said; ought we to give them a worse life, when they might have a better?

You have again forgotten, my friend, I said, the intention of the legislator, who did not aim at making any one class in the State happy above the rest; the happiness was to be in the whole State, and he held the citizens together by persuasion and necessity, making them benefactors of the State, and therefore 570 benefactors of one another; to this end he created them, not to please themselves, but to be his instruments in binding up the State.

True, he said, I had forgotten.

BOOK X: THE MYTH OF ER

Well, I said, I will tell you a tale; not one of the tales which Odysseus tells to the hero Alcinous, yet this too is a tale of a hero, Er the son of Armenius, a 575 Pamphylian by birth. He was slain in battle, and ten days afterwards, when the bodies of the dead were taken up already in a state of corruption, his body was found unaffected by decay, and carried away home to be buried. And on the twelfth day, as he was lying on the funeral pyre, he returned to life and told them what he had seen in the other world. He said that when his soul left the body he 580 went on a journey with a great company, and that they came to a mysterious place at which there were two openings in the earth; they were near together, and over against them were two other openings in the heaven above. In the intermediate space there were judges seated, who commanded the just, after they had given judgment on them and had bound their sentences in front of them, to ascend by the 585 heavenly way on the right hand; and in like manner the unjust were bidden by them to descend by the lower way on the left hand; these also bore the symbols of their deeds, but fastened on their backs. He drew near, and they told him that he was to be the messenger who would carry the report of the other world to men, and they bade him hear and see all that was to be heard and seen in that place. 590 Then he beheld and saw on one side the souls departing at either opening of heaven and earth when sentence had been given on them; and at the two other openings other souls, some ascending out of the earth dusty and worn with travel, some descending out of heaven clean and bright. And arriving ever and anon they seemed to have come from a long journey, and they went forth with gladness into 595 the meadow, where they encamped as at a festival; and those who knew one another embraced and conversed, the souls which came from earth curiously enquiring about the things above, and the souls which came from heaven about the things beneath. And they told one another of what had happened by the way, those from below weeping and sorrowing at the remembrance of the things which 600 they had endured and seen in their journey beneath the earth (now the journey lasted a thousand years), while those from above were describing heavenly delights and visions of inconceivable beauty.

The story, Glaucon, would take too long to tell; but the sum was this:—He said that for every wrong which they had done to any one they suffered tenfold; or once in a hundred years—such being reckoned to be the length of man's life, and the penalty being thus paid ten times in a thousand years. If, for example, there were any who had been the cause of many deaths, or had betrayed or enslaved cities or armies, or been guilty of any other evil behaviour, for each and all of their offences they received punishment ten times over, and the rewards of beneficence and justice and holiness were in the same proportion. I need hardly repeat what he said concerning young children dying almost as soon as they were born. Of piety and impiety to gods and parents, and of murderers, there were retributions other and greater far which he described.

He mentioned that he was present when one of the spirits asked another, "Where is Ardiaeus the Great?" (Now this Ardiaeus lived a thousand years before the time of Er: he had been the tyrant of some city of Pamphylia, and had murdered his aged father and his elder brother, and was said to have committed many other abominable crimes.) The answer of the other spirit was: "He comes not hither and will never come. And this," said he, "was one of the dreadful sights which we ourselves witnessed. We were at the mouth of the cavern, and, having completed all our experiences, were about to reascend, when of a sudden Ardiaeus appeared and several others, most of whom were tyrants; and there were also besides the tyrants private individuals who had been great criminals: they were just, as they fancied, about to return into the upper world, but the mouth, instead of admitting them, gave a roar, whenever any of these incurable sinners or some one who had not been sufficiently punished tried to ascend; and then wild men of fiery aspect, who were standing by and heard the sound, seized and carried them off; and Ardiaeus and others they bound head and foot and hand, and threw them down and flayed them with scourges, and dragged them along the road at the side, carding them on thorns like wool, and declaring to the passers-by what were their crimes, and that they were being taken away to be cast into hell." And of all the many terrors which they had endured, he said that there was none like the terror which each of them felt at that moment, lest they should hear the voice; and when there was silence, one by one they ascended with exceeding joy. These, said Er, were the penalties and retributions, and there were blessings as great.

Now when the spirits which were in the meadow had tarried seven days, on the eighth they were obliged to proceed on their journey, and, on the fourth day after, he said that they came to a place where they could see from above a line of light, straight as a column, extending right through the whole heaven and through the earth, in colour resembling the rainbow, only brighter and purer; another day's journey brought them to the place, and there, in the midst of the light, they saw the ends of the chains of heaven let down from above: for this light is the belt of heaven, and holds together the circle of the universe, like the under-girders of a trireme. From these ends is extended the spindle of Necessity, on which all the

645 revolutions turn. The shaft and hook of this spindle are made of steel, and the whorl is made partly of steel and also partly of other materials. Now the whorl is in form like the whorl used on earth; and the description of it implied that there is one large hollow whorl which is quite scooped out, and into this is fitted another lesser one, and another, and another, and four others, making eight in all, like

650 vessels which fit into one another; the whorls show their edges on the upper side, and on their lower side all together form one continuous whorl. This is pierced by the spindle, which is driven home through the centre of the eighth. The first and outermost whorl has the rim broadest, and the seven inner whorls are narrower, in the following proportions—the sixth is next to the first in size, the fourth next

655 to the sixth; then comes the eighth; the seventh is fifth, the fifth is sixth, the third is seventh, last and eighth comes the second. The largest (or fixed stars) is spangled, and the seventh (or sun) is brightest; the eighth (or moon) coloured by the reflected light of the seventh; the second and fifth (Saturn and Mercury) are in colour like one another, and yellower than the preceding; the third (Venus) has the whitest

660 light; the fourth (Mars) is reddish; the sixth (Jupiter) is in whiteness second. Now the whole spindle has the same motion; but, as the whole revolves in one direction, the seven inner circles move slowly in the other, and of these the swiftest is the eighth; next in swiftness are the seventh, sixth, and fifth, which move together; third in swiftness appeared to move according to the law of this reversed motion

665 the fourth; the third appeared fourth and the second fifth. The spindle turns on the knees of Necessity; and on the upper surface of each circle is a siren, who goes round with them, hymning a single tone or note. The eight together form one harmony; and round about, at equal intervals, there is another band, three in number, each sitting upon her throne: these are the Fates, daughters of Necessity,

670 who are clothed in white robes and have chaplets upon their heads, Lachesis and Clotho and Atropos, who accompany with their voices the harmony of the sirens—Lachesis singing of the past, Clotho of the present, Atropos of the future; Clotho from time to time assisting with a touch of her right hand the revolution of the outer circle of the whorl or spindle, and Atropos with her left hand touching

675 and guiding the inner ones, and Lachesis laying hold of either in turn, first with one hand and then with the other.

    When Er and the spirits arrived, their duty was to go at once to Lachesis; but first of all there came a prophet who arranged them in order; then he took from the knees of Lachesis lots and samples of lives, and having mounted a high pulpit,

680 spoke as follows: "Hear the word of Lachesis, the daughter of Necessity. Mortal souls, behold a new cycle of life and mortality. Your genius will not be allotted to you, but you will choose your genius; and let him who draws the first lot have the first choice, and the life which he chooses shall be his destiny. Virtue is free, and as a man honours or dishonours her he will have more or less of her; the

685 responsibility is with the chooser—God is justified." When the Interpreter had thus spoken he scattered lots indifferently among them all, and each of them took up the lot which fell near him, all but Er himself (he was not allowed), and each as he took his lot perceived the number which he had obtained. Then the Interpreter

690 placed on the ground before them the samples of lives; and there were many more lives than the souls present, and they were of all sorts. There were lives of every animal and of man in every condition. And there were tyrannies among them, some lasting out the tyrant's life, others which broke off in the middle and came to an end in poverty and exile and beggary; and there were lives of famous men, some who were famous for their form and beauty as well as for their strength and

695 success in games, or, again, for their birth and the qualities of their ancestors; and some who were the reverse of famous for the opposite qualities. And of women likewise; there was not, however, any definite character in them, because the soul, when choosing a new life, must of necessity become different. But there was every other quality, and they all mingled with one another, and also with elements of

700 wealth and poverty, and disease and health; and there were mean states also.

And here, my dear Glaucon, is the supreme peril of our human state; and therefore the utmost care should be taken. Let each one of us leave every other kind of knowledge and seek and follow one thing only, if peradventure he may be able to learn and may find some one who will make him able to learn and discern

705 between good and evil, and so to choose always and everywhere the better life as he has opportunity. He should consider the bearing of all these things which have been mentioned severally and collectively upon virtue; he should know what the effect of beauty is when combined with poverty or wealth in a particular soul, and what are the good and evil consequences of noble and humble birth, of private

710 and public station, of strength and weakness, of cleverness and dullness, and of all the natural and acquired gifts of the soul, and the operation of them when conjoined; he will then look at the nature of the soul, and from the consideration of all these qualities he will be able to determine which is the better and which is the worse; and so he will choose, giving the name of evil to the life which will make

715 his soul more unjust, and good to the life which will make his soul more just; all else he will disregard. For we have seen and know that this is the best choice both in life and after death. A man must take with him into the world below an adamantine faith in truth and right, that there too he may be undazzled by the desire of wealth or the other allurements of evil, lest, coming upon tyrannies and

720 similar villainies, he do irremediable wrongs to others and suffer yet worse himself; but let him know how to choose the mean and avoid the extremes on either side, as far as possible, not only in this life but in all that which is to come. For this is the way of happiness.

And according to the report of the messenger from the other world this was

725 what the prophet said at the time: "Even for the last comer, if he chooses wisely and will live diligently, there is appointed a happy and not undesirable existence. Let not him who chooses first be careless, and let not the last despair." And when he had spoken, he who had the first choice came forward and in a moment chose the greatest tyranny; his mind having been darkened by folly and sensuality, he

730 had not thought out the whole matter before he chose, and did not at first sight perceive that he was fated, among other evils, to devour his own children. But when he had time to reflect, and saw what was in the lot, he began to beat his

breast and lament over his choice, forgetting the proclamation of the prophet; for, instead of throwing the blame of his misfortune on himself, he accused chance and

735 the gods, and everything rather than himself. Now he was one of those who came from heaven, and in a former life had dwelt in a well-ordered State, but his virtue was a matter of habit only, and he had no philosophy. And it was true of others who were similarly overtaken, that the greater number of them came from heaven and therefore they had never been schooled by trial, whereas the pilgrims who

740 came from earth having themselves suffered and seen others suffer, were not in a hurry to choose. And owing to this inexperience of theirs, and also because the lot was a chance, many of the souls exchanged a good destiny for an evil or an evil for a good. For if a man had always on his arrival in this world dedicated himself from the first to sound philosophy, and had been moderately fortunate in the

745 number of the lot, he might, as the messenger reported, be happy here, and also his journey to another life and return to this, instead of being rough and underground, would be smooth and heavenly.

Most curious, he said, was the spectacle—sad and laughable and strange; for the choice of the souls was in most cases based on their experience of a previous

750 life. There he saw the soul which had once been Orpheus choosing the life of a swan out of enmity to the race of women, hating to be born of a woman because they had been his murderers; he beheld also the soul of Thamyras choosing the life of a nightingale; birds, on the other hand, like the swan and other musicians, wanting to be men. The soul which obtained the twentieth lot chose the life of a

755 lion, and this was the soul of Ajax the son of Telamon, who would not be a man, remembering the injustice which was done him in the judgment about the arms. The next was Agamemnon, who took the life of an eagle, because, like Ajax, he hated human nature by reason of his sufferings. About the middle came the lot of Atalanta; she, seeing the great fame of an athlete, was unable to resist the

760 temptation: and after her there followed the soul of Epeus the son of Panopeus passing into the nature of a woman cunning in the arts; and far away among the last who chose, the soul of the jester Thersites was putting on the form of a monkey. There came also the soul of Odysseus having yet to make a choice, and his lot happened to be the last of them all. Now the recollection of former toils had

765 disenchanted him of ambition, and he went about for a considerable time in search of the life of a private man who had no cares; he had some difficulty in finding this, which was lying about and had been neglected by everybody else; and when he saw it, he said that he would have done the same had his lot been first instead of last, and that he was delighted to have it. And not only did men pass into animals,

770 but I must also mention that there were animals tame and wild who changed into one another and into corresponding human natures—the good into the gentle and the evil into the savage, in all sorts of combinations.

All the souls had now chosen their lives, and they went in the order of their choice to Lachesis, who sent with them the genius whom they had severally

775 chosen, to be the guardian of their lives and the fulfiller of the choice: this genius led the souls first to Clotho, and drew them within the revolution of the spindle

impelled by her hand, thus ratifying the destiny of each; and then, when they were fastened to this, carried them to Atropos, who spun the threads and made them irreversible, whence without turning round they passed beneath the throne of

780   Necessity; and when they had all passed, they marched on in a scorching heat to the plain of Forgetfulness, which was a barren waste destitute of trees and verdure; and then towards evening they encamped by the river of Unmindfulness, whose water no vessel can hold; of this they were all obliged to drink a certain quantity, and those who were not saved by wisdom drank more than was

785   necessary; and each one as he drank forgot all things. Now after they had gone to rest, about the middle of the night there was a thunderstorm and earthquake, and then in an instant they were driven upwards in all manner of ways to their birth, like stars shooting. He himself was hindered from drinking the water. But in what manner or by what means he returned to the body he could not say; only, in the

790   morning, awaking suddenly, he found himself lying on the pyre.

And thus, Glaucon, the tale has been saved and has not perished, and will save us if we are obedient to the word spoken; and we shall pass safely over the river of Forgetfulness and our soul will not be defiled. Wherefore my counsel is, that we hold fast ever to the heavenly way and follow after justice and virtue

795   always, considering that the soul is immortal and able to endure every sort of good and every sort of evil. Thus shall we live dear to one another and to the gods, both while remaining here and when, like conquerors in the games who go round to gather gifts, we receive our reward. And it shall be well with us both in this life and in the pilgrimage of a thousand years which we have been describing.

III: ROME

13. ON FRIENDSHIP (EXCERPTS)

Cicero
(106 BCE–43 BCE)

(trans. by Evelyn S. Shuckburgh)

Marcus Tullius Cicero was involved in the major political turmoils of the Roman Republic as statesman, orator, philosopher, lawyer, and man of letters. He composed and delivered political speeches, wrote treatises on the art of writing and speaking, wrote personal letters which to this day stand as a rich source of the life and times of the late Roman Republic, and wrote philosophical essays, of which On Friendship *is one. Composed a year before Cicero's death, the dialogue is purportedly a discourse delivered by one Laelius, upon the death of his friend, Scipio Africanus. The discussion covers the origins, nature, and obligations of friendship, all the while demonstrating that a friendship is only as good as the persons involved.*

PART I

The augur Quintus Mucius Scaevola used to recount a number of stories about his father-in-law, Gaius Laelius, accurately remembered and charmingly told; and whenever he talked about him always gave him the title of "the wise" without any hesitation. I had been introduced by my father to Scaevola as soon as
5   I had assumed the toga virilis,[1] and I took advantage of the introduction never to quit the venerable man's side as long as I was able to stay and he was spared to us. The consequence was that I committed to memory many disquisitions of his, as well as many short pointed apophthegms,[2] and, in short, took as much advantage of his wisdom as I could. When he died, I attached myself to Scaevola the Pontifex,
10   whom I may venture to call quite the most distinguished of our countrymen for ability and uprightness. But of this latter I shall take other occasions to speak.

To return to Scaevola the augur: Among many other occasions I particularly remember one. He was sitting on a semicircular garden-bench, as was his custom, when I and a very few intimate friends were there, and he chanced to turn the
15   conversation upon a subject which about that time was in many people's mouths.

---

[1]**toga virilis**: the dress of a man
[2]**apophthegms (apothegm)**: a concise, pithy statement; a maxim

You must remember, Atticus,[3] for you were very intimate with Publius Sulpicius, what expressions of astonishment, or even indignation, were called forth by his mortal quarrel, as tribune, with the consul Quintus Pompeius, with whom he had formerly lived on terms of the closest intimacy and affection. Well, on this occasion, happening to mention this particular circumstance, Scaevola detailed to us a discourse of Laelius on friendship delivered to himself and Laelius' other son-in-law, Gaius Fannius, son of Marcus Fannius, a few days after the death of Africanus.[4] The points of that discussion I committed to memory, and have arranged them in this book at my own discretion. For I have brought the speakers, as it were, personally on to my stage to prevent the constant "said I" and "said he" of a narrative, and to give the discourse the air of being orally delivered in our hearing.

You have often urged me to write something on Friendship, and I quite acknowledged that the subject seemed one worth everybody's investigation, and specially suited to the close intimacy that has existed between you and me. Accordingly I was quite ready to benefit the public at your request.

As to the dramatis personae: In the treatise On Old Age,[5] which I dedicated to you, I introduced Cato as chief speaker. No one, I thought, could with greater propriety speak on old age than one who had been an old man longer than any one else, and had been exceptionally vigorous in his old age. Similarly, having learnt from tradition that of all friendships that between Gaius Laelius and Publius Scipio was the most remarkable, I thought Laelius was just the person to support the chief part in a discussion on friendship which Scaevola remembered him to have actually taken. Moreover, a discussion of this sort gains somehow in weight from the authority of men of ancient days, especially if they happen to have been distinguished. So it comes about that in reading over what I have myself written I have a feeling at times that it is actually Cato that is speaking, not I. . . .

* * *

. . . Scaevola: Well, then, what about friendship? Who could discourse on it more easily than the man whose chief glory is a friendship maintained with the most absolute fidelity, constancy, and integrity?

PART II

8. Laelius: Now you are really using force. It makes no difference what kind of force you use: force it is. For it is neither easy nor right to refuse a wish of my sons-in-law, particularly when the wish is a creditable one in itself. Well, then, it has very often occurred to me when thinking about friendship, that the chief point to be considered was this: is it weakness and want of means that make friendship desired? I mean, is its object an interchange of good offices, so that each may give

---

[3]**Atticus:** Cicero's good friend to whom he addressed many letters.
[4]**Africanus:** Scipio Africanus, a skilled Roman general who gained fame in the Punic Wars.
[5]**On Old Age:** another of Cicero's philosophical essays

that in which he is strong, and receive that in which he is weak? Or is it not rather true that, although this is an advantage naturally belonging to friendship, yet its original cause is quite other, prior in time, more noble in character, and
55 springing more directly from our nature itself? The Latin word for friendship—amicitia—is derived from that for love—amor; and love is certainly the prime mover in contracting mutual affection. For as to material advantages, it often happens that those are obtained even by men who are courted by a mere show of friendship and treated with respect from interested motives. But friendship by its
60 nature admits of no feigning, no pretence: as far as it goes it is both genuine and spontaneous. Therefore I gather that friendship springs from a natural impulse rather than a wish for help: from an inclination of the heart, combined with a certain instinctive feeling of love, rather than from a deliberate calculation of the material advantage it was likely to confer. The strength of this feeling you may
65 notice in certain animals. They show such love to their offspring for a certain period, and are so beloved by them, that they clearly have a share in this natural, instinctive affection. But of course it is more evident in the case of man: first, in the natural affection between children and their parents, an affection which only shocking wickedness can sunder: and next, when the passion of love has attained
70 to a like strength—on our finding, that is, some one person with whose character and nature we are in full sympathy, because we think that we perceive in him what I may call the beacon-light of virtue.

For nothing inspires love, nothing conciliates affection, like virtue. Why, in a certain sense we may be said to feel affection even for men we have never seen,
75 owing to their honesty and virtue. Who, for instance, fails to dwell on the memory of Gaius Fabricius and Manius Curius with some affection and warmth of feeling, though he has never seen them? Or who but loathes Tarquinius Superbus, Spurius Cassius, Spurius Maelius? We have fought for empire in Italy with two great generals, Pyrrhus and Hannibal. For the former, owing to his probity, we
80 entertain no great feelings of enmity: the latter, owing to his cruelty, our country has detested and always will detest.

9. Now, if the attraction of probity is so great that we can love it not only in those whom we have never seen, but, what is more, actually in an enemy, we need not be surprised if men's affections are roused when they fancy that they have seen
85 virtue and goodness in those with whom a close intimacy is possible. I do not deny that affection is strengthened by the actual receipt of benefits, as well as by the perception of a wish to render service, combined with a closer intercourse. When these are added to the original impulse of the heart, to which I have alluded, a quite surprising warmth of feeling springs up. And if any one thinks that this
90 comes from a sense of weakness, that each may have some one to help him to his particular need, all I can say is that, when he maintains it to be born of want and poverty, he allows to friendship an origin very base, and a pedigree, if I may be allowed the expression, far from noble. If this had been the case, a man's inclination to friendship would be exactly in proportion to his low opinion of his
95 own resources. Whereas the truth is quite the other way. For when a man's

confidence in himself is greatest, when he is so fortified by virtue and wisdom as to want nothing and to feel absolutely self-dependent, it is then that he is most conspicuous for seeking out and keeping up friendships. Did Africanus, for example, want anything of me? Not the least in the world! Neither did I of him. In 100 my case it was an admiration of his virtue, in his an opinion, maybe, which he entertained of my character, that caused our affection. Closer intimacy added to the warmth of our feelings. But though many great material advantages did ensue, they were not the source from which our affection proceeded. For as we are not beneficent and liberal with any view of extorting gratitude, and do not regard an 105 act of kindness as an investment, but follow a natural inclination to liberality; so we look on friendship as worth trying for, not because we are attracted to it by the expectation of ulterior gain, but in the conviction that what it has to give us is from first to last included in the feeling itself.

Far different is the view of those who, like brute beasts, refer everything to 110 sensual pleasure. And no wonder. Men who have degraded all their powers of thought to an object so mean and contemptible can of course raise their eyes to nothing lofty, to nothing grand and divine. Such persons indeed let us leave out of the present question.

And let us accept the doctrine that the sensation of love and the warmth of 115 inclination have their origin in a spontaneous feeling which arises directly when the presence of probity is indicated. When once men have conceived the inclination, they of course try to attach themselves to the object of it, and move themselves nearer and nearer to him. Their aim is that they may be on the same footing and the same level in regard to affection, and be more inclined to do a good 120 service than to ask a return, and that there should be this noble rivalry between them. Thus both truths will be established. We shall get the most important material advantages from friendship; and its origin from a natural impulse rather than from a sense of need will be at once more dignified and more in accordance with fact. For if it were true that its material advantages cemented friendship, it 125 would be equally true that any change in them would dissolve it. But nature being incapable of change, it follows that genuine friendships are eternal.

So much for the origin of friendship. But perhaps you would not care to hear any more.

Fannius: Nay, pray go on; let us have the rest, Laelius. I take on myself to 130 speak for my friend here as his senior.

Scaevola: Quite right! Therefore, pray let us hear.

10. Laelius: Well, then, my good friends, listen to some conversations about friendship which very frequently passed between Scipio and myself. I must begin by telling you, however, that he used to say that the most difficult thing in the 135 world was for a friendship to remain unimpaired to the end of life. So many things might intervene: conflicting interests; differences of opinion in politics; frequent changes in character, owing sometimes to misfortunes, sometimes to advancing years. He used to illustrate these facts from the analogy of boyhood, since the warmest affections between boys are often laid aside with the boyish toga; and

140   even if they did manage to keep them up to adolescence, they were sometimes broken by a rivalry in courtship, or for some other advantage to which their mutual claims were not compatible. Even if the friendship was prolonged beyond that time, yet it frequently received a rude shock should the two happen to be competitors for office. For while the most fatal blow to friendship in the majority

145   of cases was the lust of gold, in the case of the best men it was a rivalry for office and reputation, by which it had often happened that the most violent enmity had arisen between the closest friends.

    Again, wide breaches and, for the most part, justifiable ones were caused by an immoral request being made of friends, to pander to a man's unholy desires or to

150   assist him in inflicting a wrong. A refusal, though perfectly right, is attacked by those to whom they refuse compliance as a violation of the laws of friendship. Now the people who have no scruples as to the requests they make to their friends, thereby allow that they are ready to have no scruples as to what they will do for their friends; and it is the recriminations of such people which commonly not only

155   quench friendships, but give rise to lasting enmities. "In fact," he used to say, "these fatalities overhang friendship in such numbers that it requires not only wisdom but good luck also to escape them all."

    11. With these premises, then, let us first, if you please, examine the question— how far ought personal feeling to go in friendship? For instance: suppose

160   Coriolanus to have had friends, ought they to have joined him in invading his country? Again, in the case of Vecellinus or Spurius Maelius, ought their friends to have assisted them in their attempt to establish a tyranny? Take two instances of either line of conduct. When Tiberius Gracchus attempted his revolutionary measures he was deserted, as we saw, by Quintus Tubero and the friends of his

165   own standing. On the other hand, a friend of your own family, Scaevola, Gaius Blossius of Cumae, took a different course. I was acting as assessor to the consuls Laenas and Rupilius to try the conspirators, and Blossius pleaded for my pardon on the ground that his regard for Tiberius Gracchus had been so high that he looked upon his wishes as law. "Even if he had wished you to set fire to the

170   Capitol?" said I. "That is a thing," he replied, "that he never would have wished." "Ah, but if he had wished it?" said I. "I would have obeyed." The wickedness of such a speech needs no comment. And in point of fact he was as good and better than his word; for he did not wait for orders in the audacious proceedings of Tiberius Gracchus, but was the head and front of them, and was a

175   leader rather than an abettor of his madness. The result of his infatuation was that he fled to Asia, terrified by the special commission appointed to try him, joined the enemies of his country, and paid a penalty to the republic as heavy as it was deserved. I conclude, then, that the plea of having acted in the interests of a friend is not a valid excuse for a wrong action. For, seeing that a belief in a man's

180   virtue is the original cause of friendship, friendship can hardly remain if virtue be abandoned.

    But if we decide it to be right to grant our friends whatever they wish, and to ask them for whatever we wish, perfect wisdom must be assumed on both sides if

185

190

195

200

no mischief is to happen. But we cannot assume this perfect wisdom; for we are speaking only of such friends as are ordinarily to be met with, whether we have actually seen them or have been told about them—men, that is to say, of everyday life. I must quote some examples of such persons, taking care to select such as approach nearest to our standard of wisdom. We read, for instance, that Papus Aemilius was a close friend of Gaius Luscinus. History tells us that they were twice consuls together, and colleagues in the censorship. Again, it is on record that Manius Curius and Tiberius Coruncanius were on the most intimate terms with them and with each other. Now, we cannot even suspect that any one of these men ever asked of his friend anything that militated against his honour or his oath or the interests of the republic. In the case of such men as these there is no point in saying that one of them would not have obtained such a request if he had made it; for they were men of the most scrupulous piety, and the making of such a request would involve a breach of religious obligation no less than the granting it. However, it is quite true that Gaius Carbo and Gaius Cato did follow Tiberius Gracchus; and though his brother Gaius Gracchus did not do so at the time, he is now the most eager of them all.

205

210

215

220

225

12. We may then lay down this rule of friendship—neither ask nor consent to do what is wrong. For the plea "for friendship's sake" is a discreditable one, and not to be admitted for a moment. This rule holds good for all wrong-doing, but more especially in such as involves disloyalty to the republic. For things have come to such a point with us, my dear Fannius and Scaevola, that we are bound to look somewhat far ahead to what is likely to happen to the republic. The constitution, as known to our ancestors, has already swerved somewhat from the regular course and the lines marked out for it. Tiberius Gracchus made an attempt to obtain the power of a king, or, I might rather say, enjoyed that power for a few months. Had the Roman people ever heard or seen the like before? What the friends and connexions that followed him, even after his death, have succeeded in doing in the case of Publius Scipio I cannot describe without tears. As for Carbo, thanks to the punishment recently inflicted on Tiberius Gracchus, we have by hook or by crook managed to hold out against his attacks. But what to expect of the tribuneship of Gaius Gracchus I do not like to forecast. One thing leads to another; and once set going, the downward course proceeds with ever-increasing velocity. There is the case of the ballot: what a blow was inflicted first by the lex Gabinia, and two years afterwards by the lex Cassia! I seem already to see the people estranged from the Senate, and the most important affairs at the mercy of the multitude. For you may be sure that more people will learn how to set such things in motion than how to stop them. What is the point of these remarks? This: no one ever makes any attempt of this sort without friends to help him. We must therefore impress upon good men that, should they become inevitably involved in friendships with men of this kind, they ought not to consider themselves under any obligation to stand by friends who are disloyal to the republic. Bad men must have the fear of punishment before their eyes: a punishment not less severe for those who follow than for those who lead others to crime. Who was more famous and

powerful in Greece than Themistocles? At the head of the army in the Persian war
he had freed Greece; he owed his exile to personal envy: but he did not submit to
230   the wrong done him by his ungrateful country as he ought to have done. He acted
as Coriolanus had acted among us twenty years before. But no one was found to
help them in their attacks upon their fatherland. Both of them accordingly
committed suicide.

We conclude, then, not only that no such confederation of evilly disposed men
235   must be allowed to shelter itself under the plea of friendship, but that, on the
contrary, it must be visited with the severest punishment, lest the idea should
prevail that fidelity to a friend justifies even making war upon one's country. And
this is a case which I am inclined to think, considering how things are beginning to
go, will sooner or later arise. And I care quite as much what the state of the
240   constitution will be after my death as what it is now.

13. Let this, then, be laid down as the first law of friendship, that we should
ask from friends, and do for friends, only what is good. But do not let us wait to be
asked either: let there be ever an eager readiness, and an absence of hesitation. Let
us have the courage to give advice with candour. In friendship, let the influence of
245   friends who give good advice be paramount; and let this influence be used to
enforce advice not only in plain-spoken terms, but sometimes, if the case demands
it, with sharpness; and when so used, let it be obeyed.

I give you these rules because I believe that some wonderful opinions are
entertained by certain persons who have, I am told, a reputation for wisdom in
250   Greece. There is nothing in the world, by the way, beyond the reach of their
sophistry. Well, some of them teach that we should avoid very close friendships,
for fear that one man should have to endure the anxieties of several. Each man, say
they, has enough and to spare on his own hands; it is too bad to be involved in the
cares of other people. The wisest course is to hold the reins of friendship as loose
255   as possible; you can then tighten or slacken them at your will. For the first
condition of a happy life is freedom from care, which no one's mind can enjoy if it
has to travail, so to speak, for others besides itself.

Another sect, I am told, gives vent to opinions still less generous. I briefly
touched on this subject just now. They affirm that friendships should be sought
260   solely for the sake of the assistance they give, and not at all from motives of feeling
and affection; and that therefore just in proportion as a man's power and means of
support are lowest, he is most eager to gain friendships: thence it comes that weak
women seek the support of friendship more than men, the poor more than the rich,
the unfortunate rather than those esteemed prosperous. What noble philosophy!
265   You might just as well take the sun out of the sky as friendship from life; for the
immortal gods have given us nothing better or more delightful.

But let us examine the two doctrines. What is the value of this *freedom from
care*? It is very tempting at first sight, but in practice it has in many cases to be put
on one side. For there is no business and no course of action demanded from us by
270   our honour which you can consistently decline, or lay aside when begun, from a
mere wish to escape from anxiety. Nay, if we wish to avoid anxiety we must avoid

virtue itself, which necessarily involves some anxious thoughts in showing its loathing and abhorrence for the qualities which are opposite to itself—as kindness for ill nature, self-control for licentiousness, courage for cowardice.
275 Thus you may notice that it is the just who are most pained at injustice, the brave at cowardly actions, the temperate at depravity. It is then characteristic of a rightly ordered mind to be pleased at what is good and grieved at the reverse. Seeing then that the wise are not exempt from the heart-ache (which must be the case unless we suppose all human nature rooted out of their hearts), why should
280 we banish friendship from our lives, for fear of being involved by it in some amount of distress?

If you take away emotion, what difference remains I don't say between a man and a beast, but between a man and a stone or a log of wood, or anything else of that kind?

285 Neither should we give any weight to the doctrine that virtue is something rigid and unyielding as iron. In point of fact it is in regard to friendship, as in so many other things, so supple and sensitive that it expands, so to speak, at a friend's good fortune, contracts at his misfortunes. We conclude then that mental pain which we must often encounter on a friend's account is not of sufficient
290 consequence to banish friendship from our life, any more than it is true that the cardinal virtues are to be dispensed with because they involve certain anxieties and distresses.

14. Let me repeat then, *the clear indication of virtue, to which a mind of like character is naturally attracted, is the beginning of friendship.* When that is the case
295 the rise of affection is a necessity. For what can be more irrational than to take delight in many objects incapable of response, such as office, fame, splendid buildings, and personal decoration, and yet to take little or none in a sentient being endowed with virtue, which has the faculty of loving or, if I may use the expression, loving back? For nothing is really more delightful than a return of
300 affection, and the mutual interchange of kind feeling and good offices. And if we add, as we may fairly do, that nothing so powerfully attracts and draws one thing to itself as likeness does to friendship, it will at once be admitted to be true that the good love the good and attach them to themselves as though they were united by blood and nature. For nothing can be more eager, or rather greedy, for what is
305 like itself than nature. So, my dear Fannius and Scaevola, we may look upon this as an established fact, that between good men there is, as it were of necessity, a kindly feeling, which is the source of friendship ordained by nature. But this same kindliness affects the many also. For that is no unsympathetic or selfish or exclusive virtue, which protects even whole nations and consults their best
310 interests. And that certainly it would not have done had it disdained all affection for the common herd.

Again, the believers in the *interest* theory appear to me to destroy the most attractive link in the chain of friendship. For it is not so much what one gets by a friend that gives one pleasure, as the warmth of his feeling; and we only care for a
315 friend's service if it has been prompted by affection. And so far from its being true

that lack of means is a motive for seeking friendship, it is usually those who, being most richly endowed with wealth and means, and above all with virtue (which, after all, is a man's best support), are least in need of another, that are most open-handed and beneficent. Indeed I am inclined to think that friends ought at times to be in want of something. For instance, what scope would my affections have had if Scipio had never wanted my advice or co-operation at home or abroad? It is not friendship, then, that follows material advantage, but material advantage friendship.

15. We must not therefore listen to these superfine gentlemen when they talk of friendship, which they know neither in theory nor in practice. For who, in heaven's name, would choose a life of the greatest wealth and abundance on condition of neither loving or being be loved by any creature? That is the sort of life tyrants endure. They, of course, can count on no fidelity, no affection, no security for the good will of any one. For them all is suspicion and anxiety; for them there is no possibility of friendship. Who can love one whom he fears, or by whom he knows that he is feared? Yet such men have a show of friendship offered them, but it is only a fair-weather show. If it ever happens that they fall, as it generally does, they will at once understand how friendless they are. So they say Tarquin observed in his exile that he never knew which of his friends were real and which sham, until he had ceased to be able to repay either. Though what surprises me is that a man of his proud and overbearing character should have a friend at all. And as it was his character that prevented his having genuine friends, so it often happens in the case of men of unusually great means—their very wealth forbids faithful friendships. For not only is Fortune blind herself; but she generally makes those blind also who enjoy her favours. They are carried, so to speak, beyond themselves with self-conceit and self-will; nor can anything be more perfectly intolerable than a successful fool. You may often see it. Men who before had pleasant manners enough undergo a complete change on attaining power of office. They despise their old friends: devote themselves to new.

Now, can anything be more foolish than that men who have all the opportunities which prosperity, wealth, and great means can bestow, should secure all else which money can buy—horses, servants, splendid upholstering, and costly plate—but do not secure friends, who are, if I may use the expression, the most valuable and beautiful furniture of life? And yet, when they acquire the former, they know not who will enjoy them, nor for whom they may be taking all this trouble; for they will one and all eventually belong to the strongest: while each man has a stable and inalienable ownership in his friendships. And even if those possessions, which are, in a manner, the gifts of fortune, do prove permanent, life can never be anything but joyless which is without the consolations and companionship of friends.

16. To turn to another branch of our subject: We must now endeavour to ascertain what limits are to be observed in friendship—what is the boundary-line, so to speak, beyond which our affection is not to go. On this point I notice three opinions, with none of which I agree. One is that we should love our friend

360 just as much as we love ourselves, and no more; another, that our affection to friends, should exactly correspond and equal theirs to us; a third, that a man should be valued at exactly the same rate as he values himself. To not one of these opinions do I assent. The first, which holds that our regard for ourselves is to be the measure of our regard for our friend, is not true; for how many things there are
365 which we would never have done for our own sakes, but do for the sake of a friend! We submit to make requests from unworthy people, to descend even to supplication; to be sharper in invective, more violent in attack. Such actions are not creditable in our own interests, but highly so in those of our friends. There are many advantages too which men of upright character voluntarily forgo, or of
370 which they are content to be deprived, that their friends may enjoy them rather than themselves.

The second doctrine is that which limits friendship to an exact equality in mutual good offices and good feelings. But such a view reduces friendship to a question of figures in a spirit far too narrow and illiberal, as though the object
375 were to have an exact balance in a debtor and creditor account. True friendship appears to me to be something richer and more generous than that comes to; and not to be so narrowly on its guard against giving more than it receives. In such a matter we must not be always afraid of something being wasted or running over in our measure, or of more than is justly due being devoted to our friendship.

380 But the last limit proposed is the worst, namely, that a friend's estimate of himself is to be the measure of our estimate of him. It often happens that a man has too humble an idea of himself, or takes too despairing a view of his chance of bettering his fortune. In such a case a friend ought not to take the view of him which he takes of himself. Rather he should do all he can to raise his drooping
385 spirits, and lead him to more cheerful hopes and thoughts.

We must then find some other limit. But I must first mention the sentiment which used to call forth Scipio's severest criticism. He often said that no one ever gave utterance to anything more diametrically opposed to the spirit of friendship than the author of the dictum, "You should love your friend with the
390 consciousness that you may one day hate him." He could not be induced to believe that it was rightfully attributed to Aias, who was counted as one of the Seven Sages. It was the sentiment of some person with sinister motives or selfish ambition, or who regarded everything as it affected his own supremacy. How can a man be friends with another, if he thinks it possible that he may be his enemy?
395 Why, it will follow that he must wish and desire his friend to commit as many mistakes as possible, that he may have all the more handles against him; and, conversely, that he must be annoyed, irritated, and jealous at the right actions or good fortune of his friends.

This maxim, then, let it be whose it will, is the utter destruction of friendship.
400 The true rule is to take such care in the selection of our friends as never to enter upon a friendship with a man whom we could under any circumstances come to hate. And even if we are unlucky in our choice, we must put up with it—according to Scipio—in preference to making calculations as to a future breach.

17. The real limit to be observed in friendship is this: the characters of two friends must be stainless. There must be complete harmony of interests, purpose, and aims, without exception. Then if the case arises of a friend's wish (not strictly right in itself) calling for support in a matter involving his life or reputation, we must make some concession from the straight path on condition, that is to say, that extreme disgrace is not the consequence. Something must be conceded to friendship. And yet we must not be entirely careless of our reputation, nor regard the good opinion of our fellow-citizens as a weapon which we can afford to despise in conducting the business of our life, however lowering it may be to tout for it by flattery and smooth words. We must by no means abjure virtue, which secures us affection.

But to return again to Scipio, the sole author of the discourse on friendship: He used to complain that there was nothing on which men bestowed so little pains: that every one could tell exactly how many goats or sheep he had, but not how many friends; and while they took pains in procuring the former, they were utterly careless in selecting friends, and possessed no particular marks, so to speak, or tokens by which they might judge of their suitability for friendship.

Now the qualities we ought to look out for in making our selection are firmness, stability, constancy. There is a plentiful lack of men so endowed, and it is difficult to form a judgment without testing. Now this testing can only be made during the actual existence of the friendship; for friendship so often precedes the formation of a judgment, and makes a previous test impossible. If we are prudent then, we shall rein in our impulse to affection as we do chariot horses. We make a preliminary trial of horses. So we should of friendship; and should test our friends' characters by a kind of tentative friendship.

It may often happen that the untrustworthiness of certain men is completely displayed in a small money matter; others who are proof against a small sum are detected if it be large. But even if some are found who think it mean to prefer money to friendship, where shall we look for those who put friendship before office, civil or military promotions, and political power, and who, when the choice lies between these things on the one side and the claims of friendship on the other, do not give a strong preference to the former? It is not in human nature to be indifferent to political power; and if the price men have to pay for it is the sacrifice of friendship, they think their treason will be thrown into the shade by the magnitude of the reward. This is why true friendship is very difficult to find among those who engage in politics and the contest for office. Where can you find the man to prefer his friend's advancement to his own? And to say nothing of that, think how grievous and almost intolerable it is to most men to share political disaster. You will scarcely find any one who can bring himself to do that. And though what Ennius says is quite true,—"the hour of need shews the friend indeed,"—yet it is in these two ways that most people betray their untrustworthiness and inconstancy, by looking down on friends when they are themselves prosperous, or deserting them in their distress. A man, then, who has shewn a firm, unshaken, and unvarying friendship in both these contingencies we must reckon as one of a class the rarest in the world, and all but superhuman.

PART III

450

18. Now what is the quality to look out for as a warrant for the stability and permanence of friendship? It is loyalty. Nothing that lacks this can be stable. We should also in making our selection look out for simplicity, a social disposition, and a sympathetic nature, moved by what moves us. These all contribute to maintain loyalty.

455

460

You can never trust a character which is intricate and tortuous. Nor, indeed, is it possible for one to be trustworthy and firm who is unsympathetic by nature and unmoved by what affects ourselves. We may add, that he must neither take pleasure in bringing accusations against us himself, nor believe them when they are brought. All these contribute to form that constancy which I have been endeavouring to describe. And the result is, what I started by saying, that friendship is only possible between good men.

465

470

Now there are two characteristic features in his treatment of his friends that a good (which may be regarded as equivalent to a wise) man will always display. First, he will be entirely without any make-believe or pretence of feeling; for the open display even of dislike is more becoming to an ingenuous character than a studied concealment of sentiment. Secondly, he will not only reject all accusations brought against his friend by another, but he will not be suspicious himself either, nor be always thinking that his friend has acted improperly. Besides this, there should be a certain pleasantness in word and manner which adds no little flavour to friendship. A gloomy temper and unvarying gravity may be very impressive; but friendship should be a little less unbending, more indulgent and gracious, and more inclined to all kinds of good-fellowship and good nature.

475

480

485

19. But here arises a question of some little difficulty. Are there any occasions on which, assuming their worthiness, we should prefer new to old friends, just as we prefer young to aged horses? The answer admits of no doubt whatever. For there should be no satiety in friendship, as there is in other things. The older the sweeter, as in wines that keep well. And the proverb is a true one, "You must eat many a peck of salt with a man to be thorough friends with him." Novelty, indeed, has its advantage, which we must not despise. There is always hope of fruit, as there is in healthy blades of corn. But age too must have its proper position; and, in fact, the influence of time and habit is very great. To recur to the illustration of the horse which I have just now used: Every one likes (*ceteris paribus*)[6] to use the horse to which he has been accustomed, rather than one that is untried and new. And it is not only in the case of a living thing that this rule holds good, but in inanimate things also; for we like places where we have lived the longest, even though they are mountainous and covered with forest.

---

[6]**ceteris paribus**: all things being equal

But here is another golden rule in friendship: put yourself on a level with your friend. For it often happens that there are certain superiorities, as for example Scipio's in what I may call our set. Now he never assumed any airs of superiority over Philus, or Rupilius, or Mummius, or over friends of a lower rank still. For instance, he always shewed a deference to his brother Quintus Maximus because he was his senior, who, though a man no doubt of eminent character, was by no means his equal. He used also to wish that all his friends should be the better for his support. This is an example we should all follow. If any of us have any advantage in personal character, intellect, or fortune, we should be ready to make our friends sharers and partners in it with ourselves. For instance, if their parents are in humble circumstances, if their relations are powerful neither in intellect nor means, we should supply their deficiencies and promote their rank and dignity.

You know the legends of children brought up as servants in ignorance of their parentage and family. When they are recognised and discovered to be the sons of gods or kings, they still retain their affection for the shepherds whom they have for many years looked upon as their parents. Much more ought this to be so in the case of real and undoubted parents. For the advantages of genius and virtue, and in short of every kind of superiority, are never realised to their fullest extent until they are bestowed upon our nearest and dearest.

20. But the converse must also be observed. For in friendship and relationship, just as those who possess any superiority must put themselves on an equal footing with those who are less fortunate, so these latter must not be annoyed at being surpassed in genius, fortune, or rank. But most people of that sort are for ever either grumbling at something, or harping on their claims; and especially if they consider that they have services of their own to allege involving zeal and friendship and some trouble to themselves. People who are always bringing up their services are a nuisance. The recipient ought to remember them; the performer should never mention them. In the case of friends, then, as the superior are bound to descend, so are they bound in a certain sense to raise those below them. For there are people who make their friendship disagreeable by imagining themselves undervalued. This generally happens only to those who think that they deserve to be so; and they ought to be shewn by deeds as well as by words the groundlessness of their opinion.

Now the measure of your benefits should be in the first place your own power to bestow, and in the second place the capacity to bear them on the part of him on whom you are bestowing affection and help. For, however great your personal prestige may be, you cannot raise all your friends to the highest offices of the State. For instance, Scipio was able to make Publius Rupilius consul, but not his brother Lucius. But granting that you can give any one anything you choose, you must have a care that it does not prove to be beyond his powers.

As a general rule, we must wait to make up our mind about friendships till men's characters and years have arrived at their full strength and development. People must not, for instance, regard as fast friends all whom in their youthful

530 enthusiasm for hunting or football they liked for having the same tastes. By that rule, if it were a mere question of time, no one would have such claims on our affections as nurses and slave-tutors. Not that they are to be neglected, but they stand on a different ground. It is only these mature friendships that can be permanent. For difference of character leads to difference of aims, and the result of

535 such diversity is to estrange friends. The sole reason, for instance, which prevents good men from making friends with bad, or bad with good, is that the divergence of their characters and aims is the greatest possible.

  Another good rule in friendship is this: do not let an excessive affection hinder the highest interests of your friends. This very often happens. I will go

540 again to the region of fable for an instance. Neoptolemus could never have taken Troy if he had been willing to listen to Lycomedes, who had brought him up, and with many tears tried to prevent his going there. Again, it often happens that important business makes it necessary to part from friends: the man who tries to baulk it, because he thinks that he cannot endure the separation, is of a weak and

545 effeminate nature, and on that very account makes but a poor friend. There are, of course, limits to what you ought to expect from a friend and to what you should allow him to demand of you. And these you must take into calculation in every case.

  21. Again, there is such a disaster, so to speak, as having to break off

550 friendship. And sometimes it is one we cannot avoid. For at this point the stream of our discourse is leaving the intimacies of the wise and touching on the friendship of ordinary people. It will happen at times that an outbreak of vicious conduct affects either a man's friends themselves or strangers, yet the discredit falls on the friends. In such cases friendships should be allowed to die out gradually by an

555 intermission of intercourse. They should, as I have been told that Cato used to say, rather be unstitched than torn in twain; unless, indeed, the injurious conduct be of so violent and outrageous a nature as to make an instance breach and separation the only possible course consistent with honour and rectitude. Again, if a change in character and aim takes place, as often happens, or if party politics produces an

560 alienation of feeling (I am now speaking, as I said a short time ago, of ordinary friendships, not of those of the wise), we shall have to be on our guard against appearing to embark upon active enmity while we only mean to resign a friendship. For there can be nothing more discreditable than to be at open war with a man with whom you have been intimate. Scipio, as you are aware, had

565 abandoned his friendship for Quintus Pompeius on my account; and again, from differences of opinion in politics, he became estranged from my colleague Metellus. In both cases he acted with dignity and moderation, shewing that he was offended indeed, but without rancour.

  Our first object, then, should be to prevent a breach; our second, to secure

570 that, if it does occur, our friendship should seem to have died a natural rather than a violent death. Next, we should take care that friendship is not converted into active hostility, from which flow personal quarrels, abusive language, and angry recriminations. These last, however, provided that they do not pass all reasonable

575 limits of forbearance, we ought to put up with, and, in compliment to an old friendship, allow the party that inflicts the injury, not the one that submits to it, to be in the wrong. Generally speaking, there is but one way of securing and providing oneself against faults and inconveniences of this sort—not to be too hasty in bestowing our affection, and not to bestow it at all on unworthy objects.

580 Now, by "worthy of friendship" I mean those who have in themselves the qualities which attract affection. This sort of man is rare; and indeed all excellent things are rare; and nothing in the world is so hard to find as a thing entirely and completely perfect of its kind. But most people not only recognise nothing as good in our life unless it is profitable, but look upon friends as so much stock, caring most for those by whom they hope to make most profit. Accordingly they never

585 possess that most beautiful and most spontaneous friendship which must be sought solely for itself without any ulterior object. They fail also to learn from their own feelings the nature and the strength of friendship. For every one loves himself, not for any reward which such love may bring, but because he is dear to himself independently of anything else. But unless this feeling is transferred to another,

590 what a real friend is will never be revealed; for he is, as it were, a second self. But if we find these two instincts shewing themselves in animals,—whether of the air or the sea or the land, whether wild or tame, first, a love of self, which in fact is born in everything that lives alike; and, secondly, an eagerness to find and attach themselves to other creatures of their own kind; and if this natural action is

595 accompanied by desire and by something resembling human love, how much more must this be the case in man by the law of his nature? For man not only loves himself, but seeks another whose spirit he may so blend with his own as almost to make one being of two.

22. But most people unreasonably, not to speak of modesty, want such a

600 friend as they are unable to be themselves, and expect from their friends what they do not themselves give. The fair course is first to be good yourself, and then to look out for another of like character. It is between such that the stability in friendship of which we have been talking can be secured; when, that is to say, men who are united by affection learn, first of all, to rule those passions which enslave others,

605 and in the next place to take delight in fair and equitable conduct, to bear each other's burdens, never to ask each other for anything inconsistent with virtue and rectitude, and not only to serve and love but also to respect each other. I say *respect;* for if respect is gone, friendship has lost its brightest jewel. And this shews the mistake of those who imagine that friendship gives a privilege to

610 licentiousness and sin. Nature has given us friendship as the handmaid of virtue, not as a partner in guilt: to the end that virtue, being powerless when isolated to reach the highest objects, might succeed in doing so in union and partnership with another. Those who enjoy in the present, or have enjoyed in the past, or are destined to enjoy in the future such a partnership as this, must be considered to

615 have secured the most excellent and auspicious combination for reaching nature's highest good. This is the partnership, I say, which combines moral rectitude, fame, peace of mind, serenity: all that men think desirable because with them life is

happy, but without them cannot be so. This being our best and highest object, we must, if we desire to attain it, devote ourselves to virtue; for without virtue we can
620   obtain neither friendship nor anything else desirable. In fact, if virtue be neglected, those who imagine themselves to possess friends will find out their error as soon as some grave disaster forces them to make trial of them. Wherefore, I must again and again repeat, you must satisfy your judgment before engaging your affections: not love first and judge afterwards. We suffer from carelessness in many of our
625   undertakings: in none more than in selecting and cultivating our friends. We put the cart before the horse, and shut the stable door when the steed is stolen, in defiance of the old proverb. For, having mutually involved ourselves in a long-standing intimacy or by actual obligations, all on a sudden some cause of offence arises and we break off our friendships in full career.
630   23. It is this that makes such carelessness in a matter of supreme importance all the more worthy of blame. I say *supreme importance*, because friendship is the one thing about the utility of which everybody with one accord is agreed. That is not the case in regard even to virtue itself; for many people speak slightingly of virtue as though it were mere puffing and self-glorification. Nor is it the case with
635   riches. Many look down on riches, being content with a little and taking pleasure in poor fare and dress. And as to the political offices for which some have a burning desire—how many entertain such a contempt for them as to think nothing in the world more empty and trivia! And so on with the rest; things desirable in the eyes of some are regarded by very many as worthless. But of friendship all
640   think alike to a man, whether those who have devoted themselves to politics, or those who delight in science and philosophy, or those who follow a private way of life and care for nothing by their own business, or those lastly who have given themselves body and soul to sensuality—they all think, I say, that without friendship life is no life, if they want some part of it, at any rate, to be noble. For
645   friendship, in one way or another, penetrates into the lives of us all, and suffers no career to be entirely free from its influence. Though a man be of so churlish and unsociable a nature as to loathe and shun the company of mankind, as we are told was the case with a certain Timon at Athens, yet even he cannot refrain from seeking some one in whose hearing he may disgorge the venom of his bitter temper.
650   We should see this most clearly, if it were possible that some god should carry us away from these haunts of men, and place us somewhere in perfect solitude, and then should supply us in abundance with everything necessary to our nature, and yet take from us entirely the opportunity of looking upon a human being.
      Who could steel himself to endure such a life? Who would not lose in his
655   loneliness the zest for all pleasures? And indeed this is the point of the observation of, I think, Archytas of Tarentum. I have it third hand; men who were my seniors told me that their seniors had told them. It was this: "If a man could ascend to heaven and get a clear view of the natural order of the universe, and the beauty of the heavenly bodies, that wonderful spectacle would give him small
660   pleasure, though nothing could be conceived more delightful if he had but had some one to whom to tell what he had seen." So true it is that Nature abhors isolation,

and ever leans upon something as a stay and support; and this is found in its most pleasing form in our closest friend.

24. But though Nature also declares by so many indications what her wish and object and desire is, we yet in a manner turn a deaf ear and will not hear her warnings. The intercourse between friends is varied and complex, and it must often happen that causes of suspicion and offence arise, which a wise man will sometimes avoid, at other times remove, at others treat with indulgence. The one possible cause of offense that must be faced is when the interests of your friend and your own sincerity are at stake. For instance, it often happens that friends need remonstrance and even reproof. When these are administered in a kindly spirit they ought to be taken in good part. But somehow or other there is truth in what my friend Terence says in his Andria: Compliance gets us friends, plain speaking hate. Plain speaking is a cause of trouble, if the result of it is resentment, which is poison of friendship; but compliance is really the cause of much more trouble, because by indulging his faults it lets a friend plunge into headlong ruin. But the man who is most to blame is he who resents plain speaking and allows flattery to egg him on to his ruin. On this point, then, from first to last there is need of deliberation and care. If we remonstrate, it should be without bitterness; if we reprove, there should be no word of insult. In the matter of compliance (for I am glad to adopt Terence's word), though there should be every courtesy, yet that base kind which assists a man in vice should be far from us, for it is unworthy of a free-born man, to say nothing of a friend. It is one thing to live with a tyrant, another with a friend. But if a man's ears are so closed to plain speaking that he cannot bear to hear the truth from a friend, we may give him up in despair. This remark of Cato's, as so many of his did, shews great acuteness: "There are people who owe more to bitter enemies than to apparently pleasant friends: the former often speak the truth, the latter never." Besides, it is a strange paradox that the recipients of advice should feel no annoyance where they ought to feel it, and yet feel so much where they ought not. They are not at all vexed at having committed a fault, but very angry at being reproved for it. On the contrary, they ought to be grieved at the crime and glad of the correction.

25. Well, then, if it is true that to give and receive advice—the former with freedom and yet without bitterness, the latter with patience and without irritation—is peculiarly appropriate to genuine friendship, it is no less true that there can be nothing more utterly subversive of friendship than flattery, adulation, and base compliance. I use as many terms as possible to brand this vice of light-minded, untrustworthy men, whose sole object in speaking is to please without any regard to truth. In everything false pretence is bad, for it suspends and vitiates our power of discerning the truth. But to nothing is it so hostile as to friendship; for it destroys that frankness without which friendship is an empty name. For the essence of friendship being that two minds become as one, how can that ever take place if the mind of each of the separate parties to it is not single and uniform, but variable, changeable, and complex? Can anything be so pliable, so wavering, as the mind of a man whose attitude depends not only on another's feeling and wish,

but on his very looks and nods? If one says *No*, I answer *No*; if *Yes*, I answer *Yes*. In fine, I've laid this task upon myself, To echo all that's said to quote my old friend Terence again. But he puts these words into the mouth of a Gnatho. To admit such a man into one's intimacy at all is a sign of folly. But there are many

710 people like Gnatho, and it is when they are superior either in position or fortune or reputation that their flatteries become mischievous, the weight of their position making up for the lightness of their character. But if we only take reasonable care, it is as easy to separate and distinguish a genuine from a specious friend as anything else that is coloured and artificial from what is sincere and genuine. A

715 public assembly, though composed of men of the smallest possible culture, nevertheless will see clearly the difference between a mere demagogue (that is, a flatterer and untrustworthy citizen) and a man of principle, standing, and solidity. It was by this kind of flattering language that Gaius Papirius the other day endeavoured to tickle the ears of the assembled people, when proposing his

720 law to make the tribunes re-eligible. I spoke against it.

But I will leave the personal question. I prefer speaking of Scipio. Good heavens! how impressive his speech was, what a majesty there was in it! You would have pronounced him, without hesitation, to be no mere henchman of the Roman people, but their leader. However, you were there, and moreover have the

725 speech in your hands. The result was that a law meant to please the people was by the people's votes rejected. Once more to refer to myself, you remember how apparently popular was the law proposed by Gaius Licinius Crassus about the election to the College of Priests in the consulship of Quintus Maximus, Scipio's brother, and Lucius Mancinus. For the power of filling up their own vacancies on

730 the part of the colleges was by this proposal to be transferred to the people. It was this man, by the way, who began to practice of turning towards the forum when addressing the people. In spite of this, however, upon my speaking on the conservative side, religion gained an easy victory over his plausible speech. This took place in my praetorship, five years before I was elected consul, which shows

735 that the cause was successfully maintained more by the merits of the case than by the prestige of the highest office.

26. Now, if on a stage, such as a public assembly essentially is, where there is the amplest room for fiction and half-truths, truth nevertheless prevails if it be but fairly laid open and brought into the light of day, what ought to happen in the case

740 of friendship, which rests entirely on truthfulness? Friendship, in which, unless you both see and shew an open breast, to use a common expression, you can neither trust nor be certain of anything—no, not even of mutual affection, since you cannot be sure of its sincerity. However, this flattery, injurious as it is, can hurt no one but the man who takes it in and likes it. And it follows that the man to

745 open his ears widest to flatterers is he who first flatters himself and is fondest of himself. I grant you that Virtue naturally loves herself; for she knows herself and perceives how worthy of love she is. But I am not now speaking of absolute virtue, but of the belief men have that they possess virtue. The fact is that fewer people are endowed with virtue than wish to be thought to be so. It is such people that

750 take delight in flattery. When they are addressed in language expressly adapted to flatter their vanity, they look upon such empty persiflage as a testimony to the truth of their own praises. It is not then properly friendship at all when the one will not listen to the truth, and the other is prepared to lie. Nor would the servility of parasites in comedy have seemed humorous to us had there been no

755 such things as braggart captains. "Is Thais really much obliged to me?" It would have been quite enough to answer "Much," but he must needs say "Immensely." Your servile flatterer always exaggerates what his victim wishes to be put strongly. Wherefore, though it is with those who catch at and invite it that this flattering falsehood is especially powerful, yet men even of solider and steadier

760 character must be warned to be on the watch against being taken in by cunningly disguised flattery. An open flatterer any one can detect, unless he is an absolute fool: the covert insinuation of the cunning and the sly is what we have to be studiously on our guard against. His detection is not by any means the easiest thing in the world, for he often covers his servility under the guise of

765 contradiction, and flatters by pretending to dispute, and then at last giving in and allowing himself to be beaten, that the person hoodwinked may think himself to have been the clearer-sighted. Now what can be more degrading than to be thus hoodwinked? You must be on your guard against this happening to you, like the man in the Heiress: "How have I been befooled! no drivelling dotards On any

770 stage were e'er so played upon." For even on the stage we have no grosser representation of folly than that of short-sighted and credulous old men. But somehow or other I have strayed away from the friendship of the perfect, that is, of the *wise* (meaning, of course, such *wisdom* as human nature is capable of), to the subject of vulgar, unsubstantial friendships. Let us then return to our original

775 theme, and at length bring that, too, to a conclusion.

27. Well, then, Fannius and Mucius, I repeat what I said before. It is virtue, virtue, which both creates and preserves friendship. On it depends harmony of interest, permanence, fidelity. When Virtue has reared her head and shewn the light of her countenance, and seen and recognised the same light in another, she

780 gravitates towards it, and in her turn welcomes that which the other has to shew; and from it springs up a flame which you may call love or friendship as you please. Both words are from the same root in Latin; and love is just the cleaving to him whom you love without the prompting of need or any view to advantage—though this latter blossoms spontaneously on friendship, little as you may have

785 looked for it. It is with such warmth of feeling that I cherished Lucius Paulus, Marcus Cato, Gaius Gallus, Publius Nasica, Tiberius Gracchus, my dear Scipio's father-in-law. It shines with even greater warmth when men are of the same age, as in the case of Scipio and Lucius Furius, Publius Rupilius, Spurius Mummius, and myself. *En revanche*,[7] in my old age I find comfort in the affection of young men, as

790 in the case of yourselves and Quintus Tubero: nay more, I delight in the intimacy of such a very young man as Publius Rutilius and Aulus Verginius. And since the

---

[7]En revanche: in return, on the other hand

law of our nature and of our life is that a new generation is for ever springing up, the most desirable thing is that along with your contemporaries, with whom you started in the race, you may also reach what is to us the goal. But in view of the

795 instability and perishableness of mortal things, we should be continually on the look-out for some to love and by whom to be loved; for if we lose affection and kindliness from our life, we lose all that gives it charm. For me, indeed, though torn away by a sudden stroke, Scipio still lives and ever will live. For it was the virtue of the man that I loved, and that has not suffered death.

800 And it is not my eyes only, because I had all my life a personal experience of it, that never lose sight of it: it will shine to posterity also with undimmed glory. No one will ever cherish a nobler ambition or a loftier hope without thinking his memory and his image the best to put before his eyes. I declare that of all the blessings which either fortune or nature has bestowed upon me I know none to

805 compare with Scipio's friendship. In it I found sympathy in public, counsel in private business; in it too a means of spending my leisure with unalloyed delight. Never, to the best of my knowledge, did I offend him even in the most trivial point; never did I hear a word from him I could have wished unsaid. We had one house, one table, one style of living; and not only were we together on foreign service, but

810 in our tours also and country sojourns. Why speak of our eagerness to be ever gaining some knowledge, to be ever learning something, on which we spent all our leisure hours far from the gaze of the world?

If the recollection and memory of these things had perished with the man, I could not possibly have endured the regret for one so closely united with me in life

815 and affection. But these things have not perished; they are rather fed and strengthened by reflexion and memory. Even supposing me to have been entirely bereft of them, still my time of life of itself brings me no small consolation: for I cannot have much longer now to bear this regret; and everything that is brief ought to be endurable, however severe.

820 This is all I had to say on friendship. One piece of advice on parting. Make up your minds to this: Virtue (without which friendship is impossible) is first; but next to it, and to it alone, the greatest of all things is Friendship.

14. THE AENEID

Virgil
(70 BCE–19 BCE)

(trans. by Rolfe Humphries)

The greatest of the Latin poets, Virgil (70 BCE–19 BCE), set the career pattern for future epic poets: he began by composing pastoral poems, the Eclogues, *and a didactic poem on farming, the* Georgics, *which disclose the beauty and variety of the natural world. He gained Augustus' attention through a wealthy patron and by the merit of his own work which conformed to the Emperor's agrarian and moral reforms. Virgil spent most of his life on his great epic, the* Aeneid, *whose hero, Aeneas, is a flattering reflection of Augustus. In his journey from fallen Troy to Latium (a journey modeled on Homer's* Odyssey), *Aeneas moves from a place of defeat to a place of victory; from embodying Greek values and sensibilities to manifesting Roman stoic values. He is guided by the gods and encouraged by his deceased father's prophecies of the future glory of Rome; yet Aeneas also recognizes the sacrifices his mission to found Rome entails: he must put aside his love of Dido and his own happiness to achieve the greater good in the distant future. His brutal determination in the last battle to gain control of Latium (single combat against Turnus, modeled on Achilles's battle with Hector in Homer's* Iliad), *suggest the high price in human terms such heroic accomplishment exacts.*

BOOK I: THE LANDING NEAR CARTHAGE

Arms and the man I sing, the first who came,
Compelled by fate, an exile out of Troy,
To Italy and the Lavinian coast,
Much buffeted on land and on the deep
5　By violence of the gods, through that long rage,
That lasting hate, of Juno's.[1] And he suffered
Much, also, in war, till he should build his town
And bring his gods to Latium, whence, in time,
The Latin race, the Alban fathers, rose
10　And the great walls of everlasting Rome.

---

[1]**Juno's:** Juno is the Roman version of the Greek goddess Hera, who lost the beauty contest judged by the Trojan Paris to Aphrodite who had promised him the most beautiful woman in the world (Helen). Hera from thence forward hated all Trojans. She will be the patron of Carthage, the city destined to fall to Rome (Punic Wars), an event Juno hopes to divert.

Help me, O Muse, recall the reasons: why,
Why did the queen of heaven drive a man
So known for goodness, for devotion, through
So many toils and perils? Was there slight,
15   Affront, or outrage? Is vindictiveness
An attribute of the celestial mind?
      There was an ancient city, Carthage, once
Founded by Tyrians,[2] facing Italy
And Tiber's mouth, far-off, a wealthy town,
20   War-loving and aggressive; and Juno held
Even her precious Samos[3] in less regard.
Here were her arms, her chariot, and here,
Should fate at all permit, the goddess burned
To found the empire of the world forever.
25   But, she had heard, a Trojan race would come,
Some day, to overthrow the Tyrian towers,—
A race would come, imperious people, proud
In war, with wide dominion, bringing doom
For Libya. Fate willed it so. And Juno
30   Feared, and remembered: there was the old war
She fought at Troy for her dear Greeks; her mind
Still fed on hurt and anger; deep in her heart
Paris' decision rankled, and the wrong
Offered her slighted beauty; and the hatred
35   Of the whole race; and Ganymede's[4] honors—
All that was fuel to fire; she tossed and harried
All over the seas, wherever she could, those Trojans
Who had survived the Greeks and fierce Achilles,
And so they wandered over many an ocean,
40   Through many a year, fate-hounded. Such a struggle
It was to found the race of Rome!
                They were happy
Spreading the sail, rushing the foam with bronze,
And Sicily hardly out of sight, when Juno,
45   Still nourishing the everlasting wound,
Raged to herself: "I am beaten, I suppose;
It seems I cannot keep this Trojan king
From Italy. The fates, no doubt, forbid me.

---

[2]**Tyrians**: from Tyre, a city on the Syrian coast; the Carthaginians are alternately called Tyrians.

[3]**Samos**: an island in the Aegean known for its temple of Juno

[4]**Ganymede's honors**: he was selected cup bearer to the gods rather than one of Juno's children.

Pallas,[5] of course, could burn the Argive ships,
50 Could drown the sailors, all for one man's guilt,
The crazy acts of Ajax. Her own hand
Hurled from the cloud Jove's thunderbolt, and shattered
Their ships all over the sea; she raised up storm
And tempest; she spiked Ajax on the rocks,
55 Whirled him in wind, blasted his heart with fire.
And I, who walk my way as queen of the gods,
Sister of Jove, and wife of Jove, keep warring
With one tribe through the long, long years. Who cares
For Juno's godhead? Who brings sacrifice
60 Devoutly to her altars?"
                                        Brooding, burning
She sought Aeolia, the storm-clouds' dwelling,
A land that sweeps and swarms with the winds' fury,
Whose monarch, Aeolus, in his deep cave rules
65 Imperious, weighing down with bolt and prison
Those boisterous struggling roarers, who go raging
Around their bars, under the moan of the mountain.
High over them their sceptered lord sits watching,
Soothing restraining, their passionate proud spirit,
70 Lest, uncontrolled, they seize, in their wild keeping,
The land, the sea, the arch of sky, in ruin
Sweeping through space. This Jupiter feared; he hid them
Deep in dark caverns, win a mass of mountain
Piled over above them, and a king to give them
75 Most certain regulation, with a knowledge
When to hold in, when to let go. Him Juno
Approached in supplication:—"Aeolus,
Given by Jove the power to still the waters,
Or raise them with a gale, a tribe I hate
80 Is on its way to Italy, and they carry
Troy with them, and their household gods, once beaten.
Shake anger into those winds of yours, turn over
Their ships, and drown them; drive them in all directions,
Litter the sea with bodies! For such service
85 The loveliest nymph I have, Deiopea,
Shall be your bride forever, and you will father
Fair children on her fairness." Aeolus
Made answer: "Yours, O Queen, the task of seeking

---

[5]Pallas: Pallas Athene, the Greek goddess of war and wisdom (Roman Minerva), had punished Ajax for raping Cassandra, the daughter of Priam, King of Troy, and prophetess beloved by Apollo. Pallas is also a young companion of Aeneas.

Whatever it is you will; and mine the duty
90   To follow with performance. All my empire,
My sceptre, Jove's indulgence, are beholden
To Juno's favor, by whose blessing I
Attend the feasts of the gods and rule this storm-land."
    His spear-butt struck the hollow mountain-side,
95   And the winds, wherever they could, came sweeping forth,
Whirled over the land, swooped down upon the ocean.
East, South, Southwest, they heave the billows, howl,
Storm, roll the giant combers toward the shore.
Men cry; the rigging creaks and strains; the clouds
100   Darken, and men see nothing; a weight of darkness
Broods over the deep; the heavy thunder rumbles
From pole to pole; the lightning rips and dazzles;
There is no way out but death. Aeneas shudders
In the chill shock, and lifts both hands to heaven:—
105   "O happy men, thrice happy, four times happy,
Who had the luck to die, with their fathers watching
Below the walls of Troy! Ah, Diomedes,
Bravest of Greeks, why could I not have fallen,
Bleeding my life away on plains of Ilium[6]
110   In our encounter there, where mighty Hector
Went down before Achilles' spear, and huge
Sarpedon lay in dust, and Simois river
Rolled to the sea so many noble heroes,
All drowned in all their armor?" And the gale
115   Howls from the north, striking the sail, head on;
The waves are lifted to the stars; the oars
Are broken, and the prow slews round; the ship
Lies broadside on; a wall of water, a mountain,
Looms up, comes pouring down; some ride the crest,
120   Some, in the trough, can see the boil of the sand.
The South wind hurls three ships on the hidden rocks,
That sea-reef which Italians call the Altars;
The West takes three, sweeping them from the deep
On shoal and quicksand; over the stern of one,
125   Before Aeneas' eyes, a great sea falls,
Washing the helmsman overboard; the ship
Whirls thrice in the suck of the water and goes down
In the devouring gulf; and here and there
A few survivors swim, the Lycian men

---

[6]**Ilium:** Troy (*Iliad* is "the story of Troy.")

130 Whose captain was Orontes; now their arms,
Their Trojan treasures, float with the broken timbers
On the swing and slide of the waves. The storm, triumphant,
Rides down more boats, and more; there goes Achates;
Abas, Aletes, Ilioneus,

135 Receive the hostile water; the walls are broken;
The enemy pours in.
                                But meanwhile Neptune[7]
Saw ocean in a welter of confusion,
The roar of storm, and deep and surface mingled.

140 Troublesome business, this; he rose, majestic,
From under the waves, and saw the Trojan vessels
Scattered all over the sea by the might of the waves
And the wreck of sky; he recognized the anger
And cunning of his sister, and he summoned

145 The winds by name:—"What arrogance is this,
What pride of birth, you winds, to meddle here
Without my sanction, raising all this trouble?
I'll—No, the waves come first: but listen to me,
You are going to pay for this! Get out of here!

150 Go tell your king the lordship of the ocean,
The trident, are not his, but mine. His realm
Reaches no further than the rocks and caverns
You brawlers dwell in; let him rule that palace,
Big as he pleases, shut you in, and stay there!"

155   This said, he calmed the swollen sea and cloud,
Brought back the sun; Cymothoe and Triton,[8]
Heaving together, pulled the ships from the reef,
As Neptune used his trident for a lever,
Opened the quicksand, made the water smooth,

160 And the flying chariot skimmed the level surface.
Sometimes, in a great nation, there are riots
With the rabble out of hand, and firebrands fly
And cobblestones; whatever they lay their hands on
Is a weapon for their fury, but should they see

165 One man of noble presence, they fall silent,
Obedient dogs, with ears pricked up, and waiting,
Waiting his word, and he knows how to bring them
Back to good sense again. So ocean, roaring,
Subsided into stillness, as the sea-god

---

[7]**Neptune:** the equivalent of the Greek Poseidon, god of the sea.
[8]**Cymothoe and Triton:** a sea nymph and a sea god

170   Looked forth upon the waters, and clear weather
        Shone over him as he drove his flying horses.
            Aeneas' weary children make for harbor,
        Whichever lies most near, and the prows are turned
        To Libya's coast-line. In a bay's deep curve

175   They find a haven, where the water lies
        With never a ripple. A little island keeps
        The sea-swell off, and the waves break on its sides
        And slide back harmless. The great cliffs come down
        Steep to deep water, and the background shimmers,

180   Darkens and shines, the tremulous aspen moving
        And the dark fir pointing still. And there is a cave
        Under the overhanging rocks, alive
        With water running fresh, a home of the Nymphs,
        With benches for them, cut from the living stone.

185   No anchor is needed here for weary ships,
        No mooring-cable. Aeneas brings them in,
        Seven weary vessels, and the men are glad
        To be ashore again, to feel dry sand
        Under the salt-stained limbs. Achates strikes

190   The spark from the flint, catches the fire on leaves,
        Adds chips and kindling, blows and fans the flame,
        And they bring out the soaked and salty corn,
        The hand-mills, stone and mortar, and make ready,
        As best they can, for bread.

195   Meanwhile Aeneas
        Climbs to a look-out, for a view of the ocean,
        Hoping for some good luck; the Phrygian galleys
        Might meet his gaze, or Capys' boats, or a pennon
        On a far-off mast-head flying. There is nothing,

200   Nothing to see out yonder, but near the water
        Three stags are grazing, with a herd behind them,
        A long line browsing through the peaceful valley.
        He reaches for the bow and the swift arrows
        Borne by Achates,[9] and he shoots leaders,

205   High-antlered, routs the common herd, and ceases
        Only when seven are slain, a number equal
        To the ships' tally, and then he seeks the harbor,
        Divides the spoil, broaches the wine Acestes
        Had stowed for them at Drepanum on their leaving,

210   A kingly present, and he calms their trouble,

---

[9] **Achates:** Aeneas's companion, a figure and relationship similar to Achilleus' and Patroklos'

Saying: "O comrades, we have been through evil
Together before this; we have been through worse,
Scylla, Charybdis, and the Cyclops' dwelling,[10]
The sounding rocks. This, too, the god will end.
215   Call the nerve back; dismiss the fear, the sadness
Some day, perhaps, remembering even this
Will be a pleasure. We are going on
Through whatsoever chance and change, until
We come to Latium, where the fates point out
220   A quiet dwelling-place, and Troy recovered.
Endure, and keep yourself for better days."
He kept to himself the sorrow in the heart,
Wearing, for them, a mask of hopefulness.
They were ready for the feasting. Part lay bare
225   The flesh from the torn hides, part cut the meat
Impaling it, still quivering, on spits,
Setting the kettles, keeping the water boiling,
And strong with food again, sprawling stretched out
On comfortable grass, they take their fill
230   Of bread and wine and venison, till hunger
Is gone, and the board cleared. And then they talk
For a long time, of where their comrades are,
Are, or may be, hopeful and doubtful both.
Could they believe them living? or would a cry
235   Fall on deaf ears forever? All those captains,
Brave Gyas, brave Cloanthus, Amycus,
Lycus, Orontes,—in his secret heart
Aeneas mourns them.
                       Meanwhile, from the heaven
240   Jupiter watched the lands below, and the seas
With the white points of sails, and far-off people,
Turning his gaze toward Libya. And Venus[11]
Came to him then, a little sadly, tears
Brimming in those bright eyes of hers. "Great father,"
245   She said, "Great ruler of the world
Of men and gods, great wielder of the lightning,
What has my poor Aeneas done? what outrage
Could Trojans perpetrate, so that the world
Rejects them everywhere, and many a death
250   Inflicted on them over Italy?

---

[10]Scylla . . .: Cyclops' dwelling; adventures similar to those of Odysseus and his men in the *Odyssey*
[11]Venus: Aeneas has a goddess mother (Venus) and a mortal father.

There was a promise once, that as the years
Rolled onward, they would father Rome and rulers
Of Roman stock, to hold dominion over
All sea and land. That was a promise, father;
255 What changed it? Once that promise was my comfort;
Troy fell; I weighed one fate against another
And found some consolation. But disaster
Keeps on; the same ill-fortune follows after.
What end of it all, great king? One man, Antenor,
260 Escaped the Greeks, came through Illyrian waters
Safe to Liburnian regions, where Timavus
Roars underground, comes up nine times, and reaches
The floodland near the seas. One man, Antenor,
Founded a city, Padua, a dwelling
265 For Trojan men, a resting-place from labor,
And shares their quietude. But we, your children,
To whom heaven's height is granted, we are betrayed,
We have lost our ships, we are kept from Italy,
Kept far away. One enemy—I tell you
270 This is a shameful thing! Do we deserve it?
Is this our rise to power?"

        He smiled, in answer,
The kind of smile that clears the air, and kissed her.
"Fear not, my daughter; fate remains unmoved
275 For the Roman generations. You will witness
Lavinium's rise, her walls fulfill the promise;
You win bring to heaven lofty-souled Aeneas.
There has been no change in me whatever. Listen!
To ease this care, I will prophesy a little,
280 I will open the book of fate. Your son Aeneas
Will wage a mighty war in Italy,
Beat down proud nations, give his people laws,
Found them a city, a matter of three years
From victory to settlement. His son,
285 Fine boy Ascanius, named Ilus once,
When Troy was standing, and now called Iulus,[12]
Shall reign for thirty years, and great in power
Forsake Lavinium, transfer the kingdom
To Alba Longa, new-built capital.
290 Here, for three hundred years, the line of Hector
Shall govern, till a royal priestess bears

---

[12]Iulus: Ascanius and Iulus are used interchangeably for Aeneas' son (the Iulus suggesting Julius Caesar—see below, lines 299 and following).

Twin sons to Mars, and Romulus, rejoicing
In the brown wolf-skin of his foster-mother,[13]
Takes up the tribe, and builds the martial walls
295 And calls the people, after himself, the Romans.
To these I set no bounds in space or time;
They shall rule forever. Even bitter Juno
Whose fear now harries earth and sea and heaven
Will change to better counsels, and will cherish
300 The race that wears the toga, Roman masters
Of all the world. It is decreed. The time
Will come, as holy years wheel on, when Troy
Will subjugate Mycenae, vanquish Phthia,
Be lord of Argos. And from this great line
305 Will come a Trojan, Caesar, to establish
The limit of his empire at the ocean,
His glory at the stars, a man called Julius
Whose name recalls Iulus. Welcome waits
For him in heaven; all the spoils of Asia
310 Will weigh him down, and prayer be made before him.
Then wars will cease, and a rough age grow gentler,
White Faith and Vesta, Romulus and Remus,
Give law to nations. War's grim gates will close,
Tight-shut with bars of iron, and inside them
315 The wickedness of war sit bound and silent,
The red mouth straining and the hands held tight
In fastenings of bronze, a hundred hundred."
　　　With that, he sent down Mercury from heaven
That Carthage might be kindly, and her land
320 And new-built towers receive them with a welcome,
And their queen, Dido, knowing the will of fate,
Swing wide her doors. On the oarage of his wings
He flies through the wide sweep of air to Libya,
Where, at the will of the god, the folk make ready
325 In kindliness of heart, and their queen's purpose
Is gracious and gentle.
　　　　　　All night long Aeneas
Had pondered many a care, and with bright morning
Resolved to reconnoiter; the winds have brought him
330 To a new country: who lives in it, men
Or only beasts? The fields appear untended.
The fleet lies under a hollow cliff, surrounded

---

[13]foster-mother: Romulus and Remus, twin sons of Mars, were suckled by a she-wolf.

By spikes of shade, and groves arch overhead,
Ample concealment. Aeneas and Achates
335 Went forth together, armed, down the trail in the forest,
And there his mother met him, a girl, it seemed,
From Thrace or Sparta, trim as any huntress
Who rides her horses hard, or outspeeds rivers
In her swift going. A bow hung over her shoulder,
340 Her hair blew free, her knees were bare, her garments
Tucked at the waist and knotted. As she saw them,
"Ho there, young men," she cried, "have you seen my sister
Around here anywhere? She wears a quiver,
And a spotted lynx-hide; maybe you have heard her
345 Hunting the boar and shouting?

But her son
Responded: "No; we have heard no sounds of hunting,
We have seen no one here. But tell me, maiden,
What name to call you by? In voice and feature
350 You are, I think, no mortal; a goddess, surely,—
Nymph, or Apollo's sister?[14] Whoever you are,
Be kind to us, lighten our trouble, tell us
Under what sky, along what coast of the world,
We wander, knowing neither land nor people,
355 Driven by gales and billows. Many a victim
We shall make ready for your altar." Venus
Answered: "I have no title to such honor.
The Tyrian girls all wear these crimson leggings
Like mine, and carry quivers. Tyrian folk
360 Live here; their city is Carthage; over the border
Lies Libya, warlike people. Our queen, Dido,
Came here from Tyre; she was fleeing from her brother,
A long and complicated story; outrage,—
No matter; here it is, in brief. Her husband
365 Was Sychaeus, wealthiest of all Phoenicians,
At least in land, and Dido loved him dearly
Since first her father gave her to him, virgin,
And then unlucky bride. She had a brother,
Pygmalion, king of Tyre, a monster, evil
370 In wickedness, and madness came between
Those men, the two of them. Pygmalion murdered
Sychaeus at the altar; he was crazy
And blind for gold and crafty; what did he care

---

[14]**Apollo's sister:** Diana, goddess of the hunt and childbirth (similar to Greek Artemis).

About his sister's love? And he kept it quiet
375 For a long time, kept telling Dido something
To fool her with false comfort, but Sychaeus
Came to her in a dream, a ghost, unburied,
With the wounds in his breast, the story of the altar,
The pale lips blurting out the secret horror,
380 The crime in the dark of the household. *Flee*, he told her,
Forsake this land; and he told her where the treasure
Lay hidden in earth, uncounted gold and silver.
Dido was moved to flight, secured companions,
All those possessed by fear, all those whom hatred
385 Had made relentless; ships were standing ready,
As it so happened; they put the gold aboard,
And over the sea the greedy tyrant's treasure
Went sailing, with a woman for a captain.
They came here; you will see the walls arising
390 And the great citadel of the town called Carthage.
Here they bought ground; they used to call it Byrsa,
That being a word for bull's hide; they bought only
What a bull's hide could cover. And now tell me
Who you might be yourselves?
395 What land do you come from, Bound for what coast?"
                              And he began his answer
With a long sigh: "O goddess, if I told you
All from the first beginning, if you had leisure
To listen to the record of our trouble,
400 It would take me all day long. From ancient Troy,
In case that name means anything, we come
Driven over many seas, and now a storm
Has whipped us on this coast. I am Aeneas,
A good, devoted man; I carry with me
405 My household gods, saved from the Greeks; I am known
In heaven; it is Italy I seek,
A homeland for me there, and a race descended
From lofty Jove. With a score of ships we started
Over the Phrygian ocean, following fate
410 And the way my mother pointed. Only seven
Are left us now, battered survivors, after
The rage of wind and wave. And here I wander
The wastes of Libya, unknown and needy,
Driven from Europe and Asia." And his mother
415 Broke in on his complaining:—"Whoever you are,
Some god must care for you, I think, to bring you
Here to the city of Carthage. Follow on,

Go to the royal palace. For, I tell you,
Your comrades have returned, your fleet is safe,
420   Brought to good haven by the turn of the winds,
Unless the augury my parents taught me
Was foolish nonsense. In the heaven yonder
You see twelve swans, rejoicing in long column,
Scattered, a little while ago, and driven
425   By the swooping eagle, over all the sky,
But now, it seems, they light on land, or watch
Those who came down before them; as they circle
In company, and make a cheerful sound
With whir of wing or song, so, let me tell you,
430   Your ships and men already enter harbor
Or near it under full sail. Keep on, go forward
Where the path leads."
                And as she turned, her shoulders
Shone with a radiant light; her hair shed fragrance,
435   Her robes slipped to her feet, and the true goddess
Walked in divinity. He knew his mother,
And his voice pursued her flight: "Cruel again!
Why mock your son so often with false phantoms?
Why may not hand be joined to hand; and words
440   Exchanged in truthfulness?" So, still reproachful,
He went on toward the city, with Achates,
But Venus cast dark air around their going,
A veil of mist, so that no man might see them
Or lay a hand on them, or halt them, asking
445   The reasons of their coming. She soared upward
To Paphos, happily home to temple and altars
Steaming with incense, redolent with garlands.
       And they went on, where the little pathway led them
To rising ground; below them lay the city,
450   Majestic buildings now, where once were hovels,
A wonder to Aeneas, gates and bustle
And well-paved streets, the busy Tyrians toiling
With stones for walls and citadel, or marking
Foundations for their homes, drainage and furrow,
455   All under ordered process. They dredge harbors,
Set cornerstones, quarry the rock, where someday
Their theater will tower. They are like bees
In early summer over the country flowers
When the sun is warm, and the young of the hive emerge,
460   And they pack the molten honey, bulge the cells
With the sweet nectar, add new loads, and harry

The drones away from the hive, and the work glows,
And the air is sweet with bergamot and clover.
"Happy the men whose walls already rise!"

465 Exclaims Aeneas, gazing on the city,
And enters there, still veiled in cloud—a marvel!—
And walks among the people, and no one sees him.
    There was a grove in the middle of the city,
Most happy in its shade; this was the place

470 Where first the Tyrians, tossed by storm and whirlwind,
Dug up the symbol royal Juno showed them,
The skull of a war-horse, a sign the race to come
Would be supreme in war and wealth, for ages,
And Dido here was building a great temple

475 In Juno's honor, rich in gifts, and blessed
With the presence of the goddess. Lintel and rafter
Were bronze above bronze stairways, and bronze portals
Swung on bronze hinges. Here Aeneas first
Dared hope for safety, find some reassurance

480 In hope of better days: a strange sight met him,
To take his fear away. Waiting the queen,
He stood there watching, under the great temple,
Letting his eyes survey the city's fortune,
The artist's workmanship, the craftsman's labor,

485 And there, with more than wonder, he sees the battles
Fought around Troy,[15] and the wars whose fame had travelled
The whole world over; there is Agamemnon,
Priam, and Menelaus, and Achilles,
A menace to them all. He is moved to tears.

490 "What place in all the world," he asks Achates,
"Is empty of our sorrow? There is Priam!
Look! even here there are rewards for praise,
There are tears for things, and what men suffer touches
The human heart. Dismiss your fear; this story

495 Will bring some safety to you." Sighing often,
He could not turn his gaze away; it was only
A picture on a wall, but the sight afforded
Food for the spirit's need. He saw the Greeks,
Hard-pressed, in flight, and Trojans coming after,

500 Or, on another panel, the scene reversed,
Achilles in pursuit, his own men fleeing;
He saw, and tears came into his eyes again,

---

[15]**Fought around Troy:** Aeneas has entered the temple of Juno which contains a great mural depicting scenes from the Trojan War.

The tents of Rhesus, snowy-white, betrayed
In their first sleep by bloody Diomedes
505   With many a death, and the fiery horses driven
Into the camp, before they ever tasted
The grass of Troy, or drank from Xanthus' river.
Another scene showed Troilus, poor youngster,
Running away, his arms flung down; Achilles
510   Was much too good for him; he had fallen backward
Out of his car, but held the reins, and the horses
Dragged him along the ground, his hair and shoulders
Bounding in dust, and the spear making a scribble.
And there were Trojan women, all in mourning,
515   With streaming hair, on their way to Pallas' temple,
Bearing, as gift, a robe, but the stern goddess
Kept her gaze on the ground. Three times Achilles
Had dragged the body of Hector around the walls,
And was selling it for money. What a groan
520   Came from Aeneas' heart, seeing that spoil,
That chariot, and helpless Priam reaching
His hands, unarmed, across the broken body!
And he saw himself there, too, fighting in battle
Against Greek leaders, he saw the Eastern columns,
525   And swarthy Memnon's arms. Penthesilea,
The Amazon, blazes in fury, leading
Her crescent-shielded thousands, a golden buckle
Below her naked breast, a soldieress
Fighting with men.
530   And as he watched these marvels
In one long fascinated stare of wonder,
Dido, the queen, drew near; she came to the temple
With a great train, all majesty, all beauty,
As on Eurotas' riverside, or where
535   Mount Cynthus[16] towers high, Diana leads
Her bands of dancers, and the Oreads follow
In thousands, right and left, the taller goddess,
The quiver-bearing maiden, and Latona
Is filled with secret happiness, so Dido
540   Moved in her company, a queen, rejoicing,
Ordering on her kingdom's rising glory.
At Juno's portal, under the arch of the temple,

---

[16]**Mount Cynthus:** Diana, goddess of the hunt, leading wood nymphs (Oreads) and her mother (Latona, or Leto), in dance; an extended metaphor to suggest Dido's pleasure in her city environment

She took her throne, a giver of law and justice,
A fair partitioner of toil and duty,
545 And suddenly Aeneas, from the crowd,
Saw Trojan men approaching, brave Cloanthus,
Sergestus, Antheus, and all those others
Whom the black storm had driven here and yonder.
This he cannot believe, nor can Achates,
550 Torn between fear and joy. They burn with ardor
To seek their comrades' handclasp, but confusion
Still holds them in the cloud: what can have happened?
They watch from the cover of mist: men still were coming
From all the ships, chosen, it seemed, as pleaders
555 For graciousness before the temple, calling
Aloud: what fortune had been theirs, he wonders,
Where had they left the ships; why were they coming?
They were given audience; Ilioneus,
Senior to all, began: "O Queen, whom Jove
560 Has given the founding of a great new city,
Has given to bridle haughty tribes with justice,
We, pitiful Trojans, over every ocean
Driven by storm, make our appeal: keep from us
The terrible doom of fire; protect our vessels;
565 Have mercy on a decent race; consider
Our lot with closer interest. We have not come
To ravish Libyan homes, or carry plunder
Down to the shore. We lack the arrogance
Of conquerors; there is no aggression in us.
570 There is a place which Greeks have given a name,
The Land in the West; it is powerful in arms,
Rich in its soil; Oenotrians used to live there,
And now, the story goes, a younger people
Inhabit it, calling themselves Italians
575 After their leader's name. We were going there
When, big with storm and cloud, Orion rising
Drove us on hidden quicksands, and wild winds
Scattered us over the waves, by pathless rocks
And the swell of the surge. A few of us have drifted
580 Here to your shores. What kind of men are these,
What barbarous land permits such attitudes?
We have been denied the welcome of the beach,
Forbidden to set foot on land; they rouse
All kinds of war against us. You despise,
585 It may be, human brotherhood, and arms.
Wielded by men. But there are gods, remember,

Who care for right and wrong. Our king Aeneas.
May be alive; no man was ever more just,
More decent ever, or greater in war and arms.
590   If fate preserves him still, if he still breathes
The welcome air, above the world of shadows,
Fear not; to have treated us with kindly service
Need bring you no repentance. We have cities
In Sicily as well, and King Acestes
595   Is one of us, from Trojan blood. We ask you
To let us beach our battered fleet, make ready
Beams from the forest timber, mend our oarage,
Seek Italy and Latium, glad at knowing
Our king and comrades rescued. But if safety
600   Is hopeless for him now, and Libyan water
Has been his grave, and if his son Iulus
Is desperate, or lost, grant us permission
At least to make for Sicily, whence we came here,
Where king Acestes has a dwelling for us."
605   The Trojans, as he ended, all were shouting,
And Dido, looking down, made a brief answer:
"I am sorry, Trojans; put aside your care,
Have no more fear. The newness of the kingdom
And our strict need compel to me such measures—
610   Sentries on every border, far and wide.
But who so ignorant as not to know
The nation of Aeneas, manly both
In deeds and people, and the city of Troy?
We are not as dull as that, we folk from Carthage;
615   The sun shines on us here. Whether you seek
The land in the west, the sometime fields of Saturn,[17]
Or the Sicilian realms and king Acestes,
I will help you to the limit; should you wish
To settle here and share this kingdom with me,
620   The city I found is yours; draw up your ships;
Trojan and Tyrian I treat alike.
Would, also, that your king were here, Aeneas,
Driven by that same wind. I will send good men
Along the coast to seek him, under orders
625   To scour all Libya; he may be wandering
Somewhere, in woods or town, surviving shipwreck."

---

[17]**fields of Saturn:** Italy; Saturn ruled in a "golden age" before being overthrown by Jupiter.

Aeneas and Achates both were eager
To break the cloud; the queen inspired their spirit
With her address. Achates asked Aeneas:—
630 "What do we do now, goddess-born? You see
They all are safe, our vessels and our comrades,
Only one missing, and we saw him drowning,
Ourselves, beneath the waves, all other things
Confirm what Venus told us." And as he finished,
635 The cloud around them broke, dissolved in air,
Illumining Aeneas, like a god,
Light radiant around his face and shoulders,
And Venus gave him all the bloom of youth.
Its glow, its liveliness, as the artist adds
640 Luster to ivory, or sets in gold
Silver or marble. No one saw him coming
Until he spoke:—"You seek me; here I am,
Trojan Aeneas, saved from the Libyan waves.
Worn out by all the perils of land and sea,
645 In need of everything blown over the great world,
A remnant left by the Greeks, Dido, we lack
The means to thank our only pitier
For offer of a city and a home.
If there is justice anywhere, if goodness
650 Means anything to any power, if gods
At all regard good people, may they give
The great rewards you merit. Happy the age,
Happy the parents who have brought you forth!
While rivers run to sea, while shadows move
655 Over the mountains, while the stars burn on,
Always, your praise, your honor, and your name,
Whatever land I go to, will endure."
His hand went out to greet his men, Serestus,
Gyas, Cloanthus, Ilioneus,
660 The others in their turn. And Dido marveled
At his appearance, first, and all that trouble
He had borne up under; there was a moment's silence
Before she spoke: "What chance, what violence,
O goddess-born, has driven you through danger,
665 From grief to grief? Are you indeed that son
Whom Venus bore Anchises? I remember
When Teucer came to Sidon, as an exile
Seeking new kingdoms, and my father helped him,
My father, Belus, conqueror of Cyprus.
670 From that time on I have known about your city,

Your name, and the Greek kings, and the fall of Troy.
Even their enemies would praise the Trojans,
Or claim descent from Teucer's line. I bid you
Enter my house. I, too, am fortune-driven
675   Through many sufferings; this land at last
Has brought me rest. Not ignorant of evil,
I know one thing, at least,—to help the wretched."
And so she led Aeneas to the palace,
Proclaiming sacrifice at all the temples
680   In honor of his welcome, and sent presents
To his comrades at the shore, a score of bullocks,
A hundred swine, a hundred ewes and lambs
In honor of the joyous day. The palace,
Within, is made most bright with pomp and splendor,
685   The halls prepared for feasting. Crimson covers
Are laid, with fine embroidery, and silver
Is heavy on the tables; gold, engraven
Recalls ancestral prowess, a tale of heroes
From the race's first beginnings.
690   And Aeneas,
Being a thoughtful father, speeds Achates
Back to the ships, with tidings for Iulus,
He is to join them; all the father's fondness
Is centred on the son. Orders are given
695   To bring gifts with him, saved from the Trojan ruins,
A mantle stiff with figures worked in gold;
A veil with gold acanthus running through it,
Once worn by Helen, when she sailed from Sparta
Toward that forbidden marriage, a wondrous gift
700   Made by her mother Leda; and the sceptre
That Ilione, Priam's eldest daughter,
Had carried once; a necklace hung with pearls;
A crown of gold and jewels. Toward the ships
Achates sped the message.
705   Meanwhile Venus
Plotted new stratagems, that Cupid, changed
In form and feature, should appear instead
Of young Ascanius, and by his gifts
Inspire the queen to passion, with his fire
710   Burning her very bones. She feared the house
Held dubious intentions; men of Tyre
Were always two-faced people, and Juno's anger
Vexed her by night. She spoke to her winged son:—
"O my one strength and source of power, my son,

715   Disdainful of Jove's thunderbolt, to you
          I come in prayer for help. You know that Juno
          Is hateful toward Aeneas, keeps him tossing
          All over the seas in bitterness; you have often
          Grieved with me for your brother. And now Dido
720   Holds him with flattering words; I do not trust
          Juno's ideas of welcome; she will never
          Pause at a point like this. Therefore I purpose
          To take the queen by cunning, put around her
          A wall of flame, so that no power can change her,
725   So that a blazing passion for Aeneas
          Will bind her to us. Listen! I will tell you
          How you can manage this. The royal boy,
          My greatest care, has heard his father's summons
          To come to the city, bringing presents, rescued
730   From the flames of Troy and the sea; and he is ready.
          But I will make him drowsy, carry him off
          In slumber over Cythera, or hide him
          Deep on Idalium in a secret bower
          Before he learns the scheme or interrupts it.
735   You, for one night, no more, assume his features,
          The boy's familiar guise, yourself a boy,
          So that when Dido takes you to her bosom
          During the royal feast, with the wine flowing,
          And happiness abounding, you, receiving
740   The sweetness of her kiss, will overcome her
          With secret fire and poison."
                              For his mother
          Cupid put off his wings, and went rejoicing
          With young Iulus' stride; the real Iulus
745   Venus had lulled in soft repose, and borne him
          Warm in her bosom to Idalian groves,
          Where the soft marjoram cradled him with blossom
          Exhaling shadowy sweetness over his slumber.
          And, with Achates leading, Cupid came
750   Obedient to his mother, bringing gifts.
          The queen receives them, on a golden couch
          Below the royal tapestries, where spreads
          Of crimson wait Aeneas and his Trojans.
          Servants bring water for their hands, and bread
755   In baskets, and fine napkins. At the fire
          Are fifty serving-maids, to set the feast,
          A hundred more, girls, and a hundred boys
          To load the tables, and bring the goblets round,

As through the happy halls the Tyrians throng,
760   Admire the Trojan gifts, admire Iulus,
The young god with the glowing countenance,
The charming words, the robe, the saffron veil
Edged with acanthus. More than all the rest,
Disaster-bound, the unhappy queen takes fire,
765   And cannot have enough of looking moved
Alike by boy and gifts. She watches him
Cling to his father's neck, or come to her
For fondling, and her eyes, her heart, receive him,
Alas, poor queen, not knowing what a god
770   Is plotting for her sorrow. He remembers
What Venus told him; she forgets a little
About Sychaeus; the heart unused to love
Stirs with a living passion.
When the first quiet settled over the tables,
775   And the boards were cleared, they set the great bowls down,
Crowning the wine with garlands. A great hum
Runs through the halls, the voices reach the rafters,
The burning lamps below the fretted gold,
The torches flaring, put the night to rout.
780   The queen commands the loving-cup of Belus,
Heavy with gems and gold, and fills it full,
And silence fills the halls before her prayer:—
"Jupiter, giver of laws for host and guest,
Grant this to be a happy day for all,
785   Both Tyrians and travellers from Troy,
And something for our children to remember!
May Bacchus,[18] giver of joy, attend, and Juno
Be kind, and all my Tyrians be friendly!"
She poured libation on the table, touched
790   The gold rim with her lips, passed on the bowl
To Bitias, who dove deep, and other lords
Took up the challenge. And a minstrel played
A golden lyre, Iopas, taught by Atlas:
Of the sun's labors and the wandering moon
795   He sang, whence came the race of beasts and man,
Whence rain and fire, the stars and constellations,
Why suns in winter hasten to the sea,
Or what delay draws out the dawdling nights.
The Tyrians roar, applauding, and the Trojans

---

[18]**Bacchus:** god of wine and fertility (Greek Dionysus)

800   Rejoice no less, and the poor queen prolongs
        The night with conversation, drinking deep
        Of her long love, and asking many questions
        Of Priam, Hector; of the arms of Memnon;
        How big Achilles was; and Diomedes,
805   What were his horses like? "Tell us, my guest,"
        She pleads, "from the beginning, all the story,
        The treachery of the Greeks, the wanderings,
        The perils of the seven tiresome years."

BOOK II: THE FALL OF TROY

        They all were silent, watching. From his couch
        Aeneas spoke: "A terrible grief, O Queen,
        You bid me live again, how Troy went down
        Before the Greeks, her wealth, her pitiful kingdom,
5   Sorrowful things I saw myself, wherein
        I had my share and more. Even Ulysses,[19]
        Even his toughest soldiery might grieve
        At such a story. And the hour is late
        Already; night is sliding down the sky
10   And setting stars urge slumber. But if you long
        To learn our downfall, to hear the final chapter
        Of Troy, no matter how I shrink, remembering,
        And turn away in grief, let me begin it.

        Broken in war, set back by fate, the leaders
15   Of the Greek host, as years went by, contrived,
        With Pallas' help, a horse as big as a mountain.
        They wove its sides with planks of fir, pretending
        This was an offering for their safe return,
        At least, so rumor had it. But inside
20   They packed, in secret, into the hollow sides
        The fittest warriors; the belly's cavern,
        Huge as it was, was filled with men in armor.
        There is an island, Tenedos, well-known,
        Rich in the days of Priam; now it is only
25   A bay, and not too good an anchorage
        For any ship to trust. They sailed there, hid
        On the deserted shore. We thought they had gone,

---

[19]Ulysses: the Greek Odysseus

Bound for Mycenae,[20] and Troy was very happy,
Shaking off grief, throwing the gates wide open.
30   It was a pleasure, for a change, to go
See the Greek camp, station and shore abandoned;
Why, this was where Achilles camped, his minions,
The Dolopes, were here; and the fleet just yonder,
And that was the plain where we used to meet in battle
35   Some of us stared in wonder at the horse,
Astounded by its vastness, Minerva's gift
Death from the virgin goddess, had we known it.
Thymoetes, whether in treachery, or because
The fates of Troy so ordered, was the first one
40   To urge us bring it in to the heart of the city,
But Capys, and some others, knowing better,
Suspicious of Greek plotting, said to throw it
Into the sea, to burn it up with fire,
To cut it open, see what there was inside it.
45   The wavering crowd could not make up its mind.

And, at that point, Laocoön came running,
With a great throng at his heels, down from the hilltop
As fast as ever he could, and before he reached us,
Cried in alarm: 'Are you crazy, wretched people?
50   Do you think they have gone, the foe? Do you think that any
Gifts of the Greeks lack treachery? Ulysses,—
What was his reputation? Let me tell you,
Either the Greeks are hiding in this monster,
Or it's some trick of war, a spy, or engine,
55   To come down on the city. Tricky business
Is hiding in it. Do not trust it, Trojans,
Do not believe this horse. Whatever it may be,
I fear the Greeks, even when bringing presents.'
With that, he hurled the great spear at the side
60   With all the strength he had. It fastened, trembling,
And the struck womb rang hollow, a moaning sound.
He had driven us, almost, to let the light in
With the point of the steel, to probe, to tear, but something
Got in his way, the gods, or fate, or counsel,
65   Ill-omened, in our hearts; or Troy would be standing
And Priam's lofty citadel unshaken.

---

[20]Mycenae: where Agamemnon was king

Meanwhile, some Trojan shepherds, pulling and hauling,
Had a young fellow, with his hands behind him,
Tied up, and they were dragging him to Priam.
70 He had let himself be taken so, on purpose,
To open Troy to the Greeks, a stranger, ready
For death or shifty cunning, a cool intriguer,
Let come what may. They crowd around to see him,
Take turns in making fun of him, that captive.
75 Listen, and learn Greek trickiness; learn all
Their crimes from one.
He stopped in the middle, frightened and defenceless,
Looked at the Trojan ranks,—'What land, what waters,
Can take me now?' he cried, 'There is nothing, nothing
80 Left for me any more, no place with the Greeks,
And here are the Trojans howling for my blood!'
Our mood was changed. We pitied him, poor fellow,
Sobbing his heart out. We bade him tell his story,
His lineage, his news: what can he count on,
85 The captive that he is? His fear had gone
As he began: 'O King, whatever happens,
I will tell the truth; tell all of it; to start with,
I own I am a Greek. Sinon is wretched,
Fortune has made him so, but she will never
90 Make him a liar. You may perhaps have heard
Rumors of Palamedes, son of Belus,
A man of glorious fame. But the Greeks killed him,—
He was against the war, and so they killed him,
An innocent man, by perjury and lying
95 False witness. Now that he is dead they mourn him.
My father, his poor relative, had sent me
To soldier in his company; I was then
Scarcely beyond my boyhood. Palamedes
Held, for some time, some influence and standing
100 In royal councils, and we shared his glory,
But, and all men know this, Ulysses' hatred,
His cunning malice, pulled him down; thereafter
I lived in darkness, dragging out a lifetime
In sorrow for my innocent lord, and anger,
105 And in my anger I was very foolish,
I talked; I vowed, if I got home to Argos,
I would have vengeance: so I roused Ulysses
To hate me in his turn, and that began it,
Downfall and evil Ulysses always trying
110 To frighten me with hint and accusation,

With rumors planted where the crowd would listen;
Oh yes, Ulysses knew what he was doing,
He never stopped, until with Calchas[21] working
Hand in glove with him—why am I telling this,
115   And what's the use? I am stalling. All the Greeks,
You think, are all alike; what more do you want?
Inflict the punishment. That would be something
Ulysses would rejoice in, and some others
Pay handsome money for!'

120   But we were all on fire to hear him further.
Pelasgian[22] craft meant nothing to our folly.
Trembling and nervous, he resumed his lying:
'The Greeks were tired of the long war; they often
Wanted to sail from Troy for home. Oh, would
125   That they had only done it! But a storm
Would cut them off, or the wrong wind terrify them.
Especially, just after the horse was finished,
With the joined planks of maple, all the heaven
Roared loud with storm-clouds. In suspense and terror
130   We sent Eurypylus to ask Apollo
What could be done; the oracle was gloomy,
Foreboding: "Blood, O Greeks, and a slain virgin[23]
Appeased the winds when first you came here; blood
Must pay for your return, a life be given,
135   An Argive life." The word came to our ears
With terror in it, our blood ran cold in our veins,
For whom was fate preparing? who would be
The victim of Apollo? Then Ulysses
Dragged Calchas into our midst, with a great uproar,
140   Trying his best to make the prophet tell us
What the gods wanted. And there were many then
Who told me what was coming, or kept silent
Because they saw, and all too well, the scheme
Ulysses had in mind. For ten days Calchas
145   Said nothing at all, hid in his tent, refusing
To have a word of his pronounce the sentence,
And all the time Ulysses kept on shouting,

---

[21]**Calchas:** a Greek prophet
[22]**Pelasgian:** i.e., Greek
[23]**slain virgin:** Agamemnon had to sacrifice his daughter Iphigeneia to gain fair winds to sail to Troy (his wife, Clytaemnestra, will slay him for this offense upon his return home; see Aeschylus' *Oresteia, Agamemnon*).

Till Calchas broke, and doomed me to the altar.
And all assented; what each man had feared
150 In his own case, he bore with great composure
When turned another way.
The terrible day was almost on me; fillets
Were ready for my temples, the salted meal
Prepared, the altars standing. But I fled,
155 I tore myself away from death, I admit it,
I hid all night in sedge and muddy water
At the edge of the lake, hoping, forever hoping,
They might set sail. And now I hope no longer
To see my home, my parents, or my children,
160 Poor things, whom they will kill because I fled them,
Whom they will murder for my sacrilege.
But oh; by the gods above, by any power
That values truth, by any uncorrupted
Remnant of faith in all the world, have pity,
165 Have pity on a soul that bears such sorrow,
More than I ever deserved.'
He had no need to ask us. Priam said,
Untie him, and we did so with a promise
To spare his life. Our king, with friendly words,
170 Addressed him, saying, 'Whoever you are, forget
The Greeks, from now on. You are ours; but tell me
Why they have built this monstrous horse? who made it,
Who thought of it? What is it, war-machine,
Religious offering? And he, instructed
175 In every trick and artifice, made answer,
Lifting his hands, now free: 'Eternal fires,
Inviolable godhead, be my witness,
You altars, you accursed swords, you fillets
Which I as victim wore, I had the right
180 To break those solemn bonds, I had the right
To hate those men, to bring whatever they hide
Into the light and air; I am bound no longer
To any country, any laws, but, Trojans,
Keep to the promise, if I tell the truth,
185 If I pay back with interest.
All the Greek hope, since first the war began,
Rested in Pallas, always. But Ulysses,
The crime-contriver, and the son of Tydeus
Attacked Minerva's temple, stole her image
190 Out of the holy shrine, and slew the guards,
And laid their bloody hands upon the goddess,

And from that time the Danaan hopes were broken,
Faltered and failed. It was no doubtful anger
Pallas revealed; she gave them signs and portents.
195   From her image in the camp the upraised eyes
Shot fire, and sweat ran salty down the limbs,
Thrice from the ground she seemed to dash and leap
With vibrant spear and clashing shield. The priest,
Calchas, made prophecy: they must take to flight
200   Over the sea, and Troy could not be taken
Without new omens; they must go to Argos,
Bring back the goddess again, whom they have taken
In curved ships over the sea. And if they have gone,
They are bound for home, Mycenae, for new arms,
205   New gods, new soldiers; they will be here again
When least expected. Calchas' message warned them,
And so they built this image, to replace
The one they had stolen, a gigantic offering
For a tremendous sacrilege. It was Calchas,
210   Again, who bade them build a mass so mighty
It almost reached the stars, too big to enter
Through any gate, or be brought inside the walls.
For if your hands should damage it, destruction,
(May God avert it) would come upon the city,
215   But if your hands helped bring it home, then Asia
Would be invading Greece, and doom await.
Our children's children.'
                    We believed him, we
Whom neither Diomede nor great Achilles
220   Had taken, nor ten years, nor that armada,
A thousand ships of war. But Sinon did it
By perjury and guile.
                  Then something else,
Much greater and more terrible, was forced
225   Upon us, troubling our unseeing spirits.
Laocoön, allotted priest of Neptune,
Was slaying a great bull beside the altars,
When suddenly, over the tranquil deep
From Tenedos,—I shudder even now,
230   Recalling it—there came a pair of serpents
With monstrous coils, breasting the sea, and aiming
Together for the shore. Their heads and shoulders
Rose over the waves, upright, with bloody crests,
The rest of them trailing along the water,
235   Looping in giant spirals; the foaming sea

Hissed under their motion. And they reached the land,
Their burning eyes suffused with blood and fire,
Their darting tongues licking the hissing mouths.
Pale at the sight, we fled. But they went on
240 Straight toward Laocoön, and first each serpent
Seized in its coils his two young sons, and fastened
The fangs in those poor bodies. And the priest
Struggled to help them, weapons in his hand.
They seized him, bound him with their mighty coils,
245 Twice round his waist, twice round his neck they squeezed
With scaly pressure, and still towered above him.
Straining his hands to tear the knots apart,
His chaplets stained with blood and the black poison,
He uttered horrible cries, not even human,
250 More like the bellowing of a bull, when, wounded
It flees the altar, shaking from the shoulder
The ill-aimed axe. And on the pair went gliding
To the highest shrine, the citadel of Pallas,
And vanished underneath the feet of the goddess
255 And the circle of her shield.
                                    The people trembled
Again; they said Laocoön deserved it,
Having, with spear, profaned the sacred image.
It must be brought to its place, they cried, the goddess
260 Must be appeased. We broke the walls, exposing
The city's battlements, and all were busy
Helping the work, with rollers underfoot
And ropes around the neck. It climbed our walls,
The deadly engine. Boys, unwedded girls
265 Sang alleluias round it, all rejoicing
To have a hand on the tow-rope. It came nearer,
Threatening, gliding, into the very city.
O motherland! O Ilium, home of gods,
O walls of Troy! Four times it stopped, four times
270 The sound of arms came from it, and we pressed on,
Unheedful, blind in madness, till we set it,
Ill-omened thing, on the citadel we worshipped.
And even when Cassandra gave us warning,
We never believed her; so a god had ordered.
275 That day, our last, poor wretches, we were happy,
Garlanding the temples of the gods
All through the town.
                                    And the sky turned, and darkness
Came from the ocean, the great shade covering earth

280   And heaven, and the trickery of the Greeks.
        Sprawling along the walls, the Trojans slumbered,
        Sleep holding their weary limbs, and the Greek armada,
        From Tenedos, under the friendly silence
        Of a still moon, came surely on. The flagship
285   Blazed at the masthead with a sudden signal,
        And Sinon, guarded by the fates, the hostile
        Will of the gods, swung loose the bolts; the Greeks
        Came out of the wooden womb. The air received them
        The happy captains, Sthenelus, Ulysses,
290   Thessandrus, Acamas, Achilles' son
        Called Neoptolemus, Thoas, Machaon,
        Epeos, who designed the thing,—they all
        Came sliding down the rope, and Menelaus
        Was with them in the storming of a city
295   Buried in sleep and wine. The watch was murdered,
        The open doors welcome the rush of comrades,
        They marshal the determined ranks for battle.
        It was the time when the first sleep begins
        For weary mortals, heaven's most welcome gift.
300   In sleep, before my eyes, I seemed to see
        Hector, most sorrowful, black with bloody dust,
        Torn, as he had been, by Achilles' car,
        The thong-marks on his swollen feet. How changed
        He was from that great Hector who came, once,
305   Triumphant in Achilles' spoil, from hurling
        Fire at the Grecian ships. With ragged beard,
        Hair matted with his blood, wearing the wounds
        He earned around the walls of Troy, he stood there.
        It seemed that I spoke first:—'O light of Troy,
310   Our surest hope, we have long been waiting for you,
        What shores have kept you from us? Many deaths,
        Much suffering, have visited our city,
        And we are tired. Why do I see these wounds?
        What shame has caused them?' Those were foolish questions;
315   He made no answer but a sigh or a groan,
        And then: 'Alas, O goddess-born! Take flight,
        Escape these flames! The enemy has the walls,
        Troy topples from her lofty height; enough
        Has been paid out to Priam and to country.
320   Could any hand have saved them, Hector's would have.
        Troy trusts to you her household gods, commending
        Her holy things to you; take them, companions
        Of destiny; seek walls for them, and a city

To be established, a long sea-wandering over.'
325 From the inner-shrine he carried Vesta's chaplets
In his own hands, and her undying fire.
         Meanwhile, the city is all confusion and sorrow;
My father Anchises' house, remote and sheltered
Among its trees, was not so far away
330 But I could hear the noises, always clearer,
The thickening din of war. Breaking from sleep,
I climb to the roof-top, listening and straining
The way a shepherd does on the top of a mountain
When fire goes over the corn, and the winds are roaring,
335 Or the rush of a mountain torrent drowns the fields
And the happy crops and the work of men and oxen
And even drags great trees over. And then I knew
The truth indeed; the craft of the Greeks was hidden
No longer from my sight. The house of a neighbor,
340 Deiphobus, went up in flames; next door,
Ucalegon was burning. Sigeum's water
Gave back the glow. Men shouted, and the trumpets
Blared loud. I grab my arms, with little purpose,
There was no sense in it, but my heart was burning
345 To mass a band for war, rush to the hilltop
With comrades at my side. Anger and frenzy
Hurry me on. A decent death in battle
Is a helpful thought, sometimes.
         And here came Panthus, running from the weapons,
350 Priest of Apollo, and a son of Othrys,
With holy relics in his hands, and dragging
His little grandson, here came Panthus, running
In madness to my door. 'How goes it, Panthus?
What stronghold still is ours?' I had hardly spoken,
355 When he began, with a groan: 'It has come, this day
Will be our last, and we can not escape it.
Trojans we have been, Troy has been, and glory
Is ours no more. Fierce Jupiter has taken
Everything off to Argos, and Greeks lord it
360 In a town on fire. The horse, high in the city,
Pours out armed men, and Sinon, arrogant victor,
Lights up more fires. The gates are standing open,
And men are there by the thousands, ever as many
As came once from Mycenae; others block
365 The narrow streets, with weapons drawn; the blades
Flash in the dark; the point is set for murder.

A few of the guards are trying, striking blindly,
For all the good it does.'
          His words, or the gods' purpose, swept me on
370   Toward fire and arms, where the grim furies call,
And the clamor and confusion, reaching heaven.
Ripheus joined me, Epytus, mighty in arms,
Came to my side in the moonlight, Hypanis, Dymas,
And young Coroebus, Mygdon's son, poor youngster,
375   Mad with a hopeless passion for Cassandra,
He wanted to help Priam, but never heeded
The warnings of his loved one.
                    As they ranged
Themselves for battle, eager, I addressed them:
380   'O brave young hearts, it will do no good; no matter.
Even if your will is fixed, to follow a leader
Taking the final risk, you can't help seeing
The fortune of our state. The gods have gone,
They have left their shrines and altars, and the power
385   They once upheld is fallen. You are helping
A town already burnt. So let us die,
Rush into arms. One safety for the vanquished
Is to have hope of none.'
                  They were young, and angry.
390   Like wolves, marauders in black mist, whom hunger
Drives blindly on, whose whelps, abandoned, wait them
Dry-jawed, so we went on, through foes, through weapons,
To certain death; we made for the heart of the city,
Black night around us with its hollow shadow.
395   Who could explain that night's destruction, equal
Its agony with tears? The ancient city,
A power for many years, comes down, and corpses
Lie littering the streets and homes and altars.
Not only Trojans die. The old-time valor
400   Returns to the vanquished heart, and the Greek victors
Know what it is to fall. Everywhere sorrow,
Everywhere panic, everywhere the image
Of death, made manifold.
          Out of a crowd of Greeks comes one Androgeos,
405   Thinking us allies, hailing us as friendly:
'Why men, where have you been, you dawdling fellows?'
Hurry along! Here is plunder for the taking,
Others are busy at it, and you just coming
From the high ships!' And then he knew he had blundered;
410   He had fallen in with foes, who gave no answer.

He stopped, stepped back, like a man who treads on a serpent
Unseen in the rough brush, and then in panic
Draws back as the purple neck swells out in anger.
Even so, Androgeos pulled away in terror.
415 We rush them, swarm all over them; they are frightened,
They do not know their ground, and fortune favors
Our first endeavor. Coroebus, a little crazy
With nerve and luck, cries out: 'Comrades, where fortune
First shows the way and sides with us, we follow.
420 Let us change our shields, put on the Grecian emblems!
All's fair in war: we lick them or we trick them,
And what's the odds?' He takes Androgeos' helmet,
Whose plume streams over his head, takes up the shield
With proud device, and fits the sword to his side.
425 And Ripheus does the same, and so does Dymas,
And all the others, happily, being armed
With spoil new-won. We join the Greeks, all going
Under no gods of ours, in the night's darkness
Wade into many a fight, and Greeks by the dozens
430 We send to hell. And some of them in panic
Speed to the ships; they know that shore, and trust it,
And some of them—these were the abject cowards—
Climb scrambling up the horse's sides, again
Take refuge in the womb.
435   It is not for men to trust unwilling gods.
Cassandra was being dragged from Pallas' temple,
Her hair loosed to the wind, her eyes turned upward
To heaven for mercy; they had bound her hands.
Coroebus could not bear that sight; in madness
440 He threw himself upon them, and he died.
We followed, all of us, into the thick of it,
And were cut down, not only by Greeks; the rooftops,
Held by our friends, rained weapons: we were wearing
Greek crests and armor, and they did not know us.
445 And the Greeks came on, shouting with anger, burning
To foil that rescue, there was Menelaus,
And Agamemnon, and the savage Ajax,
And a whole army of them. Hurricanes
Rage the same way, when winds from different quarters
450 Clash in the sky, and the forest groans, and Neptune
Storms underneath the ocean. Those we routed
Once in the dark came back again from the byways
And alleys of the town; they mark our shields,
Our lying weapons, and our foreign voices.

455   Of course we are outnumbered. Peneleus
       It was, who slew Coroebus, at the altar
       Sacred to Pallas. Ripheus fell, a man
       Most just of all the Trojans, most fair-minded.
       The gods thought otherwise. Hypanis, Dymas,
460   Were slain by their own men, and Panthus' goodness
       Was no protection, nor his priestly office.
       I call to witness Troy, her fires, her ashes,
       And the last agonies of all our people
       That in that hour I ran from no encounter
465   With any Greek, and if the fates had been
       For me to fall in battle, there I earned it.
       The current swept me off, with two companions,
       One, Iphitus, too slow with age, the other,
       Pelias, limping from Ulysses' wound.
470   The noise kept calling us to Priam's palace.
            There might have been no fighting and no dying
       Through all the city, such a battle raged
       Here, from the ground to roof-top. At the threshold
       Waves of assault were breaking, and the Greeks
475   Were climbing, rung by rung, along the ladders,
       Using one hand, the right one up and forward
       Over the battlements, the left one thrust
       In the protecting shield. And over their heads
       The Trojans pried up towers and planking, wrecking
480   The building; gilded beams, the spoils of their fathers,
       Were ample weapons for the final moment.
       Some had the doorways blocked, others, behind them,
       Were ready with drawn swords. We had a moment
       When help seemed possible: new reinforcement
485   Might yet relieve the palace.
       There was a secret entrance there, a passage
       All the way through the building, a postern gate,
       Where, while the kingdom stood, Andromache[24]
       Would go, alone, or bring the little boy,
490   Astyanax, to Hector's father and mother.
       I climbed to the top of the roof, where the poor Trojans
       Were hurling down their unavailing darts.
       A tower stood on the very edge, a look-out
       Over all Troy, the ships and camp of the Greeks.
495   This we attacked with steel, where the joints were weakest,

---

[24]**Andromache:** Hector's wife and mother to Astyanax; Hector's father and mother are Priam and Hecube.

And pried it up, and shoved it over. It crashed,
A noisy ruin, over the hostile columns;
But more kept coming up; the shower of stones
And darts continued raining.
500   Before the entrance, at the very threshold
Stood Pyrrhus, flashing proudly in bronze light,
Sleek as a serpent coming into the open,
Fed on rank herbs, wintering under the ground,
The old slough cast, the new skin shining, rolling
505   His slippery length, reaching his neck to the sun,
While the forked tongue darts from the mouth. Automedon
Was with him, Periphas, Achilles' driver,
A giant of a man, and the host from Scyros,
All closing in on the palace, and hurling flames.
510   Among the foremost, Pyrrhus, swinging an axe,
Burst through, wrenched the bronze doors out of their hinges,
Smashed through the panelling, turned it into a window.
The long halls came to view, the inner chambers
Of Priam and the older kings; they see
515   Armed warriors at the threshold.
Within, it is all confusion, women wailing,
Pitiful noise, groaning, and blows; the din
Reaches the golden stars. The trembling mothers
Wander, not knowing where, or find a spot
520   To cling to; they would hold and kiss the doors.
Pyrrhus comes on, aggressive as his father;[25]
No barrier holds him back; the gate is battered
As the ram smashes at it; the doors come down.
Force finds a way: the Greeks pour in, they slaughter
525   The first ones in their path; they fill the courtyard
With soldiery, wilder than any river
In flood over the banks and dikes and ploughland.
I saw them, Pyrrhus, going mad with murder,
And Atreus' twin sons, and Hecuba
530   I saw, and all her daughters, and poor old Priam,
His blood polluting the altars he had hallowed.
The fifty marriage-chambers, the proud hope
Of an everlasting line, are violated,
The doors with the golden spoil are turned to splinters.
535   Whatever the fire has spared the Greeks take over.

---

[25]**his father:** Achilles; Pyrrhus is also called Neoptolemus (II. 291)

You would ask, perhaps, about the fate of Priam?
When he saw the city fall, and the doors of the palace
Ripped from the hinge, and the enemy pouring in,
Old as he was, he went and found his armor,
540   Unused so many years, and his old shoulders
Shook as he put it on. He took his sword,
A useless weapon, and, doomed to die, went rushing
Into the midst of the foe. There was an altar
In the open court-yard, shaded by a laurel
545   Whose shadow darkened the household gods, and here
Hecuba and her daughters had come thronging,
Like doves by a black storm driven. They were praying
Here at the altar, and clinging to the gods,
Whatever image was left. And the queen saw Priam
550   In the arms of his youth. 'O my unhappy husband,'
She cried, 'have you gone mad, to dress yourself
For battle, so? It is all no use; the time
Needs better help than yours; not even my Hector
Could help us now. Come to me, come to the altar;
555   It will protect us, or at least will let us
Die all together.' And she drew him to her.
      Just then through darts, through weapons, came Polites,
A son of Priam, fleeing deadly Pyrrhus,
Down the long colonnades and empty hallways,
560   Wounded, and Pyrrhus after him, vicious, eager
For the last spear-thrust, and he drives it home;
Polites falls, and his life goes out with his blood,
Father and mother watching. And then Priam,
In the very grip of death, cried out in anger:
565   'If there is any righteousness in heaven,
To care about such wickedness, the gods
Will have the right reward and thanks to offer
A man like this, who has made a father witness,
The murder of his son, the worst pollution!
570   You claim to be Achilles' son. You liar!
Achilles had some reverence, respected
A suppliant's right and trust; he gave me back
My Hector's lifeless body for the tomb,
And let me go to my kingdom.' With the word
575   He flung a feeble spear, which dropped, deflected
From the rough bronze; it had hung there for a moment,
And Pyrrhus sneered. 'So, go and tell my father
The latest news: do not forget to mention,
Old messenger-boy, my villainous behavior,

580   And what a bastard Pyrrhus is. Now die!
He dragged the old man, trembling, to the altar,
Slipping in his son's blood; he grabbed his hair
With the left hand, and the right drove home the sword,
Deep in the side, to the hilt. And so fell Priam,
585   Who had seen Troy burn and her walls come down, once monarch,
Proud ruler over the peoples and lands of Asia.
He lies, a nameless body, on the shore,
Dismembered, huge, the head torn from the shoulders.
       Grim horror, then, came home to me. I saw
590   My father when I saw the king, the life
Going out with the cruel wound. I saw Creusa
Forsaken, my abandoned home, Iulus,
My little son. I looked around. They all
Had gone, exhausted, flung down from the walls,
595   Or dead in the fire, and I was left alone.
       And I saw Helen, hiding, of all places,
At Vesta's shrine, and clinging there in silence,
But the bright flames lit the scene. That hated woman,
Fearing both Trojan anger and Greek vengeance,
600   A common fury to both lands, was crouching
Beside the altar. Anger flared up in me
For punishment and vengeance.
Should she then, I thought, come home to Sparta safe, uninjured
Walk through Mycenae, a triumphant queen?
605   See husband, home, parents and children, tended
By Trojan slave-girls? This, with Priam fallen
And Troy burnt down, and the shore soaked in blood?
Never! No memorable name, I knew,
Was won by punishing women, yet, for me,
610   There might be praise for the just abolition
Of this unholiness, and satisfaction
In vengeance for the ashes of my people.
All this I may have said aloud, in frenzy,
As I rushed on, when to my sight there came
615   A vision of my lovely mother, radiant
In the dark night, a goddess manifest,
As tall and fair as when she walks in heaven.
She caught me by the hand and stopped me:—'Son,
What sorrow rouses this relentless anger,
620   This violence? Do you care for me no longer?
Consider others first, your aged father,
Anchises; is your wife Creusa living?
Where is Iulus? Greeks are all around them,

> Only my love between them, fire and sword.
625 It is not for you to blame the Spartan woman,[26]
> Daughter of Tyndareus, or even Paris.
> The gods are the ones, the high gods are relentless
> It is they who bring this power down, who topple
> Troy from the high foundation. Look! Your vision
630 Is mortal dull, I will take the cloud away,—
> Fear not a mother's counsel. Where you see
> Rock torn from rock, and smoke and dust in billows,
> Neptune is working, plying the trident, prying
> The walls from their foundations. And see Juno,
635 Fiercest of all, holding the Scaean gates,
> Girt with the steel, and calling from the ships
> Implacable companions. On the towers,—
> Turn, and be certain—Pallas takes command
> Gleaming with Gorgon and storm-cloud. Even Jove,
640 Our father, nerves the Greeks with fire and spirit,
> And spurs the other gods against the Trojans.
> Hasten the flight, my son; no other labor
> Waits for accomplishment. I promise safety
> Until you reach your father's house.' She had spoken
645 And vanished in the thickening night of shadows.
> Dread shapes come into vision, mighty powers,
> Great gods at war with Troy, which, so it seemed,
> Was sinking as I watched, with the same feeling
> As when on mountain-tops you see the loggers
650 Hacking an ash-tree down, and it always threatens
> To topple, nodding a little, and the leaves
> Trembling when no wind stirs, and dies of its wounds
> With one long loud last groan, and dirt from the ridges
> Heaves up as it goes down with roots in air.
655 Divinity my guide, I leave the roof-top,
> I pass unharmed through enemies and blazing,
> Weapons give place to me, and flames retire.
>   At last I reached the house, I found my father,
> The first one that I looked for. I meant to take him
660 To the safety of the hills but he was stubborn
> Refusing longer life or barren exile,
> Since Troy was dead. 'You have the strength,' he told me,
> 'You are young enough, take flight. For me, had heaven
> Wanted to save my life, they would have spared

---

[26]Spartan woman: Helen, wife of Menelaus, king of Sparta. In part, Venus is protecting Helen, whom she had awarded to Paris.

665   This home for me. We have seen enough destruction,
          More than enough, survived a captured city.
          Speak to me as a corpse laid out for burial,
          A quick farewell and go. Death I shall find
          With my own hand; the enemy will pity,
670   Or look for spoil. The loss of burial
          Is nothing at all. I have been living too long
          Hated by gods and useless, since the time
          Jove blasted me with lightning wind and fire.'
          He would not move, however we wept, Creusa,
675   Ascanius, all the house, insistent, pleading
          That he should not bring all to ruin with him.
          He would not move, he would not listen. Again
          I rush to arms, I pray for death; what else
          Was left to me? 'Dear father, were you thinking
680   I could abandon you, and go? what son
          Could bear a thought so monstrous? If the gods
          Want nothing to be left of so great a city,
          If you are bound, or pleased, to add us all
          To the wreck of Troy, the way is open for it—
685   Pyrrhus will soon be here; from the blood of Priam
          He comes; he slays the son before the father,
          The sire at the altar-stone; O my dear mother,
          Was it for this you saved me, brought me through
          The fire and sword, to see our enemies
690   Here in the very house, and wife and son
          And father murdered in each other's blood?
          Bring me my arms; the last light calls the conquered.
          Let me go back to the Greeks, renew the battle,
          We shall not all of us die unavenged.'
695   Sword at my side, I was on the point of going,
          Working the left arm into the shield. Creusa
          Clung to me on the threshold, held my feet,
          And made me, see my little son:—'Dear husband,
          If you are bent on dying, take us with you,
700   But if you think there is any hope in fighting,
          And you should know, stay and defend the house
          To whom are we abandoned, your father and son,
          And I, once called your wife?' She filled the house
          With moaning outcry. And then something happened,
705   A wonderful portent. Over Iulus' head,
          Between our hands and faces, there appeared
          A blaze of gentle light; a tongue of flame,
          Harmless and innocent, was playing over

The softness of his hair, around his temples.
710 We were afraid, we did our best to quench it
With our own hands, or water, but my father
Raised joyous eyes to heaven, and prayed aloud:—
'Almighty Jupiter, if any prayer
Of ours has power to move you, look upon us,
715 Grant only this, if we have ever deserved it,
Grant us a sign, and ratify the omen!'
He had hardly spoken, when thunder on the left
Resounded, and a shooting star from heaven
Drew a long trail of light across the shadows.
720 We saw it cross above the house, and vanish
In the woods of Ida, a wake of gleaming light
Where it had sped, and a trail of sulphurous odor.
This was a victory: my father rose
In worship of the gods and the holy star,
725 Crying: 'I follow, son, wherever you lead;
There is no delay, not now; Gods of my fathers,
Preserve my house, my grandson; yours the omen,
And Troy is in your keeping. O my son,
I yield, I am ready to follow.' But the fire
730 Came louder over the walls, the flames rolled nearer
Their burning tide. 'Climb to my shoulders, father,
It will be no burden, so we are together,
Meeting a common danger or salvation.
Iulus, take my hand; Creusa, follow
735 A little way behind. Listen, you servants!
You will find, when you leave the city, an old temple
That once belonged to Ceres;[27] it has been tended
For many years with the worship of our fathers.
There's a little hill there, and a cypress tree;
740 And that's where we shall meet, one way or another.
And one thing more: you, father, are to carry
The holy objects and the gods of the household,
My hands are foul with battle and blood, I could not
Touch them without pollution:
745   I bent down
And over my neck and shoulders spread the cover
Of a tawny lion-skin, took up my burden;
Little Iulus held my hand, and trotted,
As best he could, beside me; Creusa followed.

---

[27]Ceres: goddess of the harvest

750 We went on through the shadows. I had been
Brave, so I thought, before, in the rain of weapons
And the cloud of massing Greeks. But now I trembled
At every breath of air, shook at a whisper,
Fearful for both my burden and companion.

755 I was near the gates, and thinking we had made it,
But there was a sound, the tramp of marching feet,
And many of them, it seemed; my father, peering
Through the thick gloom, cried out:—'Son, they are coming!
Flee, flee! I see their shields, their gleaming bronze.'

760 Something or other took my senses from me
In that confusion. I turned aside from the path,
I do not know what happened then. Creusa
Was lost; she had missed the road, or halted, weary,
For a brief rest. I do not know what happened,

765 She was not seen again; I had not looked back,
Nor even thought about her, till we came
To Ceres' hallowed home. The count was perfect,
Only one missing there, the wife and mother.
Whom did I not accuse, of gods and mortals,

770 Then in my frenzy? What worse thing had happened
In the city overthrown? I left Anchises,
My son, my household gods, to my companions,
In a hiding-place in the valley; and I went back
Into the city again, wearing my armor,

775 Ready, still one more time, for any danger.
I found the walls again, the gate's dark portals,
I followed my own footsteps back, but terror,
Terror and silence were all I found. I went
On to my house. She might, just might, have gone there.

780 Only the Greeks were there, and fire devouring
The very pinnacles. I tried Priam's palace;
In the empty courtyards Phoenix and Ulysses
Guarded the spoils piled up at Juno's altar.
They had Trojan treasure there, loot from the altars,

785 Great drinking bowls of gold, and stolen garments,
And human beings. A line of boys and women
Stood trembling there.
I took the risk of crying through the shadows,
Over and over, 'Creusa!' I kept calling

790 'Creusa!' and 'Creusa!' but no answer.
No sense, no limit, to my endless rushing
All through the town; and then at last I saw her,
Or thought I did, her shadow a little taller

Than I remembered. And she spoke to me
795 Beside myself with terror:—'O dear husband,
What good is all this frantic grief? The gods
Have willed it so, Creusa may not join you
Out of this city; Jupiter denies it.
Long exile lies ahead, and vast sea-reaches
800 The ships must furrow, till you come to land
Far in the West; rich fields are there, and a river
Flowing with gentle current; its name is Tiber,
And happy days await you there, a kingdom,
A royal wife. Banish the tears of sorrow
805 Over Creusa lost. I shall never see
The arrogant houses of the Myrmidons,
Nor be a slave to any Grecian woman;
I am a Dardan woman; I am the wife
Of Venus' son; it is Cybele[26] who keeps me
810 Here on these shores. And now farewell, and love
Our son.' I wept, there was more to say; she left me,
Vanishing into empty air. Three times
I reached out toward her, and three times her image
Fled like the breath of a wind or a dream on wings.
815 The night was over; I went back to my comrades.
I was surprised to find so many more
Had joined us, ready for exile, pitiful people,
Mothers, and men, and children, streaming in
From everywhere, looking for me to lead them
820 Wherever I would. Over the hills of Ida
The morning-star was rising; in the town
The Danaans held the gates, and help was hopeless.
I gave it up, I lifted up my father,
Together we sought the hills.

BOOK III: THE WANDERINGS OF AENEAS

"After the gods' decision to overthrow
The Asian world, the innocent house of Priam,
And the proud city, built by Neptune, smoked
From the ruined ground, we were driven, different ways,
5 By heaven's auguries, seeking lands forsaken.
Below Antandros, under Phrygian Ida,
We built a fleet, and gathered men, uncertain

---

[26]Cybele: a mother goddess

Of either direction or settlement. The summer
Had scarce begun, when at my father's orders,
10 We spread our sails. I wept as I left the harbor,
The fields where Troy had been. I was borne, an exile
Over the deep, with son, companions, household,
And household gods.
                    Far off there lies a land,
15 Sacred to Mars; the Thracians used to till it,
Whose king was fierce Lycurgus; they were friendly,
Of old, to Troy, when we were prosperous. Hither
I sailed, and on its curving shore established
A city site; Aeneadae, I called it.
20 This I began, not knowing fate was adverse.
    I was offering my mother proper homage,
And other gods, to bless the new beginnings,
I had a white bull ready as a victim
To the king of the gods. There was a mound nearby,
25 Bristling with myrtle and with cornel-bushes.
I needed greenery to veil the altar,
But as I struggled with the leafy branches,
A fearful portent met my gaze. Black drops
Dripped from the ends of the roots, black blood was falling
30 On the torn ground, and a cold chill went through me.
I tried again; the shoot resisted; blood
Followed again. Troubled, I prayed to the Nymphs,
To the father of the fields, to bless the vision,
Remove the curse; and down on my knees I wrestled
35 Once more against the stubborn ground, and heard;
A groan from under the hillock, and a voice crying:
'Why mangle a poor wretch, Aeneas? Spare me,
Here in the tomb, and save your hands pollution.
You know me, I am Trojan-born, no stranger,
40 This is familiar blood. Alas! Take flight,
Leave this remorseless land; the curse of greed
Lies heavy on it. I am Polydorus,
Pierced by an iron harvest; out of my body
Rise javelins and lances.' I was speechless,
45 Stunned, in my terror.
        Priam, forever unfortunate, had sent
This Polydorus on a secret mission
Once, to the king of Thrace, with gold for hiding
When the king despaired of the siege and the city's fortune.
50 And when Troy fell, and Fortune failed, the Thracian
Took Agamemnon's side, broke off his duty,

Slew Polydorus, took the gold. There is nothing
To which men are not driven by that hunger.
Once over my fear, I summoned all the leaders,
55 My father, too; I told them of the portent,
Asked for their counsel. All agreed, a land
So stained with violence and violation
Was not for us to dwell in. Southward ho!
For Polydorus we made restoration
60 With funeral rites anew; earth rose again
Above his outraged mound; dark fillets made
The altar sorrowful, and cypress boughs,
And the Trojan women loosed their hair in mourning.
We offered milk in foaming bowls, and blood
65 Warm from the victims, so to rest the spirit,
And cry aloud the voice of valediction.
       Then, when we trust the sea again, and the wind
Calls with a gentle whisper, we crowd the shores,
Launch ship again, leave port, the lands and cities
70 Fade out of sight once more.
                       There is an island
In the middle of the sea; the Nereids'[28] mother
And Neptune hold it sacred. It used to wander
By various coasts and shores, until Apollo,
75 In grateful memory, bound it fast, unmoving,
Unfearful of winds, between two other islands
Called Myconos and Gyaros. I sailed there;
Our band was weary, and the calmest harbor
Gave us safe haven. This was Apollo's city;
80 We worshipped it on landing. And their king,
Priest of Apollo also, came to meet us,
His temples bound with holy fillets, and laurel.
His name was Anius; he knew Anchises
As an old friend, and gave us joyful welcome.
85   Apollo's temple was built of ancient rock,
And there I prayed: 'Grant us a home, Apollo,
Give walls to weary men, a race, a city
That will abide; preserve Troy's other fortress,
The remnant left by the Greeks and hard Achilles.
90 Whom do we follow? where are we bidden to go
To find our settlement? An omen, father!'

-----

[28]Nereids: sea nymphs

I had scarcely spoken, when suddenly all things trembled,
The doors, and the laurel, and the whole mountain moved,
And the shrine was opened, and a rumbling sound
95   Was heard. We knelt, most humbly; and a voice
Came to our ears: 'The land which brought you forth,
Men of endurance, will receive you home.
Seek out your ancient mother. There your house
Will rule above all lands, your children's children,
100   For countless generations.' Apollo spoke,
And we were joyful and confused, together:
What walls were those, calling the wanderers home?
My father, pondering history, made answer:
'Hear, leaders; learn your hopes. There is a land
105   Called Crete, an island in the midst of the sea,
The cradle of our race; it has a mountain,
Ida, like ours, a hundred mighty cities,
Abounding wealth; if I recall correctly,
Teucer, our greatest father, came from there
110   To the Rhoetean shores to found his kingdom.
Ilium was nothing then, the towers of Troy
Undreamed of; men lived in the lowly valleys.
And Cybele, the Great Mother, came from Crete
With her clashing cymbals, and her grove of Ida
115   Was named from that original; the silence
Of her mysterious rites, the harnessed lions
Before her chariot wheels, all testify
To Cretan legend. Come, then, let us follow
Where the gods lead, and seek the Cretan kingdom.
120   It is not far; with Jupiter to favor,
Three days will see us there.' With prayer, he made
Most solemn sacrifice, a bull to Neptune,
One to Apollo, to Winter a black heifer,
A white one for fair winds.
125   The story ran
That no one lived in Crete, Idomeneus
Having left his father's kingdom, that the houses
Were empty now, dwellings vacated for us.
We sailed from Delos, flying over the water
130   Past Naxos, on whose heights the Bacchae revel
Past green Donysa, snowy Paros, skimming
The passages between the sea-sown islands.
No crew would yield to another; there is shouting,
And the cheer goes up, 'To Crete, and the land of our fathers!'
135   A stern wind follows, and we reach the land.

I am glad to be there; I lay out the walls
For the chosen city, name it Pergamea,[29]
And the people are happy. *Love your hearths*, I told them,
Build high the citadel. The ships were steadied
140 On the dry beach, the young were busy ploughing,
Or planning marriage, and I was giving laws,
Assigning homes. But the weather turned, the sky
Grew sick, and from the tainted heaven came,
Pestilence and pollution, a deadly year
145 For people and harvest. Those who were not dying
Dragged weary bodies around; the Dog-Star[30] scorched
The fields to barrenness; grass withered, corn
Refused to ripen. 'Over the sea again!'
My father said, 'let us return to Delos,
150 Consult the oracle, implore Apollo
To show us kindliness; what end awaits
Our weary destiny, where does he bid us turn
For help in trouble?'
        Sleep held all creatures over the earth at rest;
155 In my own darkness visions came, the sacred
Images of the household gods I had carried
With me from Troy, out of the burning city.
I saw them plain, in the flood of light, where the moon
Streamed through the dormers. And they eased me, saying:
160 'Apollo would tell you this, if you went over
The sea again to Delos; from him we come
To you, with willing spirit. We came with you
From the burnt city, we have followed still
The swollen sea in the ships; in time to come
165 We shall raise your sons to heaven, and dominion
Shall crown their city. Prepare to build them walls,
Great homes for greatness; do not flee the labor,
The long, long toil of flight. Crete, says Apollo,
Is not the place. There is a land in the West,
170 Called by the Greeks, Hesperia:[31] anciency
And might in arms and wealth enrich its soil.
The Oenotrians lived there once; now, rumor has it,
A younger race has called it Italy
After the name of a leader, Italus.

---

[29]**Pergamea:** named after Pergamum, the citadel of Troy

[30]**Dog Star:** Sirius, which appears in August when it is usually most hot ("dog days of summer")

[31]**Hesperia:** a westernmost terrain named for the evening star Hesperus

175   Dardanus came from there, our ancestor,
      As Iasius was. There is our dwelling-place.
      Be happy, then, waken, and tell Anchises
      Our certain message: seek the land in the West.
      Crete is forbidden country.'
180   The vision shook me, and the voice of the gods;
      (It was not a dream, exactly; I seemed to know them,
      Their features, the veiled hair, the living presence.)
      I woke in a sweat, held out my hands to heaven,
      And poured the pure libation for the altar,
185   Then, gladly, to Anchises. He acknowledged
      His own mistake, a natural confusion,
      Our stock was double, of course; no need of saying
      We had more ancestors than one. 'Cassandra,'
      Anchises said, 'alone, now I remember,
190   Foretold this fate; it seemed she was always talking
      Of a land in the West, and Italian kingdoms, always.
      But who would ever have thought that any Trojans
      Would reach the shores in the West? Or, for that matter,
      Who ever believed Cassandra? Let us yield
195   To the warning of Apollo, and at his bidding
      Seek better fortunes.' So we obeyed him,
      Leaving this place, where a few stayed, and sailing
      The hollow keels over the mighty ocean.
        We were in deep water, and the land no longer
200   Was visible, sky and ocean everywhere.
      A cloud, black-blue, loomed overhead, with night
      And tempest in it, and the water roughened
      In shadow; winds piled up the sea, the billows
      Rose higher; we were scattered in the surges.
205   Clouds took away the daylight, and the night
      Was dark and wet in the sky, with lightning flashing.
      We wandered, off our course, in the dark of ocean,
      And our pilot, Palinurus, swore he could not
      Tell day from night, nor the way among the waters.
210   For three lost days, three starless nights, we rode it,
      Saw land on the fourth, mountains and smoke arising.
      The sails came down, we bent to the oars; the sailors
      Made the foam fly, sweeping the dark blue water.
      I was saved from the waves; the Strophades[32] received me,
215   (The word means Turning-point in the Greek language),

---

[32]**Strophades:** islands off the coast of Greece in the Ionian Sea

Ionian islands where the dire Celaeno
And other Harpies live, since Phineus' house
Was closed to them, and they feared their former tables.
No fiercer plague of the gods' anger ever
220 Rose out of hell, girls with the look of birds,
Their bellies fouled, incontinent, their hands
Like talons, and their faces pale with hunger.
We sailed into the harbor, happy to see
Good herds of cattle grazing over the grass
225 And goats, unshepherded. We cut them down
And made our prayer and offering to Jove,
Set trestles on the curving shore for feasting.
Down from the mountains with a fearful rush
And a sound of wings like metal came the Harpies,
230 To seize our banquet, smearing dirtiness
Over it all, with a hideous kind of screaming
And a stinking smell. We found a secret hollow
Enclosed by trees, under a ledge of rock,
Where shade played over; there we moved the tables;
235 And lit the fire again; the noisy Harpies
Came out of somewhere, sky, or rock, and harried
The feast again, the filthy talons grabbing,
The taint all through the air. *Take arms*, I ordered,
We have to fight them. And my comrades, hiding
240 Their shields in the grass, lay with their swords beside them,
And when the birds swooped screaming, and Misenus,
Sounded the trumpet-signal, they rose to charge them,
A curious kind of battle, men with sword-blades
Against the winged obscenities of ocean.
245 Their feathers felt no blow, their backs no wound,
They rose to the sky as rapidly as ever,
Leaving the souvenirs of their foul traces
Over the ruined feast. And one, Celaeno,
Perched on a lofty rock, squawked out a warning:—
250 'Is it war you want, for slaughtered goats and bullocks,
Is it war you bring, you sons of liars, driving
The innocent Harpies from their father's kingdom?
Take notice, then, and let my words forever
Stick in your hearts; what Jove has told Apollo,
255 Apollo told me, and I, the greatest fury,
Shove down your throats; it is Italy you are after,
And the winds will help you, Italy and her harbors
You will reach, all right; but you will not wall the city
Till, for the wrong you have done us, deadly hunger

260 Will make you gnaw and crunch your very tables!'
She flew back to the forest. My companions
Were chilled with sudden fear; their spirit wavered,
They call on me, to beg for peace, not now
With arms, but vows and praying, filthy birds
265 Or ill-foreboding goddesses, no matter.
Anchises prayed with outstretched hands, appeasing
The mighty gods with sacrifice:—'Be gracious,
Great gods, ward off the threats, spare the devoted!'
He bade us tear the cable from the shore,
270 Shake loose the sails. And a wind sprang up behind us,
Driving us northward; we passed many islands,
Zacynthus, wooded, Dulichium, and Same,
The cliffs of Neritus, Laertes' kingdom,
With a curse as we went by for Ithaca,
275 Land of Ulysses. Soon Leucate's headland
Came into view, a dreadful place for sailors,
Where Apollo had a shrine. We were very weary
As we drew near the little town; the anchor
Was thrown from the prow, the sterns pulled up on the beaches.
280   This was unhoped-for land; we offered Jove
Our purifying rites, and had the altars
Burning with sacrifice. We thronged the shore
With games of Ilium. Naked, oiled for wrestling,
The young held bouts, glad that so many islands
285 Held by the Greeks, were safely passed. A year
Went by, and icy winter roughened the waves
With gales from the north. A shield of hollow bronze,
Borne once by Abas, I fastened to the door-posts,
And set a verse below it: *Aeneas won*
290 *These arms from the Greek victors.* I gave the order
To man the thwarts and leave this harbor; all
Obeyed, swept oars in rivalry. We left
Phaeacia's airy heights, coasting Epirus,
Drawn to Buthrotum, a Chaonian harbor.
295   And here we met strange news, that Helenus,
The son of Priam, was ruling Grecian cities,
Having won the wife of Pyrrhus and his crown,
And that Andromache once more had married
A lord of her own race. Amazed, I burn
300 With a strange longing to seek out that hero,
To learn his great adventures. It so happened,
Just as I left the landing, that was the day
Andromache, in a grove before the city,

By the waters of a river that resembled
305   The Simois at home, was offering homage,
Her annual mourning-gift to Hector's ashes,
Calling his ghost to the place which she had hallowed
With double altars, a green and empty tomb.
I found her weeping there, and she was startled
310   At the sight of me, and Trojan arms, a shock
Too great to bear: she was rigid for a moment,
And then lost consciousness, and a long time later
Managed to speak: 'Is it real, then, goddess-born?
What are you, living messenger or phantom,
315   Mortal or ghost? If the dear light has left you,
Tell me where Hector is.' I was moved, so deeply
I found it hard to answer to her tears
And through my own, but I did say a little:—
'I am alive; I seem to keep on living
320   Through all extremes of trouble; do not doubt me,
I am no apparition. And what has happened
To you, dear wife of Hector? Could any gain
Atone for such a loss? Has fortune tried
To even matters at all? Does Pyrrhus still
325   Presume on you as husband?' With lowered gaze
And quiet voice she answered:—'Happy the maiden
Slain at the foeman's tomb, at the foot of the walls;
Happy the daughter of Priam, who never knew
The drawing of the lots, nor came to the bed
330   Of a conqueror, his captive. After the fire
I travelled different seas, endured the pride
Achilles filled his son with, bore him children
In bondage, till he tired of me and left me
For Leda's daughter and a Spartan marriage.
335   He passed me on to Helenus, fair enough,
Slave-woman to slave-man; but then Orestes,
Inflamed with passion for his stolen bride,
And maddened by the Furies of his vengeance,
Caught Pyrrhus off-guard, and slew him at the altar
340   In his ancestral home. And Pyrrhus dying,
Part of the kingdom came to Helenus,
Who named the fields Chaonian, the land
Chaonia, after a man from Troy,
And filled the heights, as best he could, with buildings
345   To look like those we knew. But what of yourself?
What winds, what fate, have brought you here, or was it
Some god? did you know you were on our coast? How is

The boy Ascanius, living still, whom Troy
Might have—does he ever think about his mother?
350 Does he want to be a hero, a manly spirit,
Such as his father was, and his uncle Hector?'
She was in tears again, when the son of Priam,
Helenus, with an escort, came from the city,
Happy to recognize us, bringing us in
355 With tears and greeting mingled. I went on,
Seeing a little Troy, low walls that copied
The old majestic ramparts, a tiny river
In a dry bed, trying to be the Xanthus,
I found the Scaean gates, to hold and cling to.
360 My Trojans, too, were fond of the friendly town,
Whose king received them in wide halls; libations
Were poured to the gods, and feasts set on gold dishes.
     Day after day went by, and the winds were calling
And the sails filling with a good south-wester.
365 I put my questions to the king and prophet:
'O son of Troy, the god's interpreter,
Familiar with the tripod and the laurel
Of great Apollo, versed in stars and omens,
Bird-song and flying wing, be gracious to me,
370 Tell me,—for Heaven has prophesied a journey
Without mischance, and all the gods have sent me
The counsel of their oracles, to follow
Italy and a far-off country; one,
But one, Celaeno, prophesied misfortune,
375 Wrath and revolting hunger,—tell me, prophet,
What dangers first to avoid, what presence follow
To overcome disaster?'
                Bullocks slain
With proper covenant, and the chaplets loosened,
380 He led me to the temple of Apollo,
The very gates, where the god's presence awed me,
And where he spoke, with eloquent inspiration:—
'O goddess-born, the journey over the sea
Holds a clear sanction for you, under Jove,
385 Who draws the lots and turns the wheel of Fate.
I will tell you some few things, not all, that safely
You may go through friendly waters, and in time
Come to Ausonian[33] harborage; the rest

---

[33]Ausonian: Italian

Helenus does not know, or, if he did,
390 Juno would stop his speaking. First of all,
Italy, which you think is near, too fondly
Ready to enter her nearest port, is distant,
Divided from you by a pathless journey
And longer lands between. The oar must bend
395 In the Sicilian ocean, and the ships
Sail on a farther coast, beyond the lakes
Of an infernal world, beyond the isles
Where dwells Aeaean Circe,[34] not till then
Can the built city rise on friendly ground.
400 Keep in the mind the sign I give you now:
At the wave of a hidden river, you will find
Under the oaks on the shore, a sow, a white one,
Immense, with a new-born litter, thirty young
At the old one's udders; that will be the place,
405 The site of the city, the certain rest from labor.
And do not fear the eating of the tables,
The fates will find a way, Apollo answer.
Avoid this coast of Italy, the lands
Just westward of our own; behind those walls
410 Dwell evil Greeks, Narycian Locri, soldiers
Of the Cretan king, Idomeneus; the plains
Are full of them; a Meliboean captain
Governs Petelia, a tiny town
Relying on her fortress! Philoctetes
415 Commands her walls. And furthermore, remember,
Even when the ships have crossed the sea and anchored,
When the altars stand on the shore, and the vows are paid,
Keep the hair veiled, and the robe of crimson drawn
Across the eyes, so that no hostile visage
420 May interfere, to gaze on the holy fire
Or spoil the sacred omens. This rite observe
Through all the generations; keep it holy.
From that first landing, when the wind brings you down
To Sicily's coast, and narrow Pelorus widens
425 The waters of her strait, keep to the left,
Land on the left, and water on the left,
The long way round; the right is dangerous.
Avoid it. There's a story that this land
Once broke apart—(time brings so many changes)—

---

[34]Circe: a sorceress (who turned some of Odysseus' men into swine in *Odyssey*, Book X)

430 By some immense convulsion, though the lands
Had been one country once. But now between them
The sea comes in, and now the waters bound
Italian coast, Sicilian coast; the tide
Washes on severed shores, their fields, their cities.
435 Scylla keeps guard on the right; on the left Charybdis,
The unappeasable; from the deep gulf she sucks
The great waves down, three times; three times she belches
Them high up into the air, and sprays the stars.
Scylla is held in a cave, a den of darkness,
440 From where she thrusts her huge jaws out, and draws
Ships to her jagged rocks. She looks like a girl
Fair-breasted to the waist, from there, all monster,
Shapeless, with dolphins' tails, and a wolf's belly.
Better to go the long way round, make turning
445 Beyond Pachynus, than to catch one glimpse
Of Scylla the misshapen, in her cavern,
And the rocks resounding with the dark-blue sea-hounds.
And one thing more than any, goddess-born,
I tell you over and over: pray to Juno,
450 Give Juno vows and gifts and overcome her
With everlasting worship. So you will come
Past Sicily and reach Italian beaches.
You will come to a town called Cumae, haunted lakes,
And a forest called Avernus, where the leaves
455 Rustle and stir in the great woods, and there
You will find a priestess, in her wildness singing
Prophetic verses under the stones, and keeping
Symbols and signs on leaves. She files and stores them
In the depth of the cave; there they remain unmoving,
460 Keeping their order, but if a light wind stirs
At the turn of a hinge, and the door's draft disturbs them,
The priestess never cares to catch them fluttering
Around the halls of rock, put them in order,
Or give them rearrangement. Men who have come there
465 For guidance leave uncounselled, and they hate
The Sibyl's dwelling. Let no loss of time,
However comrades chide and chafe, however
The wind's voice calls the sail, postpone the visit
To this great priestess; plead with her to tell you
470 With her own lips the song of the oracles.
She will predict the wars to come, the nations
Of Italy, the toils to face, or flee from;
Meet her with reverence, and she, propitious,

Will grant a happy course. My voice can tell you
475 No more than this. Farewell; raise Troy to heaven.'
     After the friendly counsel, other gifts
Were sent to our ships, carved ivory, and gold,
And heavy silver, cauldrons from Dodona,
A triple breastplate linked with gold, a helmet
480 Shining with crested plume, the arms of Pyrrhus.
My father, too, has gifts; horses and guides
Are added, and sailing-men, and arms for my comrades.
Anchises bade the fleet prepare; the wind
Was rising, why delay? But Helenus
485 Spoke to Anchises, in compliment and honor:—
'Anchises, worthy of Venus' couch, and the blessing
Of other gods, twice saved from Trojan ruins,
Yonder behold Ausonia! Near, and far,
It lies, Apollo's offering; sail westward.
490 Farewell, made blest by a son's goodness. I
Am a nuisance with my talking.'
                And his queen,
Sad at the final parting, was bringing gifts,
Robes woven with a golden thread, a Trojan
495 Scarf for Ascanius, all courteous honor
Given with these:—'Take them, my child; these are
The work of my own hands, memorials
Of Hector's wife Andromache, and her love.
Receive these farewell gifts; they are for one
500 Who brings my own son back to me; your hands,
Your face, your eyes, remind me of him so,—
He would be just your age.'35
              I, also, wept,
As I spoke my words of parting: 'Now farewell;
505 Your lot is finished, and your rest is won,
No ocean fields to plough, no fleeing fields
To follow, you have your Xanthus and your Troy,
Built by your hands, and blest by happier omens,
Far from the path of the Greeks. But we are called
510 From fate to fate; if ever I enter Tiber
And Tiber's neighboring lands, if ever I see
The walls vouchsafed my people, I pray these shores,
Italy and Epirus, shall be one,
The life of Troy restored, with friendly towns

35Andromache and Hector's son, Astyanax, was hurled to his death by the Greeks, lest he grow up to be an avenger. (See Euripides' *Trojan Women*.)

515   And allied people. A common origin,
      A common fall, was ours. Let us remember,
      And our children keep the faith.'
      Over the sea we rode, the shortest run
      To Italy, past the Ceraunian rocks.
520   The sun went down; the hills were dark with shadow.
      The oars assigned, we drew in to the land
      For a little welcome rest; sleep overcame us,
      But it was not yet midnight when our pilot
      Sprang from his blanket, studying the winds,
525   Alert and listening, noting the stars
      Wheeling the silent heaven, the twin Oxen,
      Arcturus and the rainy Kids. All calm,
      He saw, and roused us; camp was broken; the sail
      Spread to the rushing breeze, and as day reddened
530   And the stars faded, we saw a coast, low-lying,
      And made out hills. 'Italy!', cried Achates,
      'Italy!' all the happy sailors shouted.
      Anchises wreathed a royal wine-bowl, stood
      On the high stern, calling:—'Gods of earth and ocean
535   And wind and storm, help us along, propitious
      With favoring breath!' And the breeze sprang up, and freshened;
      We saw a harbor open, and a temple
      Shone on Minerva's headland. The sails came down,
      We headed toward the land. Like the curve of a bowl
540   The port turned in from the Eastern waves; its cliffs
      Foamed with the salty spray, and towering rocks
      Came down to the sea, on both sides, double walls,
      And the temple fled the shore. Here, our first omen,
      I saw four horses grazing, white as snow,
545   And father Anchises cried:—'It is war you bring us,
      Welcoming land, horses are armed for war,
      It is war these herds portend. But there is hope
      Of peace as well. Horses will bend to the yoke
      And bear the bridle tamely.' Then we worshipped
550   The holy power of Pallas, first to hear us,
      Kept our heads veiled before the solemn altar,
      And following Helenus' injunction, offered
      Our deepest prayer to Juno.
                                 And sailed on,
555   With some misgiving past the homes of Greeks;
      Saw, next, a bay, Tarentum, and a town
      That rumor said was Hercules'; against it,
      The towers of Caulon rose, and Scylaceum,

Most dangerous to ships, and a temple of Juno.
560 Far off, Sicilian Etna rose from the waves,
And we heard the loud sea roar, and the rocks resounding,
And voices broken on the coast; the shoals
Leaped at us, and the tide boiled sand. My father
Cried in alarm:—'This must be that Charybdis
565 Helenus warned us of. Rise to the oars,
O comrades, pull from the danger!' They responded
As they did, always, Palinurus swinging
The prow to the waves on the left, and all our effort
Strained to the left, with oars and sail. One moment
570 We were in the clouds, the next in the gulf of Hell;
Three times the hollow rocks and reefs roared at us,
Three times we saw spray shower the very stars,
And the wind went down at sunset, we were weary,
Drifting, in ignorance, to the Cyclops shores.
575   There is a harbor, safe enough from wind,
But Etna thunders near it, crashing and roaring
Throwing black clouds up to the sky, and smoking
With swirling pitchy color, and white-hot ashes,
With balls of flame puffed to the stars, and boulders,
580 The mountain's guts, belched out, or molten rock
Boiling below the ground, roaring above it.
The story goes that Enceladus, a giant,
Struck by a bolt of lightning, lies here buried
Beneath all Etna's weight, with the flames pouring
585 Through the broken furnace-flues; he shifts his body,
Every so often, to rest his weariness,
And then all Sicily seems to moan and tremble
And fill the sky with smoke. We spent the night here,
Hiding in woods, enduring monstrous portents,
590 Unable to learn the cause. There were no stars,
No light or fire in the sky; the dead of the night,
The thick of the cloud, obscured the moon.
                                              And day
Arrived, at last, and the shadows left the heaven,
595 And a man came out of the woods, a sorry figure,
In hunger's final stages, reaching toward us
His outstretched hands. We looked again. His beard
Unshorn, his rags pinned up with thorns, and dirty,
He was, beyond all doubt of it, a Greek,
600 And one of those who had been at Troy in the fighting.
He saw, far off, the Trojan dress and armor,
Stopped short, for a moment, almost started back

In panic, then, with a wild rush, came on,
Pleading and crying:—'By the stars I beg you,
605   By the gods above, the air we breathe, ah Trojans,
Take me away from here, carry me off
To any land whatever; that will be plenty.
I know I am one of the Greeks, I know I sailed
With them, I warred against the gods of Ilium,
610   I admit all that; drown me for evil-doing,
Cut me to pieces, scatter me over the waves.
Kill me. If I must die, it will be a pleasure
To perish at the hands of men.' He held
Our knees and clung there, grovelling before us.
615   We urged him tell his story, his race, his fortune.
My father gave him his hand, a pledge of safety,
And his fear died down a little.
                       'I come,' he said,
'From Ithaca, a companion of Ulysses;
620   My name is Achaemenides; my father,
His name was Adamastus, was a poor man,
And that was why I came to Troy. My comrades
Left me behind here, in their terrible hurry,
To leave these cruel thresholds. The Cyclops live here
625   In a dark cave, a house of gore, and banquets
Soaking with blood. It is dark inside there, monstrous.
He hits the stars with his head—Dear gods, abolish
This creature from the world—he is not easy
To look at; he is terrible to talk to.
630   His food is the flesh of men, his drink their blood.
I saw him once myself, with two of our men,
In that huge fist of his; he lay on his back
In the midst of the cave, and smashed them on a rock,
And the whole place swam with blood; I watched him chew them
635   The limbs with black clots dripping, the muscles, warm,
Quivering as he bit them. But we got him!
Ulysses did not stand for this; he kept
His wits about him, never mind the danger.
The giant was gorged with food, and drunk, and lolling
640   With sagging neck sprawling all over the cavern
Belching and drooling blood-clots, bits of flesh,
And wine all mixed together. And we stood
Around him, praying, and drew lots,—we had found a stake,
And sharpened it at the end,—and so we bored
645   His big eye out; it glowered under his forehead
The size of a shield, or a sun. So we got vengeance

For the souls of our companions. But flee, I tell you,
Get out of here, poor wretches, cut the cables,
Forsake this shore. There are a hundred others
650 As big as he is, and just like him, keeping
Sheep in the caves of the rocks, a hundred others
Wander around this coast and these high mountains.
I have managed for three months, hiding in forests,
In the caves of beasts, on a rocky look-out, watching
655 The Cyclops, horribly frightened at their cries
And the tramp of their feet. I have lived on plants and berries,
Gnawed roots and bark. I saw this fleet come in,
And I did not care; whatever it was, I gladly
Gave myself up. At least, I have escaped them.
660 Whatever death you give is more than welcome.'
And as he finished, we saw that very giant,
The shepherd Polyphemus, looming huge
Over his tiny flock; he was trying to find
His way to the shore he knew, a shapeless monster,
665 Lumbering, clumping, blind in the dark, with a stumble,
And the step held up with trunk of a pine. No comfort
For him, except in the sheep. He reached the sand,
Wading into the sea, and scooped up water
To wash the ooze of blood from the socket's hollow,
670 Grinding his teeth against the pain, and roaring,
And striding into the water, but even so
The waves were hardly up to his sides. We fled
Taking on board our Greek; we cut the cable,
Strained every nerve at the oars. He heard, and struggled
675 Toward the splash of the wave, but of course he could not catch us,
And then he howled in a rage, and the sea was frightened,
Italy deeply shaken, and all Etna
Rumbled in echoing terror in her caverns.
Out of the woods and the thicket of the mountains
680 The Cyclops came, the others, toward the harbor,
Along the coast-line. We could see them standing
In impotent anger, the wild eye-ball glaring,
A grim assortment, brothers, tall as mountains
Where oak and cypress tower, in the groves
685 Of Jove or great Diana. In our speed
And terror, we sailed anywhere, forgetting
What Helenus had said: Scylla, Charybdis,
Were nothing to us then. But we remembered
In time, and a north wind came from strait Pelorus,
690 We passed Pantagia, and the harbor-mouth

Set in the living-rock, Thapsus, low-lying,
The bay called Megara: all these were places
That Achaemenides knew well, recalling
The scenes of former wanderings with Ulysses.
695   An island faces the Sicanian bay
Against Plemyrium, washed by waves; this island
Has an old name, Ortygia. The story
Tells of a river, Alpheus, come from Elis,
By a secret channel undersea, to join
700   The Arethusan fountains, mingling here
With the Sicilian waters. Here we worshipped
The land's great gods; went on, to pass Helorus,
A rich and marshy land; and then Pachynus
Where the cliffs rose sharp and high; and Camerina,
705   With firm foundation; the Geloan plains,
And Gela, named for a river; then Acragas,
A towering town, high-walled, and sometime famous
For its breed of horses; the city of palms, Selinus;
The shoals of Lilybaeum, where the rocks
710   Are a hidden danger; so at last we came
To Drepanum, a harbor and a shoreline
That I could not rejoice in, a survivor
Of all those storms of the sea. For here I lost
My comforter in all my care and trouble,
715   My father Anchises. All the storms and perils,
All of the weariness endured, seemed nothing
Compared with this disaster; and I had
No warning of it; neither Helenus,
Though he foretold much trouble, nor Celaeno,
720   That evil harpy, prophesied this sorrow.
There was nothing more to bear; the long roads ended
At that unhappy goal; and when I left there,
Some god or other brought me to your shores.'

And so he told the story, a lonely man
725   To eager listeners, destiny and voyage,
And made an end of it here, ceased, and was quiet.

BOOK IV: AENEAS AND DIDO

But the queen finds no rest. Deep in her veins
The wound is fed; she burns with hidden fire.
His manhood, and the glory of his race
Are an obsession with her, like his voice,

5   Gesture and countenance. On the next morning,
After a restless night, she sought her sister:
"I am troubled, Anna, doubtful, terrified,
Or am I dreaming? What new guest is this
Come to our shores? How well he talks, how brave
10   He seems in heart and action! I suppose
It must be true, he does come from the gods.
Fear proves a bastard spirit. He has been
So buffeted by fate. What endless wars
He told of! Sister, I must tell you something:
15   Were not my mind made up, once and for all,
Never again to marry, having been
So lost when Sychaeus left me for the grave,
Slain by my murderous brother at the altar,
Were not sick forever of the torch
20   And bridal bed, here is the only man
Who has moved my spirit, shaken my weak will.
I might have yielded to him. I recognize
The marks of an old fire. But I pray, rather,
That earth engulf me, lightning strike me down
25   To the pale shades and everlasting night
Before I break the laws of decency.
My love has gone with Sychaeus; let him keep it,
Keep it with him forever in the grave."
She ended with a burst of tears. "Dear sister,
30   Dearer than life," Anna replied, "why must you
Grieve all your youth away in loneliness,
Not know sweet children, or the joys of love?
Is that what dust demands, and buried shadows?
So be it. You have kept your resolution
35   From Tyre to Libya, proved it by denying
Iarbas and a thousand other suitors
From Africa's rich kingdoms. Think a little.
Whose lands are these you settle in? Getulians,
Invincible in war, the wild Numidians,
40   Unfriendly Syrtes, ring us round, and a desert
Barren with drought, and the Barcaean rangers.
Why should I mention Tyre, and wars arising
Out of Pygmalion's threats? And you, my sister,
Why should you fight against a pleasing passion?
45   I think the gods have willed it so, and Juno
Has helped to bring the Trojan ships to Carthage.
What a great city, sister, what a kingdom
This might become, rising on such a marriage!

Carthage and Troy together in arms, what glory
50   Might not be ours? Only invoke the blessing
Of the great gods, make sacrifice, be lavish
In welcome, keep them here while the fierce winter
Rages at sea, and cloud and sky are stormy,
And ships still wrecked and broken."
55   So she fanned
The flame of the burning heart; the doubtful mind
Was given hope, and the sense of guilt was lessened.
And first of all they go to shrine and altar
Imploring peace; they sacrifice to Ceres,
60   Giver of law, to Bacchus, to Apollo,
And most of all to Juno, in whose keeping
The bonds of marriage rest. In all her beauty
Dido lifts up the goblet, pours libation
Between the horns of a white heifer, slowly,
65   Or, slowly, moves to the rich altars, noting
The proper gifts to mark the day, or studies
The sacrificial entrails for the omens.
Alas, poor blind interpreters! What woman
In love is helped by offerings or altars?
70   Soft fire consumes the marrow-bones, the silent
Wound grows, deep in the heart.
Unhappy Dido burns, and wanders, burning,
All up and down the city, the way a deer
With a hunter's careless arrow in her flank
75   Ranges the uplands, with the shaft still clinging
To the hurt side. She takes Aeneas with her
All through the town, displays the wealth of Sidon,
Buildings projected; she starts to speak and falters,
And at the end of the day renews the banquet,
80   Is wild to hear the story, over and over,
Hangs on each word, until the late moon, sinking,
Sends them all home. The stars die out, but Dido
Lies brooding in the empty hall, alone,
Abandoned on a lonely couch. She hears him,
85   Sees him, or sees and hears him in Iulus,
Fondles the boy, as if that ruse might fool her,
Deceived by his resemblance to his father.
The towers no longer rise, the youth are slack
In drill for arms, the cranes and derricks rusting,
90   Walls halt halfway to heaven.
                          And Juno saw it,
The queen held fast by this disease, this passion

Which made her good name meaningless. In anger
She rushed to Venus:—"Wonderful!—the trophies,

95 The praise, you and that boy of yours are winning!
Two gods outwit one woman—splendid, splendid!
What glory for Olympus! I know you fear me,
Fear Carthage, and suspect us. To what purpose?
What good does all this do? Is there no limit?

100 Would we not both be better off, to sanction
A bond of peace forever, a formal marriage?
You have your dearest wish; Dido is burning
With love, infected to her very marrow.
Let us—why not?—conspire to rule one people

105 On equal terms; let her serve a Trojan husband;
Let her yield her Tyrian people as her dowry."
        This, Venus knew, was spoken with a purpose,
A guileful one, to turn Italian empire
To Libyan shores: not without reservation

110 She spoke in answer: "Who would be so foolish
As to refuse such terms, preferring warfare,
If only fortune follows that proposal?
I do not know, I run more than a little troubled
What fate permits: will Jupiter allow it,

115 One city for the Tyrians and Trojans,
This covenant, this mixture? You can fathom
His mind, and ask him, being his wife. I follow
Wherever you lead." And royal Juno answered:
"That I will tend to. Listen to me, and learn

120 How to achieve the urgent need. They plan,
Aeneas, and poor Dido, to go hunting
When sunlight floods the world to-morrow morning.
While the rush of the hunt is on, and the forest shaken
With beaters and their nets, I will pour down

125 Dark rain and hail and make the whole sky rumble!
With thunder and threat. The company will scatter,
Hidden or hiding in the night and shadow,
And Dido and the Trojan come for shelter
To the same cave. I will be there and join them

130 In lasting wedlock; she will be his own,
His bride, forever; this will be their marriage."
Venus assented, smiling, not ungracious—
The trick was in the open.
        Dawn, rising, left the ocean, and the youth

135 Come forth from all the gates, prepared for hunting,
Nets, toils, wide spears, keen-scented coursing hounds,

And Dido keeps them waiting; her own charger
Stands bright in gold and crimson; the bit foams,
The impatient head is tossed. At last she comes,
140 With a great train attending, gold and crimson,
Quiver of gold, and combs of gold, and manmade
Crimson with golden buckle. A Trojan escort
Attends her, with Iulus, and Aeneas
Comes to her side, more lordly than Apollo
145 Bright along Delos' ridges in the springtime
With laurel in his hair and golden weapons
Shining across his shoulders. Equal radiance
Is all around Aeneas, equal splendor.
They reach the mountain heights, the hiding-places
150 Where no trail runs; wild goats from the rocks are started,
Run down the ridges; elsewhere, in the open
Deer cross the dusty plain, away from the mountains.
The boy Ascanius, in the midst of the valley,
Is glad he has so good a horse, rides, dashing
155 Past one group or another: deer are cowards
And wild goats tame; he prays for some excitement,
A tawny lion coming down the mountain
Or a great boar with foaming mouth.
                                        The heaven
160 Darkens, and thunder rolls, and rain and hail
Come down in torrents. The hunt is all for shelter,
Trojans and Tyrians and Ascanius dashing
Wherever they can; the streams pour down the mountains.
To the same cave go Dido and Aeneas,
165 Where Juno, as a bridesmaid, gives the signal,
And mountain nymphs wail high their incantations,
First day of death, first cause of evil. Dido
Is unconcerned with fame, with reputation,
With how it seems to others. This is marriage
170 For her, not hole-and-corner guilt; she covers
Her folly with this name.
                                    Rumor goes flying
At once, through all the Libyan cities, Rumor
Than whom no other evil was ever swifter.
175 She thrives on motion and her own momentum;
Tiny at first in fear, she swells, colossal
In no time, walks on earth, but her head is hidden
Among the clouds. Her mother, Earth, was angry,
Once, at the gods, and out of spite produced her,
180 The Titans' youngest sister, swift of foot,

Deadly of wing, a huge and terrible monster,
With an eye below each feather in her body,
A tongue, a mouth, for every eye, and ears
Double that number; in the night she flies
185 Above the earth, below the sky, in shadow
Noisy and shrill; her eyes are never closed
In slumber; and by day she perches, watching
From tower or battlement, frightening great cities.
She heralds truth, and clings to lies and falsehood,
190 It is all the same to her. And now she was going
Happy about her business, filling people
With truth and lies: Aeneas, Trojan-born,
Has come, she says, and Dido, lovely woman,
Sees fit to mate with him, one way or another,
195 And now the couple wanton out the winter,
Heedless of ruling, prisoners of passion.
They were dirty stories, but the goddess gave them
To the common ear, then went to King Iarbas[36]
With words that fired the fuel of his anger.
200   This king was Ammon's son, a child of rape
Begotten on a nymph from Garamantia;
He owned wide kingdoms, had a hundred altars
Blazing with fires to Jove, eternal outposts
In the gods' honor; the ground was fat with blood,
205 The temple portals blossoming with garlands.
He heard the bitter stories, and went crazy,
Before the presences of many altars
Beseeching and imploring:—"Jove Almighty,
To whom the Moorish race on colored couches
210 Pours festive wine, do you see these things, or are we
A pack of idiots, shaking at the lightning
We think you brandish, when it is really only
An aimless flash of light, and silly noises?
Do you see these things? A woman, who used to wander
215 Around my lands, who bought a little city,
To whom we gave some ploughland and a contract,
Disdains me as a husband, takes Aeneas
To be her lord and master, in her kingdom,
And now that second Paris, with his lackeys,
220 Half-men, I call them, his chin tied up with ribbons,
With millinery on his perfumed tresses,

---

[36]**King Iarbas:** an African suitor, rejected by Dido

Takes over what he stole, and we keep bringing
Gifts to your temples, we, devout believers
Forsooth, in idle legend."
225   And Jove heard him
Making his prayer and clinging to the altars,
And turned his eyes to Carthage and the lovers
Forgetful of their better reputation.
He summoned Mercury:—"Go forth, my son,
230 Descend on wing and wind to Tyrian Carthage,
Speak to the Trojan leader, loitering there
Unheedful of the cities given by fate.
Take him my orders through the rapid winds:
It was not for this his lovely mother saved him
235 Twice from Greek arms; she promised he would be
A ruler, in a country loud with war,
Pregnant with empire; he would sire a race
From Teucer's noble line; he would ordain
Law for the world. If no such glory moves him,
240 If his own fame and fortune count as nothing,
Does he, a father, grudge his son the towers
Of Rome to be? What is the fellow doing?
With what ambition wasting time in Libya?
Let him set sail. That's all; convey the message."
245   Before he ended, Mercury made ready
To carry out the orders of his father,
He strapped the golden sandals on, the pinions
To bear him over sea and land, as swift
As the breath of the wind; he took the wand, which summons
250 Pale ghosts from Hell, or sends them there, denying
Or giving sleep, unsealing dead men's eyes,
Useful in flight through wind and stormy cloud,
And so came flying till he saw the summit
And towering sides of Atlas, rugged giant
255 With heaven on his neck, whose head and shoulders
Are dark with fir, ringed with black cloud, and beaten
With wind and rain, and laden with the whiteness
Of falling snow, with rivers running over
His aged chin, and the rough beard ice-stiffened.
260 Here first on level wing the god paused briefly,
Poised, plummeted to ocean, like a bird
That skims the water's surface, flying low
By shore and fishes' rocky breeding-ground,
So Mercury darted between earth and heaven
265 To Libya's sandy shore, cutting the wind

From the home of Maia's father.[37]
Soon as the winged sandals skim the rooftops,
He sees Aeneas founding towers, building
New homes for Tyrians; his sword is studded
270   With yellow jasper; he wears across his shoulders
A cloak of burning crimson, and golden threads
Run through it, the royal gift of the rich queen.
Mercury wastes no time:—"What are you doing,
Forgetful of your kingdom and your fortunes,
275   Building for Carthage? Woman-crazy fellow,
The ruler of the gods, the great compeller
Of heaven and earth, has sent me from Olympus
With no more word than this: what are you doing,
With what ambition wasting time in Libya?
280   If your own fame and fortune count as nothing,
Think of Ascanius at least, whose kingdom
In Italy, whose Roman land, are waiting
As promise justly due." He spoke, and vanished
Into thin air. Appalled, amazed, Aeneas
285   is stricken dumb; his hair stands up in terror,
His voice sticks in his throat. He is more than eager
To flee that pleasant land, awed by the warning
Of the divine command. But how to do it?
How get around that passionate queen? What opening
290   Try first? His mind runs out in all directions,
Shifting and veering. Finally, he has it,
Or thinks he has: he calls his comrades to him,
The leaders, bids them quietly prepare
The fleet for voyage, meanwhile saying nothing
295   About the new activity; since Dido
Is unaware, has no idea that passion
As strong as theirs is on the verge of breaking,
He will see what he can do, find the right moment,
To let her know, all in good time. Rejoicing,
300   The captains move to carry out the orders.
        Who can deceive a woman in love? The queen
Anticipates each move, is fearful even
While everything is safe, foresees this cunning,
And the same trouble-making goddess, Rumor,
305   Tells her the fleet is being armed, made ready
For voyaging. She rages through the city

---

[37]**Maia's father:** Atlas; Maia is the mother of Mercury.

Like a woman mad, or drunk, the way the Maenads
Go howling through the night-time on Cithaeron
When Bacchus' cymbals summon with their clashing.
310 She waits no explanation from Aeneas;
She is the first to speak: "And so, betrayer,
You hoped to hide your wickedness, go sneaking
Out of my land without a word? Our love
Means nothing to you, our exchange of vows,
315 And even the death of Dido could not hold you.
The season is dead of winter, and you labor
Over the fleet; the northern gales are nothing
You must be cruel, must you not? Why, even,
If ancient Troy remained, and you were seeking
320 Not unknown homes and lands, but Troy again,
Would you be venturing Troyward in this weather?
I am the one you flee from: true? I beg you
By my own tears, and your right hand—(I have nothing
Else left my wretchedness)—by the beginnings
325 Of marriage, wedlock, what we had, if ever
I served you well, if anything of mine
Was ever sweet to you, I beg you, pity
A falling house; if there is room for pleading
As late as this, I plead, put off that purpose.
330 You are the reason I am hated; Libyans,
Numidians, Tyrians, hate me; and my honor
Is lost, and the fame I had, that almost brought me
High as the stars, is gone. To whom, O guest—
I must not call you husband any longer—
335 To whom do you leave me? I am a dying woman;
Why do I linger on? Until Pygmalion,
My brother, brings destruction to this city?
Until the prince Iarbas leads me captive?
At least if there had been some hope of children
340 Before your flight, a little Aeneas playing,
Around my courts, to bring you back, in feature
At least, I would seem less taken and deserted."
　　　　There was nothing he could say. Jove bade him keep
Affection from his eyes, and grief in his heart
345 With never a sign. At last, he managed something:—
"Never, O Queen, will I deny you merit
Whatever you have strength to claim; I will not
Regret remembering Dido, while I have
Breath in my body, or consciousness of spirit.
350 I have a point or two to make. I did not,

Believe me, hope to hide my flight by cunning;
I did not, ever, claim to be a husband,
Made no such vows. If I had fate's permission
To live my life my way, to settle my troubles
355   At my own will, I would be watching over
The city of Troy, and caring for my people,
Those whom the Greeks had spared, and Priam's palace
Would still be standing; for the vanquished people,
I would have built the town again. But now,
360   It is Italy I must seek, great Italy,
Apollo orders, and his oracles
Call me to Italy. There is my love,
There is my country. If the towers of Carthage,
The Libyan citadels, can please a woman
365   Who came from Tyre, why must you grudge the Trojans
Ausonian land? It is proper for us also
To seek a foreign kingdom. I am warned
Of this in dreams: when the earth is veiled in shadow
And the fiery stars are burning I see my father,
370   Anchises, or his ghost, and I am frightened;
I am troubled for the wrong I do my son,
Cheating him out of his kingdom in the west,
And lands that fate assigns him. And a herald,
Jove's messenger—I call them both to witness—
375   Has brought me, through the rush of air, his orders;
I saw the god myself, in the full daylight,
Enter these walls, I heard the words he brought me.
Cease to inflame us both with your complainings;
I follow Italy not because I want to."
380   Out of the corner of her eye she watched him
During the first of this, and her gaze was turning
Now here, now there; and then, in bitter silence,
She looked him up and down; then blazed out at him:—
"You treacherous liar! No goddess was your mother,
385   No Dardanus the founder of your tribe,
Son of the stony mountain-crags, begotten
On cruel rocks, with a tigress for a wet-nurse!
Why fool myself, why make pretense? what is there
To save myself for now? When I was weeping
390   Did he so much as sigh? Did he turn his eyes,
Ever so little, toward me? Did he break at all,
Or weep, or give his lover a word of pity?
What first, what next? Neither Jupiter nor Juno
Looks at these things with any sense of fairness.

395   Faith has no haven anywhere in the world.
      He was an outcast on my shore, a beggar,
      I took him in, and, like a fool, I gave him
      Part of my kingdom; his fleet was lost, I found it,
      His comrades dying, I brought them back to life.
400   I am maddened, burning, burning: now Apollo
      The prophesying god, the oracles
      Of Lycia, and Jove's herald, sent from heaven,
      Come flying through the air with fearful orders,—
      Fine business for the gods, the kind of trouble
405   That keeps them from their sleep. I do not hold you,
      I do not argue, either. Go. And follow
      Italy on the wind, and seek the kingdom
      Across the water. But if any gods
      Who care for decency have any power,
410   They will land you on the rocks; I hope for vengeance,
      I hope to hear you calling the name of Dido
      Over and over, in vain. Oh, I will follow
      In blackest fire, and when cold death has taken
      Spirit from body, I will be there to haunt you,
415   A shade, all over the world. I will have vengeance,
      And hear about it; the news will be my comfort
      In the deep world below." She broke it off,
      Leaving the words unfinished; even light
      Was unendurable; sick at heart, she turned
420   And left him, stammering, afraid, attempting
      To make some kind of answer. And her servants
      Support her to her room, that bower of marble,
      A marriage-chamber once; here they attend her,
      Help her lie down.
425   And good Aeneas, longing
      To ease her grief with comfort, to say something
      To turn her pain and hurt away, sighs often,
      His heart being moved by this great love, most deeply,
      And still—the gods give orders, he obeys them;
430   He goes back to the fleet. And then the Trojans
      Bend, really, to their work, launching the vessels
      All down the shore. The tarred keel swims in the water,
      The green wood comes from the forest, the poles are lopped
      For oars, with leaves still on them. All are eager
435   For fight; all over the city you see them streaming,
      Bustling about their business, a black line moving
      The way ants do when they remember winter
      And raid a hill of grain, to haul and store it

At home, across the plain, the column moving
440   In thin black line through grass, part of them shoving
Great seeds on little shoulders, and part bossing
The job, rebuking laggards, and all the pathway
Hot with the stream of work.
                          And Dido saw them
445   With who knows what emotion: there she stood
On the high citadel, and saw, below her,
The whole beach boiling, and the water littered
With one ship after another, and men yelling,
Excited over their work, and there was nothing
450   For her to do but sob or choke with anguish.
There is nothing to which the hearts of men and women
Cannot be driven by love. Break into tears,
Try prayers again, humble the pride, leave nothing
Untried, and die in vain:—"Anna, you see them
455   Coming from everywhere; they push and bustle
All up and down the shore: the sails are swelling,
The happy sailors garlanding the vessels.
If I could hope for grief like this, my sister,
I shall be able to bear it. But one service
460   Do for me first, dear Anna, out of pity.
You were the only one that traitor trusted,
Confided in; you know the way to reach him,
The proper time and place. Give him this message,
Our arrogant enemy: tell him I never
465   Swore with the Greeks at Aulis to abolish
The Trojan race, I never sent a fleet
To Pergamus, I never desecrated
The ashes or the spirit of Anchises:
Why does he, then, refuse to listen to me?
470   What is the hurry? Let him give his lover
The one last favor: only wait a little,
Only a little while, for better weather
And easy flight. He has betrayed the marriage,
I do not ask for that again; I do not
475   Ask him to give up Latium and his kingdom.
Mere time is all I am asking, a breathing-space,
A brief reprieve, until my luck has taught me
To reconcile defeat and sorrow. This
Is all I ask for, sister; pity and help me:
480   If he grants me this, I will pay it ten times over
After my death." And Anna, most unhappy,
Over and over, told her tears, her pleading;

No tears, no pleading, move him; no man can yield
When a god stops his ears. As northern winds
485 Sweep over Alpine mountains, in their fury
Fighting each other to uproot an oak-tree
Whose ancient strength endures against their roaring
And the trunk shudders and the leaves come down
Strewing the ground, but the old tree clings to the mountain,
490 Its roots as deep toward hell as its crest toward heaven,
And still holds on even so, Aeneas, shaken
By storm-blasts of appeal, by voices calling
From every side, is tossed and torn, and steady.
His will stays motionless, and tears are vain.
495   Then Dido prays for death at last; the fates
Are terrible, her luck is out, she is tired
Of gazing at the everlasting heaven.
The more to goad her will to die, she sees—
Oh terrible!—the holy water blacken,
500 Libations turn to blood, on ground and altar,
When she makes offerings. But she tells no one,
Not even her sister. From the marble shrine,
Memorial to her former lord, attended,
Always, by her, with honor, fleece and garland,
505 She hears his voice, his words, her husband calling
When darkness holds the world, and from the house-top
An owl sends out a long funereal wailing,
And she remembers warnings of old seers,
Fearful, foreboding. In her dreams Aeneas
510 Appears to hunt her down; or she is going
Alone in a lost country, wandering
Trying to find her Tyrians, mad as Pentheus,
Or frenzied as Orestes,[38] when his mother
Is after him with whips of snakes, or firebrands,
515 While the Avengers menace at the threshold.
        She was beaten, harboring madness, and resolved
On dying; alone, she plotted time and method;
Keeping the knowledge from her sorrowing sister,
She spoke with calm composure:—"I have found
520 A way (wish me good luck) to bring him to me
Or set me free from loving him forever.
Near Ocean and the west there is a country,
The Ethiopian land, far-off, where Atlas

---

[38]Orestes: The Furies ("Avengers") pursued Orestes for having slain his mother, Clytaemnestra. (See Aeschylus' *Oresteia, The Libation Bearers*.)

Turns on his shoulders the star-studded world;
525　I know a priestess there; she guards the temple
Of the daughters of the Evening Star; she feeds
The dragon there, and guards the sacred branches,
She sprinkles honey-dew, strews drowsy poppies,
And she knows charms to free the hearts of lovers
530　When she so wills it, or to trouble others;
She can reverse the wheeling of the planets,
Halt rivers in their flowing; she can summon
The ghosts of night-time; you will see earth shaking
Under her tread, and trees come down from mountains.
535　Dear sister mine, as heaven is my witness,
I hate to take these arts of magic on me!
Be secret, then; but in the inner courtyard,
Raise up a funeral-pyre, to hold the armor
Left hanging in the bower, by that hero,
540　That good devoted man, and all his raiment,
And add the bridal bed, my doom: the priestess
Said to do this, and it will be a pleasure
To see the end of all of it, every token
Of that unspeakable knave."
545　　　　　　　　　　　　And so, thought Anna,
Things are no worse than when Sychaeus perished.
She did not know the death these rites portended,
Had no suspicion, and carried out her orders.
The pyre is raised in the court; it towers high
550　With pine and holm-oak, it is hung with garlands
And funeral wreaths, and on the couch she places
Aeneas' sword, his garments, and his image,
Knowing the outcome. Round about are altars,
Where, with her hair unbound, the priestess calls
555　On thrice a hundred gods, Erebus, Chaos,
Hecate, queen of Hell, triple Diana.
Water is sprinkled, from Avernus fountain,
Or said to be, and herbs are sought, by moonlight
Mown with bronze sickles, and the stem-ends running
560　With a black milk, and the caul of a colt, new-born.
Dido, with holy meal and holy hands,
Stands at the altar, with one sandal loosened
And robes unfastened, calls the gods to witness,
Prays to the stars that know her doom, invoking
565　Beyond them, any powers, if there are any,
Who care for lovers in unequal bondage.

    Night: and tired creatures over all the world
Were seeking slumber; the woods and the wild waters
Were quiet, and the silent stars were wheeling
570   Their course half over; every field was still;
The beasts of the field, the brightly colored birds,
Dwellers in lake and pool, in thorn and thicket,
Slept through the tranquil night, their sorrows over,
Their troubles soothed. But no such blessed darkness
575   Closes the eyes of Dido; no repose
Comes to her anxious heart. Her pangs redouble,
Her love swells up, surging, a great tide rising
Of wrath and doubt and passion. "What do I do?
What now? Go back to my Numidian suitors,
580   Be scorned by those I scorned? Pursue the Trojans?
Obey their orders? They were grateful to me,
Once, I remember. But who would let them take me?
Suppose I went. They hate me now; they were always
Deceivers: is Laomedon[39] forgotten,
585   Whose blood runs through their veins? What then? Attend them,
Alone, be their companion, the loud-mouthed sailors?
Or with my own armada follow after,
Wear out my sea-worn Tyrians once more
With vengeance and adventure? Better die.
590   Die; you deserve to; end the hurt with the sword.
It is your fault, Anna; you were sorry for me,
Won over by my tears; you put this load
Of evil on me. It was not permitted,
It seems, for me to live apart from wedlock,
595   A blameless life. An animal does better.
I vowed Sychaeus faith. I have been faithless."
So, through the night, she tossed in restless torment.
    Meanwhile Aeneas, on the lofty stern,
All things prepared, sure of his going, slumbers
600   As Mercury comes down once more to warn him,
Familiar blond young god: "O son of Venus,
Is this a time for sleep? The wind blows fair,
And danger rises all around you. Dido,
Certain to die, however else uncertain,
605   Plots treachery, harbors evil. Seize the moment
While it can still be seized, and hurry, hurry!
The sea will swarm with ships, the fiery torches

[39]Laomedon: King of Troy before Priam

Blaze, and the shore rankle with fire by morning.
Shove off, be gone! A shifty, fickle object
610 Is woman, always." He vanished into the night.
And, frightened by that sudden apparition,
Aeneas started from sleep, and urged his comrades:—
"Hurry, men, hurry; get to the sails and benches,
Get the ships under way. A god from heaven
615 Again has come to speed our flight, to sever
The mooring-ropes. O holy one, we follow,
Whoever you are, we are happy in obeying.
Be with us, be propitious; let the stars
Be right in heaven!" He drew his sword; the blade
620 Flashed shining, at the hawser; and all the men
Were seized in the same restlessness and rushing.
They have left the shore, they have hidden the sea-water
With the hulls of the ships; the white foam dies, the oars
Dip down in dark-blue water.
625   And Aurora
Came from Tithonus' saffron couch to freshen
The world with rising light, and from her watch-tower
The queen saw day grow whiter, and the fleet
Go moving over the sea, keep pace together
630 To the even spread of the sail; she knew the harbors
Were empty of sailors now; she struck her breast
Three times, four times; she tore her golden hair,
Crying, "God help me, will he go, this stranger,
Treating our kingdom as a joke? Bring arms,
635 Bring arms, and hurry! follow from all the city,
Haul the ships off the ways, some of you! Others,
Get fire as fast as you can, give out the weapons,
Pull oars! What am I saying? Or where am I?
I must be going mad. Unhappy Dido,
640 Is it only now your wickedness strikes home?
The time it should have was when you gave him power.
Well, here it is, look at it now, the honor,
The faith of the hero who, they tell me, carries
With him his household gods, who bore on his shoulders
645 His aged father! Could I not have seized him,
Torn him to pieces, scattered him over the waves?
What was the matter? Could I not have murdered
His comrades, and Iulus, and served the son
For a dainty at the table of his father?
650 But fight would have a doubtful fortune. It might have,
What then? I was going to die; whom did I fear?

I would have, should have, set his camp on fire,
Filled everything with flame, choked off the father,
The son, the accursed race, and myself with them.
655 Great Sun, surveyor of all the works of earth,
Juno, to whom my sorrows are committed,
Hecate, whom the cross-roads of the cities
Wail to by night, avenging Furies, hear me,
Grant me divine protection, take my prayer.
660 If he must come to harbor, then he must,
If Jove ordains it, however vile he is,
False, and unspeakable. If Jove ordains,
The goal is fixed. So be it. Take my prayer.
Let him be driven by arms and war, an exile,
665 Let him be taken from his son Iulus,
Let him beg for aid, let him see his people dying
Unworthy deaths, let him accept surrender
On unfair terms, let him never enjoy the kingdom,
The hoped-for light, let him fall and die, untimely,
670 Let him lie unburied on the sand. Oh, hear me,
Hear the last prayer, poured out with my last blood
And you, O Tyrians, hate, and hate forever
The Trojan stock. Offer my dust this homage.
No love, no peace, between these nations, ever!
675 Rise from my bones, O great unknown avenger,
Hunt them with fire and sword, the Dardan settlers,
Now, then, here, there, wherever strength is given.
Shore against shore, wave against wave, and war,
War after war, for all the generations."[40]
680   She spoke, and turned her purpose to accomplish
The quickest end to the life she hated. Briefly
She spoke to Barce, Sychaeus' nurse; her own
Was dust and ashes in her native country:—
"Dear nurse, bring me my sister, tell her to hurry,
685 Tell her to sprinkle her body with river water,
To bring the sacrificial beast and offerings,
And both of you cover your temples with holy fillets.
I have a vow to keep; I have made beginning
Of rites to Stygian Jove, to end my sorrows,
690 To burn the litter of that Trojan leader."
Barce, with an old woman's fuss and bustle,
Went hurrying out of sight; but Dido, trembling,

---

[40]Dido is praying for what will be the Punic Wars between Carthage and Rome.

Wild with her project, the blood-shot eyeballs rolling,
Pale at the death to come, and hectic color
695   Burning the quivering cheeks, broke into the court,
Mounted the pyre in madness, drew the sword,
The Trojan gift, bestowed for no such purpose,
And she saw the Trojan garments, and the bed
She knew so well, and paused a little, weeping,
700   Weeping, and thinking, and flung herself down on it,
Uttering her last words:—
"Spoils that were sweet while gods and fate permitted,
Receive my spirit, set me free from suffering.
I have lived, I have run the course that fortune gave me,
705   And now my shade, a great one, will be going
Below the earth. I have built a noble city,
I have seen my walls, I have avenged a husband,
Punished a hostile brother. I have been
Happy, I might have been too happy, only
710   The Trojans made their landing." She broke off,
Pressed her face to the couch, cried:—"So, we shall die,
Die unavenged; but let us die. So, so,—
I am glad to meet the darkness. Let his eyes
Behold this fire across the sea, an omen
715   Of my death going with him."
                             As she spoke,
Her handmaids saw her, fallen on the sword,
The foam of blood on the blade, and blood on the hands.
A scream rings through the house; Rumor goes reeling,
720   Rioting through the shaken town; the palace
Is loud with lamentation, women sobbing,
Wailing and howling, and the vaults of heaven
Echo the outcry, as if Tyre or Carthage
Had fallen to invaders, and the fury
725   Of fire came rolling over homes and temples.
Anna, half lifeless, heard in panic terror,
Came rushing through them all, beating her bosom,
Clawing her face:—"Was it for this, my sister?
To trick me so? The funeral pyre, the altars,
730   Prepared this for me? I have, indeed, a grievance,
Being forsaken; you would not let your sister
Companion you in death? You might have called me
To the same fate; we might have both been taken,
One sword, one hour. I was the one who built it,
735   This pyre, with my own hands; it was my voice
That called our fathers' gods, for what?—to fail you

When you were lying here. You have killed me, sister,
Not only yourself, you have killed us all, the people,
The town. Let me wash the wounds with water,
740   Let my lips catch what fluttering breath still lingers."
She climbed the lofty steps, and held her sister,
A dying woman, close; she used her robe
To try to stop the bleeding. And Dido tried
In vain to raise her heavy eyes, fell back,
745   And her wound made a gurgling hissing sound.
Three times she tried to lift herself; three times
Fell back; her rolling eyes went searching heaven
And the light hurt when she found it, and she moaned.
      At last all-powerful Juno, taking pity,
750   Sent Iris[41] from Olympus, in compassion
For the long racking agony, to free her
From the limbs' writhing and the struggle of spirit.
She had not earned this death, she had only sought it
Before her time, driven by sudden madness,
755   Therefore, the queen of Hades[42] had not taken
The golden lock, consigning her to Orcus.
So Iris, dewy on saffron wings, descending,
Trailing a thousand colors through the brightness
Comes down the sky, poises above her, saying,
760   "This lock I take as bidden, and from the body
Release the soul," and cuts the lock; and cold
Takes over, and the winds receive the spirit.

      [*After his hasty departure from Carthage, Aeneas goes to Sicily where he conducts funeral games for his father, Anchises; he sets sail for Italy, leaving the unwilling behind. On the voyage, his helmsman, Palinurus, falls overboard. Once in Italy, Aeneas consults the Sibyl of Apollo who will guide him to the underworld.*]

BOOK VI: THE LOWER WORLD

      Gods of the world of spirit, silent shadows,
Chaos and Phlegethon, areas of silence,
Wide realms of dark, may it be right and proper
To tell what I have heard, this revelation
5   Of matters buried deep in earth and darkness!

---

[41]Iris: Juno's messenger, goddess of the rainbow
[42]queen of Hades: Proserpina; Orcus is another name for Hades, or Pluto—King of the Underworld.

Vague forms in lonely darkness, they were going
Through void and shadow, through the empty realm
Like people in a forest, when the moonlight
Shifts with a baleful glimmer, and shadow covers
10   The sky, and all the colors turn to blackness.
At the first threshold, on the jaws of Orcus,
Grief and avenging Cares have set their couches,
And pale Diseases dwell, and sad Old Age,
Fear, evil-counselling Hunger, wretched Need,
15   Forms terrible to see, and Death, and Toil,
And Death's own brother, Sleep, and evil Joys,
Fantasies of the mind, and deadly War,
The Furies' iron chambers, Discord, raving,
Her snaky hair entwined in bloody bands.
20   An elm-tree loomed there, shadowy and huge,
The aged boughs outspread, beneath whose leaves,
Men say, the false dreams cling, thousands on thousands.
And there are monsters in the dooryard, Centaurs,
Scyllas, of double shape, the beast of Lerna,
25   Hissing most horribly, Briareus,
The hundred-handed giant, a Chimaera
Whose armament is fire, Harpies, and Gorgons,
A triple-bodied giant. In sudden panic
Aeneas drew his sword, the edge held forward,
30   Ready to rush and flail, however blindly,
Save that his wise companion warned him, saying
They had no substance, they were only phantoms
Flitting about, illusions without body.
From here, the road turns off to Acheron,
35   River of Hell; here, thick with muddy whirling,
Cocytus boils with sand. Charon is here,
The guardian of these mingling waters, Charon,
Uncouth and filthy, on whose chin the hair
Is a tangled mat, whose eyes protrude, are burning,
40   Whose dirty cloak is knotted at the shoulder.
He poles a boat, tends to the sail, unaided,
Ferrying bodies in his rust-hued vessel.
Old, but a god's senility is awful
In its raw greenness. To the bank come thronging
45   Mothers and men, bodies of great-souled heroes,
Their life-time over, boys, unwedded maidens,
Young men whose fathers saw their pyres burning,
Thick as the forest leaves that fall in autumn
With early frost, thick as the birds to landfall

50 From over the seas, when the chill of the year compels them
 To sunlight. There they stand, a host, imploring
 To be taken over first. Their hands, in longing,
 Reach out for the farther shore. But the gloomy boatman
 Makes choice among them, taking some, and keeping
55 Others far back from the stream's edge. Aeneas,
 Wondering, asks the Sibyl, "Why the crowding?
 What are the spirits seeking? What distinction
 Brings some across the livid stream, while others
 Stay on the farther bank?" She answers, briefly:
60 "Son of Anchises, this is the awful river,
 The Styx, by which the gods take oath; the boatman
 Charon; those he takes with him are the buried,
 Those he rejects, whose luck is out, the graceless.
 It is not permitted him to take them over
65 The dreadful banks and hoarse-resounding waters
 Till earth is cast upon their bones. They haunt
 These shores a hundred restless years of waiting
 Before they end postponement of the crossing."
 Aeneas paused, in thoughtful mood, with pity
70 Over their lot's unevenness; and saw there,
 Wanting the honor given the dead, and grieving,
 Leucaspis, and Orontes, the Lycian captain,
 Who had sailed from Troy across the stormy waters,
 And drowned off Africa, with crew and vessel
75 And there was Palinurus, once his pilot,
 Who, not so long ago, had been swept over,
 Watching the stars on the journey north from Carthage
 The murk was thick; Aeneas hardly knew him,
 Sorrowful in that darkness, but made question:
80 "What god, O Palinurus, took you from us?
 Who drowned you in the deep? Tell me. Apollo
 Never before was false, and yet he told me
 You would be safe across the seas, and come
 Unharmed to Italy; what kind of promise
85 Was this, to fool me with?" But Palinurus
 Gave him assurance:—"It was no god who drowned me,
 No falsehood on Apollo's part, my captain,
 But as I clung to the tiller, holding fast
 To keep the course, as I should do, I felt it
90 Wrenched from the ship, and I fell with it, headlong.
 By those rough seas I swear, I had less fear
 On my account, than for the ship, with rudder
 And helmsman overboard, to drift at the mercy

Of rising seas. Three nights I rode the waters,
95   Three nights of storm, and from the crest of a wave,
On the fourth morning, sighted Italy,
I was swimming to land, I had almost reached it, heavy
In soaking garments; my cramped fingers struggled
To grasp the top of the rock, when barbarous people,
100   Ignorant men, mistaking me for booty,
Struck me with swords; waves hold me now, or winds
Roll me along the shore. By the light of heaven,
The lovely air, I beg you, by your father,
Your hope of young Iulus, bring me rescue
105   Out of these evils, my unconquered leader!
Cast over my body earth—you have the power—
Return to Velia's harbor,—or there may be
Some other way—your mother is a goddess,
Else how would you be crossing this great river,
110   This Stygian swamp?—help a poor fellow, take me
Over the water with you, give a dead man
At least a place to rest in." But the Sibyl
Broke in upon him sternly:—"Palinurus,
Whence comes this mad desire? No man, unburied,
115   May see the Stygian waters, or Cocytus,
The Furies' dreadful river; no man may come
Unbidden to this bank. Give up the hope
That fate is changed by praying, but hear this,
A little comfort in your harsh misfortune:
120   Those neighboring people will make expiation,
Driven by signs from heaven, through their cities
And through their countryside; they will build a tomb,
Thereto bring offerings yearly, and the place
Shall take its name from you, Cape Palinurus."
125   So he was comforted a little, finding
Some happiness in the promise.
                      And they went on,
Nearing the river, and from the stream the boatman
Beheld them cross the silent forest, nearer,
130   Turning their footsteps toward the bank. He challenged:—
"Whoever you are, O man in armor, coming
In this direction, halt where you are, and tell me
The reason why you come. This is the region
Of shadows, and of Sleep and drowsy Night;
135   I am not allowed to carry living bodies
In the Stygian boat; and I must say I was sorry
I ever accepted Hercules and Theseus

And Pirithous, and rowed them over the lake,
Though they were sons of gods and great in courage.
140 One of them dared to drag the guard of Hell,
Enchained, from Pluto's throne, shaking in terror,
The others to snatch our queen from Pluto's chamber."
The Sibyl answered briefly: "No such cunning
Is plotted here; our weapons bring no danger.
145 Be undisturbed: the hell-hound in his cavern
May bark forever, to keep the bloodless shadows
Frightened away from trespass; Proserpine,
Untouched, in pureness guard her uncle's threshold.
Trojan Aeneas, a man renowned for goodness,
150 Renowned for nerve in battle, is descending
To the lowest shades; he comes to find his father.
If such devotion has no meaning to you,
Look on this branch at least, and recognize it"
And with the word she drew from under her mantle
155 The golden bough; his swollen wrath subsided.
No more was said; he saw the bough, and marvelled
At the holy gift, so long unseen; came sculling
The dark-blue boat to the shore, and drove the spirits,
Lining the thwarts, ashore, and cleared the gangway,
160 And took Aeneas aboard; as that big man
Stepped in, the leaky skiff groaned under the weight,
And the strained seams let in the muddy water,
But they made the crossing safely, seer and soldier,
To the far margin, colorless and shapeless,
165 Grey sedge and dark-brown ooze. They heard the baying
Of Cerberus, that great hound, in his cavern crouching
Making the shore resound, as all three throats
Belled horribly; and serpents rose and bristled
Along the triple neck. The priestess threw him
170 A sop with honey and drugged meal; he opened
The ravenous throat, gulped, and subsided, filling
The den with his huge bulk. Aeneas, crossing,
Passed on beyond the bank of the dread river
Whence none return.
175   A wailing of thin voices
Came to their ears, the souls of infants crying
Those whom the day of darkness took from the breast
Before their share of living. And there were many

Whom some false sentence brought to death. Here Minos[41]
180 Judges them once again; a silent jury
Reviews the evidence. And there are others,
Guilty of nothing, but who hated living,
The suicides. How gladly, now, they would suffer
Poverty, hardship, in the world of light!
185 But this is not permitted; they are bound
Nine times around by the black unlovely river;
Styx holds them fast.
                    They came to the Fields of Mourning
So-called, where those whom cruel love had wasted
190 Hid in secluded pathways, under myrtle,
And even in death were anxious. Procris, Phaedra,
Eriphyle, displaying wounds her son
Had given her, Caeneus, Laodamia,
Caeneus, a young man once, and now again
195 A young man, after having been a woman.
And here, new come from her own wound, was Dido,
Wandering in the wood. The Trojan hero,
Standing near by, saw her, or thought he saw her,
Dim in the shadows, like the slender crescent
200 Of moon when cloud drifts over. Weeping, he greets her:—
"Unhappy Dido, so they told me truly
That your own hand had brought you death. Was I—
Alas!—the cause? I swear by all the stars,
By the world above, by everything held sacred
205 Here under the earth, unwillingly, O queen,
I left your kingdom. But the gods' commands,
Driving me now through these forsaken places,
This utter night, compelled me on. I could not
Believe my loss would cause so great a sorrow.
210 Linger a moment, do not leave me; whither,
Whom, are you fleeing? I am permitted only
This last word with you."
                    But the queen, unmoving
As flint or marble, turned away, her eyes
215 Fixed on the ground: the tears were vain, the words,
Meant to be soothing, foolish; she turned away,
His enemy forever, to the shadows
Where Sychaeus, her former husband, took her
With love for love, and sorrow for her sorrow.

---

[41]**Minos**: king of Crete who had Daedalus build the labyrinth to hide the Minotaur monster. Minos was a judge of the dead.

220 And still Aeneas wept for her, being troubled
By the injustice of her doom; his pity
Followed her going.
They went on. They came
To the farthest fields, whose tenants are the warriors,
225 Illustrious throng. Here Tydeus came to meet him,
Parthenopaeus came, and pale Adrastus,
A fighter's ghost, and many, many others,
Mourned in the world above, and doomed in battle,
Leaders of Troy, in long array; Aeneas
230 Sighed as he saw them: Medon, Polyboetes,
The priest of Ceres; Glaucus; and Idaeus
Still keeping arms and chariot; three brothers,
Antenor's sons; Thersilochus; a host
To right and left of him, and when they see him,
235 One sight is not enough; they crowd around him,
Linger, and ask the reasons for his coming.
But Agamemnon's men, the Greek battalions,
Seeing him there, and his arms in shadow gleaming,
Tremble in panic, turn to flee for refuge,
240 As once they used to, toward their ships, but where
Are the ships now? They try to shout, in terror;
But only a thin and piping treble issues
To mock their mouths, wide-open.
One he knew
245 Was here, Deiphobus, a son of Priam,
With his whole body mangled, and his features
Cruelly slashed, and both hands cut, and ears
Torn from his temples, and his nostrils slit
By shameful wounds. Aeneas hardly knew him,
250 Shivering there, and doing his best to hide
His marks of punishment; unhailed, he hailed him:—
"Deiphobus, great warrior, son of Teucer,
Whose cruel punishment was this? Whose license
Abused you so? I heard, it seems, a story
255 Of that last night, how you had fallen, weary
With killing Greeks at last; I built a tomb,
Although no body lay there, in your honor,
Three times I cried, aloud, over your spirit,
Where now your name and arms keep guard. I could not,
260 Leaving my country, find my friend, to give him
Proper interment in the earth he came from."
And Priam's son replied:—"Nothing, dear comrade,
Was left undone; the dead man's shade was given

All ceremony due. It was my own fortune
265 And a Spartan woman's deadliness that sunk me
Under these evils; she it was who left me
These souvenirs. You know how falsely happy
We were on that last night; I need not tell you.
When that dread horse came leaping over our walls,
270 Pregnant with soldiery, she led the dancing,
A solemn rite, she called it, with Trojan women
Screaming their bacchanals; she raised the torches
High on the citadel; she called the Greeks.
Then—I was worn with trouble, drugged in slumber,
275 Resting in our ill-omened bridal chamber,
With sleep as deep and sweet as death upon me—
Then she, that paragon of helpmates, deftly
Moved all the weapons from the house; my sword,
Even, she stole from underneath my pillow,
280 Opened the door, and called in Menelaus,
Hoping, no doubt, to please her loving husband,
To win forgetfulness of her old sinning.
It is quickly told: they broke into the chamber,
The two of them, and with them, as accomplice,
285 Ulysses came, the crime-contriving bastard.
O gods, pay back the Greeks; grant the petition
If goodness asks for vengeance! But you, Aeneas,
A living man—what chance has brought you here?
Vagrant of ocean, god-inspired,—which are you?
290 What chance has worn you down, to come, in sadness,
To these confusing sunless dwelling-places?"
        While they were talking, Aurora's rosy car
Had halfway crossed the heaven; all their time
Might have been spent in converse, but the Sibyl
295 Hurried them forward:—"Night comes on, Aeneas;
We waste the hours with tears. We are at the cross-road,
Now; here we turn to the right, where the pathway leads
On to Elysium, under Pluto's ramparts.
Leftward is Tartarus, and retribution,
300 The terminal of the wicked, and their dungeon."
Deiphobus left them, saying, "O great priestess,
Do not be angry with me; I am going;
I shall not fail the roll-call of the shadows.
Pride of our race, go on; may better fortune
305 Attend you!" and, upon the word, he vanished.
        As he looked back, Aeneas saw, to his left,
Wide walls beneath a cliff, a triple rampart,

A river running fire, Phlegethon's torrent,
Rocks roaring in its course, a gate, tremendous,
310   Pillars of adamant, a tower of iron,
Too strong for men, too strong for even gods
To batter down in warfare, and behind them
A Fury, sentinel in bloody garments,
Always on watch, by day, by night. He heard
315   Sobbing and groaning there, the crack of the lash,
The clank of iron, the sound of dragging shackles.
The noise was terrible; Aeneas halted,
Asking, "What forms of crime are these, O maiden?
What harrying punishment, what horrible outcry?"
320   She answered:—"O great leader of the Trojans,
I have never crossed that threshold of the wicked;
No pure soul is permitted entrance thither,
But Hecate, by whose order I was given
Charge of Avernus' groves, my guide, my teacher,
325   Told me how gods exact the toll of vengeance.
The monarch here, merciless Rhadamanthus,
Punishes guilt, and hears confession; he forces
Acknowledgment of crime; no man in the world,
No matter how cleverly he hides his evil,
330   No matter how much he smiles at his own slyness,
Can fend atonement off; the hour of death
Begins his sentence. Tisiphone, the Fury,
Leaps at the guilty with her scourge; her serpents
Are whips of menace as she calls her sisters.
335   Imagine the gates, on jarring hinge, rasp open,
You would see her in the doorway, a shape, a sentry,
Savage, implacable. Beyond, still fiercer,
The monstrous Hydra dwells; her fifty throats
Are black, and open wide, and Tartarus
340   Is black, and open wide, and it goes down
To darkness, sheer deep down, and twice the distance
That earth is from Olympus. At the bottom
The Titans crawl, Earth's oldest breed, hurled under
By thunderbolts; here lie the giant twins,
345   Aloeus' sons, who laid their hands on heaven
And tried to pull down Jove; Salmoneus here
Atones for high presumption,—it was he
Who aped Jove's noise and fire, wheeling his horses
Triumphant through his city in Elis, cheering
350   And shaking the torch, and claiming divine homage,
The arrogant fool, to think his brass was lightning,

His horny-footed horses beat out thunder!
Jove showed him what real thunder was, what lightning
Spoke from immortal cloud, what whirlwind fury
355   Came sweeping from the heaven to overtake him.
Here Tityos, Earth's giant son, lies sprawling
Over nine acres, with a monstrous vulture
Gnawing, with crooked beak, vitals and liver
That grow as they are eaten; eternal anguish,
360   Eternal feast. Over another hangs
A rock, about to fall; and there are tables
Set for a banquet, gold with royal splendor,
But if a hand goes out to touch the viands,
The Fury drives it back with fire and yelling.
365   Why name them all, Pirithous, the Lapiths,
Ixion? The roll of crime would take forever.
Whoever, in his lifetime, hated his brother,
Or struck his father down; whoever cheated
A client, or was miserly—how many
370   Of these there seem to be!—whoever went
To treasonable war, or broke a promise
Made to his lord, whoever perished, slain
Over adultery, all these, walled in,
Wait here their punishment. Seek not to know
375   Too much about their doom. The stone is rolled,
The wheel keeps turning; Theseus forever
Sits in dejection; Phlegyas, accursed,
Cries through the halls forever: *Being warned,*
Learn justice; reverence the gods! The man
380   Who sold his country is here in hell; the man
Who altered laws for money; and a father
Who knew his daughter's bed. All of them dared,
And more than dared, achieved, unspeakable
Ambitions. If I had a hundred tongues,
385   A hundred iron throats, I could not tell
The fullness of their crime and punishment."
And then she added:—"Come: resume the journey,
Fulfill the mission; let us hurry onward.
I see the walls the Cyclops made, the portals
390   Under the archway, where, the orders tell us,
Our tribute must be set." They went together
Through the way's darkness, came to the doors, and halted,
And at the entrance Aeneas, having sprinkled

His body with fresh water, placed the bough[42]
395 Golden before the threshold. The will of the goddess
Had been performed, the proper task completed.
    They came to happy places, the joyful dwelling,
The lovely greenery of the groves of the blessed.
Here ampler air invests the fields with light,
400 Rose-colored, with familiar stars and sun.
Some grapple on the grassy wrestling-ground
In exercise and sport, and some are dancing,
And others singing; in his trailing robe
Orpheus strums the lyre; the seven clear notes
405 Accompany the dance, the song. And heroes
Are there, great-souled, born in the happier years,
Ilus, Assaracus; the city's founder,
Prince Dardanus. Far off, Aeneas wonders,
Seeing the phantom arms, the chariots,
410 The spears fixed in the ground, the chargers browsing,
Unharnessed, over the plain. Whatever, living,
The men delighted in, whatever pleasure
Was theirs in horse and chariot, still holds them
Here under the world. To right and left, they banquet
415 In the green meadows, and a joyful chorus
Rises through groves of laurel, whence the river
Runs to the upper world. The band of heroes
Dwell here, all those whose mortal wounds were suffered
In fighting for the fatherland; and poets,
420 The good, the pure, the worthy of Apollo;
Those who discovered truth and made life nobler;
Those who served others—all, with snowy fillets
Binding their temples, throng the lovely valley.
And these the Sibyl questioned, most of all
425 Musaeus, for he towered above the center
Of that great throng:—"O happy souls, O poet,
Where does Anchises dwell? For him we come here.
For him we have traversed Erebus'[43] great rivers."
And he replied:—"It is all our home, the shady
430 Groves, and the streaming meadows, and the softness
Along the river-banks. No fixed abode
Is ours at all; but if it is your pleasure,
Cross over the ridge with me; I will guide you there

---

[42]**bough**: a propitiation for Proserpina, queen of the underworld; Aeneas received the
golden bough from the Sibyl, VI. 154–55.
[43]**Erebus**: another name for the underworld; god of the dark

By easy going." And so Musaeus led them
435 And from the summit showed them fields, all shining,
And they went on over and down.
　　　　Deep in a valley of green, father Anchises
Was watching, with deep earnestness, the spirits
Whose destiny was light, and counting them over,
440 All of his race to come, his dear descendants,
Their fates and fortunes and their works and ways,
And as he saw Aeneas coming toward him
Over the meadow, his hands reached out with yearning,
He was moved to tears, and called:—"At last, my son,—
445 Have you really come, at last? and the long road nothing
To a son who loves his father? Do I, truly,
See you, and hear your voice? I was thinking so,
I was hoping so, I was counting off the days,
And I was right about it. O my son!
450 What a long journey, over land and water,
Yours must have been! What buffeting of danger!
I feared, so much, the Libyan realm would hurt you."
And his son answered:—"It was your spirit, father,
Your sorrowful shade, so often met, that led me
455 To find these portals. The ships ride safe at anchor,
Safe in the Tuscan sea. Embrace me, father;
Let hand join hand in love; do not forsake me."
And as he spoke, the tears streamed down. Three times
He reached out toward him, and three times the image
460 Fled like the breath of the wind or a dream on wings.
　　　　He saw, in a far valley, a separate grove
Where the woods stir and rustle, and a river,
The Lethe, gliding past the peaceful places,
And tribes of people thronging, hovering over,
465 Innumerable as the bees in summer
Working the bright-hued flowers, and the shining
Of the white lilies, murmuring and humming.
Aeneas, filled with wonder, asks the reason
For what he does not know, who are the people
470 In such a host, and to what river coming?
Anchises answers:—"These are spirits, ready
Once more for life; they drink of Lethe's water
The soothing potion of forgetfulness.
I have longed, for long, to show them to you, name them,
475 Our children's children; Italy discovered,
So much the greater happiness, my son."
"But, O my father, is it thinkable

That souls would leave this blessedness, be willing
A second time to bear the sluggish body,
480 Trade Paradise for earth? Alas, poor wretches,
Why such a mad desire for light?" Anchises
Gives detailed answer:[44] "First, my son, a spirit
Sustains all matter, heaven and earth and ocean,
The moon, the stars; mind quickens mass, and moves it.
485 Hence comes the race of man, of beast, of winged
Creatures of air, of the strange shapes which ocean
Bears down below his mottled marble surface.
All these are blessed with energy from heaven;
The seed of life is a spark of fire, but the body
490 A clod of earth, a clog, a mortal burden.
Hence humans fear, desire, grieve, and are joyful,
And even when life is over, all the evil
Ingrained so long, the adulterated mixture,
The plagues and pestilences of the body
495 Remain, persist. So there must be a cleansing
By penalty, by punishment, by fire,
By sweep of wind, by water's absolution,
Before the guilt is gone. Each of us suffers
His own peculiar ghost. But the day comes
500 When we are sent through wide Elysium,
The Fields of the Blessed, a few of us, to linger
Until the turn of time, the wheel of ages,
Wears off the talent, and leaves the core of spirit
Pure sense, pure flame. A thousand years pass over
505 And the god calls the countless host to Lethe
Where memory is annulled, and souls are willing
Once more to enter into mortal bodies."
      The discourse ended; the father drew his son
And his companion toward the hum, the center
510 Of the full host; they came to rising ground
Where all the long array was visible,
Anchises watching, noting, every comer.
"Glory to come, my son, illustrious spirits
Of Dardan lineage, Italian offspring,
515 Heirs of our name, begetters of our future!
These I will name for you and tell our fortunes:
First, leaning on a headless spear, and standing
Nearest the light, that youth, the first to rise

---

[44]Compare Anchises' description with Plato's Myth of Er in *The Republic*.

To the world above, is Silvius; his name
520   Is Alban; in his veins Italian blood
Will run with Trojan; he will be the son
Of your late age; Lavinia will bear him,
A king and sire of kings; from him our race
Will rule in Alba Longa. Near him, Procas,
525   A glory to the Trojan race; and Capys,
And Numitor, and Silvius Aeneas,
Resembling you in name, in arms, in goodness,
If ever he wins the Alban kingdom over.
What fine young men they are! What strength, what prowess!
530   The civic oak already shades their foreheads.
These will found cities, Gabii, Fidenae,
Nomentum; they will crown the hills with towers
Above Collatia, Inuus fortress, Bola,
Cora, all names to be, thus far ungiven.
535   "And there will be a son of Mars; his mother
Is Ilia, and his name is Romulus,
Assaracus' descendant. On his helmet
See, even now, twin plumes; his father's honor
Confers distinction on him for the world.
540   Under his auspices Rome, that glorious city,
Will bound her power by earth, her pride by heaven,
Happy in hero sons, one wall surrounding
Her seven hills, even as Cybele, riding
Through Phrygian cities, wears her crown of towers,
545   Rejoicing in her offspring, and embracing
A hundred children of the gods, her children,
Celestials, all of them, at home in heaven.
Turn the eyes now this way; behold the Romans,
Your very own. These are Iulus' children,
550   The race to come. One promise you have heard
Over and over: here is its fulfillment,
The son of a god, Augustus Caesar, founder
Of a new age of gold, in lands where Saturn
Ruled long ago; he will extend his empire
555   Beyond the Indies, beyond the normal measure
Of years and constellations, where high Atlas
Turns on his shoulders the star-studded world.
Maeotia and the Caspian seas are trembling
As heaven's oracles predict his coming,
560   And all the seven mouths of Nile are troubled.
Not even Hercules, in all his travels,
Covered so much of the world, from Erymanthus

To Lerna; nor did Bacchus, driving his tigers
From Nysa's summit. How can hesitation
565   Keep us from deeds to make our prowess greater?
What fear can block us from Ausonian land?
        "And who is that one yonder, wearing the olive,
Holding the sacrifice? I recognize him,
That white-haired king of Rome, who comes from Cures,
570   A poor land, to a mighty empire, giver
Of law to the young town. His name is Numa.
Near him is Tullus; he will rouse to arms
A race grown sluggish, little used to triumph.
Beyond him Ancus, even now too boastful,
575   Too fond of popular favor. And then the
Tarquins, And the avenger Brutus, proud of spirit,
Restorer of the balance. He shall be
First holder of the consular power; his children
Will stir up wars again, and he, for freedom
580   And her sweet sake, will call down judgment on them,
Unhappy, however future men may praise him,
In love of country and intense ambition.
        "There are the Decii, and there the Drusi,
A little farther off, and stern Torquatus,
585   The man with the axe, and Camillus, the regainer
Of standards lost. And see those two, resplendent
In equal arms, harmonious friendly spirits
Now, in the shadow of night, but if they ever
Come to the world of light, alas, what warfare,
590   What battle-lines, what slaughter they will fashion,
Each for the other, one from Alpine ramparts
Descending, and the other ranged against him
With armies from the east, father and son
Through marriage, Pompey and Caesar. O my children,
595   Cast out the thoughts of war, and do not murder
The flower of our country. O my son,
Whose line descends from heaven, let the sword
Fall from the hand, be leader in forbearing!
        "Yonder is one who, victor over Corinth,
600   Will ride in triumph home, famous for carnage
Inflicted on the Greeks; near him another,
Destroyer of old Argus and Mycenae
Where Agamemnon ruled; he will strike down
A king descended from Achilles; Pydna
605   Shall be revenge for Pallas' ruined temple,
For Trojan ancestors. Who would pass over,

Without a word, Cossus, or noble Cato,
The Gracchi, or those thunderbolts of warfare,
The Scipios, Libya's ruin, or Fabricius
610   Mighty with little, or Serranus, ploughing
The humble furrow? My tale must hurry on:
I see the Fabii next, and their great Quintus
Who brought us back an empire by delaying.
Others, no doubt, will better mould the bronze
615   To the semblance of soft breathing, draw, from marble,
The living countenance; and others plead
With greater eloquence, or learn to measure,
Better than we, the pathways of the heaven,
The risings of the stars: remember, Roman,
620   To rule the people under law, to establish
The way of peace, to battle down the haughty,
To spare the meek. Our fine arts, these, forever."
      Anchises paused a moment, and they marvelled
And he went on:—"See, how Marcellus triumphs,
625   Glorious over all with the great trophies
Won when he slew the captain of the Gauls,
Leader victorious over leading foeman.
When Rome is in great trouble and confusion
He will establish order, Gaul and Carthage
630   Go down before his sword, and triple trophies
Be given Romulus in dedication."
      There was a young man going with Marcellus,
Brilliant in shining armor, bright in beauty,
But sorrowful, with downcast eyes. Aeneas
635   Broke in, to ask his father: "Who is this youth
Attendant on the hero? A son of his?
One of his children's children? How the crowd
Murmurs and hums around him! what distinction,
What presence, in his person! But dark night
640   Hovers around his head with mournful shadow.
Who is he, father?" And Anchises answered:—
"Great sorrow for our people! O my son,
Ask not to know it. This one fate will only
Show to the world; he will not be permitted
645   Any long sojourn. Rome would be too mighty,
Too great in the gods' sight, were this gift hers.
What lamentation will the field of Mars
Raise to the city! Tiber, gliding by
The new-built tomb, the funeral state, bear witness!
650   No youth from Trojan stock will ever raise

His ancestors so high in hope, no Roman
Be such a cause for pride. Alas for goodness,
Alas for old-time honor, and the arm
Invincible in war! Against him no one,
655   Whether on foot or foaming horse, would come
In battle and depart unscathed. Poor boy,
If you should break the cruel fates; if only—
You are to be Marcellus. Let me scatter
Lilies, or dark-red flowers, bringing honor
660   To my descendant's shade; let the gift be offered,
However vain the tribute."
        So through the whole wide realm they went together,
Anchises and his son; from fields of air
Learning and teaching of the fame and glory,
665   The wars to come, the toils to face, or flee from,
Latinus' city and the Latin peoples,
The love of what would be.
                    There are two portals,
Twin gates of Sleep, one made of horn, where easy
670   Release is given true shades, the other gleaming
White ivory, whereby the false dreams issue
To the upper air. Aeneas and the Sibyl
Part from Anchises at the second portal.
He goes to the ships, again, rejoins his comrades,
675   Sails to Caieta's harbor, and the vessels
Rest on their mooring-lines.

    [*Aeneas and his men arrive at their destined place where Turnus, suitor to Lavinia, King Latinus's daughter, stirs up trouble from jealousy. Aeneas' mother, Venus, asks Vulcan, blacksmith for the gods, to make her son a new shield.*]

FROM BOOK VIII: THE SHIELD OF AENEAS

    And the bright goddess through the clouds of heaven
Came bringing gifts, seeing her son alone
By the cold river in the quiet valley,
And spoke to him:—"Behold, the gifts made ready
5   By Vulcan's promised skill. Fear not, my son,
To face the wars with Turnus and the Latins!"
After the word, the embrace. She placed the armor,
All shining in his sight, against an oak-tree,
Rejoicing in the gift, the honor, he turned
10   His eyes to these, over and over again,

Could not be satisfied, took in his hands
The helmet with the terrible plumes and flame,
The fatal sword, the breastplate, made of bronze,
Fire-colored, huge, shining the way a cloud,
15   Dark-blue, turns crimson under the slanting sun,
The greaves of gold refined and smooth electrum,
The spear, the final masterpiece, the shield.
    Hereon the great prophetic Lord of Fire
Had carved the story out, the stock to come,
20   The wars, each one in order, all the tale
Of Italy and Roman triumph.[45] Here
In Mars' green cave the she-wolf gives her udders
To the twin boys, turning half round to lick them,
And neither is afraid, and both are playing.
25   Another scene presents the Circus-games,
When Romans took their Sabine brides, and war
Broke out between old Tatius and the sons
Of Romulus, and was ended, monarchs pledging
Peace at the altars over sacrifice.
30   Mettus, the false, by the wild horses drawn
And quartered, sheds his life-blood over the brambles;
Porsena, the besieger, rings the city
For Tarquin's sake, exile and tyrant; Romans
Rush on the steel for freedom; Clelia breaks
35   Her bonds to swim the river; and Horatius
Breaks down the bridge. The guardian Manlius
Holds the high capitol and that crude palace
Fresh with the straw of Romulus; the goose
Flutters in silver through the colonnades
40   Shrieking alarm; the Gauls are near in darkness,
Golden their hair, their clothing, and their necks
Gleam white in collars of gold, and each one carries
Two Alpine javelins; they have long shields.
Near them, the Fire-god sets the priests with caps
45   Of wool, the miracle of the shields from heaven,
The Salii dancing, the Luperci naked,
And the chaste matrons riding through the city
In cushioned chariots. Far off, he adds
The seats of Hell, the lofty gates of Pluto,
50   Penance for sin: Catiline, with the Furies
Making him cower; farther off, the good,

---

[45]The following lines allude to some of the future events of Rome, a mixture of myth and history. (Compare this future account given by Anchises in the underworld.)

With Cato giving laws. And all this scene
Bound with the likeness of the swelling ocean,
Blue water and whitecap, where the dolphins playing
55   Leap with a curve of silver. In the center
Actium, the ships of bronze, Leucate burning
Hot with the glow of war, and waves on fire
With molten gold. Augustus Caesar stands
High on the lofty stern; his temples flame
60   With double fire, and over his head there dawns
His father's star. Agrippa leads a column
With favoring wind and god, the naval garland
Wreathing his temples. Antony assembles
Egypt and all the East; Antony, victor
65   Over the lands of dawn and the Red Sea,
Marshals the foes of Rome, himself a Roman,
With—horror!—an Egyptian wife. The surge
Boils under keel, the oar-blades churn the waters,
The triple-pointed beaks drive through the billows,
70   You would think that mountains swam and battled mountains,
That islands were uprooted in their anger.
Fireballs and shafts of steel are slanting showers,
The fields of Neptune redden with the slaughter.
The queen drives on her warriors, unseeing
75   The double snakes of death; rattle and cymbals
Compete with bugle and trumpet. Monstrous gods,
Of every form and fashion, one, Anubis,
Shaped like a dog, wield their outrageous weapons
In wrath at Venus, Neptune, and Minerva.
80   Mars, all in steel, storms through the fray; the Furies
Swoop from the sky; Discord exults; Bellona,
With bloody scourge, comes lashing; and Apollo
From Actium bends his bow. Egypt and India,
Sabaeans and Arabians, flee in terror.
85   And the contagion takes the queen, who loosens
The sheets to slackness, courts the wind, in terror,
Pale at the menace of death. And the Nile comes
To meet her, a protecting god, his mantle
Spread wide, to bring a beaten woman home.
90   And Caesar enters Rome triumphant, bringing
Immortal offerings, three times a hundred
New altars through the city. Streets are loud
With gladness, games, rejoicing, all the temples
Are filled with matrons praying at the altars,
95   Are heaped with solemn sacrifice. And Caesar,

Seated before Apollo's shining threshold,
Reviews the gifts, and hangs them on the portals.
In long array the conquered file, their garments,
Their speech, as various as their arms, the Nomads,
100   The naked Africans, Leleges, Carians,
Gelonians with quivers, the Morini,
Of mortals most remote, Euphrates moving
With humbler waves, the two-mouthed Rhine, Araxes,
Chafing beneath his bridge.
105   All this Aeneas
Sees on his mother's gift, the shield of Vulcan,
And, without understanding, is proud and happy
As he lifts to his shoulder all that fortune,
The fame and glory of his children's children.

FROM BOOK IX: IN THE ABSENCE OF AENEAS

While all this happened far away, queen Juno
Sent Iris down from heaven to bold Turnus.
She found him resting in a sacred valley,
Pilumnus' grove, his ancestor; all radiant
5   She spoke to him:—"No god would promise, Turnus,
This answer to your prayers, but the turn of time
Has put it in your hands. Aeneas has gone,
Leaving the town, the fleet, and his companions,
Seeking the realm of Palatine Evander,
10   And more than that: he has won some cities over,
He calls the Etruscan countrymen to arms.
What are you waiting for? Now is the time
For chariot and horse. Break off delay,
Take the bewildered camp!" She spoke, and rose
15   Skyward on even wings, and under the clouds
Cut her great soaring arc. And Turnus knew her,
And raised his hands to the sky, and followed her flight:—
"O Iris, pride of heaven, who sent you to me
Through clouds to earth? Whence comes this storm of
20   brightness?
I see the heavens part, and the stars wheeling
Across the sky. I follow these great omens,
Whoever calls to arms." And, with the word,
He went to the stream, took water up, prayed often,
25   Making his vows to all the gods of heaven.
And now, over all the plain, the army was coming,
Rich in comparison, and rich in horses,

In gold and broidered robes, Messapus leading,
And Turnus in the center, and Tyrrhus' sons
30 As captains in the rear: they stream as Ganges
Streams when his seven quiet tides flood over,
Or Nile resents his deep confining channel.
The Trojans see the sudden cloud, black dust
Thickening over the plain, and darkness rising,
35 And Caicus cries from the rampart:—"What is this,
O fellow-citizens, this rolling darkness?
Bring the swords quickly, bring weapons, climb the walls,
Here comes the enemy, yea! Hurry, hurry!"
Trojans, and noise, pour through the gates together.
40 Men fill the walls. For so, on his departure,
Aeneas had given orders: if something happened,
They should not risk a battle in the open,
They should only guard the camp, protect the ramparts.
So, much as they would love to mix in battle,
45 Anger and shame give way to prompt obedience.
They bar the gates; protected by their towers
They wait while the foe comes on. And Turnus, riding
Impatient past his dawdling column, is there
Before the city knows it. He has twenty
50 Fast riders with him, his mount a piebald Thracian,
His helmet gold with crimson crest. He cries,
"Who will be the first with me? Will anybody
Be first with me against them? Let them have it!"
And with the word, he lets the javelin fly,
55 First sign of battle; and they cheer and follow
And wonder a little at the Trojans, cowards
Who dare not fight in the open, man to man,
Who hug their walls for comfort. Round and round,
Turnus, a wild man, rides, seeking an entrance,
60 But there is no way in. He is like a wolf
Lurking about a sheep-fold, snarling at midnight
Beside the pens, enduring wind and rain,
While the bleating lambs are safe beneath the ewes,
And he, unable to get at them, rages
65 Fierce and dry-throated in the drive of hunger;
So Turnus looks at wall and camp, and passion
Burns hot within him, burns to his very bones.
How to get in? or how to yank the Trojans
Out of their cloister, smear them over the plain?
70 Ah, but the fleet is there, beside the camp,
Sheltered by earthworks and the flowing river:

There lies the chance! He calls for fire, he hurls it,
The burning torch, and his hand, almost, is burning,
And all of them pitch in—Turnus has shown them,
75   And Turnus eggs them on—they are armed with fire-
          brands,
They rob the hearths; the tar flares lurid yellow
Against the grey of the cloud, the soot and ashes.
          What god, O Muses, turned the fire? Who saved
80   The Trojan ships? Remind me—the story is old,
Men have believed it long, its glory endless.
When first Aeneas built the fleet on Ida,
Preparing for deep seas, the mother of gods,
Queen Cybele, spoke to Jove:—"Grant me, my son,
85   Lord of Olympus now, a mother's prayer.
I had a pine-wood on the mountain-top,
And men, for many years, brought offerings there,
I loved that forest, dark with fir and maple,
But when the Trojan lacked a fleet, I gave him
90   My timber gladly; now my heart is troubled.
Relieve my fear, and let a mother's pleading
Keep them from wreck on any course, unshaken
By any whirlwind. Grown upon our mountains,
They should have privilege." Her son, the swayer
95   Of the stars of the world, replied, "What call, O mother,
Is this you make on fate? What are you seeking?
Should keels laid down by mortal hand have title
To life immortal? Should Aeneas travel
Through danger, unendangered? Such power is given
100   No god in heaven. But I make this promise:
After their course is run, after the harbors
In Italy receive them, safe from the ocean,
And with Aeneas landed in Laurentum,
I will take away their mortal shape, I will make them
105   Goddesses of the sea, like Nereus' daughter,
Like Galatea, the nymphs who breast the foam."
So Jupiter promised, and, as gods do, took oath,
By the rivers of his brother under the world,
The banks that seethe with the black pitchy torrent,
110   And made Olympus tremble with his nod.
          The promised day had come, the fates had finished
The alloted span, when Turnus' desecration
Warned Cybele to keep the torch and firebrand
Far from her holy vessels. A new light blazed
115   In mortal sight, and from the east a cloud

Ran across heaven, and choirs from Ida followed,
And dread voice came down the air:—"O Trojans,
Be in no hurry to defend my vessels,
You have no need of arms; Turnus, most surely,
120   Will burn the seas before he burns these pine-trees.
Go forth in freedom, goddess of ocean,
The Mother wills it so." And each ship parted
Cable from bank, and dove to the deep water
As dolphins dive, and reappeared as maiden,—
125   Oh marvel!—and all of them bore out to the ocean.
       Rutulian hearts were stunned, their captains shaken,
Their steeds confused and frightened; even Tiber
Shrank back from the sea, and the murmuring stream
       protested.
130   But Turnus kept his nerve, his words rang loud
In challenge to their courage:—"These are portents
To make the Trojans timid; Jove has taken
Their comfort from them; the ships they always fled in
Run from Rutulian fire and sword; the oceans
135   Are pathless for the Trojans now, their hope
Of flight all gone: half of their world is taken,
And earth is in our hands, Italians, thousands,
Thousands of us in arms. I am not frightened,
However they boast of oracles from heaven.
140   Venus and fate have had their share: the Trojans
Have done enough even to touch our richness,
The Ausonian fields. I have my omens, also,
To match with theirs, a sword to slay the guilty,
Death for the rape of brides! Not Atreus' sons,
145   Not only Menelaus and Mycenae,
Know what this hurt can be, this need for vengeance,
This right to take up arms. Once to have perished,
They tell us, is enough. Once to have sinned
Ought to have been enough and more. Hereafter
150   All women should be hateful to them, cowards
Hiding behind the sheltering moat and rampart,
The little barriers that give them courage!
Have they not seen the walls that Neptune built them
Sink in the fires? Which one of you is ready,
155   Brave hearts, to slash their barriers with the sword,
To join me in the onrush? I do not need
The arms of Vulcan, nor a thousand vessels
Against the Trojans. Let them have Etruria!
One thing, at least, they need not fear,—the darkness,

160   The sneaking theft of their Palladium image,
        Guards slain in the dark, hiders in horse's belly
        I fight in open daylight, I have fire
        To put around their walls, I will teach them something,—
        Their business now is not with those Greek heroes
165   Whom Hector kept at bay for ten long years.
        Now day is almost over; you have done
        Good work; rest now; be happy, be preparing,
        Be hopeful for the battles of to-morrow."

FROM BOOK XII: THE FINAL COMBAT

                         Aeneas,
        Hearing the name of Turnus, leaves the city,
        Forsakes the lofty walls; he has no patience
        With any more delay, breaks off all projects,
5   Exults, a terrible thunderer in armor,
        As huge as Athos, or as huge as Eryx,
        Or even father Apennine, that mountain
        Roaring above the oaks, and lifting high
        His crown of shimmering trees and snowy crest.
10   Now all men turned their eyes, Rutulians, Trojans,
        Italians, those who held the lofty ramparts,
        Those battering at the wall below; their shoulders
        Were eased of armor now. And king Latinus
        Could hardly, in amazement, trust his senses
15   Seeing these two big men, born worlds apart,
        Meeting to make decision with the sword.
        The plain was cleared, and they came rushing forward,
        Hurling, far off, their spears; the fight is on,
        The bronze shields clang and ring. Earth gives a groan.
20   The swords strike hard and often; luck and courage
        Are blent in one. And as on mighty Sila
        Or on Taburnus' mountain, when two bullocks
        Charge into fight head-on, and trembling herdsmen
        Fall back in fear, and the herd is dumb with terror,
25   And heifers, hardly lowing, stare and wonder
        Which one will rule the woodland, which one the herd
        Will follow meekly after, and all the time
        They gore each other with savage horns, and shoulders
        And necks and ribs run streams of blood, and bellowing
30   Fills all the woodland,—even so, Aeneas
        And Daunus' son clash shield on shield; the clamor
        Fills heaven. And Jupiter holds the scales in balance

With each man's destiny as weight and counter,
And one the heavier under the doom of death.
35   Confident, Turnus, rising to the sword
Full height, is a flash of light; he strikes. The Trojans,
The Latins, cry aloud and come up standing.
But the sword is treacherous; it is broken off
With the blow half spent: the fire of Turnus finds
40   No help except in flight. Swift as the wind
He goes, and stares at a broken blade, a hand
Unarmed. The story is that in that hurry,
That rush of his, to arms, when the steeds were harnessed,
He took Metiscus' sword, not the one Daunus
45   Had left him. For a while it served its purpose
While the Trojans ran away, but when it met
The armor Vulcan forged, the mortal blade
Split off, like brittle ice, with glittering splinters
Like ice on the yellow sand; So Turnus flies
50   Madly across the plain in devious circles:
The Trojans ring him round, and a swamp on one side,
High walls on the other.
                      Aeneas, the pursuer,
Is none too swift: the arrow has left him hurt;
55   His knees give way, but he keeps on, keeps coming
After the panting enemy, as a hound,
Running a stag to bay, at the edge of the water
Or hedged by crimson plumes, darts in, and barks,
And snaps his jaws, closes and grips, is shaken
60   Off from the flanks again, and once more closes,
And a great noise goes up the air; the waters
Resound, and the whole sky thunders with the clamor.
Turnus has time, even in flight, for calling
Loud to Rutulians, each by name, demanding,
65   In terrible rage, the sword, the sword, the good one,
The one he knows. Let anybody bring it,
Aeneas threatens, and death and doom await him,
And the town will be a ruin. Wounded, still
He presses on. They go in five great circles,
70   Around and back: no game, with silly prizes,
Are they playing now; the life and blood of Turnus
Go to the winner.
               A wild olive-tree
Stood here, with bitter leaves, sacred to Faunus,
75   Revered by rescued sailors, who used to offer
Ex-votos to the native gods, their garments

In token of gratitude. For this the Trojans
Cared nothing, lopped the branches off to clear
The run of the field. Aeneas' spear had fastened
80   Deep in the trunk where the force of the cast had brought it,
Stuck in the grip of the root. Aeneas, stooping,
Yanks at the shaft; he cannot equal Turnus
In speed of foot, but the javelin is winged.
And Turnus, in a terrible moment of panic,
85   Cries:—"Faunus, pity me, and Earth, most kindly,
If ever I was reverent, as Aeneas
And those he leads have not been, hold the steel,
Do not let go!" He prayed, and he was answered.
Aeneas tugged and wrestled, pulled and hauled,
90   But the wood held on. And, while he strained, Juturna[46]
Rushed forward, once again Metiscus' double,
With the good sword for her brother. Then Venus, angry
Over such wanton interference, enters
And the root yields. The warriors, towering high,
95   Each one renewed in spirit, one with sword,
One with the spear, both breathing hard, are ready
For what Mars has to send.
                              And Juno, gazing
From a golden cloud to earth, watching the duel,
100   Heard the all-powerful king of high Olympus:—
"What will the end be now, O wife? What else
Remains? You know, and you admit you know it,
Aeneas is heaven-destined, the native hero
Become a god, raised by the fates, exalted.
105   What are you planning? with what hope lingering on
In the cold clouds? Was it proper that a mortal
Should wound a god? that the sword, once lost, be given
Turnus again?—Juturna, of course, is nothing
Without your help—was it proper that the beaten
110   Increase in violence? Stop it now, I tell you;
Listen to my entreaties: I would not have you
Devoured by grief in silence; I would not have you
Bring me, again, anxiety and sorrow,
However sweet the voice. The end has come.
115   To harry the Trojans over land and ocean,
To light up war unspeakable, to defile
A home with grief, to mingle bridal and sorrow,—

---

[46]Juturna: Turnus' sister, a river nymph, prompted by Juno, aids her brother in the battle.

All this you were permitted. Go no farther!
That is an absolute order." And Juno, downcast
120 In gaze, replied:—"Great Jove, I knew your pleasure:
And therefore, much against my will, left Turnus,
Left earth. Were it not so, you would not see me
Lonely upon my airy throne in heaven,
Enduring things both worthy and unworthy,
125 But I would be down there, by flame surrounded,
Fighting in the front ranks, and hauling Trojans
To battle with their enemies. Juturna,
I urged, I own, to help her wretched brother,
And I approved, I own, her greater daring
130 For his life's sake, but I did not approve,
And this I swear by Styx, that river whose name
Binds all the gods to truth, her taking weapons,
Aiming the bow. I give up now, I leave
These battles, though I hate to. I ask one favor
135 For Latium, for the greatness of your people,
And this no law of fate forbids: when, later,
And be it so, they join in peace, and settle
Their laws, their treaties, in a blessed marriage,
Do not command the Latins, native-born,
140 To change their language, to be known as Trojans,
To alter speech or garb; let them be Latium,
Let Alban kings endure through all the ages,
Let Roman stock, strong in Italian valor,
Prevail since Troy has fallen, let her name
145 Perish and be forgotten." Smiling on her,
The great creator answered:—"You are truly
True sister of Jove[47] and child of Saturn, nursing
Such tides of anger in the heart! Forget it!
Abate the rise of passion. The wish is granted.
150 I yield, and more than that,—I share your purpose.
Ausonians shall keep their old tradition,
Their fathers' speech and ways; their name shall be
Even as now it is. Their sacred laws,
Their ritual, I shall add, and make all Latins
155 Men of a common tongue. A race shall rise
All-powerful, of mingled blood; you will see them
By virtue of devotion rise to glories
Not men nor gods have known, and no race ever

---

[47]**sister of Jove**: Juno and Jove (Jupiter) were both siblings and husband and wife.

Will pay you equal honor." And the goddess
160   Gave her assent, was happy, changed her purpose,
Left heaven and quit the cloud.
                  This done, the father
Formed yet another purpose, that Juturna
Should leave her fighting brother. There are, men say,
165   Twin fiends, or triple, sisters named the Furies,
Daughters of Night, with snaky coils, and pinions
Like those of wind. They are attendant spirits
Before the throne of Jove and whet the fears
Of sickly mortals, when the king of heaven
170   Contrives disease or dreadful death, or frightens
The guilty towns in war. Now he dispatches
One of the three to earth, to meet Juturna,
An omen visible; and so from heaven
She fled with whirlwind swiftness, like an arrow
175   Through cloud from bowstring, armed with gall or poison,
Loosed from a Parthian quiver, cleaving shadows
Swifter than man may know, a shaft no power
Has power of healing over:—so Night's daughter
Came down to earth, and when she saw the Trojans
180   And Turnus' columns, she dwindled, all of a sudden,
To the shape of that small bird, which, in the night-time,
Shrills its late song, ill-omened, on the roof-tops
Or over tombs, insistent through the darkness.
And so the fiend, the little screech-owl, flying
185   At Turnus, over and over, shrilled in warning,
Beating the wings against the shield, and Turnus
Felt a strange torpor seize his limbs, and terror
Made his hair rise, and his voice could find no utterance.
       But when, far off, Juturna knew the Fury
190   By whir of those dread wings, she tore her tresses,
Clawed at her face, and beat her breast, all anguish
Over her brother:—"What can a sister do,
To help you now, poor Turnus? What remains
For me to bear? I have borne so much already.
195   What skill of mine can make the daylight longer
In your dark hour? Can I face such a portent?
Now, now, I leave the battle-line forever.
Foul birds, I fear enough; haunt me no further,
I know that beat of the wings, that deadly whirring;
200   I recognize, too well, Jove's arrogant orders,
His payment for my maidenhood. He gave me
Eternal life, but why? Why has he taken

The right of death away from me? I might have
Ended my anguish, surely, with my brother's,
205   Gone, at his side, among the fearful shadows,
But, no,—I am immortal. What is left me
Of any possible joy, without my brother?
What earth can open deep enough to take me,
A goddess, to the lowest shades?" The mantle,
210   Grey-colored, veiled her head, and the goddess, sighing,
Sank deep from sight to the greyness of the river.
      And on Aeneas presses: the flashing spear,
Brandished, is big as a tree; his anger cries:—
"Why put it off forever, Turnus, hang-dog?
215   We must fight with arms, not running. Take what shape
You will, gather your strength or craft; fly up
To the high stars, or bury yourself in earth!"
And Turnus shook his head and answered:—"Jove,
Being my enemy, scares me, and the gods,
220   Not your hot words, fierce fellow." And his vision,
Glancing about, beheld a mighty boulder,
A boundary-mark, in days of old, so huge
A dozen men in our degenerate era
Could hardly pry it loose from earth, but Turnus
225   Lifts it full height, hurls it full speed and, acting,
Seems not to recognize himself, in running,
Or moving, or lifting his hands, or letting the stone
Fly into space; he shakes at the knees, his blood
Runs chill in the veins, and the stone, through wide air going
230   Falls short, falls spent. As in our dreams at night-time,
When sleep weighs down our eyes, we seem to be running
Or trying to run, and cannot, and we falter,
Sick in our failure, and the tongue is thick
And the words we try to utter come to nothing,
235   No voice, no speech,—so Turnus finds the way
Blocked off, wherever he turns, however bravely.
All sorts of things go through his mind: he stares
At the Rutulians, at the town; he trembles,
Quails at the threat of the lance; he cannot see
240   Any way out, any way forward. Nothing.
The chariot is gone, and the charioteer,
Juturna or Metiscus, nowhere near him.
The spear, flung by Aeneas, comes with a whir
Louder than stone from any engine, louder
245   Than thunderbolt; like a black wind it flies,
Bringing destruction with it, through the shield-rim,

Its sevenfold strength, through armor, through the thigh.
Turnus is down, on hands and knees, huge Turnus
Struck to the earth. Groaning, the stunned Rutulians
250 Rise to their feet, and the whole hill resounds,
The wooded heights give echo. A suppliant, beaten,
Humbled at last, his hands reach out, his voice
Is low in pleading:—"I have deserved it, surely,
And I do not beg off. Use the advantage.
255 But if a parent's grief has any power
To touch the spirit, I pray you, pity Daunus,
(I would Anchises), send him back my body.
You have won; I am beaten and these hands go out
In supplication: everyone has seen it.
260 No more. I have lost Lavinia. Let hatred
Proceed no further."
Fierce in his arms, with darting glance, Aeneas
Paused for a moment, and he might have weakened,
For the words had moved him, when, high on the shoulder,
265 He saw the belt of Pallas, slain by Turnus,
Saw Pallas on the ground, and Turnus wearing
That belt with the bright studs, of evil omen
Not only to Pallas now, a sad reminder,
A deadly provocation. Terrible
270 In wrath, Aeneas cries:—"Clad in this treasure,
This trophy of a comrade, can you cherish
Hope that my hands would let you go? Now Pallas,
Pallas exacts his vengeance, and the blow
Is Pallas, making sacrifice!" He struck
275 Before he finished speaking: the blade went deep
And Turnus' limbs were cold in death; the spirit
Went with a moan indignant to the shadows.

15. AMORES (SELECTIONS)

Ovid
(43 BCE–18 CE)

(trans. by Peter Green)

Ovid received a traditional education as preparation for public office, but his lifelong interest was in poetry. His love poems, the Amores, Ars Amatoria *(Art of Love)* and Remedia Amoris *(Remedy for Love)* were published before 8 CE when Ovid was exiled from Rome. The amorality of his poems incurred the censure of Augustus who was endeavoring to reform the morals of Rome, but perhaps in addition, Ovid may have been having an affair with Augustus's granddaughter, Julia. The Amores, a series of witty and frankly sexual poems recounting the ups and downs of an illicit love affair with Corinna, sometimes address her with pleas and advice for keeping the spice in their relationship, and sometimes boast to male friends about the difficulties and joys of the sensual life.*

BOOK I, #4

So your man's going to be present at this dinner-party?
    I hope he drops down dead before the dessert!
Does this mean no hands, just eyes (any chance guest's
        privilege)—
5   Just to *look* at my darling, while *he*
Lies there with you beside him, in licensed embracement
    And paws your bosom or neck as he feels inclined?
I'm no longer surprised at those Centaurs[1] for horsing around
        over
10   Some cute little filly when they were full of wine—
I may not live in the forest, or be semi-equipped as a stallion,
    But still *I* can hardly keep my hands to myself
When you're around. Now listen, I've got some instructions
        for you,
15   And don't let the first breeze blow them out of your head!
Arrive before your escort. I don't see what can be managed

---

[1]**Centaurs**: mythical creatures of men with bodies of horses.

If you do—but anyway, get there first.
When he pats the couch, put on your Respectable Wife
    expression,
20   And take your place beside him—but nudge my foot
As you're passing by. Watch out for my nods and eye-talk,
    Pick up my stealthy message, send replies.
I shall speak whole silent volumes with one raised eyebrow,
    Words will spring from my fingers, words traced in wine.
25 When you're thinking about the last time we made love together,
    Touch your rosy cheek with one elegant thumb.
If you're cross with me, and can't say so, then pinch the bottom
    Of your earlobe. But when I do or say
Something that gives you especial pleasure, my darling,
30   Keep turning the ring on your finger to and fro.
When you yearn for your man to suffer some well-merited misfortune
Place your hands on the table as though in prayer.
If he mixes wine specially for you, watch out, make him drink it
    Himself. Ask the waiter for what *you* want
35 As you hand back the goblet. I'll be the first to seize it
    And drink from the place your lips have touched.
If *he* offers you tit-bits out of some dish he's tasted,
    Refuse what's been near his mouth.
Don't let him put his arms round your neck, and oh, don't lay that
40   Darling head of yours on *his* coarse breast.
Don't let his fingers roam down your dress to touch up
    Those responsive nipples. Above all, don't you dare
Kiss him, not once. If you do, I'll proclaim myself your lover,
    Lay hand upon you, claim those kisses as mine.
45 So much for what I can see. But there's plenty goes on under
    A long evening wrap. The mere thought worries me stiff.
Don't start rubbing your thigh against his, don't go playing
    Footsy under the table, keep smooth from rough.'
(I'm scared all right, and no wonder—I've been too successful
50   An operator myself, it's my own
Example I find so unnerving. I've often petted to climax
    With my darling at a party, hand hidden under her cloak—)
'—Well, *you* won't do *that*. But still, to avoid the least suspicion
    Remove such natural protection when you sit down.
55 Keep pressing fresh drinks—but no kisses—on your husband,
    Slip neat wine in his glass if you get the chance.
If he passes out comfortably, drowned in sleep and liquor,
    We must improvise as occasion dictates.
When we all (you too) get up and leave, remember
60   To stick in the middle of the crowd—

That's where you'll find me, or I you: whenever
    There's a chance to touch me, please do!'
(Yet the most I can win myself is a few hours' respite:
    At nightfall my mistress and I must part.)
65 'At nightfall he'll lock you inside, and I'll be left weeping
    On that cold front doorstep—the nearest I can come
To your longed-for embraces, while *he's* enjoying, under licence,
    The kisses, and more, that you give me on the sly.
What you *can* do is show unwilling, behave as though you're frigid,
70   Begrudge him endearments, make sex a dead loss.'
(Grant my prayer, Venus. Don't let either of them get pleasure
    Out of the act—*and certainly not her!*)
But whatever the outcome tonight, when you see me tomorrow
Just swear, through thick and thin, that you told him No.'

BOOK I, #9

Every lover's on active service, my friend, active service, believe me,
    And Cupid has his headquarters in the field.
Fighting and love-making belong to the same age-group—
    In bed as in war, old men are out of place.
5 A commander looks to his troops for gallant conduct,
    A mistress expects no less.
Soldier and lover both keep night-long vigil,
    Lying rough outside their captain's (or lady's) door.
The military life brings long route-marches—but just let his mistress
10   Be somewhere ahead, and the lover too
Will trudge on for ever, scale mountains, ford swollen rivers,
    Thrust his way through deep snow.
Come embarkation-time *he* won't talk of 'strong north easters',
    Or say it's 'too late in the season' to put to sea.
15 Who but a soldier or lover would put up with freezing
    Nights—rain, snow, sleet? The first
Goes out on patrol to observe the enemy's movements,
    The other watches his rival, an equal foe.
A soldier lays siege to cities, a lover to girls' houses,
20   The one assaults city gates, the other front doors.
Night attacks are a great thing. Catch your opponents sleeping
    And unarmed. Just slaughter them where they lie.
That's how the Greeks dealt with Rhesus and his wild Thracians
    While rustling those famous mares.
25 Lovers, too, will take advantage of slumber (her husband's),
    Strike home while the enemy sleeps: getting past
Night patrols and eluding sentries are games both soldiers

And lovers need to learn.
Love, like war, is a toss-up. The defeated can recover,
30   While some you might think invincible collapse;
So if you've got love written off as an easy option
You'd better think twice. Love calls
For guts and initiative. Great Achilles sulks for Briseis—
Quick, Trojans, smash through the Argive wall,
35   Hector went into battle from Andromache's embraces
Helmeted by his wife.
Agamemnon himself, the Supremo, was struck into raptures
At the sight of Cassandra's tumbled hair;
Even Mars was caught on the job, felt the blacksmith's meshes—
40   Heaven's best scandal in years. Then take
My own case. I was idle, born to leisure *en déshabillé*,[2]
Mind softened by lazy scribbling in the shade.
But love for a pretty girl soon drove the sluggard
To action, made him join up.
45   And just look at me now—fighting fit, dead keen on night exercises:—
If you want a cure for slackness, fall in love!

BOOK I, #11

Let me tell you about Napë. Though she's expert at setting
Unruly hair, she's no common lady's-maid.
She fixes our private assignations, arranges meetings,
Is the perfect go-between.
5   She's often fast-talked a too-hesitant Corinna
Into coming over. She's never let me down.
Hey, Napë! Here's a note I've written your mistress—
Please deliver it *now*, without delay.
You're not iron-hearted. There's no flinty streak in your nature,
10   And you're nobody's fool. You must
Have taken a hit or two yourself in the wars of passion?
Then help me—we're fighting on the same side.
If she asks how I am, say I live in longing. My letter
Provides all the details. Quick,
15   Don't let's waste time talking. Catch her at a free moment,
Give her the note—and make sure
She reads it at once. Watch her face and eyes as she does so,
Expressions can be revealing of things to come.
And take care she replies on the spot, with a good long letter—
20   Half-blank tablets drive me mad,

---

[2]*en déshabillé:* undressed

So get her to crowd up her lines, and fill the margins
    From side to side. But wait—
Why should she weary her fingers with all that scribbling?
    One single word is good enough: '*Come.*'
25   Then I'd wreathe my victorious writing-tablet with laurel
    And hang it in Venus' shrine
With this inscription: '*To Venus, from Ovid, for services rendered,*
    One cheap wooden writing tablet—now beyond price.'

BOOK I, #12

I need sympathy. I'm downhearted. That wretched writing-tablet
    Is back, with a dismal *No, can't make it today.*
There's something in omens. Just as she was departing
    Napë stubbed her toe on the doorsill, and stopped.
5   Next time you're sent out, girl, remember to be more careful
    While negotiating the threshold. Pick up your feet,
Keep off the bottle.
               To hell with that damned obstructive
    Tablet, its coffinwood frame
10 And *no*-saying wax (which I bet was extracted from hemlock
    Honey, as specially gathered by Corsican bees),
That off-red surface, dyed—I'd supposed—with a tincture
    Of cinnabar. Not true. It had tasted blood.
Cheap useless object—I'll dump you at some crossing
15   For a laden wagon to splinter with its wheels!
The craftsman who fashioned you from untrimmed timber—
    I'll swear he had guilty hands. The tree itself
Must have been used as a gibbet, then turned into crosses
    For some executioner. In its nasty shade
20 Hoarse nightjars lurked, a mass of vultures and screech-owls
    Infested its branches, hatching eggs.
Was *this* the stuff to which I entrusted such loving
    Messages for my mistress? I must have been mad.
Such a tablet would better suit the most prolix of legal
25   Documents, stuff to be droned out
By some gravel-voiced lawyer. It should lie with accounts and ledgers
    Recording the bad debts of a glum tycoon.
You in every way two-faced tablet! *Two*—that number
    Was unlucky from the start. How vent
30 My fury? Curse you, may dry rot riddle your crumbling
    Frame, and filthy white mildew blanch your wax!

BOOK II, #1

A second batch of verses by that naughty provincial poet,
    Naso,[2] the chronicler of his own
Wanton frivolities; another of Love's commissions (warning
    To puritans: *This volume is not for you*).
5   I want my works to be read by the far-from-frigid virgin
    On fire for her sweetheart, by the boy
In love for the very first time. May some fellow-sufferer,
    Perusing my anatomy of desire,
See his own passion reflected there, cry in amazement:
10   "Who told this scribbler about my private affairs?"
One time, I recall, I got started on an inflated epic
    About War in Heaven, with all
Those hundred-handed monsters, and Earth's fell-vengeance, and towering
    Ossa piled on Olympus (plus Pelion too).
15   But while I was setting up Jove—stormclouds and thunderbolts gathered
    Ready to hand, a superb defensive barrage—
My mistress staged a lock-out. I dropped Jupiter and his lightnings
    That instant, didn't give him another thought.
Forgive me, good Lord, if I found your armory useless—
20   Her shut door ran to larger bolts
Than any *you* wielded. I went back to verses and compliments,
    My natural weapons. Soft words
Remove harsh door chains. There's magic in poetry, its power
    Can pull down the bloody moon,
25   Turn back the sun, make serpents burst asunder
    Or rivers flow upstream.
Doors are no match for such spellbinding, the toughest
    Locks can be open-sesamed by its charms.
But epic's a dead loss for me. I'll get nowhere with swift-footed
30   Achilles, or with either of Atreus' sons.[3]
Old what's-his-name wasting twenty years on war and travel,
    Poor Hector dragged in the dust—
No good. But lavish fine words on some young girl's profile
    And sooner or later she'll tender herself as the fee,
35   An ample reward for your labours. So farewell, heroic
    Figures of legend—the *quid*
Pro quo[4] you offer won't tempt me. A bevy of beauties
    All swooning over my love-songs—that's what *I* want.

---

[2]**Naso**: Ovid's full name is Publius Ovidius Naso.
[3]**Atreus' sons**: Agamemnon and Menelaus
[4]**quid pro quo**: tit for tat

15. *Ovid*/Amores (Selections)

BOOK II, #4

I wouldn't attempt to defend my spotty morals, or whitewash
    My flaws with aggressive lies.
If it's any help, I confess. Admission of guilt. Then why not
    Go the whole hog, indict
5   My faults myself? I hate what I am, yet (try as I may) can't
    Not be the thing that revolts me. It's hell
Being stuck with what you can't kick. I lack all firmness
    And strength to control my moods, get whirled away
Like a skiff in a current. There's no one type of beauty
10   That arouses my longing: if I'm always in love
Blame my wide-ranging interests. Shyness and modesty spark me
    Off every time—a demurely lowered face
And I'm hooked. But it's just the same if she's pertly forward:
    Sophistication promises well in bed.
15   A primly old-fashioned appearance, then? I always suspect that's
    Mere camouflage for unacknowledged desire.
A bluestocking turns me on with her intellectual powers,
    A featherbrain ditto just by being naïve.
Then there's the girl who tells me Callimachus is a bungler
20   Compared to me—I always go for my fans—
Or the critical termagant who slates both poems and author:
    How I long to be laid by her as well!
One's got a slinky walk: *that* gets me. Another's uptight—
    She can be softened out with a little sex.
25   A fine operatic voice, for me, is a standing temptation
    To smother the singer with kisses in mid-song.
Guitar-lessons help. Watch those fingers—the chords, the glissandos!
    How fail to fall in love with such clever hands?
Then think of the floor-show dancer, arms weaving in rhythm,
30   Doing undulant bumps and grinds:
Never mind about me (I'm just omnisusceptible), make pure
    Hippolytus[5] watch her act
And even *he'd* go priapic.
            You're tall, like the heroines of legend,
35   Lie the full length of a bed;
But petite girls, too, are attractive. I'm sold on *both* sizes—
    Long and short alike are equally to my taste.
The fashionable I enjoy at their face-value, the unsmart
    For all that they *could* be, *à la mode*.
40   I'm crazy for girls who are fair-haired and pale-complexioned

---

[5]**Hippolytus:** chaste son of Phaedrus who accused him of rape.

But brunettes make marvellous lovers too:
The sight of dark tresses against a snow-white neck reminds me
That Leda was famed for her black curls,
While a flaxen poll calls up thoughts of blonde Aurora—
45   My sex-life runs the entire
Mythological gamut. My tastes are equally all-embracing:
Young girls have the looks—but when it comes to technique
Give me an older woman. In short, there's a vast cross-section
Of desirable beauties in Rome—*and I want them all!*

BOOK II, #10

It was *you*, no doubt about it, Graecinus: I clearly remember
How you said no man could possibly fall in love
With two girls at once. I believed you. I dropped my defences.
Result—double love-life. Embarrassing. All your fault.
5   There's nothing to choose between them for looks. They both dress smartly,
On performance they're just about neck and neck—
I can't make up my mind which I find more attractive,
But fancy first A, then B,
Swing to and fro like a yacht in a choppy crosswind,
10   My erotic psyche torn
Between rival claimants. Didn't one girl produce sufficient
Anxiety for me, Venus? Why double my load?
If it comes to that, why put extra stars in heaven,
Top up the sea with water, releaf the trees?
15   Still, things could be worse. At least I'm not starved for affection.
A celibate life is something I'd only wish
On my very worst enemies. Just imagine sleeping
Plumb in the middle of a double bed!
Give me some wild love-making to disrupt dull slumber,
20   With congenial company between the sheets,
And no holds barred. If one girl drains my powers
Fair enough—but if she can't, I'll take two.
I can stand the strain. My limbs may be thin, but they're wiry;
Though I'm a lightweight, I'm hard—
25   And virility feeds on sex, is boosted by practice;
No girl's ever complained about *my* technique.
Often enough I've spent the whole night in pleasure, yet still been
Fit as a fighting cock next day.
What bliss to expire in Love's duel—that, God willing,
30   Is the way *I'd* choose to die!
Let the soldier stick out his chest as a target for hostile
Arrows, purchase eternal renown with blood;

Let the cash-hungry merchant make one voyage too many
    And wash the lies down his throat
35   With the brine of the trade-routes. But I'd like to reach dissolution
    In mid-act, die on the job.
Easy enough to guess what some mourner will say at my funeral:
    "His death was all of a piece with his life."

BOOK II, #19

You may not feel any need (and more fool you) to guard that
    Girl of yours—but it sharpens *my* desire,
So would you oblige? What's allowed is a bore, it's what isn't
    That turns me on. What cold clod
5   Could woo with his rival's approval? We lovers need hope and despair in
    Alternate doses. An intermittent rebuff
Makes us promise the earth. Who wants a beautiful woman
    When she never deceives him? I can't
Love a girl who's not intermittently bitchy. Corrina spotted
10   My weakness. (full mark) and saw how
To use it against me. The times she invented a headache,
    And when I still hung around, just threw me out,
Or pretended she'd had an affair, looking horribly guilty
    When in fact she'd done nothing at all—
15   And having thus quickly rekindled my cooling ardor
    Would suddenly switch her mood
To the ultra-compliant. Her compliments, her sweet nothings,
    Her kisses—oh God, her kisses! So you too,
My latest eye-ravisher, must ensnare me at times by pretending
20   To be frightened: must—on occasion—say No,
And leave me there, prostrate on your doorstep, to suffer
    Long hours of frosty cold, the whole night through.
Act thus, and my love will endure, grow stronger with each passing
    Year—that's the way I like it, that feeds the flame,
25   Love too indulged, too compliant, will turn your stomach
    Like a surfeit of sweet rich food.
Had Danaë never been locked in that brazen turret, would Jupiter
    Ever have got her with child?
When Juno transmogrified Io into a horned heifer[6]
30   She increased the girl's sex-appeal.
If you're after what's lawful and easy, then why not gather
    Leaves from the trees, or drink
Water out of the Tiber? To prolong your dominion over

---

[6]Juno was jealous of her husband's (Jove's) love for Io.

Your lover calls for deception. (I hope I won't
35   Have cause to regret that statement.) Yet come what may, indulgence
        Irks me. I flee the eager, pursue the coy.
And as for *you*, man, so careless of your good lady,
        Why not start locking up at night?
Why not ask who it is comes tapping, ever so softly,
40   On your front door—or why it is the dogs
Start barking at midnight? What about all those to-and-fro missives
        The maid delivers? How come your wife now sleeps
Alone so often? Why can't you get really worried just
        Once in a while, allow me to display
45   My skill at deception? To covet the wife of a dummy
        Is like stealing sand off the beach.
I'm warning you: put your foot down, play the heavy husband,
        Or I'll start going cold on your wife!
I've stood it quite long enough, always hoping you'd lock her
50   Away out of sight, so that I
Could outwit you. But no. You clod, you put up with things no husband
        Should stand for a moment. Let me have the girl
And there's an end to my passion. Won't you *ever* deny me
        Entry, won't you beat me up one night?
55   Can't I ever feel scared? have insomnia? sigh in frustration?
        Won't you give me some good excuse
To wish you dead? I've no time for complaisant, pimping husbands—
        Their kinkiness spoils my fun.
Find someone else, who *likes* your easy-going habits, or if you
60   Must have me as a rival, then *get tough*!

16. METAMORPHOSES (SELECTIONS)

Ovid
(43 BCE–18 CE)

(trans. by Rolfe Humphries)

Ovid had drafted his Metamorphoses *prior to his exile (for his amoral* Amores*) in 8 CE and continued to work on the long poem in hopes that it might earn him a reprieve from Augustus. The work is a compendium of over 250 classical myths, each involving some sort of transformation. The myths are chronologically arranged beginning with cosmic transformation from chaos to order, followed by human creation, degeneration, and destruction in the flood, and our recreation from stones; the series concludes with Ovid's story of the deification of Julius Caesar, Augustus' "father." Ovid's compassionate and witty treatment of the transformation of mythic heroes' into animals or components of nature reveals his understanding of human psychology and demonstrates his poetic skill in sustaining coherent narration for a vast body of diffuse material.*

My intention is to tell of bodies changed
To different forms; the gods, who made the changes,
Will help me—or I hope so—with a poem
That runs from the world's beginning to our own days.

THE CREATION

Before the ocean was, or earth, or heaven,
Nature was all alike, a shapelessness,
Chaos, so-called, all rude and lumpy matter,
Nothing but bulk, inert, in whose confusion
5   Discordant atoms warred: there was no sun
To light the universe; there was no moon
With slender silver crescents filling slowly;
No earth hung balanced in surrounding air;
No sea reached far along the fringe of shore.
10   Land, to be sure, there was, and air, and ocean,
But land on which no man could stand, and water
No man could swim in, air no man could breathe,

Air without light, substance forever changing,
Forever at war: within a single body
15   Heat fought with cold, wet fought with dry, the hard
Fought with the soft, things having weight contended
With weightless things.
                                    Till God, or kindlier Nature,
Settled all argument, and separated
20   Heaven from earth, water from land, our air
From the high stratosphere, a liberation
So things evolved, and out of blind confusion
Found each its place, bound in eternal order.
The force of fire, that weightless element,
25   Leaped up and claimed the highest place in heaven;
Below it, air; and under them the earth
Sank with its grosser portions; and the water,
Lowest of all, held up, held in, the land.

Whatever god it was, who out of chaos
30   Brought order to the universe, and gave it
Division, subdivision, he molded earth,
In the beginning, into a great globe,
Even on every side, and bade the waters
To spread and rise, under the rushing winds,
35   Surrounding earth; he added ponds and marshes,
He banked the river-channels, and the waters
Feed earth or run to sea, and that great flood
Washes on shores, not banks. He made the plains
Spread wide, the valleys settle, and the forest
40   Be dressed in leaves; he made the rocky mountains
Rise to full height, and as the vault of Heaven
Has two zones, left and right, and one between them
Hotter than these, the Lord of all Creation
Marked on the earth the same design and pattern.
45   The torrid zone too hot for men to live in,
The north and south too cold, but in the middle
Varying climate, temperature and season.
Above all things the air, lighter than earth,
Lighter than water, heavier than fire,
50   Towers and spreads; there mist and cloud assemble,
And fearful thunder and lightning and cold winds,
But these, by the Creator's order, held
No general dominion; even as it is,
These brothers brawl and quarrel; though each one
55   Has his own quarter, still, they come near tearing

The universe apart. Eurus is monarch
Of the lands of dawn, the realms of Araby,
The Persian ridges under the rays of morning.
Zephyrus holds the west that glows at sunset,
60   Boreas, who makes men shiver, holds the north,
Warm Auster governs in the misty southland,
And over them all presides the weightless ether,
Pure without taint of earth.
                        These boundaries given,
65   Behold, the stars, long hidden under darkness,
Broke through and shone, all over the spangled heaven,
Their home forever, and the gods lived there,
And shining fish were given the waves for dwelling
And beasts the earth, and birds the moving air.

70   But something else was needed, a finer being,
More capable of mind, a sage, a ruler,
So Man was born, it may be, in God's image,
Or Earth perhaps, so newly separated
From the old fire of Heaven, still retained
75   Some seed of the celestial force which fashioned
Gods out of living clay and running water.
All other animals look downward; Man,
Alone, erect, can raise his face toward Heaven.

THE FOUR AGES

The Golden Age was first, a time that cherished
Of its own will, justice and right; no law,
No punishment, was called for; fearfulness
Was quite unknown, and the bronze tablets held
5   No legal threatening; no suppliant throng
Studied a judge's face; there were no judges,
There did not need to be. Trees had not yet
Been cut and hollowed, to visit other shores.
Men were content at home, and had no towns
10   With moats and walls around them; and no trumpets
Blared out alarums; things like swords and helmets
Had not been heard of. No one needed soldiers.
People were unaggressive, and unanxious;
The years went by in peace. And Earth, untroubled,
15   Unharried by hoe or plowshare, brought forth all
That men had need for, and those men were happy,
Gathering berries from the mountain sides,

Cherries, or blackcaps, and the edible acorns.
Spring was forever, with a west wind blowing
20 Softly across the flowers no man had planted,
And Earth, unplowed, brought forth rich grain; the field,
Unfallowed, whitened with wheat, and there were rivers
Of milk, and rivers of honey, and golden nectar
Dripped from the dark-green oak-trees.
25   After Saturn
Was driven to the shadowy land of death,
And the world was under Jove, the Age of Silver
Came in, lower than gold, better than bronze.
Jove made the springtime shorter, added winter,
30 Summer, and autumn, the seasons as we know them.
That was the first time when the burnt air glowed
White-hot, or icicles hung down in winter.
And men built houses for themselves; the caverns,
The woodland thickets, and the bark-bound shelters
35 No longer served; and the seeds of grain were planted
In the long furrows, and the oxen struggled
Groaning and laboring under the heavy yoke.

Then came the Age of Bronze, and dispositions
Took on aggressive instincts, quick to arm,
40 Yet not entirely evil. And last of all
The Iron Age succeeded, whose base vein
Let loose all evil: modesty and truth
And righteousness fled earth, and in their place
Came trickery and slyness, plotting, swindling,
45 Violence and the damned desire of having.
Men spread their sails to winds unknown to sailors,
The pines came down their mountain-sides, to revel
And leap in the deep waters, and the ground,
Free, once, to everyone, like air and sunshine,
50 Was stepped off by surveyors. The rich earth,
Good giver of all the bounty of the harvest,
Was asked for more; they dug into her vitals,
Pried out the wealth a kinder lord had hidden
In Stygian shadow, all that precious metal,
55 The root of evil. They found the guilt of iron,
And gold, more guilty still. And War came forth
That uses both to fight with; bloody hands
Brandished the clashing weapons. Men lived on plunder.
Guest was not safe from host, nor brother from brother,
60 A man would kill his wife, a wife her husband,

Stepmothers, dire and dreadful, stirred their brews
With poisonous aconite, and sons would hustle
Fathers to death, and Piety lay vanquished,
And the maiden Justice, last of all immortals,
65   Fled from the bloody earth.
                        Heaven was no safer.
Giants attacked the very throne of Heaven,
Piled Pelion on Ossa, mountain on mountain
Up to the very stars. Jove struck them down
70   With thunderbolts, and the bulk of those huge bodies
Lay on the earth, and bled, and Mother Earth,
Made pregnant by that blood, brought forth new bodies,
And gave them, to recall her older offspring,
The forms of men. And this new stock was also
75   Contemptuous of gods, and murder-hungry
And violent. You would know they were sons of blood.

JOVE'S INTERVENTION

And Jove was witness from his lofty throne
Of all this evil, and groaned as he remembered
The wicked revels of Lycaon's table,
The latest guilt, a story still unknown
5   To the high gods. In awful indignation
He summoned them to council. No one dawdled.
Easily seen when the night skies are clear,
The Milky Way shines white. Along this road
The gods move toward the palace of the Thunderer,
10   His royal halls, and, right and left, the dwellings
Of other gods are open, and guests come thronging.
The lesser gods live in a meaner section,
An area not reserved, as this one is,
For the illustrious Great Wheels of Heaven.
15   (Their Palatine Hill, if I might call it so.)

They took their places in the marble chamber
Where high above them all their king was seated,
Holding his ivory sceptre, shaking out
Thrice, and again, his awful locks, the sign
20   That made the earth and stars and ocean tremble,
And then he spoke, in outrage: "I was troubled
Less for the sovereignty of all the world
In that old time when the snake-footed giants
Laid each his hundred hands on captive Heaven.

25   Monstrous they were, and hostile, but their warfare
      Sprung from one source, one body. Now, wherever
      The sea-gods roar around the earth, a race
      Must be destroyed, the race of men. I swear it!
      I swear by all the Stygian rivers gliding
30   Under the world, I have tried all other measures.
      The knife must cut the cancer out, infection
      Averted while it can be, from our numbers.
      Those demigods, those rustic presences,
      Nymphs, fauns, and satyrs, wood and mountain dwellers,
35   We have not yet honored with a place in Heaven,
      But they should have some decent place to dwell in,
      In peace and safety. Safety? Do you reckon
      They will be safe, when I, who wield the thunder,
      Who rule you all as subjects, am subjected
40   To the plottings of the barbarous Lycaon?"

      They burned, they trembled. Who was this Lycaon,
      Guilty of such rank infamy? They shuddered
      In horror, with a fear of sudden ruin,
      As the whole world did later, when assassins
45   Struck Julius Caesar down, and Prince Augustus
      Found satisfaction in the great devotion
      That cried for vengeance, even as Jove took pleasure,
      Then, in the gods' response. By word and gesture
      He calmed them down, awed them again to silence,
50   And spoke once more:

THE STORY OF LYCAON

                  "He has indeed been punished.
      On that score have no worry. But what he did,
      And how he paid, are things that I must tell you.
      I had heard the age was desperately wicked,
5   I had heard, or so I hoped, a lie, a falsehood,
      So I came down, as man, from high Olympus,
      Wandered about the world. It would take too long
      To tell you how widespread was all that evil.
      All I had heard was grievous understatement!
10   I had crossed Maenala, a country bristling
      With dens of animals, and crossed Cyllene,
      And cold Lycaeus' pine woods. Then I came
      At evening, with the shadows growing longer,
      To an Arcadian palace, where the tyrant

15   Was anything but royal in his welcome.
      I gave a sign that a god had come, and people
      Began to worship, and Lycaon mocked them,
      Laughed at their prayers, and said: 'Watch me find out
      Whether this fellow is a god or mortal,
20   I can tell quickly, and no doubt about it.'
      He planned, that night, to kill me while I slumbered;
      That was his way to test the truth. Moreover,
      And not content with that, he took a hostage,
      One sent by the Molossians, cut his throat,
25   Boiled pieces of his flesh, still warm with life,
      Broiled others, and set them before me on the table.
      That was enough. I struck, and the bolt of lightning
      Blasted the household of that guilty monarch.
      He fled in terror, reached the silent fields,
30   And howled, and tried to speak. No use at all!
      Foam dripped from his mouth; bloodthirsty still, he turned
      Against the sheep, delighting still in slaughter,
      And his arms were legs, and his robes were shaggy hair,
      Yet he is still Lycaon, the same grayness,
35   The same fierce face, the same red eyes, a picture
      Of bestial savagery. One house has fallen,
      But more than one deserves to. Fury reigns
      Over all the fields of Earth. They are sworn to evil,
      Believe it. Let them pay for it, and quickly!
40   So stands my purpose."
                        Part of them approved
      With words and added fuel to his anger,
      And part approved with silence, and yet all
      Were grieving at the loss of humankind,
45   Were asking what the world would be, bereft
      Of mortals: who would bring their altars incense?
      Would earth be given the beasts, to spoil and ravage?
      Jove told them not to worry; he would give them
      Another race, unlike the first, created
50   Out of a miracle; he would see to it.

      He was about to hurl his thunderbolts
      At the whole world, but halted, fearing Heaven
      Would burn from fire so vast, and pole to pole
      Break out in flame and smoke, and he remembered
55   The fates had said that some day land and ocean,
      The vault of Heaven, the whole world's mighty fortress,
      Besieged by fire, would perish. He put aside

The bolts made in Cyclopean workshops; better,
He thought, to drown the world by flooding water.

THE FLOOD

So, in the cave of Aeolus, he prisoned
The North-wind, and the West-wind, and such others
As ever banish cloud, and he turned loose
The South-wind, and the South-wind came out streaming
5   With dripping wings, and pitch-black darkness veiling
His terrible countenance. His beard is heavy
With rain-cloud, and his hoary locks a torrent,
Mists are his chaplet, and his wings and garments
Run with the rain. His broad hands squeeze together
10   Low-hanging clouds, and crash and rumble follow
Before the cloudburst, and the rainbow, Iris,
Draws water from the teeming earth, and feeds it
Into the clouds again. The crops are ruined,
The farmers' prayers all wasted, all the labor
15   Of a long year, comes to nothing.
                   And Jove's anger,
Unbounded by his own domain, was given
Help by his dark-blue brother. Neptune called
His rivers all, and told them, very briefly,
20   To loose their violence, open their houses,
Pour over embankments, let the river horses
Run wild as ever they would. And they obeyed him.
His trident struck the shuddering earth; it opened
Way for the rush of waters. The leaping rivers
25   Flood over the great plains. Not only orchards
Are swept away, not only grain and cattle,
Not only men and houses, but altars, temples,
And shrines with holy fires. If any building
Stands firm, the waves keep rising over its roof-top,
30   Its towers are under water, and land and ocean
Are all alike, and everything is ocean,
An ocean with no shore-line.
                  Some poor fellow
Seizes a hill-top; another, in a dinghy,
35   Rows where he used to plough, and one goes sailing
Over his fields of grain or over the chimney
Of what was once his cottage. Someone catches
Fish in the top of an elm-tree, or an anchor
Drags in green meadow-land, or the curved keel brushes

40 Grape-arbors under water. Ugly sea-cows
   Float where the slender she-goats used to nibble
   The tender grass, and the Nereids come swimming
   With curious wonder, looking, under water,
   At houses, cities, parks, and groves. The dolphins
45 Invade the woods and brush against the oak-trees;
   The wolf swims with the lamb; lion and tiger
   Are borne along together; the wild boar
   Finds all his strength is useless, and the deer
   Cannot outspeed that torrent; wandering birds
50 Look long, in vain, for landing-place, and tumble,
   Exhausted, into the sea. The deep's great license
   Has buried all the hills, and new waves thunder
   Against the mountain-tops. The flood has taken
   All things, or nearly all, and those whom water,
55 By chance, has spared, starvation slowly conquers.

DEUCALION AND PYRRHA

   Phocis, a fertile land, while there was land,
   Marked off Oetean from Boeotian fields.
   It was ocean now, a plain of sudden waters.
   There Mount Parnassus lifts its twin peaks skyward,
5 High, steep, cloud-piercing. And Deucalion came there
   Rowing his wife. There was no other land,
   The sea had drowned it all. And here they worshipped
   First the Corycian nymphs and native powers,
   Then Themis, oracle and fate-revealer.
10 There was no better man than this Deucalion,
   No one more fond of right; there was no woman
   More scrupulously reverent than Pyrrha.
   So, when Jove saw the world was one great ocean,
   Only one woman left of all those thousands,
15 And only one man left of all those thousands,
   Both innocent and worshipful, he parted
   The clouds, turned loose the North-wind, swept them off,
   Showed earth to heaven again, and sky to land,
   And the sea's anger dwindled, and King Neptune
20 Put down his trident, calmed the waves, and Triton,
   Summoned from far down under, with his shoulders
   Barnacle-strewn, loomed up above the waters,
   The blue-green sea-god, whose resounding horn
   Is heard from shore to shore. Wet-bearded, Triton
25 Set lip to that great shell, as Neptune ordered,

Sounding retreat, and all the lands and waters
Heard and obeyed. The sea has shores; the rivers,
Still running high, have channels; the floods dwindle,
Hill-tops are seen again; the trees, long buried,
30 Rise with their leaves still muddy. The world returns.

Deucalion saw that world, all desolation,
All emptiness, all silence, and his tears
Rose as he spoke to Pyrrha: "O my wife,
The only woman, now, on all this earth,
35 My consort and my cousin and my partner
In these immediate dangers, look! Of all the lands
To East or West, we two, we two alone,
Are all the population. Ocean holds
Everything else; our foothold, our assurance,
40 Are small as they can be, the clouds still frightful.

Poor woman—well, we are not all alone—
Suppose you had been, how would you bear your fear?
Who would console your grief? My wife, believe me,
Had the sea taken you, I would have followed.
45 If only I had the power, I would restore
The nations as my father did, bring clay
To life with breathing. As it is, we two
Are all the human race, so Heaven has willed it,
Samples of men, mere specimens."
50   They wept,
And prayed together, and having wept and prayed,
Resolved to make petition to the goddess
To seek her aid through oracles. Together
They went to the river-water, the stream Cephisus,
55 Still far from clear, but flowing down its channel,
And they took river-water, sprinkled foreheads,
Sprinkled their garments, and they turned their steps
To the temple of the goddess, where the altars
Stood with the fires gone dead, and ugly moss
60 Stained pediment and column. At the stairs
They both fell prone, kissed the chill stone in prayer:
"If the gods' anger ever listens
To righteous prayers, O Themis, we implore you,
Tell us by what device our wreck and ruin
65 May be repaired. Bring aid, most gentle goddess,
To sunken circumstance."
                         And Themis heard them,

-632-

And gave this oracle: "Go from the temple,
Cover your heads, loosen your robes, and throw
70   Your mother's bones behind you!" Dumb, they stood
In blank amazement, a long silence, broken
By Pyrrha, finally: she would not do it!
With trembling lips she prays whatever pardon
Her disobedience might merit, but this outrage
75   She dare not risk, insult her mother's spirit
By throwing her bones around. In utter darkness
They voice the cryptic saying over and over,
What can it mean? They wonder. At last Deucalion
Finds the way out: "I might be wrong, but surely
80   The holy oracles would never counsel
A guilty act. The earth is our great mother,
And I suppose those bones the goddess mentions
Are the stones of earth; the order means to throw them,
The stones, behind us."

                          She was still uncertain,
85   And he by no means sure, and both distrustful
Of that command from Heaven; but what damage,
What harm, would there be in trying? They descended,
Covered their heads, loosened their garments, threw
90   The stones behind them as the goddess ordered.
The stones—who would believe it, had we not
The unimpeachable witness of Tradition?—
Began to lose their hardness, to soften, slowly,
To take on form, to grow in size, a little,
95   Become less rough, to look like human beings,
Or anyway as much like human beings
As statues do, when the sculptor is only starting,
Images half blocked out. The earthy portion,
Damp with some moisture, turned to flesh, the solid
100   Was bone, the veins were as they always had been.
The stones the man had thrown turned into men,
The stones the woman threw turned into women,
Such being the will of God. Hence we derive
The hardness that we have, and our endurance
105   Gives proof of what we have come from.
                          Other forms
Of life came into being, generated
Out of the earth: the sun burnt off the dampness,
Heat made the slimy marshes swell; as seed
110   Swells in a mother's womb to shape and substance,
So new forms came to life. When the Nile river

Floods and recedes and the mud is warmed by sunshine,
Men, turning over the earth, find living things,
And some not living, but nearly so, imperfect,
115   On the verge of life, and often the same substance
Is part alive, part only clay. When moisture
Unites with heat, life is conceived; all things
Come from this union. Fire may fight with water,
But heat and moisture generate all things,
120   Their discord being productive. So when earth
After that flood, still muddy, took the heat,
Felt the warm fire of sunlight, she conceived,
Brought forth, after their fashion, all the creatures,
Some old, some strange and monstrous.
125   One, for instance,
She bore unwanted, a gigantic serpent,
Python by name, whom the new people dreaded,
A huge bulk on the mountain-side. Apollo,
God of the glittering bow, took a long time
130   To bring him down, with arrow after arrow
He had never used before except in hunting
Deer and the skipping goats. Out of the quiver
Sped arrows by the thousand, till the monster,
Dying, poured poisonous blood on those black wounds.
135   In memory of this, the sacred games,
Called Pythian, were established, and Apollo
Ordained for all young winners in the races,
On foot or chariot, for victorious fighters,
The crown of oak. That was before the laurel,
140   That was before Apollo wreathed his forehead
With garlands from that tree, or any other.

APOLLO AND DAPHNE

Now the first girl Apollo loved was Daphne,
Whose father was the river-god Peneus,
And this was no blind chance, but Cupid's malice.
Apollo, with pride and glory still upon him
5   Over the Python slain, saw Cupid bending
His tight-strung little bow. "O silly youngster,"
He said, "What are you doing with such weapons?
Those are for grown-ups! The bow is for my shoulders;
I never fail in wounding beast or mortal,
10   And not so long ago I slew the Python
With countless darts; his bloated body covered

Acre on endless acre, and I slew him!
The torch, my boy, is enough for you to play with,
To get the love-fires burning. Do not meddle
15   With honors that are mine!" And Cupid answered:
"Your bow shoots everything, Apollo—maybe—
But mine will fix you! You are far above
All creatures living, and by just that distance
Your glory less than mine." He shook his wings,
20   Soared high, came down to the shadows of Parnassus,
Drew from his quiver different kinds of arrows,
One causing love, golden and sharp and gleaming,
The other blunt, and tipped with lead, and serving
To drive all love away, and this blunt arrow
25   He used on Daphne, but he fired the other,
The sharp and golden shaft, piercing Apollo
Through bones, through marrow, and at once he loved
And she at once fled from the name of lover,
Rejoicing in the woodland hiding places
30   And spoils of beasts which she had taken captive,
A rival of Diana, virgin goddess.
She had many suitors, but she scorned them all;
Wanting no part of any man, she travelled
The pathless groves, and had no care whatever
35   For husband, love, or marriage. Her father often
Said, "Daughter, give me a son-in-law!" and "Daughter,
Give me some grandsons!" But the marriage torches
Were something hateful, criminal, to Daphne,
So she would blush, and put her arms around him,
40   And coax him: "Let me be a virgin always;
Diana's father said she might. Dear father!
Dear father—please!" He yielded, but her beauty
Kept arguing against her prayer. Apollo
Loves at first sight; he wants to marry Daphne,
45   He hopes for what he wants—all wishful thinking!—
Is fooled by his own oracles. As stubble
Burns when the grain is harvested, as hedges
Catch fire from torches that a passer-by
Has brought too near, or left behind in the morning,
50   So the god burned, with all his heart, and burning
Nourished that futile love of his by hoping.
He sees the long hair hanging down her neck
Uncared for, says, "But what if it were combed?"
He gazes at her eyes—they shine like stars!
55   He gazes at her lips, and knows that gazing

Is not enough. He marvels at her fingers,
Her hands, her wrists, her arms, bare to the shoulder,
And what he does not see he thinks is better.
But still she flees him, swifter than the wind,
60 And when he calls she does not even listen:
"Don't run away, dear nymph! Daughter of Peneus,
Don't run away! I am no enemy,
Only your follower: don't run away!
The lamb flees from the wolf, the deer the lion,
65 The dove, on trembling wing, flees from the eagle.
All creatures flee their foes. But I, who follow,
Am not a foe at all. Love makes me follow,
Unhappy fellow that I am, and fearful
You may fall down, perhaps, or have the briars
70 Make scratches on those lovely legs, unworthy
To be hurt so, and I would be the reason.
The ground is rough here. Run a little slower,
And I will run, I promise, a little slower.
Or wait a minute: be a little curious
75 Just who it is you charm. I am no shepherd,
No mountain-dweller, I am not a ploughboy,
Uncouth and stinking of cattle. You foolish girl,
You don't know who it is you run away from,
That must be why you run. I am lord of Delphi
80 And Tenedos and Claros and Patara.
Jove is my father. I am the revealer
Of present, past and future; through my power
The lyre and song make harmony; my arrow
Is sure in aim—there is only one arrow surer,
85 The one that wounds my heart. The power of healing
Is my discovery; I am called the Healer
Through all the world: all herbs are subject to me.
Alas for me, love is incurable
With any herb; the arts which cure the others
90 Do me, their lord, no good!"
                              He would have said
Much more than this, but Daphne, frightened, left him
With many words unsaid, and she was lovely
Even in flight, her limbs bare in the wind,
95 Her garments fluttering, and her soft hair streaming,
More beautiful than ever. But Apollo,
Too young a god to waste his time in coaxing,
Came following fast. When a hound starts a rabbit
In an open field, one runs for game, one safety,

100 He has her, or thinks he has, and she is doubtful
Whether she's caught or not, so close the margin.
So ran the god and girl, one swift in hope,
The other in terror, but he ran more swiftly,
Borne on the wings of love, gave her no rest,
105 Shadowed her shoulder, breathed on her streaming hair.
Her strength was gone, worn out by the long effort
Of the long flight; she was deathly pale, and seeing
The river of her father, cried "O help me,
If there is any power in the rivers,
110 Change and destroy the body which has given
Too much delight!" And hardly had she finished,
When her limbs grew numb and heavy, her soft breasts
Were closed with delicate bark, her hair was leaves,
Her arms were branches, and her speedy feet
115 Rooted and held, and her head became a tree top,
Everything gone except her grace, her shining.
Apollo loved her still. He placed his hand
Where he had hoped and felt the heart still beating
Under the bark; and he embraced the branches
120 As if they still were limbs, and kissed the wood,
And the wood shrank from his kisses, and the god
Exclaimed: "Since you can never be my bride,
My tree at least you shall be! Let the laurel
Adorn, henceforth, my hair, my lyre, my quiver:
125 Let Roman victors, in the long procession,
Bear laurel wreaths for triumph and ovation.
Beside Augustus' portals let the laurel
Guard and watch over the oak, and as my head
Is always youthful, let the laurel always
130 Be green and shining!" He said no more. The laurel,
Stirring, seemed to consent, to be saying *Yes.*

There is a grove in Thessaly, surrounded
By woodlands with steep slopes; men call it Tempe.
Through this the Peneus River's foamy waters
135 Rise below Pindus mountain. The cascades
Drive a fine smoky mist along the tree tops,
Frail clouds, or so it seems, and the roar of the water
Carries beyond the neighborhood. Here dwells
The mighty god himself, his holy of holies
140 Is under a hanging rock; it is here he gives
Laws to the nymphs, laws to the very water.
And here came first the streams of his own country

Not knowing what to offer, consolation
Or something like rejoicing: crowned with poplars
145   Sperchios came, and restless Enipeus,
Old Apidanus, Aeas, and Amphrysos
The easy-going. And all the other rivers
That take their weary waters into oceans
All over the world, came there, and only one
150   Was absent, Inachus, hiding in his cavern,
Salting his stream with tears, oh, most unhappy,
Mourning a daughter lost. Her name was Io,
Who might, for all he knew, be dead or living,
But since he cannot find her anywhere
155   He thinks she must be nowhere, and his sorrow
Fears for the worst.[1]

THE STORY OF ORPHEUS AND EURYDICE

So Hymen left there, clad in saffron robe,
Through the great reach of air, and took his way
To the Ciconian country, where the voice
Of Orpheus called him, all in vain. He came there,
5   True, but brought with him no auspicious words,
No joyful faces, lucky omens. The torch
Sputtered and filled the eyes with smoke; when swung,
It would not blaze: bad as the omens were,
The end was worse, for as the bride went walking
10   Across the lawn, attended by her naiads,
A serpent bit her ankle, and she was gone.
Orpheus mourned her to the upper world,
And then, lest he should leave the shades untried,
Dared to descend to Styx, passing the portal
15   Men call Taenarian. Through the phantom dwellers,
The buried ghosts, he passed, came to the king
Of that sad realm, and to Persephone,
His consort, and he swept the strings, and chanted:
"Gods of the world below the world, to whom
20   All of us mortals come, if I may speak
Without deceit, the simple truth is this:
I came here, not to see dark Tartarus,
Nor yet to bind the triple-throated monster,
Medusa's offspring, rough with snakes. I came
25   For my wife's sake, whose growing years were taken

---

[1]Here would follow the story of Jove and Io and many other tales loosely woven together.

By a snake's venom. I wanted to be able
to bear this; I have tried to. Love has conquered.
This god is famous in the world above,
But here, I do not know. I think he may be

30 Or is it all a lie, that ancient story
Of an old ravishment, and how he brought
The two of you together? By these places
All full of fear, by this immense confusion,
By this vast kingdom's silences, I beg you,

35 Weave over Eurydice's life, run through too soon.
To you we all, people and things, belong,
Sooner or later, to this single dwelling
All of us come, to our last home; you hold
Longest dominion over humankind.

40 She will come back again, to be your subject,
After the ripeness of her years; I am asking
A loan and not a gift. If fate denies us
This privilege for my wife, one thing is certain:
I do not want to go back either; triumph

45 In the death of two."
                                And with his words, the music
Made the pale phantoms weep: Ixion's wheel
Was still, Tityos' vultures left the liver,
Tantalus tried no more to reach for the water,

50 And Belus' daughters rested from their urns,
And Sisyphus climbed on his rock to listen.
That was the first time ever in all the world
The Furies wept. Neither the king nor consort
Had harshness to refuse him, and they called her,

55 Eurydice. She was there, limping a little
From her late wound, with the new shades of Hell.
And Orpheus received her, but one term
Was set: he must not, till he passed Avernus,
Turn back his gaze, or the gift would be in vain.

60 They climbed the upward path, through absolute silence,
Up the steep murk, clouded in pitchy darkness,
They were near the margin, near the upper land,
When he, afraid that she might falter, eager to see her,
Looked back in love, and she was gone, in a moment.

65 Was it he, or she, reaching out arms and trying
To hold or to be held, and clasping nothing
But empty air? Dying the second time,
She had no reproach to bring against her husband,

What was there to complain of? One thing, only:
70 He loved her. He could hardly hear her calling
Farewell! when she was gone.
               The double death
Stunned Orpheus, like the man who turned to stone
At sight of Cerberus, or the couple of rock,
75 Olenos and Lethaca, hearts so joined
One shared the other's guilt, and Ida's mountain,
Where rivers run, still holds them, both together.
In vain the prayers of Orpheus and his longing
To cross the river once more; the boatman Charon
80 Drove him away. For seven days he sat there
Beside the bank, in filthy garments, and tasting
No food whatever. Trouble, grief, and tears
Were all his sustenance. At last, complaining
The gods of Hell were cruel, he wandered on
85 To Rhodope and Haemus, swept by the north winds,
Where, for three years, he lived without a woman
Either because marriage had meant misfortune
Or he had made a promise. But many women
Wanted this poet for their own, and many
90 Grieved over their rejection. His love was given
To young boys only, and he told the Thracians
That was the better way: *enjoy that springtime,*
Take those first flowers!
                 There was a hill, and on it
95 A wide-extending plain, all green, but lacking
The darker green of shade, and when the singer
Came there and ran his fingers over the strings,
The shade came there to listen. The oak-tree came,
And many poplars, and the gentle lindens,
100 The beech, the virgin laurel, and the hazel
Easily broken, the ash men use for spears,
The shining silver fir, the ilex bending
Under its acorns, the friendly sycamore,
The changing-colored maple, and the willows
105 That love the river-waters, and the lotus
Favoring pools, and the green boxwood came,
Slim tamarisks, and myrtle, and viburnum
With dark-blue berries, and the pliant ivy,
The tendrilled grape, the elms, all dressed with vines,
110 The rowan-trees, the pitch-pines, and the arbute
With the red fruit, the palm, the victor's triumph,
The bare-trunked pine with spreading leafy crest,

Dear to the mother of the gods since Attis
Put off his human form, took on that likeness,
115   And the cone-shaped cypress joined them, now a tree,
But once a boy, loved by the god Apollo
Master of lyre and bow-string, both together.

THE STORY OF PYGMALION

One man, Pygmalion, who had seen these women
Leading their shameful lives,[2] shocked at the vices
Nature has given the female disposition
Only too often, chose to live alone,
5   To have no woman in his bed. But meanwhile
He made, with marvelous art, an ivory statue,
As white as snow, and gave it greater beauty
Than any girl could have, and fell in love
With his own workmanship. The image seemed
10   That of a virgin, truly, almost living,
And willing, save that modesty prevented,
To take on movement. The best art, they say,
Is that which conceals art, and so Pygmalion
Marvels, and loves the body he has fashioned.
15   He would often move his hands to test and touch it,
Could this be flesh, or was it ivory only?
No, it could not be ivory. His kisses,
He fancies, she returns; he speaks to her,
Holds her, believes his fingers almost leave
20   An imprint on her limbs, and fears to bruise her.
He pays her compliments, and brings her presents
Such as girls love, smooth pebbles, winding shells,
Little pet birds, flowers with a thousand colors,
Lilies, and painted balls, and lumps of amber.
25   He decks her limbs with dresses, and her fingers
Wear rings which he puts on, and he brings a necklace,
And earrings, and a ribbon for her bosom,
And all of these become her, but she seems
Even more lovely naked, and he spreads
30   A crimson coverlet for her to lie on,
Takes her to bed, puts a soft pillow under
Her head, as if she felt it, calls her *Darling,*
My darling love!
                              And Venus' holiday

---

[2]reference to the previous story

35 Came round, and all the people of the island
Were holding festival, and snow-white heifers,
Their horns all tipped with gold, stood at the altars,
Where incense burned, and, timidly, Pygmalion
Made offering, and prayed: "If you can give
40 All things, O gods, I pray my wife may be—
(He almost said, *My ivory girl*, but dared not)—
One like my ivory girl." And golden Venus
Was there, and understood the prayer's intention,
And showed her presence, with the bright flame leaping
45 Thrice on the altar, and Pygmalion came
Back where the maiden lay, and lay beside her,
And kissed her, and she seemed to glow, and kissed her,
And stroked her breast, and felt the ivory soften
Under his fingers, as wax grows soft in sunshine,
50 Made pliable by handling. And Pygmalion
Wonders, and doubts, is dubious and happy,
Plays lover again, and over and over touches
The body with his hand. It is a body!
The veins throb under the thumb. And oh, Pygmalion
55 Is lavish in his prayer and praise to Venus,
No words are good enough. The lips he kisses
Are real indeed, the ivory girl can feel them,
And blushes and responds, and the eyes open
At once on lover and heaven, and Venus blesses
60 The marriage she has made. The crescent moon
Fills to full orb, nine times, and wanes again,
And then a daughter is born, a girl named Paphos,
From whom the island later takes its name.

THE TEACHINGS OF PYTHAGORAS

There was a man here, Samian born, but he
Had fled from Samos, for he hated tyrants
And chose, instead, an exile's lot. His thought
Reached far aloft, to the great gods in Heaven,
5 And his imagination looked on visions
Beyond his mortal sight. All things he studied
With watchful eager mind, and he brought home
What he had learned and sat among the people
Teaching them what was worthy, and they listened
10 In silence, wondering at the revelations
How the great world began, the primal cause,
The nature of things, what God is, whence the snows

Come down, where lightning breaks from, whether wind
Or Jove speaks in the thunder from the clouds,
15 The cause of earthquakes, by what law the stars
Wheel in their courses, all the secrets hidden
From man's imperfect knowledge. He was first
To say that animal food should not be eaten,
And learnèd as he was, men did not always
20 Believe him when he preached "Forbear, O mortals,
To spoil your bodies with such impious food!
There is corn for you, apples, whose weight bears down
The bending branches; there are grapes that swell
On the green vines, and pleasant herbs, and greens
25 Made mellow and soft with cooking; there is milk
And clover-honey. Earth is generous
With her provision, and her sustenance
Is very kind; she offers, for your tables,
Food that requires no bloodshed and no slaughter.
30 Meat is for beasts to feed on, yet not all
Are carnivores, for horses, sheep, and cattle
Subsist on grass, but those whose disposition
Is fierce and cruel, tigers, raging lions,
And bears and wolves delight in bloody feasting.
35 Oh, what a wicked thing it is for flesh
To be the tomb of flesh, for the body's craving
To fatten on the body of another,
For one live creature to continue living
Through one live creature's death. In all the richness
40 That Earth, the best of mothers, tenders to us,
Does nothing please except to chew and mangle
The flesh of slaughtered animals? The Cyclops
Could do no worse! Must you destroy another
To satiate your greedy-gutted cravings?
45 There was a time, the Golden Age, we call it,
Happy in fruits and herbs, when no men tainted
Their lips with blood, and birds went flying safely
Through air, and in the fields the rabbits wandered
Unfrightened, and no little fish was ever
50 Hooked by its own credulity: all things
Were free from treachery and fear and cunning,
And all was peaceful. But some innovator,
A good-for-nothing, whoever he was, decided,
In envy, that what lions ate was better,
55 Stuffed meat into his belly like a furnace,
And paved the way for crime. It may have been

That steel was warmed and dyed with blood through killing
Dangerous beasts, and that could be forgiven
On grounds of self-defense; to kill wild beasts
60   Is lawful, but they never should be eaten.

One crime leads to another: first the swine
Were slaughtered, since they rooted up the seeds
And spoiled the season's crop; then goats were punished
On vengeful altars for nibbling at the grape-vines.
65   These both deserved their fate, but the poor sheep,
What had they ever done, born for man's service,
But bring us milk, so sweet to drink, and clothe us
With their soft wool, who give us more while living
Than ever they could in death? And what had oxen,
70   Incapable of fraud or trick or cunning,
Simple and harmless, born to a life of labor,
What had they ever done? None but an ingrate,
Unworthy of the gift of grain, could ever
Take off the weight of the yoke, and with the axe
75   Strike at the neck that bore it, kill his fellow
Who helped him break the soil and raise the harvest.
It is bad enough to do these things; we make
The gods our partners in the abomination,
Saying they love the blood of bulls in Heaven.
80   So there he stands, the victim at the altars,
Without a blemish, perfect (and his beauty
Proves his own doom), in sacrificial garlands,
Horns tipped with gold, and hears the priest intoning:
Not knowing what he means, watches the barley
85   Sprinkled between his horns, the very barley
He helped make grow, and then is struck
And with his blood he stains the knife whose flashing
He may have seen reflected in clear water.
Then they tear out his entrails, peer, examine,
90   Search for the will of Heaven, seeking omens.
And then, so great man's appetite for food
Forbidden, then, O human race, you feed,
You feast, upon your kill. Do not do this,
I pray you, but remember: when you taste
95   The flesh of slaughtered cattle, you are eating
Your fellow-workers.
                    "Now, since the god inspires me,
I follow where he leads, to open Delphi,
The very heavens, bring you revelation

100   Of mysteries, great matters never traced
By any mind before, and matters lost
Or hidden and forgotten, these I sing.
There is no greater wonder than to range
The starry heights, to leave the earth's dull regions,

105   To ride the clouds, to stand on Atlas' shoulders,
And see, far off, far down, the little figures
Wandering here and there, devoid of reason,
Anxious, in fear of death, and so advise them,
And so make fate an open book.

110   "O mortals,
Dumb in cold fear of death, why do you tremble
At Stygian rivers, shadows, empty names,
The lying stock of poets, and the terrors
Of a false world? I tell you that your bodies

115   Can never suffer evil, whether fire
Consumes them, or the waste of time. Our souls
Are deathless; always, when they leave our bodies,
They find new dwelling-places. I myself,
I well remember, in the Trojan War

120   Was Panthous' son, Euphorbus, and my breast
Once knew the heavy spear of Menelaus.
Not long ago, in Argos, Abas' city,
In Juno's temple, I saw the shield I carried
On my left arm. All things are always changing,

125   But nothing dies. The spirit comes and goes,
Is housed wherever it wills, shifts residence
From beasts to men, from men to beasts, but always
It keeps on living. As the pliant wax
Is stamped with new designs, and is no longer

130   What once it was, but changes form, and still
Is pliant wax, so do I teach that spirit
Is evermore the same, though passing always
To ever-changing bodies. So I warn you,
Lest appetite murder brotherhood, I warn you

135   By all the priesthood in me, do not exile
What may be kindred souls by evil slaughter.
Blood should not nourish blood.
                  "Full sail, I voyage
Over the boundless ocean, and I tell you

140   Nothing is permanent in all the world.
All things are fluent; every image forms,
Wandering through change. Time is itself a river
In constant movement, and the hours flow by

Like water, wave on wave, pursued, pursuing,
145   Forever fugitive, forever new.
That which has been, is not; that which was not,
Begins to be; motion and moment always
In process of renewal. Look, the night,
Worn out, aims toward the brightness, and sun's glory
150   Succeeds the dark. The color of the sky
Is different at midnight, when tired things
Lie all at rest, from what it is at morning
When Lucifer rides his snowy horse, before
Aurora paints the sky for Phoebus' coming.
155   The shield of the god reddens at early morning,
Reddens at evening, but is white at noonday
In purer air, farther from earth's contagion.
And the Moon-goddess changes in the nighttime,
Lesser today than yesterday, if waning,
160   Greater tomorrow than today, when crescent.
Notice the year's four seasons: they resemble
Our lives. Spring is a nursling, a young child,
Tender and young, and the grass shines and buds
Swell with new life, not yet full-grown nor hardy,
165   But promising much to husbandmen, with blossom
Bright in the fertile fields. And then comes summer
When the year is a strong young man, no better time
Than this, no richer, no more passionate vigor.
Then comes the prime of Autumn, a little sober,
170   But ripe and mellow, moderate of mood,
Halfway from youth to age, with just a showing
Of gray around the temples. And then Winter,
Tottering, shivering, bald or gray, and agèd.

Our bodies also change. What we have been,
175   What we now are, we shall not be tomorrow.
There was a time when we were only seed,
Only the hope of men, housed in the womb,
Where Nature shaped us, brought us forth, exposed us
To the void air, and there in light we lay,
180   Feeble and infant, and were quadrupeds
Before too long, and after a little wobbled
And pulled ourselves upright, holding a chair,
The side of the crib, and strength grew into us,
And swiftness; youth and middle age went swiftly
185   Down the long hill toward age, and all our vigor
Came to decline, so Milon, the old wrestler,

Weeps when he sees his arms whose bulging muscles
Were once like Hercules', and Helen weeps
To see her wrinkles in the looking glass:
190   Could this old woman ever have been ravished,
Taken twice over? Time devours all things
With envious Age, together. The slow gnawing
Consumes all things, and very, very slowly.

Not even the so-called elements are constant.
195   Listen, and I will tell you of their changes.
There are four of them, and two, the earth and water,
Are heavy, and their own weight bears them downward,
And two, the air and fire (and fire is purer
Even than air) are light, rise upward
200   If nothing holds them down. These elements
Are separate in space, yet all things come
From them and into them, and they can change
Into each other. Earth can be dissolved
To flowing water, water can thin to air,
205   And air can thin to fire, and fire can thicken
To air again, and air condense to water,
And water be compressed to solid earth.
Nothing remains the same: the great renewer,
Nature, makes form from form, and, oh, believe me
210   That nothing ever dies. What we call birth
Is the beginning of a difference,
No more than that, and death is only a ceasing
Of what had been before. The parts may vary,
Shifting from here to there, hither and yon,
215   And back again, but the great sum is constant.

Nothing, I am convinced, can be the same
Forever. There was once an Age of Gold,
Later, an Age of Iron. Every place
Submits to Fortune's wheel. I have seen oceans
220   That once were solid land, and I have seen
Lands made from ocean. Often sea-shells lie
Far from the beach, and men have found old anchors
On mountain tops. Plateaus have turned to valleys,
Hills washed away, marshes become dry desert,
225   Deserts made pools. Here Nature brings forth fountains,
There shuts them in; when the earth quakes, new rivers
Are born and old ones sink and dry and vanish.
Lycus, for instance, swallowed by the earth

Emerges far away, a different stream,
230 And Erasinus disappears, goes under
The ground, and comes to light again in Argos,
And Mysus, so the story goes, was tired
Of his old source and banks and went elsewhere
And now is called Caicus. The Anigrus
235 Was good to drink from once, but now rolls down
A flood that you had better leave alone,
Unless the poets lie, because the Centaurs
Used it to wash their wounds from Hercules' arrows.
And Hypanis, rising from Scythian mountains,
240 Once fresh and sweet to the taste, is salty and brackish.

Antissa, Pharos, Tyre, all inland cities,
Were islands once, Leucas and Zancle mainland,
And Helice and Buris, should you seek them,
Those old Achaian cities, you would find them
245 Under the waves, and mariners can show you
The sloping ramps, the buried walls. Near Troezen
Stands a high treeless hill, a level plain
Until the violent winds, penned underground,
Stifled in gloomy caverns, struggled long
250 For freer air to breathe, since that black prison
Had never a chink, made the ground swell to bursting,
The way one blows a bladder or a goatskin,
And where that blister or that bubble grew
Out of the ground, the lump remained and hardened
255 With time, and now it seems a rounded hill-top.

Example on example! I could cite you
So many more that I have seen or heard of.
Just a few more. The element of water
Gives and receives strange forms. At midday Ammon
260 Is cold, but warm in the morning and the evening.
The Athamanians set wood on fire
By pouring water on it in the dark of the moon,
And the Ciconian people have a river
They never drink, for they would turn to marble.
265 Crathis and Sybaris, in our own country,
Turn hair the color of platinum or gold,
And there are other streams, more marvelous even,
Whose waters affect the mind as well as body.
You have heard about Salmacis; there are lakes
270 In Ethiopia where a swallow of the water

Will drive you raving mad or hold you rigid
In catatonic lethargy. No man
Who likes his wine should ever drink from Clytor
Or he would hate it; something in that water,
275   It may be, counteracts the heat of wine,
Or possibly, and so the natives tell us,
Melampus, when he cured the maddened daughters
Of Proetus by his herbs and magic singing,
Threw in that spring mind-clearing hellebore,
280   So that a hatred of wine stays in those waters.
Lynestis river is just the opposite;
Whoever drinks too freely there will stagger
As if he had taken undiluted wine.
At Pheneus, in Arcadia, there are springs
285   Harmless by day, injurious in the nighttime.
As lakes and rivers vary in their virtues,
So lands can change. The little island Delos
Once floated on the waters, but now stands firm,
And Jason's Argo, as you well remember,
290   Dreaded the Clashing Rocks, the high-flung spray,
Immovable now, contemptuous of the winds.
Etna, whose furnaces glow hot with sulphur,
Will not be fiery always in the future,
And was not always fiery in the past.
295   The earth has something animal about it,
Living almost, with many lungs to breathe through,
Sending out flames, but the passages of breathing
Are changeable; some caverns may be closed
And new ones open whence the fire can issue.
300   Deep caves compress the violent winds, which drive
Rock against rock, imprisoning the matter
That holds the seeds of flame, and this bursts blazing
Ignited by the friction, and the caves
Cool when the winds are spent. The tars and pitches,
305   The yellow sulphur with invisible burning,
Are no eternal fuel, so volcanoes,
Starved of their nourishment, devour no longer,
Abandon fire, as they have been abandoned.

Far to the north, somewhere around Pallene,
310   The story goes, there is a lake where men
Who plunge nine times into the chill waters
Come out with downy feathers over their bodies.
This I do not believe, nor that the women

Of Scythia sprinkle their bodies with magic juices
315 For the same purpose and effect.
                              "However,
There are stranger things that have been tried and tested
And these we must believe. You have seen dead bodies,
Rotten from time or heat, breed smaller creatures.
320 Bury the carcasses of slaughtered bullocks,
Chosen for sacrifice (all men know this),
And from the putrid entrails will come flying
The flower-culling bees, whose actions prove
Their parenthood, for they are fond of meadows,
325 Are fond of toil, and work with hopeful spirit.
The horse, being warlike, after he is buried
Produces hornets. Cut a sea-crab's claws,
Bury the rest of the body, and a scorpion
Comes from the ground. And worms that weave cocoons
330 White on the leaves of the trees, as country people
Know well, turn into moths with death's-head marking.
The mud holds seeds that generate green frogs,
Legless at first, but the legs grow, to swim with,
And take long jumps with, later. And a bear-cub,
335 New-born, is not a bear at all, but only
A lump, hardly alive, whose mother gives it
A licking into shape, herself as model.
The larvae of the honey-bearing bees,
Safe in hexagonal waxen cells, are nothing
340 But wormlike bodies; feet and wings come later.
Who would believe that from an egg would come
Such different wonders as Juno's bird, the peacock,
Jove's eagle, Venus' dove, and all the fliers?
Some people think that when the human spine
345 Has rotted in the narrow tomb, the marrow
Is changed into a serpent.
                           "All these things
Have their beginning in some other creature,
But there is one bird which renews itself
350 Out of itself. The Assyrians call it the phoenix,
It does not live on seeds nor the green grasses,
But on the gum of frankincense and juices
Of cardamon. It lives five centuries,
As you may know, and then it builds itself
355 A nest in the highest branches of a palm-tree,
Using its talons and clean beak to cover
This nest with cassia and spikes of spikenard,

And cinnamon and yellow myrrh, and there
It dies among the fragrance, and from the body
360 A tiny phoenix springs to birth, whose years
Will be as long. The fledgling, gaining strength
To carry burdens, lifts the heavy nest,
His cradle and the old one's tomb, and bears it
Through the thin air to the city of the Sun
365 And lays it as an offering at the doors
Of the Sun-god's holy temple.
                              "Wonders, wonders!
The same hyena can be male or female,
To take or give the seed of life, at pleasure,
370 And the chameleon, a little creature
Whose food is wind and air, takes on the color
Of anything it rests on. India, conquered,
Gave Bacchus, tendril-crowned, the tawny lynxes
Whose urine, when it met the air, was hardened
375 Becoming stone; so coral also hardens
At the first touch of air, while under water
It sways, a pliant weed.
                        "The day will end,
The Sun-god plunge tired horses in the ocean
380 Before I have the time I need to tell you
All of the things that take new forms. We see
The eras change, nations grow strong, or weaken,
Like Troy, magnificent in men and riches,
For ten years lavish with her blood, and now
385 Displaying only ruins and for wealth
The old ancestral tombs. Sparta, Mycenae,
Athens, and Thebes, all flourished once, and now
What are they more than names? I hear that Rome
Is rising, out of Trojan blood, established
390 On strong and deep foundations, where the Tiber
Comes from the Apennines. Rome's form is changing
Growing to greatness, and she will be, some day,
Head of the boundless world; so we are told
By oracles and seers. I can remember
395 When Troy was tottering ruinward, a prophet,
Helenus, son of Priam, told Aeneas
In consolation for his doubts and weeping
'O son of Venus, if you bear in mind
My prophecies, Troy shall not wholly perish
400 While you are living: fire and sword will give you
Safe passage through them; you will carry on

Troy's relics, till a land, more friendly to you
Than your own native soil, will give asylum.
I see the destined city for the Trojans
405 And their sons' sons, none greater in all the ages,
Past, present, or to come. Through long, long eras
Her famous men will bring her power, but one,
Sprung from Iulus' blood, will make her empress
Of the whole world, and after earth has used him
410 The heavens will enjoy him, Heaven will be
His destination.' What Helenus told Aeneas,
I have told you, I remember, and I am happy
That for our kin new walls, at last, are rising,
That the Greek victory was to such good purpose.

415 We must not wander far and wide, forgetting
The goal of our discourse. Remember this:
The heavens and all below them, earth and her creatures,
All change, and we, part of creation, also
Must suffer change. We are not bodies only,
420 But wingèd spirits, with the power to enter
Animal forms, house in the bodies of cattle.
Therefore, we should respect those dwelling-places
Which may have given shelter to the spirit
Of fathers, brothers, cousins, human beings
425 At least, and we should never do them damage,
Not stuff ourselves like the cannibal Thyestes.
An evil habit, impious preparation,
Wicked as human bloodshed, to draw the knife
Across the throat of the calf, and hear its anguish
430 Cry to deaf ears! And who could slay
The little goat whose cry is like a baby's,
Or eat a bird he has himself just fed?
One might as well do murder; he is only
The shortest step away. Let the bull plow
435 And let him owe his death to length of days;
Let the sheep give you armor for rough weather,
The she-goats bring full udders to the milking.
Have done with nets and traps and snares and springs,
Bird-lime and forest-beaters, lines and fish-hooks.
440 Kill, if you must, the beasts that do you harm,
But, even so, let killing be enough;
Let appetite refrain from flesh, take only
A gentler nourishment."

THE DEIFICATION OF CAESAR

The old god
Came to our shrines from foreign lands, but Caesar
Is god in his own city. First in war,
And first in peace, victorious, triumphant,
5   Planner and governor, quick-risen to glory,
The newest star in Heaven, and more than this,
And above all, immortal through his son.[3]
No work, in all of Caesar's great achievement,
Surpassed this greatness, to have been the father
10   Of our own Emperor. To have tamed the Britons,
Surrounded by the fortress of their ocean,
To have led a proud victorious armada
Up seven-mouthed Nile, to have added to the empire
Rebel Numidia, Libya, and Pontus
15   Arrogant with the name of Mithridates,
To have had many triumphs, and deserved
Many more triumphs: this was truly greatness,
Greatness surpassed only by being father
Of one yet greater, one who rules the world
20   As proof that the immortal gods have given
Rich blessing to the human race, so much so
We cannot think him mortal, our Augustus,
Therefore our Julius must be made a god
To justify his son.
25   And golden Venus
Saw this, and saw, as well, the murder plotted
Against her priest, the assassins in their armor,
And she grew pale with fear. "Behold," she cried
To all the gods in turn, "Behold, what treason
30   Threatens me with its heavy weight, what ambush
Is set to take Iulus' last descendant!
Must this go on forever? Once again
The spear of Diomedes strikes to wound me,
The walls of Troy fall over me in ruins,
35   Once more I see my son, long-wandering,
Storm-tossed, go down to the shades, and rise again
To war with Turnus, or to speak more truly,
With Juno. It is very foolish of me
To dwell on those old sufferings, for my fear,

---

[3]Caesar's "son" was Octavian, Caesar Augustus.

40 My present fear, has driven them from my mind.
   Look: Do you see them whetting their evil daggers?
   Avert this crime, before the fires of Vesta
   Drown in their high-priest's blood!"
                              The anxious goddess
45 Cried these complaints through Heaven, and no one listened.
   The gods were moved, and though they could not shatter
   The iron mandates of the ancient sisters,
   They still gave certain portents of the evil
   To come upon the world. In the dark storm-clouds
50 Arms clashed and trumpets blared, most terrible,
   And horns heard in the sky warned men of crime,
   And the sun's visage shone with lurid light
   On anxious lands. Firebrands were seen to flash
   Among the stars, the clouds dripped blood, rust-color
55 Blighted the azure Morning-Star, and the Moon
   Rode in a blood-red car. The Stygian owl
   Wailed in a thousand places; ivory statues
   Dripped tears in a thousand places, and wailing traveled
   The holy groves, and threats were heard. No victim
60 Paid expiation, and the liver warned
   Of desperate strife to come, the lobe found cloven
   Among the entrails. In the market place,
   Around the homes of men and the gods' temples
   Dogs howled by night, and the shadows of the silent
65 Went roaming, and great earthquakes shook the city.
   No warning of the gods could check the plotting
   Of men, avert the doom of fate. Drawn swords
   Were borne into a temple; nowhere else
   In the whole city was suitable for murder
70 Save where the senate met.
                              Then Venus beat
   Her breast with both her hands, and tried to hide him,
   Her Caesar, in a cloud, as she had rescued
   Paris from Menelaus, as Aeneas
75 Fled Diomedes' sword. And Jove spoke to her:
   "My daughter, do you think your power alone
   Can move the fates no power can ever conquer?
   Enter the home of the Three Sisters: there
   You will see the records, on bronze and solid iron,
80 Wrought with tremendous effort, and no crashing
   Of sky, no wrath of lightning, no destruction
   Shall make them crumble. They are safe, forever.
   There you will find engraved on adamant

The destinies of the race, unchangeable.
85 I have read them, and remembered; I will tell you
So you may know the future. He has finished
The time allotted him, this son you grieve for;
His debt to earth is paid. But he will enter
The Heaven as a god, and have his temples
90 On earth as well: this you will see fulfilled,
Will bring about, you and his son together.
He shall inherit both the name of Caesar
And the great burden, and we both shall help him
Avenge his father's murder. Under him
95 Mutina's conquered walls will sue for mercy,
Pharsalia know his power, and Philippi
Run red with blood again, and one more Pompey
Go down to death in the Sicilian waters.
A Roman general's Egyptian woman,
100 Foolish to trust that liaison, will perish
For all her threats that our own capitol
Would serve Canopus. Need I bring to mind
Barbarian lands that border either ocean?
Whatever lands men live on, the world over,
105 Shall all be his to rule, and the seas also.
And when peace comes to all the world, his mind
Will turn to law and order, civil justice,
And men will learn from his sublime example,
And he, still looking forward toward the future,
110 The coming generations, will give order
That his good wife's young son should take his name,
His duty when he lays the burden down,
Though he will live as long as ancient Nestor
Before he comes to Heaven to greet his kinsmen.
115 Now, in the meantime, from the murdered body
Raise up the spirit, set the soul of Julius
As a new star in Heaven, to watch over
Our market place, our Capitol."
                        He ended,
120 And Venus, all unseen, came to the temple,
Raised from the body of Caesar the fleeting spirit,
Not to be lost in air, but borne aloft
To the bright stars of Heaven. As she bore it,
She felt it burn, released it from her bosom,
125 And saw it rise, beyond the moon, a comet
Rising, not falling, leaving the long fire
Behind its wake, and gleaming as a star.

And now he sees his son's good acts, confessing
They are greater than his own, for once rejoicing
130 In being conquered. But the son refuses
To have his glories set above his father's;
Fame will not heed him, for she heeds no mortal,
Exalts him, much against his will, resists him
In this one instance only. So must Atreus
135 Defer to Agamemnon; so does Theseus
Surpass Aegeus, and Achilles Peleus,
And—(one more instance where the father's glory
Yields to the son's)—Saturn is less than Jove.
Jove rules the lofty citadels of Heaven,
140 The kingdoms of the triple world, but Earth
Acknowledges Augustus. Each is father
As each is lord. O gods, Aeneas' comrades,
To whom the fire and sword gave way, I pray you,
And you, O native gods of Italy,
145 Quirinus, father of Rome, and Mars, the father
Of Rome's unconquered sire, and Vesta, honored
With Caesar's household gods, Apollo, tended
With reverence as Vesta is, and Jove,
Whose temple crowns Tarpeia's rock, O gods,
150 However many, whom the poet's longing
May properly invoke, far be the day,
Later than our own era, when Augustus
Shall leave the world he rules, ascend to Heaven,
And there, beyond our presence, hear our prayers!

THE EPILOGUE

Now I have done my work. It will endure,
I trust, beyond Jove's anger, fire and sword,
Beyond Time's hunger. The day will come, I know,
So let it come, that day which has no power
5 Save over my body, to end my span of life
Whatever it may be. Still, part of me,
The better part, immortal, will be borne
Above the stars; my name will be remembered
Wherever Roman power rules conquered lands,
10 I shall be read, and through all centuries,
If prophecies of bards are ever truthful,
I shall be living, always.

17. "TRIMALCHIO'S BANQUET" FROM THE SATYRICON

Petronius
(d. 65 CE)

(trans. by Alfred R. Allinson)

Petronius was a Roman statesman and writer who incurred the wrath of the Emperor Nero and, according to the historian Tacitus, committed suicide by opening and closing his veins while conversing with friends. His Satyricon, *a fragmentary novel, recounts the episodic adventures of two students and their servant. In the more or less complete section, "Trimalchio's Banquet," the students crash a banquet given by a boorish self-made man whose vulgarity they mock even as they rip him off. Parodying Plato's* Symposium *which depicts an evening of good friends, good food, and good conversation, the dinner party in "Trimalchio's Banquet" reveals wealth as the yardstick of friendship, ostentatious inedible food, and boasts of bodily functions, last wills, shrouds, and tombstones. The episode is hilarious on the surface, but serves as a more serious contemporary critique of the corrosive effects of materialism.*

    . . . Whilst we were still debating sadly with ourselves how we might best escape the storm, a slave of Agamemnon's broke into our trembling conclave, crying, "What! don't you recollect whose entertainment it is this day?— Trimalchio's, a most elegant personage; he has a time-piece in his dining-room and
5   a trumpeter specially provided for the purpose keeps him constantly informed how much of his lifetime is gone." So, forgetting all our troubles, we proceed to make a careful toilette, and bid Giton, who had always hitherto been very ready to act as servant, to attend us at the bath.

    Meantime in our gala dresses, we began to stroll about, or rather to amuse
10   ourselves by approaching the different groups of ball-players. Amongst these we all of a sudden catch sight of a bald-headed old man in a russet tunic, playing ball amid a troupe of long-haired boys. It was not however so much the boys, though these were well worth looking at, that drew us to the spot, as the master himself, who wore sandals and was playing with green balls. He never stooped for a ball
15   that had once touched ground, but an attendant stood by with a sackful, and supplied the players as they required them. We noticed other novelties too. For

two eunuchs were stationed at opposite points of the circle, one holding a silver chamber-pot, while the other counted the balls, not those that were in play and flying from hand to hand, but such as fell on the floor.

We were still admiring these refinements of elegance when Menelaus runs up, saying, "See! that's the gentleman you are to dine with; why! this is really nothing else than a prelude to the entertainment." He had not finished speaking when Trimalchio snapped his fingers, and at the signal the eunuch held out the chamber-pot for him, without his ever stopping play. After easing his bladder, he called for water, and having dipped his hands momentarily in the bowl, dried them on one of the lads' hair.

Presently muffled in a wrap of scarlet felt, he was placed in a litter, preceded by four running-footmen in tinseled liveries, and a wheeled chair, in which his favorite rode, a little old young man, sore-eyed and uglier even than his master. As the latter was borne along, a musician took up his place at this head with a pair of miniature flutes, and played softly to him, as if he were whispering secrets in his ear. Full of wonder we follow the procession and arrive at the same moment as Agamemnon....

To the left hand as you entered, and not far from the porter's lodge, a huge chained dog was depicted on the wall, and written above in capital letters: 'WARE DOG! 'WARE DOG! I fell to examining the other paintings on the walls. One of these represented a slave-market, the men standing up with labels round their necks, while in another Trimalchio himself, wearing long hair, holding a caduceus[1] in his hand and led by Minerva, was entering Rome. Further on, the ingenious painter had shown him learning accounts, and presently made steward of the estate, each incident being made clear by explanatory inscriptions. Lastly, at the extreme end of the portico, Mercury was lifting the hero by the chin and placing him on the highest seat of a tribunal. Fortune stood by with her cornucopia, and the three Fates, spinning his destiny with a golden thread.

Well! at last we take our places, Alexandrian slave-boys pouring snow water over our hands, and others succeeding them to wash our feet and cleanse our toe-nails with extreme dexterity. Not even while engaged in this unpleasant office were they silent, but sang away over their work. I had a mind to try whether all the house servants were singers and accordingly asked for a drink of wine. Instantly an attendant was at my side, pouring out the liquor to the accompaniment of the same sort of shrill recitative. Demand what you would, it was the same; you might have supposed yourself among a troupe of pantomime actors rather than at a respectable citizen's table.

Then the preliminary course was served in very elegant style. For all were now at table except Trimalchio, for whom the first place was reserved, by a reversal of ordinary usage. Among the other hors d'oeuvres stood a little ass of Corinthian bronze with a packsaddle holding olives, white olives on one side, black on the other. The animal was flanked right and left by silver dishes, on the

---

[1]**caduceus:** a herald's staff, used as a symbol for physicians

60 rim of which Trimalchio's name was engraved and the weight. On arches built up
in the form of miniature bridges were dormice seasoned with honey and poppy-
seed. There were sausages, too, smoking hot on a silver grill, and underneath (to
imitate coals) Syrian plums and pomegranate seeds.

We were in the middle of these elegant trifles when Trimalchio himself was
carried in to the sound of music, and was bolstered up among a host of tiny
65 cushions, a sight that set one or two indiscreet guests laughing. And no wonder;
his bald head poked up out of a scarlet mantle, his neck was closely muffled, and
over all was laid a napkin with a broad purple stripe, and long fringes hanging
down either side. Moreover he wore on the little finger of his left hand a massive
ring of silver gilt, and on the last joint of the next finger a smaller ring, apparently
70 of solid gold, but starred superficially with little ornaments of steel. Nay! to show
this was not the whole of his magnificence, his left arm was bare, and displayed a
gold bracelet and an ivory circlet with a sparkling clasp to put it on.

After picking his teeth with a silver toothpick, "My friends," he began, "I
was far from desirous of coming to table just yet, but that I might not keep you
75 waiting by my own absence, I have sadly interfered with my own amusement. But
will you permit me to finish my game?" A slave followed him, bearing a
draughtsboard of terebinth wood[2] and crystal dice. One special bit of refinement I
noticed; instead of the ordinary black and white men he had medals of gold and
silver respectively.

80 Meantime, whilst he is exhausting the vocabulary of a tinker over the game,
and we are still at the hors d'oeuvres, a dish was brought in with a basket on it,
in which lay a wooden hen, her wings outspread round her as if she were sitting.
Instantly a couple of slaves came up, and to the sound of lively music began to
search the straw, and pulling out a lot of peafowl's eggs one after the other,
85 handed them round to the company. Trimalchio turns his head at this, saying, "My
friends, it was by my orders the hen set on the peafowl's eggs yonder; but by God!
I am very much afraid they are half-hatched. Nevertheless we can try whether they
are eatable." For our part, we take our spoons, which weighed at least half a
pound each, and break the eggs, which were made of paste. I was on the point of
90 throwing mine away, for I thought I discerned a chick inside. But when I
overheard a veteran guest saying, "There should be something good here!" I
further investigated the shell, and found a very fine fat beccafico[3] swimming in
yolk of egg flavored with pepper.

Trimalchio had by this time stopped his game and been helped to all the dishes
95 before us. He had just announced in a loud voice that any of us who wanted a
second supply of honeyed wine had only to ask for it, when suddenly at a signal
from the band, the hors d'oeuvres are whisked away by a troupe of slaves, all
singing too. But in the confusion a silver dish happened to fall and a slave picked
it up again from the floor; this Trimalchio noticed, and boxing the fellow's ears,

---

[2]**terebinth wood:** a very expensive hard wood
[3]**beccafico:** a European songbird, a delicacy

100 rated him soundly and ordered him to throw it down again. Then a groom came in
and began to sweep up the silver along with the other refuse with his [broom].

He was succeeded by two long-haired Ethiopians, carrying small leather
skins, like the fellows that water the sand in the amphitheater, who poured wine
over our hands; for no one thought of offering water.

105 After being duly complimented on this refinement, our host cried out, "Fair
play's a jewel!" and accordingly ordered a separate table to be assigned to each
guest. "In this way," he said, "by preventing any crowding, the stinking servants
won't make us so hot."

Simultaneously there were brought in a number of wine-jars of glass carefully
110 stoppered with plaster, and having labels attached to their necks reading:

FALERNIAN; OPIMIAN VINTAGE ONE HUNDRED YEARS OLD.

Then the slave brought in a silver skeleton, so artfully fitted that its
articulations and vertebrae were all movable and would turn and twist in any
direction. After he had tossed this once or twice on the table, causing the loosely
115 jointed limbs to take various postures, Trimalchio moralized thus:

Alas! how less than naught are we;
Fragile life's thread, and brief our day!
What this is now, we all shall be;
Drink and make merry while you may.

120 Our applause was interrupted by the second course. . . .

Unable to eat any more, I now turned towards my neighbor in order to glean
what information I could, and after indulging in a string of general remarks,
presently asked him, "Who is that lady bustling up and down the room yonder?"
"Trimalchio's lady," he replied; "her name is Fortunata, and she counts her coin
125 by the bushelful! Before? what was she before? Why! my dear Sir! saving your
respect, you would have been mighty sorry to take bread from her hand. Now, by
hook or by crook, she's got to heaven, and is Trimalchio's factotum. In fact if she
told him it was dark night at high noon, he'd believe her. The man's rolling in
riches, and really can't tell what he has and what he hasn't got; still his good lady
130 looks keenly after everything, and is on the spot where you least expect to see her.
She's temperate, sober and well advised, but she has a sharp tongue of her own
and chatters like a magpie between the bed-curtains. When she likes a man, she
likes him; and when she doesn't, well! she doesn't."

This agreeable gossip was here interrupted by Trimalchio; for the second
135 course had now been removed, and the company being merry with wine began to
engage in general conversation.

This lasted till fresh servants entered and spread carpets before the couches,
embroidered with pictures of fowling nets, prickers with their hunting spears, and
sporting gear of all kinds. We were still at a loss what to expect when a

140 tremendous shout was raised outside the doors, and lo and behold! a pack of Laconian dogs came careening round and round the very table. These were soon succeeded by a huge tray, on which lay a wild boar of the largest size, with a cap on its head, while from the tushes hung two little baskets of woven palm leaves, one full of Syrian dates, the other of Theban. Round it were little piglets of baked
145 sweetmeat, as if at suck, to show it was a sow we had before us; and these were gifts to be taken home with them by the guests.

At the end of this course Trimalchio left the table to relieve himself, and so finding ourselves free from the constraint of his overbearing presence, we began to indulge in a little friendly conversation. Accordingly Dama began first, after
150 calling for a cup of wine. "A day! what is a day?" he exclaimed, "before you can turn round, it's night again! So really you can't do better than go straight from bed to board. Fine cold weather we've been having; why! even my bath has hardly warmed me. But truly hot liquor is a good clothier. I've been drinking bumpers, and I'm downright fuddled. The wine has got into my head."
155 Seleucus then struck into the talk: "I don't bathe every day," he said; "your systematic bather's a mere fuller.[4] Water's got teeth, and melts the heart away, a little every day; but there! when I've fortified my belly with a cup of mulled wine, I say 'Go hang!' to the cold. Indeed I couldn't bathe today, for I've been to a funeral. A fine fellow he was too, good old Chrysanthus, but he's given up the ghost now.
160 He was calling me just this moment, only just this moment; I could fancy myself talking to him now. Alas! alas! what are we but blown bladders on two legs? We're not worth as much as flies; they are some use, but we're no better than bubbles. He wasn't careful enough in his diet, you say? I tell you, for five whole days not one drop of water, or one crumb of bread passed his lips. Nevertheless he
165 has joined the majority. The doctors killed him,—or rather his day was come; the very best of doctors is only a satisfaction to the mind. Anyhow he was handsomely buried, on his own best bed, with good blankets. The wailing was first class,—he did a trifle of manumission[5] before he died; though no doubt his wife's tears were a bit forced."
170 He was getting tiresome, and Phileros broke in: "Let's talk of living. He's got his deserts, whatever they were; he lived well and died well, what has he to complain about? He started with next to nothing, and was ready to the last to pick a farthing out of a dunghill with his teeth. So he grew and grew, like a honeycomb. Upon my word I believe he left a round hundred million behind him, and all in
175 ready money. But I'll tell you the actual facts, for I'm the soul of truth, as they say. He had a rough tongue, and a ready one, and was quarrelsomeness personified. Now his brother was a fine fellow and a true friend, with a free hand and keeping a liberal table. Just at the beginning he had a bad bird to pluck, but the very first vintage set him on his legs, for he sold his wine at his own price. But the thing that
180 chiefly made him lift up his head in the world was getting an inheritance, out of

---

[4]**fuller:** a strong smelling cleaning solvent
[5]**manumission:** freeing of slaves

which he managed to pry a good deal more than was really left him. . . . Yet it's fair to say he did well enough all his life, getting what was never meant for him. Evidently one of Fortune's favorites, in whose hands lead turns to gold. But that's simple enough, when everything runs on wheels exactly as you want it to. How
185   old, think you, was he when he died? Seventy and over. But he was as tough as horn; he carried his age well, and he was still as black as a crow. I knew him when he was a pretty loose fish, and he was lecherous to the last. Upon my soul I don't believe he left a living thing in his house alone, down to the dog. A great lover of lads, indeed a man of universal talents and tastes. Not that I blame him;
190   this was all he got out of life."

     "Alas! alas! Things get worse and worse every day, and this city of ours is growing like a cow's tail, backwards. . . . As for me, I've eaten up my duds, and if the scarcity goes on, I shall sell my bits of houses. What is to become of us, if neither gods nor men take pity on this unhappy city? As I hope for happiness, I
195   think it's all the gods' doing. For nobody any more believes heaven to be heaven, nobody keeps fast, nobody cares one straw for Jupiter, but all men shut their eyes and count up their own belongings. In former days the long-robed matrons went barefoot, with unbound hair and a pure heart, up the hill to pray Jupiter for rain; and instantly it started raining bucketfuls,—then or never,—and they all came
200   back looking like drowned rats. So the gods come stealthy-footed to our destruction, because we have no piety or reverence. The fields lie idle, and—"

     "I beseech you," cried Echion . . . . "My word! you couldn't name a better countryside, if only the inhabitants were to match. True, we are in low water for the moment, but we're not the only ones. We must not be so over particular, the
205   same heaven is over us all. If you lived elsewhere, you'd say pigs ran about here ready roasted.

     "And I tell you, we're going to have a grand show in three days from now at the festival—none of your common gangs of gladiators, but most of the chaps freedmen. Our good Titus has a heart of gold and a hot head; 'twill be do or die,
210   and no quarter. I'm in his service, he is no shirker! He'll have the best of sharp swords and no backing out; bloody butcher's meat in the middle, for the amphitheater to feast their eyes on. And he's got the wherewithal; he was left thirty million, his father came to a bad end. Suppose he does spend four hundred thousand or so, his property won't feel it, and his name will live forever. . . .

215   "You look, Agamemnon, as if you were saying to yourself, 'Whatever is that bore driving at?' I talk, because you fellows who can talk, won't talk. You're not of our stuff and so you laugh at poor men's conversation. You're a monument of learning, we all know. But there, let me persuade you one day to come down into the country and see our little place. We'll find something to eat, a pullet and a few
220   eggs; it will be grand, even though the bad weather this year has turned everything upside down. Anyway we shall find enough to fill our bellies.

     "And there's a future pupil growing up for you, my little lad at home. . . . I've just bought the lad some law books, for I want him to have a smack of law for home use. There's bread and butter in that. For as to Literature, he has been tarred

225   enough already with that brush. If he kicks, I've made up my mind to teach him a trade,—a barber, or an auctioneer, or best of all a lawyer,—which nothing but Hell can rob him of. So I impress on him every day. 'Believe me, my first-born, whatever you learn, you learn for your good. . . . Learning's a treasure, and a trade never starves.' "

230   Such were the brilliant remarks that were flashing round the board, when Trimalchio re-entered, and after wiping his brow and scenting his hands, "Pardon me, my friends," he said after a brief pause, "but for several days I have been costive.[6] My physicians were nonplused. However, pomegranate rind and an infusion of firwood in vinegar has done me good. And now I trust my belly will be
235   better behaved. At times I have such a rumbling about my stomach, you'd think I had a bull bellowing inside me! So if any of you want to relieve yourselves, there's no necessity to be ashamed about it. None of us is born solid. I don't know any torment so bad as holding it in. It's the one thing Jove himself cannot stop. What are you laughing at, Fortunata, you who so often keep me awake o' nights
240   yourself? I never hinder any man at my table from easing himself, and indeed the doctors forbid our balking nature. Even if something more presses, everything's ready outside,—water, close-stools, and the other little matters needful. Take my word for it, the vapors rise to the brain and may cause a fluxion of the whole constitution. I know many a man that's died of it, because he was too shy to speak
245   out."

    We thank our host for his generous indulgence, taking our wine in little sips the while to keep down our laughter. But little we thought we had still another hill to climb, as the saying is, and were only half through the elaboration of the meal. For when the tables had been cleared with a flourish of music, three white
250   hogs were brought in, hung with little bells and muzzled. One, so the nomenclator[7] informed us, was a two-year-old, another three, and the third six. For my part, I thought they were learned pigs, come in to perform some of those marvelous tricks you see in circuses. But Trimalchio put an end to my surmises by saying, "Which of the three will you have dressed for supper right away? Farmyard cocks and
255   pheasants are for country folks; my cooks are used to serving up calves boiled whole." So saying, he immediately ordered the cook to be summoned, and without waiting for our choice, directed the six-year-old to be killed.

    Trimalchio now turned to us and said "If you don't like the wine, I'll have it changed; otherwise please prove its quality by your drinking. Thanks to the gods'
260   goodness, I never buy it; but now I have everything that smacks good growing on a suburban estate of mine. I've not seen it yet, but they tell me it's down Terracina and Tarentum way. I am thinking at the moment of making Sicily one of my little properties, that when I've a mind to visit Africa, I may sail along my own boundaries to get there.
265   "But pray, Gaius, why is not Fortunata at table?"

---

[6]**costive**: constipated
[7]**nonmenclator**: a "master of ceremonies"

"Fortunata! Fortunata!" At this she entered at last, her frock kilted up with a yellow girdle, so as to show a cherry-colored tunic underneath, and corded anklets and gold-embroidered slippers. Then wiping her hands on a handkerchief she wore at her neck, she placed herself on the same couch beside Habinnas' wife, 270 Scintilla, kissing her while the other claps her hands, and exclaiming, "Have I really the pleasure of seeing you?"

Before long it came to Fortunata's taking off the bracelets from her great fat arms to show them to her admiring companion. Finally she even undid her anklets and her hair net, which she assured Scintilla was of the very finest gold. 275 Trimalchio observing this, ordered all the things to be brought to him. "You see this woman's fetters," he cried; "that's the way we poor devils are robbed! Six pound and a half, if it's an ounce; and yet I've got one myself of ten pound weight." Eventually to prove he was not telling a lie, he ordered a pair of scales to be brought, and had the articles carried round and the weight tested by each in turn. 280 And Scintilla was just as bad, for she drew from her bosom a little gold casket she called her Lucky Box. From it she produced a pair of ear-pendants and handed them one after the other to Fortunata to admire, saying, "Thanks to my husband's goodness, no wife has finer."

"Why truly!" remarked Habinnas, "you gave me no peace till I bought you the 285 glass bean. I tell you straight, if I had a daughter, I should cut off her ears. If there were no women in the world, we should have everything in the world dirt cheap; as it is, we've just got to piss hot and drink cold."

Meanwhile the two women, though a trifle piqued, laughed good-humoredly together and interchanged some tipsy kisses, the one praising the thrifty 290 management of the lady of the house, the other enlarging on the minions her husband kept and his unthrifty ways. While they were thus engaged in close confabulation, Habinnas got up stealthily and catching hold of Fortunata's legs, upset her on the couch. "Ah! ah!" she screeched, as her tunic slipped up above her knees. Then falling on Scintilla's bosom, she hid in her handkerchief a face all 295 afire with blushes.

After a short interval Trimalchio next ordered the dessert to be served; hereupon the servants removed all the tables and brought in fresh ones, and strewed the floor with saffron and vermilion colored sawdust and,—a refinement I had not seen before,—with specular stone reduced to powder. . . .
300 I am really ashamed to relate what followed, it was so unheard-of a piece of luxury. Long-haired slave boys brought in an unguent in a silver basin, and anointed our feet with it as we lay at table, after first wreathing our legs and ankles with garlands. Afterwards a small quantity of the same perfume was poured into the wine-jars and the lamps.
305 Then turning to Habinnas, [Trimalchio] asked him, "What say you, dear friend? are you building my monument according to my directions? I ask you particularly that at the feet of my effigy you have my little bitch put, and garlands

310 and perfume caskets and all Petraites' fights,[8] that by your good help I may live on even after death. The frontage is to be a hundred feet long, and it must reach back two hundred. For I wish to have all kinds of fruit trees growing around my ashes and plenty of vines. Surely it's a great mistake to make houses so fine for the living, yet to give never a thought to these where we have to dwell far, far longer.

315 "But I shall take good care to provide in my will against my remains being insulted. For I intend to put one of my freedmen in charge of my burial place, to see that the rabble don't come running and dirtying up my monument. I beg you to have ships under full sail carved on it, and me sitting on the tribunal, in my Senator's robes, with five gold rings on my fingers, and showering money from a bag among the public; for you remember I gave a public banquet once, two denars a head. Also there should be shown, if you approve, a banqueting-hall, and all the people

320 enjoying themselves pleasantly. On my right hand put a figure of my wife, Fortunata, holding a dove and leading a little bitch on a leash, also my little lad, and some good capacious wine-jars, stoppered so that the wine may not escape. Also you may carve a broken urn, and a boy weeping over it. Also a horologe in the center, so that anyone looking to see the time must willy-nilly read my name. As

325 for the lettering, look this over carefully and see if you think it is good enough:

HERE LIES
C. POMPEIUS TRIMALCHIO,
A SECOND MAECENAS.[9]
HE WAS NOMINATED [TO THE AUGUSTAN COLLEGE] IN HIS ABSENCE.
330 HE MIGHT HAVE BEEN A MEMBER OF EVERY [COMMITTEE] IN ROME,
BUT DECLINED.
PIOUS, BRAVE, HONORABLE, HE ROSE FROM THE RANKS.
WITHOUT LEARNING OR EDUCATION
HE LEFT A MILLION OF MONEY BEHIND HIM.
335 FAREWELL:
GO AND DO THOU LIKEWISE!"

When he had finished reading this document, Trimalchio fell to weeping copiously. Fortunata wept too; so did Habinnas; so did the servants; in fact, the whole household filled the room with lamentations. Indeed I was beginning to
340 weep myself, when Trimalchio resumed. "Well!" said he, "as we know we've got to die, why not make the most of life? As I should like to see you all happy, let's jump into the bath. I guarantee you'll be none the worse; it's as hot as an oven."

"Right! right!" cried Habinnas, "to make two days out of one; nothing I should like better," and springing up barefoot as he was, he followed Trimalchio,
345 who led the way, clapping his hands.

---

[8]**Petraites' fights:** Petraites was a popular gladiator.
[9]**Maecenas:** a wealthy patron of poets

For myself I said, turning to Ascyltos, "What think you, Ascyltos? as for me, to look at a bath now would kill me."

"Let's consent," he replied; "and then, as they are making for the bathroom, escape in the confusion."

350 This being agreed upon, Giton led the way through the colonnade, and we reached the house-door, where the watchdog greeted us with such furious barking that Ascyltos tumbled into the tank in sheer terror. I too, tipsy as I was, and having been once already scared at a painted dog, got dragged in myself in helping him out of the water.

355 At this point our mirth was disturbed, for a rather good-looking slave boy having entered along with a new lot of domestics, Trimalchio laid hold of him and started kissing him over and over again. At this Fortunata, to assert "her lawful and equitable rights" (as she put it), began abusing her husband, calling him an abomination and a disgrace, that he could not restrain his filthy passions, ending

360 up with the epithet "dog!" Trimalchio for his part was so enraged at her railing that he hurled a wine-cup in his wife's face. Fortunata screamed out, as if she had lost an eye, and clapped her trembling hands to her countenance. Scintilla was equally alarmed, and sheltered her shuddering friend in her bosom. At the same time an officious attendant applied a pitcher of cold water to her cheek, over

365 which the poor lady drooped and fell a-sighing and a-sobbing.

"However, not to forget the living, pray, my good friends, enjoy yourselves. I was once what you are now, but my own merits have made me what you see. It's gumption makes a man, all the rest's trash. 'Buy cheap, and sell dear,' that's me; one man will tell you one thing, another another, but I'm just bursting with

370 success. What! crying still, grunty pig? Mark me, I'll give you something worth crying for. But as I was saying, it was my thriftiness raised me to my present position. When first I came from Asia, I was no higher than this candle-stick. I tell you, I used to measure myself by it every day; and the sooner to get a beard under my nose, I would smear my lips with the lamp oil. But I was my master's joy for

375 fourteen years; there's nothing disgraceful in doing your master's bidding. And I satisfied my mistress in the bargain. You know what I mean; I say no more, for I'm none of your boasters.

"Eventually, it so pleased the gods, I found myself king of the castle, and behold! I could twist my master round my finger. To make a long story short, he

380 made me his co-heir with the Emperor, and I came into a senatorial fortune. Still no one is ever satisfied. I longed to be a merchant prince. So, not to be tedious, I built five ships, loaded up with wine,—it was worth its weight in gold just then,—and sent them off to Rome. . . . every one of the ships foundered, and that's a fact. In one day Neptune swallowed me up thirty millions. Do you imagine I gave in? Not I, by

385 my faith! the loss only whetted my appetite, as if it were a mere nothing. I built more ships, bigger and better and luckier, till every one allowed I was a well-plucked one. Nothing venture, nothing win, you know; and a big ship's a big venture. I loaded up again with wine, bacon, beans, perfumery and slaves. Fortunata was a real good wife to me that time; she sold all her jewelry and all her

390 clothes, and laid a hundred gold pieces in my hand; and it proved the leaven of my little property. A thing's soon done, when the gods will it. One voyage I cleared a round ten millions.

"Take my word for it,—Have a penny, good for a penny; have something, and you're thought something. So your humble servant, who was a toad once upon a
395 time, is a king now.

"Meantime, Stichus, just bring out the graveclothes I propose to be buried in; also the unguent, and a taste of the wine I wish to have my bones washed with."

Without a moment's delay, Stichus produced a white shroud and a magistrate's gown into the dining-hall, and asked us to feel if they were made of
400 good wool. Then his master added with a laugh, "Mind, Stichus, mice and moth don't get at them; else I'll have you burned alive. I wish to be buried in all my bravery, that the whole people may call down the blessings on my head." Immediately afterwards he opened a pot of spikenard, and after rubbing us all with the ointment, "I only hope," said he, "it will give me as much pleasure when
405 I'm dead as it does now when I'm alive." Further he ordered the wine vessels to be filled up, telling us to "imagine you are invited guests at my funeral feast."

The thing was getting positively sickening, when Trimalchio, now in a state of disgusting intoxication, commanded a new diversion, a company of horn-blowers, to be introduced; and then stretching himself out along the edge of a couch
410 on a pile of pillows, "Make believe I am dead," he ordered. "Play something fine." Then the horn-blowers struck up a loud funeral dirge. In particular one of these undertaker's men, the most conscientious of the lot, blew so tremendous a fanfare he roused the whole neighborhood. Hereupon the watchman in charge of the surrounding district, thinking Trimalchio's house was on fire, suddenly burst
415 open the door, and rushing in with water and axes, started the much admired confusion usual under such circumstances. For our part, we seized the excellent opportunity thus offered, snapped our fingers in Agamemnon's face, and rushed away helter-skelter just as if we were escaping from a real conflagration.

18. LIVES OF THE TWELVE CAESARS: AUGUSTUS (SELECTIONS)

Suetonius
(70–140 CE)

(trans. by Alexander Thomson and T. Forester)

Suetonius (70–140 CE) was a Roman scholar, writer, and lawyer who served as secretary to the Emperor Hadrian. Although much of his work is lost, Suetonius had a wide literary range, having composed treatises on grammar and rhetoric, biographies of famous literary figures, as well as his best known work, Lives of the Twelve Caesars *which begins with Julius Caesar and ends with Domitian. The biographies, which draw on primary material such as letters and diaries, public speeches and proclamations, as well as hearsay and anecdote, are a rich source of information on the historical era, as well as the personal lives, habits, physical aspects and defects of their subjects. Suetonius' organization of his material, a combination of chronology and topically ordered appreciation of achievement, establishes a model for later biographers (notably Einhard in his* Life of Charlemagne*).*

He lost his father when he was only four years of age; and, in his twelfth year, pronounced a funeral oration in praise of his grandmother Julia. Four years afterwards, having assumed the robe of manhood, he was honoured with several military rewards by Caesar in his African triumph, although he took no part in
5   the war on account of his youth. Upon his uncle's expedition to Spain against the sons of Pompey, he was followed by his nephew, although he was scarcely recovered from a dangerous sickness; and after being shipwrecked at sea, and travelling with very few attendants through roads that were infested with the enemy, he at last came up with him. This activity gave great satisfaction to his
10   uncle, who soon conceived an increasing affection for him, on account of such indications of character. After the subjugation of Spain, while Caesar was meditating an expedition against the Dacians and Parthians, he was sent before him to Apollonia, where he applied himself to his studies; until receiving intelligence that his uncle was murdered, and that he was appointed his heir, he
15   hesitated for some time whether he should call to his aid the legions stationed in the neighborhood; but he abandoned the design as rash and premature. However,

returning to Rome, he took possession of his inheritance, although his mother was apprehensive that such a measure might be attended with danger, and his stepfather, Marcius Philippus, a man of consular rank, very earnestly dissuaded him from it. From this time, collecting together a strong military force, he first held the government in conjunction with Mark Antony and Marcus Lepidus, then with Antony only for nearly twelve years, and at last in his own hands during a period of four and forty.

Having thus given a very short summary of his life, I shall prosecute the several parts of it, not in order of time, but arranging his acts into distinct classes, for the sake of perspicuity. He was engaged in five civil wars, namely those of Modena, Philippi, Perugia, Sicily, and Actium; the first and last of which were against Antony, and the second against Brutus and Cassius; the third against Lucius Antonius, the triumvir's brother, and the fourth against Sextus Pompeius, the son of Cneius Pompeius.

The motive which gave rise to all these wars was the opinion he entertained that both his honour and interest were concerned in revenging the murder of his uncle, and maintaining the state of affairs he had established.

* * *

The alliance between him and Antony, which had always been precarious, often interrupted, and ill cemented by repeated reconciliation, he at last entirely dissolved. And to make it known to the world how far Antony had degenerated from patriotic feelings, he caused a will of his, which had been left at Rome, and in which he had nominated Cleopatra's children, amongst others, as his heirs, to be opened and read in an assembly of the people. . . . And not long afterwards he defeated him in a naval engagement near Actium, which was prolonged to so late an hour, that, after the victory, he was obliged to sleep on board his ship.

From Actium he went to the isle of Samos to winter; but being alarmed with the accounts of a mutiny amongst the soldiers he had selected from the main body of his army sent to Brundisium after the victory, who insisted on their being rewarded for their service and discharged, he returned to Italy. . . .

He remained only twenty-seven days at Brundisium, until the demands of the soldiers were settled, and then went, by way of Asia and Syria, to Egypt, where laying siege to Alexandria, whither Antony had fled with Cleopatra, he made himself master of it in short time. He drove Antony to kill himself, after he had used every effort to obtain conditions of peace, and he saw his corpse. Cleopatra he anxiously wished to save for his triumph; and when she was supposed to have been bit to death by an asp, he sent for the Psylli[1] to endeavor to suck out the poison. He allowed them to be buried together in the same grave, and ordered a mausoleum, begun by themselves, to be completed. The eldest of Antony's two sons by Fulvia he commanded to be taken by force from the statue of Julius Caesar, to which he had fled, after many fruitless supplications for his life, and put him to death. The same fate attended Caesario, Cleopatra's son by Caesar, as he

---

[1]**Psylli**: healers who used lice or leeches.

pretended, who had fled for his life, but was retaken. The children which Antony had by Cleopatra he saved, and brought up and cherished in a manner suitable to
60   their rank, just as if they had been his own relations.

* * *

He conducted in person only two foreign wars; the Dalmatian, whilst he was yet but a youth; and, after Antony's final defeat, the Cantabrian. He was wounded in the former of these wars; in one battle he received a contusion in the right knee from a stone—and in another, he was much hurt in one leg and both arms, by the
65   fall of a bridge. His other wars he carried on by his lieutenants; but occasionally visited the army, in some of the wars of Pannonia and Germany, or remained at no great distance, proceeding from Rome as far as Ravenna, Milan, or Aquileia.

He conquered, however, partly in person, and partly by his lieutenants, Cantabria, Aquitania and Pannonia, Dalmatia, with all Illyricum and Rhaetia,
70   besides the two Alpine nations, the Vindelici and the Salassii. He also checked the incursions of the Dacians, by cutting off three of their generals with vast armies, and drove the Germans beyond the river Elbe; removing two other tribes who submitted, the Ubii and Sicambri, into Gaul, and settling them in the country bordering on the Rhine. Other nations also, which broke into revolt, he reduced to
75   submission. But he never made war upon any nation without just and necessary cause; and was so far from being ambitious either to extend the empire, or advance his own military glory, that he obliged the chiefs of some barbarous tribes to swear in the temple of Mars the Avenger, that they would faithfully observe their engagements, and not violate the peace which they had implored. Of some he
80   demanded a new description of hostages, their women, having found from experience that they cared little for their men when given as hostages; but he always afforded them the means of getting back their hostages whenever they wished it.

Even those who engaged most frequently and with the greatest perfidy in their
85   rebellion, he never punished more severely than by selling their captives, on the terms of their not serving in any neighbouring country, nor being released from their slavery before the expiration of thirty years. By the character which he thus acquired, for virtue and moderation, he induced even the Indians and Parthians, nations before known to the Romans by report only, to solicit his friendship, and
90   that of the Roman people, by ambassadors. The Parthians readily allowed his claim to Armenia; restoring, at his demand, the standards which they had taken from Marcus Crassus and Mark Antony, and offering him hostages besides. Afterwards, when a contest arose between several pretenders to the crown of that kingdom, they refused to acknowledge anyone who was not chosen by him.

* * *

95   In military affairs he made many alterations, introducing some practices entirely new, and reviving others, which had become obsolete. He maintained the strictest discipline among the troops; and would not allow even his lieutenants the liberty to visit their wives, except reluctantly, and in the winter season only. A Roman knight having cut off the thumbs of his two young sons, to render them

-670-

100   incapable of serving in the wars, he exposed both him and his estate to public sale. But upon observing the farmers of the revenue very greedy for the purchase, he assigned him to a freedman of his own, that he might send him into the country, and suffer him to retain his freedom. The tenth legion becoming mutinous, he disbanded it with ignominy; and did the same by some others which petulantly demanded

105   their discharge; withholding from them the rewards usually bestowed on those who had served their stated time in the wars. The cohorts which yielded their ground in time of action, he decimated, and fed with barley. Centurions, as well as common sentinels, who deserted their posts when on guard, he punished with death. For other misdemeanors he inflicted upon them various kinds of disgrace;

110   such as obliging them to stand all day before the praetorium,[2] sometimes in their tunics only, and without their belts, sometimes to carry poles ten feet long, or sods of turf.

* * *

He twice entertained thoughts of restoring the republic; first, immediately after he had crushed Antony, remembering that he had often charged him with

115   being the obstacle to its restoration. The second was in consequence of a long illness, when he sent for the magistrates and the senate to his own house, and delivered them a particular account of the state of the empire. But reflecting at the same time that it would be both hazardous to himself to return to the condition of a private person, and might be dangerous to the public to have the government

120   placed again under the control of the people, he resolved to keep it in his own hands, whether with the better event or intention, is hard to say. His good intentions he often affirmed in private discourse, and also published an edict in which it was declared in the following terms: "May it be permitted me to have the happiness of establishing the commonwealth on a safe and sound basis, and thus

125   enjoy the reward of which I am ambitious, that of being celebrated for moulding it into the form best adapted to present circumstances; so that, on my leaving the world, I may carry with me the hope that the foundations which I have laid for its future government, will stand firm and stable."

The city, which was not built in a manner suitable to the grandeur of the

130   empire, and was liable to inundation of the Tiber, as well as to fires, was so much improved under his administration, that he boasted, not without reason, that he "found it of brick, but left it of marble." He also rendered it secure for the time to come against such disasters, as far as could be effected by human foresight.

A great number of public buildings were erected by him, the most considerable

135   of which were a forum, containing the temple of Mars the Avenger, the temple of Apollo on the Palatine hill, and the temple of Jupiter Tonans in the capitol. The reason of his building a new forum was the vast increase in the population, and the number of causes to be tried in the courts, for which, the two already existing not affording sufficient space, it was thought necessary to have a third. It was

140   therefore opened for public use before the temple of Mars was completely finished;

---

[2]**praetorium**: residence of the Roman governor or general.

and a law was passed, that causes should be tried, and judges chosen by lot, in that place. The temple of Mars was built in fulfillment of a vow made during the war of Philippi, undertaken by him to avenge his father's murder. He ordained that the senate should always assemble there when they met to deliberate

145　respecting wars and triumphs; that hence should be dispatched all those who were sent into the provinces in the command of armies; and that in it those who returned victorious from the wars, should lodge the trophies of their triumphs. He erected the temple of Apollo in that part of his house on the Palatine hill which had been struck with lightning, and which, on that account, the soothsayers declared the

150　God to have chosen. He added porticos to it, with a library of Latin and Greek authors; and when advanced in years, used frequently there to hold the senate, and examine the rolls of the judges.

　　He dedicated the temple to Apollo Tonans, in acknowledgment of his escape from a great danger in his Cantabrian expedition; when, as he was travelling in

155　the night, his litter was struck by lightning, which killed the slave who carried a torch before him. He likewise constructed some public buildings in the name of others; for instance, his grandsons, his wife, and sister. Thus he built the portico and basilica of Lucius and Caius, and the porticos of Livia and Octavia, and the theatre of Marcellus. He also often exhorted other persons of rank to embellish the

160　city by new buildings, or repairing and improving the old, according to their means. In consequence of this recommendation, many were raised; such as the temple of Hercules and the Muses, by Marcus Philippus; a temple of Diana by Lucius Cornificius; the Court of Freedom by Asinius Pollio; a temple of Saturn by Munatius Plancus; a theatre by Cornelius Balbus; an amphitheatre by Statilius

165　Taurus; and several other noble edifices by Marcus Agrippa.

　　He divided the city into regions and districts, ordaining that the annual magistrates should take by lot the charge of the former; and that the latter should be superintended by wardens chosen out of the people of each neighbourhood. He appointed a nightly watch to be on their guard against accidents from fire; and, to

170　prevent the frequent inundation, he widened and cleansed the bed of the Tiber, which had in the course of years been almost dammed up with rubbish, and the channel narrowed by the ruins of houses. To render the approaches to the city more commodious, he took upon himself the charge of repairing the Flaminian way as far as Ariminum, and distributed the repairs of the other roads among several

175　persons who had obtained the honour of a triumph; to be defrayed out of the money arising from the spoils of war. Temples decayed by time, or destroyed by fire, he either repaired or rebuilt and enriched them, as well as many others, with splendid offerings. On a single occasion, he deposited in the cell of the temple of Jupiter Capitolinus, sixteen thousand pounds of gold, with jewels and pearls to

180　the amount of fifty millions of sesterces.

* * *

　　He restored the calendar, which had been corrected by Julius Caesar, but through negligence was again fallen into confusion, to its former regularity; and upon that occasion called the month Sextilis by his own name, August, rather than

-672-

September, in which he was born; because in it he had obtained his first consulship, and all his most considerable victories. He increased the number, dignity, and revenues of the priests, and especially those of the Vestal Virgins. And when, upon the death of one of them, a new one was to be taken, and many persons made interest that their daughters' names might be omitted in the lists for election, he replied with an oath, "If either of my own grand-daughters were old enough, I would have proposed her."

He likewise revived some old religious customs, which had become obsolete; as the augury of public health, the office of high priest of Jupiter, the religious solemnity of the Lupercalia, with the Secular, and Compitalian games. He prohibited young boys from running on the Lupercalia; and in respect of the Secular games, issued an order, that no young persons of either sex should appear at any public diversions in the night-time, unless in the company of some elderly relation. He ordered the household gods to be decked twice a year with spring and summer flowers, in the Compitalian festival.

Next to the immortal gods, he paid the highest honours to the memory of those generals who had raised the Roman state from its low origin to the highest pitch of grandeur. He accordingly repaired or rebuilt the public edifices erected by them; preserving the former inscriptions, and placing statues of them all, with triumphal emblems, in both the porticos of his forum, issuing an edict on the occasion, in which he made the following declaration: "My design in so doing is, that the Roman people may require from me, and all succeeding princes, a conformity to those illustrious examples." He likewise removed the statue of Pompey from the senate-house, in which Caius Caesar had been killed, and placed it under a marble arch, fronting the palace attached to Pompey's theatre.

He corrected many ill practices, which, to the detriment of the public, had either survived the licentious habits of the late civil wars, or else originated in the long peace. Bands of robbers shewed themselves openly, completely armed, under colour of self-defence; and in different parts of the country, travellers, freemen and slaves without distinction, were forcibly carried off, and kept to work in the houses of correction. Several associations were formed under the specious name of a new college, which banded together for the perpetration of all kinds of villany. The banditti he quelled by establishing posts of soldiers in suitable stations for the purpose; the houses of correction were subjected to a strict superintendence; all associations, those only excepted which were of ancient standing, and recognised by the laws, were dissolved.

He burnt all the notes of those who had been a long time in arrears with the treasury, as being the principal source of vexatious suits and prosecutions. Places in the city claimed by the public where the right was doubtful, he adjudged to the actual possessors. He struck out of the list of criminals the names of those over whom prosecutions had been long impending, where nothing further was intended by the informers than to gratify their own malice, by seeing their enemies humiliated; laying it down as a rule, that if anyone chose to renew a prosecution, he should incur the risk of the punishment which he sought to inflict. And that

230 crimes might not escape punishment, nor business be neglected by delay, he ordered the courts to sit during the thirty days which were spent in celebrating honorary games. . . .

He was himself assiduous in his functions as a judge, and would sometimes prolong his sittings even into the night: if he were indisposed, his litter was placed before the tribunal, or he administered justice reclining on his couch at home; displaying always not only the greatest attention, but extreme lenity. To save a
235 culprit, who evidently appeared guilty of parricide, from the extreme penalty of being sewn up in a sack, because none were punished in that manner but such as confessed the fact, he is said to have interrogated him thus: "Surely you did not kill your father, did you?" And when, in a trial of a cause about a forged will, all those who had signed it were liable to the penalty of the Cornelian law, he
240 ordered that his colleagues on the tribunal should not only be furnished with the two tablets by which they decided, "guilty or not guilty," but with a third likewise, ignoring the offence of those who should appear to have given their signatures through any deception or mistake. All appeals in causes between inhabitants of Rome, he assigned every year to the praetor of the city; and where
245 provincials were concerned, to men of consular rank, to one of whom the business of each province was referred.

Some laws he abrogated, and he made some new ones; such as the sumptuary law,[3] that relating to adultery and the violation of chastity, the law against bribery in elections, and likewise that for the encouragement of marriage. Having
250 been more severe in his reform of this law than the rest, he found the people utterly averse to submit to it, unless the penalties were abolished or mitigated, besides allowing an interval of three years after a wife's death, and increasing the premiums on marriage. . . . But finding that the force of the law was eluded by marrying girls under the age of puberty and by frequent change of wives, he limited
255 the time for consummation after espousals, and imposed restrictions on divorce.

By two separate scrutinies he reduced to their former number and splendor the senate, which had been swamped by a disorderly crowd; for they were now more than a thousand and some of them very mean persons, who, after Caesar's death, had been chosen by dint of interest and bribery, so that they had the
260 nickname of Orcini[4] among the people. The first of these scrutinies was left to themselves, each senator naming another; but the last was conducted by himself and Agrippa. On this occasion he is believed to have taken his seat as he presided, with a coat of mail under his tunic, and a sword by his side, and with ten of the stoutest men of senatorial rank, who were his friends, standing round his chair.
265 Cordus Cremutius relates that no senator was suffered to approach him, except singly, and after having his bosom searched [for secreted daggers]. Some he obliged to have the grace of declining the office; these he allowed to retain the privileges of

---

[3]sumptuary law: regulating extravagent expenditure on food or clothing
[4]Orcini: derived from the Latin for whale, designating ogres of horrid form and habit.

wearing the distinguishing dress, occupying the seats at the solemn spectacles, and of feasting publicly, reserved to the senatorial order.

270   That those who were chosen and approved of, might perform their functions under more solemn obligations, and with less inconvenience, he ordered that every senator, before he took his seat in the house, should pay his devotions, with an offering of frankincense and wine, at the altar of that God in whose temple the senate then assembled, and that their stated meetings should be only twice in the
275   month, namely, on the calends and ides;[5] and that in the months of September and October, a certain number only, chosen by lot, which as the law required to give validity to a decree, should be required to attend. For himself, he resolved to choose every six months a new council, with whom he might consult previously upon such affairs as he judged proper at any time to lay before the full senate. He
280   also took the votes of the senators upon any subject of importance, not according to custom, nor in regular order, but as he pleased; that every one might hold himself ready to give his opinion, other than a mere vote of assent.

* * *

Having thus regulated the city and its concerns, he augmented the population of Italy by planting in it no less than twenty-eight colonies, and greatly improved
285   it by public works, and a beneficial application of revenues. In rights and privileges, he rendered it in a measure equal to the city itself, by inventing a new kind of suffrage, which the principal officers and magistrates of the colonies might take at home, and forward under seal to the city, against the time of the elections. To increase the number of persons of condition, and of children among the lower
290   ranks, he granted the petitions of all those who requested the honour of doing military service on horseback as knights, provided their demands were seconded by the recommendation of the town in which they lived; and when he visited the several districts of Italy, he distributed a thousand sesterces a head to such of the lower class as presented him with sons or daughters.

295   The more important provinces, which could not with ease or safety be entrusted to the government of annual magistrates, he reserved for his own administration: the rest he distributed by lot amongst the proconsuls: but sometimes he made exchanges, and frequently visited most of both kinds in person. Some cities in alliance with Rome, but which by their great licentiousness were
300   hastening to ruin, he deprived of their independence. Others, which were much in debt, he relieved, and rebuilt such as had been destroyed by earthquakes. To those that could produce any instance of their having deserved well of the Roman people, he presented the freedom of Latium, or even that of the City. There is not, I believe, a province, except Africa and Sardinia, which he did not visit. . . .

305   Kingdoms, of which he had made himself master by the right of conquest, a few only excepted, he either restored to their former possessors, or conferred upon aliens. Between kings in alliance with Rome, he encouraged most intimate union;

---

[5]**calends and ides:** the first day, and the mid-point (either the 15th or 13th) of Roman months, respectively.

being always ready to promote or favour any proposal of marriage or friendship
amongst them; and, indeed, treated them all with the same consideration, as if they
310 were members and parts of the empire. To such of them as were minors or lunatics
he appointed guardians, until they arrived at age, or recovered their senses; and
the sons of many of them he brought up and educated with his own.

With respect to the army, he distributed the legions and auxiliary troops
throughout the several provinces. He stationed a fleet at Misenum, and another at
315 Ravenna, for the protection of the Upper and Lower Seas. A certain number of the
forces were selected, to occupy the posts in the city, and partly for his own bodyguard; but he dismissed the Spanish guard, which he retained about him until the
fall of Antony; and also the Germans, whom he had amongst his guards, until the
defeat of Varus. Yet he never permitted a greater force than three cohorts in the
320 city, and had no (praetorian) camps. The rest he quartered in the neighbourhood of
the nearest towns, in winter and summer camps.

All the troops throughout the empire he reduced to one fixed model with
regard to their pay and their pensions; determining these according to their rank in
the army, the time they had served, and their private means; so that after their
325 discharge, they might not be tempted by age or necessities to join the agitators for a
revolution. For the purpose of providing a fund always ready to meet their pay
and pensions, he instituted a military exchequer, and appropriated new taxes to
that object. In order to obtain the earliest intelligence of what was passing in the
provinces, he established posts, consisting at first of young men stationed at
330 moderate distances along the military roads, and afterwards of regular couriers
with fast vehicles; which appeared to him the most commodious, because the
persons who were the bearers of dispatches, written on the spot, might then be
questioned about the business, as occasion occurred.

* * *

He always abhorred the title of *Lord*, as ill-omened and offensive. And when,
335 in a play, performed at the theatre, at which he was present, these words were
introduced, "O just and gracious lord," and the whole company, with joyful
acclamations, testified their approbation of them, as applied to him, he instantly
put a stop to their indecent flattery, by waving his hand, and frowning sternly,
and next day publicly declared his displeasure, in a proclamation. He never
340 afterwards would suffer himself to be addressed in that manner, even by his own
children or grand-children, either in jest or earnest, and forbade them the use of all
such complimentary expressions to one another.

He rarely entered any city or town, or departed from it, except in the evening
or the night, to avoid giving any person the trouble of complimenting him. During
345 his consulships, he commonly walked the streets on foot; but at other times, rode in
a closed carriage. He admitted to court even plebeians, in common with people of
the higher ranks; receiving the petitions of those who approached him with so
much affability, that he once jocosely rebuked a man, by telling him, "You present
your memorial with as much hesitation as if you were offering money to an
350 elephant." On senate days, he used to pay his respects to the Conscript Fathers

only in the house, addressing them each by name as they sat, without any prompter; and on his departure, he bade each of them farewell, while they retained their seats. In the same manner, he maintained with many of them a constant intercourse of mutual civilities, giving them his company upon occasions of any particular festivity in their families; until he became advanced in years, and was incommoded by the crowd at a wedding.

* * *

How much he was beloved for his worthy conduct in all these respects, it is easy to imagine. I say nothing of the decrees of the senate in his honour, which may seem to have resulted from compulsion or deference. The Roman knights voluntarily, and with one accord, always celebrated his birth for two days together; and all ranks of the people, yearly, in performance of a vow they had made, threw a piece of money into the Curtian lake, as an offering for his welfare. They likewise, on the calends of January, presented for his acceptance new-year's gifts in the capitol, though he was not present: with which donations he purchased some costly images of the Gods, which he erected in several streets of the city; as that of Apollo Sandaliarius, Jupiter Tragoedus, and others.

When his house on the Palatine hill was accidentally destroyed by fire, the veteran soldiers, the judges, the tribes, and even the people individually, contributed, according to the ability of each, for rebuilding it; but he would accept only some small portion out of the several sums collected, and refused to take from any one person more than a single denarius. Upon his return home from any of the provinces, they attended him not only with joyful acclamations, but with songs. It is also remarked, that as often as he entered the city, the infliction of punishment was suspended for the time.

The whole body of the people, upon a sudden impulse, and with unanimous consent, offered him the title of Father of His Country. It was announced to him first at Antium, by a deputation from the people, and upon his declining the honour, they repeated their offer on his return to Rome, in a full theatre, when they were crowned with laurel. The senate soon afterwards adopted the proposal.

* * *

Having thus given an account of the manner in which he filled his public offices, both civil and military, and his conduct in the government of the empire, both in peace and war, I shall now describe his private and domestic life.

* * *

He ate sparingly (for I must not omit even this), and commonly used a plain diet. He was particularly fond of coarse bread, small fishes, new cheese made of cow's milk, and green figs of the sort which bear fruit twice a year. He did not wait for supper, but took food at any time, and in any place, when he had an appetite. The following passages relative to this subject, I have transcribed from his letters. "I ate a little bread and some small dates, in my carriage." Again. "In returning home from the palace in my litter, I ate an ounce of bread, and a few raisins." Again. "No Jew, my dear Tiberius, ever keeps such strict fast upon the Sabbath, as I have to-day; for while in the bath, and after the first hour of the

night, I only ate two biscuits, before I began to be rubbed with oil." From this great indifference about his diet, he sometimes supped by himself, before his company began, or after they had finished, and would not touch a morsel at table with his
395   guests.

He was by nature extremely sparing in the use of wine. Cornelius Nepos says that he used to drink only three times at supper in the camp at Modena; and when he indulged himself the most, he never exceeded a pint; or if he did, his stomach rejected it. Of all wines, he gave preference to the Rhaetian, but scarcely ever
400   drank any in the day-time. Instead of drinking, he used to take a piece of bread dipped in cold water, or a slice of cucumber, or some leaves of lettuce, or a green, sharp, juicy apple.

After a slight repast at noon, he used to seek repose, dressed as he was, and with his shoes on, his feet covered, and his hand held before his eyes. After supper
405   he commonly withdrew to his study, a small closet, where he sat late, until he had put down in his diary all or most of the remaining transactions of the day, which he had not before registered. He would then go to bed, but never slept above seven hours at most, and that not without interruption; for he would wake three or four times during that time. If he could not again fall asleep, as sometimes happened, he
410   called for some one to read or tell stories to him, until he became drowsy, and then his sleep was usually protracted till after day-break. He never liked to lie awake in the dark, without somebody to sit by him. Very early rising was apt to disagree with him. On which account, if he was obliged to rise betimes, for any civil or religious functions, in order to guard as much as possible against the
415   inconvenience resulting from it, he used to lodge in some apartment near the spot, belonging to any of his attendants. If at any time a fit of drowsiness seized him in passing along the streets, his litter was set down while he snatched a few moments' sleep.

In person he was handsome and graceful, through every period of his life. But
420   he was negligent in his dress; and so careless about dressing his hair, that he usually had it done in great haste by several barbers at a time. His beard he sometimes clipped, and sometimes shaved; and either read or wrote during the operation. His countenance, either when discoursing or silent, was so calm and serene that a Gaul of the first rank declared amongst his friends that he was so
425   softened by it, as to be restrained from throwing him down a precipice, in his passage over the Alps, when he had been admitted to approach him, under pretense of conferring with him. His eyes were bright and piercing; and he was willing it should be thought that there was something of a divine vigour in them. He was likewise not a little pleased to see people, upon his looking stedfastly at them,
430   lower their countenances, as if the sun shone in their eyes. But in his old age, he saw very imperfectly with his left eye. His teeth were thin set, small and scaly, his hair a little curled, and inclining to a yellow color. His eye-brows met; his ears were small, and he had an aquiline nose. His complexion was betwixt brown and fair; his stature but low; though Julius Marathus, his freedman, says he was five
435   feet and nine inches in height. This, however, was so much concealed by the just

proportion of his limbs that it was only perceivable upon comparison with some taller person standing by him.

He is said to have been born with many spots upon his breast and belly, answering to the figure, order, and number of the stars in the constellation of the
440   Bear. He had besides several callosities resembling scars, occasioned by an itching in his body, and the constant and violent use of the strigil in being rubbed. He had a weakness in his left hip, thigh, and leg, insomuch that he often halted on that side; but he received much benefit from the use of sand and reeds. He likewise sometimes found the fore-finger of his right hand so weak that, when it was
445   benumbed and contracted with cold, to use it in writing he was obliged to have recourse to a circular piece of horn. He had occasionally a complaint in the bladder; but upon voiding some stones in his urine, he was relieved from that pain.

IV: EARLY MIDDLE AGES

19. THE CONFESSIONS (SELECTIONS)

Augustine of Hippo
(354–430 CE)

(trans. by Albert C. Outler)

Augustine stands as one of the greatest of the Church Fathers, shaping Christian doctrine and spiritual outlook for the next thousand years, and thus earning the epithet "architect of the Middle Ages." By experience and intellect, he represents the last of the great classical writers trained in logic and rhetoric, and the first of the great medieval theologians recognizing human weakness and the absolute necessity of God's Grace. His theology is informed by his own long struggle to achieve spiritual repose which is recorded in his Confessions, *composed ten years after the fact when he was appointed Bishop of Hippo. The autobiography, the first known in the West, represents his first great teaching as bishop by opening his own life for examination; he establishes the metaphor of life being a journey with God as guide and goal. Crafted along biblical lines, it is a confession of his sinful past, a profession of his profound faith, and a theology of a caring, providential God.*

BOOK ONE

In God's searching presence, Augustine undertakes to plumb the depths of his memory to trace the mysterious pilgrimage of grace which his life has been—and to praise God for his constant and omnipotent grace. In a mood of sustained prayer, he recalls what he can of his infancy, his learning to speak, and his childhood experiences in school. He concludes with a paean of grateful praise to God.

"Great art thou, O Lord, and greatly to be praised; great is thy power, and infinite is thy wisdom." And man desires to praise thee, for he is a part of thy creation; he bears his mortality about with him and carries the evidence of his sin and the proof that thou dost resist the proud. Still he desires to praise thee, this man who is only a small part of thy creation. Thou hast prompted him, that he should delight to praise thee, for thou hast made us for thyself and restless is our heart until it comes to rest in thee. Grant me, O Lord, to know and understand whether first to invoke thee or to praise thee; whether first to know thee or call upon thee. But who can invoke thee, knowing thee not? For he who knows thee not may invoke thee as another than thou art. It may be that we should invoke thee

in order that we may come to know thee. But "how shall they call on him in whom they have not believed? Or how shall they believe without a preacher?" Now, "they shall praise the Lord who seek him," for "those who seek shall find him,"
15 and, finding him, shall praise him. I will seek thee, O Lord, and call upon thee. I call upon thee, O Lord, in my faith which thou hast given me, which thou hast inspired in me through the humanity of thy Son, and through the ministry of thy preacher.

Who shall bring me to rest in thee? Who will send thee into my heart so to
20 overwhelm it that my sins shall be blotted out and I may embrace thee, my only good? What art thou to me? Have mercy that I may speak. What am I to thee that thou shouldst command me to love thee, and if I do it not, art angry and threatenest vast misery?. . . . The house of my soul is too narrow for thee to come in to me; let it be enlarged by thee. It is in ruins; do thou restore it. There is much about it which
25 must offend thy eyes; I confess and know it. But who will cleanse it? Or, to whom shall I cry but to thee? "Cleanse thou me from my secret faults," O Lord, "and keep back thy servant from strange sins." "I believe, and therefore do I speak." But thou, O Lord, thou knowest. Have I not confessed my transgressions unto thee, O my God; and hast thou not put away the iniquity of my heart? I do not contend in
30 judgment with thee, who art truth itself; and I would not deceive myself, lest my iniquity lie even to itself. I do not, therefore, contend in judgement with thee, for "if thou, Lord, shouldst mark iniquities, O Lord, who shall stand?"

Still, dust and ashes as I am, allow me to speak before thy mercy. Allow me to speak, for, behold, it is to thy mercy that I speak and not to a man who scorns me.
35 Yet perhaps even thou mightest scorn me; but when thou dost turn and attend to me, thou wilt have mercy upon me. For what do I wish to say, O Lord my God, but that I know not whence I came hither into this life-in-death. Or should I call it death-in-life? I do not know. And yet the consolations of thy mercy have sustained me from the very beginning, as I have heard from my fleshly parents, from whom and
40 in whom thou didst form me in time—for I cannot myself remember. Thus even though they sustained me by the consolation of woman's milk, neither my mother nor my nurses filled their own breasts but thou, through them, didst give me the food of infancy according to thy ordinance and thy bounty which underlie all things. For it was thou who didst cause me not to want more than thou gavest and
45 it was thou who gavest to those who nourished me the will to give me what thou didst give them. And they, by an instinctive affection, were willing to give me what thou hadst supplied abundantly. It was, indeed, good for them that my good should come through them, though, in truth, it was not from them but by them. For it is from thee, O God, that all good things come—and from my God is all my health. This is
50 what I have since learned, as thou hast made it abundantly clear by all that I have seen thee give, both to me and to those around me. For even at the very first I knew how to suck, to lie quiet when I was full, and to cry when in pain—nothing more.

Afterward I began to laugh—at first in my sleep, then when waking. For this I have been told about myself and I believe it—though I cannot remember it—for I
55 see the same things in other infants. Then, little by little, I realized where I was

and wished to tell my wishes to those who might satisfy them, but I could not! For my wants were inside me, and they were outside, and they could not by any power of theirs come into my soul. And so I would fling my arms and legs about and cry, making the few and feeble gestures that I could, though indeed the signs were not much like what I inwardly desired and when I was not satisfied—either from not being understood or because what I got was not good for me—I grew indignant that my elders were not subject to me and that those on whom I actually had no claim did not wait on me as slaves—and I avenged myself on them by crying. That infants are like this, I have myself been able to learn by watching them; and they, though they knew me not, have shown me better what I was like than my own nurses who knew me.

"Hear me, O God! Woe to the sins of men!" When a man cries thus, thou showest him mercy, for thou didst create the man but not the sin in him. Who brings to remembrance the sins of my infancy? For in thy sight there is none free from sin, not even the infant who has lived but a day upon this earth. Who brings this to my remembrance? Does not each little one, in whom I now observe what I no longer remember of myself? In what ways, in that time, did I sin? Was it that I cried for the breast? If I should now so cry—not indeed for the breast, but for food suitable to my condition—I should be most justly laughed at and rebuked. What I did then deserved rebuke but, since I could not understand those who rebuked me, neither custom nor common sense permitted me to be rebuked. As we grow we root out and cast away from us such childish habits. Yet I have not seen anyone who is wise who cast away the good when trying to purge the bad. Nor was it good, even in that time, to strive to get by crying what, if it had been given me, would have been hurtful; or to be bitterly indignant at those who, because they were older—not slaves, either, but free—and wiser than I, would not indulge my capricious desires. Was it a good thing for me to try, by struggling as hard as I could, to harm them for not obeying me, even when it would have done me harm to have been obeyed? Thus, the infant's innocence lies in the weakness of his body and not in the infant mind. I have myself observed a baby to be jealous, though it could not speak; it was livid as it watched another infant at the breast.

Who is ignorant of this?. . . .

I am loath to dwell on this part of my life of which, O Lord, I have no remembrance, about which I must trust the word of others and what I can surmise from observing other infants, even if such guesses are trustworthy. For it lies in the deep murk of my forgetfulness and thus is like the period which I passed in my mother's womb. But if "I was conceived in iniquity, and in sin my mother nourished me in her womb," where, I pray thee, O my God, where, O Lord, or when was I, thy servant, ever innocent? But see now, I pass over that period, for what have I to do with a time from which I can recall no memories?

And yet I sinned, O Lord my God, thou ruler and creator of all natural things—but of sins only the ruler—I sinned, O Lord my God, in acting against the precepts of my parents and of those teachers. For this learning which they wished me to acquire no matter what their motives were—I might have put to good account

100 afterward. I disobeyed them, not because I had chosen a better way, but from a
sheer love of play. I loved the vanity of victory, and I loved to have my ears tickled
with lying fables, which made them itch even more ardently, and a similar
curiosity glowed more and more in my eyes for the shows and sports of my elders.

Even as a boy I had heard of eternal life promised to us through the humility
105 of the Lord our God, who came down to visit us in our pride, and I was signed
with the sign of his cross, and was seasoned with his salt even from the womb of
my mother, who greatly trusted in thee. Thou didst see, O Lord, how, once, while I
was still a child, I was suddenly seized with stomach pains and was at the point
of death—thou didst see, O my God, for even then thou wast my keeper, with what
110 agitation and with what faith I solicited from the piety of my mother and from thy
Church (which is the mother of us all) the baptism of thy Christ, my Lord and my
God. The mother of my flesh was much perplexed, for, with a heart pure in thy
faith, she was always in deep travail for my eternal salvation. If I had not quickly
recovered, she would have provided forthwith for my initiation and washing by
115 thy life-giving sacraments, confessing thee, O Lord Jesus, for the forgiveness of
sins. So my cleansing was deferred, as if it were inevitable that, if I should live, I
would be further polluted; and, further, because the guilt contracted by sin after
baptism would be still greater and more perilous.

Thus, at that time, I "believed" along with my mother and the whole
120 household, except my father. But he did not overcome the influence of my mother's
piety in me, nor did he prevent my believing in Christ, although he had not yet
believed in him. For it was her desire, O my God, that I should acknowledge thee
as my Father rather than him. In this thou didst aid her to overcome her husband,
to whom, though his superior, she yielded obedience. In this way she also yielded
125 obedience to thee, who dost so command.

But in this time of childhood—which was far less dreaded for me than my
adolescence—I had no love of learning, and hated to be driven to it. Yet I was
driven to it just the same, and good was done for me, even though I did not do it
well, for I would not have learned if I had not been forced to it. For no man does
130 well against his will, even if what he does is a good thing. Neither did they who
forced me do well, but the good that was done me came from thee, my God. For they
did not care about the way in which I would use what they forced me to learn, and
took it for granted that it was to satisfy the inordinate desires of a rich beggary
and a shameful glory. But thou, Lord, by whom the hairs of our head are
135 numbered, didst use for my good the error of all who pushed me on to study: but my
error in not being willing to learn thou didst use for my punishment. And I—
though so small a boy yet so great a sinner—was not punished without warrant.
Thus by the instrumentality of those who did not do well, thou didst well for me;
and by my own sin thou didst justly punish me. For it is even as thou hast
140 ordained: that every inordinate affection brings on its own punishment.

. . . I was compelled to learn about the wanderings of a certain Aeneas,
oblivious of my own wanderings, and to weep for Dido dead, who slew herself
for love. And all this while I bore with dry eyes my own wretched self dying to

145 thee, O God, my life, in the midst of these things. For what can be more wretched than the wretch who has no pity upon himself, who sheds tears over Dido, dead for the love of Aeneas, but who sheds no tears for his own death in not loving thee, O God, light of my heart, and bread of the inner mouth of my soul, O power that links together my mind with my inmost thoughts? I did not love thee, and thus committed fornication against thee. Those around me, also sinning, thus cried out:
150 "Well done! Well done!"

However, O Lord, to thee most excellent and most good, thou Architect and Governor of the universe, thanks would be due thee, O our God, even if thou hadst not willed that I should survive my boyhood. For I existed even then; I lived and felt and was solicitous about my own well-being—a trace of that most mysterious
155 unity from whence I had my being. I kept watch, by my inner sense, over the integrity of my outer senses, and even in these trifles and also in my thoughts about trifles, I learned to take pleasure in truth. I was averse to being deceived; I had a vigorous memory; I was gifted with the power of speech, was softened by friendship, shunned sorrow, meanness, ignorance. Is not such an animated
160 creature as this wonderful and praiseworthy? But all these are gifts of my God; I did not give them to myself.

Moreover, they are good, and they all together constitute myself. Good, then, is he that made me, and he is my God; and before him will I rejoice exceedingly for every good gift which, even as a boy, I had. But herein lay my sin, that it was not
165 in him, but in his creatures—myself and the rest—that I sought for pleasures, honors, and truths. And I fell thereby into sorrows, troubles, and errors.

BOOK TWO

Augustine concentrates here on his sixteenth year, a year of idleness, lust, and adolescent mischief. The memory of stealing some pears prompts a deep probing of the motives and aims of sinful acts. "I became to myself a wasteland."

I wish now to review in memory my past wickedness and the carnal corruptions of my soul—not because I still love them, but that I may love thee, O my God. For love of thy love I do this, recalling in the bitterness of self-examination my wicked ways, that thou mayest grow sweet to me, thou sweetness
5 without deception! Thou sweetness happy and assured! Thus thou mayest gather me up out of those fragments in which I was torn to pieces, while I turned away from thee, O Unity, and lost myself among "the many." For as I became a youth, I longed to be satisfied with worldly things, and I dared to grow wild in a succession of various and shadowy loves. My form wasted away, and I became
10 corrupt in thy eyes, yet I was still pleasing to my own eyes—and eager to please the eyes of men.

But what was it that delighted me save to love and to be loved? Still I did not keep the moderate way of the love of mind to mind—the bright path of friendship. Instead, the mists of passion steamed up out of the puddly concupiscence of the

15   flesh, and the hot imagination of puberty, and they so obscured and overcast my heart that I was unable to distinguish pure affection from unholy desire.

Where was I, and how far was I exiled from the delights of thy house, in that sixteenth year of the age of my flesh, when the madness of lust held full sway in me—that madness which grants indulgence to human shamelessness, even though it
20   is forbidden by thy laws—and I gave myself entirely to it? Meanwhile, my family took no care to save me from ruin by marriage, for their sole care was that I should learn how to make a powerful speech and become a persuasive orator.

Now, in that year my studies were interrupted. I had come back from Madaura, a neighboring city where I had gone to study grammar and rhetoric; and
25   the money for a further term at Carthage was being got together for me. This project was more a matter of my father's ambition than of his means, for he was only a poor citizen of Tagaste.

To whom am I narrating all this? Not to thee, O my God, but to my own kind in thy presence—to that small part of the human race who may chance to come
30   upon these writings. And to what end? That I and all who read them may understand what depths there are from which we are to cry unto thee. For what is more surely heard in thy ear than a confessing heart and a faithful life?

Who did not extol and praise my father, because he went quite beyond his means to supply his son with the necessary expenses for a far journey in the
35   interest of his education? For many far richer citizens did not do so much for their children. Still, this same father troubled himself not at all as to how I was progressing toward thee nor how chaste I was, just so long as I was skillful in speaking—no matter how barren I was to thy tillage, O God, who art the one true and good Lord of my heart, which is thy field.

40   During that sixteenth year of my age, I lived with my parents, having a holiday from school for a time—this idleness imposed upon me by my parents' straitened finances. The thornbushes of lust grew rank about my head, and there was no hand to root them out. Indeed, when my father saw me one day at the baths and perceived that I was becoming a man, and was showing the signs of
45   adolescence, he joyfully told my mother about it as if already looking forward to grandchildren, rejoicing in that sort of inebriation in which the world so often forgets thee, its Creator, and falls in love with thy creature instead of thee—the inebriation of that invisible wine of a perverted will which turns and bows down to infamy. But in my mother's breast thou hadst already begun to build thy temple
50   and the foundation of thy holy habitation—whereas my father was only a catechumen, and that but recently. She was, therefore, startled with a holy fear and trembling: for though I had not yet been baptized, she feared those crooked ways in which they walk who turn their backs to thee and not their faces.

What is worse, I took pleasure in [. . .] exploits, not for the pleasure's sake
55   only but mostly for praise. What is worthy of vituperation except vice itself? Yet I made myself out worse than I was, in order that I might not go lacking for praise. And when in anything I had not sinned as the worst ones in the group, I would still say that I had done what I had not done, in order not to appear contemptible

60   because I was more innocent than they; and not to drop in their esteem because I was more chaste.

The Pear Tree

Theft is punished by thy law, O Lord, and by the law written in men's hearts, which not even ingrained wickedness can erase. For what thief will tolerate another thief stealing from him? Even a rich thief will not tolerate a poor thief who is driven to theft by want. Yet I had a desire to commit robbery, and did so,
65   compelled to it by neither hunger nor poverty, but through a contempt for well-doing and a strong impulse to iniquity. For I pilfered something which I already had in sufficient measure, and of much better quality. I did not desire to enjoy what I stole, but only the theft and the sin itself.

There was a pear tree close to our own vineyard, heavily laden with fruit,
70   which was not tempting either for its color or for its flavor. Late one night—having prolonged our games in the streets until then, as our bad habit was—a group of young scoundrels, and I among them, went to shake and rob this tree. We carried off a huge load of pears, not to eat ourselves, but to dump out to the hogs, after barely tasting some of them ourselves.
75   Doing this pleased us all the more because it was forbidden. Such was my heart, O God, such was my heart—which thou didst pity even in that bottomless pit. Behold, now let my heart confess to thee what it was seeking there, when I was being gratuitously wanton, having no inducement to evil but the evil itself. It was foul, and I loved it. I loved my own undoing. I loved my error not that for
80   which I erred but the error itself. A depraved soul, falling away from security in thee to destruction in itself, seeking nothing from the shameful deed but shame itself.

What was it in you, O theft of mine, that I, poor wretch, doted on—you deed of darkness—in that sixteenth year of my age? Beautiful you were not, for you
85   were a theft. But are you anything at all, so that I could analyze the case with you? Those pears that we stole were fair to the sight because they were thy creation, O Beauty beyond compare, O Creator of all, O thou good God—God the highest good and my true good. Those pears were truly pleasant to the sight, but it was not for them that my miserable soul lusted, for I had an abundance of better
90   pears. I stole those simply that I might steal, for, having stolen them, I threw them away. My sole gratification in them was my own sin, which I was pleased to enjoy; for, if any one of these pears entered my mouth, the only good flavor it had was my sin in eating it. And now, O Lord my God, I ask what it was in that theft of mine that caused me such delight; for behold it had no beauty of its own.
95   Thus the soul commits fornication when she is turned from thee, and seeks apart from thee what she cannot find pure and untainted until she returns to thee.

BOOK THREE

The story of his student days in Carthage, his discovery of Cicero's Hortensius, the enkindling of his philosophical interest, his infatuation with the Manichean heresy, and his mother's dream which foretold his eventual return to the true faith and to God.

I came to Carthage, where a caldron of unholy loves was seething and bubbling all around me. I was not in love as yet, but I was in love with love; and, from a hidden hunger, I hated myself for not feeling more intensely a sense of hunger. I was looking for something to love, for I was in love with loving, and I

5   hated security and a smooth way, free from snares. Within me I had a dearth of that inner food which is thyself, my God—although that dearth caused me no hunger. And I remained without any appetite for incorruptible food—not because I was already filled with it, but because the emptier I became the more I loathed it. Because of this my soul was unhealthy; and, full of sores, it exuded itself forth,

10   itching to be scratched by scraping on the things of the senses. Yet, had these things no soul, they would certainly not inspire our love.

To love and to be loved was sweet to me, and all the more when I gained the enjoyment of the body of the person I loved. Thus I polluted the spring of friendship with the filth of concupiscence and I dimmed its luster with the slime of

15   lust. Yet, foul and unclean as I was, I still craved, in excessive vanity, to be thought elegant and urbane. And I did fall precipitately into the love I was longing for. My God, my mercy, with how much bitterness didst thou, out of thy infinite goodness, flavor that sweetness for me! For I was not only beloved but also I secretly reached the climax of enjoyment; and yet I was joyfully bound with

20   troublesome tics, so that I could be scourged with the burning iron rods of jealousy, suspicion, fear, anger, and strife.

Stage plays also captivated me, with their sights full of the images of my own miseries: fuel for my own fire. Now, why does a man like to be made sad by viewing doleful and tragic scenes, which he himself could not by any means

25   endure? Yet, as a spectator, he wishes to experience from them a sense of grief, and in this very sense of grief his pleasure consists. What is this but wretched madness? For a man is more affected by these actions the more he is spuriously involved in these affections. Now, if he should suffer them in his own person, it is the custom to call this "misery." But when he suffers with another, then it is called

30   "compassion." But what kind of compassion is it that arises from viewing fictitious and unreal sufferings? The spectator is not expected to aid the sufferer but merely to grieve for him. And the more he grieves the more he applauds the actor of these fictions. If the misfortunes of the characters—whether historical or entirely imaginary—are represented so as not to touch the feelings of the

35   spectator, he goes away disgusted and complaining. But if his feelings are deeply touched, he sits it out attentively, and sheds tears of joy.

But at that time, in my wretchedness, I loved to grieve; and I sought for things to grieve about. In another man's misery, even though it was feigned and impersonated on the stage, that performance of the actor pleased me best and attracted me most powerfully which moved me to tears. What marvel then was it that an unhappy sheep, straying from thy flock and impatient of thy care, I became infected with a foul disease? This is the reason for my love of griefs: that they would not probe into me too deeply (for I did not love to suffer in myself such things as I loved to look at), and they were the sort of grief which came from hearing those fictions, which affected only the surface of my emotion. Still, just as if they had been poisoned fingernails, their scratching was followed by inflammation, swelling, putrefaction, and corruption. Such was my life! But was it life, O my God?

And still thy faithful mercy hovered over me from afar.

Those studies I was then pursuing, generally accounted as respectable, were aimed at distinction in the courts of law—to excel in which, the more crafty I was, the more I should be praised. Such is the blindness of men that they even glory in their blindness. And by this time I had become a master in the School of Rhetoric, and I rejoiced proudly in this honor and became inflated with arrogance.

. . . in that unstable period of my life, I studied the books of eloquence, for it was in eloquence that I was eager to be eminent, though from a reprehensible and vainglorious motive, and a delight in human vanity. In the ordinary course of study I came upon a certain book of Cicero's, whose language almost all admire, though not his heart. This particular book of his contains an exhortation to philosophy and was called Hortensius. Now it was this book which quite definitely changed my whole attitude and turned my prayers toward thee, O Lord, and gave me new hope and new desires. Suddenly every vain hope became worthless to me, and with an incredible warmth of heart I yearned for an immortality of wisdom and began now to arise that I might return to thee. It was not to sharpen my tongue further that I made use of that book. I was now nineteen; my father had been dead two years, and my mother was providing the money for my study of rhetoric. What won me in it [i.e., the Hortensius] was not its style but its substance.

How ardent was I then, my God, how ardent to fly from earthly things to thee! Nor did I know how thou wast even then dealing with me. For with thee is wisdom. In Greek the love of wisdom is called "philosophy," and it was with this love that that book inflamed me.

I was delighted with Cicero's exhortation, at least enough so that I was stimulated by it, and enkindled and inflamed to love, to seek, to obtain, to hold, and to embrace, not this or that sect, but wisdom itself, wherever it might be. Only this checked my ardor: that the name of Christ was not in it. For this name, by thy mercy, O Lord, this name of my Saviour thy Son, my tender heart had piously drunk in, deeply treasured even with my mother's milk. And whatsoever was lacking that name, no matter how erudite, polished, and truthful, did not quite take complete hold of me.

I resolved, therefore, to direct my mind to the Holy Scriptures, that I might see what they were. And behold, I saw something not comprehended by the proud, not disclosed to children, something lowly in the hearing, but sublime in the doing, and veiled in mysteries. Yet I was not of the number of those who could enter into it or
85   bend my neck to follow its steps. For then it was quite different from what I now feel. When I then turned toward the Scriptures, they appeared to me to be quite unworthy to be compared with the dignity of Tully [Cicero]. For my inflated pride was repelled by their style, nor could the sharpness of my wit penetrate their inner meaning. Truly they were of a sort to aid the growth of little ones, but I
90   scorned to be a little one and, swollen with pride, I looked upon myself as fully grown.

   . . . And so it was that I was subtly persuaded to agree with these foolish deceivers [Manicheans] when they put their questions to me: "Whence comes evil?" and, "Is God limited by a bodily shape, and has he hairs and nails?" and,
95   "Are those patriarchs to be esteemed righteous who had many wives at one time, and who killed men and who sacrificed living creatures?" In my ignorance I was much disturbed over these things and, though I was retreating from the truth, I appeared to myself to be going toward it, because I did not yet know that evil was nothing but a privation of good (that, indeed, it has no being); and how should I
100   have seen this when the sight of my eyes went no farther than physical objects, and the sight of my mind reached no farther than to fantasms?. . . . And I was entirely ignorant as to what is that principle within us by which we are like God, and which is rightly said in Scripture to be made "after God's image."

   And now thou didst "stretch forth thy hand from above" and didst draw up
105   my soul out of that profound darkness [of Manicheism] because my mother, thy faithful one, wept to thee on my behalf more than mothers are accustomed to weep for the bodily deaths of their children. For by the light of the faith and spirit which she received from thee, she saw that I was dead. And thou didst hear her, O Lord, thou didst hear her and despised not her tears when, pouring down, they
110   watered the earth under her eyes in every place where she prayed. Thou didst truly hear her.

   For what other source was there for that dream by which thou didst console her, so that she permitted me to live with her, to have my meals in the same house at the table which she had begun to avoid, even while she hated and detested the
115   blasphemies of my error? In her dream she saw herself standing on a sort of wooden rule, and saw a bright youth approaching her, joyous and smiling at her, while she was grieving and bowed down with sorrow. But when he inquired of her the cause of her sorrow and daily weeping (not to learn from her, but to teach her, as is customary in visions), and when she answered that it was my soul's
120   doom she was lamenting, he bade her rest content and told her to look and see that where she was there I was also. And when she looked she saw me standing near her on the same rule.

Whence came this vision unless it was that thy ears were inclined toward her heart? O thou Omnipotent Good, thou carest for every one of us as if thou didst care for him only, and so for all as if they were but one!

125

Nearly nine years passed in which I wallowed in the mud of that deep pit and in the darkness of falsehood, striving often to rise, but being all the more heavily dashed down. But all that time this chaste, pious, and sober widow—such as thou dost love was now more buoyed up with hope, though no less zealous in her weeping and mourning; and she did not cease to bewail my case before thee, in all the hours of her supplication. Her prayers entered thy presence, and yet thou didst allow me still to tumble and toss around in that darkness.

130

Meanwhile, thou gavest her yet another answer, as I remember—for I pass over many things, hastening on to those things which more strongly impel me to confess to thee—and many things I have simply forgotten. But thou gavest her then another answer, by a priest of thine, a certain bishop reared in thy Church and well versed in thy books. When that woman had begged him to agree to have some discussion with me, to refute my errors, to help me to unlearn evil and to learn the good—for it was his habit to do this when he found people ready to receive it—he refused, very prudently, as I afterward realized. For he answered that I was still unteachable, being inflated with the novelty of that heresy, and that I had already perplexed divers inexperienced persons with vexatious questions, as she herself had told him. "But let him alone for a time," he said, "only pray God for him. He will of his own accord, by reading, come to discover what an error it is and how great its impiety is." He went on to tell her at the same time how he himself, as a boy, had been given over to the Manicheans by his misguided mother and not only had read but had even copied out almost all their books. Yet he had come to see, without external argument or proof from anyone else, how much that sect was to be shunned—and had shunned it. When he had said this she was not satisfied, but repeated more earnestly her entreaties, and shed copious tears, still beseeching him to see and talk with me. Finally the bishop, a little vexed at her importunity, exclaimed, "Go your way; as you live, it cannot be that the son of these tears should perish." As she often told me afterward, she accepted this answer as though it were a voice from heaven.

135

140

145

150

BOOK FOUR

This is the story of his years among the Manicheans. It includes the account of his teaching at Tagaste, his taking a mistress, the attractions of astrology, the poignant loss of a friend which leads to a searching analysis of grief and transience. He reports on his first book, De pulchro et apto, *and his introduction to Aristotle's* Categories *and other books of philosophy and theology, which he mastered with great ease and little profit.*

During this period of nine years, from my nineteenth year to my twenty-eighth, I went astray and led others astray. I was deceived and deceived others, in varied

lustful projects—sometimes publicly, by the teaching of what men style "the liberal
arts"; sometimes secretly, under the false guise of religion. In the one, I was proud
5   of myself; in the other, superstitious; in all, vain! In my public life I was striving
after the emptiness of popular fame, going so far as to seek theatrical applause,
entering poetic contests, striving for the straw garlands and the vanity of
theatricals and intemperate desires.

In those years I had a mistress, to whom I was not joined in lawful marriage.
10   She was a woman I had discovered in my wayward passion, void as it was of
understanding, yet she was the only one; and I remained faithful to her and with
her I discovered, by my own experience, what a great difference there is between
the restraint of the marriage bond contracted with a view to having children and
the compact of a lustful love, where children are born against the parents' will—
15   although once they are born they compel our love.

In those years, when I first began to teach rhetoric in my native town, I had
gained a very dear friend, about my own age, who was associated with me in the
same studies. Like myself, he was just rising up into the flower of youth. He had
grown up with me from childhood and we had been both school fellows and
20   playmates. But he was not then my friend, nor indeed ever became my friend, in the
true sense of the term; for there is no true friendship save between those thou dost
bind together and who cleave to thee by that love which is "shed abroad in our
hearts through the Holy Spirit who is given to us." Still, it was a sweet friendship,
being ripened by the zeal of common studies. Moreover, I had turned him away
25   from the true faith—which he had not soundly and thoroughly mastered as a
youth—and turned him toward those superstitious and harmful fables which my
mother mourned in me. With me this man went wandering off in error and my soul
could not exist without him. But behold thou wast close behind thy fugitives—at
once a God of vengeance and a Fountain of mercies, who dost turn us to thyself by
30   ways that make us marvel. Thus, thou didst take that man out of this life when he
had scarcely completed one whole year of friendship with me, sweeter to me than
all the sweetness of my life thus far.

Who can show forth all thy praise for that which he has experienced in
himself alone? What was it that thou didst do at that time, O my God; how
35   unsearchable are the depths of thy judgments! For when, sore sick of a fever, he
long lay unconscious in a death sweat and everyone despaired of his recovery, he
was baptized without his knowledge. And I myself cared little, at the time,
presuming that his soul would retain what it had taken from me rather than what
was done to his unconscious body. It turned out, however, far differently, for he
40   was revived and restored. Immediately, as soon as I could talk to him—and I did
this as soon as he was able, for I never left him and we hung on each other
overmuch—I tried to jest with him, supposing that he also would jest in return
about that baptism which he had received when his mind and senses were
inactive, but which he had since learned that he had received. But he recoiled from
45   me, as if I were his enemy, and, with a remarkable and unexpected freedom, he
admonished me that, if I desired to continue as his friend, I must cease to say such

things. Confounded and confused, I concealed my feelings till he should get well and his health recover enough to allow me to deal with him as I wished. But he was snatched away from my madness, that with thee he might be preserved for my
50   consolation. A few days after, during my absence, the fever returned and he died.

And what did it profit me that I could read and understand for myself all the books I could get in the so-called "liberal arts," when I was actually a worthless slave of wicked lust? I took delight in them, not knowing the real source of what it was in them that was true and certain. For I had my back toward the light, and my
55   face toward the things on which the light falls, so that my face, which looked toward the illuminated things, was not itself illuminated. Whatever was written in any of the fields of rhetoric or logic, geometry, music, or arithmetic, I could understand without any great difficulty and without the instruction of another man. All this thou knowest, O Lord my God, because both quickness in
60   understanding and acuteness in insight are thy gifts. Yet for such gifts I made no thank offering to thee. Therefore, my abilities served not my profit but rather my loss, since I went about trying to bring so large a part of my substance into my own power. And I did not store up my strength for thee, but went away from thee into the far country to prostitute my gifts in disordered appetite.

BOOK FIVE

A year of decision. Faustus comes to Carthage and Augustine is disenchanted in his hope for solid demonstration of the truth of Manichean doctrine. He decides to flee from his known troubles at Carthage to troubles yet unknown at Rome. His experiences at Rome prove disappointing and he applies for a teaching post at Milan. Here he meets Ambrose, who confronts him as an impressive witness for Catholic Christianity and opens out the possibilities of the allegorical interpretation of Scripture. Augustine decides to become a Christian catechumen.

Meeting the Manichean Faustus

Let me now lay bare in the sight of God the twenty-ninth year of my age. There had just come to Carthage a certain bishop of the Manicheans, Faustus by name, a great snare of the devil; and many were entangled by him through the charm of his eloquence. Now, even though I found this eloquence admirable, I was
5   beginning to distinguish the charm of words from the truth of things, which I was eager to learn. Nor did I consider the dish as much as I did the kind of meat that their famous Faustus served up to me in it. His fame had run before him, as one very skilled in an honorable learning and pre-eminently skilled in the liberal arts.

For almost the whole of the nine years that I listened with unsettled mind to
10   the Manichean teaching I had been looking forward with unbounded eagerness to the arrival of this Faustus. For all the other members of the sect that I happened to meet, when they were unable to answer the questions I raised, always referred me to his coming. They promised that, in discussion with him, these and even greater

15 difficulties, if I had them, would be quite easily and amply cleared away. When at last he did come, I found him to be a man of pleasant speech, who spoke of the very same things they themselves did, although more fluently and in a more agreeable style. But what profit was there to me in the elegance of my cupbearer, since he could not offer me the more precious draught for which I thirsted? My ears had already had their fill of such stuff, and now it did not seem any better because it

20 was better expressed nor more true because it was dressed up in rhetoric.

That eagerness, therefore, with which I had so long awaited this man, was in truth delighted with his action and feeling in a disputation, and with the fluent and apt words with which he clothed his ideas. I was delighted, therefore, and I joined with others—and even exceeded them—in exalting and praising him. Yet it

25 was a source of annoyance to me that, in his lecture room, I was not allowed to introduce and raise any of those questions that troubled me, in a familiar exchange of discussion with him. As soon as I found an opportunity for this, and gained his ear at a time when it was not inconvenient for him to enter into a discussion with me and my friends, I laid before him some of my doubts. I discovered at once that he

30 knew nothing of the liberal arts except grammar, and that only in an ordinary way. He had, however, read some of Tully's [Cicero's] orations, a very few books of Seneca, and some of the poets, and such few books of his own sect as were written in good Latin. With this meager learning and his daily practice in speaking, he had acquired a sort of eloquence which proved the more delightful

35 and enticing because it was under the direction of a ready wit and a sort of native grace. Was this not even as I now recall it, O Lord my God, Judge of my conscience? My heart and my memory are laid open before thee, who wast even then guiding me by the secret impulse of thy providence and wast setting my shameful errors before my face so that I might see and hate them.

40 For as soon as it became plain to me that Faustus was ignorant in those arts in which I had believed him eminent, I began to despair of his being able to clarify and explain all these perplexities that troubled me.

Thus the zeal with which I had plunged into the Manichean system was checked, and I despaired even more of their other teachers, because Faustus who

45 was so famous among them had turned out so poorly in the various matters that puzzled me.

To Rome and to Skepticism

Thou didst so deal with me, therefore, that I was persuaded to go to Rome and teach there what I had been teaching at Carthage. And how I was persuaded to do this I will not omit to confess to thee, for in this also the profoundest workings of

50 thy wisdom and thy constant mercy toward us must be pondered and acknowledged. I did not wish to go to Rome because of the richer fees and the higher dignity which my friends promised me there—though these considerations did affect my decision. My principal and almost sole motive was that I had been informed that the students there studied more quietly and were better kept under

55   the control of stern discipline, so that they did not capriciously and impudently rush into the classroom of a teacher not their own—indeed, they were not admitted at all without the permission of the teacher. At Carthage, on the contrary, there was a shameful and intemperate license among the students. They burst in rudely and, with furious gestures, would disrupt the discipline which the teacher
60   had established for the good of his pupils. Many outrages they perpetrated with astounding effrontery, things that would be punishable by law if they were not sustained by custom.

         I was now half inclined to believe that those philosophers whom they call "The Academics" were wiser than the rest in holding that we ought to doubt
65   everything, and in maintaining that man does not have the power of comprehending any certain truth, for, although I had not yet understood their meaning, I was fully persuaded that they thought just as they are commonly reputed to do. And I did not fail openly to dissuade my host from his confidence which I observed that he had in those fictions of which the works of Mani are
70   full. For all this, I was still on terms of more intimate friendship with these people than with others who were not of their heresy. I did not indeed defend it with my former ardor; but my familiarity with that group—and there were many of them concealed in Rome at that time—made me slower to seek any other way. This was particularly easy since I had no hope of finding in thy Church the truth from
75   which they had turned me aside, O Lord of heaven and earth, Creator of all things visible and invisible. And it still seemed to me most unseemly to believe that thou couldst have the form of human flesh and be bounded by the bodily shape of our limbs. And when I desired to meditate on my God, I did not know what to think of but a huge extended body—for what did not have bodily extension did not seem to
80   me to exist—and this was the greatest and almost the sole cause of my unavoidable errors.

         And thus I also believed that evil was a similar kind of substance, and that it had its own hideous and deformed extended body—either in a dense form which they called the earth or in a thin and subtle form as, for example, the substance of
85   the air, which they imagined as some malignant spirit penetrating that earth. And because my piety—such as it was—still compelled me to believe that the good God never created any evil substance, I formed the idea of two masses, one opposed to the other, both infinite but with the evil more contracted and the good more expansive. And from this diseased beginning, the other sacrileges followed after.
90   And I believed that our Saviour himself also—thy Only Begotten—had been brought forth, as it were, for our salvation out of the mass of thy bright shining substance. So that I could believe nothing about him except what I was able to harmonize with these vain imaginations. I thought, therefore, that such a nature could not be born of the Virgin Mary without being mingled with the flesh, and I
95   could not see how the divine substance, as I had conceived it, could be mingled thus without being contaminated. I was afraid, therefore, to believe that he had been born in the flesh, lest I should also be compelled to believe that he had been

contaminated by the flesh. Now will thy spiritual ones smile blandly and lovingly at me if they read these confessions. Yet such was I.

100   I set about diligently to practice what I came to Rome to do—the teaching of rhetoric. The first task was to bring together in my home a few people to whom and through whom I had begun to be known. And lo, I then began to learn that other offenses were committed in Rome which I had not had to bear in Africa. Just as I had been told, those riotous disruptions by young blackguards were not

105   practiced here. Yet, now, my friends told me, many of the Roman students— breakers of faith, who, for the love of money, set a small value on justice—would conspire together and suddenly transfer to another teacher, to evade paying their master's fees.

To Milan and Ambrose

    When, therefore, the officials of Milan sent to Rome, to the prefect of the city,

110   to ask that he provide them with a teacher of rhetoric for their city and to send him at the public expense, I applied for the job through those same persons, drunk with the Manichean vanities, to be freed from whom I was going away—though neither they nor I were aware of it at the time. They recommended that Symmachus, who was then prefect, after he had proved me by audition, should appoint me.

115   And to Milan I came, to Ambrose the bishop, famed through the whole world as one of the best of men, thy devoted servant. His eloquent discourse in those times abundantly provided thy people with the flour of thy wheat, the gladness of thy oil, and the sober intoxication of thy wine. To him I was led by thee without my knowledge, that by him I might be led to thee in full knowledge. That man of

120   God received me as a father would, and welcomed my coming as a good bishop should. And I began to love him, of course, not at the first as a teacher of the truth, for I had entirely despaired of finding that in thy Church—but as a friendly man. And I studiously listened to him—though not with the right motive—as he preached to the people. I was trying to discover whether his eloquence came up to

125   his reputation, and whether it flowed fuller or thinner than others said it did. And thus I hung on his words intently, but, as to his subject matter, I was only a careless and contemptuous listener. I was delighted with the charm of his speech, which was more erudite, though less cheerful and soothing, than Faustus' style. As for subject matter, however, there could be no comparison, for the latter was

130   wandering around in Manichean deceptions, while the former was teaching salvation most soundly. But "salvation is far from the wicked," such as I was then when I stood before him. Yet I was drawing nearer, gradually and unconsciously.

    For, although I took no trouble to learn what he said, but only to hear how he said it—for this empty concern remained foremost with me as long as I despaired

135   of finding a clear path from man to thee—yet, along with the eloquence I prized, there also came into my mind the ideas which I ignored; for I could not separate them. And, while I opened my heart to acknowledge how skillfully he spoke, there also came an awareness of how *truly* he spoke—but only gradually. First of all,

his ideas had already begun to appear to me defensible; and the Catholic faith, for which I supposed that nothing could be said against the onslaught of the Manicheans, I now realized could be maintained without presumption. This was especially clear after I had heard one or two parts of the Old Testament explained allegorically—whereas before this, when I had interpreted them literally, they had "killed" me spiritually.

BOOK SIX

Turmoil in the twenties. Monica follows Augustine to Milan and finds him a catechumen in the Catholic Church. Both admire Ambrose but Augustine gets no help from him on his personal problems. Ambition spurs and Alypius and Nebridius join him in a confused quest for the happy life. Augustine becomes engaged, dismisses his first mistress, takes another, and continues his fruitless search for truth.

O Hope from my youth, where wast thou to me and where hadst thou gone away? For hadst thou not created me and differentiated me from the beasts of the field and the birds of the air, making me wiser than they? And yet I was wandering about in a dark and slippery way, seeking thee outside myself and thus not finding the God of my heart. I had gone down into the depths of the sea and had lost faith, and had despaired of ever finding the truth.

By this time my mother had come to me, having mustered the courage of piety, following over sea and land, secure in thee through all the perils of the journey. For in the dangers of the voyage she comforted the sailors—to whom the inexperienced voyagers, when alarmed, were accustomed to go for comfort—and assured them of a safe arrival because she had been so assured by thee in a vision.

She found me in deadly peril through my despair of ever finding the truth. But when I told her that I was now no longer a Manichean, though not yet a Catholic Christian, she did not leap for joy as if this were unexpected; for she had already been reassured about that part of my misery for which she had mourned me as one dead, but also as one who would be raised to thee. She had carried me out on the bier of her thoughts, that thou mightest say to the widow's son, "Young man, I say unto you, arise!" and then he would revive and begin to speak, and thou wouldst deliver him to his mother. Therefore, her heart was not agitated with any violent exultation when she heard that so great a part of what she daily entreated thee to do had actually already been done that, though I had not yet grasped the truth, I was rescued from falsehood. Instead, she was fully confident that thou who hadst promised the whole would give her the rest, and thus most calmly, and with a fully confident heart, she replied to me that she believed, in Christ, that before she died she would see me a faithful Catholic. And she said no more than this to me. But to thee, O Fountain of mercy, she poured out still more frequent prayers and tears that thou wouldst hasten thy aid and enlighten my darkness, and she hurried all the more zealously to the church and hung upon the words of Ambrose, praying

30   for the fountain of water that springs up into everlasting life. For she loved that man as an angel of God, since she knew that it was by him that I had been brought thus far to that wavering state of agitation I was now in, through which she was fully persuaded I should pass from sickness to health, even though it would be after a sharper convulsion which physicians call "the crisis."

35   Nor had I come yet to groan in my prayers that thou wouldst help me. My mind was wholly intent on knowledge and eager for disputation. Ambrose himself I esteemed a happy man, as the world counted happiness, because great personages held him in honor. Only his celibacy appeared to me a painful burden. But what hope he cherished, what struggles he had against the temptations that beset his high station, what solace in adversity, and what savory joys thy bread possessed

40   for the hidden mouth of his heart when feeding on it, I could neither conjecture nor experience.

    And I listened with delight to Ambrose, in his sermons to the people, often recommending this text most diligently as a rule: "The letter kills, but the spirit gives life," while at the same time he drew aside the mystic veil and opened to view

45   the spiritual meaning of what seemed to teach perverse doctrine if it were taken according to the letter. I found nothing in his teachings that offended me, though I could not yet know for certain whether what he taught was true. For all this time I restrained my heart from assenting to anything, fearing to fall headlong into error.

    If I could have believed, I might have been cured, and, with the sight of my soul

50   cleared up, it might in some way have been directed toward thy truth, which always abides and fails in nothing. But, just as it happens that a man who has tried a bad physician fears to trust himself with a good one, so it was with the health of my soul, which could not be healed except by believing. But lest it should believe falsehoods, it refused to be cured, resisting thy hand, who hast prepared

55   for us the medicines of faith and applied them to the maladies of the whole world, and endowed them with such great efficacy.

    Still, from this time forward, I began to prefer the Catholic doctrine. I felt that it was with moderation and honesty that it commanded things to be believed that were not demonstrated—whether they could be demonstrated, but not to everyone,

60   or whether they could not be demonstrated at all.

    After that, O Lord, little by little, with a gentle and most merciful hand, drawing and calming my heart, thou didst persuade me that, if I took into account the multitude of things I had never seen, nor been present when they were enacted—such as many of the events of secular history; and the numerous reports

65   of places and cities which I had not seen; or such as my relations with many friends, or physicians, or with these men and those—that unless we should believe, we should do nothing at all in this life.

    Thus, since we are too weak by unaided reason to find out truth, and since, because of this, we need the authority of the Holy Writings, I had now begun to

70   believe that thou wouldst not, under any circumstances, have given such eminent authority to those Scriptures throughout all lands if it had not been that through them thy will may be believed in and that thou mightest be sought. For, as to those

passages in the Scripture which had heretofore appeared incongruous and offensive to me, now that I had heard several of them expounded reasonably, I could see that they were to be resolved by the mysteries of spiritual interpretation. The authority of Scripture seemed to me all the more revered and worthy of devout belief because, although it was visible for all to read, it reserved the full majesty of its secret wisdom within its spiritual profundity.

How wretched I was at that time, and how thou didst deal with me so as to make me aware of my wretchedness, I recall from the incident of the day on which I was preparing to recite a panegyric on the emperor. In it I was to deliver many a lie, and the lying was to be applauded by those who knew I was lying. My heart was agitated with this sense of guilt and it seethed with the fever of my uneasiness. For, while walking along one of the streets of Milan, I saw a poor beggar—with what I believe was a full belly—joking and hilarious. And I sighed and spoke to the friends around me of the many sorrows that flowed from our madness, because in spite of all our exertions—such as those I was then laboring in, dragging the burden of my unhappiness under the spur of ambition, and, by dragging it, increasing it at the same time—still and all we aimed only to attain that very happiness which this beggar had reached before us; and there was a grim chance that we should never attain it! For what he had obtained through a few coins, got by his begging, I was still scheming for by many a wretched and tortuous turning—namely, the joy of a passing felicity. He had not, indeed, gained true joy, but, at the same time, with all my ambitions, I was seeking one still more untrue. Anyhow, he was now joyous and I was anxious. He was free from care, and I was full of alarms.

Behold, I was now getting close to thirty, still stuck fast in the same mire, still greedy of enjoying present goods which fly away and distract me; and I was still saying, "Tomorrow I shall discover it; behold, it will become plain, and I shall see it; behold, Faustus will come and explain everything."

Or I would say: "O you mighty Academics, is there no certainty that man can grasp for the guidance of his life? No, let us search the more diligently, and let us not despair. See, the things in the Church's books that appeared so absurd to us before do not appear so now, and may be otherwise and honestly interpreted. I will set my feet upon that step where, as a child, my parents placed me, until the clear truth is discovered."

Active efforts were made to get me a wife. I wooed; I was engaged; and my mother took the greatest pains in the matter. For her hope was that, when I was once married, I might be washed clean in health-giving baptism for which I was being daily prepared, as she joyfully saw, taking note that her desires and promises were being fulfilled in my faith. Yet, when, at my request and her own impulse, she called upon thee daily with strong, heartfelt cries, that thou wouldst, by a vision, disclose unto her a leading about my future marriage, thou wouldst not. She did, indeed, see certain vain and fantastic things, such as are conjured up by the strong preoccupation of the human spirit, and these she supposed had some reference to me. And she told me about them, but not with the confidence she usually had when thou hadst shown her anything. For she always said that she could distinguish, by a certain feeling impossible to describe, between thy revelations and the dreams of her own soul. Yet the matter was pressed forward, 120 and proposals were made for a girl who was as yet some two years too young to marry. And because she pleased me, I agreed to wait for her.

Meanwhile my sins were being multiplied. My mistress was torn from my side as an impediment to my marriage, and my heart which clung to her was torn and wounded till it bled. And she went back to Africa, vowing to thee never to know 125 any other man and leaving with me my natural son by her. But I, unhappy as I was, and weaker than a woman, could not bear the delay of the two years that should elapse before I could obtain the bride I sought. And so, since I was not a lover of wedlock so much as a slave of lust, I procured another mistress—not a wife, of course. Thus in bondage to a lasting habit, the disease of my soul might be nursed 130 up and kept in its vigor or even increased until it reached the realm of matrimony. Nor indeed was the wound healed that had been caused by cutting away my former mistress; only it ceased to burn and throb, and began to fester, and was more dangerous because it was less painful.

BOOK SEVEN

The conversion to Neoplatonism. Augustine traces his growing disenchantment with the Manichean conceptions of God and evil and the dawning understanding of God's incorruptibility. But his thought is still bound by his materialistic notions of reality. He rejects astrology and turns to the study of Neoplatonism. There follows an analysis of the differences between Platonism and Christianity and a remarkable account of his appropriation of Plotinian wisdom and his experience of a Plotinian ecstasy. From this, he comes finally to the diligent study of the Bible, especially the writings of the apostle Paul. His pilgrimage is drawing toward its goal, as he begins to know Jesus Christ and to be drawn to him in hesitant faith.

The Problem of Evil

But as yet, although I said and was firmly persuaded that thou our Lord, the true God, who madest not only our souls but our bodies as well—and not only our souls and bodies but all creatures and all things—wast free from stain and alteration and in no way mutable, yet I could not readily and clearly understand 5 what was the cause of evil. Whatever it was, I realized that the question must be so analyzed as not to constrain me by any answer to believe that the immutable God was mutable, lest I should myself become the thing that I was seeking out.

And I directed my attention to understand what I now was told, that free will is the cause of our doing evil and that thy just judgment is the cause of our having 10 to suffer from its consequences. But I could not see this clearly. So then, trying to draw the eye of my mind up out of that pit, I was plunged back into it again, and trying often was just as often plunged back down. But one thing lifted me up toward thy light: it was that I had come to know that I had a will as certainly as I knew that I had life. When, therefore, I willed or was unwilling to do something, I was utterly certain that it was none but myself who willed or was unwilling—and immediately I realized that there was the cause of my sin.

For in my struggle to solve the rest of my difficulties, I now assumed henceforth as settled truth that the incorruptible must be superior to the corruptible, and I did acknowledge that thou, whatever thou art, art incorruptible. For there never yet was, nor will be, a soul able to conceive of anything better than thee, who art the highest and best good. And since most truly and certainly the incorruptible is to be placed above the corruptible—as I now admit it—it followed that I could rise in my thoughts to something better than my God, if thou wert not incorruptible. When, therefore, I saw that the incorruptible was to be preferred to the corruptible, I saw then where I ought to seek thee, and where I should look for the source of evil: that is, the corruption by which thy substance can in no way be profaned. For it is obvious that corruption in no way injures our God, by no inclination, by no necessity, by no unforeseen chance because he is our God, and what he wills is good, and he himself is that good.

But, then, whence does it [evil] come, since God who is good has made all these things good? Indeed, he is the greatest and chiefest Good, and hath created these lesser goods; but both Creator and created are all good. Whence, then, is evil? Or, again, was there some evil matter out of which he made and formed and ordered it, but left something in his creation that he did not convert into good? But why should this be? Was he powerless to change the whole lump so that no evil would remain in it, if he is the Omnipotent? Finally, why would he make anything at all out of such stuff? Why did he not, rather, annihilate it by his same almighty power? Could evil exist contrary to his will?

Such perplexities I revolved in my wretched breast, overwhelmed with gnawing cares lest I die before I discovered the truth. And still the faith of thy Christ, our Lord and Saviour, as it was taught me by the Catholic Church, stuck fast in my heart. As yet it was unformed on many points and diverged from the rule of right doctrine, but my mind did not utterly lose it, and every day drank in more and more of it.

And it was made clear to me that all things are good even if they are corrupted. They could not be corrupted if they were supremely good; but unless they were good they could not be corrupted. If they were supremely good, they would be incorruptible; if they were not good at all, there would be nothing in them to be corrupted. For corruption harms; but unless it could diminish goodness, it could not harm. Either, then, corruption does not harm—which cannot be—or, as is certain, all that is corrupted is thereby deprived of good.

Evil, then, the origin of which I had been seeking, has no substance at all; for if it were a substance, it would be good. For either it would be an incorruptible substance and so a supreme good, or a corruptible substance, which could not be corrupted unless it were good. I understood, therefore, and it was made clear to me that thou madest all things good, nor is there any substance at all not made by thee.

And I asked what wickedness was, and I found that it was no substance, but a perversion of the will bent aside from thee, O God, the supreme substance. . . .

60 By having thus read the books of the Platonists, and having been taught by them to search for the incorporeal Truth, I saw how thy invisible things are understood through the things that are made. And, even when I was thrown back, I still sensed what it was that the dullness of my soul would not allow me to contemplate. I was assured that thou wast, and wast infinite, though not diffused in finite space or infinity; that thou truly art, who art ever the same, varying

65 neither in part nor motion; and that all things are from thee, as is proved by this sure cause alone: that they exist.

Of all this I was convinced, yet I was too weak to enjoy thee. I chattered away as if I were an expert; but if I had not sought thy Way in Christ our Saviour, my knowledge would have turned out to be not instruction but destruction. For

70 now full of what was in fact my punishment, I had begun to desire to seem wise. I did not mourn my ignorance, but rather was puffed up with knowledge. For where was that love which builds upon the foundation of humility, which is Jesus Christ? Or, when would these books teach me this? I now believe that it was thy pleasure that I should fall upon these books before I studied thy Scriptures, that it

75 might be impressed on my memory how I was affected by them; and then afterward, when I was subdued by thy Scriptures and when my wounds were touched by thy healing fingers, I might discern and distinguish what a difference there is between presumption and confession—between those who saw where they were to go even if they did not see the way, and the Way which leads. . . .

BOOK EIGHT

Conversion to Christ. Augustine is deeply impressed by Simplicianus' story of the conversion to Christ of the famous orator and philosopher, Marius Victorinus. He is stirred to emulate him, but finds himself still enchained by his incontinence and preoccupation with worldly affairs. He is then visited by a court official, Ponticianus, who tells him and Alypius the stories of the conversion of Anthony and also of two imperial "secret service agents." These stories throw him into a violent turmoil, in which his divided will struggles against himself. He almost succeeds in making the decision for continence, but is still held back. Finally, a child's song, overheard by chance, sends him to the Bible; a text from Paul resolves the crisis; the conversion is a fact. Alypius also makes his decision, and the two inform the rejoicing Monica.

Of thy eternal life I was now certain, although I had seen it "through a glass darkly." And I had been relieved of all doubt that there is an incorruptible substance and that it is the source of every other substance. Nor did I any longer crave greater certainty about thee, but rather greater steadfastness in thee.

5 But as for my temporal life, everything was uncertain, and my heart had to be purged of the old leaven. "The Way"—the Saviour himself—pleased me well, but

as yet I was reluctant to pass through the strait gate. Now, indeed, my passions had ceased to excite me as of old with hopes of honor and wealth, and it was a grievous burden to go on in such servitude. For, compared with thy sweetness and

10 the beauty of thy house—which I loved—those things delighted me no longer. But I was still tightly bound by the love of women; nor did the apostle forbid me to marry, although he exhorted me to something better, wishing earnestly that all men were as he himself was. . . . But I was weak and chose the easier way, and for this single reason my whole life was one of inner turbulence and listless indecision. . . .

15 I went, therefore, to Simplicianus, the spiritual father of Ambrose (then a bishop), whom Ambrose truly loved as a father. I recounted to him all the mazes of my wanderings, but when I mentioned to him that I had read certain books of the Platonists which Victorinus—formerly professor of rhetoric at Rome, who died a Christian, as I had been told—had translated into Latin, Simplicianus

20 congratulated me that I had not fallen upon the writings of other philosophers, which were full of fallacies and deceit. . . .

Then, to encourage me to copy the humility of Christ, which is hidden from the wise and revealed to babes, he told me about Victorinus himself, whom he had known intimately at Rome. And I cannot refrain from repeating what he told me

25 about him. For it contains a glorious proof of thy grace, which ought to be confessed to thee.

He used to read the Holy Scriptures, as Simplicianus said, and thought out and studied all the Christian writings most studiously. He said to Simplicianus— not openly but secretly as a friend—"You must know that I am a Christian." To

30 which Simplicianus replied, "I shall not believe it, nor shall I count you among the Christians, until I see you in the Church of Christ." Victorinus then asked, with mild mockery, "Is it then the walls that make Christians?" Thus he often would affirm that he was already a Christian, and as often Simplicianus made the same answer; and just as often his jest about the walls was repeated. He was fearful of

35 offending his friends, proud demon worshipers, from the height of whose Babylonian dignity, as from the tops of the cedars of Lebanon which the Lord had not yet broken down, he feared that a storm of enmity would descend upon him.

But he steadily gained strength from reading and inquiry, and came to fear lest he should be denied by Christ before the holy angels if he now was afraid to

40 confess him before men. Thus he came to appear to himself guilty of a great fault, in being ashamed of the sacraments of the humility of thy Word, when he was not ashamed of the sacrilegious rites of those proud demons, whose pride he had imitated and whose rites he had shared. From this he became bold-faced against vanity and shamefaced toward the truth. Thus, suddenly and unexpectedly, he

45 said to Simplicianus—as he himself told me—"Let us go to the church; I wish to become a Christian." Simplicianus went with him, scarcely able to contain himself for joy. He was admitted to the first sacraments of instruction, and not long afterward gave in his name that he might receive the baptism of regeneration. At this Rome marveled and the Church rejoiced. The proud saw and were enraged;

50   they gnashed their teeth and melted away! But the Lord God was thy servant's hope and he paid no attention to their vanity and lying madness.

     Finally, when the hour arrived for him to make a public profession of his faith—which at Rome those who are about to enter into thy grace make from a platform in the full sight of the faithful people, in a set form of words learned by
55   heart—the presbyters offered Victorinus the chance to make his profession more privately, for this was the custom for some who were likely to be afraid through bashfulness. But Victorinus chose rather to profess his salvation in the presence of the holy congregation. For there was no salvation in the rhetoric which he taught: yet he had professed that openly. Why, then, should he shrink from naming
60   thy Word before the sheep of thy flock, when he had not shrunk from uttering his own words before the mad multitude?

     Now when this man of thine, Simplicianus, told me the story of Victorinus, I was eager to imitate him. Indeed, this was Simplicianus' purpose in telling it to me. But when he went on to tell how, in the reign of the Emperor Julian, there was a
65   law passed by which Christians were forbidden to teach literature and rhetoric; and how Victorinus, in ready obedience to the law, chose to abandon his "school of words" rather than thy Word, by which thou makest eloquent the tongues of the dumb—he appeared to me not so much brave as happy, because he had found a reason for giving his time wholly to thee. For this was what I was longing to do;
70   but as yet I was bound by the iron chain of my own will. The enemy held fast my will, and had made of it a chain, and had bound me tight with it. For out of the perverse will came lust, and the service of lust ended in habit, and habit, not resisted, became necessity. By these links, as it were, forged together—which is why I called it "a chain"—a hard bondage held me in slavery. But that new will
75   which had begun to spring up in me freely to worship thee and to enjoy thee, O my God, the only certain Joy, was not able as yet to overcome my former willfulness, made strong by long indulgence. Thus my two wills—the old and the new, the carnal and the spiritual—were in conflict within me; and by their discord they tore my soul apart.

80   And now I will tell and confess unto thy name, O Lord, my helper and my redeemer, how thou didst deliver me from the chain of sexual desire by which I was so tightly held, and from the slavery of worldly business. With increasing anxiety I was going about my usual affairs, and daily sighing to thee. I attended thy church as frequently as my business, under the burden of which I groaned, left
85   me free to do so.

     On a certain day, then, when Nebridius was away—for some reason I cannot remember—there came to visit Alypius and me at our house one Ponticianus, a fellow countryman of ours from Africa, who held high office in the emperor's court. What he wanted with us I do not know; but we sat down to talk together.

90   He then told us how, on a certain afternoon, at Trier, when the emperor was occupied watching the gladiatorial games, he and three comrades went out for a walk in the gardens close to the city walls. There, as they chanced to walk two by two, one strolled away with him, while the other two went on by themselves. As

95 they rambled, these first two came upon a certain cottage where lived some of thy
servants, some of the "poor in spirit" ("of such is the Kingdom of Heaven"), where
they found the book in which was written the life of Anthony! One of them began
to read it, to marvel and to be inflamed by it. While reading, he meditated on
embracing just such a life, giving up his worldly employment to seek thee alone.
These two belonged to the group of officials called "secret service agents." Then,
100 suddenly being overwhelmed with a holy love and a sober shame and as if in
anger with himself, he fixed his eyes on his friend, exclaiming: "Tell me, I beg you,
what goal are we seeking in all these toils of ours? What is it that we desire?
What is our motive in public service? Can our hopes in the court rise higher than
to be 'friends of the emperor'? But how frail, how beset with peril, is that pride!
105 Through what dangers must we climb to a greater danger? And when shall we
succeed? But if I chose to become a friend of God, see, I can become one now. . . . .
Now I have broken loose from those hopes we had, and I am determined to serve
God; and I enter into that service from this hour in this place. If you are reluctant
to imitate me, do not oppose me." The other replied that he would continue bound
110 in his friendship, to share in so great a service for so great a prize. So both became
thine, and began to "build a tower," counting the cost—namely, of forsaking all
that they had and following thee. Shortly after, Ponticianus and his companion,
who had walked with him in the other part of the garden, came in search of them to
the same place, and having found them reminded them to return, as the day was
115 declining. But the first two, making known to Ponticianus their resolution and
purpose, and how a resolve had sprung up and become confirmed in them,
entreated them not to take it ill if they refused to join themselves with them. But
Ponticianus and his friend, although not changed from their former course, did
nevertheless (as he told us) bewail themselves and congratulated their friends on
120 their godliness, recommending themselves to their prayers. And with hearts
inclining again toward earthly things, they returned to the palace. But the other
two, setting their affections on heavenly things, remained in the cottage. Both of
them had affianced brides who, when they heard of this, likewise dedicated their
virginity to thee.
125 Such was the story Ponticianus told. But while he was speaking, thou, O
Lord, turned me toward myself, taking me from behind my back, where I had put
myself while unwilling to exercise self-scrutiny. And now thou didst set me face to
face with myself, that I might see how ugly I was, and how crooked and sordid,
bespotted and ulcerous. And I looked and I loathed myself; but whither to fly from
130 myself I could not discover. And if I sought to turn my gaze away from myself, he
would continue his narrative, and thou wouldst oppose me to myself and thrust me
before my own eyes that I might discover my iniquity and hate it.
But now, the more ardently I loved those whose wholesome affections I heard
reported—that they had given themselves up wholly to thee to be cured—the more
135 did I abhor myself when compared with them. For many of my years—perhaps
twelve—had passed away since my nineteenth, when, upon the reading of Cicero's
Hortensius, I was roused to a desire for wisdom. And here I was, still postponing

the abandonment of this world's happiness to devote myself to the search. For not
just the finding alone, but also the bare search for it, ought to have been preferred
140   above the treasures and kingdoms of this world; better than all bodily pleasures,
though they were to be had for the taking. But, wretched youth that I was—
supremely wretched even in the very outset of my youth—I had entreated chastity
of thee and had prayed, "Grant me chastity and continence, but not yet." For I was
afraid lest thou shouldst hear me too soon, and too soon cure me of my disease of
145   lust which I desired to have satisfied rather than extinguished.

Then, as this vehement quarrel, which I waged with my soul in the chamber of
my heart, was raging inside my inner dwelling, agitated both in mind and
countenance, I seized upon Alypius and exclaimed: "What is the matter with us?
What is this? What did you hear? The uninstructed start up and take heaven, and
150   we—with all our learning but so little heart—see where we wallow in flesh and
blood! Because others have gone before us, are we ashamed to follow, and not
rather ashamed at our not following?" I scarcely knew what I said, and in my
excitement I flung away from him, while he gazed at me in silent astonishment. For
I did not sound like myself: my face, eyes, color, tone expressed my meaning more
155   clearly than my words.

Conversion in the Garden

There was a little garden belonging to our lodging, of which we had the use—
as of the whole house—for the master, our landlord, did not live there. The tempest
in my breast hurried me out into this garden, where no one might interrupt the fiery
struggle in which I was engaged with myself, until it came to the outcome that thou
160   knewest though I did not. But I was mad for health, and dying for life; knowing
what evil thing I was, but not knowing what good thing I was so shortly to
become.

I fled into the garden, with Alypius following step by step; for I had no secret
in which he did not share, and how could he leave me in such distress? We sat
165   down, as far from the house as possible. I was greatly disturbed in spirit, angry at
myself with a turbulent indignation because I had not entered thy will and
covenant, O my God, while all my bones cried out to me to enter, extolling it to the
skies.

While I was deliberating whether I would serve the Lord my God now, as I
170   had long purposed to do, it was I who willed and it was also I who was
unwilling. In either case, it was I. I neither willed with my whole will nor was I
wholly unwilling. And so I was at war with myself and torn apart by myself. And
this strife was against my will; yet it did not show the presence of another mind,
but the punishment of my own. Thus it was no more I who did it, but the sin that
175   dwelt in me—the punishment of a sin freely committed by Adam, and I was a son of
Adam.

Thus I was sick and tormented, reproaching myself more bitterly than ever,
rolling and writhing in my chain till it should be utterly broken. By now I was

180 held but slightly, but still was held. And thou, O Lord, didst press upon me in my inmost heart with a severe mercy, redoubling the lashes of fear and shame; lest I should again give way and that same slender remaining tie not be broken off, but recover strength and enchain me yet more securely.

I kept saying to myself, "See, let it be done now; let it be done now." And as I said this I all but came to a firm decision. I all but did it—yet I did not quite.

185 Now when deep reflection had drawn up out of the secret depths of my soul all my misery and had heaped it up before the sight of my heart, there arose a mighty storm, accompanied by a mighty rain of tears. That I might give way fully to my tears and lamentations, I stole away from Alypius, for it seemed to me that solitude was more appropriate for the business of weeping. I went far enough

190 away that I could feel that even his presence was no restraint upon me. This was the way I felt at the time, and he realized it. I suppose I had said something before I started up and he noticed that the sound of my voice was choked with weeping. And so he stayed alone, where we had been sitting together, greatly astonished. I flung myself down under a fig tree—how I know not—and gave free course to my

195 tears. The streams of my eyes gushed out an acceptable sacrifice to thee. And, not indeed in these words, but to this effect, I cried to thee: "And thou, O Lord, how long? How long, O Lord? Wilt thou be angry forever? Oh, remember not against us our former iniquities." For I felt that I was still enthralled by them. I sent up these sorrowful cries: "How long, how long? Tomorrow and tomorrow? Why not

200 now? Why not this very hour make an end to my uncleanness?"

I was saying these things and weeping in the most bitter contrition of my heart, when suddenly I heard the voice of a boy or a girl I know not which— coming from the neighboring house, chanting over and over again, "Pick it up, read it; pick it up, read it." Immediately I ceased weeping and began most earnestly to

205 think whether it was usual for children in some kind of game to sing such a song, but I could not remember ever having heard the like. So, damming the torrent of my tears, I got to my feet, for I could not but think that this was a divine command to open the Bible and read the first passage I should light upon. For I had heard how Anthony, accidentally coming into church while the gospel was being read,

210 received the admonition as if what was read had been addressed to him: "Go and sell what you have and give it to the poor, and you shall have treasure in heaven; and come and follow me." By such an oracle he was forthwith converted to thee.

So I quickly returned to the bench where Alypius was sitting, for there I had put down the apostle's [Paul] book when I had left there. I snatched it up, opened

215 it, and in silence read the paragraph on which my eyes first fell: "Not in rioting and drunkenness, not in chambering and wantonness, not in strife and envying, but put on the Lord Jesus Christ, and make no provision for the flesh to fulfill the lusts thereof." I wanted to read no further, nor did I need to. For instantly, as the sentence ended, there was infused in my heart something like the light of full

220 certainty and all the gloom of doubt vanished away.

Closing the book, then, and putting my finger or something else for a mark I began—now with a tranquil countenance—to tell it all to Alypius. And he in turn

225

230

disclosed to me what had been going on in himself, of which I knew nothing. He asked to see what I had read. I showed him, and he looked on even further than I had read. I had not known what followed. But indeed it was this, "Him that is weak in the faith, receive." This he applied to himself, and told me so. By these words of warning he was strengthened, and by exercising his good resolution and purpose—all very much in keeping with his character, in which, in these respects, he was always far different from and better than I—he joined me in full commitment without any restless hesitation.

235

240

Then we went in to my mother, and told her what happened, to her great joy. We explained to her how it had occurred—and she leaped for joy triumphant; and she blessed thee, who art "able to do exceedingly abundantly above all that we ask or think." For she saw that thou hadst granted her far more than she had ever asked for in all her pitiful and doleful lamentations. For thou didst so convert me to thee that I sought neither a wife nor any other of this world's hopes, but set my feet on that rule of faith which so many years before thou hadst showed her in her dream about me. And so thou didst turn her grief into gladness more plentiful than she had ventured to desire, and dearer and purer than the desire she used to cherish of having grandchildren of my flesh.

BOOK NINE

The end of the autobiography. Augustine tells of his resigning from his professorship and of the days at Cassiciacum in preparation for baptism. He is baptized together with Adeodatus and Alypius. Shortly thereafter, they start back for Africa. Augustine recalls the ecstasy he and his mother shared in Ostia and then reports her death and burial and his grief. The book closes with a moving prayer for the souls of Monica, Patricius, and all his fellow citizens of the heavenly Jerusalem.

Now that the vintage vacation was ended, I gave notice to the citizens of Milan that they might provide their scholars with another word-merchant. I gave as my reasons my determination to serve thee and also my insufficiency for the task, because of the difficulty in breathing and the pain in my chest.

5

And by letters I notified thy bishop, the holy man Ambrose, of my former errors and my present resolution.

10

15

When the time arrived for me to give in my name, we left the country and returned to Milan. Alypius also resolved to be born again in thee at the same time. He was already clothed with the humility that befits thy sacraments, and was so brave a tamer of his body that he would walk the frozen Italian soil with his naked feet, which called for unusual fortitude. We took with us the boy Adeodatus, my son after the flesh, the offspring of my sin. Thou hadst made of him a noble lad. He was barely fifteen years old, but his intelligence excelled that of many grave and learned men. I confess to thee thy gifts, O Lord my God, creator of all, who hast power to reform our deformities—for there was nothing of me in that boy but the sin.

His talent was a source of awe to me. And who but thou couldst be the worker of such marvels? And thou didst quickly remove his life from the earth, and even now I recall him to mind with a sense of security, because I fear nothing
20 for his childhood or youth, nor for his whole career. We took him for our companion, as if he were the same age in grace with ourselves, to be trained with ourselves in thy discipline. And so we were baptized and the anxiety about our past life left us.

We cast about for some place where we might be most useful in our service to
25 thee, and had planned on going back together to Africa. And when we had got as far as Ostia on the Tiber, my mother died.

Augustine's Account of the Life of Monica

I am passing over many things, for I must hasten. Receive, O my God, my confessions and thanksgiving for the unnumbered things about which I am silent. But I will not omit anything my mind has brought back concerning thy handmaid
30 who brought me forth—in her flesh, that I might be born into this world's light, and in her heart, that I might be born to life eternal. I will not speak of her gifts, but of thy gift in her; for she neither made herself nor trained herself. Thou didst create her, and neither her father nor her mother knew what kind of being was to come forth from them. And it was the rod of thy Christ, the discipline of thy only
35 Son, that trained her in thy fear, in the house of one of thy faithful ones who was a sound member of thy Church. Yet my mother did not attribute this good training of hers as much to the diligence of her own mother as to that of a certain elderly maidservant who had nursed her father, carrying him around on her back, as big girls carried babies. Because of her long-time service and also because of her
40 extreme age and excellent character, she was much respected by the heads of that Christian household. The care of her master's daughters was also committed to her, and she performed her task with diligence. She was quite earnest in restraining them with a holy severity when necessary and instructing them with a sober sagacity. Thus, except at mealtimes at their parents' table—when they were
45 fed very temperately—she would not allow them to drink even water, however parched they were with thirst. In this way she took precautions against an evil custom and added the wholesome advice:

"You drink water now only because you don't control the wine; but when you are married and mistresses of pantry and cellar, you may not care for water,
50 but the habit of drinking will be fixed." By such a method of instruction, and her authority, she restrained the longing of their tender age, and regulated even the thirst of the girls to such a decorous control that they no longer wanted what they ought not to have.

And yet, as thy handmaid related to me, her son, there had stolen upon her a
55 love of wine. For, in the ordinary course of things, when her parents sent her as a sober maiden to draw wine from the cask, she would hold a cup under the tap; and then, before she poured the wine into the bottle, she would wet the tips of her lips

60

with a little of it, for more than this her taste refused. She did not do this out of any craving for drink, but out of the overflowing buoyancy of her time of life, which bubbles up with sportiveness and youthful spirits, but is usually borne down by the gravity of the old folks. And so, adding daily a little to that little— for "he that contemns small things shall fall by a little here and a little there"—she slipped into such a habit as to drink off eagerly her little cup nearly full of wine.

65

70

75

Where now was that wise old woman and her strict prohibition? Could anything prevail against our secret disease if thy medicine, O Lord, did not watch over us? Though father and mother and nurturers are absent, thou art present, who dost create, who callest, and who also workest some good for our salvation, through those who are set over us. What didst thou do at that time, O my God? How didst thou heal her? How didst thou make her whole? Didst thou not bring forth from another woman's soul a hard and bitter insult, like a surgeon's knife from thy secret store, and with one thrust drain off all that putrefaction? For the slave girl who used to accompany her to the cellar fell to quarreling with her little mistress, as it sometimes happened when she was alone with her, and cast in her teeth this vice of hers, along with a very bitter insult: calling her "a drunkard." Stung by this taunt, my mother saw her own vileness and immediately condemned and renounced it.

80

As the flattery of friends corrupts, so often do the taunts of enemies instruct. Yet thou repayest them, not for the good thou workest through their means, but for the malice they intended. That angry slave girl wanted to infuriate her young mistress, not to cure her; and that is why she spoke up when they were alone. Or perhaps it was because their quarrel just happened to break out at that time and place; or perhaps she was afraid of punishment for having told of it so late.

85

90

Thus modestly and soberly brought up, she was made subject to her parents by thee, rather more than by her parents to thee. She arrived at a marriageable age, and she was given to a husband whom she served as her lord. And she busied herself to gain him to thee, preaching thee to him by her behavior, in which thou madest her fair and reverently amiable, and admirable to her husband. For she endured with patience his infidelity and never had any dissension with her husband on this account. For she waited for thy mercy upon him until, by believing in thee, he might become chaste.

95

100

Moreover, even though he was earnest in friendship, he was also violent in anger; but she had learned that an angry husband should not be resisted, either in deed or in word. But as soon as he had grown calm and was tranquil, and she saw a fitting moment, she would give him a reason for her conduct, if he had been excited unreasonably. As a result, while many matrons whose husbands were more gentle than hers bore the marks of blows on their disfigured faces, and would in private talk blame the behavior of their husbands, she would blame their tongues, admonishing them seriously—though in a jesting manner—that from the hour they heard what are called the matrimonial tablets read to them, they should think of them as instruments by which they were made servants. So, always being mindful of their condition, they ought not to set themselves up in opposition to

105 their lords. And, knowing what a furious, bad-tempered husband she endured, they marveled that it had never been rumored, nor was there any mark to show, that Patricius had ever beaten his wife, or that there had been any domestic strife between them, even for a day. And when they asked her confidentially the reason for this, she taught them the rule I have mentioned. Those who observed it confirmed the wisdom of it and rejoiced; those who did not observe it were bullied and vexed. Even her mother-in-law, who was at first prejudiced against her by the whisperings of malicious servants, she conquered by submission, persevering in it

110 with patience and meekness; with the result that the mother-in-law told her son of the tales of the meddling servants which had disturbed the domestic peace between herself and her daughter-in-law and begged him to punish them for it. In conformity with his mother's wish, and in the interest of family discipline to insure the future harmony of its members, he had those servants beaten who were

115 pointed out by her who had discovered them; and she promised a similar reward to anyone else who, thinking to please her, should say anything evil of her daughter-in-law. After this no one dared to do so, and they lived together with a wonderful sweetness of mutual good will.

This other great gift thou also didst bestow, O my God, my Mercy, upon that

120 good handmaid of thine, in whose womb thou didst create me. It was that whenever she could she acted as a peacemaker between any differing and discordant spirits, and when she heard very bitter things on either side of a controversy—the kind of bloated and undigested discord which often belches forth bitter words, when crude malice is breathed out by sharp tongues to a

125 present friend against an absent enemy—she would disclose nothing about the one to the other except what might serve toward their reconciliation. This might seem a small good to me if I did not know to my sorrow countless persons who, through the horrid and far-spreading infection of sin, not only repeat to enemies mutually enraged things said in passion against each other, but also add some things that

130 were never said at all. It ought not to be enough in a truly humane man merely not to incite or increase the enmities of men by evil-speaking; he ought likewise to endeavor by kind words to extinguish them. Such a one was she—and thou, her most intimate instructor, didst teach her in the school of her heart.

Finally, her own husband, now toward the end of his earthly existence, she

135 won over to thee. Henceforth, she had no cause to complain of unfaithfulness in him, which she had endured before he became one of the faithful. She was also the servant of thy servants. All those who knew her greatly praised, honored, and loved thee in her because, through the witness of the fruits of a holy life, they recognized thee present in her heart. For she had "been the wife of one man," had

140 honored her parents, had guided her house in piety, was highly reputed for good works, and brought up her children, travailing in labor with them as often as she saw them swerving from thee. Lastly, to all of us, O Lord—since of thy favor thou allowest thy servants to speak—to all of us who lived together in that association before her death in thee she devoted such care as she might have if she had been

145 mother of us all; she served us as if she had been the daughter of us all.

As the day now approached on which she was to depart this life—a day which thou knewest, but which we did not—it happened (though I believe it was by thy secret ways arranged) that she and I stood alone, leaning in a certain window from which the garden of the house we occupied at Ostia could be seen.

150 Here in this place, removed from the crowd, we were resting ourselves for the voyage after the fatigues of a long journey.

We were conversing alone very pleasantly and "forgetting those things which are past, and reaching forward toward those things which are future." We were in the present—and in the presence of Truth (which thou art)—discussing together

155 what is the nature of the eternal life of the saints: which eye has not seen, nor ear heard, neither has entered into the heart of man. We opened wide the mouth of our heart, thirsting for those supernal streams of thy fountain, "the fountain of life" which is with thee, that we might be sprinkled with its waters according to our capacity and might in some measure weigh the truth of so profound a mystery.

160 And when our conversation had brought us to the point where the very highest of physical sense and the most intense illumination of physical light seemed, in comparison with the sweetness of that life to come, not worthy of comparison, nor even of mention, we lifted ourselves with a more ardent love toward the Selfsame, and we gradually passed through all the levels of bodily

165 objects, and even through the heaven itself, where the sun and moon and stars shine on the earth. Indeed, we soared higher yet by an inner musing, speaking and marveling at thy works.

And we came at last to our own minds and went beyond them, that we might climb as high as that region of unfailing plenty where thou feedest Israel forever

170 with the food of truth, where life is that Wisdom by whom all things are made, both which have been and which are to be. Wisdom is not made, but is as she has been and forever shall be; for "to have been" and "to be hereafter" do not apply to her, but only "to be," because she is eternal and "to have been" and "to be hereafter" are not eternal. And while we were thus speaking and straining after

175 her, we just barely touched her with the whole effort of our hearts. Then with a sigh, leaving the first fruits of the Spirit bound to that ecstasy, we returned to the sounds of our own tongue, where the spoken word had both beginning and end.

Still, O Lord, thou knowest that on that day we were talking thus and that this world, with all its joys, seemed cheap to us even as we spoke. Then my mother

180 said: "Son, for myself I have no longer any pleasure in anything in this life. Now that my hopes in this world are satisfied, I do not know what more I want here or why I am here. There was indeed one thing for which I wished to tarry a little in this life, and that was that I might see you a Catholic Christian before I died. My God hath answered this more than abundantly, so that I see you now made his

185 servant and spurning all earthly happiness. What more am I to do here?"

I do not well remember what reply I made to her about this. However, it was scarcely five days later—certainly not much more—that she was prostrated by fever. While she was sick, she fainted one day and was for a short time quite unconscious. We hurried to her, and when she soon regained her senses, she

190   looked at me and my brother as we stood by her, and said, in inquiry, "Where was I?" Then looking intently at us, dumb in our grief, she said, "Here in this place shall you bury your mother." I was silent and held back my tears; but my brother said something, wishing her the happier lot of dying in her own country and not abroad. When she heard this, she fixed him with her eye and an anxious

195   countenance, because he savored of such earthly concerns, and then gazing at me she said, "See how he speaks." Soon after, she said to us both: "Lay this body anywhere, and do not let the care of it be a trouble to you at all. Only this I ask: that you will remember me at the Lord's altar, wherever you are." And when she had expressed her wish in such words as she could, she fell silent, in heavy pain

200   with her increasing sickness.

       I heard later on that, during our stay in Ostia, she had been talking in maternal confidence to some of my friends about her contempt of this life and the blessing of death. When they were amazed at the courage which was given her, a woman, and had asked her whether she did not dread having her body buried so

205   far from her own city, she replied: "Nothing is far from God. I do not fear that, at the end of time, he should not know the place whence he is to resurrect me." And so on the ninth day of her sickness, in the fifty-sixth year of her life and the thirty-third of mine, that religious and devout soul was set loose from the body.

       I closed her eyes; and there flowed in a great sadness on my heart and it was

210   passing into tears, when at the strong behest of my mind my eyes sucked back the fountain dry, and sorrow was in me like a convulsion. As soon as she breathed her last, the boy Adeodatus burst out wailing; but he was checked by us all, and became quiet. Likewise, my own childish feeling which was, through the youthful voice of my heart, seeking escape in tears, was held back and silenced. For we did

215   not consider it fitting to celebrate that death with tearful wails and groanings. This is the way those who die unhappy or are altogether dead are usually mourned. But she neither died unhappy nor did she altogether die. For of this we were assured by the witness of her good life, her "faith unfeigned," and other manifest evidence.

220   And then, little by little, there came back to me my former memories of thy handmaid: her devout life toward thee, her holy tenderness and attentiveness toward us, which had suddenly been taken away from me—and it was a solace for me to weep in thy sight, for her and for myself, about her and about myself. Thus I set free the tears which before I repressed, that they might flow at will,

225   spreading them out as a pillow beneath my heart. And it rested on them, for thy ears were near me—not those of a man, who would have made a scornful comment about my weeping. But now in writing I confess it to thee, O Lord! Read it who will, and comment how he will, and if he finds me to have sinned in weeping for my mother for part of an hour—that mother who was for a while dead to my eyes,

230   who had for many years wept for me that I might live in thy eyes—let him not laugh at me; but if he be a man of generous love, let him weep for my sins against thee, the Father of all the brethren of thy Christ.

235

Therefore, let her rest in peace with her husband, before and after whom she was married to no other man; whom she obeyed with patience, bringing fruit to thee that she might also win him for thee. And inspire, O my Lord my God, inspire thy servants, my brothers; thy sons, my masters, who with voice and heart and writings I serve, that as many of them as shall read these confessions may also at thy altar remember Monica, thy handmaid, together with Patricius, once her husband; by whose flesh thou didst bring me into this life, in a manner I know not.

240

May they with pious affection remember my parents in this transitory life, and remember my brothers under thee our Father in our Catholic mother; and remember my fellow citizens in the eternal Jerusalem, for which thy people sigh in their pilgrimage from birth until their return. So be fulfilled what my mother desired of me—more richly in the prayers of so many gained for her through these

245

confessions of mine than by my prayers alone.

BOOK TEN

From autobiography to self-analysis. Augustine turns from his memories of the past to the inner mysteries of memory itself. In doing so, he reviews his motives for these written "confessions," and seeks to chart the path by which men come to God. But this brings him into the intricate analysis of memory and its relation to the self and its powers. This done, he explores the meaning and mode of true prayer. In conclusion, he undertakes a detailed analysis of appetite and the temptations to which the flesh and the soul are heirs, and comes finally to see how necessary and right it was for the Mediator between God and man to have been the God-Man.

BOOK ELEVEN

The eternal Creator and the Creation in time. Augustine ties together his memory of his past life, his present experience, and his ardent desire to comprehend the mystery of creation. This leads him to the questions of the mode and time of creation. He ponders the mode of creation and shows that it was de nihilo and involved no alteration in the being of God. He then considers the question of the beginning of the world and time and shows that time and creation are cotemporal. But what is time? To this Augustine devotes a brilliant analysis of the subjectivity of time and the relation of all temporal process to the abiding eternity of God. From this, he prepares to turn to a detailed interpretation of Gen. 1:1, 2.

BOOK TWELVE

The mode of creation and the truth of Scripture. Augustine explores the relation of the visible and formed matter of heaven and earth to the prior matrix from which it was formed. This leads to an intricate analysis of "unformed matter" and the primal "possibility" from which God created, itself created de nihilo. He finds a reference to this in the misconstrued Scriptural phrase "the heaven of heavens." Realizing that his interpretation of Gen. 1:1, 2, is not self-evidently the only possibility, Augustine turns to an elaborate discussion of the multiplicity of perspectives in hermeneutics and, in the course of this, reviews the various possibilities of true interpretation of his Scripture text. He emphasizes the importance of tolerance where there are plural options, and confidence where basic Christian faith is concerned.

20. THE RULE (SELECTIONS)

Benedict of Nursia
(480–547 CE)

(trans. by Ernest F. Henderson)

Benedict of Nursia composed a Rule *(c. 530) for "beginners" in monastic living that would become the standard Rule in the West; it is characterized by moderation and serves as a compendium of practical self-sufficient communal living in a time when security in the Western world was scarce and options for survival few. The monastery offered a safe haven, a life of mutual support, the comfort of daily routine, and hope of ultimate salvation. Benedict sets reasonable prescripts for every aspect of monastic living from governance, to living conditions, and, of course, for study, prayer and work; and he recognizes human limitations and, most importantly, that one should never despair of the mercy of God.*

PROLOGUE

... We are about to found therefore a school for the Lord's service; in the organization of which we trust that we shall ordain nothing severe and nothing burdensome. But even if, the demands of justice dictating it, something a little irksome shall be the result, for the purpose of amending vices or preserving
5   charity;—thou shalt not therefore, struck by fear, flee the way of salvation, which can not be entered upon except through a narrow entrance. But as one's way of life and one's faith progresses, the heart becomes broadened, and, with the unutterable sweetness of love, the way of the mandates of the Lord is traversed. Thus, never departing from His guidance, continuing in the monastery in his
10 teaching until death, through patience we are made partakers in Christ's passion, in order that we may merit to be companions in His kingdom.

1. Concerning the Kinds of Monks and Their Manner of Living

It is manifest that there are four kinds of monks. The cenobites are the first kind; that is, those living in a monastery, serving under a rule or an abbot. Then the second kind is that of the anchorites; that is, the hermits—those who, not by
15 the new fervour of a conversion but by the long probation of life in a monastery, have learned to fight against the devil, having already been taught by the solace of

many. They, having been well prepared in the army of brothers for the solitary fight of the hermit, being secure now without the consolation of another, are able, God helping them, to fight with their own hand or arm against the vices of the flesh or of their thoughts.

But a third very bad kind of monks are the sarabaites, approved by no rule, experience being their teacher, as with the gold which is tried in the furnace. But, softened after the manner of lead, keeping faith with the world by their works, they are known through their tonsure to lie to God. These being shut up by twos or threes, or, indeed, alone, without a shepherd, not in the Lord's but in their own sheep-folds—their law is the satisfaction of their desires. For whatever they think good or choice, this they call holy; and what they do not wish, this they consider unlawful. But the fourth kind of we are about to found, therefore, a school for the monks is the kind which is called gyratory. During their whole life they are guests, for three or four days at a time, in the cells of the different monasteries, throughout the various provinces; always wandering and never stationary, given over to the service of their own pleasures and the joys of the palate, and in every way worse than the sarabaites. Concerning the most wretched way of living of all such monks it is better to be silent than to speak. These things therefore being omitted, let us proceed, with the aid of God, to treat of the best kind, the cenobites.

2. What the Abbot Should Be Like

An abbot who is worthy to preside over a monastery ought always to remember what he is called, and carry out with his deeds the name of a Superior. For he is believed to be Christ's representative, since he is called by His name, the apostle saying: "Ye have received the spirit of adoption of sons, whereby we call Abba, Father." And so the abbot should not—grant that he may not—teach, or decree, or order, any thing apart from the precept of the Lord; but his order or teaching should be sprinkled with the ferment of divine justice in the minds of his disciples. Let the abbot always be mindful that, at the tremendous judgment of God, both things will be weighed in the balance: his teaching and the obedience of his disciples. And let the abbot know that whatever the father of the family finds of less utility among the sheep is laid to the fault of the shepherd. Only in a case where the whole diligence of their pastor shall have been bestowed on an unruly and disobedient flock, and his whole care given to their morbid actions, shall that pastor, absolved in the judgment of the Lord, be free to say to the Lord with the prophet: "I have not hid Thy righteousness within my heart, I have declared Thy faithfulness and Thy salvation, but they despising have scorned me." And then at length let the punishment for the disobedient sheep under his care be death itself prevailing against them. Therefore, when any one receives the name of abbot, he ought to rule over his disciples with a double teaching; that is, let him show forth all good and holy things by deeds more than by words. So that to ready disciples he may propound the mandates of God in words; but, to the hard-hearted and the more simpleminded, he may show forth the divine precepts by his deeds. But as to

60

65

70

75

80

all the things that he has taught to his disciples to be wrong, he shall show by his deeds that they are not to be done; lest, preaching to others, he himself shall be found worthy of blame, and lest God may say at some time to him a sinner: "What hast thou to do to declare my statutes or that thou should'st take my covenant in thy mouth. Seeing that thou hatest instruction and casteth my words behind thee; and why beholdest thou the mote that is in thy brother's eye, but considerest not the beam that is in thine own eye?" He shall make no distinction of persons in the monastery. One shall not be more cherished than another, unless it be the one whom he finds excelling in good works or in obedience. A free-born man shall not be preferred to one coming from servitude, unless there be some other reasonable cause. But if, justice demanding that it should be thus, it seems good to the abbot, he shall do this no matter what the rank shall be. But otherwise they shall keep their own places; for whether we be bond or free we are all one in Christ; and, under one God, we perform an equal service of subjection; for God is no respecter of persons. Only in this way is a distinction made by Him concerning us: if we are found humble and surpassing others in good works. Therefore let him [the abbot] have equal charity for all: let the same discipline be administered in all cases according to merit. In his teaching indeed the abbot ought always to observe that form laid down by the apostle when he says: "reprove, rebuke, exhort." That is, mixing seasons with seasons, blandishments with terrors, let him display the feeling of a severe yet devoted master. He should, namely, rebuke more severely the unruly and the turbulent. The obedient, moreover, and the gentle and the patient, he should exhort, that they may progress to higher things. But the negligent and scorners, we warn him to admonish and reprove. . . .

3. About Calling in the Brethren to Take Council

85

As often as anything especial is to be done in the monastery, the abbot shall call together the whole congregation, and shall himself explain the question at issue. And, having heard the advice of the brethren, he shall think it over by himself, and shall do what he considers most advantageous.

5. Concerning Obedience

90

The first grade of humility is obedience without delay. This becomes those who, on account of the holy service which they have professed, or on account of the fear of hell or the glory of eternal life, consider nothing dearer to them than Christ: so that, so soon as anything is commanded by their superior, they may not know how to suffer delay in doing it, even as if it were a divine command. Concerning whom the Lord said: "As soon as he heard of me he obeyed me."

7. Concerning Humility

The sixth grade of humility is, that a monk be contented with all lowliness or extremity, and consider himself, with regard to everything which is enjoined on him, as a poor and unworthy workman; saying to himself with the prophet: "I was reduced to nothing and was ignorant; I was made as the cattle before thee, and I am always with thee." The seventh grade of humility is, not only that he, with his tongue, pronounce himself viler and more worthless than all; but that he also believe it in the inner-most workings of his heart; humbling himself and saying with the prophet, etc. The eighth degree of humility is that a monk do nothing except what the common rule of the monastery, or the example of his elders, urges him to do. The ninth degree of humility is that a monk restrain his tongue from speaking; and, keeping silence, do not speak until he is spoken to. The tenth grade of humility is that he be not ready, and easily inclined, to laugh. . . . The eleventh grade of humility is that a monk, when he speaks, speak slowly and without laughter, humbly with gravity, using few and reasonable words; and that he be not loud of voice. . . . The twelfth grade of humility is that a monk shall, not only with his heart but also with his body, always show humility to all who see him: that is, when at work, in the oratory, in the monastery, in the garden, on the road, in the fields. And everywhere, sitting or walking or standing, let him always be with head inclined, his looks fixed upon the ground; remembering every hour that he is guilty of his sins. Let him think that he is already being presented before the tremendous judgment of God, saying always to himself in his heart what the publican of the gospel, fixing his eyes on the earth, said: "Lord I am not worthy, I a sinner, so much as to lift mine eyes unto Heaven."

8. Concerning the Divine Offices at Night

In the winter time, that is from the Calends of November until Easter, according to what is reasonable, they must rise at the eighth hour of the night, so that they rest a little more than half the night, and rise when they have already digested. But let the time that remains after vigils be kept for meditation by those brothers who are in any way behind hand with the psalter or lessons. From Easter, moreover, until the aforesaid Calends of November, let the hour of keeping vigils be so arranged that, a short interval being observed in which the brethren may go out for the necessities of nature, the matins, which are always to take place with the dawning light, may straightway follow.

9. How Many Psalms Are to Be Said at Night

In the winter first of all the verse shall be said: "Make haste oh God to deliver me; make haste to help me oh God." Then, secondly, there shall be said three times: "Oh Lord open Thou my lips and my mouth shall show forth Thy praise." To which is to be subjoined the third psalm and the Gloria. After this the

ninety-fourth psalm is to be sung antiphonally or in unison. The Ambrosian chant shall then follow: then six psalms antiphonally. These having been said, the abbot
130   shall, with the verse mentioned, give the blessing. And all being seated upon the benches, there shall be read in turn from the Scriptures—following out the analogy—three lessons; between which also three responses shall be sung. Two responses shall be said without the Gloria; but, after the third lesson, he who chants shall say the Gloria. And, when the cantor begins to say this, all shall
135   straightway rise from their seats out of honour and reverence for the holy Trinity. Books, moreover, of the old as well as the New Testament of Divine authority shall be read at the vigils; but also expositions of them which have been made by the most celebrated orthodox teachers and catholic Fathers. Moreover, after these three lessons with their responses, shall follow other six psalms to be sung with
140   the Alleluia. After this a lesson of the Apostle shall follow, to be recited by heart; and verses and the supplication of the Litany, that is the Kyrie eleison: and thus shall end the nocturnal vigils.

16. How Divine Service Shall Be Held Through the Day

As the prophet says: "Seven times in the day so I praise Thee." Which sacred number of seven will thus be fulfilled by us if, at matins, at the first, third, sixth,
145   ninth hours, at vesper time and at "completorium" we perform the duties of our service; for it is of these hours of the day that he said: "Seven times in the day do I praise Thee." For, concerning nocturnal vigils, the same prophet says: "At midnight I arose to confess unto thee." Therefore, at these times, let us give thanks to our Creator concerning the judgments of his righteousness; that is, at matins,
150   etc. . . . . and at night we will rise and confess to him. . . .

22. How the Monks Shall Sleep

They shall sleep separately in separate beds. They shall receive positions for their beds, after the manner of their characters, according to the dispensation of their abbot. If it can be done, they shall all sleep in one place. If, however, their number do not permit it, they shall rest, by tens or twenties, with elders who will
155   concern themselves about them. A candle shall always be burning in that same cell until early in the morning. They shall sleep clothed, and girt with belts or with ropes; and they shall not have their knives at their sides while they sleep, lest perchance in a dream they should wound the sleepers. And let the monks be always on the alert; and, when the signal is given, rising without delay, let them
160   hasten to mutually prepare themselves for the service of God with all gravity and modesty, however. The younger brothers shall not have beds by themselves, but interspersed among those of the elder ones. And when they rise for the service of God, they shall exhort each other mutually with moderation on account of the excuses that those who are sleepy are inclined to make.

31. Concerning the Cellarer of the Monastery, What Sort of a Person He Shall Be

165   As a cellarer of the monastery there shall be elected from the congregation one who is wise, mature in character, sober, not given to much eating, not proud, not turbulent, not an upbraider, not tardy, not prodigal, but fearing God: a father, as it were, to the whole congregation. He shall take care of everything, he shall do nothing without the order of the abbot. He shall have charge of what things are

170   ordered: he shall not rebuff the brethren. If any brother by chance demand anything unreasonably from him, he shall not, by spurning, rebuff him; but reasonably, with humility, shall deny to him who wrongly seeks.

33. Whether the Monks Should Have Anything of Their Own

    More than anything else is this special vice to be cut off root and branch from the monastery, that one should presume to give or receive anything without the

175   order of the abbot, or should have anything of his own. He should have absolutely not anything: neither a book, nor tablets, nor a pen—nothing at all.—For indeed it is not allowed to the monks to have their own bodies or wills in their own power. But all things necessary they must expect from the Father of the monastery; nor is it allowable to have anything which the abbot did not give or permit. All things

180   shall be common to all, as it is written: "Let not any man presume or call anything his own." But if any one shall have been discovered delighting in this most evil vice: being warned once and again, if he do not amend, let him be subjected to punishment.

39. Concerning the Amount of Food

    We believe, moreover, that, for the daily refection of the sixth as well as of the

185   ninth hour, two cooked dishes, on account of the infirmities of the different ones, are enough for all tables: so that whoever, perchance, can not eat of one may partake of the other. Therefore let two cooked dishes suffice for all the brothers: and, if it is possible to obtain apples or growing vegetables, a third may be added. One full pound of bread shall suffice for a day, whether there be one refection, or

190   a breakfast and a supper. But if they are going to have supper, the third part of that same pound shall be reserved by the cellarer, to be given back to those who are about to sup. But if, perchance, some greater labour shall have been performed, it shall be in the will and power of the abbot, if it is expedient, to increase anything; surfeiting above all things being guarded against, so that indigestion

195   may never seize a monk: for nothing is so contrary to every Christian as surfeiting, as our Lord says: "Take heed to yourselves, lest your hearts be overcharged with surfeiting. " But to younger boys the same quantity shall not be served, but less than that to the older ones; moderation being observed in all things. But the eating

200   of the flesh of quadrupeds shall be abstained from altogether by every one, excepting alone the weak and the sick.

40. Concerning the Amount of Drink

Each one has his own gift from God, the one in this way, the other in that. Therefore it is with some hesitation that the amount of daily sustenance for others is fixed by us. Nevertheless, in view of the weakness of the infirm we believe that a hemina [just less than half a liter] of wine a day is enough for each one. Those 205 moreover to whom God gives the ability of bearing abstinence shall know that they will have their own reward. But the prior shall judge if either the needs of the place, or labour or the heat of summer, requires more; considering in all things lest satiety or drunkenness creep in. Indeed we read that wine is not suitable for monks at all. But because, in our day, it is not possible to persuade the monks of 210 this, let us agree at least as to the fact that we should not drink till we are sated, but sparingly. For wine can make even the wise to go astray. Where, moreover, the necessities of the place are such that the amount written above can not be found— but much less or nothing at all—those who live there shall bless God and shall not murmur. And we admonish them to this above all: that they be without murmuring.

45. Concerning Those Who Make Mistakes in the Oratory

215   If any one, in saying a psalm, response, or antiphone or lesson, make a mistake; unless he humble himself there before all, giving satisfaction, he shall be subjected to greater punishment, as one who was unwilling to correct by humility that in which he had erred by neglect. But children, for such a fault, shall be whipped.

48. Concerning the Daily Manual Labour

220   Idleness is the enemy of the soul. And therefore, at fixed times, the brothers ought to be occupied in manual labour; and again, at fixed times, in sacred reading. . . . there shall certainly be appointed one or two elders, who shall go round the monastery at the hours in which the brothers are engaged in reading, and see to it that no troublesome brother chance to be found who is open to 225 idleness and trifling, and is not intent on his reading; being not only of no use to himself, but also stirring up others.

55. Concerning Clothes and Shoes

Vestments shall be given to the brothers according to the quality of the places where they dwell, or the temperature of the air. For in cold regions more is required; but in warm, less. This, therefore, is a matter for the abbot to decide. We 230 nevertheless consider that for ordinary places there suffices for the monks a cowl and a gown apiece—the cowl, in winter hairy, in summer plain or old—and a working garment, on account of their labours. As clothing for the feet, shoes and boots.

58. Concerning the Manner of Receiving Brothers

When any new comer applies for conversion, an easy entrance shall not be granted him: but, as the apostle says, "Try the spirits if they be of God." Therefore, if he who comes perseveres in knocking, and is seen after four or five days to patiently endure the insults inflicted upon him, and the difficulty of ingress, and to persist in his demand: entrance shall be allowed him, and he shall remain for a few days in the cell of the guests. After this, moreover, he shall be in the cell of the novices, where he shall meditate and eat and sleep. And an elder shall be detailed off for him who shall be capable of saving souls, who shall altogether intently watch over him, and make it a care to see if he reverently seek God, if he be zealous in the service of God, in obedience, in suffering shame. And all the harshness and roughness of the means through which God is approached shall be told him in advance. If he promise perseverance in his steadfastness, after the lapse of two months this Rule shall be read to him in order, and it shall be said to him: Behold the law under which thou dost wish to serve; if thou canst observe it, enter; but if thou canst not, depart freely. If he have stood firm thus far, then he shall be led into the aforesaid cell of the novices; and again he shall be proven with all patience. And, after the lapse of six months, the Rule shall be read to him; that he may know upon what he is entering. And, if he stand firm thus far, after four months the same Rule shall again be re-read to him. And if, having deliberated with himself, he shall promise to keep everything, and to obey all the commands that are laid upon him: then he shall be received in the congregation; knowing that it is decreed, by the law of the Rule, that from that day he shall not be allowed to depart from the monastery, nor to shake free his neck from the yoke of the Rule, which, after such tardy deliberation, he was at liberty either to refuse or receive.

64. Concerning the Ordination of an Abbot

In ordaining an abbot this consideration shall always be observed: that such a one shall be put into office as the whole congregation, according to the fear of God, with one heart—or even a part, however small, of the congregation with more prudent counsel—shall have chosen. He who is to be ordained, moreover, shall be elected for merit of life and learnedness in wisdom; even though he be the lowest in rank in the congregation. But even if the whole congregation with one consent shall have elected a person consenting to their vices—which God forbid;—and those vices shall in any way come clearly to the knowledge of the bishop to whose diocese that place pertains, or to the neighbouring abbots or

Christians: the latter shall not allow the consent of the wicked to prevail, but shall set up a dispenser worthy of the house of God; knowing that they will receive a good reward for this, if they do it chastely and with zeal for God. just so they shall know, on the contrary, that they have sinned if they neglect it.

270

21. BEOWULF
(c. 8th c. CE)

(trans. by Charles W. Kennedy)

Composed between the 8th–10th centuries by a Christian in the Midlands of England, this long heroic poem is based on an oral Germanic tradition brought over from the Continent in the 5th century by the pagan Anglo-Saxon tribes. Despite the very different perspectives of poet and subject, Beowulf's heroic actions and deeds and his boasts and concern with fame and treasure, are treated with respect by the Christian poet. The skilled poet, or scop [shaper], preserves the integrity of his own ancestral traditions while indicating the limitations of those values, and subtly coloring his material with Christian import. The three great battles Beowulf faces, his moral sensibility in giving and receiving treasure, and his acceptance of his responsibility as savior of his people, earn him praise both from his men and from his poet:

> So it is proper a man should praise
> His friendly lord with a loving heart,
> When his soul must forth from the fleeting flesh.

THE DANISH COURT AND THE RAIDS OF GRENDEL

Lo! we have listened to many a lay
Of the Spear-Danes' fame, their splendor of old,
Their mighty princes, and martial deeds!
Many a mead-hall Scyld, son of Sceaf,
5   Snatched from the forces of savage foes.
From a friendless foundling, feeble and wretched,
He grew to a terror as time brought change.
He throve under heaven in power and pride
Till alien peoples beyond the ocean
10   Paid toll and tribute. A good king he!
       To him thereafter an heir was born,
A son of his house, whom God had given
As stay to the people; God saw the distress
The leaderless nation had long endured.
15   The Giver of glory, the Lord of life,

Showered fame on the son of Scyld;
His name was honored, Beowulf[1] known,
To the farthest dwellings in Danish lands.
So must a young man strive for good
20   With gracious gifts from his father's store,
That in later seasons, if war shall scourge,
A willing people may serve him well.
'Tis by earning honor a man must rise
In every state. Then his hour struck,
25   And Scyld passed on to the peace of God.
      As their leader had bidden, whose word was law
In the Scylding realm which he long had ruled,
His loving comrades carried him down
To the shore of ocean; a ring-prowed ship,
30   Straining at anchor and sheeted with ice,
Rode in the harbor, a prince's pride.
Therein they laid him, their well-loved lord,
Their ring-bestower, in the ship's embrace,
The mighty prince at the foot of the mast
35   Amid much treasure and many a gem
From far-off lands. No lordlier ship
Have I ever heard of, with weapons heaped,
With battle-armor, with bills and byrnies.
On the ruler's breast lay a royal treasure
40   As the ship put out on the unknown deep.
With no less adornment they dressed him round,
Or gift of treasure, than once they gave
Who launched him first on the lonely sea
While still but a child. A golden standard
45   They raised above him, high over head,
Let the wave take him on trackless seas.
Mournful their mood and heavy their hearts;
Nor wise man nor warrior knows for a truth
Unto what haven that cargo came.
50   Then Beowulf ruled o'er the Scylding realm,
Beloved and famous, for many a year—
The prince, his father, had passed away—
Till, firm in wisdom and fierce in war,
The mighty Healfdene held the reign,
55   Ruled, while he lived, the lordly Scyldings.

---

[1]**Beowulf:** this is not the titular hero but rather the son of Scyld, father of Healfdene, and grandfather of Hrothgar, the Danish king whose kingdom is being ravaged by the monster Grendel. It is our titular hero Beowulf who will come to the rescue of Hrothgar and his people.

Four sons and daughters were seed of his line,
Heorogar and Hrothgar, leaders of hosts,
And Halga, the good. I have also heard
A daughter was Onela's consort and queen,
60   The fair bed-mate of the Battle-Scylfing.

      To Hrothgar was granted glory in war,
Success in battle; retainers bold
Obeyed him gladly; his band increased
To a mighty host. Then his mind was moved
65   To have men fashion a high-built hall,
A mightier mead-hall than man had known,
Wherein to portion to old and young
All goodly treasure that God had given,
Save only the folk-land, and lives of men.
70   His word was published to many a people
Far and wide o'er the ways of earth
To rear a folk-stead richly adorned;
The task was speeded, the time soon came
That the famous mead-hall was finished and done.
75   To distant nations its name was known,
The Hall of the Hart;[2] and the king kept well
His pledge and promise to deal out gifts,
Rings at the banquet. The great hall rose
High and horn-gabled, holding its place
80   Till the battle-surge of consuming flame
Should swallow it up;[3] the hour was near
That the deadly hate of a daughter's husband
Should kindle to fury and savage feud.

      Then an evil spirit who dwelt in the darkness
85   Endured it ill that he heard each day
The din of revelry ring through the hall,
The sound of the harp, and the scop's sweet song.
A skillful bard sang the ancient story
Of man's creation; how the Maker wrought
90   The shining earth with its circling waters;
In splendor established the sun and moon
As lights to illumine the land of men;
Fairly adorning the fields of earth

---

[2]**Hart,** also called by its Anglo-Saxon name, Heorot.

[3]**swallow it up:** the mead hall will be destroyed by fire in the future as a result of a failed attempt to establish peace among enemies via intermarriage. This will not occur in the poem, but the allusion serves as a general reminder that "all good things come to an end," and serves as a specific reference to a real or legendary event known to perhaps some of the audience.

With leaves and branches; creating life
95   In every creature that breathes and moves.
So the lordly warriors lived in gladness,
At ease and happy, till a fiend from hell
Began a series of savage crimes.
They called him Grendel, a demon grim
100   Haunting the fen-lands, holding the moors,
Ranging the wastes, where the wretched wight
Made his lair with the monster kin,
He bore the curse of the seed of Cain
Whereby God punished the grievous guilt
105   Of Abel's murder. Nor ever had Cain
Cause to boast of that deed of blood;
God banished him far from the fields of men;
Of his blood was begotten an evil brood,
Marauding monsters and menacing trolls,
110   Goblins and giants who battled with God
A long time. Grimly He gave them reward!
     Then at the nightfall the fiend drew near
Where the timbered mead-hall towered on high,
To spy how the Danes fared after the feast.
115   Within the wine-hall he found the warriors
Fast in slumber, forgetting grief,
Forgetting the woe of the world of men.
Grim and greedy the gruesome monster,
Fierce and furious, launched attack,
120   Slew thirty spearmen asleep in the hall,
Sped away gloating, gripping the spoil,
Dragging the dead men home to his den.
Then in the dawn with the coming of daybreak
The war-might of Grendel was widely known.
125   Mirth was stilled by the sound of weeping;
The wail of the mourner awoke with day.
And the peerless hero, the honored prince,
Weighed down with woe and heavy of heart,
Sat sorely grieving for slaughtered thanes,
130   As they traced the track of the cursed monster.
From that day onward the deadly feud
Was a long-enduring and loathsome strife.
     Not longer was it than one night later
The fiend returning renewed attack
135   With heart firm-fixed in the hateful war,
Feeling no rue for the grievous wrong.
'Twas easy thereafter to mark the men

Who sought their slumber elsewhere afar,
Found beds in the bowers, since Grendel's hate
140   Was so baldly blazoned in baleful signs.
He held himself at a safer distance
Who escaped the clutch of the demon's claw.
So Grendel raided and ravaged the realm,
One against all, in an evil war
145   Till the best of buildings was empty and still.
'Twas a weary while! Twelve winters' time
The lord of the Scyldings had suffered woe,
Sore affliction and deep distress.
And the malice of Grendel, in mournful lays,
150   Was widely sung by the sons of men,
The hateful feud that he fought with Hrothgar—
Year after year of struggle and strife,
An endless scourging, a scorning of peace
With any man of the Danish might.
155   No strength could move him to stay his hand,
Or pay for his murders; the wise knew well
They could hope for no halting of savage assault.
Like a dark death-shadow the ravaging demon,
Night-long prowling the misty moors,
160   Ensnared the warriors, wary or weak.
No man can say how these shades of hell
Come and go on their grisly rounds.
        With many an outrage, many a crime,
The fierce lone-goer, the foe of man,
165   Stained the seats of the high-built house,
Haunting the hall in the hateful dark.
But throne or treasure he might not touch,
Finding no favor or grace with God.
Great was the grief of the Scylding leader,
170   His spirit shaken, while many a lord
Gathered in council considering long
In what way brave men best could struggle
Against these terrors of sudden attack.
From time to time in their heathen temples
175   Paying homage they offered prayer
That the Slayer of souls would send them succor
From all the torment that troubled the folk.
Such was the fashion and such the faith
Of their heathen hearts that they looked to hell,
180   Not knowing the Maker, the mighty Judge,
Nor how to worship the Wielder of glory,

The Lord of heaven, the God of hosts.
Woe unto him who in fierce affliction
Shall plunge his soul in the fiery pit
185   With no hope of mercy or healing change;
But well with the soul that at death seeks God,
And finds his peace in his Father's bosom.
        The son of Healfdene was heavy-hearted,
Sorrowfully brooding in sore distress,
190   Finding no help in a hopeless strife;
Too bitter the struggle that stunned the people,
The long oppression, loathsome and grim.

THE COMING OF BEOWULF

        Then tales of the terrible deeds of Grendel
Reached Hygelac's thane[4] in his home with the Geats;
195   Of living strong men he was the strongest,
Fearless and gallant and great of heart.
He gave command for a goodly vessel
Fitted and furnished; he fain would sail
Over the swan-road to seek the king
200   Who suffered so sorely for need of men.
And his bold retainers found little to blame
In his daring venture, dear though he was;
They viewed the omens, and urged him on.
Brave was the band he had gathered about him,
205   Fourteen stalwarts seasoned and bold,
Seeking the shore where the ship lay waiting,
A sea-skilled mariner sighting the landmarks.
Came the hour of boarding; the boat was riding
The waves of the harbor under the hill.
210   The eager mariners mounted the prow;
Billows were breaking, sea against sand.
In the ship's hold snugly they stowed their trappings,
Gleaming armor and battle-gear;
Launched the vessel, the well-braced bark,
215   Seaward bound on a joyous journey.
Over breaking billows, with bellying sail
And foamy beak, like a flying bird
The ship sped on, till the next day's sun
Showed sea-cliffs shining, towering hills
220   And stretching headlands. The sea was crossed,

---

[4]**Hygelac's thane:** Beowulf

The voyage ended, the vessel moored.
And the Weder people[5] waded ashore
With clatter of trappings and coats of mail;
Gave thanks to God that His grace had granted
225   Sea-paths safe for their ocean journey.
        Then the Scylding coast-guard watched from the sea-cliff
Warriors bearing their shining shields,
Their gleaming war-gear, ashore from the ship.
His mind was puzzled, he wondered much
230   What men they were. On his good horse mounted,
Hrothgar's thane made haste to the beach,
Boldly brandished his mighty spear
With manful challenge: 'What men are you,
Carrying weapons and clad in steel,
235   Who thus come driving across the deep
On the ocean-lanes in your lofty ship?
Long have I served as the Scylding outpost,
Held watch and ward at the ocean's edge
Lest foreign foemen with hostile fleet
240   Should come to harry our Danish home,
And never more openly sailed to these shores
Men without password, or leave to land.
I have never laid eyes upon earl on earth
More stalwart and sturdy than one of your troop,
245   A hero in armor; no hall-thane he
Tricked out with weapons, unless looks belie him,
And noble bearing. But now I must know
Your birth and breeding, nor may you come
In cunning stealth upon Danish soil.
250   You distant-dwellers, you far sea-farers,
Hearken, and ponder words that are plain:
'Tis best you hasten to have me know
Who your kindred and whence you come.'
        The lord of the seamen gave swift reply,
255   The prince of the Weders unlocked his word-hoard:
'We are sprung of a strain of the Geatish stock,
Hygelac's comrades and hearth-companions.
My father was famous in many a folk-land,
A leader noble, Ecgtheow his name!
260   Many a winter went over his head
Before death took him from home and tribe;
Well nigh every wise man remembers him well

---

[5]**Weder people:** alternate name for the Geats

Far and wide on the ways of earth.
With loyal purpose we seek your lord,
265 The prince of your people, great Healfdene's son.
Be kindly of counsel; weighty the cause
That leads us to visit the lord of the Danes;
Nor need it be secret, as far as I know!
You know if it's true, as we've heard it told,
270 That among the Scyldings some secret scather,
Some stealthy demon in dead of night,
With grisly horror and fiendish hate
Is spreading unheard-of havoc and death.
Mayhap I can counsel the good, old king
275 What way he can master the merciless fiend,
If his coil of evil is ever to end
And feverish care grow cooler and fade—
Or else ever after his doom shall be
Distress and sorrow while still there stands
280 This best of halls on its lofty height.'
   Then from the saddle the coast-guard spoke,
The fearless sentry: 'A seasoned warrior
Must know the difference between words and deeds,
If his wits are with him. I take your word
285 That your band is loyal to the lord of the Scyldings.
Now go your way with your weapons and armor,
And I will guide you; I'll give command
That my good retainers may guard your ship,
Your fresh-tarred floater, from every foe,
290 And hold it safe in its sandy berth,
Till the curving prow once again shall carry
The loved man home to the land of the Geat.
To hero so gallant shall surely be granted
To come from the swordplay sound and safe.'
295   Then the Geats marched on; behind at her mooring,
Fastened at anchor, their broad-beamed boat
Safely rode on her swinging cable.
Boar-heads glittered on glistening helmets
Above their cheek-guards, gleaming with gold;
300 Bright and fire-hardened the boar held watch
Over the column of marching men.
Onward they hurried in eager haste
Till their eyes caught sight of the high-built hall,
Splendid with gold, the seat of the king,
305 Most stately of structures under the sun;
Its light shone out over many a land.

The coast-guard showed them the shining hall,
The home of heroes; made plain the path;
Turned his horse; gave tongue to words:
310 'It is time to leave you! The mighty Lord
In His mercy shield you and hold you safe
In your bold adventure. I'll back to the sea
And hold my watch against hostile horde.'

BEOWULF'S WELCOME AT HROTHGAR'S COURT

The street had paving of colored stone;
315 The path was plain to the marching men.
Bright were their byrnies, hard and hand-linked;
In their shining armor the chain-mail sang
As the troop in their war-gear tramped to the hall.
The sea-weary sailors set down their shields,
320 Their wide, bright bucklers along the wall,
And sank to the bench. Their byrnies rang.
Their stout spears stood in a stack together
Shod with iron and shaped of ash.
'Twas a well-armed troop! Then a stately warrior
325 Questioned the strangers about their kin:
'Whence come you bearing your burnished shields,
Your steel-gray harness and visored helms,
Your heap of spears? I am Hrothgar's herald,
His servant-thane. I have never seen strangers,
330 So great a number, of nobler mien.
Not exiles, I ween, but high-minded heroes
In greatness of heart have you sought out Hrothgar.'
Then bold under helmet the hero made answer,
The lord of the Weders, manful of mood,
335 Mighty of heart: 'We are Hygelac's men,
His board-companions; Beowulf is my name.
I will state my mission to Healfdene's son,
The noble leader, your lordly prince,
If he will grant approach to his gracious presence.'
340 And Wulfgar answered, the Wendel prince,
Renowned for merit in many a land,
For war-might and wisdom: 'I will learn the wish
Of the Scylding leader, the lord of the Danes,
Our honored ruler and giver of rings,
345 Concerning your mission, and soon report
The answer our leader thinks good to give.'
He swiftly strode to where Hrothgar sat

Old and gray with his earls about him;
Crossed the floor and stood face to face
350   With the Danish king; he knew courtly custom.
Wulfgar saluted his lord and friend:
'Men from afar have fared to our land
Over ocean's margin—men of the Geats,
Their leader called Beowulf—seeking a boon,
355   The holding of parley, my prince, with thee.
O gracious Hrothgar, refuse not the favor!
In their splendid war-gear they merit well
The esteem of earls; he's a stalwart leader
Who led this troop to the land of the Danes.'
360   Hrothgar spoke, the lord of the Scyldings:
'Their leader I knew when he still was a lad.
His father was Ecgtheow; Hrethel the Geat
Gave him in wedlock his only daughter.
Now is their son come, keen for adventure,
365   Finding his way to a faithful friend.
Sea-faring men who have voyaged to Geatland
With gifts of treasure as token of peace,
Say that his hand-grip has thirty men's strength.
God, in His mercy, has sent him to save us—
370   So springs my hope—from Grendel's assaults.
For his gallant courage I'll load him with gifts!
Make haste now, marshal the men to the hall,
And give them welcome to Danish ground.'
        Then to the door went the well-known warrior,
375   Spoke from the threshold welcoming words:
'The Danish leader, my lord, declares
That he knows your kinship; right welcome you come,
You stout sea-rovers, to Danish soil.
Enter now, in your shining armor
380   And vizored helmets, to Hrothgar's hall.
But leave your shields and the shafts of slaughter
To wait the issue and weighing of words.'
        Then the bold one rose with his band around him,
A splendid massing of mighty thanes;
385   A few stood guard as the Geat gave bidding
Over the weapons stacked by the wall.
They followed in haste on the heels of their leader
Under Heorot's roof. Full ready and bold
The helmeted warrior strode to the hearth;
390   Beowulf spoke; his byrny glittered,
His war-net woven by cunning of smith:

'Hail! King Hrothgar! I am Hygelac's thane,
Hygelac's kinsman. Many a deed
Of honor and daring I've done in my youth.
395   This business of Grendel was brought to my ears
On my native soil. The sea-farers say
This best of buildings, this boasted hall,
Stands dark and deserted when sun is set,
When darkening shadows gather with dusk.
400   The best of my people, prudent and brave,
Urged me, King Hrothgar, to seek you out;
They had in remembrance my courage and might.
Many had seen me come safe from the conflict,
Bloody from battle; five foes I bound
405   Of the giant kindred, and crushed their clan.
Hard-driven in danger and darkness of night
I slew the nicors[6] that swam the sea,
Avenged the woe they had caused the Weders,
And ended their evil—they needed the lesson!
410   And now with Grendel, the fearful fiend,
Single-handed I'll settle the strife!
Prince of the Danes, protector of Scyldings,
Lord of nations, and leader of men,
I beg one favor—refuse me not,
415   Since I come thus faring from far-off lands—
That I may alone with my loyal earls,
With this hardy company, cleanse Hart-Hall.
I have heard that the demon in proud disdain
Spurns all weapons; and I too scorn—
420   May Hygelac's heart have joy of the deed—
To bear my sword, or sheltering shield,
Or yellow buckler, to battle the fiend.
With hand-grip only I'll grapple with Grendel;
Foe against foe I'll fight to the death,
425   And the one who is taken must trust to God's grace!
The demon, I doubt not, is minded to feast
In the hall unaffrighted, as often before,
On the force of the Hrethmen, the folk of the Geats.
No need then to bury the body he mangles!
430   If death shall call me, he'll carry away
My gory flesh to his fen-retreat
To gorge at leisure and gulp me down,
Soiling the marshes with stains of blood.

---

[6]nicors: sea monsters

There'll be little need longer to care for my body!
435 If the battle slays me, to Hygelac send
This best of corselets that covers my breast,
Heirloom of Hrethel, and Wayland's work,[7]
Finest of byrnies. Fate goes as Fate must!'
    Hrothgar spoke, the lord of the Scyldings:
440 'Deed of daring and dream of honor
Bring you, friend Beowulf, knowing our need!
Your father once fought the greatest of feuds,
Laid Heatholaf low, of the Wylfing line;
And the folk of the Weders refused him shelter
445 For fear of revenge. Then he fled to the South-Danes,
The Honor-Scyldings beyond the sea.
I was then first governing Danish ground,
As a young lad ruling the spacious realm,
The home-land of warriors. Heorogar was dead,
450 The son of Healfdene no longer living,
My older brother, and better than I!
Thereafter by payment composing the feud,
O'er the water's ridge I sent to the Wylfing
Ancient treasure; he swore me oaths!
455 It is sorrow sore to recite to another
The wrongs that Grendel has wrought in the hall,
His savage hatred and sudden assaults.
My war-troop is weakened, my hall-band is wasted;
Fate swept them away into Grendel's grip.
460 But God may easily bring to an end
The ruinous deeds of the ravaging foe.
Full often my warriors over their ale cups
Boldly boasted, when drunk with beer,
They would bide in the beer-hall the coming of battle,
465 The fury of Grendel, with flashing swords.
Then in the dawn, when the daylight strengthened,
The hall stood reddened and reeking with gore,
Bench-boards wet with the blood of battle;
And I had the fewer of faithful fighters,
470 Beloved retainers, whom Death had taken.
Sit now at the banquet, unbend your mood,
Speak of great deeds as your heart may spur you!'
    Then in the beer-hall were benches made ready
For the Geatish heroes. Noble of heart,
475 Proud and stalwart, they sat them down

---

[7]**Wayland's work:** Wayland was the skilled blacksmith of the gods.

And a beer-thane served them; bore in his hands
The patterned ale-cup, pouring the mead,
While the scop's sweet singing was heard in the hall.
There was joy of heroes, a host at ease,
480   A welcome meeting of Weder and Dane.

UNFERTH TAUNTS BEOWULF

Then out spoke Unferth, Ecglaf's son,
Who sat at the feet of the Scylding lord,
Picking a quarrel—for Beowulf's quest,
His bold sea-voyaging, irked him sore;
485   He bore it ill that any man other
In all the earth should ever achieve
More fame under heaven than he himself:
'Are you the Beowulf that strove with Breca
In a swimming match in the open sea,
490   Both of you wantonly tempting the waves,
Risking your lives on the lonely deep
For a silly boast? No man could dissuade you,
Nor friend nor foe, from the foolhardy venture
Of ocean-swimming; with outstretched arms
495   You clasped the sea-stream, measured her streets,
With plowing shoulders parted the waves.
The sea-flood boiled with its wintry surges,
Seven nights you toiled in the tossing sea;
His strength was the greater, his swimming the stronger!
500   The waves upbore you at break of day
To the stretching beach of the Battle-Ræmas;
And Breca departed, beloved of his people,
To the land of the Brondings, the beauteous home,
The stronghold fair, where he governed the folk,
505   The city and treasure; Beanstan's son
Made good his boast to the full against you!
Therefore, I ween, worse fate shall befall,
Stout as you are in the struggle of war,
In deeds of battle, if you dare to abide
510   Encounter with Grendel at coming of night.'
Beowulf spoke, the son of Ecgtheow:
'My good friend Unferth, addled with beer
Much have you made of the deeds of Breca!
I count it true that I had more courage,
515   More strength in swimming than any other man.
In our youth we boasted—we were both of us boys—

We would risk our lives in the raging sea.
And we made it good! We gripped in our hands
Naked swords, as we swam in the waves,
520 Guarding us well from the whales' assault.
In the breaking seas he could not outstrip me,
Nor would I leave him. For five nights long
Side by side we strove in the waters
Till racing combers wrenched us apart,
525 Freezing squalls, and the falling night,
And a bitter north wind's icy blast.
Rough were the waves; the wrath of the sea-fish
Was fiercely roused; but my firm-linked byrny,
The gold-adorned corselet that covered my breast,
530 Gave firm defense from the clutching foe.
Down to the bottom a savage sea-beast
Fiercely dragged me and held me fast
In a deadly grip; none the less it was granted me
To pierce the monster with point of steel.
535 Death swept it away with the swing of my sword.
The grisly sea-beasts again and again
Beset me sore; but I served them home
With my faithful blade as was well-befitting.
They failed of their pleasure to feast their fill
540 Crowding round my corpse on the ocean-bottom!
Bloody with wounds, at the break of day,
They lay on the sea-beach slain with the sword.
No more would they cumber the mariner's course
On the ocean deep. From the east came the sun,
545 Bright beacon of God, and the seas subsided;
I beheld the headlands, the windy walls.
Fate often delivers an undoomed earl
If his spirit be gallant! And so I was granted
To slay with the sword-edge nine of the nicors.
550 I have never heard tell of more terrible strife
Under dome of heaven in darkness of night,
Nor of man harder pressed on the paths of ocean.
But I freed my life from the grip of the foe
Though spent with the struggle. The billows bore me,
555 The swirling currents and surging seas,
To the land of the Finns. And little I've heard
Of any such valiant adventures from you!
Neither Breca nor you in the press of battle
Ever showed such daring with dripping swords—
560 Though I boast not of it! But you stained your blade

With blood of your brothers, your closest of kin;
And for that you'll endure damnation in hell,
Sharp as you are! I say for a truth,
Son of Ecglaf, never had Grendel
565 Wrought such havoc and woe in the hall,
That horrid demon so harried your king,
If your heart were as brave as you'd have men think!
But Grendel has found that he never need fear
Revenge from your people, or valiant attack
570 From the Victor-Scyldings; he takes his toll,
Sparing none of the Danish stock.
He slays and slaughters and works his will
Fearing no hurt at the hands of the Danes!
But soon will I show him the stuff of the Geats,
575 Their courage in battle and strength in the strife;
Then let him who may go bold to the mead-hall
When the next day dawns on the dwellings of men,
And the sun in splendor shines warm from the south.'
Glad of heart was the giver of treasure,
580 Hoary-headed and hardy in war;
The lordly leader had hope of help
As he listened to Beowulf's bold resolve.
        There was revel of heroes and high carouse,
Their speech was happy; and Hrothgar's queen,[8]
585 Of gentle manners, in jewelled splendor
Gave courtly greeting to all the guests.
The high-born lady first bore the beaker
To the Danish leader, lord of the land,
Bade him be blithe at the drinking of beer;
590 Beloved of his people, the peerless king
Joined in the feasting, had joy of the cup.
Then to all alike went the Helming lady
Bearing the beaker to old and young,
Till the jewelled queen with courtly grace
595 Paused before Beowulf, proffered the mead.
She greeted the Geat and to God gave thanks,
Wise of word, that her wish was granted;
At last she could look to a hero for help,
Comfort in evil. He took the cup,
600 The hardy warrior, at Wealhtheow's hand
And, eager for battle, uttered his boast;
Beowulf spoke, the son of Ecgtheow:

---

[8]**Hrothgar's queen:** Wealtheow, whose name means "welfare of the people."

'I had firm resolve when I set to sea
With my band of earls in my ocean-ship,
605   Fully to work the will of your people
Or fall in the struggle slain by the foe.
I shall either perform deeds fitting an earl
Or meet in this mead-hall the coming of death!'
Then the woman was pleased with the words he uttered,
610   The Geat-lord's boast; the gold-decked queen
Went in state to sit by her lord.

BEOWULF SLAYS GRENDEL

In the hall as of old were brave words spoken,
There was noise of revel; happy the host
Till the son of Healfdene would go to his rest.
615   He knew that the monster would meet in the hall
Relentless struggle when light of the sun
Was dusky with gloom of the gathering night,
And shadow-shapes crept in the covering dark,
Dim under heaven. The host arose.
620   Hrothgar graciously greeted his guest,
Gave rule of the wine-hall, and wished him well,
Praised the warrior in parting words:
'Never to any man, early or late,
Since first I could brandish buckler and sword,
625   Have I trusted this ale-hall save only to you!
Be mindful of glory, show forth your strength,
Keep watch against foe! No wish of your heart
Shall go unfulfilled if you live through the fight.'
Then Hrothgar withdrew with his host of retainers,
630   The prince of the Scyldings, seeking his queen,
The bed of his consort. The King of Glory
Had stablished a hall-watch, a guard against Grendel,
Dutifully serving the Danish lord,
The land defending from loathsome fiend.
635   The Geatish hero put all his hope
In his fearless might and the mercy of God!
He stripped from his shoulders the byrny of steel,
Doffed helmet from head; into hand of thane
Gave inlaid iron, the best of blades;
640   Bade him keep well the weapons of war.
Beowulf uttered a gallant boast,
The stalwart Geat, ere he sought his bed:
'I count myself nowise weaker in war

Or grapple of battle than Grendel himself.
645 Therefore I scorn to slay him with sword,
Deal deadly wound, as I well might do!
Nothing he knows of a noble fighting,
Of thrusting and hewing and hacking of shield,
Fierce as he is in the fury of war.
650 In the shades of darkness we'll spurn the sword
If he dares without weapon to do or to die.
And God in His wisdom shall glory assign,
The ruling Lord, as He deems it right.'
Then the bold in battle bowed down to his rest,
655 Cheek pressed pillow; the peerless thanes
Were stretched in slumber around their lord.
Not one had hope of return to his home,
To the stronghold or land where he lived as a boy.
For they knew how death had befallen the Danes,
660 How many were slain as they slept in the wine-hall.
But the wise Lord wove them fortune in war,
Gave strong support to the Weder people;
They slew their foe by the single strength
Of a hero's courage. The truth is clear,
665 God rules forever the race of men.
      Then through the shades of enshrouding night
The fiend came stealing; the archers slept
Whose duty was holding the horn-decked hall—
Though one was watching—full well they knew
670 No evil demon could drag them down;
To shades under ground if God were not willing.
But the hero watched awaiting the foe,
Abiding in anger the issue of war.
      From the stretching moors, from the misty hollows,
675 Grendel came creeping, accursed of God,
A murderous ravager minded to snare
Spoil of heroes in high-built hall.
Under clouded heavens he held his way
Till there rose before him the high-roofed house,
680 Wine-hall of warriors gleaming with gold.
Nor was it the first of his fierce assaults
On the home of Hrothgar; but never before
Had he found worse fate or hardier hall-thanes!
Storming the building he burst the portal,
685 Though fastened of iron, with fiendish strength;
Forced open the entrance in savage fury
And rushed in rage o'er the shining floor.

A baleful glare from his eyes was gleaming
Most like to a flame. He found in the hall
690 Many a warrior sealed in slumber,
A host of kinsmen. His heart rejoiced;
The savage monster was minded to sever
Lives from bodies ere break of day,
To feast his fill of the flesh of men.
695 But he was not fated to glut his greed
With more of mankind when the night was ended!
      The hardy kinsman of Hygelac waited
To see how the monster would make his attack.
The demon delayed not, but quickly clutched
700 A sleeping thane in his swift assault,
Tore him in pieces, bit through the bones,
Gulped the blood, and gobbled the flesh,
Greedily gorged on the lifeless corpse,
The hands and the feet. Then the fiend stepped nearer,
705 Sprang on the Sea-Geat lying outstretched,
Clasping him close with his monstrous claw.
But Beowulf grappled and gripped him hard,
Struggled up on his elbow; the shepherd of sins
Soon found that never before had he felt
710 In any man other in all the earth
A mightier hand-grip; his mood was humbled,
His courage fled; but he found no escape!
He was fain to be gone; he would flee to the darkness,
The fellowship of devils. Far different his fate
715 From that which befell him in former days!
The hardy hero, Hygelac's kinsman,
Remembered the boast he had made at the banquet;
He sprang to his feet, clutched Grendel fast,
Though fingers were cracking, the fiend pulling free.
720 The earl pressed after; the monster was minded
To win his freedom and flee to the fens.
He knew that his fingers were fast in the grip
Of a savage foe. Sorry the venture,
The raid that the ravager made on the hall.
725   There was din in Heorot. For all the Danes,
The city-dwellers, the stalwart Scyldings,
That was a bitter spilling of beer!
The walls resounded, the fight was fierce,
Savage the strife as the warriors struggled.
730 The wonder was that the lofty wine-hall
Withstood the struggle, nor crashed to earth,

The house so fair; it was firmly fastened
Within and without with iron bands
Cunningly smithied; though men have said
735 That many a mead-hall gleaming with gold
Sprang from its sill as the warriors strove.
The Scylding wise men had never weened
That any ravage could wreck the building,
Firmly fashioned and finished with bone,
740 Or any cunning compass its fall,
Till the time when the swelter and surge of fire
Should swallow it up in a swirl of flame.
Continuous tumult filled the hall;
A terror fell on the Danish folk
745 As they heard through the wall the horrible wailing,
The groans of Grendel, the foe of God
Howling his hideous hymn of pain,
The hell-thane shrieking in sore defeat.
He was fast in the grip of the man who was greatest
750 Of mortal men in the strength of his might,
Who would never rest while the wretch was living,
Counting his life-days a menace to man.
Many an earl of Beowulf brandished
His ancient iron to guard his lord,
755 To shelter safely the peerless prince.
They had no knowledge, those daring thanes,
When they drew their weapons to hack and hew,
To thrust to the heart, that the sharpest sword,
The choicest iron in all the world,
760 Could work no harm to the hideous foe.
On every sword he had laid a spell,
On every blade; but a bitter death
Was to be his fate; far was the journey
The monster made to the home of fiends.
765 Then he who had wrought such wrong to men,
With grim delight as he warred with God,
Soon found that his strength was feeble and failing
In the crushing hold of Hygelac's thane.
Each loathed the other while life should last!
770 There Grendel suffered a grievous hurt,
A wound in the shoulder, gaping and wide;
Sinews snapped and bone-joints broke,
And Beowulf gained the glory of battle.
Grendel, fated, fled to the fens,
775 To his joyless dwelling, sick unto death.

He knew in his heart that his hours were numbered,
His days at an end. For all the Danes
Their wish was fulfilled in the fall of Grendel.
The stranger from far, the stalwart and strong,
780   Had purged of evil the hall of Hrothgar,
And cleansed of crime; the heart of the hero
Joyed in the deed his daring had done.
The lord of the Geats made good to the East-Danes
The boast he had uttered; he ended their ill,
785   And all the sorrow they suffered long
And needs must suffer—a foul offense.
The token was clear when the bold in battle
Laid down the shoulder and dripping claw—
Grendel's arm—in the gabled hall!

THE JOY OF THE DANES AND THE LAY OF SIGEMUND

790   When morning came, as they tell the tale,
Many a warrior hastened to hall,
Folk-leaders faring from far and near
Over wide-running ways, to gaze at the wonder,
The trail of the demon. Nor seemed his death
795   A matter of sorrow to any man
Who viewed the tracks of the vanquished monster
As he slunk weary-hearted away from the hall,
Doomed and defeated and marking his flight
With bloody prints to the nicors' pool.
800   The crimson currents bubbled and heaved
In eddying reaches reddened with gore;
The surges boiled with the fiery blood.
But the monster had sunk from the sight of men.
In that fenny covert the cursed fiend
805   Not long thereafter laid down his life,
His heathen spirit; and hell received him.
        Then all the comrades, the old and young,
The brave of heart, in a blithesome band
Came riding their horses home from the mere.
810   Beowulf's prowess was praised in song;
And many men stated that south or north,
Over all the world, or between the seas,
Or under the heaven, no hero was greater,
More worthy of rule. But no whit they slighted
815   The gracious Hrothgar, their good old king.
Time and again they galloped their horses,

Racing their roans where the roads seemed fairest;
Time and again a gleeman chanted,
A minstrel mindful of saga and lay.
820 He wove his words in a winsome pattern,
Hymning the burden of Beowulf's feat,
Clothing the story in skillful verse.

All tales he had ever heard told he sang of Sigemund's glory,[9]
Deeds of the Wælsing forgotten, his weary roving and wars,
825 *Feuds and fighting unknown to men, save Fitela only,*
Tales told by uncle to nephew when the two were companions,
What time they were bosom-comrades in battle and bitter strife.
Many of monster blood these two had slain with the sword-edge;
Great glory Sigemund gained that lingered long after death,
830 *When he daringly slew the dragon that guarded the hoard of gold.*
Under the ancient rock the warrior ventured alone,
No Fitela fighting beside him; but still it befell
That his firm steel pierced the worm, the point stood fast in the wall;
The dragon had died the death! And the hero's daring
835 *Had won the treasure to have and to hold as his heart might wish.*
Then the Wælsing loaded his sea-boat, laid in the breast of the ship
Wondrous and shining treasure; the worm dissolved in the heat.
Sigemund was strongest of men in his deeds of daring,
Warrior's shield and defender, most famous in days of old
840 *After Heremod's might diminished, his valor and vigor in war,*
Betrayed in the land of the Jutes to the hands of his foemen, and slain.
Too long the surges of sorrow swept over his soul; in the end
His life was a lingering woe to people and princes.
In former days his fate was mourned by many a warrior
845 *Who had trusted his lord for protection from terror and woe,*
Had hoped that the prince would prosper, wielding his father's wealth,
Ruling the tribe and the treasure, the Scylding city and home.
Hygelac's kinsman had favor and friendship of all mankind,
But the stain of sin sank deep into Heremod's heart.

850 Time and again on their galloping steeds
Over yellow roads they measured the mile-paths;
Morning sun mounted the shining sky
And many a hero strode to the hall,
Stout of heart, to behold the wonder.
855 The worthy ruler, the warder of treasure,

---

[9]The court poet (scop, gleeman) tells of the feats of Sigemund ("victory mind")—which very roughly parallel Beowulf's—and goes on to contrast the positive example with a negative one about Heremod ("war mind").

Set out from the bowers with stately train;
The queen with her maidens paced over the mead-path.
    Then spoke Hrothgar; hasting to hall
He stood at the steps, stared up at the roof
860 High and gold-gleaming; saw Grendel's hand:
'Thanks be to God for this glorious sight!
I have suffered much evil, much outrage from Grendel,
But the God of glory works wonder on wonder.
I had no hope of a haven from sorrow
865 While this best of houses stood badged with blood,
A woe far-reaching for all the wise
Who weened that they never could hold the hall
Against the assaults of devils and demons.
But now with God's help this hero has compassed
870 A deed our cunning could no way contrive.
Surely that woman may say with truth,
Who bore this son, if she still be living,
Our ancient God showed favor and grace
On her bringing-forth! O best of men,
875 I will keep you, Beowulf, close to my heart
In firm affection; as son to father
Hold fast henceforth to this foster-kinship.
You shall know not want of treasure or wealth
Or goodly gift that your wish may crave,
880 While I have power. For poorer deeds
I have granted guerdon, and graced with honor
Weaker warriors, feebler in fight.
You have done such deeds that your fame shall flourish
Through all the ages! God grant you still
885 All goodly grace as He gave before.'
    Beowulf spoke, the son of Ecgtheow:
'By the favor of God we won the fight,
Did the deed of valor, and boldly dared
The might of the monster. I would you could see
890 The fiend himself lying dead before you!
I thought to grip him in stubborn grasp
And bind him down on the bed of death,
There to lie straining in struggle for life,
While I gripped him fast lest he vanish away.
895 But I might not hold him or hinder his going
For God did not grant it, my fingers failed.
Too savage the strain of his fiendish strength!
To save his life he left shoulder and claw,
The arm of the monster, to mark his track.

900 But he bought no comfort; no whit thereby
Shall the wretched ravager racked with sin,
The loathsome spoiler, prolong his life.
A deep wound holds him in deadly grip,
In baleful bondage; and black with crime
905 The demon shall wait for the day of doom
When the God of glory shall give decree.'
　　　Then slower of speech was the son of Ecglaf,[10]
More wary of boasting of warlike deeds,
While the nobles gazed at the grisly claw,
910 The fiend's hand fastened by hero's might
On the lofty roof. Most like to steel
Were the hardened nails, the heathen's hand-spurs,
Horrible, monstrous; and many men said
No tempered no excellent iron,
915 Could have harried the monster or hacked away
The demon's battle-claw dripping with blood.

THE FEAST AND THE LAY OF FINNSBURG

　　　In joyful haste was Heorot decked
And a willing host of women and men
Gaily dressed and adorned the guest-hall.
920 Splendid hangings with sheen of gold
Shone on the walls, a glorious sight
To eyes that delight to behold such wonders.
The shining building was wholly shattered
Though braced and fastened with iron bands;
925 Hinges were riven; the roof alone
Remained unharmed when the horrid monster,
Foul with evil, slunk off in flight,
Hopeless of life. It is hard to flee
The touch of death, let him try who will;
930 Necessity urges the sons of men,
The dwellers on earth, to their destined place
Where the body, bound in its narrow bed,
After the feasting is fast in slumber.
　　　Soon was the time when the son of Healfdene
935 Went to the wine-hall; he fain would join
With happy heart in the joy of feasting.
I never have heard of a mightier muster
Of proud retainers around their prince.

---

[10]**son of Ecglaf:** Unferth ("lacking spirit"), the jealous thane of Hrothgar.

All at ease they bent to the benches,
940 Had joy of the banquet; their kinsmen bold,
Hrothgar and Hrothulf, happy of heart,
In the high-built hall drank many a mead-cup.
The hall of Hrothgar was filled with friends;
No treachery yet had troubled the Scyldings.
945 Upon Beowulf, then, as a token of triumph,
Hrothgar bestowed a standard of gold,
A banner embroidered, a byrny and helm.
In sight of many, a costly sword
Before the hero was borne on high;
950 Beowulf drank of many a bowl.
No need for shame in the sight of heroes
For gifts so gracious! I never have heard
Of many men dealing in friendlier fashion,
To others on ale-bench, richer rewards,
955 Four such treasures fretted with gold!
On the crest of the helmet a crowning wreath,
Woven of wire-work, warded the head
Lest tempered swordblade, sharp from the file,
Deal deadly wound when the shielded warrior
960 Went forth to battle against the foe.
Eight horses also with plated headstalls
The lord of heroes bade lead into hall;
On one was a saddle skillfully fashioned
And set with jewels, the battle-seat
965 Of the king himself, when the son of Healfdene
Would fain take part in the play of swords;
Never in fray had his valor failed,
His kingly courage, when corpses were falling.
And the prince of the Ingwines gave all these gifts
970 To the hand of Beowulf, horses and armor;
Bade him enjoy them! With generous heart
The noble leader, the lord of heroes,
Rewarded the struggle with steeds and with treasure,
So that none can belittle, and none can blame,
975 Who tells the tale as it truly happened.
　　Then on the ale-bench to each of the earls
Who embarked with Beowulf, sailing the sea-paths,
The lord of princes dealt ancient heirlooms,
Gift of treasure, and guerdon of gold
980 To requite his slaughter whom Grendel slew,
As he would have slain others, but all-wise God
And the hero's courage had conquered Fate.

The Lord ruled over the lives of men
As He rules them still. Therefore understanding
985   And a prudent spirit are surely best!
He must suffer much of both weal and woe
Who dwells here long in these days of strife.
      Then song and revelry rose in the hall;
Before Healfdene's leader the harp was struck
990   And hall-joy wakened; the song was sung,
Hrothgar's gleeman rehearsed the lay
Of the sons of Finn when the terror befell them:[11]

Hnæf of the Scyldings, the Half-Dane, fell in the Frisian slaughter;
Nor had Hildeburh cause to acclaim the faith of the Jutish folk,
995   *Blameless, bereft of her brothers in battle, and stripped of her sons*
Who fell overcome by their fate and wounded with spears!
Not for nothing Hoc's daughter bewailed death's bitter decree,
In the dawn under morning skies, when she saw the slaughter of kinsmen
      In the place where her days had been filled with the fairest delights of the
1000   *world.*
Finn's thanes were slain in the fight, save only a few;
Nor could he do battle with Hengest or harry his shattered host;
And the Frisians made terms with the Danes, a truce, a hall for their dwelling,
A throne, and a sharing of rights with the sons of the Jutes,
1005   *And that Finn, the son of Folcwalda, each day would honor the Danes,*
The host of Hengest, with gifts, with rings and guerdon of gold,
Such portion of plated treasure as he dealt to the Frisian folk
When he gladdened their hearts in the hall. So both were bound by the truce.
And Finn swore Hengest with oaths that were forceful and firm
1010   *He would rightfully rule his remnant, follow his council's decree,*
And that no man should break the truce, or breach it by word or by will,
Nor the lordless in malice lament they were fated to follow
The man who had murdered their liege; and, if ever a Frisian
Fanned the feud with insolent speech, the sword should avenge it.
1015   *Then a funeral pyre was prepared, and gold was drawn from the hoard,*
The best of the Scylding leaders was laid on the bier;
In the burning pile was a gleaming of blood-stained byrnies,
The gilded swine and the boar-helm hard from the hammer,
Many a warrior fated with wounds and fallen in battle.
1020   *And Hildeburh bade that her son be laid on the bier of Hnæf,*
His body consumed in the surging flame at his uncle's shoulder.
Beside it the lady lamented, singing her mournful dirge.
The hero was placed on the pyre; the greatest of funeral flames

---

[11]The story of Finn is the longest and most complete of the digressions the poet incorporates in *Beowulf.*

Rolled with a roar to the skies at the burial barrow.
1025   *Heads melted and gashes gaped, the mortal wounds of the body,*
Blood poured out in the flames; the fire, most greedy of spirits,
Swallowed up all whom battle had taken of both their peoples.
Their glory was gone! The warriors went to their homes,
Bereft of their friends, returning to Friesland, to city and strong-hold.
1030   *Then Hengest abode with Finn all the slaughter-stained winter,*
But his heart longed ever for home, though he could not launch on the sea
His ring-stemmed ship, for the billows boiled with the storm,
Strove with the wind, and the winter locked ocean in bonds of ice;
Till a new Spring shone once more on the dwellings of men,
1035   *The sunny and shining days which ever observe their season.*
The winter was banished afar, and fair the bosom of earth.
Then the exile longed to be gone, the guest from his dwelling,
But his thoughts were more on revenge than on voyaging over the wave,
Plotting assault on the Jutes, renewal of war with the sword.
1040   *So he spurned not the naked hint when Hunlafing laid in his lap*
The battle-flasher, the best of blades, well known to the Jutes!
In his own home death by the sword befell Finn, the fierce-hearted,
When Guthlaf and Oslaf requited the grim attack,
The woe encountered beyond the sea, the sorrow they suffered,
1045   *Nor could bridle the restive spirits within their breasts!*
Then the hall was reddened with blood and bodies of foemen,
Finn killed in the midst of his men, and the fair queen taken.
The Scylding warriors bore to their ships all treasure and wealth,
Such store as they found in the home of Finn of jewels and gems.
1050   *And the noble queen they carried across the sea-paths,*
Brought her back to the Danes, to her own dear people.

So the song was sung, the lay recited,
The sound of revelry rose in the hall.
Stewards poured wine from wondrous vessels;
1055   And Wealhtheow, wearing a golden crown,
Came forth in state where the two were sitting,
Courteous comrades, uncle and nephew,
Each true to the other in ties of peace.
Unferth, the orator, sat at the feet
1060   Of the lord of the Scyldings; and both showed trust
In his noble mind, though he had no mercy
On kinsmen in swordplay; the Scylding queen spoke:
'My sovereign lord, dispenser of treasure,
Drink now of this flagon, have joy of the feast!
1065   Speak to the Geats, O gold-friend of men,
In winning words as is well-befitting;

Be kind to the Geat-men and mindful of gifts
From the gold you have garnered from near and far.
You have taken as son, so many have told me,
1070   This hardy hero. Heorot is cleansed,
The gleaming gift-hall. Rejoice while you may
In lavish bounty, and leave to your kin
People and kingdom when time shall come,
Your destined hour, to look on death.
1075   I know the heart of my gracious Hrothulf,
That he'll safely shelter and shield our sons
When you leave this world, if he still is living.
I know he will favor with gracious gifts
These boys of ours, if he bears in mind
1080   The many honors and marks of love
We bestowed upon him while he still was a boy.'
      She turned to the bench where her boys were sitting,
Hrethric and Hrothmund, the sons of heroes,
The youth together; there the good man sat,
1085   Beowulf of the Geats, beside the two brothers.
Then the cup was offered with gracious greeting,
And seemly presents of spiraled gold,
A corselet, and rings, and the goodliest collar
Of all that ever were known on earth.
1090   I have never heard tell of a worthier treasure
In the hoarding of heroes beneath the sky
Since Hama bore off to the shining city
The Brosings' jewel, setting and gems,
Fled from Eormenric's cruel craft
1095   And sought the grace of eternal glory.
Hygelac, the Geat, grandson of Swerting
Wore the ring in the last of his raids,
Guarding the spoil under banner in battle,
Defending the treasure. Overtaken by Fate,
1100   In the flush of pride he fought with the Frisians
And met disaster. The mighty prince
Carried the ring o'er the cup of the waves,
The precious jewel, and sank under shield.
Then his body fell into Frankish hands,
1105   His woven corselet and jewelled collar,
And weaker warriors plundered the dead
After the carnage and welter of war.
The field of battle was covered with corpses
Of Geats who had fallen, slain by the sword.
1110   The sound of revelry rose in the hall;

Wealhtheow spoke to the warrior host:
'Take, dear Beowulf, collar and corselet,
Wear these treasures with right good will!
Thrive and prosper and prove your might!
1115 Befriend my boys with your kindly counsel;
I will remember and I will repay.
You have earned the undying honor of heroes
In regions reaching as far and wide
As the windy walls that the sea encircles.
1120 May Fate show favor while life shall last!
I wish you wealth to your heart's content;
In your days of glory be good to my sons!
Here each hero is true to other,
Gentle of spirit, loyal to lord,
1125 Friendly thanes and a folk united,
Wine-cheered warriors who do my will.'

THE TROLL-WIFE AVENGES GRENDEL

Then she went to her seat. At the fairest of feasts
Men drank of the wine-cup, knowing not Fate,
Nor the fearful doom that befell the earls
1130 When darkness gathered, and gracious Hrothgar
Sought his dwelling and sank to rest.
A host of heroes guarded the hall
As they oft had done in the days of old.
They stripped the benches and spread the floor
1135 With beds and bolsters. But one of the beer-thanes
Bowed to his hall-rest doomed to death.
They set at their heads their shining shields,
Their battle-bucklers; and there on the bench
Above each hero his towering helmet,
1140 His spear and corselet hung close at hand.
It was ever their wont to be ready for war
At home or in field, as it ever befell
That their lord had need. 'Twas a noble race!
Then they sank to slumber. But one paid dear
1145 For his evening rest, as had often happened
When Grendel haunted the lordly hall
And wrought such ruin, till his end was come,
Death for his sins; it was easily seen,
Though the monster was slain, an avenger survived
1150 Prolonging the feud, though the fiend had perished.
The mother of Grendel, a monstrous hag,

Brooded over her misery, doomed to dwell
In evil waters and icy streams
From ancient ages when Cain had killed
1155   His only brother, his father's son.
Banished and branded with marks of murder
Cain fled far from the joys of men,
Haunting the barrens, begetting a brood
Of grisly monsters; and Grendel was one,
1160   The fiendish monster who found in the hall
A hero on watch, and awaiting the fray.
The monster grappled; the Geat took thought
Of the strength of his might, that marvelous gift
Which the Lord had given; in God he trusted
1165   For help and succor and strong support,
Whereby he humbled the fiend from hell,
Destroyed the demon; and Grendel fled,
Harrowed in heart and hateful to man,
Deprived of joy, to the place of death.
1170   But rabid and raging his mother resolved
On a dreadful revenge for the death of her son!
     She stole to the hall where the Danes were sleeping,
And horror fell on the host of earls
When the dam of Grendel burst in the door.
1175   But the terror was less as the war-craft is weaker,
A woman's strength, than the might of a man
When the hilted sword, well shaped by the hammer,
The blood-stained iron of tempered edge,
Hews the boar from the foeman's helmet.
1180   Then in the hall was the hard-edged blade,
The stout steel, brandished above the benches;
Seizing their shields men stayed not for helmet
Or ample byrny, when fear befell.
As soon as discovered, the hag was in haste
1185   To fly to the open, to flee for her life.
One of the warriors she swiftly seized,
Clutched him fast and made off to the fens.
He was of heroes the dearest to Hrothgar,
The best of comrades between two seas;
1190   The warrior brave, the stout-hearted spearman,
She slew in his sleep. Nor was Beowulf there;
But after the banquet another abode
Had been assigned to the glorious Geat.
There was tumult in Heorot. She tore from its place
1195   The blood-stained claw. Care was renewed!

It was no good bargain when both in turn
Must pay the price with the lives of friends!
    Then the white-haired warrior, the aged king,
Was numb with sorrow, knowing his thane
1200   No longer was living, his dearest man dead.
Beowulf, the brave, was speedily summoned,
Brought to the bower; the noble prince
Came with his comrades at dawn of day
Where the wise king awaited if God would award
1205   Some happier turn in these tidings of woe.
The hero came tramping into the hall
With his chosen band—the boards resounded—
Greeted the leader, the Ingwine lord,
And askèd if the night had been peaceful and pleasant.
1210   Hrothgar spoke, the lord of the Scyldings:
'Ask not of pleasure; pain is renewed
For the Danish people. Æschere is dead!
Dead is Yrmenlaf's elder brother!
He was my comrade, closest of counsellors,
1215   My shoulder-companion as side by side
We fought for our lives in the welter of war,
In the shock of battle when boar-helms crashed.
As an earl should be, a prince without peer,
Such was Æschere, slain in the hall
1220   By the wandering demon! I know not whither
She fled to shelter, proud of her spoil,
Gorged to the full. She avenged the feud
Wherein yesternight you grappled with Grendel
And savagely slew him because so long
1225   He had hunted and harried the men of my folk.
He fell in the battle and paid with his life.
But now another fierce ravager rises
Avenging her kinsman, and carries it far,
As it seems to many a saddened thane
1230   Who grieves in his heart for his treasure-giver.
This woe weighs heavy! The hand lies still
That once was lavish of all delights.
    Oft in the hall I have heard my people,
Comrades and counsellors, telling a tale
1235   Of evil spirits their eyes have sighted,
Two mighty marauders who haunt the moors.
One shape, as clearly as men could see,
Seemed woman's likeness, and one seemed man,
An outcast wretch of another world,

1240 And huger far than a human form.
   Grendel my countrymen called him, not knowing
   What monster-brood spawned him, what sire begot.
   Wild and lonely the land they live in,
   Wind-swept ridges and wolf-retreats,
1245 Dread tracts of fen where the falling torrent
   Downward dips into gloom and shadow
   Under the dusk of the darkening cliff.
   Not far in miles lies the lonely mere
   Where trees firm-rooted and hung with frost
1250 Overshroud the wave with shadowing gloom.
   And there a portent appears each night,
   A flame in the water; no man so wise
   Who knows the bound of its bottomless depth.
   The heather-stepper, the horned stag,
1255 The antlered hart hard driven by hounds,
   Invading that forest in flight from afar
   Will turn at bay and die on the brink
   Ere ever he'll plunge in that haunted pool.
   'Tis an eerie spot! Its tossing spray
1260 Mounts dark to heaven when high winds stir
   The driving storm, and the sky is murky,
   And with foul weather the heavens weep.
   On your arm only rests all our hope!
   Not yet have you tempted those terrible reaches
1265 The region that shelters that sinful wight.
   Go if you dare! I will give requital
   With ancient treasure and twisted gold,
   As I formerly gave in guerdon of battle,
   If out of that combat you come alive.'
1270   Beowulf spoke, the son of Ecgtheow:
   'Sorrow not, brave one! Better for man
   To avenge a friend than much to mourn.
   All men must die; let him who may
   Win glory ere death. That guerdon is best
1275 For a noble man when his name survives him.
   Then let us rise up, O ward of the realm,
   And haste us forth to behold the track
   Of Grendel's dam. And I give you pledge
   She shall not in safety escape to cover,
1280 To earthy cavern, or forest fastness,
   Or gulf of ocean, go where she may.
   This day with patience endure the burden
   Of every woe, as I know you will.'

Up sprang the ancient, gave thanks to God
1285   For the heartening words the hero had spoken.

BEOWULF SLAYS THE TROLL-WIFE

Quickly a horse was bridled for Hrothgar,
A mettlesome charger with braided mane;
In royal splendor the king rode forth
Mid the trampling tread of a troop of shieldmen.
1290   The tracks lay clear where the fiend had fared
Over plain and bottom and woodland path,
Through murky moorland making her way
With the lifeless body, the best of thanes
Who of old with Hrothgar had guarded the hall.
1295   By a narrow path the king pressed on
Through rocky upland and rugged ravine,
A lonely journey, past looming headlands,
The lair of monster and lurking troll.
Tried retainers, a trusty few,
1300   Advanced with Hrothgar to view the ground.
Sudden they came on a dismal covert
Of trees that hung over hoary stone,
Over churning water and blood-stained wave.
Then for the Danes was the woe the deeper,
1305   The sorrow sharper for Scylding earls,
When they first caught sight, on the rocky sea-cliff,
Of slaughtered Æschere's severed head.
The water boiled in a bloody swirling
With seething gore as the spearmen gazed.
1310   The trumpet sounded a martial strain;
The shield-troop halted. Their eyes beheld
The swimming forms of strange sea-dragons,
Dim serpent shapes in the watery depths,
Sea-beasts sunning on headland slopes;
1315   Snakelike monsters that oft at sunrise
On evil errands scour the sea.
Startled by tumult and trumpet's blare,
Enraged and savage, they swam away;
But one the lord of the Geats brought low,
1320   Stripped of his sea-strength, despoiled of life,
As the bitter bow-bolt pierced his heart.
His watery-speed grew slower, and ceased,
And he floated, caught in the clutch of death.
Then they hauled him in with sharp-hooked boar-spears,

1325 By sheer strength grappled and dragged him ashore,
   A wondrous wave-beast; and all the array
   Gathered to gaze at the grisly guest.
     Beowulf donned his armor for battle,
   Heeded not danger; the hand-braided byrny,
1330 Broad of shoulder and richly bedecked,
   Must stand the ordeal of the watery depths.
   Well could that corselet defend the frame
   Lest hostile thrust should pierce to the heart.
   Or blows of battle beat down the life.
1335 A gleaming helmet guarded his head
   As he planned his plunge to the depths of the pool
   Through the heaving waters—a helm adorned
   With lavish inlay and lordly chains,
   Ancient work of the weapon-smith
1340 Skillfully fashioned, beset with the boar,
   That no blade of battle might bite it through.
   Not the least or the worst of his war-equipment
   Was the sword the herald of Hrothgar loaned
   In his hour of need—Hrunting its name—
1345 An ancient heirloom, trusty and tried;
   Its blade was iron, with etched design,
   Tempered in blood of many a battle.
   Never in fight had it failed the hand
   That drew it daring the perils of war,
1350 The rush of the foe. Not the first time then
   That its edge must venture on valiant deeds.
   But Ecglaf's stalwart son was unmindful
   Of words he had spoken while heated with wine,
   When he loaned the blade to a better swordsman.
1355 He himself dared not hazard his life
   In deeds of note in the watery depths;
   And thereby he forfeited honor and fame.
   Not so with that other undaunted spirit
   After he donned his armor for battle.
1360 Beowulf spoke, the son of Ecgtheow:
   'O gracious ruler, gold-giver to men,
   As I now set forth to attempt this feat,
   Great son of Healfdene, hold well in mind
   The solemn pledge we plighted of old,
1365 That if doing your service I meet my death
   You will mark my fall with a father's love.
   Protect my kinsmen, my trusty comrades,
   If battle take me. And all the treasure

You have heaped on me bestow upon Hygelac,
1370   Hrothgar beloved! The lord of the Geats,
The son of Hrethel, shall see the proof,
Shall know as he gazes on jewels and gold,
That I found an unsparing dispenser of bounty,
And joyed, while I lived, in his generous gifts.
1375   Give back to Unferth the ancient blade,
The sword-edge splendid with curving scrolls,
For either with Hrunting I'll reap rich harvest
Of glorious deeds, or death shall take me.'
       After these words the prince of the Weders
1380   Awaited no answer, but turned to the task,
Straightway plunged in the swirling pool.
Nigh unto a day he endured the depths
Ere he first had view of the vast sea-bottom.
Soon she found, who had haunted the flood,
1385   A ravening hag, for a hundred half-years,
Greedy and grim, that a man was groping
In daring search through the sea-troll's home.
Swift she grappled and grasped the warrior
With horrid grip, but could work no harm,
1390   No hurt to his body; the ring-locked byrny
Cloaked his life from her clutching claw;
Nor could she tear through the tempered mail
With her savage fingers. The she-wolf bore
The ring-prince down through the watery depths
1395   To her den at the bottom; nor could Beowulf draw
His blade for battle, though brave his mood.
Many a sea-beast, strange sea-monsters,
Tasked him hard with their menacing tusks,
Broke his byrny and smote him sore.
1400   Then he found himself in a fearsome hall
Where water came not to work him hurt,
But the flood was stayed by the sheltering roof.
There in the glow of firelight gleaming
The hero had view of the huge sea-troll.
1405   He swung his war-sword with all his strength,
Withheld not the blow, and the savage blade
Sang on her head its hymn of hate.
But the bold one found that the battle-flasher
Would bite no longer, nor harm her life.
1410   The sword-edge failed at his sorest need.
Often of old with ease it had suffered
The clash of battle, cleaving the helm,

The fated warrior's woven mail.
That time was first for the treasured blade
1415   That its glory failed in the press of the fray.
But fixed of purpose and firm of mood
Hygelac's earl was mindful of honor;
In wrath, undaunted, he dashed to earth
The jewelled sword with its scrolled design,
1420   The blade of steel; staked all on strength,
On the might of his hand, as a man must do
Who thinks to win in the welter of battle
Enduring glory; he fears not death.
The Geat-prince joyed in the straining struggle,
1425   Stalwart-hearted and stirred to wrath,
Gripped the shoulder of Grendel's dam
And headlong hurled the hag to the ground.
But she quickly clutched him and drew him close,
Countered the onset with savage claw.
1430   The warrior staggered, for all his strength,
Dismayed and shaken and borne to earth.
She knelt upon him and drew her dagger,
With broad bright blade, to avenge her son,
Her only issue. But the corselet's steel
1435   Shielded his breast and sheltered his life
Withstanding entrance of point and edge.
      Then the prince of the Geats would have gone his journey,
The son of Ecgtheow, under the ground;
But his sturdy breast-net, his battle-corselet,
1440   Gave him succor, and holy God,
The Lord all-wise, awarded the mastery;
Heaven's Ruler gave right decree.
      Swift the hero sprang to his feet;
Saw mid the war-gear a stately sword,
1445   An ancient war-brand of biting edge,
Choicest of weapons worthy and strong,
The work of giants, a warrior's joy,
So heavy no hand but his own could hold it,
Bear to battle or wield in war.
1450   Then the Scylding warrior, savage and grim,
Seized the ring-hilt and swung the sword,
Struck with fury, despairing of life,
Thrust at the throat, broke through the bone-rings;
The stout blade stabbed through her fated flesh.
1455   She sank in death; the sword was bloody;
The hero joyed in the work of his hand.

The gleaming radiance shimmered and shone
As the candle of heaven shines clear from the sky.
Wrathful and resolute Hygelac's thane
1460 Surveyed the span of the spacious hall;
Grimly gripping the hilted sword
With upraised weapon he turned to the wall.
The blade had failed not the battle-prince;
A full requital he firmly planned
1465 For all the injury Grendel had done
In numberless raids on the Danish race,
When he slew the hearth-companions of Hrothgar,
Devoured fifteen of the Danish folk
Clasped in slumber, and carried away
1470 As many more spearmen, a hideous spoil.
All this the stout-heart had stern requited;
And there before him bereft of life
He saw the broken body of Grendel
Stilled in battle, and stretched in death,
1475 As the struggle in Heorot smote him down.
The corpse sprang wide as he struck the blow,
The hard sword-stroke that severed the head.
     Then the tried retainers, who there with Hrothgar
Watched the face of the foaming pool,
1480 Saw that the churning reaches were reddened,
The eddying surges stained with blood.
And the gray, old spearmen spoke of the hero,
Having no hope he would ever return
Crowned with triumph and cheered with spoil.
1485 Many were sure that the savage sea-wolf
Had slain their leader. At last came noon.
The stalwart Scyldings forsook the headland;
Their proud gold-giver departed home.
But the Geats sat grieving and sick in spirit,
1490 Stared at the water with longing eyes,
Having no hope they would ever behold
Their gracious leader and lord again.
     Then the great sword, eaten with blood of battle,
Began to soften and waste away
1495 In iron icicles, wonder of wonders,
Melting away most like to ice
When the Father looses the fetters of frost,
Slackens the bondage that binds the wave,
Strong in power of times and seasons;
1500 He is true God! Of the goodly treasures

From the sea-cave Beowulf took but two,
The monster's head and the precious hilt
Blazing with gems; but the blade had melted,
The sword dissolved, in the deadly heat,
1505   The venomous blood of the fallen fiend.

BEOWULF RETURNS TO HEOROT

Then he who had compassed the fall of his foes
Came swimming up through the swirling surge.
Cleansed were the currents, the boundless abyss,
Where the evil monster had died the death
1510   And looked her last on this fleeting world.
With sturdy strokes the lord of the seamen
To land came swimming, rejoiced in his spoil,
Had joy of the burden he brought from the depths.
And his mighty thanes came forward to meet him,
1515   Gave thanks to God they were granted to see
Their well-loved leader both sound and safe.
From the stalwart hero his helmet and byrny
Were quickly loosened; the lake lay still,
Its motionless reaches reddened with blood.
1520   Fain of heart men fared o'er the footpaths,
Measured the ways and the well-known roads.
From the sea-cliff's brim the warriors bore
The head of Grendel, with heavy toil,
Four of the stoutest, with all their strength,
1525   Could hardly carry on swaying spear
Grendel's head to the gold-decked hall.
Swift they strode, the daring and dauntless,
Fourteen Geats, to the Hall of the Hart;
And proud in the midst of his marching men
1530   Their leader measured the path to the mead-hall.
The hero entered, the hardy in battle,
The great in glory, to greet the king;
And Grendel's head by the hair was carried
Across the floor where the feasters drank—
1535   A terrible sight for lord and for lady—
A gruesome vision whereon men gazed!
Beowulf spoke, the son of Ecgtheow:
'O son of Healfdene, lord of the Scyldings!
This sea-spoil wondrous, whereon you stare,
1540   We joyously bring you in token of triumph!
Barely with life surviving the battle,

The war under water, I wrought the deed
Weary and spent; and death had been swift
Had God not granted His sheltering strength.
1545 My strong-edged Hrunting, stoutest of blades,
Availed me nothing. But God revealed—
Often His arm has aided the friendless—
The fairest of weapons hanging on wall,
An ancient broadsword; I seized the blade,
1550 Slew in the struggle, as fortune availed,
The cavern-warders. But the war-brand old,
The battle-blade with its scrolled design,
Dissolved in the gush of the venomous gore;
The hilt alone I brought from the battle.
1555 The record of ruin, and slaughter of Danes,
These wrongs I avenged, as was fitting and right.
Now I can promise you, prince of the Scyldings,
Henceforth in Heorot rest without rue
For you and your nobles; nor need you dread
1560 Slaughter of follower, stalwart or stripling
Or death of earl, as of old you did.'
Into the hand of the aged leader,
The gray-haired hero, he gave the hilt,
The work of giants, the wonder of gold.
1565 At the death of the demons the Danish lord
Took in his keeping the cunning craft,
The wondrous marvel, of mighty smiths;
When the world was freed of the ravaging fiend,
The foe of God, and his fearful dam
1570 Marked with murder and badged with blood,
The bound hilt passed to the best of kings
Who ever held sceptre beside two seas,
And dealt out treasure in Danish land!
        Hrothgar spoke, beholding the hilt,
1575 The ancient relic whereon was etched
An olden record of struggle and strife,
The flood that ravaged the giant race,
The rushing deluge of ruin and death.
That evil kindred were alien to God,
1580 But the Ruler avenged with the wrath of the deep!
On the hilt-guards, likewise, of gleaming gold
Was rightly carven in cunning runes,
Set forth and blazoned, for whom that blade
With spiral tooling and twisted hilt,
1585 That fairest of swords, was fashioned and smithied.

Then out spoke Hrothgar, Healfdene's son,
And all the retainers were silent and still:
'Well may he say, whose judgment is just,
Recalling to memory men of the past,
1590 That this earl was born of a better stock!
Your fame, friend Beowulf, is blazoned abroad
Over all wide ways, and to every people.
In manful fashion have you showed your strength,
Your might and wisdom. My word I will keep,
1595 The plighted friendship we formerly pledged.
Long shall you stand as a stay to your people,
A help to heroes, as Heremod was not
To the Honor-Scyldings, to Ecgwela's sons!
Not joy to kindred, but carnage and death,
1600 He wrought as he ruled o'er the race of the Danes.
In savage anger he slew his comrades,
His table-companions, till, lawless and lone,
An odious outcast, he fled from men.
Though God had graced him with gifts of strength,
1605 Over all men exalting him, still in his breast
A bloodthirsty spirit was rooted and strong.
He dealt not rings to the Danes for glory;
His lot was eternal torment of woe,
And lasting affliction. Learn from his fate!
1610 Strive for virtue! I speak for your good;
In the wisdom of age I have told the tale.
        'Tis a wondrous marvel how mighty God
In gracious spirit bestows on men
The gift of wisdom, and goodly lands,
1615 And princely power! He rules over all!
He suffers a man of lordly line
To set his heart on his own desires,
Awards him fullness of worldly joy,
A fair home-land, and the sway of cities,
1620 The wide dominion of many a realm,
An ample kingdom, till, cursed with folly,
The thoughts of his heart take no heed of his end.
He lives in luxury, knowing not want,
Knowing no shadow of sickness or age;
1625 No haunting sorrow darkens his spirit,
No hatred or discord deepens to war;
The world is sweet, to his every desire,
And evil assails not—until in his heart
Pride overpowering gathers and grows!

1630   The warder slumbers, the guard of his spirit;
    Too sound is that sleep, too sluggish the weight
    Of worldly affairs, too pressing the Foe,
    The Archer who looses the arrows of sin.
        Then is his heart pierced, under his helm,
1635   His soul in his bosom, with bitter dart.
    He has no defense for the fierce assaults
    Of the loathsome Fiend. What he long has cherished
    Seems all too little! In anger and greed
    He gives no guerdon of plated rings.
1640   Since God has granted him glory and wealth
    He forgets the future, unmindful of Fate.
    But it comes to pass in the day appointed
    His feeble body withers and fails;
    Death descends, and another seizes
1645   His hoarded riches and rashly spends
    The princely treasure, imprudent of heart.
    Beloved Beowulf, best of warriors,
    Avoid such evil and seek the good,
    The heavenly wisdom. Beware of pride!
1650   Now for a time you shall feel the fullness
    And know the glory of strength, but soon
    Sickness or sword shall strip you of might,
    Or clutch of fire, or clasp of flood,
    Or flight of arrow, or bite of blade,
1655   Or relentless age; or the light of the eye
    Shall darken and dim, and death on a sudden,
    O lordly ruler, shall lay you low.
        A hundred half-years I've been head of the Ring-Danes,
    Defending the folk against many a tribe
1660   With spear-point and sword in the surges of battle
    Till not one was hostile 'neath heaven's expanse.
    But a loathsome change swept over the land,
    Grief after gladness, when Grendel came,
    That evil invader, that ancient foe!
1665   Great sorrow of soul from his malice I suffered;
    But thanks be to God who has spared me to see
    His bloody head at the battle's end!
    Join now in the banquet; have joy of the feast,
    O mighty in battle! And the morrow shall bring
1670   Exchange of treasure in ample store.'
        Happy of heart the Geat leader hastened,
    Took seat at the board as the good king bade.
    Once more, as of old, brave heroes made merry

And tumult of revelry rose in the hall.
1675   Then dark over men the night shadows deepened;
The host all arose, for Hrothgar was minded,
The gray, old Scylding, to go to his rest.
On Beowulf too, after labor of battle,
Came limitless longing and craving for sleep.
1680 A hall-thane graciously guided the hero,
Weary and worn, to the place prepared,
Serving his wishes and every want
As befitted a mariner come from afar.
The stout-hearted warrior sank to his rest;
1685 The lofty building, splendid and spacious,
Towered above him. His sleep was sound
Till the black-coated raven, blithesome of spirit,
Hailed the coming of Heaven's bliss.

THE PARTING OF BEOWULF AND HROTHGAR

Then over the shadows uprose the sun.
1690 The Geats were in haste, and eager of heart
To depart to their people. Beowulf longed
To embark in his boat, to set sail for his home.
The hero tendered the good sword Hrunting
To the son of Ecglaf, bidding him bear
1695 The lovely blade; gave thanks for the loan,
Called it a faithful friend in the fray,
Bitter in battle. The greathearted hero
Spoke no word in blame of the blade!
Arrayed in war-gear, and ready for sea,
1700 The warriors bestirred them; and, dear to the Danes,
Beowulf sought the high seat of the king.
The gallant in war gave greeting to Hrothgar;
Beowulf spoke, the son of Ecgtheow:
'It is time at last to tell of our longing!
1705 Our homes are far, and our hearts are fain
To seek again Hygelac over the sea.
You have welcomed us royally, harbored us well
As a man could wish; if I ever can win
Your affection more fully, O leader of heroes,
1710 Swift shall you find me to serve you again!
If ever I learn, o'er the levels of ocean,
That neighboring nations beset you sore,
As in former days when foemen oppressed,
With thanes by the thousand I will hasten to help.

1715 For I know that Hygelac, lord of the Geats,
　　　 Prince of the people, though young in years,
　　　 Will favor and further by word and deed
　　　 That my arm may aid you, and do you honor,
　　　 With stout ash-spear and succor of strength
1720 In the press of need. And if princely Hrethric
　　　 Shall purpose to come to the court of the Geats,
　　　 He will find there a legion of loyal friends.
　　　 That man fares best to a foreign country
　　　 Who himself is stalwart and stout of heart.'
1725 　　　Hrothgar addressed him, uttered his answer:
　　　 'Truly, these words has the Lord of wisdom
　　　 Set in your heart, for I never have harkened
　　　 To speech so sage from a man so young.
　　　 You have strength, and prudence, and wisdom of word!
1730 I count it true if it come to pass
　　　 That point of spear in the press of battle,
　　　 Or deadly sickness, or stroke of sword,
　　　 Shall slay your leader, the son of Hrethel,
　　　 The prince of your people, and you still live,
1735 The Sea-Geats could have no happier choice
　　　 If you would be willing to rule the realm,
　　　 As king to hold guard o'er the hoard and the heroes.
　　　 The longer I know you, the better I like you,
　　　 Beloved Beowulf! You have brought it to pass
1740 That between our peoples a lasting peace
　　　 Shall bind the Geats to the Danish-born;
　　　 And strife shall vanish, and war shall cease,
　　　 And former feuds, while I rule this realm.
　　　 And many a man, in the sharing of treasure,
1745 Shall greet another with goodly gifts
　　　 O'er the gannet's bath. And the ring-stemmed ship
　　　 Shall bear over ocean bountiful riches
　　　 In pledge of friendship. Our peoples, I know,
　　　 Shall be firm united toward foe and friend,
1750 Faultless in all things, in fashion of old.'
　　　 　　　Then the son of Healfdene, shelter of earls,
　　　 Bestowed twelve gifts on the hero in hall,
　　　 Bade him in safety with bounty of treasure
　　　 Seek his dear people, and soon return.
1755 The peerless leader, the Scylding lord,
　　　 Kissed the good thane and clasped to his bosom
　　　 While tears welled fast from the old man's eyes.
　　　 Both chances he weighed in his wise, old heart,

But greatly doubted if ever again
1760 They should meet at council or drinking of mead.
Nor could Hrothgar master—so dear was the man—
His swelling sorrow; a yearning love
For the dauntless hero, deep in his heart,
Burned through his blood. Beowulf, the brave,
1765 Prizing his treasure and proud of the gold,
Turned away, treading the grassy plain.
The ring-stemmed sea-goer, riding at anchor,
Awaited her lord. There was loud acclaim
Of Hrothgar's gifts, as they went their way.
1770 He was a king without failing or fault,
Till old age, master of all mankind,
Stripped him of power and pride of strength.

BEOWULF RETURNS TO GEATLAND

Then down to the sea came the band of the brave,
The host of young heroes in harness of war,
1775 In their woven mail; and the coast-warden viewed
The heroes' return, as he heeded their coming!
No uncivil greeting he gave from the sea-cliff
As they strode to ship in their glistening steel;
But rode toward them and called their return
1780 A welcome sight for their Weder kin.
There on the sand the ring-stemmed ship,
The broad-bosomed bark, was loaded with war-gear,
With horses and treasure; the mast towered high
Over the riches of Hrothgar's hoard.
1785 A battle-sword Beowulf gave to the boatwarden
Hilted with gold; and thereafter in hall
He had the more honor because of the heirloom,
The shining treasure. The ship was launched.
Cleaving the combers of open sea
1790 They dropped the shoreline of Denmark astern.
A stretching sea-cloth, a bellying sail,
Was bent on the mast; there was groaning of timbers;
A gale was blowing; the boat drove on.
The foamy-necked plunger plowed through the billows,
1795 The ring-stemmed ship through the breaking seas,
Till at last they sighted the sea-cliffs of Geatland,
The well-known headlands; and, whipped by the wind,
The boat drove shoreward and beached on the sand.
Straightway the harbor-watch strode to the seashore;

1800   Long had he watched for the well-loved men,
       Scanning the ocean with eager eyes!
       The broad-bosomed boat he bound to the shingle
       With anchor ropes, lest the rip of the tide
       Should wrench from its mooring the comely craft.
1805   From the good ship Beowulf bade them bear
       The precious jewels and plated gold,
       The princely treasure. Not long was the path
       That led to where Hygelac, son of Hrethel,
       The giver of treasure, abode in his home
1810   Hard by the sea-wall, hedged by his thanes.
       Spacious the castle, splendid the king
       On his high hall-seat; youthful was Hygd,
       Wise and well-born—though winters but few
       Hæreth's daughter had dwelt at court.
1815   She was noble of spirit, not sparing in gifts
       Of princely treasure to the people of the Geats.

           Of the pride of Thryth, and her crimes, the fair folk-queen was free;
           Thryth, of whose liegemen none dared by day, save only her lord,
           Lift up his eyes to her face, lest his fate be a mortal bondage,
1820   *Seizure and fetters and sword, a blow of the patterned blade*
           Declaring his doom, and proclaiming the coming of death.
           That is no way of a queen, nor custom of lovely lady,
           Though peerless her beauty and proud, that a weaver of peace
           Should send a dear man to his death for a feigned affront.
1825   *But the kinsman of Hemming at last made an end of her evil.*
           For men at the drinking of mead tell tale of a change,
           How she wrought less ruin and wrong when, given in marriage
           Gleaming with jewels and gold, to the high-born hero and young,
           Over the fallow flood she sailed, at her father's bidding
1830   *Seeking the land of Offa, and there while she lived,*
           Famed for goodness, fulfilled her fate on the throne.
           She held high love for her lord, the leader of heroes,
           The best, I have heard, of mankind or the children of men
           Between the two seas; for Offa, the stalwart, was honored
1835   *For his gifts and his greatness in war. With wisdom he governed;*
           And from him Eomær descended, Hemming's kinsman, grandson of Garmund,
           Stalwart and strong in war, and the helper of heroes.

           Then the hero strode with his stalwart band
       Across the stretches of sandy beach,
1840   The wide sea-shingle. The world-candle shone,
       The hot sun hasting on high from the south.

Marching together they made their way
To where in his stronghold the stout young king,
Ongentheow's slayer, protector of earls,
1845   Dispensed his treasure. Soon Hygelac heard
Of the landing of Beowulf, bulwark of men,
That his shoulder-companion had come to his court
Sound and safe from the strife of battle.
       The hall was prepared, as the prince gave bidding,
1850   Places made ready for much travelled men.
And he who came safe from the surges of battle
Sat by the side of the king himself,
Kinsman by kinsman; in courtly speech
His liege lord greeted the loyal thane
1855   With hearty welcome. And Hæreth's daughter
Passed through the hall-building pouring the mead,
With courtesy greeting the gathered host,
Bearing the cup to the hands of the heroes.
In friendly fashion in high-built hall
1860   Hygelac questioned his comrade and thane;
For an eager longing burned in his breast
To hear from the Sea-Geats the tale of their travels.
'How did you fare in your far sea-roving,
Beloved Beowulf, in your swift resolve
1865   To sail to the conflict, the combat in Heorot,
Across the salt waves? Did you soften at all
The sorrows of Hrothgar, the weight of his woe?
Deeply I brooded with burden of care
For I had no faith in this far sea-venture
1870   For one so beloved. Long I implored
That you go not against the murderous monster,
But let the South Danes settle the feud
Themselves with Grendel. To God be thanks
That my eyes behold you unharmed and unhurt.'
1875   Beowulf spoke, the son of Ecgtheow:
'My dear lord Hygelac, many have heard
Of that famous grapple 'twixt Grendel and me,
The bitter struggle and strife in the hall
Where he formerly wrought such ruin and wrong,
1880   Such lasting sorrow for Scylding men!
All that I avenged! Not any on earth
Who longest lives of that loathsome brood,
No kin of Grendel cloaked in his crime,
Has cause to boast of that battle by night!
1885   First, in that country, I fared to the hall;

With greeting for Hrothgar; Healfdene's kinsman
Learned all my purpose, assigned me a place
Beside his own son. 'Twas a happy host!
I never have seen under span of heaven
1890   More mirth of heroes sitting at mead!
The peerless queen, the peace-pledge of peoples,
Passed on her round through the princely hall;
There was spurring of revels, dispensing of rings,
Ere the noble woman went to her seat.
1895   At times in the host the daughter of Hrothgar
Offered the beaker to earls in turn;
Freawaru men called her, the feasters in hall,
As she held out to heroes the well-wrought cup.
Youthful and gleaming with jewels of gold
1900   To the fair son of Froda the maiden is plighted.
For the Scylding leader, the lord of the land,
Deems it wise counsel, accounting it gain,
To settle by marriage the murderous feud,
The bloody slaughter! But seldom for long
1905   Does the spear go ungrasped when a prince has perished,
Though the bride in her beauty be peerless and proud!
Ill may it please the Heathobard prince
And all his thanes, when he leads his lady
Into the hall, that a Danish noble
1910   Should be welcomed there by the Heathobard host.
For on him shall flash their forefathers' heirlooms,
Hard-edged, ring-hilted, the Heathobards' hoard
When of old they had war-might, nor wasted in battle
Their lives and the lives of their well-loved thanes.
1915   Then an aged spearman shall speak at the beer-feast,
The treasure beholding with sorrow of heart,
Remembering sadly the slaughter of men,
Grimly goading the young hero's spirit,
Spurring to battle, speaking this word:
1920   "Do you see, my lord, the sword of your father,
The blade he bore to the last of his fights,
The pride of his heart as, under his helmet,
The Scyldings slew him, the savage Danes,
When Withergyld fell, and after the slaughter,
1925   The fall of heroes, they held the field?
And now a son of those bloody butchers,
Proud in his trappings, tramps into hall
And boasts of the killing, clothed with the treasure
That is yours by your birthright to have and to hold?"

-772-

1930   Over and over the old man will urge him,
       With cutting reminders recalling the past
       Till it comes at last that the lady's thane,
       For the deeds of his father, shall forfeit his life
       In a bloody slaughter, slain by the sword,
1935   While the slayer goes scatheless knowing the land.
       On both sides then shall sword-oaths be broken
       When hate boils up within Ingeld's heart,
       And his love of his lady grows cooler and lessens
       Because of his troubles. I count not true
1940   Heathobard faith, nor their part in the peace,
       Nor their friendship firm to the Danish folk.

         I must now speak on, dispenser of treasure,
       Further of Grendel, till fully you know
       How we fared in that fierce and furious fight!
1945   When the jewel of heaven had journeyed o'er earth,
       The wrathful demon, the deadly foe,
       Stole through the darkness spying us out
       Where still unharmed we guarded the gold-hall.
       But doom in battle and bitter death
1950   Were Handscio's fate! He was first to perish
       Though girded with weapon and famous in war.
       Grendel murdered him, mangled his body,
       Bolted the dear man's bloody corpse.
       No sooner for that would the slaughterous spirit,
1955   Bloody of tooth and brooding on evil,
       Turn empty-handed away from the hall!
       The mighty monster made trial of my strength
       Clutching me close with his ready claw.
       Wide and wondrous his huge pouch hung
1960   Cunningly fastened, and fashioned with skill
       From skin of dragon by devil's craft.
       Therein the monster was minded to thrust me
       Sinless and blameless, and many beside.
       But it might not be, when I rose in wrath,
1965   And fronted the hell-fiend face to face.
       Too long is the tale how I took requital
       On the cursed foe for his every crime,
       But the deeds I did were a lasting honor,
       Beloved prince, to your people's name.
1970   He fled away, and a fleeting while
       Possessed his life and the world's delights;
       But he left in Heorot his severed hand,
       A bloody reminder to mark his track.

Humbled in spirit and wretched in heart
1975   Down he sank to the depths of the pool.
      When the morrow fell, and we feasted together,
The Scylding ruler rewarded me well
For the bloody strife, in guerdon bestowing
Goodly treasure of beaten gold.
1980   There was song and revel. The aged Scylding
From well-stored mind spoke much of the past.
A warrior sang to the strains of the glee-wood,
Sometimes melodies mirthful and joyous,
Sometimes lays that were tragic and true.
1985   And the great-hearted ruler at times would tell
A tale of wonder in fitting words.
Heavy with years the white-haired warrior
Grieved for his youth and the strength that was gone;
And his heart was moved by the weight of his winters
1990   And many a memory out of the past.
All the long day we made merry together
Till another night came to the children of men,
And quickly the mother of Grendel was minded
To wreak her vengeance; raging with grief
1995   She came to the hall where the hate of the Weders
Had slain her son. But the hideous hag
Avenged his killing; with furious clutch
She seized a warrior—the soul of Æschere,
Wise and aged, went forth from the flesh!
2000   Not at all could the Danes, when the morrow dawned,
Set brand to his body or burn on the bale
Their well-loved comrade. With fiendish clasp
She carried his corpse through the fall of the force.
That was to Hrothgar, prince of the people,
2005   Sorest of sorrows that ever befell!
For your sake the sad-hearted hero implored me
To prove my valor and, venturing life,
To win renown in the watery depths.
He promised reward. Full well is it known
2010   How I humbled the horrible guard of the gulf.
Hand to hand for a space we struggled
Till the swirling eddies were stained with blood;
With cleaving sword-edge I severed the head
Of Grendel's hag in that hall of strife.
2015   Not easily thence did I issue alive,
But my death was not fated; not yet was I doomed!
      Then the son of Healfdene, the shelter of earls,

Gave many a treasure to mark the deed.
The good king governed with courtly custom;
2020   In no least way did I lose reward,
The meed of my might; but he gave me treasure,
Healfdene's son, to my heart's desire.
These riches I bring you, ruler of heroes,
And warmly tender with right good will.
2025   Save for you, King Hygelac, few are my kinsmen,
Few are the favors but come from you.'
       Then he bade men bring the boar-crested headpiece,
The towering helmet, and steel-gray sark,
The splendid war-sword, and spoke this word:
2030   'The good king Hrothgar gave me this gift,
This battle-armor, and first to you
Bade tell the tale of his friendly favor.
He said King Heorogar, lord of the Scyldings,
Long had worn it, but had no wish
2035   To leave the mail to his manful son,
The dauntless Heoroweard, dear though he was!
Well may you wear it! Have joy of it all.'
As I've heard the tale, he followed the trappings
With four bay horses, matched and swift,
2040   Graciously granting possession of both,
The steeds and the wealth. 'Tis the way of a kinsman,
Not weaving in secret the wiles of malice
Nor plotting the fall of a faithful friend.
To his kinsman Hygelac, hardy in war,
2045   The heart of the nephew was trusty and true;
Dear to each was the other's good!
To Hygd, as I've heard, he presented three horses
Gaily saddled, slender and sleek,
And the gleaming necklace Wealhtheow gave,
2050   A peerless gift from a prince's daughter.
With the gracious guerdon, the goodly jewel,
Her breast thereafter was well bedecked.
       So the son of Ecgtheow bore himself bravely,
Known for his courage and courteous deeds,
2055   Strove after honor, slew not his comrades
In drunken brawling; nor brutal his mood.
But the bountiful gifts which the Lord God gave him
He held with a power supreme among men.
He had long been scorned, when the sons of the Geats
2060   Accounted him worthless; the Weder lord
Held him not high among heroes in hall.

Laggard they deemed him, slothful and slack.
But time brought solace for all his ills!
    Then the battle-bold king, the bulwark of heroes,
2065   Bade bring a battle-sword banded with gold,
The heirloom of Hrethel; no sharper steel,
No lovelier treasure, belonged to the Geats.
He laid the war-blade on Beowulf's lap,
Gave him a hall and a stately seat
2070   And hides seven thousand. Inherited lands
Both held by birth-fee, home and estate.
But one held rule o'er the spacious realm,
And higher therein his order and rank.

THE FIRE-DRAGON AND THE TREASURE

    It later befell in the years that followed
2075   After Hygelac sank in the surges of war,
And the sword slew Heardred under his shield
When the Battle-Scylfings, those bitter fighters,
Invaded the land of the victor-folk
Overwhelming Hereric's nephew in war,
2080   That the kingdom came into Beowulf's hand.
For fifty winters he governed it well,
Aged and wise with the wisdom of years,
Till a fire-drake flying in darkness of night
Began to ravage and work his will.
2085   On the upland heath he guarded a hoard,
A stone barrow lofty. Under it lay
A path concealed from the sight of men.
There a thief broke in on the heathen treasure,
Laid hand on a flagon all fretted with gold,
2090   As the dragon discovered, though cozened in sleep
By the pilferer's cunning. The people soon found
That the mood of the dragon was roused to wrath!
    Not at all with intent, of his own free will,
Did he ravish the hoard, who committed the wrong;
2095   But in dire distress the thrall of a thane,
A guilty fugitive fleeing the lash,
Forced his way in. There a horror befell him!
Yet the wretched exile escaped from the dragon,
Swift in retreat when the terror arose.
2100   A flagon he took. There, many such treasures
Lay heaped in that earth-hall where the owner of old
Had carefully hidden the precious hoard,

The countless wealth of a princely clan.
Death came upon them in days gone by
2105   And he who lived longest, the last of his line,
Guarding the treasure and grieving for friend,
Deemed it his lot that a little while only
He too might hold that ancient hoard.
A barrow new-built near the ocean billows
2110   Stood cunningly fashioned beneath the cliff;
Into the barrow the ring-warden bore
The princely treasure, the precious trove
Of golden wealth, and these words he spoke:
'Keep thou, O Earth, what men could not keep—
2115   This costly treasure—it came from thee!
Baleful slaughter has swept away,
Death in battle, the last of my blood;
They have lived their lives; they have left the mead-hall.
Now I have no one to wield the sword,
2120   No one to polish the plated cup,
The precious flagon—the host is fled.
The hard-forged helmet fretted with gold
Shall be stripped of its inlay; the burnishers sleep
Whose charge was to brighten the battle-masks.
2125   Likewise the corselet that countered in war
Mid clashing of bucklers the bite of the sword—
Corselet and warrior decay into dust;
Mailed coat and hero are moveless and still.
No mirth of gleewood, no music of harp,
2130   No good hawk swinging in flight through the hall;
No swift steed stamps in the castle yard;
Death has ravished an ancient race.'
So sad of mood he bemoaned his sorrow,
Lonely and sole survivor of all,
2135   Restless by day and wretched by night
Till the clutch of death caught at his heart.
Then the goodly treasure was found unguarded
By the venomous dragon enveloped in flame,
The old naked night-foe flying in darkness,
2140   Haunting the barrows; a bane that brings
A fearful dread to the dwellers of earth.
His wont is to hunt out a hoard under ground
And guard heathen gold, growing old with the years.
But no whit for that is his fortune more fair!
2145   For three hundred winters this waster of peoples
Held the huge treasure-hall under the earth

Till the robber aroused him to anger and rage,
Stole the rich beaker and bore to his master,
Imploring his lord for a compact of peace.
2150 So the hoard was robbed and its riches plundered;
To the wretch was granted the boon that he begged;
And his liege-lord first had view of the treasure,
The ancient work of the men of old
Then the worm awakened and war was kindled,
2155 The rush of the monster along the rock,
When the fierce one found the tracks of the foe;
He had stepped too close in his stealthy cunning
To the dragon's head. But a man undoomed
May endure with ease disaster and woe
2160 If he has His favor who wields the world.
Swiftly the fire-drake sought through the plain
The man who wrought him this wrong in his sleep.
Inflamed and savage he circled the mound,
But the waste was deserted—no man was in sight.
2165 The worm's mood was kindled to battle and war;
Time and again he returned to the barrow
Seeking the treasure-cup. Soon he was sure
That a man had plundered the precious gold.
Enraged and restless the hoard-warden waited
2170 The gloom of evening. The guard of the mound
Was swollen with anger; the fierce one resolved
To requite with fire the theft of the cup.
Then the day was sped as the worm desired;
Lurking no longer within his wall
2175 He sallied forth surrounded with fire,
Encircled with flame. For the folk of the land
The beginning was dread as the ending was grievous
That came so quickly upon their lord.
          Then the baleful stranger belched fire and flame,
2180 Burned the bright dwellings—the glow of the blaze
Filled hearts with horror. The hostile flier
Was minded to leave there nothing alive.
From near and from far the war of the dragon,
The might of the monster, was widely revealed
2185 So that all could see how the ravaging scather
Hated and humbled the Geatish folk.
Then he hastened back ere the break of dawn
To his secret den and the spoil of gold.
He had compassed the land with a flame of fire,
2190 A blaze of burning; he trusted the wall

The sheltering mound, and the strength of his might—
But his trust betrayed him! The terrible news
Was brought to Beowulf, told for a truth,
That his home was consumed in the surges of fire,
2195 The goodly dwelling and throne of the Geats.
The heart of the hero was heavy with anguish,
The greatest of sorrows; in his wisdom he weened
He had grievously angered the Lord Everlasting,
Blamefully broken the ancient law.
2200 Dark thoughts stirred in his surging bosom,
Welled in his breast, as was not his wont.
The flame of the dragon had levelled the fortress,
The people's stronghold washed by the wave.
But the king of warriors, prince of the Weders,
2205 Exacted an ample revenge for it all.
The lord of warriors and leader of earls
Bade work him of iron a wondrous shield,
Knowing full well that wood could not serve him
Nor linden defend him against the flame.
2210 The stalwart hero was doomed to suffer
The destined end of his days on earth;
Likewise the worm, though for many a winter
He had held his watch o'er the wealth of the hoard.
The ring-prince scorned to assault the dragon
2215 With a mighty army, or host of men.
He feared not the combat, nor counted of worth
The might of the worm, his courage and craft,
Since often aforetime, beset in the fray,
He had safely issued from many an onset,
2220 Many a combat and, crowned with success,
Purged of evil the hall of Hrothgar
And crushed out Grendel's loathsome kin.
        Nor was that the least of his grim engagements
When Hygelac fell, great Hrethel's son;
2225 When the lord of the people, the prince of the Geats,
Died of his wounds in the welter of battle,
Perished in Friesland, smitten with swords.
Thence Beowulf came by his strength in swimming;
Thirty sets of armor he bore on his back
2230 As he hasted to ocean. The Hetware men
Had no cause to boast of their prowess in battle
When they gathered against him with linden shields.
But few of them ever escaped his assault
Or came back alive to the homes they had left;

2235 So the son of Ecgtheow swam the sea-stretches,
Lonely and sad, to the land of his kin.
Hygd then tendered him kingdom and treasure,
Wealth of riches and royal throne,
For she had no hope with Hygelac dead
2240 That her son could defend the seat of his fathers
From foreign foemen. But even in need,
No whit the more could they move the hero
To be Heardred's liege, or lord of the land.
But he fostered Heardred with friendly counsel,
2245 With honor and favor among the folk,
Till he came of age and governed the Geats.
Then the sons of Ohthere fleeing in exile;
Sought out Heardred over the sea.
They had risen against the lord of the Scylfings,
2250 Best of the sea-kings, bestower of rings,
An illustrious prince in the land of the Swedes.
So Heardred fell. For harboring exiles
The son of Hygelac died by the sword.
Ongentheow's son, after Heardred was slain,
2255 Returned to his home, and Beowulf held
The princely power and governed the Geats.
He was a good king, grimly requiting
In later days the death of his prince.
Crossing the sea with a swarming host
2260 He befriended Eadgils, Ohthere's son,
In his woe and affliction, with weapons and men;
He took revenge in a savage assault,
And slew the king. So Ecgtheow's son
Had come in safety through all his battles,
2265 His bitter struggles and savage strife,
To the day when he fought with the deadly worm.
With eleven comrades, kindled to rage
The Geat lord went to gaze on the dragon.
Full well he knew how the feud arose,
2270 The fearful affliction; for into his hold
From hand of finder the flagon had come.
The thirteenth man in the hurrying throng
Was the sorrowful captive who caused the feud.
With woeful spirit and all unwilling
2275 Needs must he guide them, for he only knew
Where the earth-hall stood near the breaking billows
Filled with jewels and beaten gold.
The monstrous warden, waiting for battle,

Watched and guarded the hoarded wealth.
2280 No easy bargain for any of men
To seize that treasure! The stalwart king,
Gold-friend of Geats, took seat on the headland,
Hailed his comrades and wished them well.
Sad was his spirit, restless and ready
2285 And the march of Fate immeasurably near;
Fate that would strike, seek his soul's treasure,
And deal asunder the spirit and flesh.
Not long was his life encased in the body!
    Beowulf spoke, the son of Ecgtheow:
2290 'Many an ordeal I endured in youth,
And many a battle. I remember it all.
I was seven winters old when the prince of the people,
The lord of the treasure-hoard, Hrethel the king,
From the hand of my father had me and held me,
2295 Recalling our kinship with treasure and feast.
As long as he lived I was no less beloved,
As thane in his hall, than the sons of his house,
Herebeald and Hæthcyn and Hygelac, my lord.
For the eldest brother the bed of death
2300 Was foully fashioned by brother's deed
When Hæthcyn let fly a bolt from his horn-bow,
Missed the mark, and murdered his lord;
Brother slew brother with bloody shaft—
A tragic deed and beyond atonement,
2305 A foul offense to sicken the heart!
Yet none the less was the lot of the prince
To lay down his soul and his life, unavenged.
    Even so sad and sorrowful is it,
And bitter to bear, to an old man's heart,
2310 Seeing his young son swing on the gallows.
He wails his dirge and his wild lament
While his son hangs high, a spoil to the raven;
His aged heart can contrive no help.
Each dawn brings grief for the son that is gone
2315 And his heart has no hope of another heir,
Seeing the one has gone to his grave.
In the house of his son he gazes in sorrow
On wine-hall deserted and swept by the wind,
Empty of joy. The horsemen and heroes
2320 Sleep in the grave. No sound of the harp,
No welcoming revels as often of old!
He goes to his bed with his burden of grief;

To his spirit it seems that dwelling and land
Are empty and lonely, lacking his son.
2325   So the helm of the Weders yearned after Herebeald
And welling sadness surged in his heart.
He could not avenge the feud on the slayer
Nor punish the prince for the loathsome deed,
Though he loved him no longer, nor held him dear.
2330   Because of this sorrow that sore befell
He left life's joys for the heavenly light,
Granting his sons, as a good man will,
Cities and land, when he went from the world.
         Then across the wide water was conflict and war,
2335   A striving and struggle of Swedes and Geats,
A bitter hatred, when Hrethel died.
Ongentheow's sons were dauntless and daring,
Cared not for keeping of peace overseas;
But often around Hreosnabeorh slaughtered and slew.
2340   My kinsmen avenged the feud and the evil,
As many have heard, though one of the Weders
Paid with his life—a bargain full bitter!
Hæthcyn's fate was to fall in the fight.
It is often recounted, a kinsman with sword-edge
2345   Avenged in the morning the murderer's deed
When Ongentheow met Eofor. Helm split asunder;
The aged Scylfing sank down to his death.
The hand that felled him remembered the feud
And drew not back from the deadly blow.
2350   For all the rich gifts that Hygelac gave me
I repaid him in battle with shining sword,
As chance was given. He granted me land,
A gracious dwelling and goodly estate.
Nor needed he seek of the Gifths, or the Spear-Danes,
2355   Or in Swedish land, a lesser in war
To fight for pay; in the press of battle
I was always before him alone in the van.
So shall I bear me while life-days last,
While the sword holds out that has served me well
2360   Early and late since I slew Dæghrefn,
The Frankish hero, before the host.
He brought no spoil from the field of battle,
No corselet of mail to the Frisian king.
Not by the sword the warden of standards,
2365   The stalwart warrior, fell in the fight.
My battle-grip shattered the bones of his body

And silenced the heart-beat. But now with the sword,
With hand and hard blade, I must fight for the treasure.'

BEOWULF AND WIGLAF SLAY THE DRAGON

For the last time Beowulf uttered his boast:
2370 'I came in safety through many a conflict
In the days of my youth; and now even yet,
Old as I am, I will fight this feud,
Do manful deeds, if the dire destroyer
Will come from his cavern to meet my sword.'
2375 The king for the last time greeted his comrades,
Bold helmet-bearers and faithful friends:
'I would bear no sword nor weapon to battle
With the evil worm, if I knew how else
I could close with the fiend, as I grappled with Grendel.
2380 From the worm I look for a welling of fire,
A belching of venom, and therefore I bear
Shield and byrny. Not one foot's space
Will I flee from the monster, the ward of the mound.
It shall fare with us both in the fight at the wall
2385 As Fate shall allot, the lord of mankind.
Though bold in spirit, I make no boast
As I go to fight with the flying serpent.
Clad in your corselets and trappings of war,
By the side of the barrow abide you to see
2390 Which of us twain may best after battle
Survive his wounds. Not yours the adventure,
Nor the mission of any, save mine alone,
To measure his strength with the monstrous dragon
And play the part of a valiant earl.
2395 By deeds of daring I'll gain the gold
Or death in battle shall break your lord.'
Then the stalwart rose with his shield upon him,
Bold under helmet, bearing his sark
Under the stone-cliff; he trusted the strength
2400 Of his single might. Not so does a coward!
He who survived through many a struggle,
Many a combat and crashing of troops,
Saw where a stone-arch stood by the wall
And a gushing stream broke out from the barrow.
2405 Hot with fire was the flow of its surge,
Nor could any abide near the hoard unburned,
Nor endure its depths, for the flame of the dragon.

Then the lord of the Geats in the grip of his fury
Gave shout of defiance; the strong-heart stormed.
2410   His voice rang out with the rage of battle,
Resounding under the hoary stone.
Hate was aroused; the hoard-warden knew
'Twas the voice of a man. No more was there time
To sue for peace; the breath of the serpent,
2415   A blast of venom, burst from the rock.
The ground resounded; the lord of the Geats
Under the barrow swung up his shield
To face the dragon; the coiling foe
Was gathered to strike in the deadly strife.
2420   The stalwart hero had drawn his sword,
His ancient heirloom of tempered edge;
In the heart of each was fear of the other!
The shelter of kinsmen stood stout of heart
Under towering shield as the great worm coiled;
2425   Clad in his war-gear he waited the rush.
In twisting folds the flame-breathing dragon
Sped to its fate. The shield of the prince
For a lesser while guarded his life and his body
Than heart had hoped. For the first time then
2430   It was not his portion to prosper in war;
Fate did not grant him glory in battle!
Then lifted his arm the lord of the Geats
And smote the worm with his ancient sword
But the brown edge failed as it fell on bone,
2435   And cut less deep than the king had need
In his sore distress. Savage in mood
The ward of the barrow countered the blow
With a blast of fire; wide sprang the flame.
The ruler of Geats had no reason to boast;
2440   His unsheathed iron, his excellent sword,
Had weakened as it should not, had failed in the fight.
It was no easy journey for Ecgtheow's son
To leave this world and against his will
Find elsewhere a dwelling! So every man shall
2445   In the end give over this fleeting life.
        Not long was the lull. Swiftly the battlers
Renewed their grapple. The guard of the hoard
Grew fiercer in fury. His venomous breath
Beat in his breast. Enveloped in flame
2450   The folk-leader suffered a sore distress.
No succoring band of shoulder-companions,

No sons of warriors aided him then
By valor in battle. They fled to the forest
To save their lives; but a sorrowful spirit
2455   Welled in the breast of one of the band.
The call of kinship can never be stilled
In the heart of a man who is trusty and true.
     His name was Wiglaf, Weohstan's son,
A prince of the Scylfings, a peerless thane,
2460   Ælfhere's kinsman; he saw his king
Under his helmet smitten with heat.
He thought of the gifts which his lord had given,
The wealth and the land of the Wægmunding line
And all the folk-rights his father had owned;
2465   Nor could he hold back, but snatched up his buckler,
His linden shield and his ancient sword,
Heirloom of Eanmund, Ohthere's son,
Whom Weohstan slew with the sword in battle,
Wretched and friendless and far from home.
2470   The brown-hewed helmet he bore to his kinsmen,
The ancient blade and the byrny of rings.
These Onela gave him—his nephew's arms—
Nor called for vengeance, nor fought the feud,
Though Weohstan had slaughtered his brother's son.
2475   He held the treasures for many half-years,
The byrny and sword, till his son was of age
For manful deeds, as his father before him.
Among the Geats he gave him of war-gear
Countless numbers of every kind;
2480   Then, full of winters, he left the world,
Gave over this life. And Wiglaf, the lad,
Was to face with his lord the first of his battles,
The hazard of war. But his heart did not fail
Nor the blade of his kinsman weaken in war,
2485   As the worm soon found when they met in the fight!
     Wiglaf spoke in sorrow of soul,
With bitter reproach rebuking his comrades:
'I remember the time, as we drank in the mead-hall,
When we swore to our lord who bestowed these rings
2490   That we would repay for the war-gear and armor,
The hard swords and helmets, if need like this
Should ever befall him. He chose us out
From all the host for this high adventure,
Deemed us worthy of glorious deeds,
2495   Gave me these treasures, regarded us all

As high-hearted bearers of helmet and spear—
Though our lord himself, the shield of his people,
Thought single-handed to finish this feat,
Since of mortal men his measure was most
2500   Of feats of daring and deeds of fame.
Now is the day that our lord has need
Of the strength and courage of stalwart men.
Let us haste to succor his sore distress
In the horrible heat and the merciless flame.
2505   God knows I had rather the fire should enfold
My body and limbs with my gold-friend and lord.
Shameful it seems that we carry our shields
Back to our homes ere we harry the foe
And ward the life of the Weder king.
2510   Full well I know it is not his due
That he alone, of the host of the Geats,
Should suffer affliction and fall in the fight.
One helmet and sword, one byrny and shield,
Shall serve for us both in the storm of strife.'
2515   Then Wiglaf dashed through the deadly reek
In his battle-helmet to help his lord.
Brief were his words: 'Beloved Beowulf,
Summon your strength, remember the vow
You made of old in the years of youth
2520   Not to allow your glory to lessen
As long as you lived. With resolute heart,
And dauntless daring, defend your life
With all your force. I fight at your side!'
      Once again the worm, when the words were spoken,
2525   The hideous foe in a horror of flame,
Rushed in rage at the hated men.
Wiglaf's buckler was burned to the boss
In the billows of fire; his byrny of mail
Gave the young hero no help or defense.
2530   But he stoutly pressed on under shield of his kinsman
When his own was consumed in the scorching flame.
Then the king once more was mindful of glory,
Swung his great sword-blade with all his might
And drove it home on the dragon's head.
2535   But Nægling broke, it failed in the battle,
The blade of Beowulf, ancient and gray.
It was not his lot that edges of iron
Could help him in battle; his hand was too strong,
Overtaxed, I am told, every blade with its blow.

2540   Though he bore a wondrous hard weapon to war,
No whit the better was he thereby!
    A third time then the terrible scather,
The monstrous dragon inflamed with the feud,
Rushed on the king when the opening offered,
2545   Fierce and flaming; fastened its fangs
In Beowulf's throat; he was bloodied with gore;
His life-blood streamed from the welling wound.
    As they tell the tale, in the king's sore need
His shoulder-companion showed forth his valor,
2550   His craft and courage, and native strength.
To the head of the dragon he paid no heed,
Though his hand was burned as he helped his king.
A little lower the stalwart struck
At the evil beast, and his blade drove home
2555   Plated and gleaming. The fire began
To lessen and wane. The king of the Weders
Summoned his wits; he drew the dagger
He wore on his corselet, cutting and keen,
And slit asunder the worm with the blow.
2560   So they felled the foe and wrought their revenge;
The kinsmen together had killed the dragon.
So a man should be when the need is bitter!
That was the last fight Beowulf fought;
That was the end of his work in the world.

BEOWULF'S DEATH

2565   The wound which the dragon had dealt him began
To swell and burn; and soon he could feel
The baneful venom inflaming his breast.
The wise, old warrior sank down by the wall
And stared at the work of the giants of old,
2570   The arches of stone and the standing columns
Upholding the ancient earth-hall within.
His loyal thane, the kindest of comrades,
Saw Beowulf bloody and broken in war;
In his hands bore water and bathed his leader,
2575   And loosened the helm from his dear lord's head.
    Beowulf spoke, though his hurt was sore,
The wounds of battle grievous and grim.
Full well he weened that his life was ended,
And all the joy of his years on earth;
2580   That his days were done, and Death most near:

'My armor and sword I would leave to my son
Had Fate but granted, born of my body,
An heir to follow me after I'm gone.
For fifty winters I've ruled this realm,
2585   And never a lord of a neighboring land
Dared strike with terror or seek with sword.
In my life I abode by the lot assigned,
Kept well what was mine, courted no quarrels,
Swore no false oaths. And now for all this
2590   Though my hurt is grievous, my heart is glad.
When life leaves body, the Lord of mankind
Cannot lay to my charge the killing of kinsmen!
Go quickly, dear Wiglaf, to gaze on the gold
Beneath the hoar stone. The dragon lies still
2595   In the slumber of death, despoiled of his hoard.
Make haste that my eyes may behold the treasure,
The gleaming jewels, the goodly store,
And, glad of the gold, more peacefully leave
The life and the realm I have ruled so long.'
2600   Then Weohstan's son, as they tell the tale,
Clad in his corselet and trappings of war,
Hearkened at once to his wounded lord.
Under roof of the barrow he broke his way.
Proud in triumph he stood by the seat,
2605   Saw glittering jewels and gold on the ground,
The den of the dragon, the old dawn-flier,
And all the wonders along the walls.
Great bowls and flagons of bygone men
Lay all unfurnished and barren of gems,
2610   Many a helmet ancient and rusted,
Many an arm-ring cunningly wrought.
Treasure and gold, though hid in the ground,
Override man's wishes, hide them who will!
High o'er the hoard he beheld a banner,
2615   Greatest of wonders, woven with skill,
All wrought of gold; its radiance lighted
The vasty ground and the glittering gems.
But no sign of the worm! The sword-edge had slain him.
As I've heard the tale, the hero unaided
2620   Rifled those riches of giants of old,
The hoard in the barrow, and heaped in his arms
Beakers and platters, picked what he would
And took the banner, the brightest of signs.
The ancient sword with its edge of iron

2625   Had slain the worm who watched o'er the wealth,
        In the midnight flaming, with menace of fire
        Protecting the treasure for many a year
        Till he died the death. Then Wiglaf departed
        In haste returning enriched with spoil.
2630   He feared, and wondered if still he would find
        The lord of the Weders alive on the plain,
        Broken and weary and smitten with wounds.
        With his freight of treasure he found the prince,
        His dear lord, bloody and nigh unto death.
2635   With water he bathed him till words broke forth
        From the hoard of his heart and, aged and sad,
        Beowulf spoke, as he gazed on the gold:
        'For this goodly treasure whereon I gaze
        I give my thanks to the Lord of all,
2640   To the Prince of glory, Eternal God,
        Who granted me grace to gain for my people
        Such dower of riches before my death.
        I gave my life for this golden hoard.
        Heed well the wants, the need of my people;
2645   My hour is come, and my end is near.
        Bid warriors build, when they burn my body,
        A stately barrow on the headland's height.
        It shall be for remembrance among my people
        As it towers high on the Cape of the Whale,
2650   And sailors shall know it as Beowulf's Barrow,
        Sea-faring mariners driving their ships
        Through fogs of ocean from far countries.'
        Then the great-hearted king unclasped from his throat
        A collar of gold, and gave to his thane;
2655   Gave the young hero his gold-decked helmet,
        His ring and his byrny, and wished him well.
        'You are the last of the Wægmunding line.
        All my kinsmen, earls in their glory,
        Fate has sent to their final doom,
2660   And I must follow.' These words were the last
        The old king spoke ere the pyre received him,
        The leaping flames of the funeral blaze,
        And his breath went forth from his bosom, his soul
        Went forth from the flesh, to the joys of the just.
2665   Then bitter it was for Beowulf's thane
        To behold his loved one lying on earth
        Suffering sore at the end of life.
        The monster that slew him, the dreadful dragon,

Likewise lay broken and brought to his death.
2670 The worm no longer could rule the hoard,
But the hard, sharp sword, the work of the hammer,
Had laid him low; and the winged dragon
Lay stretched near the barrow, broken and still.
No more in the midnight he soared in air,
2675 Disclosing his presence, and proud of his gold;
For he sank to earth by the sword of the king.
But few of mankind, if the tales be true,
Has it prospered much, though mighty in war
And daring in deed, to encounter the breath
2680 Of the venomous worm or plunder his wealth,
When the ward of the barrow held watch o'er the mound.
Beowulf bartered his life for the treasure;
Both foes had finished this fleeting life.
        Not long was it then till the laggards in battle
2685 Came forth from the forest, ten craven in fight,
Who had dared not face the attack of the foe
In their lord's great need. The shirkers in shame
Came wearing their bucklers and trappings of war
Where the old man lay. They looked upon Wiglaf
2690 Weary he sat by the side of his leader
Attempting with water to waken his lord.
It availed him little; the wish was vain!
He could not stay his soul upon earth,
Nor one whit alter the will of God.
2695 The Lord ruled over the lives of men
As He rules them still. With a stern rebuke
He reproached the cowards whose courage had failed.
Wiglaf addressed them, Weohstan's son;
Gazed sad of heart on the hateful men:
2700 'Lo ! he may say who would speak the truth
That the lord who gave you these goodly rings,
This warlike armor wherein you stand—
When oft on the ale-bench he dealt to his hall-men
Helmet and byrny, endowing his thanes
2705 With the fairest he found from near or from far—
That he grievously wasted these trappings of war
When battle befell him. The king of the folk
Had no need to boast of his friends in the fight.
But the God of victory granted him strength
2710 To avenge himself with the edge of the sword
When he needed valor. Of little avail
The help I brought in the bitter battle!

Yet still I strove, though beyond my strength,
To aid my kinsman. And ever the weaker
2715 The savage foe when I struck with my sword;
Ever the weaker the welling flame!
Too few defenders surrounded our ruler
When the hour of evil and terror befell.
Now granting of treasure and giving of swords,
2720 Inherited land-right and joy of the home,
Shall cease from your kindred. And each of your clan
Shall fail of his birthright when men from afar
Hear tell of your flight and your dastardly deed.
Death is better for every earl
2725 Than life besmirched with the brand of shame!'

THE MESSENGER FORETELLS THE DOOM OF THE GEATS

Then Wiglaf bade tell the tidings of battle
Up over the cliff in the camp of the host
Where the linden-bearers all morning long
Sat wretched in spirit, and ready for both,
2730 The return, or the death, of their dear-loved lord.
Not long did he hide, who rode up the headland,
The news of their sorrow, but spoke before all:
'Our leader lies low, the lord of the Weders,
The King of the Geats, on the couch of death
2735 He sleeps his last sleep by the deeds of the worm.
The dreadful dragon is stretched beside him
Slain with dagger-wounds. Not by the sword
Could he quell the monster or lay him low.
And Wiglaf is sitting, Weohstan's son,
2740 Bent over Beowulf, living by dead.
Death watch he keeps in sorrow of spirit
Over the bodies of friend and foe.

Now comes peril of war when this news is rumored abroad,
The fall of our king known afar among Frisians and Franks!
2745 *For a fierce feud rose with the Franks when Hygelac's warlike host*
Invaded the Frisian fields, and the Hetware vanquished the Geats,
Overcame with the weight of their hordes, and Hygelac fell in the fray;
It was not his lot to live on dispensing the spoils of war.
And never since then of the Franks had we favor or friend.
2750 *And I harbor no hope of peace or faith from the Swedish folk,*
For well is it known of men that Ongentheow slew with the sword
Hæthcyn, the son of Hrethel, near Ravenswood, in the fight

When the Swedish people in pride swept down on the Geats.
And Ohthere's aged father, old and a terror in battle,
2755 *Made onslaught, killing their king, and rescued his queen,*
Ohthere's mother and Onela's, aged, bereft of her gold.
He followed the flying foe till, lordless and lorn,
They barely escaped into Ravenswood. There he beset them,
A wretched remnant of war, and weary with wounds.
2760 *And all the long hours of the night he thundered his threats*
That some on the morrow he would slay with the edge of the sword,
And some should swing on the gallows for food for the fowls!
But hope returned with the dawn to the heavy-hearted
When they heard the sound of the trumpets and Hygelac's horn,
2765 *As the good king came with his troops marching up on their track.*
     Then was a gory meeting of Swedes and Geats;
On all sides carnage and slaughter, savage and grim,
As the struggling foemen grappled and swayed in the fight.
And the old earl Ongentheow, crestfallen and cowed,
2770 *Fled with his men to a fastness, withdrew to the hills.*
He had tasted Hygelac's strength, the skill of the hero in war,
And he had no hope to resist or strive with the sea-men,
To save his hoard from their hands, or his children, or wife.
So the old king fled to his fortress; but over the plain
2775 *Hygelac's banners swept on in pursuit of the Swedes,*
Stormed to the stronghold's defenses, and old Ongentheow
Was brought to bay with the sword, and subject to Eofor's will!
Wulf, son of Wonred, in wrath then struck with his sword,
And the blood in streams burst forth from under the old man's hair.
2780 *Yet the aged Scylfing was all undaunted and answered the stroke*
With a bitter exchange in the battle; and Wonred's brave son
Could not requite the blow, for the hero had cleft his helmet,
And, covered with blood, he was forced to bow; befell to the earth.
But his death was not doomed, and he rallied, though the wound was deep.
2785 *Then Hygelac's hardy thane, when his brother lay low,*
Struck with his ancient blade, a sturdy sword of the giants,
Cut through the shield-wall, cleaving the helmet. The king,
The folk-defender, sank down. He was hurt unto death.
Then were many that bound Wulf's wounds when the fight was won,
2790 *When the Geats held the ground of battle; as booty of war*
Eofor stripped Ongentheow of iron byrny and helm,
Of sword-blade hilted and hard, and bore unto Hygelac
The old man's trappings of war. And Hygelac took the treasures,
Promising fair rewards, and this he fulfilled.
2795 *The son of Hrethel, the king of the Geats, when he came to his home,*
Repaid with princely treasure the prowess of Eofor and Wulf;

Gave each an hundred thousand of land and linked rings,
And none could belittle or blame. They had won the honor in war.
He gave to Eofor also the hand of his only daughter
2800 *To be a pledge of good will, and the pride of his home.*

This is the fighting and this the feud,
The bitter hatred, that breeds the dread
Lest the Swedish people should swarm against us
Learning our lord lies lifeless and still.
2805 His was the hand that defended the hoard,
Heroes, and realm against ravaging foe,
By noble counsel and dauntless deed.
Let us go quickly to look on the king
Who brought us treasure, and bear his corpse
2810 To the funeral pyre. The precious hoard
Shall burn with the hero. There lies the heap
Of untold treasure so grimly gained,
Jewels and gems he bought with his blood
At the end of life. All these at the last
2815 The flames shall veil and the brands devour.
No man for remembrance shall take from the treasure,
Nor beauteous maiden adorn her breast
With gleaming jewel; bereft of gold
And tragic-hearted many shall tread
2820 A foreign soil, now their lord has ceased
From laughter and revel and rapture of joy.
Many a spear in the cold of morning
Shall be borne in hand uplifted on high.
No sound of harp shall waken the warrior,
2825 But the dusky raven despoiling the dead
Shall clamor and cry and call to the eagle
What fare he found at the carrion-feast
The while with the wolf he worried the corpses.'
    So the stalwart hero had told his tidings,
2830 His fateful message; nor spoke amiss
As to truth or telling. The host arose;
On their woeful way to the Eagles' Ness
They went with tears to behold the wonder.
They found the friend, who had dealt them treasure
2835 In former days, on the bed of death,
Stretched out lifeless upon the sand.
The last of the good king's days was gone;
Wondrous the death of the Weder prince!
They had sighted first, where it lay outstretched,

2840 The monstrous wonder, the loathsome worm,
      The horrible fire-drake, hideous-hued,
      Scorched with the flame. The spread of its length
      Was fifty foot-measures! Oft in the night
      It sported in air, then sinking to earth
2845 Returned to its den. Now moveless in death
      It had seen the last of its earthly lair.
      Beside the dragon were bowls and beakers,
      Platters lying, and precious swords
      Eaten with rust, where the hoard had rested
2850 A thousand winters in the womb of earth.
      That boundless treasure of bygone men,
      The golden dower, was girt with a spell
      So that never a man might ravage the ring-hall
      Save as God himself, the Giver of victory—
2855 He is the Shelter and Shield of men—
      Might allow such man as seemed to Him meet,
      Might grant whom He would, to gather the treasure.
          His way of life, who had wickedly hoarded
      The wealth of treasure beneath the wall,
2860 Had an evil end, as was widely seen.
      Many the dragon had sent to death,
      But in fearful fashion the feud was avenged!
      'Tis a wondrous thing when a warlike earl
      Comes to the close of his destined days,
2865 When he may no longer among his kinsmen
      Feast in the mead-hall. So Beowulf fared
      When he sought the dragon in deadly battle!
      Himself he knew not what fate was in store
      Nor the coming end of his earthly life.
2870 The lordly princes who placed the treasure
      Had cursed it deep to the day of doom,
      That the man who plundered and gathered the gold
      Might pay for the evil imprisoned in hell,
      Shackled in torment and punished with pain,
2875 Except the invader should first be favored
      With the loving grace of the Lord of all!
          Then spoke Wiglaf, Weohstan's son:
      'Often for one man many must sorrow
      As has now befallen the folk of the Geats.
2880 We could not persuade the king by our counsel,
      Our well-loved leader, to shun assault
      On the dreadful dragon guarding the gold;
      To let him lie where he long had lurked

In his secret lair till the world shall end.
2885   But Beowulf, dauntless, pressed to his doom.
The hoard was uncovered; heavy the cost;
Too strong the fate that constrained the king!
I entered the barrow, beholding the hoard
And all the treasure throughout the hall;
2890   In fearful fashion the way was opened,
An entrance under the wall of earth.
Of the hoarded treasure I heaped in my arms
A weighty burden, and bore to my king.
He yet was living; his wits were clear.
2895   Much the old man said in his sorrow;
Sent you greeting, and bade you build
In the place of burning a lofty barrow,
Proud and peerless, to mark his deeds;
For he was of all men the worthiest warrior
2900   In all the earth, while he still might rule
And wield the wealth of his lordly land.
Let us haste once more to behold the treasure,
The gleaming wonders beneath the wall.
I will show the way that you all may see
2905   And closely scan the rings and the gold.
Let the bier be ready, the pyre prepared,
When we come again to carry our lord,
Our leader beloved, where long he shall lie
In the kindly care of the Lord of all.'

BEOWULF'S FUNERAL

2910   Then the son of Weohstan, stalwart in war,
Bade send command to the heads of homes
To bring from afar the wood for the burning
Where the good king lay: 'Now glede shall devour,
As dark flame waxes, the warrior prince
2915   Who has often withstood the shower of steel
When the storm of arrows, sped from the string,
Broke over shield, and shaft did service,
With feather-fittings guiding the barb.'
      Then the wise son of Weohstan chose from the host
2920   Seven thanes of the king, the best of the band;
Eight heroes together they hied to the barrow
In under the roof of the fearful foe;
One of the warriors leading the way
Bore in his hand a burning brand.

2925   They cast no lots who should loot the treasure
        When they saw unguarded the gold in the hall
        Lying there useless; little they scrupled
        As quickly they plundered the precious store.
        Over the sea-cliff into the ocean
2930   They tumbled the dragon, the deadly worm,
        Let the sea-tide swallow the guarder of gold.
        Then a wagon was loaded with well-wrought treasure,
        A countless number of every kind;
        And the aged warrior, the white-haired king,
2935   Was borne on high to the Cape of the Whale.
            The Geat folk fashioned a peerless pyre
        Hung round with helmets and battle-boards,
        With gleaming byrnies as Beowulf bade.
        In sorrow of soul they laid on the pyre
2940   Their mighty leader, their well-loved lord.
        The warriors kindled the bale on the barrow,
        Wakened the greatest of funeral fires.
        Dark o'er the blaze the wood-smoke mounted;
        The winds were still, and the sound of weeping
2945   Rose with the roar of the surging flame
        Till the heat of the fire had broken the body.
        With hearts that were heavy they chanted their sorrow,
        Singing a dirge for the death of their lord;
        And an aged woman with upbound locks
2950   Lamented for Beowulf, wailing in woe.
        Over and over she uttered her dread
        Of sorrow to come, of bloodshed and slaughter,
        Terror of battle, and bondage, and shame.
        The smoke of the bale-fire rose to the sky!
2955   The men of the Weder folk fashioned a mound
        Broad and high on the brow of the cliff,
        Seen from afar by seafaring men.
        Ten days they worked on the warrior's barrow
        Inclosing the ash of the funeral flame
2960   With a wall as worthy as wisdom could shape.
        They bore to the barrow the rings and the gems,
        The wealth of the hoard the heroes had plundered.
        The olden treasure they gave to the earth,
        The gold to the ground, where it still remains
2965   As useless to men as it was of yore.
        Then round the mound rode the brave in battle,
        The sons of warriors, twelve in a band,
        Bemoaning their sorrow and mourning their king.

They sang their dirge and spoke of the hero
2970   Vaunting his valor and venturous deeds.
So is it proper a man should praise
His friendly lord with a loving heart,
When his soul must forth from the fleeting flesh.
So the folk of the Geats, the friends of his hearth,
2975   Bemoaned the fall of their mighty lord;
Said he was kindest of worldly kings,
Mildest, most gentle, most eager for fame.